MW01616298

TEN THEORIES OF RELIGION

FOURTH EDITION

Daniel L. Pals

University of Miami

New York Oxford
OXFORD UNIVERSITY PRESS

Oxford University Press is a department of the University of Oxford.
It furthers the University's objective of excellence in research, scholarship,
and education by publishing worldwide. Oxford is a registered trademark of
Oxford University Press in the UK and certain other countries.

Published in the United States of America by Oxford University Press
198 Madison Avenue, New York, NY 10016, United States of America.

Copyright © 2022, 2015, 2006, 1996 by Oxford University Press.

For titles covered by Section 112 of the US Higher Education
Opportunity Act, please visit www.oup.com/us/he for the latest
information about pricing and alternate formats.

All rights reserved. No part of this publication may be reproduced, stored in
a retrieval system, or transmitted, in any form or by any means, without the
prior permission in writing of Oxford University Press, or as expressly permitted
by law, by license, or under terms agreed with the appropriate reproduction
rights organization. Inquiries concerning reproduction outside the scope of the
above should be sent to the Rights Department, Oxford University Press,
at the address above.

You must not circulate this work in any other form
and you must impose this same condition on any acquirer.

Library of Congress Control Number: 2021937886
978-0-19-093508-5

Printing number: 9 8 7 6 5 4 3 2 1

Printed by Sheridan Books, Inc., United States of America

Again and always: To Phyllis and Katharine,
the lights of my life ever-shining

CONTENTS

PREFACE

Several years back, when Robert Miller first suggested a new edition of this book, I was of course willing to listen. His earlier wise advice had brought *Seven Theories of Religion* into print initially and through two editions beyond the first, keeping it current and available to readers for two decades. But when he shared what he now had in mind, I was hesitant. Among the commentaries Oxford had solicited on the third edition, some pointed to an unfilled gap. Although nine theories were better than seven or eight, some readers felt that what the book still lacked was an address to feminist theory. The point was well taken, but the prospect was a bit clouded. There were two related complications: the identification of a theorist, and the identity of the author: that is, myself.

The issue of choosing a theorist came first. When the second wave of feminism emerged in the decades after World War II, it soon generated a rich profusion of advocates and activists, all with compelling voices—articulate and intellectually aggressive, as well as historically and culturally informed. Simone de Beauvoir in the late 1940s, Betty Friedan in the 1960s, and Germaine Greer after 1970 were prominent, but they were hardly alone. Feminism could not be readily traced to the study of a single scholar, as was possible with certain other theories in the book. So who should be its signature voice? There were too many to choose from. Gradually, however, and on further reflection, one name, Mary Daly, came foremost to mind, and for two reasons: her pivotal place in the movement and her purist stance as a theorist. Daly was not America's first feminist, but she was placed among the very first to address, in no uncertain terms, the troubled convergence of feminism and traditional religion. That clearly was significant. Secondly, as a theorist within the feminist orbit, she gave to advocacy for women the very last full measure of her aggression. She boldly embraced feminist thinking in what may fairly be called its purest, most militant form—feminism without moderation or compromise, confronting male supremacy with no quarter given. To some in the circles of women's liberation, she reached too far and assumed a focus too narrow. But from the standpoint of ideological purity, nothing could be more illuminating. And from the perspective of pedagogy and comparative analysis, nothing could be more welcome.

Mary Daly, then, provided the solution to identifying the theorist, but she created a problem of a different kind for this author. Throughout her career she expressed a deep distrust of men, especially men in academia. As it happens, I am—unfortunately—an academic, and I am—inescapably—male. This complication cannot be fully resolved, though it can perhaps be alleviated slightly by here asking her posthumous forgiveness, which I do. Beyond that, I can do no more than affirm that I have tried to wrestle honestly with any implicit male bias and stay alert to its silent workings at every phase of the new chapter's exposition. I have also asked my wife Phyllis, whose feminist attachments are deep and longstanding, to read the text with an eye to that bias wherever she might be able to detect the first signs of it. In the end, though, and for good or ill, the verdict on my efforts must be left to the book's readers—especially its female readers—to render. The proof will need to be found in their reading.

NEW IN THIS EDITION

A note about changes associated with the new, tenth theory is in order. The interval between this fourth edition and the previous has been somewhat shorter than between the second and third, so I have not updated the lists of "Suggestions for Further Reading" in the chapters other than the new one devoted to Mary Daly. They stand as they did in *Nine Theories.* I have, however, updated the discussion of recent theories as outlined in the conclusion by citing some of the more noteworthy new contributions to the literature engaged with theories of religion. Finally, in addition to the main discussion of Daly and feminist theory, the concluding chapter, which offers a comparison and appraisal of theories, has naturally been updated to include Mary Daly's work in the conversation.

ACKNOWLEDGMENTS

Although I have already had occasion to mention the help she has given in the form of feminist discernment, I need also to thank in the warmest way my wife Phyllis, once again, for her skills as proofreader and diction expert. As with each of this book's previous editions, she has read every new page and paragraph with her extraordinarily keen eye for my too-habitual typos, as well errors of diction and general linguistic malfeasance. I must also record a substantial debt to two of my professional colleagues at the University of Miami. Professors David Kling and Dexter Callender read my account of Mary Daly as theorist with exceedingly close attention and keen insight. That does not show, of course, because what they found and corrected or amended has now vanished, leaving the manuscript and its author much the better in multiple ways for their efforts. In a few instances, they were especially astute in discovering even slight lapses from the special standard of objective exposition I have tried to set for this chapter on feminism in particular.

In 2019, Robert Miller, whose sustained support I have already acknowledged, retired from his post as one of Oxford's senior editors. To say that I have missed his counsel is beyond obvious. But I am now doubly privileged to have worked with his successor, Andrew Blitzer, and to have come at once to appreciate his comparable wisdom and exceptional patience over this past year—the year of COVID-19—especially. Andrew is the very soul of collegial affirmation—the trait that few authors will admit they silently most prize in an editor, but only find in the best. I would like, finally, to thank in equal measure assistant editor Anna Deen and editorial assistant Lacey Harvey, who have assisted me through the several phases of the publication process and the tedious labors—too little thanked—that it entails.

For their feedback throughout the writing process, I would also like to thank the following reviewers:

- Robert Stephens, Clemson University
- Henry Delcore, California State University, Fresno
- Kaine Fini, Golden West College
- Quinton Dixie, Duke Divinity School
- Pamela Winfield, Elon University
- Adrienne Ambrose, University of the Incarnate Word
- Adil Khan, Loyola University New Orleans
- Christel Manning, Sacred Heart University

This edition is dedicated, as was the first, a quarter-century ago, to Phyllis and Katharine, who have taught me how much learning is enhanced by living and being loved.

Introduction

On a February day in the winter of 1870, a personable, middle-aged German scholar rose to the stage of London's prestigious Royal Institution to deliver a public lecture. At the time, German professors were famous for their deep learning, and this one was no exception, though as it happened he had also become very English. His name was Friedrich Max Müller. He had first come to Britain as a young man destined for Oxford, where his plan was to study the ancient texts of India's Vedas, its books of sacred knowledge. He soon settled in, married a proper English wife, and managed to acquire a position at the University. Müller was admired for his knowledge of Sanskrit, the language of early India, but he also acquired a mastery of English, which he employed with admirable skill in popular writings on language and mythology that appealed widely to Victorian readers. On this occasion, however, he proposed a different subject: he wished to promote "the science of religion."

Those words in that sequence doubtless struck some in Müller's audience as puzzling in the extreme. After all, he was speaking at the end of a decade marked by furious debate over Charles Darwin's *Origin of Species* (1859) and its startling theory of evolution by natural selection. Thoughtful Victorians had heard so much of science pitted *against* religion that a science *of* religion could only fall on the ears as a quite curious combination. How could the age-old certainties of faith ever mix with a program of study devoted to experiment, revision, and change? How could these two apparently mortal enemies meet without one destroying the other? These were understandable concerns, but Müller was of a different mind: he was quite certain that the two enterprises could meet and that a truly scientific study of religion had much to offer to both sides in that controversy. His lecture, the first in a series later published as an *Introduction to the Science of Religion* (1873), was designed to prove just that point. He reminded his listeners that the words of the poet Goethe on language could also be applied to religion: "He who knows one, knows none."[1] If that is so, then perhaps it was time indeed for a new and objective look at this very old subject. Instead of following the theologians, who wanted only to prove their own religion true and others false, the time had come to take a less partisan approach, seeking out those elements, patterns, and principles that could be found uniformly in the religions of all times and places. Much could be gained by proceeding as a good scientist, by gathering various facts—customs, rituals, and beliefs—of religions throughout the world and then offering theories that compare and account for them, just as a biologist or chemist might explain the workings of nature.

Certainly not everyone, even among scholars, agreed that something of value could be gained from the study of many religions. Back in Germany, Adolf von Harnack, the foremost Church historian of the age, insisted that Christianity alone is what matters; other faiths do not. "Whoever does not know this religion knows none," he wrote in pointed rejection of Müller's view, "and whoever knows it and its history, knows all."[2] He added, with more than a trace of disdain, that it was pointless to go to the Indians, the Chinese, still less the Africans or Papuans: Christian civilization alone was destined to endure, so there was little need to bother. Harnack was unusually blunt, but his view itself was not unusual. There was a fairly wide consensus among theologians and historians across Europe that Christian ideals and values, which formed the spiritual center of the West, expressed the highest in human moral and cultural achievement. To imagine that something significant could be learned from others was to think inferiors can tutor their betters. None of this could discourage Müller, however: he was confident that serious study would show how certain shared spiritual intuitions link the sages of Asia and other distant lands to the saints and martyrs of the Church.

Ancient Theories

Müller's program may have been unwelcome to some and new to others, but elements of what he proposed in his lecture were in fact very old. Questions as to what religion is and why different people practice it as they do doubtless reach back as far as the human race itself. The earliest theories would have been framed when the first traveler ventured outside the local clan or village and discovered that neighbors had other gods with different names. When on his travels the ancient historian Herodotus (484–425 BCE) tried to explain that the gods Amon and Horus, whom he met in Egypt, were the equivalents of Zeus and Apollo in his native Greece, he was actually offering at least the beginning of a general theory of religion. So was the writer Euhemerus (330–260 BCE) when he claimed that the gods were simply outstanding personages from history who began to be worshipped after their death. According to Cicero of Rome, the Stoic Chrysippus (280–206 BCE) was a thoroughly systematic student of the customs and beliefs of as many tribes and races as his travels led him to encounter. Some Stoic philosophers accounted for the gods as personifications of the sky, the sea, or other natural forces. After viewing the facts of religion, they and others sought, often quite creatively, to explain how it had come to be what it was.[3]

Judaism and Christianity

These philosophers lived in the classical civilizations of ancient Greece and Rome, where many divinities were worshipped and the idea of comparing or connecting one god with another was a natural habit of mind. Both Judaism and Christianity, however, took a very different view of things. To Isaiah and other prophets of Israel, there was no such thing as a variety of gods and rituals, each with a different and perhaps equal claim on our interest or devotion: there was only the one true God, the Lord of the covenant, who had appeared to Abraham, Isaac, and Jacob and had revealed the divine law to Moses on Mt. Sinai. As this God alone was real and all others were mere figments of the human imagination, there was little about religion that needed either comparison or explanation. The people of Israel were to trust in Yahweh, who had chosen only them and had spoken to them directly; other nations worshipped idols, their eyes being darkened by ignorance, wickedness, or both. Christianity, which arose out of later Judaism, took over this perspective of Isaiah almost without change. For the apostles and theologians of the early Church, God had put himself on clear display in the human person of Jesus the Christ. Those who believed in him had found the truth; those who did not were victims of the great deceiver Satan—their souls destined to pay a bitter eternal price in Hell. As Christianity spread across the ancient world and later to the peoples of Europe, this view came to dominate Western civilization. There were occasional exceptions, of course, but the prevailing attitude was expressed most clearly in the great struggle against Islam during the age of the Crusades. Christians, the children of light, were commanded to struggle against the children of darkness. The beauty and truth of God's revelation explained the faith of Christendom; the machinations of the Devil and his hosts explained the perversions of its enemies.[4]

For the better part of a thousand years after the Roman empire had become Christian, this militant perspective on religions outside the creed of the Church did not significantly change. But around the year 1500, as the epoch of world explorations and the age of the Protestant Reformation arrived, the beginnings of a new outlook began to take shape. The voyages of explorers, traders, missionaries, and adventurers to the New World and to the Orient brought Christians into direct encounters with alien peoples who were neither Jews nor Muslims, both of whose religions were readily dismissed (the first as a mere preface to Christianity, the second as a perversion of it). Missionaries, traveling with those who explored and conquered, were at the leading edge of the engagement. Their aim was to bring "heathen nations" to Christ, and so they certainly did. Many were converted, but the process also brought surprises. When the scholarly Jesuit Matteo Ricci (1552–1610) took residence at the court of the emperor in China, the missionary very nearly became the convert.

The Chinese, Ricci discovered, had a real civilization, with art, ethics, and literature. Their ways were rational, and they followed the impressive moral wisdom of their own Moses, the ancient teacher Confucius. Another Jesuit, Roberto di Nobili (1577–1656), had a similar experience in India. The spiritual wisdom of the Hindu sages captured his imagination; he studied the sacred books so intensively that he became known as "the white Brahmin." Still other missionaries, at work in the New World, discovered something like belief in a Supreme Being among America's "Indians." As these reports filtered back to Europe, it occurred to some in thoughtful circles that the condemnation of such peoples as disciples of the Devil just might be premature. China's Confucians may not have known Christ, but somehow, without a Bible to guide them, they had produced a civilization of mild manners and high morals. Had the apostles visited, they too might have admired it.

At the very same moment that these contacts were being made, the Christian civilization that the Prince of Peace presumably *had* established found itself plunged into bloody and violent turmoil. Led by Martin Luther in Germany and John Calvin in Switzerland and France, the new Protestant movements of Northern Europe challenged the power of the Church and rejected its interpretations of biblical truth. While the explorers traveled, their homelands often came ablaze with the fires of persecution and war. Communities were split apart by ferocious quarrels over theology, first between Catholics and Protestants and later among the scores and more of different religious sects that began to appear in once-unified Christendom. Amid the religious storms and political struggles that gripped the sixteenth and seventeenth centuries, it is no surprise that concerned believers on all sides grew less certain that they alone held God's final truth in their hands. The deadly, destructive wars of religion, which persisted for more than a hundred years in some lands, led some people to believe that the truth about religion cannot possibly be found in sects that were prepared to torture and execute opponents, confident their work was God's will. Surely, they said, the truth of religion must be found beyond the quarrels of the churches, beyond the tortures of the stake and the rack. Surely, the faiths of Europe could find a pure and common form, a simpler and more universal framework of belief and values that could be shared across the borders of confessions.[5]

The Enlightenment and Natural Religion

It was this quest for a shared, simpler religion, set against the bloody background of the previous era, that inspired thinkers of the eighteenth century, the Age of Enlightenment. They embarked on a mission that led them to the idea of a true and ancient "natural religion" shared by the entire human race.

Natural religion formed the basic creed of Deism, as it commonly came to be called. It enlisted the most articulate voices and celebrated names of the age: philosophers such as John Toland and Matthew Tindal in Britain, the American colonial statesmen Thomas Jefferson and Ben Franklin, and brilliant men of letters such as Denis Diderot and the great Voltaire in France, as well as the dramatist Gotthold Lessing and philosopher Immanuel Kant in Germany. Nearly all in this circle, who saw themselves as voices of reason, endorsed the idea of a universal, natural religion. They affirmed belief in a Creator God who made the world and then left it to its own natural laws, instituted a parallel set of moral laws to guide the conduct of humanity, and offered the promise of an afterlife of rewards for good and punishments for evil. To the Deists this elegantly simple creed was the faith of the very first human beings, the common philosophy of all races. The best hope of humanity was to recover this original creed and to live by it in a universal brotherhood of all peoples—Christians, Jews, Muslims, Hindus, Confucians, and all others—under their one Creator God.

In addition to its commendable work in promoting tolerance, the Deist notion of an original natural religion of humanity opened the door to a new way of explaining the many forms of religion in all their conflict and confusion. Whatever the different beliefs of the various Christian sects, the rituals of native Americans, the ancestral rites of the Chinese, or the teachings of the Hindu sages, all could ultimately be traced back to the natural religion of the first human beings and then followed forward as that ancient wisdom was gradually transformed and dispersed into its modern versions and variations. China especially offered proof of this point. As trading ships from the Orient began to return regularly in the 1700s, fascination attended all forms of *chinoiserie*. Fabrics, spices, porcelains, teas, and furnishings gave evidence of China's civility and elegance, its prosperity, deference, and piety, all plainly acquired without any help from the Bible. These graces, and the ethics of Confucius especially, displayed the virtues of natural religion.

Modern Theories

There was, of course, another side to the Deist agenda. To praise natural religion was also to blame revealed religion, which by the Deists' estimate was little more than the twisted handiwork of priests and theologians. By and large, the Christian Church was seen by Deists as filled with retailers of ignorance and superstition, revelations and ceremonies, miracles, confessions, sacraments, saints, and sacred texts in a language few could understand. Natural religion, on the other hand, was emphatically not a set of truths revealed directly by God to the Church and withheld from the rest of humanity. True religion was natural and primeval—the one universal faith of humanity long before it had been corrupted by churches, dogmas, and clerics. Moreover, because it was natural rather than supernatural, religion could also be explained rationally, just as the laws of motion and gravitation had been shown by Newton the physicist to be implanted in the world as it came from the Creator's hand.[6]

Deists prized rationality but showed little appreciation for the deep emotions that give life to religion or for the enchantments of its rich history and its wealth of diverse cultural forms. That posture deeply alienated those who saw traditional devotion as the very heart of religion. Faithful Catholics, fervent Protestants (called Pietists), and revivalists such as John Wesley protested the Deist program by celebrating a religion of the heart rather than a dry, rationalistic religion of the head. Their appreciation of the emotions was shared by religious Romantic writers, scholars, and poets who joined to it a deep appreciation of just what Deists despised—the glory of churches and temples, the surpassing beauty of rituals and ceremonies, the power of sacraments and prayers: the entire rich and colorful history of religious faith, especially (but not only) the Christian faith. The historical forms and institutions of religion, they contended, are not enemies of the religious spirit; they are its guardians and they bear its torch. The accents of this Romantic reaction are perhaps best illustrated in the great French historical novelist Vicomte de Chateaubriand, whose book *The Genius of Christianity* (1802) savors the beauty and history of old Catholicism.

It is fair to say that both of these historical streams—the cold current of Enlightenment Deism and the warm waters of religious Romanticism—converged in the mind of Max Müller and others. As a thinker, Müller was a virtual Deist. He relied on the philosopher Immanuel Kant, Germany's voice of Enlightenment, who centered religion on the two cardinal doctrines of Deism: belief in God above and in "the moral law within." As a personality, however, Müller was a Romantic. His young life overlapped the later years of Chateaubriand, and though he was a German Protestant rather than a French Catholic, he was just as deeply affected by the same mystical spirit and attuned to the presence of the divine wherever it could be discerned, either in the beauty of nature or in the spiritual strivings of humanity. Wherever in nature or history clues to the divine might appear, he was prepared to find them.

This blend of contrasting perspectives—Deist and Romantic—furnished Müller and others like him with both a motive and rationale for the study of all religions. They believed that it was possible to find the root impulse of religion everywhere, and they made use of methods that were mainly historical. By sustained and diligent inquiry, they would reach far back in time to discover the earliest religious ideas and practices of the human race; that accomplished, it was a natural next step to trace their development onward and upward to the present day. Müller and his associates believed not just that they could do such a thing, but that in their time it could be done better than the Deists ever imagined, largely because of great advances made in the study of archaeology, history, language, and mythology, complemented by the newfound disciplines of ethnology and anthropology.[7] In addition to his knowledge of the Vedas and mythology, Müller was himself one of Europe's foremost names in the field of comparative philology, or linguistics; the Hindu Vedas that he edited were then thought to be the oldest religious documents of the human race. Archaeologists in the first decades of the nineteenth century had made significant discoveries by excavating the early layers of human civilization; historians had pioneered new critical methods for studying ancient texts; students of folklore were gathering information on the customs and tales of Europe's peasants; and the first anthropologists could draw on reports from those who had observed societies of apparently primitive people still surviving in the modern world. In addition, there was now the very successful model of the natural sciences to imitate. Instead of just guessing about the origins and development of religion or naively assuming with some Deists that to know the writings of Confucius was to know all of Chinese religion, inquirers could now systematically assemble facts—rituals, beliefs, customs—from a wide sample of the world's religions. With these in hand and properly classified, they could infer the general principles—the scientific "laws of development"—that would explain how such belief systems arose and what purposes they served.

By the middle decades of the 1800s, then, a small circle mainly of French, German, and British scholars felt that both the methods and materials were on hand to leave speculation behind and offer instead systematic theories about religion's origins that could claim the authority of science. Not only in Müller's lectures but in other writings of the time as well, we can notice an optimism, an energy, and confidence about the tasks ahead. The aim was not just to guess about origins, but to frame theories based on evidence. Like their counterparts in the physical sciences, students of religion would work from a solid foundation of facts and frame generalizations that could be tested, revised, and improved. To all appearances, this scientific method had the further advantage that it could be applied independently of one's personal religious commitments. Müller was a deeply devout, almost sentimental Christian who believed that the truth of his faith had nothing to fear from science and would in fact shine more brightly if it were explained in the context of other religions. As we shall soon see, E. B. Tylor, Müller's contemporary and critic, took a different view, convinced that his scientific inquiry gave support to his personal stance of agnostic skepticism. Both, however, believed that a theory of religion could be developed from a common ground of objective facts that would provide both evidentiary support and a final test of truth. Both also believed that they could reach theories that were comprehensive and general in nature. Such was the confidence they had in both their science and the body of facts at their disposal that they felt no hesitation in claiming they could explain the entire phenomenon of religion—not just this ritual or that belief, not just religion in one place or time, but the worldwide story of its origin, development, and diversity. In stating this bold ambition, they laid out the issues that the major theorists of the twentieth century (those who occupy center stage in this book) would later need to address.[8]

When we look back on it from the perspective of the present day, this hope of forming a single theory of all religions somewhat astonishes by its vaulting ambition. We are inclined now to be far more modest. Impressive books have been written just to explain one belief of one religion or to compare a single feature—a specific custom or ritual—of one religion with something similar in another. Nonetheless, the hope of one day discovering some broad pattern or general principle that explains all (or even most) religious behavior has not been given up easily. As will be clear in some of the chapters to come, several important theorists of the twentieth century have been inspired by this very same ideal, and for understandable reasons. Physicists have not given up on Einstein's unified field theory, even though finding it has proved more difficult than many of them imagined. In the same way, religionists, despite the difficulties, have also been inspired by the scientific ideal of a general theory that can draw many different phenomena into one coherent, widely illuminating pattern. Moreover, explanations need not be valid to be of value: in religion, as in other fields of inquiry, a suggestive and original theory can, even in failure, spur new inquiry or reformulate issues in such a way as to promote fruitful new understandings. Thus, even if most of what they say were found to be in error, the theorists who appear in these pages would still deserve our time and attention. Their ideas and interpretations are original. Further, they diffuse themselves beyond the sphere of religion to affect our literature, philosophy, history, politics, art, psychology, and indeed almost every realm of modern culture.

It is interesting in this connection to notice how well hidden are the origins and first advocates of ideas now regarded as belonging to the stock of common knowledge. How many people who casually refer to religion as a superstitious belief in spirits realize that they are essentially repeating E. B. Tylor's famous theory of animism as explained in *Primitive Culture*, a work midway into its second century since publication? Would they today recognize the name of either the author or his once-revered book? Who among those who claim that science replaces religion can recall the fame of James Frazer at the turn of the twentieth century, when he placed that thesis at the center of his monumental *Golden Bough*? How many general readers with a curiosity about religion would recognize the unusual name and provocative theory of Mircea Eliade, even though his institutional influence on the study of religion in the American academy over the past half century and more has been remarkably widespread? How many know the role that anthropologist E. E. Evans-Pritchard has played in philosophical debates over rationality and relativism? How readily can people who refer to the Protestant work ethic in everyday conversation identify German sociologist Max Weber, who first defined it? The views associated with the leading radical thinkers, especially Marx and Freud, tend to be better known, of course, but often in ways that are vague, fragmentary, or distorted. In consequence, a great deal of current debate *about* such theories often goes on without a very firm grasp of the assumptions, evidence, and logic to be found *in* them. One service this book can render is to help readers relatively new to this subject avoid making just that mistake.

Ten Theories

The following chapters consider ten of the most important theories of religion that have been put forward since the idea of a scientific approach to religion first caught the imagination of serious scholars in the nineteenth century. In each case, the theory is presented first by discussing the life and background of its proponent, then by treating its key ideas as presented in certain central texts, and finally by noticing its distinctive features in comparison with other theories and recording the main objections raised by its critics.

Principle of Selection

Out of a number of theories that might have been chosen for the purpose, this book selects those that have exercised a shaping influence not only on religion but on the whole intellectual culture of the twentieth century. In sequence, their authors are as follows: (1) E. B. Tylor and J. G. Frazer, (2) Sigmund Freud, (3) Émile Durkheim, (4) Karl Marx, (5) Max Weber, (6) William James, (7) Mircea Eliade, (8) E. E. Evans-Pritchard, (9) Clifford Geertz, and (10) Mary Daly. Knowledgeable readers will notice at once that several highly regarded figures, including the Swiss psychologist Carl Jung and even Max Müller himself, fall outside this group. Omissions as large as these are not easy to justify; indeed, another author might well have chosen differently. But the choices do have a rationale. Important as he was in promoting the idea of a science of religion, Max Müller has been left aside because his own theory was for the most part rejected in his day and has had only limited influence thereafter. Again, the influential French philosopher Lucien Lévy-Bruhl, who is noticed briefly in Chapter 8, is a theorist who some would say deserves admission here, but Lévy-Bruhl too is a complex figure—of more indirect influence—whose views changed significantly over time; moreover, since the major issues he took up were also considered by E. E. Evans-Pritchard, who had the further benefit of grounding his views in sustained fieldwork among tribal peoples, the latter seems for our purposes the better of the two to select. The same is true to a degree in the case of Carl Jung. It is well known that Jung took a subtle, sympathetic, and textured approach to religion and that he made extensive use of religious materials in his psychological research. For just that reason, however, he offers a somewhat less rigorously consistent example of a psychologically functional interpretation than what we find in Freud. Further, Jung's long-term influence on the field of psychology, though great, was less extensive, so Freud seems the right choice. The better theorist to place in this text along with Freud is the American William James, considered in Chapter 6. In addition to taking a position on religion quite different from Freud's, he illustrates well how in its early decades psychology certainly was more than psychoanalysis. In the end any book must have limits, and some choices may well appear to some readers more arbitrary than astute. The important thing is to note that these classic theorists offer models of how some—admittedly not all—of the most influential interpretations of religion have made their mark over the past century and more.

Definition of Terms

Before we begin, some comment is needed on the two terms that are most basic to the discussions that follow: "religion" and "theory." Most people, even if they are coming to this subject for the first time, have some idea of what the term "religion" means. They are likely to think of belief in a God or gods, in supernatural spirits, or in an afterlife. Or they are likely to name one of the great world religions, such as Hinduism, Christianity, Buddhism, Judaism, or Islam. They probably also have some general idea of what the term "theory" means. Having heard the term most often in the context of science, they think of it as a kind of explanation—an attempt to account for something that is not at first understood. It answers the question "Why?". Most of us readily admit that we do not understand the theory of relativity, but we do recognize that it somehow accounts for the connection between space and time in a way that no one had imagined before. At the start of things, there is no need for us to go beyond everyday notions such as these. Whatever their limitations, ordinary understandings of general terms such as "religion" and "theory" are indispensable for a book such as this—not only at the starting point but to offer guideposts as we proceed. At the same time, we should also notice that few of the theorists we shall consider are content to stay with these intuitions of common sense once they have seriously worked their way into the issues.

When discussing the term "religion," some observers find that "belief in a God or gods" is far too specific, far too theological a definition to use for certain people such as Buddhists, who worship no God, or for specific groups such as some Jews, who think of their faith chiefly as a matter of activities rather than beliefs. To accommodate such instances, which clearly belong to the sphere of religion, a theorist might better follow the path chosen by Durkheim and Eliade, who both prefer a broad concept like "the sacred" as the essential defining feature. They note that the Buddhist who does not believe in God does, after all, have a sense of things that are sacred. So they find this abstract term more suitable when considering the entire span and story of religion in the world rather than traditions of just one place or time or type. Again, some theorists strongly prefer *substantive* definitions, which closely resemble the common sense approach. They define religion in terms of the beliefs or the ideas that religious people affirm. Others think this approach just too restrictive and offer instead a more *functional* definition. They leave the content, the ideas, of religion off to the side and define it solely in terms of how it operates in human life. They want to know what a religion does for an individual person psychologically or for a group socially. Less concerned with the content of people's beliefs or practices, they are inclined to describe religion, *whatever its specific content*, as that which brings a sense of comfort or well-being to an individual or provides support for a group. As we proceed, it will be wise to keep in mind that the matter of defining religion is closely linked to the matter of explaining it and that the issue of definitions is considerably more difficult than common sense leads us on first look to believe.

The same can be said for the term "theory." At first glance, the idea of an explanation of religion is not hard to understand, but again, the more deeply we move into the actual business of explaining, the more complex it becomes. Two brief illustrations can show why. First, a theorist who proposes to explain religion by showing its "origin" can mean by this word any of several things: its *prehistorical* origin—how, at the dawn of history, the first human beings acquired a religion; its *psychological* or *social* origin—how, at all times in human history, it arises in response to certain group or individual needs; its *intellectual* origin—how, at one time or all times, certain perceived truths about the world have led people to believe certain religious claims; or its *historical* origin—how, at a known specific time and place in the past, a certain prophetic personality or a special sequence of events has created a religion and given it a distinctive character or form. Both in describing and in evaluating a theory, it is important to know what kind of origin it is addressing and what connection one type of origin may have with the other types.

The second case has already been partly noticed: theories of religion, no less than definitions, may also be either substantive or functional in character. Theorists who advocate substantive approaches tend to explain religion intellectually in terms of the ideas that guide and inspire people. They stress human intention, emotions, and agency. People are religious, they say, because certain ideas strike them as true and valuable and therefore ought to be followed in the framing of their lives. Theorists who stress this role of human thought and feeling are sometimes described as interpretive rather than explanatory in their approach. Religions, they contend, are adopted by persons and are about things that have meaning to human beings; accordingly, interpretations, which take account of conscious human intent, best explain religion, which after all is the product of human thoughts and purposes. Interpretive theorists tend to reject "explanations" because they are about things, not persons. They appeal only to impersonal processes rather than to humanly meaningful purposes. Functional theorists, by contrast, strongly disagree. They think that though explanations are of course good for things—for physical objects and natural processes—they are just as useful in understanding people. Functional theorists strive to look beneath or behind the conscious thoughts of religious people to find something deeper and more hidden. They routinely contend that certain underlying social structures or unnoticed psychological pressures are the real causes of religious behavior. Whether they are individual, social, or even biological, these compelling forces—and *not* the ideas that religious people themselves imagine to be governing their actions—form the real sources of religion wherever we find it. We will be able to trace these differences in some detail later on in our discussion.[9] For the moment, however, they serve notice that with theories of religion, no less than with definitions, the seemingly simple often masks the deceptively complex.

In the chapters to follow, we will attend to the definitions as well as the explanations and interpretations advanced by our theorists, taking note of the links that in each case connect the latter with the former. Along the way, it should become apparent how and why each theorist is moved to consider both the obvious and the unnoticed, the surface and the substrate, in the effort to understand religion. It should also be clear that these theories have been placed in a sequence, partly chronological and partly conceptual, that is meant to suggest a pattern. After starting with the classic intellectualist theories of Tylor and Frazer, we move next to explanatory approaches, tracing the lines of psychological, economic, and social functionalism through Freud, Marx, and Durkheim, respectively. We then turn to Weber and James, who offer qualified departures from functionalist theories, and to Eliade, who registers a more assertive protest against their explanatory reductionism. We finish with the more recent theories of Evans-Pritchard, Geertz, and Daly, the first two of whom make efforts to overcome the interpretive/explanatory divide, while the third takes a decidedly new turn, putting the challenge of radical feminism to the entire sequence of (undeniably male) theorists who have preceded her. The conclusion will offer a brief review of what has happened among theorists in the interval since these classic theories came into currency, and it will ask some final comparative and analytical questions.

Notes

1. F. Max Müller, *Lectures on the Science of Religion* (New York: Charles Scribner and Company, 1872), p. 11. This was also published under the title *Introduction to the Science of Religion*. On Müller's interesting life, see Nirad Chaudhuri, *Scholar Extraordinary: The Life of Professor the Rt. Hon. Friedrich Max Müller* (London: Chatto & Windus, 1974).

2. Cited in Helwig Schmidt-Glintzer, "The Economic Ethics of the World Religions," in Hartmut Lehman and Guenther Roth, *Weber's Protestant Ethic: Origins, Evidence, Contexts* (Cambridge: Cambridge University Press, 1993), p. 350.

3. On these ancient precursors of the modern theory of religion, see Eric J. Sharpe, *Comparative Religion: A History* (New York: Charles Scribner's Sons, 1975), pp. 1–7.

4. Sharpe, *Comparative Religion*, pp. 7–13.

5. On the connection between the wars of religion in Europe and the effort to explain religion comparatively, without theological judgments, see J. Samuel Preus, *Explaining Religion: Criticism and Theory from Bodin to Freud* (New Haven, CT: Yale University Press, 1987), pp. 3–20.

6. On early Deism and later skepticism in the Age of Enlightenment, see the discussions of Herbert of Cherbury and David Hume in Preus, *Explaining Religion*, pp. 23–39, 84–103.

7. On the rise of anthropology in the mid-Victorian years, see (among others) Richard M. Dorson, *The British Folklorists: A History* (Chicago: University of Chicago Press, 1968); Paul Bohannan, *Social Anthropology* (New York: Holt, Rinehart & Winston, 1969), pp. 311–315; J. W. Burrow, *Evolution and Society* (Cambridge: Cambridge University Press, 1970); George W. Stocking, Jr., *Victorian Anthropology* (New York: Free Press, 1987); and Timothy Larsen, *The Slain God: Anthropologists and the Christian Faith* (New York: Oxford University Press, 2014), pp. 13–79.

8. On these early efforts to develop theories of religion with the help of anthropological and other research, see Brian Morris, *Anthropological Studies of Religion* (Cambridge: Cambridge University Press, 1987), pp. 91–105.

9. The most important and provocative analyses of this division are to be found in two collections of trenchant essays by Robert A. Segal: *Religion and the Social Sciences: Essays on the Confrontation* (Atlanta: Scholars Press, 1989) and *Explaining and Interpreting Religion: Essays on the Issue* (New York: Peter Lang Publishing, 1992).

Suggestions for Further Reading

Bellah, Robert. *Religion in Human Evolution: From the Paleolithic to the Axial Age*. Cambridge, MA: Harvard University Press, 2011. The last major effort of an eminent American sociologist, this ambitious survey engages the difficult, seldom-ventured task of reconstructing the early history of religion—from human beginnings through the great civilizations of antiquity.

Chaudhuri, Nirad C. *Scholar Extraordinary: The Life of Professor the Rt. Hon. Friedrich Max Müller*. London: Chatto & Windus, 1974. A detailed study of the life and some consideration of the theories of Friedrich Max Müller.

Eliade, Mircea, Editor in Chief. *The Macmillan Encyclopedia of Religion*. New York: Macmillan, 1987. At present the most useful and comprehensive English-language reference work on religion.

Evans-Pritchard, E. E. *Theories of Primitive Religion*. Oxford: Clarendon Press, 1965. A brief and penetrating analysis of certain classic approaches to the explanation of religion.

Fitzgerald, Timothy. *The Ideology of Religious Studies*. New York: Oxford University Press, 2000. A controversial critique of the study of religion on the grounds that the term "religion" is impossible to define, so explanations that appeal to the concept are neither meaningful nor useful.

Harrison, Peter. *"Religion" and the Religions in the English Enlightenment*. Cambridge: Cambridge University Press, 1990. An informative study that shows how the thinkers and ideas of the Enlightenment in England contributed to the rise of the scientific study of religion.

Larsen, Timothy. *The Slain God: Anthropologists and the Christian Faith.* New York: Oxford University Press, 2014. An in-depth comparative assessment of influential British anthropologists and their varying engagements with Christian belief.

Masuzawa, Tomoko. *In Search of Dreamtime: The Quest for the Origin of Religion*. Chicago: University of Chicago Press, 1993. An original but difficult book that examines the presuppositions behind the keen interest of earlier, evolutionary theorists in the historical origin of religion.

McCutcheon, Russell T. *Manufacturing Religion: The Discourse on Sui Generis Religion and the Politics of Nostalgia*. New York: Oxford University Press, 1997. A critique of some recent approaches to the study of religion and similar research pursued in Religious Studies departments of American universities.

Morris, Brian. *Anthropological Studies of Religion*. Cambridge: Cambridge University Press, 1987. A comprehensive survey of scientific theories of religion in the nineteenth and twentieth centuries.

Preus, J. Samuel. *Explaining Religion: Criticism and Theory from Bodin to Freud*. New Haven, CT: Yale University Press, 1987. A much-praised study that follows the history of thinking about religion over most of the past three centuries.

Segal, Robert A. *Religion and the Social Sciences: Essays on the Confrontation*. Brown Studies in Religion, no. 8. Atlanta: Scholars Press, 1989. Trenchant essays by a keenly analytical theorist who sees an inescapable conflict between the theories of those who personally sympathize with religion and the critical explanatory methods of the social sciences.

Sharpe, Eric J. *Comparative Religion: A History*. New York: Charles Scribner's Sons, 1975. A wide-ranging overview of theories and theorists of religion. Helpful both as an introduction to the field and for short accounts of the lives and thought of its leading figures.

Stausberg, Michael, Editor. *Contemporary Theories of Religion: A Critical Companion*. New York: Routledge: 2009. Critical assessments of leading newer theories and approaches offered in the two decades on either side of the year 2000.

Van den Bosch, Lourens. *Friedrich Max Müller: A Life Devoted to the Humanities*. Numen Book Series 94. Leiden: E. J. Brill, 2002. This recent in-depth study is now the definitive account of Müller's life and work.

1

Animism and Magic: E. B. Tylor and J. G. Frazer

> Are the forces which govern the world conscious and personal, or unconscious and impersonal? Religion, as a conciliation of the superhuman powers, assumes the former. . . . [I]t stands in fundamental antagonism to magic as well as to science [which holds that] the course of nature is determined, not by the passions or caprice of personal beings, but by the operation of immutable laws acting mechanically.
>
> James Frazer, *The Golden Bough*[1]

Our survey begins with not one but two theorists whose writings are related and whose ideas closely resemble each other. The first is Edward Burnett Tylor (1832–1917), a self-educated Englishman who never attended a university but, through his travels and independent study, arrived at the theory of animism, which in his view held the key to the origin of religion. The second is James George Frazer (1854–1941), a shy, scholarly Scotsman who, unlike Tylor, spent virtually all of his life in a book-lined apartment at Cambridge University. Frazer is often associated with what is sometimes called the "magic" theory of religion, rather than with Tylor's animism, but in fact he was a disciple of Tylor, who readily took over his mentor's main ideas and methods while adding certain new touches of his own. As we shall see in our discussion, the two theories are so closely related that we can more helpfully consider them as differing versions—an earlier and later form—of the same general point of view. Tylor is perhaps the more original thinker, while Frazer enjoys the greater fame and influence.

E. B. Tylor

E. B. Tylor's first interest was not religion but the study of human culture, or social organization. Some, in fact, consider him the founder of cultural, or social, anthropology as that science is now practiced in Britain and North America. He was born in 1832 to a family of prosperous Quakers who owned a London brass factory.[2] The Quakers originally were an extreme, almost fanatical group of English Protestants who dressed in plain, unfashionable clothes and lived by the inspiration of a personal "inner light." By the 1800s most had discarded their unusual dress, earned social respect, and moved all the way over to very liberal, even nonreligious views. This perspective is clearly present in Tylor's writings, which show a strong distaste for traditional Christianity, especially Roman Catholicism.

Because both of Tylor's parents died when he was a young man, he planned to assist in managing the family business, only to discover his own health failing when he showed signs of developing tuberculosis. Advised to spend time in a warmer climate, he chose to travel to Central America and left home in 1855, at the young age of twenty-three. This American experience proved decisive in his life, for it kindled his keen interest in the study of unfamiliar cultures. As he traveled, he took careful notes on the customs and beliefs of the people he saw, publishing the results of his work in a book entitled *Anahuac: Or Mexico and the Mexicans, Ancient and Modern* (1861). On his journeys, Tylor also met a fellow Quaker, the archaeologist Henry Christy, who sparked his interest in prehistoric studies. Though he did not travel again, Tylor began to study the customs and beliefs of all peoples who lived in "primitive" conditions, whether from prehistoric ages (insofar as they could be known from archaeological finds) or from tribal communities of the present day. Soon he published a second book, *Researches into the Early History of Mankind and the Development of Civilization* (1865). Six years later, after much more work on these subjects, he published *Primitive Culture* (1871), a large two-volume study that became the masterwork of his career and a landmark in the study of human civilization. This important book not only appealed to a wide audience of general readers but also cast a spell over a number of brilliant younger men who were to become Tylor's enthusiastic disciples. Through their further outstanding work, the systematic study of folklore and the newly developing science of anthropology made great strides in the later years of the nineteenth century.[3] Though it was not the only such book, *Primitive Culture* served as a virtual Bible for all who were inspired by what was called "Mr. Tylor's science."

Tylor continued his work, and in 1884 was appointed Oxford University's first reader in the new field of anthropology. Later on he became its first professor in the discipline, enjoying a long career that extended all the way to World War I. Even so, none of his later writing matched the importance of *Primitive Culture*. Since this influential book presents his theory of animism in definitive form, it is the natural centerpiece for our examination of Tylor's views.

Primitive Culture

Background

The significance of Tylor's work is best appreciated within its historical and religious context. *Primitive Culture* was published in Victorian Britain at a time when thoughtfully religious people were wrestling with more than a few disturbing challenges to their faith. Since the early years of the century, a number of philosophers, historians, and naturalists in the field of geology found themselves drawn to the idea of very long-term development both in nature and human society. To some, the Earth and human life were beginning to look far older than the mere 6,000 years that theologians had computed from their readings in the biblical book of Genesis. The young Tylor was acquainted with these discussions and strongly disposed to think in similar terms.[4] Then, in 1859, Charles Darwin published his famous *Origin of Species*, perhaps the most important single book in science or any other field during the entire nineteenth century. His theory of evolution by natural selection struck many as contrary to the scriptures but irresistibly persuasive nonetheless. It was followed in 1871 by *The Descent of Man*, a work just as controversial because of its startling thesis about the animal origins of the human race. After the *Origin* the controversy over "evolution" was on almost everyone's lips, and the idea of development took an even stronger hold on Tylor's thought. Moreover, while these disputes raged, other thinkers were raising further troublesome questions about some of the most basic elements of Christian belief, including the historical accuracy of the Bible, the reality of miracles, and the divinity of Christ. Thus, when *Primitive Culture* appeared, with its new theory on the origin of *all* religious belief systems including the Christian one, it seemed to send yet another tremor of doubt through an already unsettled populace.

Tylor also drew upon new trends in research. He placed a pioneering emphasis on "ethnography" and "ethnology." These were the labels he and his associates gave to a distinctive new kind of study: the description (ethno*graphy*: from the Greek *grapho*, "to write") and scientific analysis (ethno*logy*: from the Greek *logos*, "study") of an individual society, culture, or racial group (from the Greek *ethnos*, a "nation" or "people") in all of its many component parts. They also used the term "anthropology," the scientific study of mankind (from the Greek *anthropos*, "man"). In addition, as a personally nonreligious man, Tylor refused to settle any question by an appeal to the divine authority of the Church or the Bible.

Prior to Tylor's day and still during much of his career, people of traditional views insisted that the origin of the Christian religion, at least, had to be understood as something miraculous in character, primarily because it had been revealed as such by God in the scriptures and affirmed in Church traditions.

Over against this orthodox view, Christian scholars of liberal inclinations pursued a more naturalistic understanding of things, but still in a manner quite supportive of traditional religious beliefs. They were led by Friedrich Max Müller, the learned and eloquent German whom we met in our opening pages.

Müller and Tylor shared the view that appeals to the supernatural should be left out of their discussions, but they disagreed strongly on the value of Tylor's ethnological research. Müller felt that the key to religion, myth, and other aspects of culture lay in language. He and other students of comparative philology (the forerunner of today's linguistics) had shown that the forms of speech in India and most of Europe belonged to a group of languages that originated with a single ancient people known as Aryans.[5] By comparing word parallels across these languages, they tried to show that the thought patterns of all these "Indo-European" Aryans were largely the same, and that, in this large portion of the human race, religion began when people reacted to the great and powerful workings of nature. In awesome natural processes like the sunrise and sunset, these ancient Aryans experienced a dim "perception of the infinite," the sense of a singular divinity behind the world. Unfortunately, when they expressed this feeling in their prayers and poems, their speech betrayed them. They personified things. The Greeks, for example, belong to the Aryan family; for them the word "Apollo" once simply meant "sun" and "Daphne," the "dawn." Over time these simple original meanings came to be forgotten; further, because the words were nouns with either masculine or feminine gender and because they were used with verbs expressing activity, the names for these natural objects came gradually to suggest personal beings. As Müller put it in a clever wordplay of his own, the *nomina* (Latin for "names") became *numina* (Latin for "gods"). Instead of noticing that every day as the dawn fades the sun rises, people began to tell fanciful tales of the goddess Daphne dying in the arms of the god Apollo. Through this process, which Müller called a "disease of language," words meant to describe nature and hint at the infinite power behind it degenerated into silly stories of many different gods, along with their misdeeds and comical misadventures. Instead of framing a pure, natural religion drawn from an inspired and beautiful perception of the infinite, people succumbed to the absurd stories of mythology.

Tylor, who had little training in languages, thought a few of Müller's ideas made sense and even incorporated them into his own. But he strongly disagreed with Müller's method of building a theory almost entirely on little more than language habits and word derivations. One needed more than mere verbal misunderstandings of events like the sunrise to explain the beginnings of the complex systems of belief and ritual that go under the name of religion—or even the tales of mythology, for that matter. One purpose of *Primitive Culture*, accordingly, was to present Tylor's decidedly different approach. Even without knowing the language, he felt, it was far better to study a given culture in *all* of its component parts—to explore the actual deeds, habits, ideas, and customs that language *describes*—than to make far-fetched guesses based only on the analogies and origins of certain words. Ethnology was clearly better than etymology.

Aims and Assumptions

It was against this backdrop—of evolutionary ideas at odds with the Bible and ethnologists opposed to philology—that Tylor introduced his book, announcing it in quite grand fashion as an attempt to pursue a new "science of culture." The proper subject of such an inquiry, he claimed, is not just language, but the whole network of elements that go into the making of what is commonly called human civilization. Ethnology assumes that any organized community or culture must be understood as a whole—as a complex network made up of knowledge and beliefs, of art and morals, tools and technology, language, laws, customs, legends, myths, and other components, all fused into a unitary system. Ethnology tries to find patterns, or laws, of human culture and expects these laws to be "as definite as those which govern the motion of waves" and "the growth of plants and animals."[6] Like the chemist or biologist, the ethnologist gathers facts, classifies and compares them, and searches for underlying principles to explain what has been found. Tylor was further convinced that when this work is properly done, and when the whole span of the human past is placed under observation, two great laws of culture come clearly into view. They are (1) the principle of psychic unity, or uniformity, within the human race and (2) the pattern of intellectual evolution, or improvement, over time.

With regard to psychic unity, Tylor maintained that throughout the world many things done or said by human beings at different times and places quite obviously resemble each other. Though some of these likenesses may have come from "diffusion"—from one people managing to teach another its good ideas—it is more often the case that different people discover the same ideas and invent the same customs quite independently. In other words, the similarities are not coincidental; they demonstrate the fundamental uniformity of the human mind. Unlike the "racialists" of his day, who saw fixed and unalterable differences separating various groups within the human race, Tylor and his associates contended that all human beings are in essence the same, especially with regard to their basic mental capacity. When in different cultures we observe very similar things, they may be presumed to be products of a single, universal rationality. With respect to logic—that is, the capacity to follow certain formal and necessary procedures of reasoning—humans of all places and times are the same. For Tylor, as one observer has put it, "all the world is a single country."[7]

But if this is true (and here the second principle plays its role), then whenever variations *do* occur, they cannot be evidence of a difference in kind, only of a difference in degree, or a change in the level of development. When two societies are seen to diverge, it is because one must be higher and the other lower on the scale of cultural evolution. Tylor thought evidence of these grades of development could be found everywhere. Because in all cultures each generation learns from the last, he believed he could trace through human history a long pattern of social and intellectual improvement, from the first savages, who hunted and gathered their food, through the cultures of the ancient world and the Middle Ages, which were based on farming, up to the modern era of trade, science, and industry. In history, each generation improves upon the last by standing on its shoulders and starting where the earlier has left off. In brief, civilization tells the story of "the ascent of man."

The Doctrine of "Survivals"

With his assumptions in place, Tylor proceeds to the evidence. We cannot speak of progress, he says, without noticing in some cultures certain things that do not look progressive at all. If a London physician prescribes surgery for an ailment while a doctor in a rural village advises bloodletting, we can hardly say that all of modern English medicine is progressive. We must account also for what is backward. Tylor does so by outlining his much-discussed "doctrine of survivals."[8] He notes that not all cultures and not all things in any one culture evolve at the same pace. Some practices, fitting in their day, linger long after the march of progress has passed them by. Among these are curious pastimes, quaint customs, folklore, folk medicine, and assorted superstitions found in almost every sphere of human endeavor. For example, no serious modern hunter would still use a bow and arrow to kill game, but the skills of archery are still with us—now as a sport or hobby. Archery "survives" from a bygone age when hunting game was crucial to sustaining life. Again, nothing is more common than to give a blessing after a sneeze; it seems trivial. Yet this was once a serious gesture, governed by the belief that at that very moment a spirit, or demon, had come out of the body. Today the blessing survives, but as a habitual response whose original intent has been long forgotten. Again, in many lands, people urge, strangely, that one should never try to save a drowning person. Though to us such advice seems cruel and selfish, it was in earlier cultures perfectly rational, for it was widely held that the river or sea, deprived of its almost captured victim, would take revenge on the very person who made the rescue! Tylor observes that the record of human history is filled with superstitions such as these, which show that while the stream of social evolution is real and its current strong, a trail of cultural "leftovers" floats in its wake.

If the principle of evolution shows why survivals exist, then it is the companion principle of uniformity that enables us to understand and explain them. Since—regardless of race, language, or culture—all human beings reason the same, we can always enter the minds of people in other cultures, even though the level of their knowledge may be very different from our own. Modern primitives, like ancient peoples, know less than we do and fail to test their opinions sufficiently, but they still think with the same mental mechanism as ours. So even amid great differences, uniformity of the mind unites the human race.

Aspects of Human Culture

For Tylor the connection between basic rational thinking and social evolution is apparent in all aspects of a culture if we only take time to look at them closely enough. He furnishes as a prime example the use of magic, which is common everywhere among primitive peoples. Magic is based upon the association of ideas, a tendency that "lies at the very foundation of human reason."[9] If somehow in thought people can connect one idea with another, then their logic moves them to find the same connection in reality. Primitive people believe that, even at a distance, they can hurt or heal others just by acting on a fingernail, a lock of hair, a piece of clothing, or anything else that has been in contact with their persons. Or they think that a symbolic resemblance matters. Some tribal peoples imagine that because certain diseases tint the skin yellow and because gold is of the same color, jaundice in the body can be cured with a golden ring. Others who practice primitive agriculture have been known to torture human victims in the belief that their tears of pain will bring showers of rain to the fields. To us such actions may seem stupid or cruel; to believers in magic, they are rational efforts to influence the world.

Tylor finds the same pattern of rationality in two of humanity's most basic and significant accomplishments: the development of language and discovery of mathematics. In each case, the process starts simply, with single words that mimic the sounds of nature and with counting systems based on fingers and toes. Over time, these concepts are slowly built up to produce the very complicated systems of speech and number that today we master even in childhood and apply with ease in everyday affairs. Across the long span of history, Tylor explains, this process has required countless trials and ended in many errors, but through them all the line of progress makes itself visible. Even mythology, that storehouse of seemingly irrational ideas and amusing stories, is governed by the logic of rational thinking. Myths arise from the natural tendency to "clothe every idea in a concrete shape, and whether created by primitives of the remote past or those of modern times, they tend to follow orderly laws of development."[10] Myths originate in the logical association of ideas. They account for the facts of nature and life with the aid of analogies and comparisons, as when the Samoans recall the ancient battle of the plantains and bananas to explain why the winners now grow upright while the losers hang down their heads. In the same vein, a myth may connect suitable imaginary events to the lives of legendary or historical figures; it may grow logically out of a play on words; or it may try, through stories, to teach a moral lesson. In some cases—and here Tylor includes an idea of Müller's—myths arise under the influence of language, which has gender, and out of the natural inclination to make analogies between human activities and processes in nature. If the noise of a storm sounds like an angry human outburst and rainfall suggests tears of sorrow, it is easy to see how, in myth, these great forces of nature lend themselves to tales in which their activities are made to resemble those of animals and human beings. Thus earthquakes are attributed by the Scandinavians to the underground writhings of their god Loki, by the Greeks to the struggles of Prometheus, and by Caribbean peoples to the dancing of Mother Earth. Though partly works of the imagination, these personifications are just as clearly exercises in rational thought; they are meant to explain how things happen. When primitives animate the sun, moon, or stars, they honestly think of these objects as having personal characteristics.

The Origin of Religion

Tylor's comments on myth are important, for in his eyes they mark the path of inquiry that must also be followed in searching for the origin of religion. He recognizes, of course, that we cannot explain something unless we know what it is; so religion must first be defined. He further observes that we cannot casually follow the natural impulse to describe religion simply as belief in God, though that is what his mostly Christian readers might want to do. That approach would exclude a large portion of the human race—people who are plainly religious but believe in more and other gods than do Christians and Jews. He therefore proposes, as a more suitable place to start, his own minimal definition: religion is "belief in spiritual beings."[11] This formula, which others, following Tylor, have adopted as well, has the merit of being simple, straightforward, and suitably wide in scope. For though we can find other similarities, Tylor feels the one characteristic shared by all religions, great or small, ancient or modern, is the belief in spirits who think, act, and feel like human persons. The essence of religion, like mythology, seems to be animism (from the Latin *anima*, meaning "spirit")—the belief in living, personal powers behind all things. Animism further is a very old form of thought, which is found throughout the entire history of the human race. So, Tylor suggests, if we truly wish to explain religion, the question we must answer is this: How and why did the human race first come to believe that such things as spiritual beings actually exist?

Asking this question is easy; answering it is another matter. Devout people will want to say that they believe in a spiritual being, such as God, because that being has actually spoken to them, supernaturally, through the Bible or the Quran or some other scripture. For Tylor, however, as for Müller, appeals to divine revelation are not acceptable. Such statements may be pleasing as personal confessions, but they are not science. He insists that any account of how a human being, or the whole human race, came to believe in spiritual beings must appeal only to natural causes, only to considerations of the kind that scientists and historians would use in explaining an occurrence of any sort, nonreligious as well as religious. We must presume that early peoples acquired their first religious ideas through the same reasoning process they applied to other aspects of their lives. Like us, they simply observed their world and tried to explain it.

What observations, then, did these primitives make? And what explanations did they choose? Tylor at this point peers backward, deep into prehistoric times, to reconstruct the thoughts of the very first human beings:

> It seems as though thinking men, as yet at a low level of culture, were deeply impressed by two groups of biological problems. In the first place, what is it that makes a difference between a living body and a dead one; what causes waking, sleep, trance, disease, death? In the second place, what are those human shapes which appear in dreams and visions? Looking at these two groups of phenomena, the ancient savage philosophers probably made their first step by the obvious inference that every man has two things belonging to him, namely, a life and a phantom as being its image or second self; both, also, are perceived to be things separable from the body. . . . The second step would seem also easy for savages to make, seeing how extremely difficult civilized men have found it to unmake. It is merely to combine the life and the phantom . . . the result is that well-known conception . . . the personal soul, or spirit.[12]

From their vivid encounters with both death and dreams, early peoples reasoned first to a simple theory of their own lives: that each of us is animated by a soul, a spiritual principle. They thought of this soul as "a thin, unsubstantial human image, in its nature a sort of vapour, film, or shadow; the cause of life and thought in the individual it animates."[13] From this premise, they next reasoned, as we all do, by analogy and extension. If the concept of a soul explains the movements, activities, and changes of the human person, why should it not also be applied more widely to explain the rest of the natural world? Why should not plants and trees, the rivers, winds, and animals, even the stars and planets also be moved by souls? Further, since souls are separable from the objects they animate, why should there not also be, behind the visible scene of nature, beings who do not even need to be connected to physical objects—why not spirits, pure and simple? If there are souls in humans, could there not also be such powerful beings as demons and angels who have no necessary attachment to normal physical objects, though they certainly can enter and "possess" them if they wish? Last, and above all, could there not perhaps be certain supreme spirits, the beings we call gods?

Through this natural, almost childlike chain of reasoning, early humans arrived at their first religious beliefs. Like their myths, their religious teachings arose from a rational effort to explain how nature worked. From this perspective, all seemed quite clear: as souls animate persons, so spirits must animate the world.

Tylor further argues that the value of this animistic theory to primitive peoples is apparent from the great variety of early beliefs and customs it could readily explain. Doctrines of a future life provide an example. In Oriental cultures there is widespread belief in reincarnation, while in religions of the Western world, like Christianity and Islam, there are the doctrines of resurrection and immortality of the soul. Animism explains both as ways of extending the life of the soul beyond the death of the body. Being separable from the flesh, the soul has an afterlife and destiny of its own. Animism also explains why sacred objects and trinkets—things called "fetishes"—are important to primitives. Such people are not "idol-worshippers," as narrow-minded Christian missionaries used to describe them. They do not worship sticks and stones; they adore the "anima" within, the spirit that—not wholly unlike the god of Christians themselves—gives the wood of the stick or substance of the stone its life and power. Knowing the nature of animism, we can also make sense of tribal medicine. When a man shakes uncontrollably with fever, he knows that he does not himself do this; he is "possessed" by a demon within. To be cured, he needs an exorcism, not a medicine. The evil spirit must be driven out.

Throughout most of the entire second volume of *Primitive Culture*, Tylor fills his pages with examples to illustrate the full scope and scale of animism in earlier centuries of human civilization. It was a system that spread worldwide, becoming the first "general philosophy of man and nature" ever devised.[14] As it was absorbed by a tribe or clan or culture, it spread into every aspect of daily life. If one asks why, across almost all cultures, the gods have human personalities, the answer is that they are spirits modeled on the souls of human persons. If we want to know why gifts are given to the dead at primitive funerals and why the services, especially for great and powerful men, sometimes even include human sacrifice, animism gives the answers. The gifts provide support for the soul in its new residence beyond the grave; the sacrifices furnish the king or prince with the souls of servants to wait upon him in the realm of death, just as they did in life. Why do the Indians of America talk to animals as they would to each other? Because, like themselves, animals too have souls. Why does the water move, or the tree grow? Because nature spirits inhabit them. Why does the medicine man fast or use drugs? To qualify himself "for intercourse with the . . . ghosts, from whom he is to obtain direction in his craft."[15]

In this systematic, sequential fashion, with scores of examples at his disposal, Tylor explores the whole range of primitive life, thought, and custom. At each point he shows how the doctrine of animism makes sense of ideas and behaviors that otherwise would strike us as nothing more than irrational and incomprehensible nonsense.

The Growth of Religious Thought

Tylor further explains that once these spiritual ideas acquired their grip on the minds of ancient peoples, they did not remain in a fixed form. Like everything else in history, animism exhibits growth and development. At first people think of individual spirits as small and specific, associated with each tree, river, or animal they happen to see. Later on, their power widens. The spirit of one tree grows in power to become the spirit of the forest or of trees in general. In time, that same spirit is gradually considered separable from the object it controls, acquiring its own identity and character. At this stage, when people worship, say, the goddess of the forest, they recognize the woodlands as her home, but they know she can also leave this home if she wishes. Among the very earliest Greeks, for example, Poseidon was at first simply the spirit of the "divine sea"; later he acquired his trident, beard, and distinctive character, so that by the time of the poet Homer, he had become a mighty and personal deity who could leave the sea and travel swiftly to Mount Olympus when Zeus assembled the gods in council.

Interestingly, Tylor approaches this later growth of a belief in the personal gods of mythology much the way Max Müller does, though he refuses to see it as arising from some unfortunate disease of language. In the animistic view, the more complex polytheism that we see among the Greeks belongs to an age of cultural progress rather than linguistic decay. From about the time of Homer forward, a new era of civilization—Tylor calls it the "barbaric" stage—takes over from the earlier "savage" stage. In the savage era, people hunted, gathered, lived in small clans, and never got beyond their first simple ideas of spirits. With the coming of the barbaric age, we find agriculture, cities, and literacy—all the main elements of the great civilizations built by the Babylonians, Greeks and Romans, native Americans, Hindus, and Chinese. In these "higher" cultures, there are divisions of labor and complex structures of power and authority, and their religions show the same characteristics. We find the spirits of local trees and rivers on one level, while above them stand the much greater spirits of the wind, rain, and sun. The local spirit of the river can do nothing about it if the god of the sun should decide to bake dry the streams that feed him or the goddess of rain should transform him into a raging flood. Just as a king and council of nobles rule their subjects, so the sun (or Heaven) as king and the Earth as queen rule the natural world with the wind, rain, and seasons as their powerful agents or advisers.

Such complex polytheistic systems are quite typical of the barbaric age. They reach their highest form, however, when they are organized in such a way that one god, one supreme being, stands at the top of the divine society. And gradually, by different paths, most civilizations do move to this last, highest stage of animism—belief in one supreme divinity. Needless to say, Judaism and Christianity are the leading examples of the last stage. Monotheism forms the logical end to the process of development that began in the dark mists of prehistory, when the man whom Tylor calls the first "savage philosopher" concluded that souls like his own must animate the world around him.

The Decline of Animism and Progress of Thought

In one sense the story of animism is an encouraging one. Religion can be seen to have gradually evolved upward from the first primitive belief in the spirits of the trees and rocks to the later high plain of monotheism and ethics exhibited in Judaism and Christianity. Higher civilization correlates with "higher religions." But that is not the full story. A clear-eyed look at animism and its history in the dry light of science suggests a less cheerful view. Whatever progress we find has been severely limited. For however great its spread and wide its appeal through history, we cannot forget that animism at bottom is a grand mistake. As we all know, the world is *not* animated by invisible spirits. As any modern geologist can tell us, rocks do *not* have phantoms within them. Any botanist can explain that plants are *not* moved to grow by some secret *anima* in their stem. Science shows that the real sun and sea owe nothing to the adventures of Apollo and Poseidon, that plants grow by the reactions of chemicals within their fibers, and that the wind and water are only names for powerful flows of molecules governed by iron laws of cause and effect.

In its time, the animist explanation of things was reasonable enough. But the better methods of today's science show us that the reasoning of early peoples has always had its element of unreason as well. Though they can think rationally, one must also note that primitives think rationally only as children do. Savages, Tylor reminds us, are

> exceedingly ignorant as regards both physical and mental knowledge; want of discipline makes their opinions crude and their action ineffective . . . the tyranny of tradition at every step imposes upon them . . . much of what they believe to be true, must be set down as false.[16]

It follows from this that whereas the course of reason once led people naturally toward the system of animism, in the modern era, the age of science, that same course of reason ought now to lead away from it. Intellectual progress today must be measured by an opposite movement—the retreat of animist theory from all of those very realms of life it was once thought to explain. Gradually, but none the less certainly, the falsehoods of savage and barbaric peoples must withdraw before the spreading truths of the sciences. In sphere after sphere of nature, animist spirits and deities must bow and defer to modern science's impersonal causes and effects. In the modern era, religion's advance, like that of its close friends magic and myth, "has been checked by science, it is dying of weights and measures, of proportions and specimens."[17] We now understand our world only to the degree that we can pull ourselves away from animism's powerful but misguided embrace. A few of its ethical principles may linger as still useful, but its gods must die and disappear.

In the end, then, Tylor's theory provides a mixed portrait of religion and its development. As an effort of early peoples to understand the world, as a response to its mysteries and uncertain events, animistic religion presents a natural parallel to science. Both are inspired by the human search for understanding—the deep urge to know just how things work. But clearly religion is earlier, more primitive, less effective than science. Belief in spiritual beings represents a natural stage in the evolution of human reason, but it is not the end stage, and it is certainly no longer the most rational response to the world now that the program and methods of empirical science have come our way. Like the other odd customs and superstitions people are unwilling to part with, religion is now a "survival." In that connection, Tylor insists that the double mission of ethnology, "the reformer's science," requires not only that it point the way of progress but that it also take on "the harsher task" of clearing away the clutter of animism that still persists. Destined to disappear, religion can only slow the progress of mind for those who persist, unwisely, in clinging to its comforts. In the final analysis, animist ideas belong properly to the childhood of the human race, not to its maturity. And having entered adulthood, we must put away childish things.

Further on, we can examine and assess this theory, along with the judgment on the future of religion that follows from it. But first, we need to consider how these ideas were adopted and further developed in the work of James Frazer, Tylor's most famous and influential disciple.

J. G. Frazer

Early in his career, while still a promising young student in classics at Cambridge University, James George Frazer became a "convert" to Tylor's ideas and methods. Thereafter, he devoted immense effort to anthropological research, and through the rest of his long life, he promoted his own amplified version of the animistic theory. The centerpiece of Frazer's many labors was *The Golden Bough* (1890–1915), a monumental study of primitive customs and beliefs. As we shall see in chapters to come, this important book has exercised a lasting influence on subsequent thinking about religion. More than that, in the early years of the twentieth century it left a large imprint on almost every field of modern thought, from anthropology and history to literature, philosophy, sociology, and even natural science.[18]

Like Tylor, Frazer came from a Protestant Christian family, but his was not a home of liberal, affluent Quakers.[19] Born on New Year's Day, 1854, in Glasgow, Scotland, he was raised by stern and devout Scottish Presbyterian parents. His father's daily habit of reading the Bible in family worship left him steeped in its sacred stories and permanently affected by the beautiful imagery and the stately rhythms of its language. Of course, the truth of the Bible—as well as the Calvinist theology of his parents—was quite another matter. Frazer rejected both. Early in life he took the stance of an atheist, or at least an agnostic, in regard not only to Christian beliefs, but any religion. For him, religion was to be always an interest but never a creed. During the years of his early schooling, he much preferred to immerse himself in the non-Christian world of ancient Greek and Roman civilization. He studied classical languages intensively, winning multiple prizes in Latin and Greek at his preparatory school and at Glasgow University while later earning a scholarship to Trinity College, Cambridge. Eventually he became a fellow of Trinity, where he was to marry a very protective spouse, remain childless, and live the quiet, private life of a university don for the rest of his days. If ever a man fit the description of an "ivory tower" scholar, it was James Frazer.

While at Cambridge, Frazer pursued his first interest: classical literature. He wrote on the philosopher Plato and began to translate the writings of the ancient Greek traveler Pausanias, who had compiled a rich record of Greek legend, folklore, and popular custom. Pausanias would prove useful in considering primitive religion.

At just about the time he was starting his work on Pausanias, two unexpected encounters changed the course of Frazer's thought—as well as his career. While on a walking tour, a friend gave him a copy of *Primitive Culture*. As he began to read, he was attracted at once to Tylor's account of animism and its importance to primitive thought. Just as important, Frazer found his eyes suddenly opened to the possibilities of anthropological research and the use of the comparative method. The second encounter was not with a book but a person. In 1883, the very same year that he came upon Tylor's work, Frazer met William Robertson Smith (1846–1894), a brilliant and controversial Scottish biblical scholar, who soon became his mentor and very close friend.[20] Intellectually, Smith was a perfect soulmate. Like Frazer, he was fascinated by the way in which anthropology, through its study of modern tribal societies, could shed light on an ancient subject, in his case the story of the ancient Israelites as told in the Bible. Ahead of his time, Smith actually traveled to Arabia to observe the customs of desert communities and apply them in his research. In particular, he felt that the use of "totems" by these tribal peoples was extremely important. Totem use was associated with the tribal custom of dividing into different clans, or kinship groups. Each of these clans commonly attached itself to a specific animal (or occasionally a plant), which it recognized as its totem, according it worship as a kind of divinity. Totemism was also linked to exogamy, the practice of marrying only "outside" the clan. If within a large tribe a man belonged, say, to the smaller clan of the bear, he was obliged to marry only a woman from another clan (say, of the eagle or deer) and not from his own totem group. In addition, because the totem was sacred, members of the clan were not allowed to kill or eat their chosen animal—except (as Smith supposed, though there was no evidence) on certain special occasions, when the rule might have been purposely broken, perhaps for some ceremonial totem animal sacrifice. In *The Religion of the Semites* (1890), his most important book, Smith drew on his observations in Arabia and on Tylor's concept of evolutionary survivals to argue that ancient Hebrew practices, especially their sacrifices, fit with uncanny precision into the category of tribal totemism that he observed in modern Arabia.

Frazer, for his part, was captivated by both the originality of Smith's ideas and the intellectual excitement that came through his personality in almost every scholarly conversation. In return, Smith, who at this very moment was editing the *Encyclopaedia Britannica*, wisely used his new position to encourage his friend. He asked Frazer to write the articles on the subjects of "totem" and "taboo." Frazer accepted, so long as Smith would help. It was not long before Frazer's work in preparing these articles won him over fully to the anthropological perspective—and laid the groundwork for most of his later research. Soon the two men were sharing research on primitive customs and beliefs, each relying on the other in almost equal measure.

The Golden Bough

As he began his turn to anthropology, Frazer did not leave his classical studies behind. His aim was still to read the Greeks and Romans, but now with an eye also on anthropology, looking for traces of the older, primitive world behind the cultivated poetry, drama, and philosophical writings of the classical authors. Helped by Tylor's doctrine of survivals, he felt that classical civilization could be seen with new a clarity if one noticed the earlier primitive ideas and habits that persisted within it. He was convinced that a blend of classics and anthropology, of the well worn and the as yet untried, offered the prospect of a virtual revolution in understanding the ancient world. This perspective was to guide the broad research project that would become *The Golden Bough*. The publication of this ever-expanding book occupied Frazer for most of his adult years and became his definitive statement on the origin and nature of religion. In time, *The Golden Bough* grew to three editions and twelve thick volumes, requiring over twenty-five years of Frazer's long days in his study to bring to completion. It was first published in two volumes in 1890. A second, three-volume edition appeared in 1900. New installments were added regularly until it reached its full length in 1915. By then, what began as a book had ended as an encyclopedia. Fortunately for us, in 1922 Frazer abridged *The Golden Bough* into one very long single volume; in the discussion that follows, we can take advantage of this helpful shorter version.[21]

The Golden Bough begins like a good mystery. It offers a riddle, some tantalizing clues, and a striking description of long-forgotten scenes and events. Frazer explains that along the Appian Way, the ancient road that runs from Rome to the villages of central Italy, there is a small town named Aricia; near it, in a wooded grove by a lake called Nemi, stands the ruin of a temple dedicated by the Romans to Diana, goddess of the hunt, as well as of both fertility and childbirth. In the happy days of the empire, this lakeside shrine with its woodland was both a country resort and a place of pilgrimage. Citizens of Rome traveled often to the site, especially at midsummer, to celebrate a yearly festival of fire. It was to all appearances a restful, civilized, and lovely place. But the woods at the lakeshore also held a secret. The Roman poets told of a second god, Virbius, who was also worshipped at the temple. He was sometimes identified with the young Greek hero Hippolytus, who, according to other myths, had been murdered by one of the gods in a fit of anger, only to be restored to life by Diana, who then chose to hide him here at her temple. Virbius was represented by a very mysterious figure, a man who was understood actually to live in the woods and was said to be both a priest and a king. He took it as his duty to keep constant watch not only over Diana's temple but also over a sacred tree that grew in the forest—an oak with a distinctive yellow branch, or "golden bough." The man bore the title Rex Nemorensis, "Nemi's King of the Wood." Though obviously human, this king was thought also to be a god; he was at once both the divine lover of the goddess Diana and the animating spirit of the sacred oak tree near which he stood guard.

Strange as this King of the Wood himself may seem, the way in which he acquired his position was still stranger. It came by way of a murder. Legend held that this priest-king had taken over the wood by putting to death the previous one, and that he too would keep his power only as long as he remained vigilant and strong, ready in a moment to defend his very life against other would-be kings who might try to seize his place and power. To keep his life and rule, the king had to walk the temple woods constantly, sword in hand, waiting for the approach of any would-be assailant. Should his guard fail or his strength weaken, an intruder might at any moment break through, duel the king to his death, and tear away the golden bough, which then entitled the victor to both the sexual favors of the goddess Diana and the priestly rule of the woodland. On the victor also, however, fell the same wearying burden of vigilant self-defense—the need to guard the oak without rest and to search the forest for the threatening form of any new rival who might approach, ready to kill, and eager himself to become the next King of the Wood.

With an opening scene such as this, so haunted with mystery and hidden danger, curious readers found it hard to resist following Frazer into the long trail of his narrative. But the reason for all of this drama was not just the wish to tell an unusual story. Frazer's purpose was rather to set the stage for his study by unfolding a single, sharp contrast—one that discloses the outline of an earlier, more brutal state of humanity lying just below the surface of the societies we like to think of as civilized. How, he asks, could there be a place as beautiful as the grove at Nemi, a temple and grounds so loved by visitors for its peace and healing renewal, yet at the same time so steeped in a heritage of savage violence? How is it that a center given over to the comforts of religion could be the stage for a ritual murder? That is a riddle we should very much like to see explained. In searching for solutions Frazer tells us that we will get nowhere if we keep only to the evidence available from the days of classical Greek and Roman civilization. The pastimes of cultivated Romans who visited Diana's temple offer no clues to explain the shadowy, foreboding personage of the King of the Wood. To account for such a figure, we must look elsewhere—into the deeper prehistoric past, when savage ancestors of the Romans walked the very same woods and shores centuries before Diana's temple was ever built. If it should be that among these much earlier peoples we can find an obscure custom or belief that continued down to Roman times, if we should discover one of Tylor's "survivals," then we might very well have a way to identify the King of the Wood and solve his deadly mystery. Doing so, however, requires a great deal of searching and comparing, for prehistoric peoples have left us no documents. The only thing we can do is reach out everywhere into the folklore, legends, and practices of the most primitive peoples we know to see if among them there can be found any old patterns or traditions into which the Roman legends may fit. If we can penetrate the system of primitive ideas that lies behind it, the dark riddle of the King of the Wood and his murder can perhaps be understood. But that task is not uncomplicated. It turns out that primitive thinking (and here Frazer somewhat departs from Tylor) is governed by two quite different systems of ideas: the one is magic, the other religion. Understanding both of these, and the connection between them, is the key that gives entry to the primitive mind.

Magic and Religion

Once introduced, the subjects of magic and religion become a central theme of *The Golden Bough*, and though Frazer does finally return to it, the mystery of the King of the Wood recedes into the background. *A Study in Magic and Religion* is in fact the subtitle given to the book in its second edition. To appreciate the importance of these enterprises to primitive peoples, we must notice a fundamental fact of early human life, whether lived in Diana's woodland or any other place on the globe. It centered on the struggle to survive. Hunters needed animals to kill; farmers needed the sun and suitable rains for their crops. Whenever natural circumstances did not accommodate these needs, primitive peoples, being capable of thought, made every effort they could to understand the world and change it. The very first of these efforts took the form of magic. Frazer's full name for it is "sympathetic magic," since the primitive mind assumes that nature works by sympathies, or influences. In words that closely resemble Tylor's, he explains that "savages" (like Tylor, he preferred this word for prehistoric peoples) always suppose that when two things can in some way be mentally associated—when to the mind they appear "sympathetic"—they must also be physically associated in the outside world. Mental connections mirror physical ones. Going beyond Tylor, however, he finds in magic something more systematic, and even "scientific," than his mentor did. He points out that the main connections made by the sympathetic magician are basically of two types: imitative, the magic that connects things on the principle of similarity; and contagious, the magic of contact, which connects on the principle of attachment. In the one case, we might say "like affects like," in the other, "part affects part." When Russian peasants pour water through a screen in a time of drought, they imagine that because the filtered falling water *looks* like a rain shower, sprinkling of this sort will actually force rain to fall from the sky. When a voodoo priest pushes a pin through the heart of a doll decorated with the fingernails and hair of his enemy, he imagines that merely by contact—by contagious transmission—he can bring death to his victim.

Frazer explains that evidence of this magical thinking can be multiplied in countless examples drawn from primitive life around the globe, and he supplies them in great number. When, as traders report, the Pawnee Indians touched the blood of a sacrificed maiden to their field tools, they firmly believed that, merely by contact, its life-giving power would be transferred to their seeds of maize. When drought strikes certain villages of India, the people dress up a boy in leaves, name him the Rain King, and at each house sprinkle him with water, all in the belief that this ritual will bring the rains, making green plants to grow again. When the Indians of South America bury lighted sticks in the ground during an eclipse of the moon, they believe the darkening of its fire will also put out all fires on earth, unless some, at least, are hidden from its influence. In each of these cases, and many, many others that he cites, Frazer shows how simple peoples everywhere assume that nature operates on the principles of imitation and contact. They think of these principles as constant, universal, and unbreakable—as firm and certain as any modern scientific law of cause and effect. In India, when the Brahmin priest makes his morning offering to the sun, he firmly believes it will not rise without his ritual. In ancient Egypt, the Pharaoh, who represented the sun, routinely made a solemn journey around the temple to ensure that the real sun would complete its daily journey as well. Magic is thus built on the assumption that once a proper ritual or action is completed, its natural effects *must* occur as prescribed. Such rites form a kind of science for primitive peoples. They offer knowledge of the natural world and control of its processes.

Frazer also goes beyond Tylor, who tends to speak of magical knowledge as its own reward, in emphasizing the social power that accrues to people who have command of the magical art. It is not by accident that in primitive cultures the person who can claim mastery of its techniques—whether called a magician, medicine man, or witch doctor—routinely holds a position of considerable prestige and power. Usually the magician rises to the role of king, since he best knows how to control the natural world for the good of the tribe or for the evil of its enemies. Evidence from around the globe shows that among tribal peoples, nothing is more common than for the magician to be also the village chieftain or king.

Of course the power that magical skills confer ought not blind us to a quite fundamental problem: Magic may look like science, but it is a false science. Primitives are deceived, but moderns are not. As every modern person certainly knows, the laws of imitation and contact do not apply to the real world. Magic cannot work. The primitive magician, for all his shrewd magical skills, is simply wrong. The real world does not operate by the pattern of sympathies and similarities he mistakenly applies to it. Over time, therefore, the more critical and thoughtful minds even in primitive communities draw the reasonable conclusion that magic is, at bottom, nonsense. The magician can try to explain away failures or even take the blame upon himself, but the facts cry out loudly that it is the system, not the man, that is mistaken. The general recognition of that failure is for Frazer a momentous development in the history of human thought; for as magic declines, religion comes to fill its place.

Religion follows a path quite different from that of magic. Here we may recall that Tylor, after defining religion as belief in spiritual beings, found it generally to resemble magic, both being built upon the uncritical association of ideas. Frazer is perfectly content with Tylor's definition of religion, but he is more interested in the contrasts than the similarities it shows with magic. For him the interesting thing about religion is precisely its rejection of the principles of magic. Instead of magical laws of contact and imitation, religious people claim that the real powers behind the natural world are not principles at all; they are personalities—the supernatural beings we call the gods. Accordingly, when truly religious people want to control or change the course of nature, they do not normally use magical spells but rather prayers and pleadings addressed to their favorite god or goddess. Just as if they were dealing with another human person, they ask favors, plead for help, call down revenge, and make vows of love, loyalty, or obedience. These things are crucially important, for the personalities of the gods control nature; it is their anger that can start a storm, their favor that can save a life, their compassion that can calm a troubled sea. For Frazer, wherever there is belief in these supernatural beings and wherever there are human efforts to win their help by prayers or rituals, we have moved out of the realm of magic and into that of religion.

In addition, and though it may not seem so at first, this turn to religion should be read as a sign of progress because it improves on magic and marks an intellectual advance for the human race. Why? For the simple reason that religious explanations are better than magical ones in describing the world as we actually experience it. Magic, we must recognize, asserts laws that are impersonal, constant, and universal. If the rain ritual is done correctly, rain *must* actually come; the rules of imitation and contact do not allow exceptions. Religion is quite different. From the start it never claims to have iron-clad principles of explanation. To the contrary, it confesses that the world is in the hands of the gods, who control nature's forces for *their* interests, not ours. Moreover, the gods are many, with different personalities and often competing aims and agendas. We worship the gods, we pray and sacrifice to them in the hope that they will bring rain, or give us children, or heal the sick, but we cannot force them to do these things. Religion offers no guarantees. And yet as Frazer sees it, this very uncertainty is in its way commendable. Is it not a fact that most of nature's processes, great and small, *do* fall outside our control? To offer prayers that sometimes are answered and sometimes are not, to ask favors that are granted one day and denied the next—is not such a view of the world, which places all things under the control of great and powerful beings beyond ourselves, very close to the facts of our existence as we actually find them? Does it not actually fit far better than magic to life as we actually encounter it, filled with both its surprise pleasures and unexpected misfortunes? Like the gods, the world sometimes gives us what we want—and sometimes it does not.

Magic, Religion, and the Divinity of Kings

With the coming of religion, there also appear certain related changes in society. Gradually, the old magician-king gives way to the new priest-king, whose power lies in the new religious type of thought—specifically, in his ability to communicate with the gods or, just as often, in possessing a kind of divinity himself. Divine kings are as natural to the age of religion as magician-kings are to the age of magic, though we ought not to consider this transition between the two periods to have been sharp or sudden. Frazer reminds us that cultures evolve slowly and often unevenly through time. Even as they were gradually turning over the control of the natural processes from the principles of magic to the personalities of the gods, primitive peoples usually combined the two systems. Even as they embraced the gods, they still reserved a place for magic; in fact, they often used magic *on* the gods, trying, as it were, to force them to act favorably on human requests. Frazer finds magic and religion to have been mixed so often and in so many cultures around the world that, in the mountains of evidence he supplies, he scarcely even tries to disentangle the two.

Examples of magic and religion in combination play a key role in some of Frazer's most important discussions. Ritual prostitution is an instance. Primitive people, he says, believe that if the sexual encounter reproduces human life, a ritual act of intercourse performed in the house of the gods will, by the law of imitation, actually *compel* the divine Sky Father and Earth Mother to do the same. With that, the rains will come, and crops will grow for another season. Royal personages are seen in a similar light. While many tribal societies think of their king in religious terms, as a god, they conceive of his powers and his relation to the tribe as magical. The king is seen as the divine center of the world. His mere words become law. From his person an energy radiates in all directions, so that any of his actions, or any change in his state of being, can affect the whole balance of the natural order and the whole life of the tribe. At the same time, it should be noted that this divine power is more magical than personal in nature—so thoroughly magical, in fact, that even the king himself must bow to it. Frazer notes how some African peoples do not allow the king to leave his house, because the mere movement of his body would affect the weather. In ancient Ireland, kings were forbidden to be in a certain town at sunrise or in another on Wednesdays or to sail their ships on certain Mondays—all for fear of the effects of their magical powers on specific places at specific times.

The magical charge carried by the person of the king also explains why monarchs are often surrounded by taboos—sacred prohibitions meant as life preservers for souls. In some cases, the king may not be allowed to touch certain persons or things because of the effect his powers may have on them; in others, persons must avoid the king for just the opposite reason—because of the ill effects *they* may have on *his* use of his powers. Even into recent times, the emperor of Japan, the divine Mikado, was seen as so filled with magical power that his feet were not allowed to touch the ground.

In more general terms primitive peoples often insist that because the king is a god, measures must be taken to preserve his divine energy, transferring it to a new person whenever he shows signs of sickness, injury, or age. Nothing was more startling to Victorian readers of *The Golden Bough* than the evidence it furnished to show that when in some tribal cultures kings age or grow ill, they must be ritually put to death, so that their divine spirit can be conveyed in full strength to a new ruler. Hardly less shocking were its demonstrations that to the primitive mind, such executions are not immoral acts of cruelty; they are sacred acts of magical necessity. This was true, moreover, even though the form of the ritual was subject to change. Since many kings did not relish the prospect of being executed, often a slave or captive, an animal, an image, or even a son was put forward as the king's substitute. Indeed, Frazer at one point suggests that the Jewish festival of Purim and the Christian remembrance of Christ's crucifixion at Passover both fall into the category of these royal substitutions. It is of interest, he suggests, that both involve the sacrifice of a "pretend" king and both show a similar intent: to preserve by magical transfer the power of the divine life.[22]

The Gods of Vegetation

Of all the places where magic and religion converge, none is for Frazer more common than the great, seasonal cults of vegetation and agriculture that are found so widely around the world. Worship of vegetation gods like Osiris, Tammuz, Attis, and Adonis was widespread not only in the ancient civilizations of Egypt, Greece, and Rome but almost everywhere that people practiced the arts of agriculture. These agrarian cults were steeped in symbols of sexuality and the cycle of birth and death. Ancient Cyprus provides an instance. There the god Adonis was routinely paired with the goddess Aphrodite/Astarte, whose rituals included prostitution and a bizarre sexual law requiring all virgins to sleep with a complete stranger at the temple before their marriage. Strange as it may seem, says Frazer, it was not perversion that inspired this practice but the sacred rules of imitative magic. The purpose of the rite was to compel the gods also to mate, so that all of nature could be reborn.

Rituals of death and rebirth served a similar purpose. In the cult of Attis, the myth that recounted the bloody death of the god had to be reenacted each year because it ensured the death of the crop at harvest time; then each spring the god was to be ritually reborn, so the plants could once again come to life and grow. As Frazer explains it, worshippers in these religions "thought that by performing certain magical rites they could aid the god who was the principle of life, in his struggle with the opposing principle of death. They imagined that they could recruit his failing energies and even raise him from the dead."[23] When the rites were performed, all of nature could be expected to benefit from the return of life and growth. In Egyptian traditions, the god Osiris clearly was a personification of the grain; the story of how, after death, his mangled body was scattered across the land offers a mythical counterpart to the process of planting, in which dead seeds are sown across the fields, later to be reborn and rise as growing plants. For nearly all who participate in these religious cults, the sacrifice of some sacred animal identified with a deity, such as the bull of Dionysus, is a way of pushing the gods, and thus the crops, forward in their natural cycle. Similarly, when primitives sacrifice an actual human king as a divinity, that horrible rite mirrors myths like those of Attis and Osiris, where the magic of imitation is reinforced by the magic of contact. As in the myths, so in the ritual: the body of the victim may be torn apart or burnt, while the flesh and blood, or bones and ashes, are spread on the fields, releasing their magical power to fertilize the soil.

In additional volumes of his study, Frazer brings forward still other primitive customs that fit this magical-religious pattern of thought, most notably those associated with the totem and the scapegoat. Robertson Smith, as we saw, first called Frazer's attention to the primitive practice of totemism, and this practice was the focus of pioneering research at the very time the second edition of *The Golden Bough* was in preparation. Working among Australian aboriginal tribesmen, two field investigators, Baldwin Spencer and F. J. Gillen, made the remarkable discovery that on certain special occasions the sacred totem animal was indeed killed and eaten by its clan—just as Robertson Smith had earlier guessed![24] The Aborigines called the ritual of eating the *intichiuma* ceremony. In it, says Frazer, we can see in perhaps their earliest form the rites of religious sacrifice and the concept of the dying god. By killing the totem, primitives protect against the decline of power in their animal god; by eating it, they take its divine energy into themselves. A similar pattern is to be found in the custom of the tribal "scapegoat." Anyone familiar with the Bible knows how the scapegoat was used by the Hebrews, who each year chose an animal for the specific purpose of being sent away from the community in a solemn ritual and left to wander until it died. Seen in the light of magical principles, this practice arises from the belief that sins or illnesses can somehow be physically driven out of the community by attaching them to an object like a stick or leaf and allowing them to be carried on the animal's back as it travels away. When placed in the context of totem practice and royal executions, the underlying purpose of the ritual becomes apparent: since the animal represents the divine, its banishment is another way of killing the tribal god.

Tree Spirits, Fire Festivals, and the Myth of Balder

In explaining the role played by magical-religious ideas in the worship of vegetation gods, Frazer draws most of his evidence from the ancient Mediterranean world. He was convinced, however, that these ideas and practices could be found in the European countries as well. To prove this point, he relied heavily on the work of a German student of folklore, Wilhelm Mannhardt (1831–1880), who had gathered evidence of the archaic customs, rituals, and mythology of European peasants into several important books.[25] Among these, Frazer made special note of certain traditions observed by the Celtic peoples of the British Isles and by the Nordic cultures of Scandinavia. In northern Europe, the worship of tree spirits was prevalent; perhaps because of its great size, the oak tree in particular was held sacred. Among the early Celts there were also dramatic fire festivals like the great Beltane ceremony, which was celebrated every spring and fall and called for human images to be thrown into its raging sacred flames. In Norse tradition, again, there was the tragic myth of Balder, the beautiful young god killed by an arrow made of mistletoe, the only thing in all of nature that could do him harm. As with Osiris in Egypt, Nordic mythology presented his death as an immense tragedy, and at the funeral, when Balder's body was burnt aboard his own ship in a huge fire at the ocean's edge, there was deep mourning in the assembly of the gods.

In general terms, these sagas and stories from the North provide still further evidence of magic and religion in close association. But they also serve a second purpose; they bring the long narrative of *The Golden Bough* to its end. With these stories in hand, the riddle that began the tale can at last be solved, though even at this point the path to the solution is not a simple one. It follows a sequence of comparisons and connections too complicated to trace in detail, so we shall have to be content with a short summary sketch.

If we look closely at the myths and rituals of the North, Frazer explains, it is clear that Virbius, the king of Diana's woodland, and the Norse god Balder, who also may have been once a real person, are both human embodiments of the great tree spirit, the soul of the sacred oak. This is not surprising, for among primitives the spirit, or soul, of an object can always exist in external form. The spirit of the tree need not remain in its trunk; it can also exist, outside its wooden body, in these human forms. Conversely, the souls of deities like Balder and Virbius are capable of traveling outside *their* quite human bodies as well; when they do, they lodge, naturally enough as tree spirits, in the ever-green mistletoe, which grows on the trunk of the oak even in the coldest winter. In this telltale clue, says Frazer, we have at last an explanation for the golden bough said to grow from the tree at Nemi; it is simply a poetic name for the mistletoe, which turns a definite shade of yellow when cut from its tree. Further, the action we find in the Nordic myth, the shooting of the arrow at Balder, closely parallels that of the Roman tale, where the bough is broken by the assailant and in the moment of challenge probably hurled (just like Balder's arrow) at the King of the Wood. Both stories thus describe the same kind of act: an assault on the god in which his own soul (in the form of the mistletoe) is seized from him and turned against his body to secure his death. The god is killed in order magically to take from him his divine power.

If these parallels are valid, then anthropology can step in to make the final connection. It seems clear to Frazer that the tales of Balder and Virbius alike must have originated in real events: the prehistoric murder of a tribal king to transfer his divine powers as commanded by the laws of early magic and religion. So it is nothing less than the sacrificial murders of real human kings from the deep past that lie behind the mortal figures of Balder and Lake Nemi's King of the Wood. The midsummer festivals of fire that the Romans so innocently enjoyed at Diana's temple only confirm the connection. It is no accident that these rites bear a striking resemblance to the midsummer fire rituals found also in Scandinavia. In both there is the common fact of a fire ceremony held at precisely the same time of year—and fueled probably by the sacred wood of fallen oaks. In addition, there are, especially in the northern rites, those curious hints of a victim in the fire: the ritual burning of Balder's body and those human images thrown into the flames of the Irish Beltane fires. Such clues tell us that however innocent on their surface, these ceremonies too are survivals recalling the hideous sacrifice of human beings envisioned as dying gods. Frazer intimates that in the earliest centuries of human life together, there were countless occasions when fires such as these were solemnly lit to welcome the bodies of those unfortunate kings (or their unhappy substitutes) who were human predecessors of Balder and Virbius—gods who had to be slain so that the powers of nature would not weaken but be renewed.

From all of this it should be indisputably clear that the earliest humans lived their lives by a system of ideas that was rational enough for them but fearfully distant from our own. Behind the rites of Diana's temple and the Roman legend of the King of the Wood lies the grim ordeal of human sacrifice, the ceremonial murder of a man thought to be a god.[26] Barbaric to us, such actions were nonetheless rational in the ages that knew them, for the laws of nature were seen to require nothing less than this ultimate sacrifice. Better to kill the one than risk the death of all. To the primitive mind, it was the voice not of revolution but of religion and reason that first uttered the cry: "The king is dead; long live the [new] king."[27]

Conclusion

Looking back on it when he had finished, Frazer described his book as a great "voyage of discovery," a journey backward in time to explore the mind of prehistoric humanity. A long voyage it certainly was! Though he rarely left his study, his investigations had taken him—in thought at least—to nearly every place, time, and culture known to the human race. No corner of undiscovered humanity could escape the global reach of his discussions. He gathered information, seemingly, from everyone and everywhere, and he had the great good fortune of being himself at the right place and time to do so. Writing in Cambridge during the golden last decades of the British empire, he was ideally positioned to gather stories from missionaries and soldiers, from traders and diplomats, from travelers, scholars, and explorers who passed on personal observations from every odd and lonely corner of the world. Through their letters, reports, and responses to Frazer's own questionnaire, these sources—some reliable, others less so—provided him with all that he could need and, indeed, more even than he could want.[28]

This vast fund of information Frazer had at his disposal gave him great confidence in the scientific merits of his theory and, with it, his account of the origin of religion. In his view, worship of the gods had arisen, as Tylor first suggested, in the earliest human attempts to explain the world, and it was driven by the human desire to control the powers of nature—to avoid its hazards and win its favors. Magic was the first such attempt, and it failed. As it declined, belief in the gods arose, subtly combined with it, and over the centuries moved more and more fully into its place. Religion put its hopes in prayers and pleadings. But in the end, it too has been found wanting; its claims about the gods have been found to hold no more truth than the laws of magic. Accordingly, says Frazer, just as the age of magic was replaced by that of religion, so too the present era of belief in the gods, one or many, must yield to the third and next era of human thought—the age of science, which is now upon us. Like magic, religion must be assigned to the category of Tylor's survivals. Though it clings to life among backward peoples, as a kind of intellectual fossil, its time has passed. In its place has come science, a way of thought now very much alive, which offers knowledge of the world that is both rational and faithful to facts. Like a new and better magic, science abandons the belief in supernatural beings and once again tries to explain the world by appealing to general and impersonal principles. In the present age these principles are no longer the secret sympathies of imitation and contact but the valid laws of physical cause and effect. As religion fades, science inevitably assumes its place, for it is the rationality of the present, and it knows the true laws of nature. For Frazer, it is magic without the mistakes.

Analysis

If we stand back to observe the theories of Tylor and Frazer in broad outline, several key themes come clearly into view:

1. Science and Anthropology

In terms of method, Tylor and Frazer both see themselves as *scientific* theorists. They assume from the outset that any explanation of religion which appeals to claims of miraculous events or to some supernatural revelation must be ruled out. They will not allow a theory that might claim, for example, that the ancient Hebrews followed the Ten Commandments because they were revealed by God. Only natural explanations can be seriously considered. Accordingly, such scientific study requires the wide collection of facts, followed by comparison and classification; only after that can one formulate a general theory that accounts for all the instances. Both men feel they can do this best through their new sciences of ethnology and anthropology, which gather samples of behavior from every culture in the world and thus seem ideally suited to the purpose of framing something so broad as a general theory of religion. Not surprisingly, both *Primitive Culture* and *The Golden Bough* are very large books, their pages crowded and bursting with examples, instances, parallels, and variations, all meant to support the broad generalizations that are central to the theories they advance.

2. Evolution and Origins

Tylor and Frazer both are committed to explaining religion primarily in terms of its prehistoric origin, its beginning in ages long past and its gradual evolution to present form in the centuries thereafter. They believe that the key thing is to discover how it began, to observe it in its earliest, simplest form, and then to follow the path from its beginnings to the present day. Further, they are convinced that, broadly speaking, this origin is something we *can* actually discover, though not in any single event.[29] Religion, they say, arose in a set of circumstances faced by all prehistoric peoples, who responded in ways that, though mistaken, were the best their reason could manage, given the limitations of their knowledge. Further, having arisen in the past, religion has seen its status, along with its claims of truth and usefulness, change significantly over the long process of its intellectual evolution. Through their own hard efforts, human beings have slowly improved themselves by creating ever more civilized communities, by learning the limits of their knowledge, and by treating each other with greater measures of decency and dignity. To be sure, religion—an agent of progress insofar as it once took the mind of humanity a step beyond magic—has played its role in this great evolutionary drama, but only for a time. With the arrival of science, that role now is ended.

3. Intellectualism and Individualism

Theorists today often refer to Tylor and Frazer as advocates of an "intellectualist" approach to religion.[30] By this they mean that both men think of religion as first of all a matter of beliefs, of ideas that people develop to account for what they find in the world. Religion is not seen as in the first instance about group needs, feelings, structures, or activities. On the contrary, it originates in the mind of the individual "savage philosopher," as Tylor calls him, the lone prehistoric thinker who tries to solve the riddles of life and then passes his ideas on. Religion becomes communal or social only when an idea seen to be valid by one person comes gradually to be shared by others. Religious groups, accordingly, are in the first instance viewed as collections of individuals who happen to share the same beliefs.

Critique

In the prime years of their influence, which came in the last decades of the Victorian era, Tylor and Frazer won many disciples within anthropology and even more admirers outside of it—among them people who enjoyed the fascinating application of their ideas to literature, art, history, philosophy, and even popular opinion. To those who read them at the time, these two talented authors seemed capable of shedding new light on almost every feature of religion or society one might want to address. Even so, there were a few, like Max Müller, who had serious doubts about how far one could really go with the methods of anthropology and the principles of intellectual evolutionism. As the years have passed, the ranks of the skeptics have grown, and the severity of the criticisms has increased as well. Ironically, the most serious doubts now surround precisely those things noted above as the key elements of the intellectualist program. They include the following:

1. Anthropological Method

Though both Tylor and Frazer were pioneers in using anthropological data, their methods have not worn well over time. Professional anthropologists in particular grimace at the way in which these enterprising Victorians bring together supposedly similar customs of different peoples in different times and places with only minimal regard for their original social context.[31] It is this method, for example, that allows Frazer to associate Celtic fire festivals with Scandinavian ones, and then to assume conveniently that a practice found only in the former (tossing human images into the fires) must at some point have occurred also in the latter. All the while, he overlooks that while the Nordic fires occur in midsummer, as in the festival of Diana, the Celtic festival occurs only in the spring and fall. After a close look at such loosely made connections, we find ourselves asking what it is, apart from the coincidence of fire in each, that enables Frazer to connect these festivals at all. Similar stretchings occur throughout the argument of *The Golden Bough*, though less often in the pages of *Primitive Culture*.

2. Evolutionism

This habit of using evidence loosely raises complications also for the doctrine of intellectual progress, which Tylor and Frazer both make central to their theories. When Tylor finds an example of religious monotheism, he assumes it reflects a stage of thought later than polytheism. Yet the evidence brought forward seldom shows such a sequence because it is mostly "timeless" in character. Its source is an undatable oral tradition, which may be recent or ancient; no one knows. Often it is impossible to tell whether, say, belief in one high god developed in earlier or later centuries of a people's history, or perhaps somewhere in between. When Frazer finds a report of purely magical practices, for example, he naturally assumes that they are rooted in an era that historically precedes the age of religion. But how does he know this? The evidence usually cannot tell him. Most of his examples show magic and religion existing together, as if both arose in a long single span of history that was both magical and religious at the same time. It is not surprising that Tylor and Frazer found it difficult to respond when other scholars of the time, most notably critics like Andrew Lang and Wilhelm Schmidt, pointed out the uncomfortable fact that monotheism, supposedly the "higher" form of religion, was more common in the simpler cultures of people who hunted and gathered food than in the later, advanced communities of those who farmed and kept herds of domestic animals while almost everywhere embracing polytheism.

3. The Individual and the Social

Finally, as we shall see in the chapters immediately following, strong doubts have been raised about the intellectualist individualism that Tylor and Frazer endorse. Is it really true that religious behavior arises only, or chiefly, from intellectual motives, as the work of solitary thinkers seeking to explain life's riddles and mysteries? Is it true that the social and ritual elements of religion are purely secondary—always dependent upon the intellectual factor, which is supposedly more fundamental? Further, if the origin of religion lies in ages and peoples far beyond the reach of the historical record and must be creatively reconstructed from legends and folkways, how do we prove such speculations? They seem to lie beyond either proof or disproof. It was this issue that led a theorist we shall meet later, E. E. Evans-Pritchard, to say that most explanations of the sort given by Tylor and Frazer are "just so stories"—imaginative reconstructions of what *might have happened*, but nothing more.[32]

However all of this stands, there is little doubt that, historically considered, the intellectualist theories of Tylor and Frazer are of great importance. As we shall see further on, their work has served as the starting point for most other theorists both in their time and afterward. Their theories of animism and magic have come to represent a theoretical stance that rival thinkers have felt free to reject, endorse, or revise, but never to ignore.

Notes

1. Abridged ed., p. 51; see n. 21.

2. The only full-length biography of Tylor is R. R. Marett, *Tylor* (London: Chapman and Hall, 1936). There is a short appreciation of Tylor's life and work prepared in honor of his seventy-fifth birthday by Andrew Lang, who regarded himself as more an associate and peer of Tylor than a follower; see "Edward Burnett Tylor," in *Anthropological Essays Presented to Edward Burnett Tylor* (Oxford: Clarendon Press, 1907), pp. 1–15.

3. For Tylor's associates, disciples, and influence on the study of folklore, see Richard M. Dorson, *The British Folklorists: A History* (Chicago: University of Chicago Press, 1968); on Tylor's work in particular, see pp. 167–197.

4. On the influence of early evolutionary ideas on Tylor's thought, see George W. Stocking, Jr., *Victorian Anthropology* (New York: Free Press, 1987), pp. 46–109, and Robert A. Segal, "Victorian Anthropology," *Journal of the American Academy of Religion* 58, no. 3 (Fall 1990): 469–477.

5. Müller developed his views over a period of more than four decades from the late 1850s to the end of the century. Among his most important works were the influential essay "Comparative Mythology" in the *Oxford Magazine* (1856), *Lectures on the Origin*

and Growth of Religion: As Illustrated by the Religions of India (1878), and the Gifford Lectures, published as *Natural Religion* (1881). Müller's subsequent works develop in more detail the general themes of natural religion—deity, morality, and immortality. Articles that Müller published to the end of the century echo or offer variations of themes developed in the books.

6. E. B. Tylor, *Primitive Culture: Researches into the Development of Mythology, Philosophy, Religion, Language, Art, and Custom*, 2 vols., 4th ed., rev. (London: John Murray, [1871], 1903), 1: 2.

7. Stocking, *Victorian Anthropology*, p. 162.

8. On the general doctrine of "survivals," see Margaret T. Hogden, *The Doctrine of Survivals: A Chapter in the History of Scientific Method in the Study of Man* (London: Allenson, 1936).

9. *Primitive Culture*, 1: 115–116; on the association of ideas, see J. W. Burrow, *Evolution and Society* (Cambridge: Cambridge University Press, 1970), pp. 248–251.

10. *Primitive Culture*, 1: 408.

11. *Primitive Culture*, 1: 424.

12. *Primitive Culture*, 1: 429.

13. *Primitive Culture*, 1: 429.

14. *Primitive Culture*, 2: 356.

15. *Primitive Culture*, 1: 414.

16. E. B. Tylor, "The Religion of Savages," *Fortnightly Review* 6 (August 15, 1866): 86.

17. *Primitive Culture*, 1: 317.

18. For Frazer's influence on historical studies and his role in the development of anthropology, see Eric Sharpe, *Comparative Religion: A History* (New York: Charles Scribner's Sons, 1975), pp. 87–96; Brian Morris, *Anthropological Studies of Religion* (Cambridge: Cambridge University Press, 1987), pp. 103–106; and Robert Ackerman, *The Myth and Ritual School: J. G. Frazer and the Cambridge Ritualists* (New York: Garland, 1991). On the relevance of his work to issues in philosophy and science, especially questions of epistemology, see Ludwig Wittgenstein, *Remarks on Frazer's Golden Bough*, ed. Rush Rhees, tr. A. C. Miles (Nottinghamshire, England: Brynmill, 1979). The two most important studies of Frazer's great influence on literature in the twentieth century are John B. Vickery, *The Literary Impact of* The Golden Bough (Princeton, NJ: Princeton University Press, 1973), and the collection of essays in Robert Fraser, ed., *Sir James Frazer and the Literary Imagination: Essays in Affinity and Influence* (New York: St. Martin's Press, 1990). An interesting study of *The Golden Bough* as *itself* a work of literature more than science is Stanley Edgar Hyman, *The Tangled Bank: Darwin, Marx, Frazer & Freud as Imaginative Writers* (New York: Athenaeum, 1974), pp. 233–291.

19. There is an excellent biography of Frazer by Robert Ackerman, *J. G. Frazer: His Life and Work* (Cambridge: Cambridge University Press, 1987); see also *The Macmillan Encyclopedia of Religion*, under "Frazer, James, G."

20. On the encounter with Robertson Smith and his influence on Frazer, see Ackerman, *J. G. Frazer*, pp. 53–69, and Robert Alun Jones, "Robertson Smith and James Frazer on Religion: Two Traditions in British Social Anthropology," in George W. Stocking, Jr., ed.,

Functionalism Historicized: Essays on British Social Anthropology, History of Anthropology, vol. 2 (Madison: University of Wisconsin Press, 1984), pp. 31–58.

21. James George Frazer, *The Golden Bough: A Study in Magic and Religion*, abridged edition (hereafter cited as *The Golden Bough*) (New York: The Macmillan Company, 1924). It needs to be pointed out that over the years of its composition, Frazer changed his views on a number of important issues considered in *The Golden Bough*. Myth proved an especially troublesome topic, as did totemism. On the latter, he wavered from one theory to another and had to accommodate new information that kept coming in from ethnographic field studies. On the differences between *The Golden Bough*'s three editions, see Ackerman, *J. G. Frazer*, pp. 95–100, 164–179, 236–257, and Fraser, *The Making of the Golden Bough*, pp. 117–155, 156–202.

22. On this thesis, which was developed chiefly in the second edition, see Ackerman, *J. G. Frazer*, pp. 167–169.

23. *The Golden Bough*, p. 324.

24. On the work of Spencer and Gillen, see Ackerman, *J. G. Frazer*, pp. 154–157; also Chapter 3 of the present volume, where the research of Émile Durkheim is considered.

25. These were *Die Korndämonen (Spirits of the Corn)* (1868); *Der Baumkultus der Germanen (The Tree-Worship of the Germans)* (1875); and *Antike Wald- und Feldkulte (The Ancient Worship of Forest and Field)* (1875–77). On Mannhardt's influence on British anthropology and the work of Frazer, see Sharpe, *Comparative Religion: A History*, pp. 50–51.

26. For further analysis of human sacrifice in religion, see René Girard, *Violence and the Sacred*, tr. Patrick Gregory (Baltimore: Johns Hopkins University Press, 1977) and *The Scapegoat*, tr. Yvonne Freccero (Baltimore: Johns Hopkins University Press, 1986).

27. *The Golden Bough*, p. 714.

28. For examples of Frazer's correspondence and methods of research, see Fraser, *The Making of The Golden Bough*, pp. 75–85, and throughout. On Frazer's questionnaire and the critical comment that he did not rely on it nearly as much as on the work of other scholars, see two articles by Edmund Leach, "Golden Bough or Gilded Twig," *Daedalus* 90 (1961): 371–399, especially p. 384, n. 4, and "On the 'Founding Fathers': Frazer and Malinowski," *Encounter* 25 (1965): 24–36.

29. On the scholarly search for the origins of religion, see the study by Tomoko Masuzawa, *In Search of Dreamtime: The Quest for the Origin of Religion* (Chicago: University of Chicago Press, 1993).

30. On the intellectualism of Tylor and Frazer, see my "Max Müller, E. B. Tylor, and the 'Intellectualist' Origins of the Science of Religion," *International Journal of Comparative Religion*, 1, no. 2 (June 1995): 69–83; for an assessment of recent attempts to restate the Tylorian position, see Gillian Ross, "Neo-Tylorianism: A Reassessment," *Man*, n.s. 6, no. 1 (March 1971): 105–116.

31. These criticisms have come from many quarters of modern anthropology, and they are the main reason why Frazer's views, especially, have been almost universally discarded. There is more respect for Tylor. For an appreciation of his work and a criticism of the doctrine of "survivals," see Burrow, *Evolution and Society*, pp. 244–245.

For a particularly stringent criticism of Frazer, see two articles by Edmund Leach cited in n. 28.

32. E. E. Evans-Pritchard, *Theories of Primitive Religion* (Oxford: Clarendon Press, 1965), p. 25.

Suggestions for Further Reading

Ackerman, Robert. *J. G. Frazer: His Life and Work*. Cambridge: Cambridge University Press, 1987. The definitive intellectual biography of Frazer.

Ackerman, Robert. *The Myth and Ritual School: J. G. Frazer and the Cambridge Ritualists*. London: Routledge, 2002. Explores Frazer's association with the famous and influential circle of classical scholars at Cambridge University.

Burrow, J. W. *Evolution and Society*. Cambridge: Cambridge University Press, 1970. A close study of E. B. Tylor and other early Victorian anthropological thinkers who argued for a pattern of evolutionary growth in both society and religion.

Clack, Brian R. *Wittgenstein, Frazer and Religion*. Houndmills, Basingstoke, Hampshire, UK: Palgrave Macmillan, 1999. Examines the influence of *The Golden Bough* on one of the most important philosophers of the twentieth century.

Dorson, Richard M. *The British Folklorists: A History*. Chicago: University of Chicago Press, 1968. Still the best study of the circle of learned amateurs whose work provided a context for the researches of Tylor and Frazer and helped lay the foundations for modern scientific anthropology.

Fraser, Robert. *The Making of The Golden Bough: The Origins and Growth of an Argument*. New York: St. Martin's Press, 1990. Published on the centennial anniversary of the first printing of *The Golden Bough* in 1890, this study examines ideas and influences that found their way into its pages as well as the changes that occurred over the long interval of its composition.

Fraser, Robert, ed. *Sir James Frazer and the Literary Imagination: Essays in Affinity and Influence*. New York: St. Martin's Press, 1990. A collection of essays also published on the centennial anniversary of *The Golden Bough*, it explores Frazer's wide impact on modern literature and other spheres of intellectual life.

Horton, Robin. *Patterns of Thought in Africa and the West: Essays on Magic, Religion, and Science*. Cambridge: Cambridge University Press, 1993. A collection of illuminating essays by the best-known current neo-Tylorian theorist.

Hyman, Stanley Edgar. *The Tangled Bank: Darwin, Marx, Frazer & Freud as Imaginative Writers*. New York: Athenaeum, 1974. An interesting study of *The Golden Bough* as a work whose greatest impressions were made in the arts and culture rather than anthropology and social science.

Lang, Andrew. "Edward Burnett Tylor." In *Anthropological Essays Presented to Edward Burnett Tylor*, edited by Andrew Lang. Oxford: Clarendon Press, 1907, pp. 1–15. A short appreciation of Tylor's life and work by a brilliant contemporary of Tylor, who also wrote extensively on the matter of explaining religion.

Larsen, Timothy. *The Slain God: Anthropologists and the Christian Faith*. Oxford: Oxford University Press. Chapters on Tylor and Frazer explore their rationalist rejections of Christianity.

Leach, Edmund. "Golden Bough or Gilded Twig." *Daedalus* 90 (1961): 371–399. A severe critique of Frazer by a leading contemporary British anthropologist.

Marett, R. R. *Tylor*. London: Chapman and Hall, 1936. Though now dated, the only available biography of Tylor. Marett was one of Tylor's disciples and an important theorist of religion in his own right.

Rivière, Peter, ed. *A History of Oxford Anthropology.* New York: Berghahn Books, 2007. An instructive collection of essays charting the rise of anthropology in Britain; discusses the university's role in the early efforts and the later rise of field anthropology.

Stocking, George W., Jr. *Victorian Anthropology*. New York: Free Press, 1987. A perceptive and detailed study of the early British anthropologists in their nineteenth-century social and intellectual context.

Vickery, John B. *The Literary Impact of* The Golden Bough. Princeton, NJ: Princeton University Press, 1973. A study of the surprisingly wide and deep influence Frazer's book had on some of the greatest writers of the early twentieth century, including, among others, T. S. Eliot and James Joyce.

Wheeler-Barclay, Marjorie. *The Science of Religion in Britain, 1860–1915.* Charlottesville: University of Virginia Press, 2010. A thorough and thoughtful account of the pioneers—Müller, Tylor, Frazer, Lang, and others—in the science of religion as it took shape in the context of mid- and late-Victorian intellectual change and cultural debate.

2

Religion and Personality: Sigmund Freud

Religion would thus be the universal obsessional neurosis of humanity.
Freud, *The Future of an Illusion*[1]

Few thinkers in modern times have stirred more episodes of fierce debate than Sigmund Freud (1856–1939), the psychologist from Vienna, Austria, who at the turn of the twentieth century stunned not only the field of medicine but society at large with his unsettling new analyses of the human personality. To this day, almost anyone who hears the name "Freud" associates it with two things: psychotherapy and sex. That impression is not inaccurate as far as it goes, but it does not go very far. Freud was a most unusual man, driven by ceaseless curiosity, towering ambition, and a remarkably wide range of intellectual interests. His original profession was medicine, especially brain research. But the more he traveled this path of specialized study, the more it branched in new and different directions. His neurological inquiries quickly widened to an interest in the nature of mental illness and other puzzles of the mind. Before long he had proposed a provocative new concept of the human personality. From this platform, he moved confidently ahead, searching out the psychological dimension in almost every aspect of human life, from seemingly insignificant things like dreams, jokes, and personal quirks to the deep, complex emotions that steer personal relationships and shape social customs. Wherever he turned, he found yet another application of his ideas. They illuminated questions about the nature of the family and social life; they offered clues to the explanation of mythology, folklore, and history; and they suggested new interpretations of drama, literature, and art. To Freud and his followers, it seemed at times as if he had found an explanatory golden key. Analysis of the psyche opened a door on the innermost motives of human thought and action, from the stresses placed on the individual personality to the great forces that drive and shape civilizations. It could uncover the smallest secret of a single, troubled self while at the same time offering a new perspective on the great endeavors of human history, among them society, morals, philosophy, and—not least—religion.

Background: Freud's Life and Work

Freud was born in 1856 in Moravia, a part of central Europe that then belonged to the sprawling Austro-Hungarian empire.[2] His family was Jewish, and his father, a widowed merchant, already had two grown sons when he chose to remarry. Freud was the first child born to his father's much younger second wife; he thus grew up in a complex extended family. His playmates as a child were his own nephew and a niece, Pauline, a girl whom he liked to torment but to whom he was also attracted. Looking back later on his childhood, Freud found this experience to be evidence of ambivalence, a state of divided emotion, which appears as a key theme in his writings, especially when he considers religion. Human beings, he believed, are often driven by contradictory feelings of both love and aggression directed toward the same object or person.

While still a boy, Freud moved with his family to the capital of the empire, Vienna, where he was to live and work almost all of his years. As a Jew, he found it impossible to develop any real love for this predominantly Catholic city, but his family did become comfortable in it. For almost his entire life, in fact, he would remain there, raising his own children to adulthood and leaving only in the year before his death, when the coming of the Nazis to Austria forced him to take refuge in England. Freud's parents were conscious of their Jewish identity, observing Passover and giving the children some synagogue instruction, but in other respects they were religiously indifferent. They did not follow Jewish dietary laws, and they adapted to Christian holidays, such as Christmas.

In secondary school Freud was a gifted student who took courses in Greek, Latin, and Hebrew and finished at the top of his class. Alongside his native German, he became fluent in both French and English, then went on to teach himself Spanish and Italian. In 1873, when he was seventeen, he became a medical student at the University of Vienna, where he began research in anatomy and physiology. After graduating as a doctor of medicine in 1881, he began working in the Vienna General Hospital, where he continued his brain research. A few years later, he married Martha Bernays, who became the mother to their six children and a loyal companion throughout their long married life.

During his earlier years of medical work, Freud encountered Josef Breuer, a man who had done careful case studies of mental illness and soon became a close friend. In addition, in 1885 he visited Paris to study nervous disorders with Jean-Martin Charcot, a famous French physician. This visit was a turning point, for it sparked Freud's permanent interest in the psychological study of the mind rather than purely physiological research on the brain. After Paris, he returned to Vienna, continued his work with the mentally ill, and published his first book, *Studies on Hysteria* (1895), which was written with his colleague Breuer. Significantly for Freud's later work, the two authors described in this study a process of *repression*, by which troubled people seem to force themselves to forget painful experiences. Freud also reported success in treating neurosis—the irrational behavior of these troubled people—by using hypnotism or simply by engaging them in discussions of their illnesses. With one patient in particular, a woman he called Anna O., he claimed success in curing her of hysteria by working back through word associations to an event that was the cause of her problem. This use of a conversational approach was a key step. Out of it Freud would develop a way of investigating—and treating—the human mind, which he put at the center of all his work. He chose to call it "psychoanalysis."

As Freud envisioned it, the clinical practice of psychoanalysis consisted mainly of listening to a patient, who at regular appointments was encouraged to feel comfortable saying whatever came to mind, in whatever way it came, without any logical sequence or storyline. Patients were to speak simply by "free association" of ideas and memories. To many people (in Freud's day and ours), such a technique seems little more than a waste of a good physician's time. But Freud felt differently; he found in psychoanalytic conversation an unexpected avenue into the most hidden part of his patients' personalities. He began also to analyze himself, making special note of the things that came up when he was dreaming, and he asked his patients to do the same. Working in this vein with patients over a full five years of practice and research, he listened, read, reflected, and then drew conclusions that were put into a work entitled *The Interpretation of Dreams* (1900). It was this epoch-making book, published on the very edge of the new century, that launched the great "Freudian revolution" in modern thought. Among other things, this study outlined for the first time Freud's remarkable concept of "the unconscious"—a notion to be examined more closely in a moment.

Though at first severely criticized by the medical establishment, Freud's work readily attracted a small circle of interested followers. In 1902 he formed a professional organization that became the Vienna Psychological Society. Included were several men who gained followers alongside Freud: Otto Rank, Karl Abraham, Alfred Adler, Carl Jung, Ernest Jones, and others. Several journals were established, and psychoanalysis found itself gradually transformed from a method and a few creative ideas to a path-breaking new field of scholarly investigation.

During this same interval and through the hardships of World War I, Freud continued to work. In several highly productive years just after the turn of the century, he explored the wider implications of psychoanalytic theory, publishing such works as *The Psychopathology of Everyday Life* (1901) and *Three Essays on the Theory of Sexuality* (1905). A number of journal articles also appeared in the decade, including one on religion and neurosis and several others on primitive religion.[3] The latter efforts became the book *Totem and Taboo* (1913). In the following years, while fighting raged elsewhere in Europe, he completed his *Introductory Lectures on Psychoanalysis* (1916–1917). As peace returned, he added new works, among them *Beyond the Pleasure Principle* (1920), *The Ego and the Id* (1923), and *The Question of Lay Analysis* (1926). All along, he energetically promoted the field of psychoanalytic study by continuing to see patients, corresponding with colleagues, arranging scholarly congresses, and supporting two academic journals.

In the last two decades of his life, Freud added to his more specifically psychoanalytic studies several controversial works on general subjects related to society, science, and religion. They included *The Future of an Illusion* (1927) and *Moses and Monotheism* (1938), two books that, along with the earlier *Totem and Taboo*, express his main ideas on religion. We will consider them here.

Freudian Theory: Psychoanalysis and the Unconscious

We can best understand Freud by beginning where he himself does—with the discoveries reported in *The Interpretation of Dreams* (1900).[4] In this important book he observes that human dreams have always attracted curiosity, figuring widely in myth, literature, folklore, and magic. Tylor, as we saw, thought it was the experience of dreams that led primitive people to believe in souls. Freud accepts these claims but makes it clear that he is prepared to say more. He insists that dreams are more significant than mere curiosity or even theories of the soul would ever lead us to guess. Among other things, dreams show just how much more there is to the activity of the mind than what appears on the surface. We all can grasp the role of everyday consciousness; when we speak to a friend, write a check, play a game, or read a book, we not only use our minds but know that we are doing so. We also recognize that beneath our surface awareness lie other ideas and concepts that seem best described as "preconscious." These are memories, ideas, or intentions that we are not aware of at the moment but can easily call upon as needed—things like the ages of our children, what was served for dinner yesterday, or where we intend to be on the weekend. Though not immediately aware of such things, we can easily retrieve them as needed. In the experience of dreams, however, Freud contends that we come upon something quite unlike either conscious or preconscious mental activity. We draw upon another layer, a different region of the mind that is deep, hidden, huge, and strangely powerful. This is the realm of the unconscious. Like the great underside of an iceberg, this deep sector of the self, though unrecognized, is enormously important. It is the source, first, of our most basic physical urges, our desires for food and sexual activity. Second, bundled together with these drives is a quite extraordinary assemblage of ideas, impressions, and emotions associated with everything a person has ever experienced or done or wished to do, from the first days of life up to the most recent minute. If we want an image of it, we might call this realm of the unconscious the mind's mysterious cellar, a dark storehouse necessary for life upstairs, but filled down below with a jumble of half-formed urges that blend with images, impressions, and trace memories of past experience. Up above, the conscious mind is unaware of these things, but they do exist, and they exercise a powerful indirect influence on all that we think and do.

When he first wrote of it, Freud acknowledged that his idea of an unconscious mind was not entirely new. "Everywhere I go," he once said, "I find the poet has been there before me." Since antiquity, philosophers too have suggested a hidden dimension of the mind, but their writings were intuitive, not scientific. Though they perceived something mysterious that was deep in the self and sensed its power, they had no way of explaining why such a thing should exist or how it might work. Psychoanalysis is very different. It proposes a rational method for discovering the contents of this hidden realm and explaining what purpose it serves. Freud claimed that basic biological drives, for example, are found there because they cannot be anywhere else; they are by nature without consciousness. Images and emotions, on the other hand, sink down into it from the conscious mind up above. They come into the unconscious in two ways: either they drift in quietly as a kind of faint transcript of past experience, or they are forced down, as it were, for quite specific and unusual reasons. In this second case they have traveled down into hiding because of a complex sequence of events that first occurred up on the plane of conscious thought. The forcing mechanism is repression, the remarkable process Freud and Breuer managed to identify in their intense conversations with distressed patients.[5] Most of these people possessed a common characteristic. Some earlier event or circumstance in their lives produced an emotional response so powerful that it could not be expressed openly; it was therefore pushed down into the unconscious and out of mental view. On the surface, says Freud, an event repressed is an event forgotten, but in fact it has not disappeared. Unconsciously it remains very much in the mind, only to work itself back out in quite puzzling ways. Repressed thoughts and emotions release themselves in forms of action that no rational person would engage in: pointless movements, unfounded fears, irrational attachments, obsessive personal rituals, and other strange behaviors. Freud labeled them "neurotic." Victims of such neuroses cannot be treated with medicines, but they could be helped by psychoanalysis. A skilled therapist can bring the repressed thought up into consciousness, allow all of the neurotic emotions to be properly released, and through this process bring the behavior to a level of awareness that allows it to be controlled.

In first framing these central concepts of repression and the unconscious, Freud relied heavily on his early encounters with neurotic people, some of whom were suffering from serious personality disorders. But the evidence he drew from dreams, which, of course, everyone experiences, suggested to him that *all* human activity—normal as well as abnormal—could be shown to be powerfully affected by the unconscious. Dreams indicated that to a degree, all persons are neurotic. Freud chose to describe dreams as "wish fulfillments." They are states of mind created by the fact that we feel certain powerful drives—such as the craving for a sexual encounter—that are rooted in the needs of the body. These drives naturally have no sense of time; they want satisfaction immediately. And though we might like to accommodate them exactly as felt, the rules of normal life usually make this impossible. In most waking hours, when the conscious mind is in control, they must be repressed—driven down into the unconscious. And yet so powerful are these urges and emotions that, as soon as we sleep, as soon as our consciousness fades, they begin to "leak out" in the form of dreams—just as the mentally disturbed person's repressions leak out as neurotic behavior. For the psychoanalyst, then, the interpretation of a dream achieves a purpose similar to that of a conversation with a neurotic person; both offer paths into the secret corridors of the unconscious.

Nor is this all. Freud came to believe that many things we do even in waking life are ruled by the hidden energies of the unconscious. In further books like *The Psychopathology of Everyday Life* (1901) and *Wit and Its Relation to the Unconscious* (1905), he sought to show that such routine happenings as jokes, slips of the tongue (the well-known "Freudian slip"), absentmindedness, memory lapses, doodling, and even bodily quirks and gestures all originate in the unconscious. He pointed also to the power of the unconscious in the achievements of great artists, dramatists, and writers. In the light of psychoanalysis, the works of Leonardo da Vinci, Michelangelo, Dostoyevsky, Sophocles, and Shakespeare all could be seen as affected by forces rising up from the unconscious.[6] It is no accident that the familiar stories found in mythology and folklore and the recurring themes of art, literature, and religion bear a strong resemblance to the subjects and images that keep returning in human dreams. All testify to the secret, subterranean power of the unconscious.

The Personality in Conflict

In these writings Freud traces so many different things to the unconscious that one may wonder whether the idea is pressed to an unbalanced extreme. But he insists not. The unconscious is central to thought because it serves as the crucial link between what is physical and what is mental in the human person. After all, there are no pure spirits in the human race. Every personality is rooted in a physical body, which is driven by certain basic biological instincts, or drives. Hunger is instinctive and so is the sex drive; these physical impulses preserve both the self and the species, the human individual and the race. Both operate on the "pleasure principle." We feel a need, and we feel pleasure when it is satisfied. By our very nature as physical beings, we seek pleasure and turn away from the opposite.

In themselves the physical drives are simple things. Strains and tensions arise, however, because these drives are of different kinds: they can come into conflict when they collide with each other or when they meet the unchangeable set of facts that make up the outside world. If I see an apple when hungry, I eat it and satisfy the pleasure principle in doing so. But should another person, also hungry, be holding the apple, then I face a conflict. The circumstance forces me to repress my urge. Since the risk of losing the apple altogether is too great, I must agree to share it. In the face of reality or the claims of other drives, it is unavoidable that some drives on some occasions must be repressed. Such repressions feed the unconscious.

Freud struggled long and hard to determine just what were the most basic human drives and to describe how they operated. At first he thought there were only the "ego instinct," represented by hunger, and the *libido* (the Latin word for "desire"), which represented sexuality. Later on he spoke of both of these as forms of one drive he called *eros* (the Greek for "love") and suggested an opposite drive, aggression, as the other. Later still, and without discarding the idea of aggression, he settled upon *eros* as the drive to continue life and *thanatos* (the Greek for "death") as the drive to end it.

Whatever the labels, the fundamental thing about the drives is the idea of conflict, of struggle that takes place both among the drives and between the drives and the outside world. This idea of an unavoidable tension at the center of the self is what led Freud to come up with perhaps the best known of all his concepts—the threefold division of the human personality into the ego (Latin for "I"), the superego (Latin for the "I above"), and the id (Latin for "it").[7] In this scheme, the id is considered the earliest and most basic of the three elements. Rooted in the early, animal stage of human evolution, it is unconscious and unaware of itself; it is where the raw, physical drives of the body translate themselves into wishes—to eat, to kill, or to engage in sex. At the other extreme, the top of the personality so to speak, lies the superego. It represents a collection of influences that, from the moment of birth, begin to be imposed on the personality by the outside world. These are the expectations of society as framed first by the family and then by larger groups, such as the tribe, the city, or the nation. Finally, suspended in a position between the demands of society and the desires of the body, we find the third element of the self—the ego, or "reality principle." The ego might best be called the "choosing center" of the human person. Its delicate task is to perform a continual balancing act within. It must, on the one hand, satisfy the desires of the id and, on the other, be ready to curb or deny them whenever they clash with the hard facts of the physical world or the social restraints imposed by the superego.

As some have noticed, this sketch of the mind bears an interesting resemblance to that of Plato, the Greek philosopher who explained the self on the analogy of a charioteer trying to control the contending horses of reason and passion. Freud, too, suggests that the personality is the scene of a continuing struggle. "Action by the ego," he writes, "is as it should be if it satisfies simultaneously the demands of the id, of the superego, and of reality—that is to say, if it can reconcile their demands with one another."[8]

Infantile Sexuality and the Oedipus Complex

The most fascinating application of this conflict model of the personality appears in Freud's now-famous theories of infantile sexuality and the Oedipus complex. As most know, Freudian theory places great importance on childhood, especially the earliest years—from birth to age six. If he had merely claimed that this is the age when much of what he calls the superego is formed—that is, the age when parents plant the rules of reality, family, and society in the child's mind—Freud would have pleased many and disturbed no one; that only confirms common sense. What he actually puts forward, however, is a stunning idea that many people found not just wrong but perverse. He boldly insists that early childhood, no less than adult life, is strongly shaped by the sexual desires of the id. In *Three Essays on the Theory of Sexuality* (1905), he argues that from the moment of birth onward, physical, sexual urges govern much of the behavior of an infant child. In the first eighteen months of life, there is an oral phase, in which sexual pleasure comes along with nourishment from sucking at a mother's breast; from that time up to age three, there is an anal phase, when pleasure comes from control of excretion; from age three onward, the genital organs assume importance. This phallic stage (from the Greek *phallos*, meaning "penis"), which includes masturbation and sexual fantasies, reaches to the age of six, at which point a nonsexual stage of latency sets in. This phase lasts until the early teens and the arrival of full adult sexual capacities.

As a person passes through this development, the earlier sexual stages do not completely disappear; they are instead overlaid by the new ones. Accordingly, cases of abnormal behavior are best understood as fixations, as the failure to move on to the next level of growth, or in other cases as regressions, in which people move backward into earlier stages. A person obsessed with ordering the trivial details of life, for example, might be described as suffering a fixation in the anal stage, when behavior is excessively control-oriented, and could conceivably even regress to the infantile oral stage. This view of human development turns out to be especially important when Freud turns to religion, for one of his main concerns is to find the place of religious belief in the sequence of normal emotional growth: Does it belong to an adult stage of personality development or to an earlier phase? A great deal, obviously, hinges on the answer to this question. Moreover, when Freud discusses the history of human civilizations, he prefers to use the analogy of individual growth, as if he were talking about an individual person. Clearly, anyone who accepts Freud's pattern will be inclined to take one view of religion if it is seen as belonging to the childhood of the human race and quite another if it is taken as a mark of adulthood, of civilization in its maturity.

Probably no one needs to be told that infantile sexuality—and its link to religion—is on clearest display in what Freud calls the Oedipus complex. This well-known term comes from the celebrated tragedy (which Freud translated as a schoolboy) by Sophocles, the great dramatist of ancient Greece. It tells the story of King Oedipus, a proud, good man whose fate it was quite unknowingly to kill his father and then marry his own mother. In a way that is remarkably parallel to the story of Oedipus, Freud tells us, children in the phallic stage experience a desire to displace one of their parents and become the lover of the other. The boy, discovering the pleasure given him by his penis, wants to become the sexual partner of his mother, thereby taking the place of his father, whom in a sense he "hates" as his rival. Sensing these feelings, the mother, with supporting threats from the father, discourages her son from touching his sexual organ; there is even the threat it could be cut off. The son, in turn, is genuinely frightened, and surmising from girls' lack of a penis that such a thing could actually happen to him, experiences a castration complex—"the severest trauma of his young life."[9] The son therefore finds that he must submit to his father, give up hope of possessing his mother, and get his satisfaction from sexual fantasies instead. Still, he never entirely gives up his desire for his mother or ends his jealous rivalry with his father. Young girls experience similar emotions but along a different path. They envy the male penis, imagine they have the same organ, and at first seek a similar encounter with the mother, only later to accept their feminine role and acknowledge the rightful authority of their father.

Even after the contemporary sexual revolution, Freud's account of the Oedipus complex still comes to many people as something of a shock. They find it inconceivable that the innocence of childhood could be shaded by such powerful drives and dark emotions. But Freud is convinced of it. Even more, he feels that the Oedipus complex is actually "the central experience of the years of childhood, the greatest problem of early life, and the main source of later inadequacy."[10] Indeed, Oedipal conflicts are a problem for society as well as the individual. If this deep incestuous urge were to be acted upon, it would be exceedingly damaging to the entire family unit, which is crucial to the child's own survival. If carried out, the urge toward incest would ultimately be destructive of both the self and society, just as it certainly was for King Oedipus in the play. It follows, then, that already in the earliest phase of life, a struggle arises in the child between the drive for sex and the need of a family. In their very first years, all human beings begin to discover that unless they find a balance, unless they can control their colliding desires, there can be neither a family nor society and hence no framework of security for the self. Restraints must be placed on our urges, for without them we cannot have a civilization, and without civilization we cannot survive.

Later Developments and Writings

In his mature years, Freud developed and refined his theories, looking always for new dimensions and wider applications of his core ideas: the unconscious, the Oedipus complex, neurosis, and the three-part framework of human personality. In *Beyond the Pleasure Principle* (1920), he revised his earlier understanding of the basic drives, which to him centered on sex and self-preservation—the two urges that create and sustain life—and elaborated on *thanatos,* the "death instinct," as the backward urge to restore the world to its primal state, to the time when there was no life at all. Such a concept, he felt, was the only thing to account for such behaviors as masochism and sadism, in which people avoid pleasure and actively seek pain. In *Group Psychology and the Analysis of the Ego* (1921), he expanded the concept of the *libido*, or sexual desire, to include the broader idea of diffused emotional attachment, such as is found in a family. Then he applied it to explain how an organized community like a church depends on personal attachments to a leader; in Christianity, for example, devotion to the person of Christ shared with one's fellow believers is what gives this huge, varied community such a sense of binding solidarity.

With the outbreak of World War I and the difficult decades afterward, Freud reflected at length on the themes of death, human weakness, and the limits of civilization. His commitment to psychoanalysis remained strong, and he placed great faith in the progress of science. Still, a general sense of melancholy, of pessimism about the plight of humanity began to come forward. We find this attitude especially in *Civilization and Its Discontents* (1930), where he explores the unhappy conflict between our instinctive personal desires, most notably the power of human aggression, and the strong restraints that society must place upon them if humanity is to survive.

Freud and Religion

Once he had developed the basic ideas of psychoanalysis, Freud found religion a most promising subject of study.[11] In childhood, of course, he had gained a basic acquaintance with the teachings of Judaism. Although his family was largely nonreligious, he knew well the stories and favorite texts of the Hebrew Bible. He also developed a useful working knowledge of Christianity, drawn partly from the facts of life in staunchly Catholic Vienna and partly from his own wide reading in the history and literature of Western civilization. Further, religious ideas, imagery, and parallels figured prominently in the neuroses of some of his first patients. His personal stance, however, was one of complete rejection of religious belief. The biographer who knew him best tells us bluntly that "he went through life from beginning to end a natural atheist."[12] Freud found no reason to believe in God and therefore saw no value or purpose in the rituals of religious life.

In light of this background, it is not surprising that Freud's approach to religion, like that of Tylor and Frazer, is quite the opposite of that taken by people who are themselves religious. In most cases, religious believers say that they believe as they do because their God has spoken in a sacred book, or because what their church or synagogue teaches is the truth. Freud, by contrast, is quite sure that religious ideas do not come from the Judeo-Christian God or other gods, for gods do not exist. Nor do religious teachings arise from the sort of sound thinking about the world that normally leads to truth. Like Tylor and Frazer, he is certain that religious beliefs are superstitions. At the same time, he notes that they are interesting superstitions, which raise important questions about human nature. Why, if they are so obviously false, do so many people persist in holding these beliefs, and with such deep conviction? If religion is not rational, how do people acquire it? And why do they keep to it? Tylor shows almost no interest in these questions, and Frazer, though he does somewhat explore the attractions of magic, largely ignores them as well. Freud, however, does consider them—and with good reason: in psychoanalysis he claims to have found the answers.

In an early article published under the title "Obsessive Actions and Religious Practices" (1907), we can find a first clue to Freud's approach. He observes that there is a close resemblance between the activities of religious people and the behaviors of his neurotic patients. Both, for example, place great emphasis on doing things in a patterned, ceremonial fashion; both also feel guilty unless they follow their rituals to perfection. In both cases too, the ceremonies are associated with the repression of basic instincts: psychological neuroses often arise from repression of the sex drive; religion demands the same, as well as repression of selfishness in general and control of the ego-instinct. Thus, just as sexual repression results in an individual obsessional neurosis, religion, which is practiced widely in the human race, seems to be "a universal obsessional neurosis."[13] This comparison suggests a theme that is fundamental to almost everything Freud writes on religion. In his view, religious behavior always resembles mental illness; accordingly, the concepts most suited to explaining it are those that have been developed by psychoanalysis.

All three of the books Freud devotes to religion take this basic approach, but they do so in distinctive ways. As it happens, all three are also fairly brief. So instead of choosing just one, we can give some consideration to each of them, all the while noticing the pattern of psychoanalytic explanation that is common throughout.

Totem and Taboo

Totem and Taboo (1913) is a book Freud regarded as one of his best. It presents a psychological interpretation of the life of primitive peoples. It employs the concepts of psychoanalysis, but like other books of the time, it is also influenced by evolutionary thinking—not just Darwin's theory of biological evolution but the general ideas of intellectual and social evolution as well. Freud accepts the opinion of his age that more than just our physical selves can be attributed to evolution; he also adopts the idea, shared by Tylor and Frazer, that we have evolved intellectually; through the ages our social institutions, like our animal species, have traced an unsteady but still upward line of progress. Consequently, just as we find clues to the personality of individual adults in their earlier character as children, so we find in the character of past cultures important clues to the nature of civilization in the present. This past, moreover, includes not just our civilized ancestors like the Greeks and Romans but—now that Darwin has shown the connection—even prehistoric cultures and peoples, those communities of humans who first descended from their animal ancestors.

With this premise in hand, Freud turns next to two practices of primitive peoples that strike modern minds as especially strange: the use of animal "totems" and the custom of "taboo." Tylor, Frazer, and other anthropologists were fascinated by these customs, as we have noticed. In the first case, a tribe or clan chooses to associate itself with a specific animal (or plant), which serves as its sacred object, its "totem." In the second, some person or thing is called "taboo" if a tribe wants to declare it "off limits" or forbidden. According to the oldest and strongest known taboos, most early societies seem to have strictly prohibited two things. The first is incest: marriage must always be "exogamous" (i.e., outside the immediate family or clan). Among primitives there is almost always what Freud calls a "horror of incest." Second, there could be no killing or eating of the totem animal; eating the "totem" was also "taboo." Freud then goes beyond other theorists to add that there could be no point in making taboos unless somehow, at some time, people *wanted* to do what they prohibit. Presumably, these are crimes that people did try to commit. But if so, why make them crimes in the first place? Why make everyone miserable by creating rules that no one really wanted to keep?

Here in specific form we meet the kind of question that does not appear in the works of theorists like Tylor and Frazer. From their intellectualist standpoint, human religious behavior is a conscious endeavor; it represents an effort to use reason to understand the world while, at the same time, it demonstrates a failure to reason correctly. Religious people try to be rational but do not succeed; their rites of "taboo" and rituals of totemism cannot achieve what they suppose. But then the question remains: If it is a mistake to believe in totems and taboos, why should anyone continue to do so? Freud finds the answer in the unconscious. He claims that experience with neurotic patients shows the personalities of both disturbed and normal people alike to be strongly marked by ambivalence—by the clash of powerful opposing desires. Obsessively neurotic people, for example, will sometimes feel extreme grief when a loved one, a father or mother, dies. Yet on probing the unconscious, we often find that it is not love but guilt and hate that actually cause their emotion. Remarkably, tribal peoples show just this trait, thinking of their dead ancestors as demons, or "wicked spirits," who deserve their hate. In their use of magic, too, they imagine that the world is just an extension of their own selves. By thinking about the sound of thunder and imitating it, they suppose they can make real rain.

The practices of totemism and taboo thus present us with a particularly striking display of psychic ambivalence—one that opens a window on the power of human emotions in the very earliest age of humanity. After all, says Freud, if Darwin is right about our descent from the apes, we should think of the first human beings as living, like their animal ancestors, in "primal hordes"—extended families of women and children dominated by one powerful male.

Within these groups there would have been loyalty, affection, and security against danger; for the young males, however, there was also something else: frustration and envy. Though they feared and respected the stronger father, they also sexually desired the females, all of whom were his wives. Torn between their need for the security of the horde and their suppressed sexual urges, they were at length driven to a fateful act. In a fearsome turn of events, which undoubtedly occurred many times in different hordes, the sons banded together, murdered their father, and (since they were cannibals) consumed his body, even as they proceeded to take possession of his wives. At first, this murder in the primeval horde brought a sense of joy and liberation, but grave second thoughts soon followed. The sons were overcome with guilt and remorse. Wanting desperately to restore the master they had killed, they found in the totem animal a "father substitute" and symbol; they agreed to worship it, and before it they then swore the oldest of all taboos: "Thou shalt not kill the totem." Over time, this rule was generalized to the entire clan and became the universal commandment against all murder. "Thou shalt not kill" thus undoubtedly became the first moral rule of the human race.

The same powerful feelings of remorse led to the second taboo, the commandment against incest. Regretting their act and recognizing at once that seizing the father's wives would only create new conflict among themselves, the sons agreed to a second commandment: "Thou shalt not take thy father's wives." To live together, the sons had to agree to find any new wives only "outside the clan." Freud suggests that these prehistoric agreements of the brothers may have been the real events that lie behind the mythical "social contract" that philosophers have often presented as the foundation of human society.

The case of the first taboo is more complicated than the second, and to explain it Freud draws on the work of William Robertson Smith, the very same biblical scholar who influenced Frazer and first suggested the idea of the primitive "totem sacrifice."[14] Though normally the totem's life was sacred, the newer Australian research had shown that there were certain sacred occasions on which the pattern was reversed: the totem animal then *was* killed and consumed by all in a ritual feast. From the standpoint of psychoanalysis, says Freud, this too is highly significant. The totem sacrifice makes sense only as a deeply emotional ceremony in which the community reenacts the primeval murder of the first father, who, through death, has now become its god. In the ritual, the sons publicly reaffirm their love for him and—quite unconsciously—also release the hate caused by the sexual renunciation they now endure.

The totem sacrifice thus confirms that the original murder of the father—a crime committed, fittingly, in the childhood of the human race—is nothing less than the acting out in history of the powerful, double human emotions that converge in every male's infancy to form the Oedipus complex. The brothers' assault upon their father is in essence the crime of Oedipus enacted thousands of years before Sophocles ever wrote his play! Out of jealous desire for their father's wives—a desire for their own mothers—the first sons committed a murder that was followed by a great ritual of remorse and affection. To the human race, these extraordinary events have left a legacy of profound emotional ambivalence. On the level of conscious activity, the members of the tribe identify the animal in the totem sacrifice with their dead father and, by projection, give him the status of divinity; they confess that they are all his children and offer him their worship by eating the totem flesh and restraining their sexual desire. On the deeper plane of the unconscious, however, they express quite the opposite emotions, for the ritual by its very nature recreates their original deed of rebellious murder and cannibalism, thereby releasing the frustration and hate that arise from the ongoing denial of their Oedipal urges.

Seen in this light, moreover, a modern sacrament like the Christian communion shows its true character. Like the ancient totem ritual, it reenacts, and seeks to reverse, the original crime of humanity. In the communion, the flesh and blood of Christ, God's son (symbolizing the eldest brother, leader of the rebellion), are eaten in remembrance of his crucifixion, a death suffered as punishment for the "original sin" of the primeval rebellion. On behalf of his brothers, Christ atones for their prehistoric crime. Yet the atonement is also reenactment. Since, in Christian theology, the father and son are one, the sacrament of the son's death is symbolically at the same moment the sacrament of the father's murder. Thus the communion secretly recalls Oedipal hate as well as love.

Freud of course recognizes that a long process of evolution stands between the totem rites of early cannibals and the communion meal of Christianity. He suggests that, over time, the totem animal was reduced to a simple sacrificial gift. Its place was taken by others, first by animal-human deities, later by the gods of polytheism, and finally by the father God of Christianity. But these are details. Freud's main concern, like Frazer's, but now from the standpoint of emotions rather than intellect, is to show the striking connection between present-day religion and the dark ceremonies of the primitive past. If we want to find the origin of religion, he insists, we need look no farther than these grim prehistoric events and deep psychological tensions. The birth of belief is to be found in the Oedipus complex, in the powerful, divided emotions that led humanity to its first great crime, then turned a murdered father into a god and promised sexual renunciation as a way to serve him. In Freud's own words, "Totemic religion arose from the filial sense of guilt, in an attempt to allay that feeling and appease the father by deferred obedience to him. All later religions are seen to be attempts at solving the same problem."[15]

For Freud the murder in the prehistoric herd is an event of momentous importance in the history of human social life. In the powerful emotions it produced, we find the origin of religion. In the incest taboo—the agreement to protect the clan in its aftermath—we can see the origin of morality and the social contract. Taken together, totem and taboo thus form the very foundation of all that has come to be called civilization.

The Future of an Illusion

Totem and Taboo met with approval from Freud's associates in psychoanalysis—and with outrage from just about everyone else. Christian critics found the book particularly insulting. For his part, Freud ignored much of the debate and turned to other interests. Not until fourteen years later did he return to the subject of religion in *The Future of an Illusion* (1927), a book he chose to describe as a continuation of the earlier study. He notes that while *Totem and Taboo* looks backward into the prehistoric past, *The Future of an Illusion* considers religion in the present and looks forward. It centers not on an event hidden in prehistoric times but on the "manifest motives" of religion in all places and times. In addition, the second book puts a focus less on rituals than on ideas and beliefs—particularly Western monotheistic belief in God.

Freud begins *The Future of an Illusion* with certain facts recognized by almost everyone. Human life has arisen, or evolved, out of the natural world, an arena that is not necessarily friendly to our enterprises. Though it has produced our species, nature constantly threatens also to destroy us, whether through predators, disasters, disease, or physical decline. For protection, therefore, we have from the first joined into clans and communities, thereby creating what we call civilization. Through it we gain security, but at a price. As the events recounted in *Totem and Taboo* show us, society can survive only if we bend our personal desires to its rules and restraints. We cannot just kill when anger seizes us, take what we do not own, or satisfy sexual desires as we want. We must restrain our instincts, compensating ourselves (though never enough) with other satisfactions we can hope to find in, say, the joys of art and leisure or the ties of family and community. Yet even with these sacrifices and comforts, civilization cannot fully protect us. In the face of disease and death, we are all ultimately helpless. In the battle between nature and culture, nature's laws of decay and death will always finally win.

Freud next observes that none of us finds this unhappy truth easy to accept; it runs counter to all we treasure most. We would rather face things as we did in the sunnier days of our childhood. Then there was always a father to reassure us against the dangers of the storm or darkness of the night. Then there was always a voice of strength to say that all would be well in the end. As adults, in fact, we all continue to crave that childhood security, though in reality we can no longer have it. Or can we? The voice of religion makes us think that indeed we can. Following the childhood pattern, religious belief projects onto the external world a God, who through his power dispels the terrors of nature, gives us comfort in the face of death, and rewards us for accepting the moral restrictions imposed by civilization. Religious belief claims that "over each one of us there watches a benevolent providence which . . . will not suffer us to become a plaything of the over-mighty and pitiless forces of nature."[16] In the eyes of such faith, even death loses its sting, for we can be certain that our immortal spirits will one day be released from our bodies and live on with God. In denying our desires, therefore, we can be sure we are not just helping society; we are obeying the eternal laws of a just and righteous Lord.

The best word we can use to describe such beliefs, Freud contends, is "illusion." By this he means something quite specific. An illusion for him is a belief whose main characteristic is that we very much want it to be true. My belief that I am destined for greatness would be a case in point. It could turn out someday to be true, but that is not why I hold it. I hold it because I strongly *wish* it to be true. An illusion is not the same as a delusion, which is something I may also want to be true but which everyone else knows is not, and perhaps never could be so. If I were to claim that I will one day be eight feet tall (which, being now fully grown, I most certainly will not), I would be holding to a delusion. Rather shrewdly, Freud claims that he is not here calling belief in God as Father a delusion; in fact, he insists otherwise: "To assess the truth-value of religious doctrines does not lie within the scope of the present enquiry. It is enough for us that we have recognized them as being, in their psychological nature, illusions."[17]

Religious teachings, therefore, are not truths revealed by God, nor are they logical conclusions based on scientifically confirmed evidence. They are, on the contrary, ideas whose main feature is that we dearly want them to be true. They are "fulfillments of the oldest, strongest and most urgent wishes of mankind. The secret of their strength lies in the strength of those wishes."[18]

We should notice here that, though it may be helpful for some, for Freud himself this distinction between "illusion" and "delusion" comes to very little. In his view, it hardly makes a difference which term we use, because even if they cannot be absolutely proven such, religious beliefs are in the end delusions; they are teachings we have no right to believe because they cannot pass the test of the scientific method, which is the only way we have of reliably determining what is true and what is not. It is the habit of believers to draw on mere personal feelings and intuitions, and these are notorious for being often mistaken. Hence, we ought never to put our trust in religion, even if its teachings can be shown to have provided certain services for humanity in the past. Freud concedes that, at times, religious beliefs may have been of some small assistance in the growth of civilization. Certainly the early totem made a contribution through its role in the denunciation of murder and incest, and later religion did its part when these and similar crimes were discouraged by presenting them as offenses deserving of punishment in Hell. But civilization is now mature and established. We would no more want to build today's society on such superstition and repression than we would want to force grown men and women to obey the rules of behavior we lay down for children.

Religious teachings should be seen in this same light—as beliefs and rules suitable to the childhood of the human race. In the earlier history of humanity, "the times of its ignorance and intellectual weakness," religion was inescapable, like an episode of neurosis that individuals pass through in their childhood. However, when there is a failure to overcome the traumas and repressions of earlier life and the neurosis persists into adulthood, then psychoanalysis knows that the personality is in disorder. The same is true for the growth of civilization. Religion that persists into the present age of human history can only be a sign of illness; to begin to leave it behind is the first signal of health. In Freud's words:

> Religion would thus be the universal obsessional neurosis of humanity; like the obsessional neuroses of children, it arose out of the Oedipus Complex, out of the relation to the father. If this view is right, it is to be supposed that a turning-away from religion is bound to occur with the fatal inevitability of a process of growth, and that we find ourselves at this very juncture in the middle of that phase of development.[19]

Echoing Tylor, Freud concludes it is best "to view religious teachings . . . as neurotic relics, and we may now argue that the time has probably come, as it does in an analytic treatment, for replacing the effects of repression by the results of the rational operation of the intellect."[20] In short, as humanity grows into adult life, it must discard religion and replace it with forms of thought suitable to maturity. Mature people are guided by reason and by science, not by superstition and faith.

An interesting feature of *The Future of an Illusion* is its dialogue format. Freud routinely stops along the way of his discussion to answer the objections of an imaginary critic who takes the side of religion. Among other things, this critic insists that it is wrong to talk of religion as arising merely from our emotional needs, that religion ought to be believed on the basis of tradition, and—perhaps most important—that if religion is discarded as the ground for morals, society will collapse into violence and chaos. These criticisms are of course designed to strengthen Freud's case; and in each instance he offers a skillful and persuasive reply. In one of these objections, Freud is asked why he seems to have changed his theme since *Totem and Taboo*. That book was also about the origin of religion, but its subject was totemism and the father–son relationship; this one talks mainly about human helplessness. Has the theory now changed? Freud's answer to this question is instructive if not quite convincing. He explains that *Totem and Taboo* explored only one element, though it was deeply concealed, of what goes into religion. That was the two-sided feeling of both love for and fear of the father, who ruled the primeval horde. The present book, he says, explores "the other, less deeply concealed part"—the realization of adults that in the face of nature's crushing power, they will always be as weak as children and in need of a loving Father to defend them. Freud does not address the puzzling fact that while God is presented in the first book as a figure about whom human beings have very mixed emotions, in the second He is the Father who only loves—and is only loved in return. Still, whatever the motives, the result in Freud's eyes is always the same. The God whom people call upon in prayer is not a being who belongs to reality; he is an image, an illusion projected outward from the self and onto the external world out of the deep need to overcome our guilt or allay our fears.

Moses and Monotheism

Freud's interest in religion did not end with *The Future of an Illusion*, even though it offers perhaps the most important statement of his views. At the very end of his career, while struggling with the cancer that eventually took his life and finding himself driven from Vienna by the Nazi takeover of Austria, he returned to the subject for one final effort—writing this time on Judaism, his own religious tradition. In a series of essays undertaken between 1934 and 1937, he focused his attention on the figure of Moses, examining his foundational role in Jewish life and thought. These essays were then brought together in a single volume and published as *Moses and Monotheism* (1937) two years before his death.

As in *Totem and Taboo*, so in this quite unusual book, Freud puts forward a set of startling new claims about certain events in religious history—in particular Jewish history—and tries to show how the concepts and comparisons drawn from psychoanalysis can help to explain them. In the Bible, he observes, we learn that Moses is the great Hebrew prophet who inspired the people of Israel by his leadership and shaped their lives by giving them the law of God. True enough perhaps, but how do we know that Moses was really a Hebrew? A close look at the texts gives reason to believe that he was actually an Egyptian prince, a ruler and follower of the radical Pharaoh Akhenaten, who tried to replace the many gods of ancient Egypt with a strict devotion to one and only one deity—the sun god Aten. Unlike the other cults, the worship of Aten employed neither images nor superstitious rituals; it stressed a purely spiritual God of love and goodness, who was also revered as the strong guardian of an eternal moral law.

When Akhenaten died, his new religion failed in Egypt, but not entirely. It was kept alive by this same man Moses, who adopted the Hebrew slaves as his people, united them behind the new faith, and with great courage led them out of their captivity.

Initially Moses' followers prospered under his leadership. Later on, however, buffeted by their misfortunes in the desert, his chosen people rebelled against his leadership, renounced his God, and put him to death. His monotheistic religion was then overlaid by a new cult dedicated to a violent volcano-deity named Yahweh, whom Israelites chose to worship as they fought bloody battles to win the land of promise. Later, in writing their scriptures, Jewish scribes attached the name of Moses also to the founder of this second faith, but this sleight of hand could not disguise the differences between the new religion and the monotheism of the original Moses, their first and true spiritual leader. The new faith replaced the pure spirituality and morals of the earlier creed with the rituals, superstitions, and bloody sacrifices we find in Israel during the age of the great Hebrew kings. Degraded as it was, says Freud, the new religion managed almost completely to push out the old, leaving behind little more than a faint memory of the original Moses and his faith.

Yet that is not where the story ends. Centuries later in the life of the community, and against all probability, the people of Israel found themselves confronted by the great monotheistic prophets, men seized with the mission to recover and revive the old faith of the tribe. These prophets—Amos, Isaiah, and others—denounced the religion of sacrifices; they demanded worship of the one universal God announced by the first Moses, and they called again for obedience to his stern moral law. Their words thus marked a decisive turn that affected not just Jewish history but the entire world. For it was out of the soil of this revived Jewish monotheism that Christianity would one day rise to become a great world religion. From the time of the Hebrew prophets forward, faith in the awesome, righteous God of Moses took its place as the immovable center of both Jewish and Christian belief.

There is no question that this quite extraordinary retelling of Hebrew history as Freud sees it rests on a number of adventurous connections and eye-opening historical conjectures that would trouble both the historian and the biblical scholar. It is not easy to find in the Bible any clear proof that Moses was an Egyptian, that he was murdered, that two persons were given his name, or that the early Hebrews ever had two different religions. To Freud, however, these problems are not a concern. Much more interesting to him is the mystery of how, over many centuries, a true monotheism was somehow born, apparently died, and then came back to life. How can it be, he asks, that the faith of the original Moses virtually disappeared from the life of his people, only to return centuries later in dramatic fashion and win back the hearts and minds of the entire Jewish community? Theologians may be at a loss to answer such a question, but psychoanalysis certainly is not. Freud asks us to suppose once again that a parallel can be found between what happens psychologically to an individual person over the course of a life and what happens in history, over a much longer time, to an entire community of people like the Jews. And he restates his view that religion is best conceived along the lines of a neurosis. That said, he offers the following ingenious argument.

Psychoanalytic theory has clearly demonstrated that cases of personal neurosis follow a familiar pattern. They start, often in early childhood, with a traumatic, disturbing event that is pushed out of memory for a time. There follows a period of "latency," when nothing shows; all seems normal. Then at a later point—often at the onset of puberty or in early adulthood—the irrational behavior that is the sign of neurosis suddenly makes its appearance. We find that there is a "return of the repressed." Now if these stages are indeed identifiable, Freud suggests that we can compare them with the sequences discovered in the history of Judaism. And as we do, let us recall as well the points made in the earlier books about ambivalent emotions, tribal murder, and religion as childlike desire for the figure of a father. Do they not fit with an almost uncanny accuracy? The message of monotheism spoke to the Jews' natural human longing for a divine father. The powerful personality of Moses, whom the people may even have identified with his God, recalled the imposing figure of the first father in the primeval horde. His death in a desert rebellion was more than a mere historical accident; it can be read as a reenactment of the primeval murder of the great father, an event no less traumatic for the Jews than the first murder was for the sons and brothers in the prehistoric human tribe. Fittingly, once the murder had been committed, the Hebrew community, in an act of collective repression, sought to relieve its guilt by striving to erase the entire memory of Moses—both the monotheism and the murder—from community life, thereby allowing the crude Yahweh religion of the second Moses to take its place. For the true Mosaic religion, this was the period of its latency, a long era when it lay submerged and almost forgotten in the Judaic communal mind. And yet the law of neurosis is clear: Whatever is repressed must return. After centuries in eclipse, the pure and ancient creed of the founder made its powerful return in the oracles of the prophets. Henceforth, pure monotheism, the religion of loving devotion to the Lord of the Covenant, became again the faith of all Jews, who on those terms rightfully and to the present day claim the honor of being his chosen people.

Significantly, Freud adds, even the role of Christianity as Judaism's successor comes into clearer focus once we read its history through the eyes of psychoanalysis. It is clear from the discussion in *Totem and Taboo* that the revolt in the primeval horde had a two-sided emotional outcome: love and fear.

Judaism recalls the urge to idealize the Father, to make him into a loving God and repress the guilt left behind by his murder. Christianity feels the same mix of affection and guilt but responds by declaring the need for atonement. As framed by its chief thinker, the Jewish rabbi Paul, Christian theology centers not on God the Father but on Christ the Son and his death—in other words, on God who, in the form of the firstborn Son, goes to his death to atone for the original sin committed by the first sons in the prehistoric horde.

Never modest in his claims, Freud here offers a psychoanalytic portrait of both Jewish and Christian monotheism that few theologians or historians would dare attempt. Along the same bold lines of analogy laid out in his earlier works, he argues that the appeal of these—and other—religions lies not in the truth of their teachings about a god or a savior, their claims about miracles or a chosen people, or their hopes of a life after death. Those doctrines are empty because they lie beyond any chance of proof. The concepts of psychoanalytic science, however, are very different. And they show in ever-so-interesting ways that the real power of religions is to be found beyond their doctrines, in the deep psychological needs they fill and the unconscious emotions they express.

Analysis

1. Psychology and Religion

In commenting on the twentieth century, the great English poet W. H. Auden once said, "We are all Freudians now." This remark pays tribute to the enormous influence that Freud's ideas have had on all spheres of thought in our time. Religion is no exception. Freud's analysis of the hidden forces within the human personality has compelled not just those concerned with the theory of religion but almost everyone associated with its practice—theologians, clergy, counselors, and teachers—to look beneath the surface of accepted doctrines and discover the deep, unnoticed elements of personality that shape human religious faith and are in turn shaped by it. Interestingly, though Freud himself takes a decidedly negative view of religious behavior, other leaders in psychoanalysis—and even entire schools of thought in contemporary psychology—have been eager to adapt his insights to their own much more sympathetic views. Among others, perhaps the most notable figure in this tradition has been the Swiss psychologist Carl Jung (1875–1961), one of the most important voices in the circle of Freud's earliest associates. For Jung, religion draws on a deep fund of images and ideas that belong collectively to the human race and find expression in mythology, folklore, philosophy, and literature. Religion, like these other endeavors, draws on the resources of this "collective unconscious" not as a form of neurosis but as the healthy expression of true and deep humanity.

Others, such as contemporary ego psychologists and object relation theorists, have followed a similar path, developing an entire field of studies in religion and personality and producing a rich literature of theory and therapy. It seems to matter little on this account whether analysts share Freud's distaste for belief or Jung's approval; both perspectives have contributed greatly to the contemporary understanding of religion.

2. Freud's Explanation of Religion

The importance of Freud's theory of religion is closely connected to the context in which he wrote. His views actually follow a line of thought developed early in the 1800s by Ludwig Feuerbach, a German philosopher who gained fame in his day for a book called *The Essence of Christianity* (1841). In this controversial study, he claimed that all of religion is just a psychological device by which we attach our own hopes, virtues, and ideals to an imaginary supernatural being we call "God" and in the process only diminish ourselves. Feuerbach, whom we shall meet again in this book because of his impact on Karl Marx, might well be called the first modern thinker to offer a purely "projectionist" explanation of religion. That is to say, he explains religion by showing not what truth or rationality believers find in their ideas but rather what is the psychological mechanism that creates religious beliefs, *regardless* of whether they are true or false, rational or irrational. Though briefly popular, Feuerbach was not able to keep his following, and his theory faded from view. Marx developed it further, as we shall see, but he too was largely ignored in his age. By Freud's day, however, the time for just such a functional projectionist theory was again ripe. And that was largely because of the work of Tylor and Frazer. As we saw previously, both of these thinkers conclude that religion is something primarily "intellectual"; it is a system of ideas once sincerely believed and now known to be mistaken and absurd. But again, assuming all of this to be so, we must still try to explain how and why the human race has held so firmly to this collection of superstition and error throughout its history and into the scientific present. Why, if it is so absurd, do people insist upon religion? In the eyes of some, that is the puzzle that Freud, who knew well the work of these English anthropological writers, brilliantly managed to solve. On his view, if we want to know why religion persists even when it has been discredited by science or better philosophy, we need only turn to psychoanalysis, which tells us quite clearly that the true source of religion's appeal is not the rational mind but the unconscious. Religion arises from emotions and conflicts that originate early in childhood and lie deep beneath the rational, normal surface of the personality. It is best seen as an obsessional neurosis. Accordingly, we can no more suppose that believers would give up their faith because it has been proved irrational than that a neurotic would give up continuous hand-washing because it has been pointed out that his hands are already quite clean. The normal causes we see on the surface of things are not the real causes of the behavior.

Freud is quite prepared to push this functional account of religion as far as it can possibly go. He does not just say that, *among other things*, religion seems to have certain psychological functions. He asserts that religion arises *only* in response to deep emotional conflicts and weaknesses; he insists that these are in fact its true, fundamental causes and, consequently, that once psychoanalysis has scientifically resolved such problems, we can expect the illusion of religion quite naturally to disappear from the human scene. Freud thus presents us with a particularly vivid instance of an explanatory strategy that has had great influence in the twentieth century—the approach theorists today describe as functionalist *reductionism*. In what he sees as a radical unmasking of the real truth about religion, Freud claims not just to explain it but to explain it away. In his view, religion in its entirety can be "reduced" to little more than a by-product of psychological distress, dismissed as a collection of ideas and beliefs that, once their surface appearance has been penetrated, turn out to be illusory wish fulfillments generated by the unconscious.

We do need to add here that Freud is not always consistent in his judgments; in some places he seems not quite so exclusively committed to this psychological reductionism as in others. But in the main, he furnishes us with a clear and outspoken version of the reductionist approach, which strongly insists that religion is never a reality on its own terms; it is always an appearance, an expression of something else. It is not a genuine agent in human behavior or thought because its fundamental character is always passive; its nature is to reflect other realities—more powerful and more basic—that underlie it. Outspoken and influential as he has been, moreover, Freud is by no means alone in pursuing this particularly aggressive functionalist strategy. As we shall see in the chapters that immediately follow, the same kind of approach is evident in the work of two other theorists whose views on religion have been of major importance to the present day. We find versions of it both in the sociology of Émile Durkheim, Freud's French contemporary, and in the economic materialism of Karl Marx.

Critique

Any appraisal of Freud requires comment not only on his theory of religion but also on the larger framework of psychoanalytic science that serves as its support. We have space here to raise just a few pertinent questions about the first, then to note an ongoing, animated debate about the merits of the second.

1. The Problem of Theistic and Nontheistic Religions

The first thing to observe is that Freud offers us not so much a theory of religion in general as a theory of Judeo-Christian, or at least monotheistic, religion in particular. In all three of the works we have examined, the ideas of the Oedipus complex and the need for a father image are so central to the discussion that it is hard to see how the arguments could be applied to any form of religion that is not monotheistic. Though he does mention them in a few places, religions that affirm many gods, that propose mother gods, or that articulate a faith in divine powers that are not personal in character fall largely outside the embrace of Freud's discussion. Since he chooses not to consider such religions, we cannot say for certain how Freud would have explained them had he made the attempt. But even if we were to try, on his behalf, to extend his explanations to cover them, it is not easy to see how this could be done. Much of his theory seems constructed specifically to account for those religions that affirm one, and only one, all-powerful Father God. Others just do not fit.

2. The Problems of Analogy and History

Assuming we could find a way past the focus on monotheism, there is the issue of Freud's reasoning by analogy. For example, as we have seen in *Totem and Taboo* and *Moses and Monotheism*, the argument of both books turns on an extended comparison between the psychological growth of an individual and the historical development of a large social group. The one takes place over at most the sequence of decades that makes up the life of a single individual; the other takes place over the course of centuries in the history of an entire community. What ground do we have, logically, to assume any real similarity or clear connection between these two quite different things? It may be true that from childhood onward a neurotic person passes through the several stages Freud depicts. But outside of coincidence and Freud's ingenuity, what grounds do we have to suppose that the entire history of the Jews conforms to the pattern of development found in a single disturbed human personality?

Again, by what logic do we conclude, as Freud does in *Totem and Taboo*, that the Christian rite of communion is somehow created from the hidden communal memory of an Oedipal murder that took place thousands of years earlier in the first animal-like hordes of humans? We can perhaps understand how an early trauma could stay with one person for the rest of a life. But how can an ancient murder be unconsciously "remembered" by the whole human race? Freud feels that there are such collective memories, but that is mainly because he relies on a version of evolutionary theory, put forward by the French scientist Lamarck, who held that an experience acquired during one's life can be biologically inherited by descendants. Unfortunately, in the decades after Darwin, this version of evolution came under severe challenge from those who saw far better grounds for concluding that natural selection was the key to the evolutionary process. It is disconcerting to discover that Freud, who often advertised his solemn commitment to science, rested his analyses of religion so heavily on a form of evolutionism that other important scientists of his day had given good reasons to reject.

A further point also needs notice here. Even if we were to grant everything Freud says about human individuals in his analogical arguments, very large historical questions remain about their cultural side. From almost their first encounters with *Moses and Monotheism*, historical critics have found in the biblical and archaeological evidence little support for Freud's highly imaginative reconstruction of the early history of the Jews. If anything, anthropologists have been even more skeptical of the conjectures about the original human hordes and the murder of the first fathers. The plain fact is that most of these events are simply lost in the fog of prehistory; reconstructing them requires a great deal of imaginative guesswork. It is not a matter of uncertainty, as if some evidence supports Freud and the rest does not; it is really a matter of ignorance and inaccessibility. About such matters we often have little evidence of any kind to support a theory of the sort Freud advances.

3. The Problem of Circularity

As we saw in his very first essay on religion and at the core of the argument in *The Future of an Illusion*, Freud argues that religion is very similar to a neurosis. Just as neurotic people believe and do irrational things, so religious people also believe and do irrational things. The kind of obsessional neurosis discovered by psychoanalysis appears mainly in individual persons. The kind of obsessional neurosis seen in religion afflicts entire cultures; it is universal. Here again, however, we must inquire about Freud's curious uses of analogy, for context is crucial in explaining behavior. As even a number of critics friendly to Freud have pointed out, a nun who spends hours at devotions moving her prayer beads and a neurotic who spends hours counting the buttons on his shirt are both engaged in the same form of behavior, but only one is mentally disturbed. For nuns it is normal, not neurotic, to pray. Freud chooses to find unconscious motives for such action only because *from the start* he has assumed that prayer is an abnormal behavior. But of course he cannot do that without claiming that it arises not from rational motives but from irrational ones located in the unconscious—the very thing he sets out to prove. To put the matter bluntly, some of Freud's discussions wear the look of arguments that are decidedly circular.

Furthermore, the idea of projection itself is open to some question. The mere fact that people project things from their minds out onto the world is hardly proof that they are engaged in neurotic wish fulfillment. The symbols of science and mathematics belong, strictly speaking, to numerical and conceptual systems that we project upon the world not out of neurosis but simply because they help us describe and understand that real world better. The obvious fact that every day these "projections" of ourselves are successfully applied to real life shows that they do, in fact, reflect something of the character of the world as we experience it. But if that is true for the conceptions of mathematics and natural science, there is no reason why, in principle at least, we cannot allow that certain religious projections might also be true and might originate not from neurosis but from a reasonable and appropriate understanding of the real world as we perceive it.

4. Psychoanalysis as Science

We must finish this brief critique by raising finally the problematic position of psychoanalysis itself as a form of science. Freud was trained in the natural sciences; he began his career with research on the physiology of the brain. When he turned to psychoanalysis, he stressed from the beginning, and in definitive terms, that its methods were those of science. Psychoanalysis was to be built on in-depth consultations with patients, on the careful framing and testing of hypotheses, on the search for general theories, and on the exchange of criticism in scholarly journals. In *The Future of an Illusion* Freud proudly compares the slow, steady progress of sciences like psychoanalysis with the backward dogmatism of religion. And today, certainly, the wide acceptance of psychoanalysis rests mainly on the common view that it is a *science* of the mind.

It is just this accepted view, however, that in recent decades has come under severe scientific attack. Over the past forty years especially, critics in many quarters have subjected the entire enterprise of psychoanalysis—from Freud onward—to a rigorous and searching reassessment. Their common verdict, which is not friendly, can be summarized in two sentences: Whatever his talents, Freud was not a scientist. And whatever its claims, psychoanalysis is not a science. The weightiest charges against the discipline were leveled by an American philosopher of science, Adolf Grünbaum, who argues that psychoanalysts regularly assume the very things they hope to prove in their work with patients, that their techniques for gathering evidence are scientifically unsound, and that when usable evidence is, in fact, brought forward, it does not support the elaborate Freudian conclusions conventionally drawn from it. Grünbaum does not say that the field is unscientific in principle, but he does state that it has yet to establish truly scientific methods for testing its claims.[21] Others, looking on from a different perspective, have joined in these criticisms, noticing that the principles at the core of the science—Freud's theories of the personality and neurosis—are constructed out of vague comparisons and questionable inferences, most of which cannot be either proved or disproved because, again, there is simply no scientific way even to test them.[22] Still other observers have turned a sternly critical eye upon Freud himself, only to find someone quite different from the man his disciples presented to the world as a disinterested, pioneering scientist, the spokesman for truth in a world of Victorian repression. They point out that while his talents of imagination and persuasion were certainly quite formidable, Freud was also a shrewd promoter of his own interests as well as a man willing to bend evidence, ignore valid criticism, and even misuse people when such actions served the purpose of his program.[23]

In the light of these criticisms, it must be said that the scientific future of psychoanalysis does not look especially promising. Freud's theory of religion is unlikely to fare better—unless (and that is always a possibility) it is refitted to a new frame and placed on a less uncertain footing. At the same time, it should be duly noted that psychoanalysis is only one strand of modern psychology. Later in these pages we will trace a different strand in Freud's contemporary William James, honored by some as "the father of psychology" in America.

Notes

1. *The Future of an Illusion*, in *The Standard Edition of the Complete Psychological Works of Sigmund Freud*, ed. James Strachey with Anna Freud (London: Hogarth Press, 1961), 21: 43.

2. The classic older biography of Freud, written by an Englishman who belonged to the circle of his original followers, is Ernest Jones, *The Life and Work of Sigmund Freud*, 3 vols. (New York: Basic Books, 1953–1957). An authoritative later biography is Peter Gay, *Freud: A Life for our Times* (New York: W. W. Norton, 1988). There are also numerous thematic and shorter biographical studies.

3. "Obsessive Actions and Religious Practices," in *Standard Edition*, 9: 116–127.

4. Much in this book was based on self-analysis, especially Freud's interpretations of his own dream experiences. See Gerald Levin, *Sigmund Freud* (Boston: Twayne Publishers, 1975), p. 28.

5. Much has been written on Freud's concept of repression. A good, brief account of this idea and its place in Freud's thought can be found in Philip Rieff's *Freud: The Mind of the Moralist*, 3rd ed. (Chicago: University of Chicago Press, 1979), pp. 37–44, 314–320.

6. Freud's study *Leonardo da Vinci and a Memory of His Childhood* (1910) and his articles on "The Moses of Michelangelo" (1914) and "Dostoyevsky and Parricide" (1928) continue to fascinate historians of art and literature.

7. Freud first presented this formulation in *The Ego and the Id* in 1923.

8. See Freud, *An Outline of Psychoanalysis*, in *Standard Edition*, 23: 146.

9. Freud, *An Outline of Psychoanalysis*, in *Standard Edition*, 23: 190.

10. Freud, *An Outline of Psychoanalysis*, in *Standard Edition*, 23: 191.

11. Among a number of instructive works on Freud's Jewish background and his religious opinions, see Howard Littleton Philp, *Freud and Religious Belief* (New York: Pitman, 1956); G. Zillboorg, *Freud and Religion: A Restatement of an Old Controversy* (Westminster, MD: Newman Press, 1958); Earl A. Grollman, *Judaism in Sigmund Freud's World* (New York: Appleton-Century, 1965); Hans Küng, *Freud and the Problem of God* (New Haven, CT: Yale University Press, 1979); Edwin R. Wallace IV, "Freud and Religion," in Werner Muensterberger et al., eds., *The Psychoanalytic Study of Society*, vol. 10 (Hillsdale, NJ: The Analytic Press, 1984), pp. 113–161; and Peter Gay, *A Godless Jew: Freud, Atheism, and the Making of Psychoanalysis* (New Haven, CT: Yale University Press, 1987). Wallace and Gay also provide substantial recent bibliographies.

12. Jones, *Life and Work of Freud*, 3: 351.

13. Freud, "Obsessive Actions and Religious Practices" (1907), in *Standard Edition*, 9: 126; this famous phrase, which heads this chapter, appears again in *The Future of an Illusion*.

14. *Totem and Taboo*, in *Standard Edition*, 13: 132–142.

15. *Totem and Taboo*, in *Standard Edition*, 13: 145.

16. Freud, *The Future of an Illusion*, in *Standard Edition*, 21: 19.

17. *The Future of an Illusion*, in *Standard Edition*, 21: 33.

18. *The Future of an Illusion*, in *Standard Edition*, 21: 30.

19. *The Future of an Illusion*, in *Standard Edition*, 21: 43.

20. *The Future of an Illusion*, in *Standard Edition*, 21: 44.

21. See his important work, *The Foundations of Psychoanalysis* (Berkeley: University of California Press, 1984).

22. See especially Malcolm Macmillan, *Freud Evaluated: The Completed Arc* (New York: North Holland, 1991).

23. On Freud's literary talents, especially in the area of expository nonfiction, see Patrick J. Mahony, *Freud as a Writer* (New Haven, CT: Yale University Press, 1987). The scientific criticisms, along with appreciations, of Freud are put with special force in Frank Sulloway, *Freud, Biologist of the Mind: Beyond the Psychoanalytic Legend* (New York: Basic Books, 1979); see also Jeffrey Moussaieff Masson, *The Assault upon Truth: Freud's Suppression of the Seduction Theory* (New York: Farrar, Straus, and Giroux, 1984), and Frederick C. Crews, *Skeptical Engagements* (New York: Oxford University Press, 1986). For summaries of these criticisms and the heated debates they have elicited, see Paul Robinson, *Freud and His Critics* (Berkeley: University of California Press, 1993), and Frederick C. Crews, "The Unknown Freud," *New York Review of Books* 40, no. 19 (November 18, 1993): 55–66.

Suggestions for Further Reading

Bernstein, Richard J. *Freud and the Legacy of Moses*. Cambridge: Cambridge University Press, 1998. Reappraises *Moses and Monotheism*, claiming this much-criticized book is Freud's most important because it offers a new conception of religion.

Capps, Donald, ed. *Freud and Freudians on Religion: A Reader*. New Haven, CT: Yale University Press, 2001. Assembles writings on religion from the perspective of psychoanalysis as advanced by both Freud and a number of his most prominent followers.

Crews, Frederick, ed. *Unauthorized Freud: Doubters Confront a Legend*. New York: Viking Press, 1998. One of Freud's harshest contemporary critics collects further challenges from prominent figures who continue to place the methods of both Freud and psychoanalysis under scrutiny.

Dufresne, Todd. *Against Freud: Critics Talk Back*. Stanford, CA: Stanford University Press, 2007. A collection of interviews with the leading contemporary critics of Freud, his methods, and Freudian theory.

Flem, Lydia. *Freud the Man*. Translated by Susan Fairfield. New York: Other Press, 2003. A newer biography that centers on the personal interests and concerns of Freud alongside his professional work in psychology.

Gay, Peter. *A Godless Jew: Freud, Atheism, and the Making of Psychoanalysis*. New Haven, CT: Yale University Press, 1987. A brief, insightful assessment of Freud's perspective on religion by an authoritative biographer.

Grünbaum, Adolf. *Validation in the Clinical Theory of Psychoanalysis: A Study in the Philosophy of Psychoanalysis*. Madison, CT: International Universities Press, 1993. An amplification of the critique first advanced by Grünbaum with *The Foundations of Psychoanalysis* in 1984.

Kerr, John. *A Most Dangerous Method: The Story of Jung, Freud, and Sabina Spielrein*. New York: Alfred A. Knopf, 1993. Raises questions, both moral and scientific, about the aims and methods of Freud and Jung in dealing with one of their first patients.

Kramer, Peter D. *Freud: Inventor of the Modern Mind*. New York: Harper Collins, 2006. A recent reappraisal of Freud that steers a middle path between disciples and critics.

Küng, Hans. *Freud and the Problem of God*. New Haven, CT: Yale University Press, 1979. A thoughtful analysis of Freud's theological opinions by a distinguished modern Catholic theologian.

Lear, Jonathan. *Freud*. New York: Routledge, 2005. A reinterpretation of Freud's career with particular focus on his achievement in creating psychoanalysis and the status of his work viewed from the perspective of philosophy.

MacIntyre, Alasdair C. *The Unconscious: A Conceptual Analysis*. London: Routledge & Kegan Paul, 1958. Now quite dated, but uniquely valuable as a clear and brief study of the idea that gave birth to psychoanalysis. Written by an influential philosopher in the tradition of language analysis.

Masson, Jeffrey Moussaieff. *The Assault upon Truth: Freud's Suppression of the Seduction Theory*. New York: Farrar, Straus, and Giroux, 1984. A controversial exposé of Freud's methods that attempts to show how he mishandled one of his early patients in psychoanalysis.

Merlino, Joseph P. et al., *Freud at 150: 21st Century Essays on a Man of Genius.* Lanham, MD: Jason Aronson, Inc., 2007. Lectures measuring Freud's world stature and achievement; contributed to a conference sponsored by the Austrian government on the 150th anniversary of Freud's birth.

Neu, Jerome, ed. *The Cambridge Companion to Freud.* New York: Cambridge University Press, 1991. Instructive essays on Freud by various scholars of strong pedigree active in writing on his life and thought.

Palmer, Michael. *Freud and Jung on Religion.* London: Routledge, 1997. Explores the fundamentally opposite appraisals of religion offered by the two founders of psychoanalysis.

Rieff, Philip. *Freud: The Mind of the Moralist.* 3rd ed. Chicago: University of Chicago Press, 1979. A widely read and much appreciated study of Freud's ideas in their biographical and cultural context.

Rizzuto, Ana-Maria. *Why Did Freud Reject God? A Psychodynamic Interpretation.* New Haven, CT: Yale University Press, 1998. Argues that Freud's childhood development and family circumstances made serious consideration of belief in God impossible for him.

Roazen, Paul. *Encountering Freud: The Politics and Histories of Psychoanalysis.* New Brunswick, NJ: Transaction Publishers, 1990. An exploration of the controversies surrounding the aims of both Freud and his new field of study.

Robinson, Paul. *Freud and His Critics.* Berkeley: University of California Press, 1993. Summarizes and evaluates issues in the heated debate over Freud and the validity of psychoanalysis as a science.

Sulloway, Frank. *Freud, Biologist of the Mind: Beyond the Psychoanalytic Legend.* New York: Basic Books, 1979. A comprehensive study by a scholar who, since this book, has gradually grown more critical of Freud's science.

3

Society as Sacred: Émile Durkheim

The idea of society is the soul of religion.

Durkheim, *The Elementary Forms of the Religious Life*[1]

In the very years during which Freud put forward his controversial views in Vienna, an equally original thinker in France, Émile Durkheim, set to work on a theory of religion that was just as revolutionary, though in quite a different way. If Freud is the first name that people associate with modern psychology, then that of Durkheim—though less widely known—should be one of the first that comes to mind at the mention of sociology. Durkheim championed the central importance of society—of social structures, relationships, and institutions—in understanding human thought and behavior. His distinct perspective consists in his determination to see almost every major enterprise of human life—our laws and morality, labor and recreation, family and personality, science, art, and certainly religion—through the lens of their social dimension. Without a society to give them birth and shape them, he claimed, none of these things could exist.

At a first glance, of course, a theorist who sounds this social theme hardly seems revolutionary. In the present climate of thought, few discussions of any kind take place without some reference to the "social environment." Hardly a day passes without some comment on "social decay," "social engineering," "social reform," or "social justice." A century ago, however, such language would have been almost as rare as it is common now. "Society" was a word mostly associated with upper-class manners and the dinner parties of the wealthy. The leading systems of thought were quite individualistic, with a tendency to see any social arrangement—from a single family to a village, a church, or an entire nation—as little more than a collection of separate persons who happened to be brought together by a common location or shared interests. Durkheim's view was emphatically different. He went so far as to say that social facts are more fundamental than individual ones—that they are, in their way, as real as physical objects, and that individuals are more often than not *mis*understood when the powerful imprint of society upon them is ignored or insufficiently noticed. Human beings, after all, are never just individuals; they always *belong* to something—to parents or relatives, a town or city, a race, a political party, an ethnic tradition, or some other group. In Durkheim's view, it is futile to think that we can really comprehend what a person is by appealing only to biological instinct, individual psychology, or isolated self-interest. We must explain individuals in and through society.

In accord with this social premise, Durkheim insisted, very much like Freud, that his subject required nothing less than a new scientific discipline to investigate it. This field he chose to call "sociology," even though he was not the first to use the word and was not himself very fond of it. Simply put, sociology was to be the science of society. In a significant measure it is because of Durkheim's strong advocacy and guiding influence that social science holds such a prominent place in modern life, whether we appeal to it in matters of government, economics, education, or in any other forum of public discussion, from the university lecture room to the television reality show. Today, our instinctively social view of the world is an index of just how thoroughly successful Durkheim's revolution in thought has turned out to be.[2]

Durkheim actually presents us with two parallels to Freud. Not only did both men feel the need to promote special fields of study—psychology in the one case and sociology in the other—but both also found that their new perspectives led them unavoidably back to the very old question of religious behavior and belief. Like Freud, Durkheim too was driven to ask: What is religion? Why has it been so important and central in human affairs? What does it do for both the individual and society? Freud, as we saw, thought he could not fully explain the individual personality without also accounting for the appeal of religion. Durkheim felt precisely the same about society. In the course of trying to understand "the social" in all of its hidden and powerful dimensions, he found himself drawn steadily and repeatedly to "the religious." For Durkheim, religion and society are inseparable and—to each other—virtually indispensable.

Life and Career

Durkheim was born in 1858 in the town of Epinal, near Strasbourg in northeastern France.[3] His father was a rabbi, and as a young boy he was also strongly affected by a schoolteacher who was Roman Catholic. These influences may have contributed something to his general interest in religious endeavors, but they did not make him personally a believer. By the time he was a young man, he had become an avowed agnostic.

In secondary school Durkheim was a brilliant student, and at the age of twenty-one he was admitted to the demanding École Normale Supérieure, one of France's finest centers of learning, where he studied both history and philosophy. His experience there was not a completely happy one, in part because he did not like the rigid way in which the programs of study were designed. Yet his response at the time, which offers a clue to his temperament, was not to withdraw or complain; he had too keen an appreciation for social order to abandon an institution just because he was personally unsuited to its rules. After finishing his program and writing the two dissertations required of all students at the École Normale, he began teaching at secondary schools in the vicinity of Paris. He also took a year to study in Germany with the noted psychologist Wilhelm Wundt. In 1887 he married Louise Dreyfus, a woman who devoted herself lifelong to his career and their two children. In the same year he became a professor at the University of Bordeaux, which created a new chair of social science and education specifically for his sociological research.

Over the next fifteen years, while working at Bordeaux, Durkheim diligently pursued his sociological inquiries and developed his ideas. His first major book was *The Division of Labor*, published in 1893. It was followed in 1895 by *The Rules of Sociological Method*, a theoretical work that stirred a great deal of debate. He also published an important study, *Suicide* (1897), which looked for the public, social factors behind what others of his day commonly regarded as a strictly private act of despair. At about the same time, he established with other scholars *L'Année sociologique*, a new academic journal that published articles and reviewed other writings from a sociological perspective. This journal, which became famous throughout France and the world, did as much as any of Durkheim's own books to promote the discipline of sociology. Other talented scholars were drawn to contribute their work to its pages and in the process developed Durkheim's perspective into an identifiable "school of thought." Not surprisingly, on the strength of these impressive achievements (and with the help of some political maneuvering in the government), Durkheim was named a professor at the University of Paris. At the age of forty-four, he could boast the supreme achievement of a French academic career.

At Paris, Durkheim passed through years of triumph and later of tragedy. Already in Bordeaux his interests had begun to turn strongly toward an exploration of religion's role in social life, but after his move, new commitments and tasks slowed the progress of this research. Nonetheless, he kept to his plan and a decade later published *The Elementary Forms of the Religious Life* (1912), his best-known and most important book. Durkheim's chief claim to importance as a theorist of religion—and his great influence on other thinkers—rests largely on this impressive study, which we shall examine closely in this chapter. As its date indicates, *The Elementary Forms* appeared just two years before Europe was shaken by World War I. This enormous catastrophe fell hardest on Belgium and France, where much of the fighting took place, and it left its sad mark on Durkheim's personal life, as it did on so many others. Though he believed that scholars should preserve their scientific objectivity by avoiding comment on current affairs, he made an exception during the war, speaking out fiercely for the cause of France against Germany. Then, early in 1916, he learned that his only son, André, himself a promising young scholar, had been killed on a military campaign in Serbia. Broken by grief, Durkheim struggled to work and write, only to suffer a debilitating stroke some months later. His own death came just over a year thereafter, in 1917, at the relatively young age of fifty-nine.

Ideas and Influences

Durkheim's great interest in society was not some sudden creation of his own. As he would have been the first to point out, a sequence of French thinkers before him had shown similar interests, and his ideas could be seen as a development of theirs.[4] One of his two dissertations had been written on the Baron de Montesquieu, the French philosopher of the eighteenth century who carefully observed and analyzed European culture and political institutions. Montesquieu's work showed that social structures could be examined in a critical scientific fashion. Durkheim also read the writings of the Comte de Saint-Simon, a socialist thinker of the early 1800s who believed that all private property should be given over to the state. And he was equally impressed by the most famous French thinker of the early nineteenth century, August Comte (1798–1857), who proposed, like Tylor and Frazer, an evolutionary pattern of civilization. In this grand scheme, earlier stages of human thinking, governed first by theology and then by the abstract ideas of philosophers, are eventually surpassed by the current, "positive" age of scientific thought, in which close study only of observable facts provides the key to all knowledge. During the present epoch of science, a new "religion of humanity" replaces the discredited religions and philosophies of the past. From Comte, Durkheim took an appreciation of the human need for communal ties and a deep commitment to scientific analysis of social phenomena. He was somewhat less taken with the notion of evolutionary social progress.

In addition to these earlier figures, we must not forget two of the most celebrated scholars in France during Durkheim's youth: the great biblical critic

Ernest Renan, who took a keenly social interest in both ancient Judaism and early Christianity, and an extraordinarily gifted classical historian who was one of Durkheim's own greatly admired university teachers at the École Normale. This was Numa Denys Fustel de Coulanges, whose influential book *The Ancient City* (1864) was to become a classic study of social life in the ancient world. In this fascinating work, Coulanges presented his readers with a close social analysis of the Greek and Roman city-states, showing not only how ordinary life was governed by deeply cherished traditions and rooted in conservative moral values but also how thoroughly these traditions and values were steeped in classical polytheistic religion.

Durkheim built naturally upon the ideas of these thinkers in framing his own perspective, but the circumstances of modern French life contributed something as well. As most well know, by the later 1800s France and Europe had passed through two great revolutions. One was economic (the Industrial Revolution); the other was political (the French Revolution and its several successors). In Durkheim's estimate, the joint impact of these two momentous developments permanently changed the pattern of life in Western civilization. Europe had long relied for stability on its agriculture, its well-defined social classes, its property-owning aristocracies and monarchies, and the intimate community ties of its villages and towns, along with the overarching truths, traditions, and structures of the Christian church. In the aftermath of the twin revolutions, these fixtures of Western culture were shaken as never before and so altered as never again to be the same. The effect was to create a new and different kind of civilization, which saw its people moving to factories and cities, its wealth moving from titled lords to enterprising merchants, its power shifting from the old privileged classes to radical movements or popular causes, and its religion everywhere facing disputes, indifference, or open disbelief. In specific terms, Durkheim noticed especially the following four trends, or patterns:

1. In place of Europe's traditional social system, laced together as it was by ties of family, community, and religious faith, a new "contractual" order was emerging, in which private concerns and money-related interests seemed to predominate.
2. In the realm of morals and behavior, the sacred values once sanctioned by the Church were now challenged by newer ideals, which stressed reason over religious faith and a desire for a happiness in this life over any hope of Heaven (or fear of Hell) in the life to come.
3. In the sphere of politics, the emergence of the democratic masses at the bottom of society and a powerful central state at the top had changed the nature of social control. Individuals were finding themselves disconnected

from their old moral teachers—the family, village, and Church—and were left to find what guidance they could from political parties, mass movements, and the state.

4. In the area of personal affairs, this new freedom of individuals released from their old frameworks presented great opportunity *and* great risk. With it came the chance of greater prosperity and self-realization but also the serious threat of loneliness and personal isolation.

Sociology and "the Social"

Looking over these momentous changes, Durkheim felt that there was only one way to approach them—scientifically. Only a fully scientific sociology could help people comprehend the tremors of an entire world that was moving beneath their feet. Accordingly, he laid down for his scholarly investigations two fixed and fundamental principles: (1) that the nature of society is the most suitable and promising subject for systematic investigation, especially at the present moment in history, and (2) that all such "social facts" should be investigated by the most purely objective scientific methods attainable.

The Nature of Society

In *The Division of Labor*, Durkheim's first major book, he shows how easily one can go wrong by ignoring the first of these principles. Social life, he explains, has shaped the most fundamental features of human culture, but that is not how previous thinkers tended to see it. If they considered it at all, they did so as a kind of afterthought. When they looked at the past, they proposed ideas like the famous "social contract," which held that society began when some individuals agreed to hand power to another, stronger individual—the king—in return for his protection. When this primeval agreement was sealed, society was born. Such stories offer an interesting exercise in imaginative fiction, says Durkheim, but the real history of humanity was never so. Even in prehistoric times, individuals were always born *first* into groups—into families, clans, tribes, nations—and raised in that context. Their languages, habits, beliefs, and emotional responses—even the very concept they had of their individual selves—always came from a social framework that was there to shape them from the first moment they appeared in the world. Ancient contracts, for example, always had to be sworn with a sacred religious oath, which showed that such agreements were not just a matter of convenience between the parties involved but were to be enforced by the gods, for all of the community had an interest in the outcome. So too with the concept of private property. It too is thought to have developed individually; conventional thinking holds that the idea of a person's right to own an object or piece of ground arose because these things could be seen as extensions of the individual self. But again, Durkheim claims the facts of history show otherwise. The first possessions were not individual but communal in character, starting with the sacred ground that early peoples regarded as belonging not to the priest or any other single person but to the whole tribe. These *common* holdings provided the earliest ideas of property and ownership. Only out of the notion of *public* rights to things owned or possessed by all—things sacred to the whole clan—did cultures ever develop the idea of something that could be privately possessed by one person alone or by some apart.

Social solidarity, then, has always been primary. Out of an underlying sense of the group have come such basic structures of life as moral obligation and ownership of personal property. That having been said, Durkheim observes that the main difference between ancient and modern societies pertains to the ways in which they try to achieve their unity. Study of legal codes, for example, shows that early communities tend to rely on "mechanical solidarity." Good behavior is secured by punishments (often severe) for anyone who breaks the moral code of the group. This is external enforcement. In more modern times, on the other hand, a different pattern of "organic solidarity" tends to take over. Because there is the division of labor, because different people can do different things, the sense of moral commitment develops in another way; it comes not from the threat of punishment but from the need that each person acquires for the work of the others. Here enforcement must become internal. A wrong done by any one person must be seen as damaging to the others on whom that person depends. Ancient societies also have a broad and strong "collective conscience"; in them, there is uniform agreement as to what is right and what is wrong in almost all matters of human conduct. Modern societies, by contrast, are marked by moral individualism; they still need a foundation, a common moral basis, but because they allow for more individual diversity and personal freedom, their collective conscience is smaller in scope. It is limited to a few commands and obligations rather than many.

This last fact is especially significant because Durkheim believes firmly that morality, the obligation of each to others and all to the standards of the group, is inseparable from religion. Further, as we shall shortly see, both religion and morals are inseparable from a social framework. We cannot have either without a social context, and as that changes, so must they. When, as has happened especially in Western civilization, a society gives up the collective conscience it had in more primitive times and through division of labor replaces it with a morally individualistic system like that of the present, we should not be surprised to see that religion and morals have changed right along with the rest of the social order.

The Scientific Study of Society

The second of Durkheim's two principles of inquiry is developed in *The Rules of Sociological Method* (1895), where he explains how sociology must be pursued as an objective, independent science. In France, many people knew the perceptive analyses of society carried out by Montesquieu, Alexis de Tocqueville, and August Comte; these were admirable and insightful narratives in the style of traditional historical study. When Durkheim, in contrast, insisted that his "science" of society was really quite another thing, reasonable people naturally wondered: What kind of other thing? How can there be a science of an abstraction like the social order, of something we really cannot see or touch in the way a chemist or botanist can observe the visible, solid objects of nature? Durkheim's answer was to think of society in a manner similar to that of Tylor and the British anthropologists when they spoke of "culture" but then to go even further. He insisted that social facts, no less than stones or seashells, are real things, as solid in their way as physical objects are in theirs. A society is not just a passing thought in someone's head; it is an accumulated body of facts—of language, laws, customs, ideas, values, traditions, techniques, and products—all of which are connected to one another and exist in a manner quite "external" to individual human minds. They are in the world before we individuals arrive; the moment we are born, they impose themselves on us; as we grow through childhood, they mold us; in adulthood, they animate and guide us; and, just as surely, in death they survive us. Moreover, it stands to reason that if there indeed are such real and independent social facts surrounding us, then there ought to be a distinct scientific discipline devoted to the study of them. We do not imagine that we can explain a living organism only through physics or chemistry; we also need biology. In the same way, we cannot explain society if we look only to biology and psychology or even economics. Society requires sociology; other disciplines are not sufficient.

None of this means for Durkheim that the actual methods of sociological study will be dramatically different from those of other sciences. The key to any science, physical or social, is the gathering of evidence, followed by comparison, classification into groups, and finally the framing of general principles, or "laws," that can in some way be tested for their validity. In this connection, sociology not only does what other sciences do but in some ways hopes even to do it better. For example, Durkheim takes care to separate himself from the well-known comparative method as it was practiced by Tylor, Frazer, and the other Victorian British anthropologists. We have seen how, in their searches for significant patterns, they preferred to travel globally, choosing customs or ideas at will and placing them into a general category, such as "imitative magic," with little attention to their context. Such determined gathering of facts from the remotest ends and ages of the world does make for large, impressive books like *The Golden Bough*, but in Durkheim's view it is not science. It rests everything on surface similarities and very little on substance. Sociology is more cautious. It knows that comparisons can be made, and general laws laid down, only when two societies are very closely examined and can be seen to fit clearly into a common type.

Though we cannot here follow his account of sociology's methods in detail, we can briefly take note of at least some of the categories Durkheim puts into play in his approach to religion. Among other things, he believes that we can determine, for any society, what is *normal* behavior and, consequently, what is also *pathological*, or abnormal, behavior. This is certainly not a matter of absolute values, of what is good or evil at all times and places. The normal is always determined from within a group, never from outside of it. Suicide, for example, is more "normal" for some societies, like Japan, than for others. Polygamy is more normal for primitive societies than for modern ones. We must always judge the normal from within the social. In addition, whether normal or not, the category of *function* in a society is for Durkheim also extremely important in explaining behavior. And it must be kept separate from the idea of cause. The *cause* of an inner-city religious revival might be the spellbinding sermons of a storefront preacher, but the revival's social *function* may be something that goes entirely unnoticed by those who join it. From the sociologist's standpoint, the preacher's success can be traced not to the number of sinners brought to conversion but to something wholly unnoticed by those who are kneeling in prayer: the event as a whole has restored a sense of community, of shared identity and purpose, to a neighborhood of otherwise poor, isolated, even disillusioned individuals.

A good illustration of these categories can be found in Durkheim's famous study *Suicide* (1895), which was published not long after *The Rules.* After examining and closely comparing the suicide rates in the major countries of Europe, he noticed that the figures were highest in Protestant countries, were lowest in Catholic ones, and fell in between for countries of mixed religious population. In light of these ratios, it is possible to say that a certain kind of suicide, which Durkheim labels "egoistic," is more normal—that is, more typical—for Protestant countries than Catholic ones. We cannot account for this circumstance, he says, directly from the differing religious belief systems because both groups think suicide is wrong. Sociologically, however, there are certain definite and interesting differences. Protestant societies offer the individual greater freedom of thought and life; in them, people are "on their own" before God. Catholics, by contrast, belong to a more strongly integrated social community, where priests mediate between God and the believer and ties within the parish are strong. It would seem, therefore, that the rate of suicide in a community is inversely correlated to the degree of its social integration: the tighter the social ties, the lower the rate of suicide. Another kind of suicide—Durkheim called it "anomic" (from the Greek *anomia*: "lawlessness") to suggest a feeling of dislocation and aimlessness—tends to occur most in times of great economic and social instability. Clearly, to the trained sociologist the phenomenon of suicide appears in a light very different from that which strikes the eye of the ordinary observer.

Politics, Education, and Morals

Durkheim felt that his sociological perspective offered special insight into the nature of political systems, education, morals, and especially religion. In the sphere of political philosophy he gave lectures on socialism and communism, describing both as responses to the unsettlement of modern life but rejecting their ideas of class struggle and their theories of a powerful state.[5] In other lectures, especially *Professional Ethics and Civic Morals* (published after his death), he recognized that the state does need certain extensive powers, which can even be good for the lives of individuals. At the same time he stressed the importance also of what he called "secondary," intermediate groups, such as local brotherhoods and professional associations, to help protect the rights and well-being of individuals lest national governments become too strong. A key task of the state is the promotion of moral values, which is why it must also play a central role in a society's system of education. Durkheim addressed this subject often, writing, among other works, a two-volume history of education in France. As he describes it, the purpose of schools is not just to give technical training in certain skills but also to pass along the values of self-discipline and community welfare and to promote them over the selfish personal interests of individuals. Such instruction in moral values is not a luxury or an option; it is vital to the health and harmonious operation of any society. These opinions, which have had considerable influence on modern French educational theory, are at least partly responsible for the wry observation that, on any given day, the minister of education in Paris knows precisely what page in their textbooks all the children of France are reading. Against this backdrop, it is not surprising to find that alongside his treatments of both politics and education, Durkheim also makes the analysis of moral theory and legal traditions a key part of his program.[6]

The question of morals, as we have already noticed, is in Durkheim's view impossible to answer without at some point turning also to the question of religion. This he had done in the earlier years of his career indirectly, through essays, articles, and reviews of the work of others. But he reserved his complete and definitive discussion of religion for his last and most important book,

their systems of belief as quite logical responses to the world as they encounter it. The most prominent of these theories are the naturism of Friedrich Max Müller, whom we met in our introduction, and the animism of E. B. Tylor. Müller holds that people came to believe in gods by trying to describe the great objects and events of nature. Tylor, as we have seen, holds that belief in gods developed out of the idea of the soul. In framing these views both of these theorists have tried to go backward in time to the earliest peoples and guess how they thought. But this is really an impossible enterprise. If we truly want to be scientific about religion, we must try to look instead for "the ever-present causes" on which it rests, the factors that shape it at all times and places. Instead of making a grand guess about the distant past, we should look firsthand at a real example of religion in action. And for this purpose, what better method could there be than to locate the simplest society we know of and rely on someone who has actually observed it? A religion linked to the simplest social system that exists might well be regarded as "the most elementary religion we can possibly know."[10] If we can explain this religion, we have a start on explaining all religion. We will have in hand religion's "elementary forms."

Australian Tribal Religion: Totemism

Durkheim further thought that on just this point—finding a specimen of a truly simple civilization—recent researchers had provided a remarkable breakthrough. We have already noticed how Frazer took an interest in the work of Baldwin Spencer and F. J. Gillen, two field anthropologists who had been able to observe closely certain primitive aboriginal tribes in the remote hinterlands of Australia. Their work—along with that of the German fieldworker Carl von Strehlow and others—furnished a detailed portrait of social life in these extremely simple communities. And to all appearances they found that the religion of these peoples was none other than totemism, the very practice that so captivated Robertson Smith, Frazer, Freud, and others.

Durkheim was no less fascinated than the others by this new Australian research, but he felt also that they had not grasped its full importance. None had really appreciated how fundamental to primitive culture totemism really is. All recognized that tribal peoples divide themselves into different clans, each of which claims its separate totem animal or plant. And all noticed that the totem itself, whether it be the bear or the crow, the kangaroo or the tea tree, is tightly bound to its clan. But none had detected the genuinely important thing: how totemism impressively illustrates the concepts of the sacred and the profane.

In each of these primitive societies, Durkheim observes, animals other than the totem, which are profane, can ordinarily be killed and eaten by the clan; the totem animal cannot. Because it is sacred, it is absolutely forbidden to the clan—except on those select occasions when, as a part of specially designated ceremonies, it is ritually sacrificed and eaten. In addition, the clan itself is regarded as sacred because it is considered to be one with its totem. And perhaps most important, the emblem, or logo, of the totem animal is always extremely important; it is not just sacred but the very model, the perfect example, of a sacred thing. When the clan gathers, it is always the totem symbol, carved into a piece of wood or rock, that holds center stage. The totem is supremely sacred and communicates its sacred character to all around it.

Totem beliefs, moreover, are so fundamental to the life of these simple societies that everything of importance is ultimately shaped by them. One can hardly find anything more basic than the very categories of human thought and experience. Among the Aborigines, these are provided by totemism. For example, totemic concepts govern their most basic perceptions of nature, so that not only groups of people but the entire world of natural objects is divided into categories based on totem clans, or clusters of clans, called phratries. One tribe, for example, places the sun in the clan of the white cockatoo, while the moon and stars are assigned to the clan of its black counterpart. In addition, natural objects are placed in a hierarchy of power, which could only have been devised on the basis of the levels of authority that primitives experience first in the structures of the family and clan. The concepts of the totem and the clan thus find their way into every significant aspect of tribal life. There are even cases of individual totems—those that a clan member can choose as a sort of personal friend—and sexual totems, which group people by gender. Both of these types undoubtedly derive from more basic and general clan totems.

In casting about for explanations of totemism, earlier theorists have followed their own quite predictable paths. Tylor, as we might have guessed, insists that the custom arises out of animism; others derive it from nature worship; still others, like Frazer, have claimed that it is magical, or that it may have no connection at all to either religion or magic. Where these theories go wrong is for Durkheim not hard to see: each attempts to trace totemism to *something else* that is supposedly earlier and more fundamental. But that is a critical mistake. Finding a form of religion older than totemism is quite impossible, for the simple reason that there is none. Totemism, which appears in the very simplest societies, is itself the simplest, most basic, and original form of religion; all other forms can only grow out of *it*. Totemism is not a product, not a derivative of some more basic form of religion; it is itself the source from which all other kinds of religious worship—whether it be of spirits, gods, animals, planets, or stars—ultimately arise.

It is true that at first glance totemism seems to be merely another of the usual religious types: a kind of animal or plant worship and nothing more. But

Durkheim insists that when we look at it in detail, it turns out to be something considerably different. Followers of totem cults do not actually adore the crow, the frog, or the white cockatoo; they commit to the worship "of an anonymous and impersonal force, found in each of these beings but not to be confounded with any of them. No one possesses it entirely and all participate in it." If we want, we can of course speak loosely of a "god" adored in the totem cult, but "it is an impersonal god, without name or history, immanent in the world and diffused in an innumerable multitude of things."[11] To speak accurately we should call it "the totemic principle," which stands at the center of all of the clan's beliefs and rituals. Behind the totem is an impersonal force that possesses enormous power, both physical and moral, over the life of the clan. People respect it; they feel a moral obligation to observe its ceremonies; and through it they feel tightly bound to each other in deep and abiding loyalty.

Here we can see why Durkheim thinks it misleading, at least at the outset, for theorists to define religion as belief in gods or supernatural beings. In his view, before we ever get to belief in gods, there is always this first and more basic thing, the sense of a hidden, impersonal, and powerful force—the totemic principle—that is the original focus of the clan's worship. It is significant, moreover, that the evidence we find for this totemic principle is by no means limited to Australia. Under different names, Durkheim claims to find it as well in other tribal societies. Among the Melanesians, there is the similar concept of *mana*; and among native Americans, we find it described in such words as *wakan*, *manitou*, and *orenda*, all of which convey the same idea of an all-pervading, impersonal force, a dominating power that is the real center of clan or tribe worship. It follows, then, that if we want to account for religion, we must explain more than surface beliefs in the gods or spirits; we need to explain this more fundamental reality. We must show what this worship of "the totemic principle" really is.

Society and the Totem

The totem is in the first instance a symbol—but a symbol of what? An initial answer, as we now see, is the totemic principle, the hidden force worshipped by the clan. At the same time—and here Durkheim makes his pivotal turn—the totem is also the concrete, visible image of the clan. It is its flag, its banner or logo, its very self in a symbol, just as one might say that the American eagle, "Old Glory," or "Uncle Sam" is the visible emblem of the United States. But if the totem "is at once the symbol of the god and of the society, is that not because the god and the society are only one?" "The god of the clan, the totemic principle, can therefore be nothing else than the clan itself, personified and represented to the imagination under the visible form of the animal or vegetable which serves as totem."[12] The totem, in brief, is simultaneously the symbol of both the god *and* the clan, because both the god and the clan are in reality the same thing. Devotion to a god or gods is how primitive peoples express and reinforce their devotion to the clan.

It is true, of course, that in their rituals, which are always communal, the members of these aboriginal clans themselves think they are worshipping some divinity, some animal or plant, "out there" in the world, who can control the rain or make them prosper. But what is really happening is something else, something that can best be grasped in terms of social function. Society needs the commitment of the individual. It "cannot exist," Durkheim observes, "except in and through individual consciousness"; that is why the totem principle must somehow always "penetrate and organize itself within us."[13] Moreover, we can know exactly when and how this occurs; it happens on those awe-inspiring ceremonial occasions when the whole community assembles for its general rites of the clan or tribe. In these great and unforgettable ceremonies, the worshippers seal their commitment to the clan. In their moments of great excitement, in the wild emotional ecstasies of chanting and dancing, individuals manage to lose themselves in the heaving mass of the crowd; they allow their private—that is, profane—selves to sink into the great single self of the clan. In the middle of these thrilling assemblies, individuals acquire sentiments and undertake actions they would never be capable of embracing on their own. They leave behind what is most distinctively their own and merge their identities joyfully into the common self of the clan. In such moments they leave the everyday, the humdrum, the selfish; they move with elation into the domain of what is great and general. They enter the solemn sphere of the sacred.

Durkheim vividly describes the sentiments that "bubble up" in the excitement of these group ceremonies. They are filled with energy, enthusiasm, joy, selfless commitment, and complete security. "It is in the midst of these effervescent social environments and out of this effervescence itself that the religious idea seems to be born."[14] At such moments the profane is left behind; only the sacred exists.

The Implications of Totemism

Once Durkheim has made his key point—the idea that worship of the totem is nothing less than worship of society itself—he feels that all other pieces in the puzzle of Australian religion fall naturally into place. The role of the totem symbol, for example, now seems clear. Carved in wood or stone, it is a concrete object that conveys to each person the fact that the clan, which claims the loyalty of all, is not just something imagined; it is a real thing, which imposes itself on everyone's life and thoughts. The totem symbol also conveys the sentiment that society, like itself, is something fixed and permanent; it remains as a focus of inspiration long after the excitement of the religious ceremonies is over. If we ask why animals and plants should be the most common totems, that too is clear. The clan does not want as its symbol something distant and vague; it needs an object that is specific, concrete, and near at hand, something closely tied to its daily experience. If we ask how such primitive societies developed their systems of thought, their ways of ordering and classifying the world, that process too becomes clear. The aim of totemism is to notice the interconnectedness of things, the intricate web of ties that bind each person to the next in the clan, the clan as a whole to the natural world, and different parts of the natural world to each other. This urge to embrace and connect all things is in fact so strong that it enables primitive totemism, simple as it is, to lay the groundwork for the closely connected systems of language, logic, and science that develop in later stages of civilization.

Properly understood, the totemic principle can account for the components of religion as well. Totemism shows how beliefs in souls and spirits have developed. The idea of the soul is really just the totemic principle implanted in each individual. Since the clan exists only because individuals think about it in their minds, it is only natural for its members to think of the totemic principle as somehow infusing itself into each one of them. As it distributes itself throughout the clan, the fragment of it that each individual comes to own serves as his or her separate soul; it is "the clan within."[15]

This "social" idea of the soul is quite enlightening, Durkheim adds, when we think of the age-old religious (and philosophical) problem of its relation to the body. If the soul is, in effect, the clan idealized and implanted within the self, then in that capacity its task is to represent society's demands and ideals to the individual. The soul is the conscience of the self, the voice of the clan within, informing each of his or her personal obligation to the group. The body, on the other hand, naturally asserts its own self-centered desires, which can and often do clash sharply with the constraints of social life. No wonder, then, that religion has always been suspicious of the desires of the flesh! They satisfy the individual and are profane; religion asserts the claims of the social and is therefore sacred.

The doctrine of the immortality of the soul is also a natural development from totemism. To speak of the soul as immortal is for totem peoples only another way of saying that while individuals die, the clan lives on. Ancestral spirits appear as fragments from the clan's past that have survived into the present. Interestingly, these spirits often associate themselves with living members of the clan in a way that gives each person a kind of double soul: "one which is within us, or rather, which is us; the other [in the form of the ancestral spirit] which is above us, and whose function it is to control and assist the first one" in doing its duty to the clan. Over time, these guardian spirits begin to grow in power and prestige. They become more important; their sphere of influence widens; and they acquire "mythical personalities of a superior order." In short, as the concept of the soul and its immortality gradually arises out of the worship of the totemic principle, so, over time, the worship of the gods arises in its turn from the immortality of ancestral souls.

With the emergence of the gods from original totemism, Durkheim comes at last to the realm of religion as it has been more traditionally understood. Even in Australia, he admits, clan religion has developed to the point where it has numerous gods, most of whom are associated not with the smaller clan ceremonies but with the larger tribal rites of initiation, which make young men and women full members of adult society. The best way to understand these greater gods, in fact, is to think of them as personifications of these wider tribal units. And the same is true for that other well-known feature of primitive religion that is on exhibit in Australia: the belief in a high god who rules over all. Modern scholars have been fascinated to find among early peoples a belief such as this, which is so strikingly similar to the Jewish and Christian faith in a creator and moral ruler of the world. But in Australia, says Durkheim, the idea of such a god is just a natural extension of the same thinking that accounts for tribal gods. As contacts increased among tribes that lived in a certain region, and as they exchanged ideas, they began to suppose that there was one ancestor of special importance whom they all shared. That ancestor was the high god. His status is grand, but he comes into being like all other gods—as a further extension of the original totemic principle. For whatever the level we observe, the process that gives rise to belief in the gods has left us clear traces of its operation. The gods grow out of the totemic principle as it filters gradually through the clan, first into souls, next to ancestors who become clan spirits, and finally beyond them to the higher and highest of gods.

Totemism and Ritual

The last part of the *Elementary Forms* turns from the matter of beliefs to take up the other side of Australian religion: its ritual performances. Here we must note Durkheim's earlier observation that religious sentiments and emotions first arise not in private moments but in the great group ceremonials of the clan. It follows from this that the beliefs found in totemism are not the most important thing about it; rituals are. In Durkheim's view, the "cult" (from the Latin *cultus*: "worship"), which consists of emotional group ceremonies held on set occasions, is the core of the clan's life together. Whenever they occur and however they are performed, these cultic acts of worship are of supreme importance. They are sacred; all else is profane. Their purpose is always to promote the clan, to make people feel a part of it, and to keep it in every way apart from the profane.

In totem practice, the cult breaks into two main forms, negative and positive, while a third type, called "piacular" (from the Latin *piaculum*: "atonement"), plays a role of its own alongside the first two. The rituals of the negative cult have one main task: insulating the sacred from the profane. They consist chiefly of prohibitions, or taboos. Taboos of location protect certain sacred places, usually rocks or caves. They are the source of the belief, common in later religions, that a temple or church stands on holy ground or encloses a sacred space. The sacred and the profane must also be kept from colliding in time. The negative cult therefore sets aside certain holy days for sacred festivals; one of the most common taboos on such days is the prohibition of any routine activities from profane life. Normal work and play are prohibited; only rest or sacred activity is permitted, just as more developed religions like Judaism and Christianity require on the Sabbath or Sunday. If such rules have often seemed inconvenient and annoying, no one should be surprised, for that is what they should be. Their role is to press upon everyone the need to deny the self, or even endure pain, for the sake of the group. Indeed, Durkheim continues, that is precisely why almost all religions point with pride to certain people—"ascetics" as they are commonly called—who make a point of extreme self-denial. Invariably such people are highly respected. Their excessive pain and self-restraint, their refusal to enjoy sex, good food, or other luxuries, is meant to serve as an ideal for everyone. They are models of what, to a lesser degree, is required of everyone for the good of the clan. Without sacrifice of self, the clan can neither prosper nor survive.

Normally, then, the sacred is off limits, and the point of the negative cult is to keep it so. When the time and place are right, however, and the clan does move into the realm of the sacred, the means for doing so are then provided by the rituals Durkheim describes as belonging to the positive cult. For Australians, the central rite is the *intichiuma*, the ceremony that, as we may recall, Robertson Smith, Frazer, and Freud found so uncannily similar to the Christian communion meal. At the beginning of every rainy season, men of the clan start a sequence of ceremonies to promote the welfare of their totem. They begin with rituals done over certain consecrated stones; a period of keen religious excitement comes next; then amid a solemn ritual the totem creature itself is seized, killed, and eaten in a sacred meal. Why is this done? asks Durkheim. It is, as Robertson Smith correctly saw, the earliest form of the rite of sacrifice, which has assumed such a central place in so many later religions. In worshipping the totem, each person publicly celebrates its existence and declares that he or she will be loyal to it; in return, by eating the totem, each receives back from the god an infusion of divine power and a renewal of the divine life in the soul. Durkheim describes it, ingeniously, as a sacred exchange. In the *intichiuma* rite, the worshippers give life to their god, and the god returns it to them.

On the level of appearances, there can of course be little doubt that the Australian *intichiuma* is a strictly religious ritual—a transaction between the people of the clan and their god. Underneath, however, and in reality, it is none other than the social renewal of the life of the clan. Beneath the surface of theology lies the substrate of sociology. Durkheim explains it thus:

> If the sacred principle is nothing more nor less than society transfigured and personified, it should be possible to interpret the ritual in lay and social terms. And, as a matter of fact, social life, just like the ritual, moves in a circle. On the one hand, the individual gets from society the best part of himself, all that gives him a distinct character and a special place among other beings, his intellectual and moral culture. . . . But, on the other hand, society exists and lives only in and through individuals. If the idea of society were extinguished in individual minds and the beliefs, traditions and aspirations of the group were no longer felt and shared by the individuals, society would die. We can say of it what we just said of the divinity: it is real only insofar as it has a place in human consciousness, and this place is whatever one we may give it. We now see the real reason why the gods cannot do without their worshippers any more than these can do without their gods; it is because society, of which the gods are only a symbolic expression, cannot do without individuals any more than these can do without society.[16]

In this important paragraph, we can see as clearly as anywhere else in *The Elementary Forms* the thesis that stands at the heart of Durkheim's theory. Religious beliefs and rituals are in the last analysis *symbolic expressions of social realities.* Worship of the totem is really a statement of loyalty to the clan. Eating the totem is really an affirmation and reinforcement of the group, a symbolic way for each member to say that the clan matters more than the individual selves that it comprises.

Totem rituals thus put us in a position to explain religious practice in the same way that totem ideas can explain religious belief. The concept of society once again furnishes the key. The function of religious rituals, which are more fundamental than beliefs, is to provide occasions where individuals renew their commitment to the community, reminding themselves in the most solemn fashion that they depend on the clan, just as it depends on them. Feast days and festivals exist to put society, the community, back in the foreground of people's minds, and to push personal, self-oriented concerns back into a secondary place, where they belong.

Other rituals besides the *intichiuma* ceremony are included in the positive cult. There are, for instance, imitative rituals of the sort Frazer classified as a type of magic. In the rites of certain clans, people mimic the cries of their totem birds, thinking that this will make them reproduce and thrive. In other cases, there are what Durkheim calls "representative" rites, or rituals of remembrance, in which one clan member simply recites the myth of a great ancestor to a group of listeners, apparently just to provide entertainment and instruction. But even so, the underlying motive is social. Telling the story of an ancestor is a way of binding the past members of the community to those alive in the present. And people naturally believe that certain rituals can make the totem magically reproduce precisely *because of* the power those ceremonies have already shown in uniting the clan. The social effects of ritual lead to the thought that it has physical effects as well.

Piacular Rites

In addition to both the positive and negative cult there are, finally, certain important rituals Durkheim calls "piacular." These are the clan's rites of atonement and mourning, which follow upon a death or other tragic event. Tylor thought that primitive peoples held such rituals in order to make peace with the spirits of the dead, who were angry that their life had ended. But once again, Durkheim provides a social reason. In cultures where funeral mourners weep loudly and beat themselves in despair, these acts are not spontaneous. They are quite formal gestures, required by custom from all clan members, even those who hardly knew the deceased person. Why? Because when someone dies, it is not just the immediate family that has been weakened; the whole clan has lost a member, a portion of its strength. At such a time, it needs, through the cult, to regroup, revive, and reaffirm itself. In the earliest ages, the rites performed—processions, wailings, breast-beatings—were not even directed to spirits or gods. Belief in these supernatural beings actually developed later in time and only *as a result* of the ritual, just to give people a better mental image for their action. Originally, there were no gods to command a ritual; there was only the ritual, which over time itself created the gods.

Piacular rites, finally, show the double-sided power of the sacred, which can be dark and distressed as well as bright and affirming. Just as the positive cult is a celebration of the clan in the full vigor of its joy and confidence, it falls to the piacular cult to carry it through its shadowed passages—the moments of grief, catastrophe, fear, or uncertainty that can descend on a community at any place or time. An example of Durkheim's point can here be supplied from American political history. Few Americans who were living in November 1963, when President John F. Kennedy was assassinated, can ever forget the overwhelming emotional impact on the nation of the elegant, somber funeral procession that moved through the streets of the capital and was followed by the heartbreaking rites of burial at Arlington National Cemetery. For those in every town and state who watched on television, it could well have seemed that an entire nation was a single, grieving family. Durkheim's concept of a piacular rite well explains why this should have been so. Whatever the mood of society, the rites of religion will invariably reflect and reinforce it.

Conclusion

Durkheim contends that if his analysis is correct, there is a great deal to be learned from the primitive peoples of Australia. In the totemism of their tribes and clans, one finds on clear display all of the truly "elementary forms" of the religious life: a separation between the sacred and the profane; ideas of souls and spirits; the beginnings of mythology and the gods; and a full array of rituals, including those of prohibition (taboo), celebration, imitation, remembrance, and sorrow. With these building blocks in hand, it becomes possible to construct a theory that can be applied throughout history and across cultures to explain religious behavior of any kind wherever we may find it. Durkheim holds that no matter where we look for the determining causes of religion—all religions—those causes invariably turn out to be social. Though more subtle to detect in the great religions of the world, they are as unmistakably present in these complex traditions as they are in the simplest totemism. East or West, ancient or modern, beliefs and rituals always express a society's needs—its constant call upon all members to think first of the group, to sense its importance, feel its power, and sacrifice personal pleasures for its continued welfare. Religion's role, accordingly, is not to make claims about "the outside world," not to teach what it thinks are truths about the creation of the cosmos, the existence of a god, or a life after death. On all of these subjects, which people once thought proper for faith, it has had to yield to science, a more valid system of thought that, in fact, religion helped to create. Religion's true purpose is not intellectual but social. It serves as the carrier of social sentiments, providing symbols and rituals that enable people to express the deep emotions that anchor them to their community. Insofar as it does this, religion, or some substitute for it, will always be with us. For then it stands on its true home ground, preserving and protecting the very "soul of society."

Analysis

In following Durkheim's approach to religion, we have naturally had to pass over certain details, but the main outlines of his theory should now be fairly clear. From almost the moment it appeared, *The Elementary Forms* stirred keen interest, especially in France, where Durkheim had associates and disciples already disposed to look at religion through sociological lenses. Even beyond France, however, Durkheim's originality was widely recognized. In Britain, the study of anthropology was shaped by his influence, as was the new field of social psychology in the United States. Across the social sciences, Durkheim's work has been able to win new admirers and open fresh lines of inquiry to the present day.

Why all of this recognition? The answer lies partly in the scope of his ideas; like Freud, Durkheim is a wide-ranging theorist. He finds in sociology a new way of understanding almost every aspect of human behavior. In the case of religion his analyses offer a variety of fertile and intriguing insights, at least four of which deserve notice here.

1. Society and Religion

As we have seen throughout this discussion, the core of Durkheim's view lies in his claim that "religion is something eminently social."[17] He insists that although as individuals all of us make choices in our lives, we make them within a social framework that is a "given" for us from the day of birth. "We speak a language that we did not make; we use instruments that we did not invent; we invoke rights that we did not found; a treasury of knowledge is transmitted to each generation that it did not gather itself."[18] Religion is in all cultures the most prized part of that social treasury. It serves society by providing from infancy onward the ideas, rituals, and sentiments that guide the life of every person within it. In the present circumstance, discussions of "social influence" exerted on or by religion are so routine as to seem habitual; everyone speaks in such terms. But to see the originality in this perspective, we need only remind ourselves of how Tylor wrote on religion less than half a century before Durkheim. When he considers primitive religion, Tylor speaks of a single "savage philosopher," thinking his way all alone to the ideas of the soul and the gods. Similarly for Freud: though he does grasp the roles of family and society, his focus, too, is primarily on the personality of the individual. Durkheim's view, however, is decidedly different. He is not the first or only thinker of his age to have glimpsed the power of "the social" in human life, but he is unique in understanding its full importance and in pushing it to the forefront of study.

2. Scientific Method

Durkheim takes great pride in being scientific. Like earlier theorists, he wants to gather data, compare it, classify it, and make generalizations, or laws, to explain it. In a quite limited way, he also embraces social evolution. He assumes human societies do evolve from the elementary to the complex. And he agrees that the best place to start is with cultures that are simple—with so-called primitive peoples. He does not, of course, like the idea of some broad scheme of human progress, mostly rejecting this idea when he met it in the philosophy of Comte. He also dismisses Frazer's version, which presents the portrait of humanity marching steadily upward through the ages of magic, religion, and science. Against the British anthropologists, he insists that we must not use the comparative method to pick out customs and beliefs casually from around the world and then arrange them, out of their contexts, into some predetermined scheme of historical progress. That will not work. What he says we must do—and here *The Elementary Forms* serves as a model—is center on a single society, examine it carefully, and attend to details. Only *after* that close work has been done may theorists begin to make very limited comparisons with other societies, and even then, only if they are societies of the same type. True science, he insists, works slowly—from a few specimens carefully examined, not from many gathered in haste.

In the years after World War I, this important feature of Durkheim's method was taken very much to heart in the field of anthropology, especially in Britain and America. In England, it was promoted especially by the social theorist A. R. Radcliffe-Brown and by the field anthropologist Bronislaw Malinowski, who wrote on religion and other features of primitive cultures in the South Pacific. The principle of investigating one and only one society in depth before going on to comparisons is now widely approved in social science. It has brought a kind of final closure to the grand ambitions of Tylor, Frazer, and the Victorian age of anthropology.

3. Ritual and Belief

Durkheim also parts from the ways of Tylor and Frazer on the question of the relation between religious ritual and belief. Their "intellectualist" approach holds that beliefs and ideas about the world are the primary elements in the religious life. Religion's practices—its customs and rituals—are seen as secondary; they follow from the beliefs and depend upon them. The belief is the cause of the practice. In Durkheim's thinking, just the opposite holds. For him rituals have priority; they are basic and occasion the beliefs that accompany them. If there is anything "eternal" about religion, it is that a society always needs rites—ceremonial activities of renewal and rededication. Through them, people are reminded that the group always matters more than any of its single members. Beliefs, by contrast, are not so eternal. While the social function of religious rituals has always remained constant, the intellectual content of religious beliefs has always been changeable. Beliefs are the "speculative side" of religion. They may

serve to separate the Christian from the Jew and the Hindu
particular ideas they assert make little difference. Ideas alwa
ligion to religion and even from age to age in the same religio
ceremonies always remains; they are the true source of social
society they are the real ties that bind. They disclose the esse

4. Functional Explanation

The matter of ritual takes us to the heart of Durkheim's theory: the functional explanation of religion. Durkheim, like Freud, sees himself as presenting not just a different theory but a theory different in *kind* from those that came before him. In explaining religion, he thinks he can go beneath the surface of things. Tylor and Frazer try to explain religion as it appears; they take more or less at face value the beliefs that religious people hold and then ask how those beliefs explain their lives and deeds. In this intellectualist approach, ideas and beliefs—what Durkheim calls the speculative side of religion—are the key to explaining other cultures. For the follower of Tylor, a primitive ritual makes sense once we know that the Indian rainmaker believes an imitation of thunder can create a storm and send showers on his fields. The principle of imitative magic may be absurd to us, but not to him; it explains why he acts as strangely as he does. Like Freud, however, Durkheim wants to ask another question. If we agree that these beliefs are absurd, then why do people hold them? If such ideas are silly superstitions, why do they survive?

For Durkheim, the answer to this riddle can be found only in one place: not in the content of the beliefs, not in what they claim about gods or the world, but in their *function*—in what they *do*, socially, for those who live by them. The true nature of religion is to be found not on its surface but underneath. As the case of Australian totemism clearly shows, religion's key value lies in the ceremonies through which it inspires and renews the allegiance of individuals to the group. Ritual is primary, symbolism secondary. Moreover, if a society truly needs such rites to survive and flourish, it follows that there can never be a community without either a religion or something similar to fill its place. Religious ideas can be discarded and changed, but religious rituals, or something very much like them, must endure. Society cannot exist without ceremony; community requires religiosity.

Critique

Needless to say, Durkheim's ambitiously social approach presents us with a most original and intriguing theory of religion. Unlike Tylor's animism, it claims to show how the roots of religious behavior run much deeper than purely intellectual need to understand how the world works. And unlike Freudian personality theory, it appreciates in all its wide scope the powerful shaping influence that social structures exert when people declare some things sacred and others profane. Yet compelling as it appears in these respects, Durkheim's argument is less persuasive in others. The very first reviewers of *The Elementary Forms* were quick to notice some of these difficulties, and more recent critics have not hesitated to multiply the complaints. The criticisms tend to cluster about three main issues: Durkheim's assumptions about the nature of religion, his Australian evidence, and his reductionist conclusions. We can examine each in its turn.

1. Assumptions

With Durkheim, as with our other theorists, a great deal depends on what the Greek thinker Archimedes called his *pou sto*, the place "where I stand" at the start of the argument. Consider in this connection the definition of religion laid out in the opening pages of *The Elementary Forms*. Religion, we are told, is rooted in the basic distinction all societies make between the sacred and the profane. The main concern of religious rites is with the first (that is, with the sacred), which is to be kept separate from the profane. Further, the sacred is always tied up with the great social events of the clan, while the profane is the realm of private affairs. This root conception serves as the foundation on which the full framework of Durkheim's imposing theory is then erected. If we look at it very closely, however, surely the pivotal role of this definition in the theory creates something of a problem. If, already at the start of the discussion, Durkheim envisions the sacred as the social, is it not quite easy—rather too easy—to reach the conclusion that religion is nothing more than the expression of social needs? The inquiry would seem to begin at the very place where Durkheim wants to finish. The sacred is the social, he writes, and the religious is the sacred; therefore, the religious is the social. To be sure, Durkheim is not the only theorist whose reasoning tends toward a certain circularity; we have seen something of the same in Freud, and others too are inclined to offer definitions that most easily accommodate the theory they hope to defend. But Durkheim's way of starting the analysis very near the place where it ought to end is, logically, a cause for some concern.

This problem becomes more pressing when we recall Durkheim's own rather summary dismissal of other definitions. He tells us, for instance, that we may not define religion as belief in the realm of the supernatural because primitive peoples of the world, who are clearly religious, have no such concept. For them, all events are the same; there is no supernatural realm separate from the natural. But more than a few scholars both in Durkheim's day and since then have insisted—with evidence—that this is just not so; primitive peoples may not have exactly *our* concept of the supernatural, but they *do* hold ideas about mystical or extraordinary kinds of events that are quite similar to our modern conceptions. At the same time, interestingly enough, many of them *do not* in all cases manage to separate the sacred from the profane, especially in the absolute way that Durkheim says they must. Considerations such as these, which tend to count in favor of more traditional notions of religion and against Durkheim's conception, could perhaps be dismissed if the questions of the supernatural and the sacred were minor matters. Unfortunately, they are not. Durkheim's choice of definitions is quite central to his entire strategy of explanation. It does not meet us at the fringes of the theory, where adjustments could be made without loss. It stands out in front and at the center.

2. Evidence

Durkheim contends that the great merit of his study, unlike those of earlier theorists, is his determination to study only one type of culture, the Aborigine communities of Australia, and explain religion in that context. He relies on the widely acclaimed ethnographical reports of Spencer and Gillen, along with those of other firsthand observers, and he rests his theory squarely on the evidence they provide. The scientific value of such an approach is clear and undisputed—but so is its potential weakness. Should reason arise to question the value of these reports, or Durkheim's readings of them, what would be left of his theory, linked as closely as it is to this Australian evidence? Significantly, several of the very first critics to comment on *The Elementary Forms* made this point in forcible terms. One, a sociologist named Gaston Richard, who had earlier worked with Durkheim, carefully examined the Australian reports and showed how, in a number of places, the evidence could be read to prove quite the opposite of what Durkheim concludes. Richard also claimed, rather persuasively, that most of Durkheim's theory had been assembled before he ever looked at the Australian reports.[19] Other critics now question whether even the Australian reports themselves were completely accurate.[20] Perhaps the harshest words on this subject were to come from Arnold van Gennep, the famed Dutch anthropologist of Africa. In a strongly worded review written soon after *The Elementary Forms* appeared, he wrote, "In ten years the whole of his analysis of the Australian material will be completely rejected." He then added that it was based on "the most unsound group of ethnographical facts I have ever encountered."[21] Though overstated, these words have proven at least partly prophetic. Today, more than a little of the evidence and more than a few of the inferences drawn from it have come to be questioned.[22]

3. Reductionism

Just as psychological functionalism is the cornerstone of Freudian theory, sociological functionalism is the key to Durkheim's explanatory method. In a certain sense, of course, the value of such an approach seems beyond question. Who can really doubt that, beneath the surface of things, religious beliefs and rituals often accomplish social purposes that believers themselves may not be aware of? Who would wish to deny that for devout Catholics, a requiem mass, which on its face is a plea to God to save the souls of the dead from Hell, is, underneath that surface, also a powerful ritual of group solidarity and renewal? Such socially functional readings of religion seem so natural and appropriate that no one is any longer likely to dispute them.

But even if we agree in a general way that religion and society are thus functionally inseparable, we need still to ask how this relationship really works. In discussing this matter, Durkheim invariably claims that society determines, while religion is the thing determined. Society controls; religion reflects. In each Australian instance he considers, Durkheim insists that social need powerfully shapes religion, while religion seems unable to do the reverse. In each instance social structure is reality, while religion is appearance. It seems at least reasonable to ask why this should have to be so. It is one thing to say that *alongside* its other claims and purposes, religion *also* has a social function; it is quite another to say that religion has *only* a social function. As we saw in the case of Freud, "reductionism" is the theoretical term for this particularly aggressive form of functionalist explanation. Freud explains religion as "nothing but" a surface appearance, a set of neurotic symptoms produced by an underlying psychological trauma. Durkheim's agenda is similar; he accounts for religion as nothing but the surface foam—his own word actually is "effervescence"—given off by an underlying social reality. He differs from Freud, of course, in that he is much more reluctant to pass a negative judgment on religion from this perspective. Freud sees religion as a sign of disorder, a symptom of mental dysfunction. Durkheim is not so sure; even if we may find the beliefs mistaken, religion and its rites would seem indispensable to social health.

Despite that difference, Durkheim's theory, like Freud's, fits the mold of an aggressively reductionist functionalism; his program essentially reduces religion to something other than what its adherents think it to be. Although functionalist explanations have proven their merits through the years, the question of such reductionist versions of functionalism is a different matter—one that leaves present-day theorists sharply divided. Some applaud such approaches, finding in reductionist theories the very model of a strong scientific method.[23] Others find them one-sided and fundamentally misleading.[24] In that connection, it should not come as a surprise that most actual religious believers find the reductionist theories of both Freud and unacceptable. In the eyes of religious faith, these approa offer insight into *aspects* of belief, simply misundersta tom is all about. Even at that, however, the views of Freu probably less offensive to religious ears than those expresse theirs, in one of the most militant and aggressive of all reductionist th that of the German socialist philosopher Karl Marx. His unsparing and combative account of religion is the one we consider next.

Notes

1. Émile Durkheim, *The Elementary Forms of the Religious Life*, tr. Joseph Ward Swain (New York: The Macmillan Company, 1915), p. 419.

2. Durkheim was, of course, not the only contributor to the "sociological revolution" in modern thinking. On the matter of Durkheim's influence, see Albert Salomon, "Some Aspects of the Legacy of Durkheim," in Kurt H. Wolff, ed., *Essays on Sociology and Philosophy: Durkheim, et al. with Appraisals of His Life and Thought* (New York: Harper Torchbooks, [1960] 1964), pp. 247–266.

3. The authoritative biography of Durkheim is now Marcel Fournier, *Émile Durkheim: A Biography*, tr. David Macey (Malden: MA: Polity Press, 2013); prior to Fournier the best English biography was Steven Lukes, *Émile Durkheim, His Life and Work: A Historical and Critical Study* (New York: Harper & Row, 1972). An excellent in-depth study of Durkheim's thought on religion is W. S. F. Pickering, *Durkheim's Sociology of Religion: Themes and Theories* (London: Routledge & Kegan Paul, 1984).

4. For Durkheim's own appreciation of the French sociological tradition in which he stood, see his "Sociology in France in the Nineteenth Century," tr. Mark Traugott, in Robert N. Bellah, ed., *Émile Durkheim: Morality and Society: Selected Writings* (Chicago: University of Chicago Press, 1973), pp. 3–22.

5. On Durkheim as a political theorist, see Steve Fenton, *Durkheim and Modern Sociology* (Cambridge: Cambridge University Press, 1984), pp. 81–115.

6. See Ernest Wallwork, *Durkheim: Morality and Milieu* (Cambridge, MA: Harvard University Press, 1972).

7. Durkheim, *Elementary Forms*, p. 47. On the importance of this distinction, see Nisbet, *The Sociology of Émile Durkheim* (New York: Oxford University Press, 1974), pp. 172–176.

8. Durkheim, *Elementary Forms*, p. 47.

9. Durkheim, *Elementary Forms*, p. 44.

10. Durkheim, *Elementary Forms*, p. 168.

11. Durkheim, *Elementary Forms*, p. 188.

12. Durkheim, *Elementary Forms*, p. 206; on this crucial linkage between the clan, the totem, and the totem symbol, with each as sacred, see Anthony Giddens, *Émile Durkheim* (New York: Viking Press, 1978), p. 94.

13. Durkheim, *Elementary Forms*, p. 209.

14. Durkheim, *Elementary Forms*, pp. 218–219.

Giddens, Anthony. *Émile Durkheim.* New York: Viking Press, 1978. An insightful, brief study by a leading modern sociological theorist.

Jensen, Henrik. *Weber and Durkheim: A Methodological Comparison.* New York: Routledge, 2012 [2005]. A detailed comparison of the quite different methods adopted by the two founding figures in modern sociology; examines general questions about the aims and limits of sociology and the nature of sociological explanation in light of these differences.

Jones, Robert Alun. *Émile Durkheim.* Beverly Hills, CA: Sage, 1986. An illuminating short study by a scholar familiar with Robertson Smith, Frazer, and other early interpreters of religion.

Jones, Susan Stedman. *Durkheim Reconsidered.* Cambridge: Polity Press, 2001. A reappraisal of Durkheim that seeks to clear away misconceptions and place his achievement in the context of French society and the politics of the day.

Lukes, Steven. *Emile Durkheim: His Life and Work: A Historical and Critical Study.* New York: Harper and Row, 1972. Though no longer definitive, still a valuable resource.

Mestrovic, Stjepan G. *Émile Durkheim and the Reformation of Sociology.* Totowa, NJ: Rowman & Littlefield, 1988. An assessment particularly of Durkheim's role in creating the modern discipline of sociology.

Nisbet, Robert. *The Sociology of Émile Durkheim.* New York: Oxford University Press, 1974. Excellent on the historical context of Durkheim's work and on the social thinkers, especially in France, who preceded Durkheim and influenced his thought.

Pickering, W. S. F. *Durkheim's Sociology of Religion: Themes and Theories.* London: Routledge & Kegan Paul, 1984. An excellent in-depth study of Durkheim on religion.

Pickering, W. S. F., and Massimo Rosati, eds. *Suffering and Evil: The Durkheimian Legacy: Essays in Commemoration of the 90th Anniversary of Durkheim's Death.* New York: Berghan Books, 2008. A milestone collection of essays recognizing Durkheim's significance while also addressing an issue often overlooked in studies of Durkheim; considers also the views of Durkheim's colleagues and followers associated with *L'Année sociologique.*

Tiryakian, Edward A., ed., *For Durkheim.* Farnham, UK: Ashgate, 2009. An international collection of essays reflecting the current state of scholarly discussion within the lineage of Durkheim and engaged especially with current issues of religion, morality, and society.

Turner, Bryan. *Religion and Modern Society: Citizenship, Secularisation, and the State.* New York: Cambridge University Press, 2011. A general discussion by an accomplished British sociologist that addresses the theories of both Durkheim and Weber in connection with debates over secularization and religious revival.

4

Religion as Alienation: Karl Marx

> Marx discovered . . . the simple fact . . . that mankind must first of all eat, drink, have shelter and clothing, before it can pursue politics, science, art, religion.
>
> Friedrich Engels, "Speech at the Graveside of Karl Marx"[1]

If the order of this book were strictly chronological, the theorist we take up in this chapter would have appeared at the beginning, not here in the middle. Karl Marx (1818–1883), the German social philosopher and guiding spirit of the movement that has come to be known as communism, had lived much of his life before the other figures in our survey had even begun their work. His major writings were completed well before Tylor published *Primitive Culture* in 1871, and Frazer's *Golden Bough* did not appear until some seven years after Marx's death in 1883. It would be still another twenty years before Freud and Durkheim developed their leading ideas. Nonetheless, it makes sense to consider Marx here and not earlier in our survey. For though he wrote in the middle years of the nineteenth century, his ideas drew little notice in his day beyond a small circle of his own radical associates—and the suspicious eyes of public authorities. Only late in his life, after he published *Das Kapital*[2] (in English, *Capital*), the first volume of his imposing critical study of economics, did people in the mainstream of thought begin to pay closer attention to his views. From that point on, however, his influence did begin to grow enormously, as anyone now alive certainly knows. In Russia, he won a convert in Vladimir Lenin, the moving force behind the Russian Revolution of 1917, which destroyed an empire and shocked the world. Later, in the 1940s, the same shock went through China when another Marxist, Mao Tse-tung, led an army of poor peasants to an equally shattering victory. As similar revolts unfolded around the world in lesser lands, intellectuals in both Europe and America found themselves compelled to grapple with Marx's explosive and all-embracing vision of society. Some have been strongly attracted, others thoroughly repelled. In the present circumstance, even after the major communist systems have suffered to collapse, all would readily agree on at least one thing: Marx's own century could ignore him, but its successors cannot.[3]

About Marx, two things must be noticed from the very start. First, as the shaper of communism, he presents us less with a theory of religion than a total system of thought that itself resembles a religion. Though some have said the same even of Freud's psychoanalysis, the impact of the Marxist creed around the world has been much greater. For a time in the last century, Marxist thought in one form or other was the ruling philosophy of governments in many parts of the world, though—since the great collapse of communism in Eastern Europe and the Soviet Union—just a few major outposts remain. Marx's writings are as sacred to some communists as is the Bible to the most sincere and devout of Christians. Communism offers a system of doctrines with authorized interpretations. It has its own ceremonies, sacred places, and sacred persons. It has missionaries who in the space of one century have won (and now lost) millions of converts; and it has conducted persecutions more fearsome even than those of the Middle Ages or Wars of Religion. Communism in essence claims to present not just a broad theory of politics, society, and economics but a compelling total vision of human life, complete with a philosophical stance on humanity's place in the natural world, an explanation of all that is past in history, and a prophecy of what is still to come.

Second, because Marx's philosophy is so far-reaching, what he offers as a "theory" of traditional religion makes up a rather small—and not necessarily central—part of his thinking. In this respect, he is quite unlike Durkheim or Freud or our other theorists. The views he held were clear and outspoken, as we shall shortly see; they have also had tremendous influence in the modern world, especially in officially communist societies. But among all of Marx's voluminous writings, it is significant that none addresses specifically or in systematic fashion the subject of religion. Though he touches on it often enough in his many books, letters, and articles on other subjects, he almost always does so in indirect fashion, commenting here on religion in general, there on churches, sacraments, or clergy, and at other places on this belief or that practice. Consequently, this chapter calls for a plan slightly different from the one we followed in the others. Instead of tracing the argument of a single book, as we could do with figures like Tylor and Durkheim, we will have to reconstruct Marx's view of religion mainly from certain early philosophical and social writings, where he addresses the subject most explicitly, and from occasional comments he makes in later books on politics and economics. With that exception out of the way, we can still keep to our pattern. We shall look first at Marx's life and intellectual background, next at the overall framework of his thinking, and then at his view of religion. After that, we can devote the remaining space to analysis and criticism.

Background: Marx's Life, Activities, and Writings

Karl Marx was born on May 5, 1818, the second of eight children in the family of Heinrich Marx, a Jewish lawyer who lived in the small and beautiful Rhineland city of Trier.[4] During this era, when Germany was not yet a single nation, Trier was under the control of Prussia, the most powerful in a cluster of separate German states ruled by Christian noble families. Marx's grandfathers on both sides were rabbis, but because of Prussia's anti-Jewish laws, his father had converted to Christianity, in name at least, shortly before Marx was born. The father's gentle temperament contrasted sharply with that of his son, who was intellectually gifted but also stubborn, blunt, and fiercely independent; he rarely showed personal emotion. Though his secondary school record was unspectacular, Marx found an informal mentor in a cultivated Prussian state official and family friend, Baron von Westphalen, who kindled his early interest in literary classics. Marx later married the baron's daughter Jenny, with whom he was to have six children.

For a year Marx studied philosophy and law at the University of Bonn, where he did his share of drinking and dueling. He was able to avoid military service on grounds of bad health. He did not become a truly serious student until he transferred to the University of Berlin, where he adapted at once to its thriving cultural life. The university was a great center of learning in a large city, which was itself a gathering place for scholars, government officials, and serious intellectuals, some with very radical ideas. Berlin and most other German universities were at the time dominated by the towering figure of one man, the philosopher Georg Wilhelm Friedrich von Hegel (1770–1831). Hegel's system of thought is extremely important for understanding Marx, but it is not easy to explain in simple terms; we will need to return to it later on. Here we can say, in a word, that Hegel was an idealist, a thinker who solved the age-old philosopher's question of matter and mind by deciding that mental things—ideas, or concepts—are fundamental to the world, while material things are always secondary; they are the physical expressions of an underlying universal Spirit, or absolute Idea. Any thinker who wished to be taken seriously in Germany had to respond in some fashion to this idealist system. Marx did so by placing himself in a circle of thinkers—known as the Young Hegelians—who were not just disciples but also critics of their master. Also known as Hegelians of the left wing, they claimed that though Hegel was right to see the problem of matter and mind as fundamental, his solution was precisely the reverse of the truth. Matter is primary, while mind—the realm of concepts and ideas so important to thinkers—is, in fact, just the reflection, like the color red in an apple, of a world that is fundamentally material in nature. Marx defended this view with vigor. In 1841 he completed a doctoral dissertation devoted—significantly—to two decidedly "materialist" ancient Greek philosophers, Democritus and Epicurus.

This general principle, that what is fundamentally real about the world can be found in material forces rather than mental concepts, became the philosophical anchor for all of Marx's later thinking. In particular, it underlies two themes that took center stage as his thought developed: (1) the conviction that economic realities determine human behavior and (2) the thesis that human history is the story of class struggle, the scene of a perpetual conflict in every society between those who own things—the rich—and those who must work to survive—the poor.

Marx had hoped for a career as a university professor, but his association with the Young Hegelians and his own increasingly radical ideas made that impossible. He turned therefore to journalism, first writing for a German political newspaper, then moving to Paris, where he read the works of French social and economic thinkers and began to develop his own theories in depth. This early period was, in fact, the key phase of his career as a thinker. Over an interval of about seven years from 1843 to 1850, during which he moved from Paris over to Brussels, then back to Germany, Marx wrote a cluster of his most important political essays and philosophical treatises. Among these were *On the Jewish Question* (1843), *Toward the Critique of Hegel's Philosophy of Right: Introduction* (1843), *Economic and Philosophic Manuscripts* (1844), *The Holy Family: Or a Critique of All Critiques* (1845), and others. In these writings he formulated his overarching materialist view of human nature and destiny. In them he also framed his key ideas on history and society, on economics and politics, on law, morals, philosophy, and religion. As for the general perspective he adopted, we can take a clue from the motto on the masthead of one of the newspapers he edited: "The reckless criticism of all that exists."[5]

What Marx wrote in this period was truly decisive for the rest of his life, but he did not do it entirely on his own. For at just this key moment he met and began a lifelong friendship with Friedrich Engels, the son of a German factory owner. Living in England, where he observed the depressing lives of factory workers, Engels had independently developed materialist economic and social views that closely resembled those of Marx. In 1845, Marx and Engels found their way to something that rarely happens among intellectuals: a nearly perfect collaboration. They were men of like minds, but with very different talents. Marx, the more original thinker, served as the philosopher and oracle, on occasion obscure but also profound. Engels was the interpreter and communicator, readily able to express ideas in ways that were clear, direct, and persuasive. Over the years, they visited factories together; they shared the results of their studies; they criticized each other's ideas; they joined in writing for their common cause; and they combined to support and advise new political parties. Together in 1848 they wrote the celebrated *Communist Manifesto*.

Consequently, it is not really Marx alone, but Marx and Engels jointly, who are the fathers of "Marxism" as we know it today. Together they promoted their message of materialism, class struggle, communism, and revolution in a way that neither could have managed as effectively on his own.

Though ordinary people knew little about them, the "revolutionary" ideas of Marx and Engels were no secret to authorities. When in 1848 revolutions broke out across Europe, Marx came under immediate suspicion. Arrested and expelled from Belgium, he returned to Germany to take part in the revolution that was beginning there; arrested again, he had the good fortune to be acquitted of all charges in court. In 1849 he left the European continent for London. There he chose to live for the rest of his life—in exile but emphatically not in retirement. Despite grinding poverty and a family not far from the edge of starvation, he worked tirelessly on further studies in politics and economics. Returning regularly to a favorite chair in the reading room of the British Museum (where today a plaque marks his place), he wrote two works on French revolutionary politics, two more on political economy, and several others on economic history and theory. *Capital* (1867) was of course the most important of these studies. In it Marx assembles a wealth of factual data, subjects it to social analysis, and adds his acute insight into political and social structures—all to show how the facts of economic activity support his materialist view of history and point the way to a revolutionary communist future.

During this time Marx also tried to remain active in what he regarded as the ongoing class struggle, the battle of workers against their capitalist oppressors. He gave advice and assistance to socialist parties in France and Germany. He was a leader in organizing the Workingmen's International Association (more simply, "the International"), whose aim was to represent the common interests of the workers, regardless of their national home. All the while he continued his writing. *Capital* was the first of three volumes on that subject. He continued work on two others, which were in manuscript but not complete, and which were to be part of the great project he envisioned under the general title *Economics.* His work habits were strange. Some days he would be drunk or asleep, while on others he would work fanatically through the night and into the day despite a house full of noisy children. He was fortunate to have almost limitless energy, and when he wished, he could apply it with a mental discipline made of iron. Only during the last ten years of his life did his energies abate, as illness began to take its toll. A timely inheritance and some financial help from Engels had at least taken his family out of poverty. Although he continued to read and correspond with friends, all of his major writing was by then behind him. His wife, Jenny, died in 1881, and two years later he followed. With Engels at the graveside, he was buried in London—largely unmourned and unnoticed in the land where he lived, studied, and wrote for the last thirty years of his life.

Marxism: Economics and the Theory of Class Struggle

Few thinkers have ever presented their main thesis in words as blunt or as disturbing as those of Marx and Engels in the *Communist Manifesto*:

> The history of all hitherto existing society is the history of class struggles.
>
> Freeman and slave, patrician and plebeian, lord and serf, guild-master and journeyman, in a word, oppressor and oppressed, stood in constant opposition to one another, carried on an uninterrupted, now hidden, now open fight, a fight that each time ended, either in a revolutionary re-constitution of society at large, or in the common ruin of the contending classes.[6]

The message of these ringing sentences is unmistakably clear. If we wish to understand what humanity and its history are all about, we must recognize what is truly fundamental. And what is fundamental is the following: from their first emergence on earth human beings have been motivated not by grand ideas but by very basic material concerns, the elementary needs of survival. This is the first fact in the materialist view of history. Everyone needs food, clothing, and shelter. Once these needs are met, others, like the drive for sex, join them. Reproduction then leads to families and communities, which create still other material desires and demands. These can be met only by developing what Marx calls a "mode of production."[7] The necessities and even comforts of life must in some way be produced—by hunting and gathering foods, by fishing, growing grain, or entering on some other labor. Moreover, because various people are involved in these activities in different ways, they sooner or later fall into a division of labor; different people do different things. Marx calls the ties or connections among those who divide their labor in this fashion "relations of production." I may be a boat maker; you may make nets to fish with. In the earliest, simplest form of society, the kind Marx calls primitive communist, both the boat and the net are commonly owned by everyone in the village, where each shares all things as need may arise.

For Marx this original tribal communism was in a sense the most natural of human organizations. It allowed people to enjoy variety in their lives by participating in a healthy mix of meaningful work and refreshing leisure. They belonged to the group but also knew the worth of their separate selves. A fateful turn occurred, however, once the notion of private property was introduced, and its effects are most markedly evident in the stage of history known as classical civilization. Here, Marx explains, the relations of production are greatly changed. The maker of the boat claims it as his own property, as does the maker of the net. They can deal with each other only by exchanging what they have made—that is, by selling the products of their labor. And before long, by talent, crime, or good fortune, some acquire more and better private property while others are left with little or nothing. In addition, as the mode of production changes from hunting and gathering to the growing of grain, those who happen to hold property find themselves in a position of great advantage. They own not just products but also the very means of production—the land on which crops are grown. Since others do not, the landowners are masters; the rest must fall in as their dependents, assistants, or even slaves. Private property and agriculture—two hallmarks of early civilization—thus help to frame the central conflict of all humanity: the separation of classes by power and wealth, and with it the beginnings of permanent social unrest. Later, in the medieval era, the mode of production remains largely the same. It is agricultural, and the strains of class conflict continue largely unaltered. The feudal lord and serf simply replace the ancient master and slave. Even among craftsmen, the master artisan and his lowly apprentice reenact the old conflict between the Roman patrician and plebeian.

In the final, modern stage of development, this age-old conflict of classes persists, but it acquires a new intensity and a darker coloring. Modern capitalism introduces a new mode of production: commercial manufacturing; and with it comes also a profound change in the relations of production. Owner and worker are still with us, but the conflict between them becomes more intense. By introducing commercial activity and the profit motive on a large scale, capitalism produces great wealth for some, for those whom Marx calls the bourgeoisie, or "middle class." (By this term Marx means what we would call today the affluent upper middle class, the owners and managers of corporations.) Meanwhile workers, those whom Marx calls "the proletariat," are left with almost nothing; they must sell their precious daily labor to the owner-managers in return for wages on which they simply subsist. This grim situation is made even worse because capitalism has also become industrial. It has given birth to the factory, the place where workers spend long, exhausting hours at machines that make objects in huge quantities and bring a fabulous return of wealth—but of course only to their owners. The spread of this industrial capitalism thus raises the conflict between classes to a fever pitch, ushering in its last and most desperate phase—a period of proletarian misery so great that workers find their only hope in revolution. They lash out, bitterly, in an attempt to overthrow by force the entire social and economic order that oppresses them. Violence in this situation is to be expected, for the rich will never give up what they have unless it is taken by force. Confrontation is unavoidable, for it is driven by deep historical forces that no one group, nation, or class can resist.

In such a world, it is quite clear that communism has a double mission. Part of its job is education: it must explain these realities to people who cannot see them. The other part is action: it calls proletarians everywhere to prepare for revolution. With the commanding voice of an ancient Hebrew prophet, the Communist Party denounces the state and the ruling class. It urges workers to organize, to swim with history's powerful current, to add their weight to its waves, and to throw themselves forward until the day comes for them to crash down upon the edifice of capitalism, shattering its frame and very foundation. Only then, only after this stormy surge of destruction, will justice and peace return to the social order of humanity. To achieve this paradise, there will first have to be a phase of transition, a preliminary interval marked by what Marx calls the "dictatorship of the proletariat." The poor, once powerless, will be truly in control. Their rule will then gradually give way to the final phase of history, in which true human harmony arrives and the evils of class division and private property cease any longer to exist.

Materialism, Alienation, and the Dialectic of History

In outlining his great scheme, Marx did not himself invent the concept of social classes or even social struggle; he did feel, however, that he had discovered *the connection* between the social class divisions and certain stages of economic development, and he believed that he alone had seen how, in the future, this struggle would lead to revolution and the end of classes altogether. But if so, where did he get these ideas? How did he reach the unusual notion of human history moving toward a happy future, but only after passing through a sequence of oppositions marked by ever more bitter and violent episodes of struggle?

To answer this question we must recall Marx's early years in Berlin and, again, the influence of Hegel. We have already noticed Hegel's idealism; he found material objects to be secondary things. He spoke of ultimate reality as "the absolute Spirit," or "absolute Idea"—what religious people call God. In his system, this "Absolute" is a being that constantly strives to become ever more aware, more conscious, of itself. It does so by pouring itself into material forms and events, just as, let us say, the mind of an architect might express itself in a beautiful building. But because the actual never fully captures the ideal (as every dissatisfied architect knows), the material form is always inadequate, or, in Hegel's language, "alien" to Spirit. Try as it may, the material cannot match the ideal. So over against the initial event, which Hegel calls a "thesis," the Absolute generates an opposed event—an "antithesis"—to correct it. The tension is then resolved by yet a third event, the "synthesis," which blends elements of both, only to serve as the new thesis for yet another sequence of opposition and resolution. Again, think of an architect who adjusts and readjusts his design. Hegel calls this process the “dialectic” of history—the “give and take”—of absolute Spirit and its rial forms. He thought of this alternation as happening not just in small but in very large social patterns. In his scheme, an entire culture, such as civilization of classical Greece or that of Renaissance Europe, can serve as a great, single expression of the Absolute—a thesis that, after an interval, calls forth as its antithesis a new form of civilization, their conflict being resolved by yet another form as the synthesis. The entire world unfolds through this great alternating sequence that ties nature, history, and absolute Spirit into a grand, unitary whole.

We noted above that Marx rejected Hegel’s idealism. However, he did not reject either the concept of alienation or the idea that history moves along by a vast process of conflict. On the contrary, he folded both of these ideas into his materialism and put them at the very center of his own view of the human story. History, he says, is indeed a great scene of conflict, and Hegel is right to see “alienation” at the core of it. But he fails to see just how deeply alienation is rooted not in ideas but in the basic material realities of life. When Hegel speaks of alienation, he thinks chiefly of how the physical world never lives up to the perfection of its spiritual source, the Absolute. But in fact things are just the other way around; it is concrete, actual, working human beings who create their own alienation, and precisely by attributing to others the very things that properly belong to themselves. That is the *real* alienation and the true injustice. In religion, God is always being given the praise, the worship that properly belongs to human beings. In philosophy, Hegel credits his Absolute for what human sweat and toil actually accomplish. Even in politics he makes this mistake; he sees government—the modern nation-state—as a great and recent expression of Spirit, with the naturally conservative conclusion that human beings must resign their individual interests and desires to those of a king or some ruling elite. But why should people give all this glory to God or Spirit and all this power to kings? Not because there really is a God or because there are people deserving to be called royal, but because something is fundamentally wrong with human thinking—because at the very core of our being, we suffer from *self*-alienation, a deep sense of inner separation from our natural humanity.

If we truly want to understand alienation, Marx continues, we must notice how singularly important the everyday economic fact of labor is to everyone who lives. Labor is the free activity of human beings as they generate and support their social lives over against the world of nature. It ought to be rich, creative, varied, and satisfying—an expression of the whole personality. But unfortunately, it is not. It has in fact become something apart, something alien to ourselves, partly because of the evil notion of private property. As we noticed with the boatman and the net maker, alienation begins once I think of the as an object apart, as something *other than* the natural onality for the benefit of a community. From that moment ny product; it is something I can sell and another person ienated from my own self; rather than expressing my ving of nets is just the making of a commodity, some- use to barter or buy other commodities. The net maker is also further alienated from what Marx calls the "species-life" of humanity: dealing in a mere product, I have nothing meaningfully human to show for my work. And finally, I am alienated from other individual people because my personality, the thing that is essentially human about me, no longer engages yours; we just trade the objects each of us has made. In these multiple forms of alienation we find the true misery of the human condition.

Exploitation of Labor: Capitalism and Surplus Value

The cure for this corrosive alienation cannot be applied without first finding the cause. And here it is plain that however bad in itself, alienation has been made cruelly worse by the coming of modern industrial capitalism. Marx tries to provide an explanation for all of this in the many pages of *Capital.* Though no short summary of this long book can be fair to it, we can at least notice what Marx says in it about labor and value. He explains that the value of something I make or want to buy is created by the amount of work that goes into it. If it takes a day to make a pair of shoes and twenty days to make a precision clock, the value, or cost, of the clock will be twenty times that of the shoes. The shoemaker who needs a timepiece will have to make at least twenty pairs in order to buy or barter for one clock. This sort of example offers a fairly close approximation of how, in the past, economics actually tended to work—by even exchange of value for value.

Unfortunately, capitalism and property ownership are all about *profit,* rather than the equal exchange of value; they are about trading and investing to come out ahead rather than coming out even. And if we ask, "Where does this profit come from?" there can be only one answer. In capitalism the very thing about the clock or shoes that gives them their worth—the quantity of human labor they carry within them—is being *under-*valued. Of this sober truth there is abundant evidence almost anywhere one looks. While workers must put into goods at least enough value to earn wages that will support their families, modern machinery allows them to do this in the mere fraction of a day. But they actually work a *full* day, or even (in the London Marx knew) much more than a full day. In addition, entire families often worked for as many as ten, twelve, or more hours at machines; yet they were extremely poor. What was happening? Each day, Marx claims, each of these workers was creating an enormous amount of *surplus value* for the capitalist factory owner. After working a short time to earn their wages, they continued to create value—surplus value—all of which was taken directly from them and sold for profit by the factory owner. Surplus value, in other words, is quite simply that which is left over after the workers' wages (which they use to pay for shelter, clothing, and food) are subtracted from the much greater value they produce in their daily work. In each of the farms and factories of Marx's Europe, therefore, one owner who possessed fields or operated a plant was each day harvesting the surplus value created by scores or hundreds of workers, taking it as his profit and using it to build a country estate complete with servants, foxes, and hounds. All the while, his workers were squeezed into cramped, dirty apartments in the city center, befriended by boredom, disease, and virtual starvation.

Regrettably, this unjust circumstance is not just a matter of personal greed. Even if he did not like foxes and hounds, the owner's hand would still be forced by the brutal competition of the capitalist market. To keep his company alive, he *must* take most of the surplus funds it generates in order to invest in new, bigger factories that will exploit still more workers, so another factory owner does not begin to undersell and ruin him. Since he must keep his costs down to compete, every capitalist tries to use better and bigger machines; and he tries to center everything in one bigger and better company—into a trust or monopoly—so as to produce and sell his products on ever more favorable terms. The effect of these actions on the worker is not hard to notice. His life becomes ever more dismal as his position weakens in the brutal economic arena. As population grows and factories become more efficient, workers find that they themselves are a surplus; there is always a "reserve" of unemployed proletarians reminding those who do have jobs that they can be replaced—and more cheaply—at any moment.

To make matters worse, even the excess of workers is not the most serious problem. The fierce rule of competition in capitalism, the drive to get greater production from workers, leads eventually to a strange new dilemma—the "overproduction of capital." Workers and machines make more products than can actually be sold. Owners in that unfortunate circumstance then have no choice but to reverse their path and reduce production, thereby bringing on periods of economic crisis marked by layoffs, downturns, and crippling unemployment. Here is how Marx describes the circumstance:

> Within the capitalist system . . . all means for the development of production transform themselves into means of domination over, and exploitation of, the producers; they mutilate the laborer into a fragment of a man, degrade him to the level of an appendage of a machine, destroy every remnant of charm in his

> work and turn it into a hated toil; they estrange from him the intellectual potentialities of the labor-process . . . they distort the conditions under which he works, subject during the labor-process to a despotism the more hateful for its meanness; they transform his life-time into working-time, and drag his wife and child beneath the wheels of the Juggernaut of capital.[8]

In this way, the excesses and misfortunes of economic life fuel the fires of social conflict and lead capitalism finally to its own self-destruction. Amid their awful degradation and economic misery, says Marx, the proletarians discover something: they "have nothing to lose but their chains." Out of their fury, and with all the weight of history on their side, the workers are finally driven to plan, to organize, and in the end to act against the entire capitalist system. When the time is right, they can be expected to revolt. In that moment, the day of reckoning for the capitalist world will at last have arrived.

Base and Superstructure

For Marx, then, the central drama of history is the struggle of classes, a conflict controlled from below by the hard realities of economic life. In a world of private property, the rich own the means of production, while the rest—overwhelmingly the poor—do not. But even so, economics is not all of existence. What about the types of activity that form the other dimensions of our social life? What about politics and law? What about morality, the arts, literature, and various other intellectual endeavors? And what about religion? Where do all of these fit in?

Marx has much to say on each of these topics, and his starting point for all of them is to make a distinction between what he calls the "base" of society and its "superstructure." Throughout history, he insists, economic facts have formed the foundation of social life; they are the base that generates the division of labor, the struggle of classes, and human alienation. By contrast, the other spheres of activity, the things that are so visible in daily life, belong to the superstructure. They not only arise from the economic base but are in significant ways shaped by it. They are created by the underlying energies and emotions of the class struggle. The institutions we associate with cultural life—family, government, the arts, most of philosophy, ethics, and religion—must be understood as structures whose main role is to suppress or provide a controlled release of the bitter animosities arising from the clash between the powerful and powerless.

Consider the case of government. The state exists in all ages to represent the wishes of the ruling class, the dominant group. In a capitalist society built on the principle of private property, it therefore passes strict laws against theft, so that the mother of a starving child can be jailed for stealing a loaf of bread even from a factory owner so wealthy that he has enough food to feed a village. Government creates and pays a police force to make sure that the laws are enforced; thieves must be caught and brought to trial. And it establishes a judiciary to make certain that those laws are upheld; the accused must be convicted and sentenced for her offense. The breakdown of law is a constant threat to any society that, like the capitalist order, is made up of just a few oppressors and so many who are oppressed. So the presence of a strong state, one that will impose laws and crush any threat of deviation, is essential.

Although the state uses force to achieve control, other authorities in the cultural superstructure achieve the same end by distraction or persuasion. In each age of the past, ethical leaders—theologians, philosophers, and moralists—have helped to control the poor simply by preaching to them, by telling them what is right and what is wrong. The particular virtues they promote depend, naturally, on the kind of society they live in, for "the ideas of the ruling class are in every epoch the ruling ideas."[9] In the Middle Ages, when farming was the chief means of production, all lands were owned by bishops of the Church or by feudal lords, who defended their property with armies of vassals and serfs sworn to their service. Should we be surprised, then, that the moral code of the day stressed devotion to the Church, along with warrior virtues such as obedience, honor, and loyalty to one's feudal master? In modern industrial society, capitalist owners need a huge pool of movable workers, people with few ties beyond their immediate family and no claim to social privilege or status. Should we be shocked, then, that in the present era the moral watchwords are individual freedom and social equality? Modern philosophers and theologians promote these new moral values because they serve the new economy. Like their medieval counterparts, they claim that the morals they preach are eternal truths, that they belong to a fixed order of nature when in fact they are determined by the economic realities of their own specific place and time. Nor are the creative arts much different. For all their talk of individualism and originality, writers and artists depend on the accepted ideas of the age for their success, so even when they seem to protest, they in reality give unwitting, silent approval to society under the oppressors' control.

For historical support of these views, Marx turns to the recent revolutions in modern Europe: the English Civil War of the 1600s and the later revolutions in France, which he studied all of his life and discussed in three separate works.[10] On the surface, these fierce conflicts seem to be purely matters of politics and religion; the underlying realities, however, look considerably different. In seventeenth-century England dawning capitalist motives led the London merchants and middle-class gentry to challenge the political authority of the king, whose power lay with established landowners. It is capitalism that leads the rising middle class to adopt a new form of religion, Protestantism, which is much better suited to its interests in trade, investment, and individual enterprise. And, we might add, it is urban capitalism that leads artists like Rembrandt and Frans Hals to paint portraits of Dutch townsmen and their families instead of the saints, princes, and kings whom we find in the frescoes of medieval chapels. In France of 1789 it is the rising middle class (the urban bourgeoisie) of professionals and bureaucrats who engineer the overthrow of the king and lead the attack on the Church in the name of human rights. Once the upheaval subsides, economic interests again prevail as the same middle class unites to hold back the revolutionary aspirations of the impoverished masses. In each case we can see that the superstructure of politics and religion is really controlled by the economic base and the dynamics of class warfare.

Marx has a special word for all of the intellectual activity that makes up this superstructure: the endeavors of artists, politicians, and theologians all amount to "ideology."[11] Such people produce systems of ideas and creative works of art that in *their* minds seem to spring from the desire for truth or love of beauty. But in reality these products are mere expressions of class interest; they reflect the hidden social need to justify things as they stand. The thinkers are always the servants of the rulers.

Critique of Religion

Mention of such things as ideology and superstructure brings us at last to the sphere of religion, where by now Marx's basic view should hardly come as a surprise. There are, in truth, few subjects on which he is as brief or as blunt. Religion, he says, is pure illusion. Worse, it is an illusion with most definitely evil consequences. It is the most extreme example of ideology, of a belief system whose chief purpose is simply to provide reasons—excuses, really—for keeping things in society just the way the oppressors like them. As a matter of fact, religion is so fully determined by economics that it is pointless to consider any of its doctrines or beliefs on their own merits. These doctrines differ from one religion to the next, to be sure, but because religion is always ideological, the specific form it takes in one society or another is in the end largely dependent on one thing: the shape of social life as determined by the material forces in control of it at any given place and time. Marx asserts that belief in a god or gods is an unhappy byproduct of the class struggle, something that should not just be dismissed, but dismissed with scorn. In fact, no thinker considered in this book—not even Freud—discusses religion in quite the same mood of sarcastic contempt as that of Marx.

The settled hostility in this attitude undoubtedly has roots that go bey mere intellectual disagreement. Marx's first steps toward a fierce rejection religion were taken in his youth. Early on, he made clear in absolute terms that he was an atheist. Whether the reasons for this original stance were social, intellectual, purely personal, or some combination of several such factors is hard to know. He may well have resented his father's weakness in converting to Christianity just to save his law practice, and certainly he had no love for the often anti-Semitic, militantly Christian ethos of the Prussian communities. Yet his absolute repudiation of belief ran deeper than his denial of Christianity. In the preface to his doctoral dissertation, he took as his own the motto of the Greek hero Prometheus, "I hate all the gods," adding as his reason that they "do not recognize man's self-consciousness as the highest divinity."[12]

Of course a simple rejection of religion is one thing; a full intellectual campaign to unmask its falsehood is quite another. Marx did not begin to develop an explanatory account—what he called a "critique"—of religion until the decade of the 1840s, which was, as noted, the decisive period in his thinking and the time when he read the important writings of Ludwig Feuerbach, who was closely associated with the Young Hegelians in Berlin. Feuerbach, like the others, was at first a disciple of Hegel, but later he reversed course to become a stern critic of idealism. In 1841, he created a sensation with *The Essence of Christianity*, a frontal attack on orthodox religion. The furor over this book was still going strong when he astonished German opinion with two other works that proceeded to launch a parallel attack on the almost equally sacred system of Hegel.[13] Predictably, Feuerbach at once became a cult hero to the more radical students in the German universities.

Though he too wrote in the difficult philosophical language of his day, which spoke of "consciousness" and "alienation," Feuerbach's basic point was not hard to grasp. Both Hegel and Christian theology, he said, make the same error. Both talk about some alien being—about God or the Absolute—when what they are really talking about is humanity, and nothing more. Christian theologians notice all of the personal qualities we most dearly admire—ideals like goodness, beauty, truthfulness, wisdom, love, steadfastness, and strength of character—and then proceed to strip them from their human owners and project them onto the screen of heaven, where they are worshipped—now in a form separate from ourselves—under the name of a supernatural being called God. Hegel does the same thing. He notices abstract ideas like freedom, reason, and goodness, then feels he must "objectify" them by claiming they are really expressions of the Absolute, which operates as an invisible stage manager behind the scenes of the world. But this too is mistaken: concepts like "rationality" and "freedom" merely describe features of our own natural human life. Christian theology and Hegelian philosophy are thus both guilty of "alienating" our consciousness. They take what is properly human and assign it, quite wrongly, to some alien being called the Absolute or to God.

When he read these arguments of Feuerbach, Marx found himself completely convinced; in fact, they merely expressed in greater detail the view that he had already begun to adopt. He hailed Feuerbach as "the true conqueror of the old philosophy of Hegel" and described his books as "the only writings since Hegel's . . . which contain a real theoretical revolution."[14] And in his own *Critique of Hegel's Philosophy of Right: Introduction*, written a year after Feuerbach's book, he followed him almost to the letter: "Man, who looked for a superman in the fantastic reality of heaven . . . found nothing there but the *reflexion* of himself." He then added: "The basis of irreligious criticism is: *Man makes religion*, religion does not make man."[15]

Persuasive as Feuerbach's arguments were, Marx saw two places where they could be made still stronger. First, if we ask *why* human beings refuse to take credit for their own accomplishments, if we ask why they insist on calling themselves miserable sinners and offer instead all praise and glory to God, Feuerbach really has no answer beyond an empty generality. He tends to say, in effect, that is just the way people are; it is human nature to be alienated—unhappy with ourselves yet pleased with God. This will not do for Marx. There is a real answer to the question of alienation, he insists, and it fairly leaps out at us the moment we look at things from a materialist *and* economic perspective.

Marx observes that there is a parallel between religious and socio-economic activity. Both are marked by alienation. Religion takes qualities—moral ideals—out of our natural human life and gives them, unnaturally, to an imaginary and alien being we call God. Capitalist economies take another expression of our natural humanity—our productive labor—and transform it just as unnaturally into a material object, something that is bought, sold, and owned by others. In the one case, we hand over a part of our selves—our virtue and sense of self-worth—to a wholly imaginary being. In the other, we just as readily deliver our labor for nothing more than wages to get other things that money will buy. As religion robs us of our human merits and gives them to God, so the capitalist economy robs us of our labor, our true self-expression, and gives it, as a mere commodity, into the hands of the those—the rich—who are able to buy it. Nor is this unhappy combination just a coincidence. Religion, remember, is part of the superstructure of society. Economic realities form its base. The alienation we see in religion is, in actuality, just the *expression* of our more basic unhappiness, which is always economic. The surface alienation evident in religion is simply a mirror image of the real and underlying alienation of humanity, which is economic and material.

In these terms it is easy to understand why for many people religion has such a powerful and lasting appeal. Better than anything else in the social superstructure, it addresses the emotional needs of an alienated, unhappy humanity. Here is how Marx puts it in the famous lines that, depending on the reader, are now among the most widely hated or admired in all of his writings:

> *Religious* distress is at the same time the *expression* of real [economic] distress and the *protest* against real distress. Religion is the sigh of the oppressed creature, the heart of a heartless world, just as it is the spirit of a spiritless situation. It is the *opium* of the people.
>
> The abolition of religion as the *illusory* happiness of the people is required for their *real* happiness. The demand to give up the illusion about its condition is the *demand to give up a condition which needs illusions.*[16]

It is not clear how much Marx understood about opium use in his day, but certainly he knew it was a narcotic and hallucinogenic substance; it eased pain even as it created fantasies. And that, for him, is precisely the role of religion in the life of the poor. Through it, the pain people suffer in a world of cruel exploitation is eased by the fantasy of a heavenly world where all sorrows cease, all oppression disappears. Are the poor without jewels? No matter; the gates of Heaven are inlaid with pearl. Are the oppressed without money? The very streets of Heaven are paved with gold. Are the poor jealous of the rich? They can read Jesus' parable of poor Lazarus, who died and went to father Abraham, while the soul of the rich man who ignored him in life traveled down to Hades at his death. To "fly away" one day and go home to live with God, as the old slave spiritual declares, is to enjoy in the next life a well-deserved consolation for the sufferings endured in this one.

From Marx's standpoint, it is just this unreality, this leap into an imaginary world, that makes religion such a wickedly comforting business. After all, if the truth is that there is neither a God nor a supernatural world, being religious is no different from being addicted to a drug, like opium. It is pure escapism. Worse, in terms of the struggle against exploitation in the world, it is also fundamentally destructive. What energies will the poor ever put into changing their circumstance if they are perfectly content with the thought of the next life? How will they organize, plan their attack, and begin their revolt if their hope of heaven leaves them no more wish to change their life than the "sigh of protest" we find in otherworldly rituals and ceremonies? Religion shifts their gaze upward to God when it should really be turned downward to the injustice of their material, physical situation.

It is in just this connection that Marx offers his other improvement on Feuerbach, whose major problem is that, like most thinkers, he prefers restricting himself merely to the life of the mind, passively commenting on the human situation. He rightly observes that human beings are alienated and therefore turn to religion. But mere observation is not enough. Feuerbach and other intellectuals must be awakened to the fact that the purpose of analyzing the problem of religion is not just to have a new subject for discussion; the purpose is to find an active strategy that will solve the problem. This emphasis on *action*, in contrast to the purely theoretical concerns of so many thinkers in his day (and ours), is a crucial point in Marx's communist program. As he puts it in the last of his famous *Theses on Feuerbach*, "The philosophers have only *interpreted* the world, in various ways; the point, however, is to *change* it."[17]

Escape, then, is the main thing religion offers the oppressed. For those who are not oppressed, for those lucky enough to control the means of production, it offers something far better. Religion provides the ideology, the system of ideas that they can call upon to remind the poor of God's will: that the owning rich and laboring poor remain where they are, which is just where they belong. Religion's role in history has been to offer a divine justification for the status quo, for life just as we find it. "The social principles of Christianity," Marx insists,

> justified the slavery of Antiquity, glorified the serfdom of the Middle Ages and equally know, when necessary, how to defend the oppression of the proletariat, although they make a pitiful face over it.
>
> The social principles of Christianity preach the necessity of a ruling and an oppressed class, and all they have for the latter is the pious wish [that] the former will be charitable. . . .
>
> The social principles of Christianity declare all vile acts of the oppressors against the oppressed to be either the just punishment of original sin and other sins or trials that the Lord in his infinite wisdom imposes on those redeemed.
>
> The social principles of Christianity preach cowardice, self-contempt, abasement, submission, dejection.[18]

There is nothing half-hearted about Marx's verdict on religion, as these scathing words clearly show. For him, belief in God and in some heavenly salvation is not just an illusion; it is an illusion that paralyzes and imprisons. It paralyzes workers by drawing off into fantasy the very motives of anger and frustration they need to organize a revolt. Expectation of Heaven makes them content with Earth. At the same time, religion also imprisons: it promotes oppression by presenting a system of belief that declares poverty and misery to be unavoidable facts of life: realities that ordinary people must simply accept and embrace.

It must be noted here that for all the force of Marx's original words and judgments on these matters, Marxism does exhibit variations in doctrine not unlike those found within a broad economic system like capitalism or a religion like Christianity. Engels, for example, and the later Marxist historian Karl Kautsky, in his *Foundations of Christianity* (1908), both suggested that communism could be the friend of religion, not just its enemy. The rise of Christianity in the ancient world could be seen as the expression of a proletarian revolutionary protest against privileged Roman oppressors. Since the later decades of the last century, theologians in Latin America also have drawn on Marxist analysis to frame the protest against economic injustice known as "liberation theology."

While these forms of Marxism that are more in sympathy with religion have come into existence, it is unlikely that Marx himself would have thought much of them. He would have wondered why anyone should even try such salvage efforts, for his own final verdict is as much dismissive as it is contemptuous. Fierce as the fury of his rhetoric may be, it is significant that Marx does not try to make religion into communism's great public enemy, as religious people, conversely, often have done with communism. And that is because in his view of things, religion, for all its evil doings, really does not matter very much. Though it certainly aids the oppressors, there is no need to launch hysterical crusades against it, for it is just not that important. It is merely the symptom of a disease, not the disease itself. It belongs to society's superstructure, not to its base—and the base is the real field of battle for the oppressed. As Marx puts the plight of the poor in one of his characteristic reversals of phrase, "The call to abandon their illusions about their condition is a *call to abandon a condition which requires illusions*."[19]

He is fully confident that, in time, the attack on those conditions will succeed. And when it does, religion, like the state and everything else in the superstructure of oppression, will "wither away" entirely on its own.

Analysis

Marx's explanation of religion has exerted wide influence in our century, in part because it is not just another remote scholarly theory. It is tied to a philosophy of political action that, until recently, was embraced by nearly a third of the contemporary world, including not only nations as great as the Soviet Union and mainland China but multiple smaller ones as well. For countless people born in these cultures, Marxism and its relentless critique of religion are the only philosophy of life they have ever known. It is partly because of this political success, of course, that Marxism has had its equally great impact on modern intellectual life. During most of the last century, Marxist thinkers and theorists have played a leading role in virtually every modern field of study outside the natural sciences. Fifty years ago, more than a few serious intellectuals were convinced that communism had caught the flow of history's irreversible tide. To them, its ultimate triumph was assured. Over the last three decades, however, the world communist experiment has come into considerable eclipse. The not surprising consequence is that, in the current moment, communism's own "ideology"—including its view of religion—stands under a cloud of doubt. Marx himself might not have been as disturbed by all of this as we may suppose, for in his dialectical view of history, any one episode of capitalist success can still be read as preface to its later collapse amid the great proletarian revolution of a more distant future. Nonetheless, the almost blindly enthusiastic approval Marxist theory once enjoyed has been replaced by a comparable scale of current misgiving.

Between these two extremes, objectivity about either Marx or his view of religion is difficult to achieve.[20] Perhaps the best that one can do, at least at the start, is to lay aside the issue of praise or blame and try to be merely descriptive. In that regard, two elements of Marx's theory deserve our notice: (1) his strategy of functional explanation, which ends in its own distinctive form of reductionism, and (2) his stress on the ties that link religion to economics.

1. Functional Explanation and Reductionism

Although he began writing more than half a century before either of them, Marx's general approach to religion is similar in form to the functional explanations we have observed in both Freud and Durkheim. What interests him is not so much the content of religious beliefs—not so much what people actually say is true about God, Heaven, or the Bible as the role these beliefs play in the social struggle. He agrees with Tylor and Frazer that the main religious beliefs are, of course, absurd superstitions. But he also agrees with Freud and Durkheim that we still have to explain why people hold to them. Like them, he insists that we find the key to religion only when we discover what its *function* is. Marx's stress on society puts his view in one respect closer to Durkheim than to Freud, for Freud's emphasis, as we saw, falls mainly on the individual rather than the group. Even so, the contrast is not a sharp one because Freud's theory also has social features, with the individual personality being shaped by the influences of the family and community.

At the same time, Marx and Freud are closer together—and farther from Durkheim—on another side of the issue. Since for Durkheim religion is in a very real sense simply the worship of society, he thinks it impossible to imagine human social life without *some* set of either religious rituals or their near equivalent. Marx and Freud, by contrast, believe no such thing; both think religion expresses a false need for comfort and security, and they are perfectly happy to predict the disappearance of religion once the cause of its fantasies has been detected and removed. Freud thinks people would be much better off without the neurotic illusions of faith, but he seems to realize many will still cling to them. Marx goes farther; he thinks people *cannot* be better off *until* they are without them—that is, until revolution has done away with the exploitation and misery that have created religion in the first place. Because religion endorses a social order that is deeply unjust, he cannot just dismiss it, with Freud, as neurosis in need of cure; it is an evil that must be destroyed.

2. Economics and Religion

Whatever our judgment on Marx's reductionism, one thing is beyond debate. His emphasis on economic realities has now made it impossible to understand religious life anywhere without exploring its close ties to economic and social realities. In the century and more since his death, Marx's disciples have brought great insight to our understanding of relationships between the spiritual and material dimensions of life. They have cast a whole new light on the connections between economic needs, social classes, and religious beliefs, especially in the case of such pivotal events in history as the Protestant Reformation, the English Civil War, the French Revolution, and similar, more recent social upheavals. In addition, they have produced provocative studies of the connections between religion and such subjects as modern imperialism, colonialism, and slavery. In this respect, whatever happens to Marxist political regimes, Marx's materialist economic perspective will no doubt continue to furnish insight wherever theorists address the role of religion in economic, social, and political affairs.

Critique

Marx's economic reductionism offers a wealth of insight into the ties that bind religion to socioeconomic life. Insight, however, is not persuasion. Insofar as Marx gives us a theory of religion, how compelling is it? That question is an especially large one in this case, because Marx's judgment on religion is almost impossible to separate from the other aspects of his thought. We saw this to some degree also in the case of Freud, whose conclusions about religion rest heavily on his claims about psychology. In the same way, it is very hard to evaluate Marx's theory of religion without at the same time making judgments on his claims about economy, politics, and society. So, in the following, we start with some critical comments on the role of religion as Marx sees it but then move to the broader contours of his thinking on nature, history, and human social endeavor.

1. Christianity and Religion

If we focus specifically on the theory of religion as explained earlier, two problem areas in Marxist thought require special notice. First, what Marx actually presents is not an account of religion in general but an analysis of Christianity—and of similar faiths that stress belief in God and an afterlife. In part, this may be due to the influence of Hegel, who saw Christianity as the highest form of religion and felt that whatever he said about Christianity applied automatically to all "lesser" religions as well. Feuerbach took this position, and Marx, as we saw, closely follows Feuerbach's analysis. But, more importantly, the main focus of Marx's thinking is not so much world civilization as the culture and economy of Western Europe, which is of course the historical homeland of Christianity.

It is chiefly Christianity that Marx has in mind when he depicts religion as an opium-like escape for the poor from economic misery and oppression. We can of course imagine a similarly Marxist explanation of, say, the Hindu doctrine of rebirth, which also offers people hope of a better next life, or the teachings of certain Buddhists who stress the joys of sheer nirvana over the miseries of the present world and life.[21] But Marx's thesis cannot be very well applied to certain primitive tribal religions, which have almost no meaningful doctrine of an afterlife, or to the religions of ancient Greece and Rome, which were disposed to offer hope of an afterlife on terms just the opposite of Marx's: immortality for the great and powerful and a mere shadow existence for simple folk. Further, according to Marx, the phenomenon of alienation—which creates religion—came about only as human societies were introduced to the division of labor and private property. It would seem to follow that there was a time in human history before all of these things when human beings needed no religion and, in fact, had none. But while it is possible that in some deep prehistoric age this was true, there is no historical evidence to support such an idea. Nor is there any evidence available from modern tribal peoples, whose form of life often comes closest to Marx's idea of an original communism, that would show them to be without religion or even exhibit less of an inclination to it than others.

2. Religion, Reduction, and the Superstructure

Whether Christian or not, religion in Marx's view is an ideology. Like the state, the arts, moral discourse, and certain other intellectual endeavors, it belongs to the superstructure of society, and it depends in a fundamental way on the economic base. Thus, if there is a change in economic life, a change in religion must follow. The problem with this position as stated is that Marx explicates it in an extremely elusive fashion. He insists that his own research is strictly scientific in nature, yet when he reduces religion to economics and the class struggle, he does so in terms so broad and variable that his theorems are exceedingly difficult to test in any systematically scientific fashion. For example, we could agree with Marx's view that the rise of capitalism at the end of the Middle Ages caused a shift away from Catholicism and toward Protestantism. But then, what about more specific, small-scale changes? Does the religious superstructure change with *them* as well? When in certain areas of Europe we find evidence of capitalism earlier on, say in the medieval period, why are there no developments of a Protestant sort in the social superstructure to reflect *that* change as well? And why, after the rise of capitalism, do we find this new bourgeois economic system in some cities and countries that clearly did *not* become Protestant? Throughout the later Middle Ages and early modern era, certain Italian city-states moved toward capitalism, but they did not give up Catholicism. Why? Moreover, even in those countries where Protestantism did arise, can we be sure it was economics that changed the religion? Could it not be that the new religion actually changed the economics? Two decades after Marx's death, German sociologist Max Weber, whom we will meet in our next chapter, framed an intriguing argument for just this point. We can consider it more carefully later, but at a minimum it suggests that few such historical connections are as clear or certain as Marx supposes them to be. Outside the realm of religion as well, there are multiple cases in which ideas from the spheres of art, literature, and morals as well as from politics and law have changed or shaped economics in important ways, rather than the reverse, as Marx contends. Indeed, the whole formulation of the problem, which suggests that in these complex cultural interactions one element—economics—must always be the cause while all of the others are simply effects, seems overly simplified. Religion fits into society as part of an intricate network of causes and effects that act and react on each other in complicated ways. To suggest, as Marx does, that economics is always the agent in these transactions and that ideologies are always mere expressions of it is to take a stance that does not fit easily with the record of either culture or economics as they have evolved even in the Western civilization Marx knows, quite apart from the paths of development that may have been followed in other societies.

3. Marxist Political Theory: A Contradiction

A theory is only as strong as its assumptions. Since Marxist thinking reduces religion to economics, we cannot leave it without examining, at least briefly, the general theory of economy and society on which it rests. This is, to be sure, no simple task. In both communist and noncommunist countries, entire libraries are needed to hold all the appreciations and critiques of Marx and Marxism in their multiple variations. What we can do briefly is point to at least two central difficulties that bear on the issue of religion and seem knitted to the inner fabric of Marxism. These are not just charges hurled by political enemies but apparently congenital disabilities that in candid moments Marxists themselves recognize the need to overcome.

The first is a fundamentally social and political problem, and to see it we must remember that Marx recommends his system not just as a theory but as a living course of action. The working class—the proletariat—is the great agent of revolution; out of its desperation, it must rise up to destroy bourgeois capitalism. Its leaders, whether they be the members of a communist party, self-styled revolutionary strongmen, or elected representatives, embody the singular, uniform interest of "the people" as a whole. They and they alone speak and act for the revolution. Moreover, because there can be only one such "collective will" of the people, there is no place for disagreement about its purposes. Though it is elected, there can be only one political party. Nor can there be such a thing as "individual freedom" for artists, scientists, and intellectuals, since the only purpose in any of these pursuits is to serve the will of the proletariat. Though families exist, parents too must recognize that their children belong ultimately to the state. Religion, of course, cannot be tolerated because it saps revolutionary energies and demands an ultimate loyalty that should be given only to the cause of revolution.

If this is a fair portrait of Marx's revolutionary social program, then it is very hard to see how it could ever achieve the end of a perfectly classless, harmonious community that he sets for it. Marx seems to assume that the workers in all of their millions will, on any important social issue, have only *one* point of view—a stance determined fully by their fate as the oppressed class. But why should this necessarily be so? At the outbreak of World War I, some communist leaders expected that proletarians in each of the European nations involved would actually refuse to fight their fellow workers in enemy lands. But this obviously did not happen: French, German, and British workers discovered that the ties of language, nation, and culture were stronger than class solidarity. They fought for country, not class.

Second, and more alarmingly, Marxist theory seems to assume that some smaller group—some elite, elected or otherwise—will, in fact, be making the important decisions in the name of the workers, but apparently without any institution in the society that has a right to examine or question that claim. If I as Communist Party leader say, "You must die because the cause of revolution demands it," the one question that apparently no one—no artist, theologian, opposing politician, or ordinary citizen—has a protected right to ask me is: "Why do *you alone* speak for the cause of revolution?" Since I assume I speak for the party, the mere fact that someone questions me already suggests that she or he is an enemy of the revolution. I must respond to such challenging questions not with an answer or a persuasive argument but with force. The practical consequence of this impossible situation, borne out in almost every modern communist state, is the dark turn toward absolute rule by parties or dictators, along with the willing destruction of basic human rights. And why not? Marx himself was never swayed by appeals to human rights, for, as he pointed out in the case of the French Revolution, they are only bourgeois values—ideals imposed on all by the middle class, the group that, in modern Western nations, happens now to hold the power. In other ages, other masters did the teaching, but always it has been power, the "might" of wealth, that determined the "right" of morals. Ironically, however, this unsparingly radical view of moral rights as relative has grave consequences for the very workers whose interests Marx supposedly has at heart. Since it places no independent moral restraints upon those people who, now in the name of the revolution, have acquired power and claim to speak on its behalf, it leaves ordinary people just as open as before to brutalization, though now under the new banner of revolution and their own (future) well-being. All of which is troubling. There seems to be a basic conflict at the heart of Marxist social theory, a paradox some critics have perceptively described as the problem of "totalitarian democracy."[22]

4. Marxist Economic Theory: A Contradiction

Marx spent the latter portion of his life writing on economics in the several volumes of *Capital* and other books. He regarded this as extremely important work, providing the solid foundation in economic fact and theory for his doctrines of the class struggle and worker exploitation. In *Capital*, as we have seen, he argues that human labor creates the only real value to be found in products and that exploitation occurs when capitalists pay workers just enough to stay barely alive and then "steal" for themselves the remaining surplus value in the products the workers have made. To Marxist theoreticians, this analysis seems fundamentally correct. Others are not so sure.

Writing just over a decade after Marx's death, Eugen Böhm-Bawerk, an Austrian economist, discovered in *Capital* what he regarded as a "massive contradiction" between its theories of value and the actual facts of capitalist life as we see it.[23] In simple terms, he argued as follows: Marx holds a labor theory of value; only workers (and never machines) create the value that goes into their products. If that is so, it should be the case that very labor-intensive industries will always create more value (that is, be more profitable) than others; they provide more surplus value for the owner to steal. The actual facts of capitalism, however, show that regardless of the industries we consider, their rate of return on investment—that is, their profit—is almost always just about the same. It makes no difference whether they have a few workers running many machines or many workers and few machines; the profit margin remains basically constant. Toward the end of the first volume of *Capital*, Marx himself appears to have realized this problem and promised a solution. Ill health, however, prevented him from ever fully addressing the issue, though he did what he could and in later volumes actually moved away from his notion that value is defined solely by the amount of human labor in products. Nonetheless, as Böhm-Bawerk observes, this labor theory of value is crucial to Marx's related theory of surplus value; the one cannot be given up without losing the other. But the theory of surplus value is the very pivot on which Marx's central claim of worker exploitation is made to turn. Without it, his fundamentally moral complaint against capitalism seems weakened, with a problematic result for all that follows from it. In brief, if Marx's theories of value must be given up, if the footing crumbles, it is hard to see what could remain of the rest of Marxist economic theory. The doctrine of exploitation, the thesis of class struggle, the claims about base and superstructure, and certainly also the theory of religion as a dire, dismal symptom of alienation—all of these become difficult to defend. If Böhm-Bawerk is right, it would seem that the contradiction he notices cannot be dismissed as a side issue. Later Marxists have worked hard to refute this critique or revise Marx, but without notable success.

We thus end our encounter with Marx at a place that seems considerably removed from religion—in the details of economic theory. From the materialist perspective, however, any distance we claim to see between the two realms is mostly a matter of appearances and not reality. Marx, in fact, is certain of their connection. For him, the key to religion clearly is to be found in economics. He follows what is to him a clear and direct path from religious belief down through alienation and exploitation to the class struggle and from there to the root evils of private property and the theft of surplus value. If this explanatory road shows turns and twists similar to those followed by Durkheim and Freud, that should hardly surprise us. Like them, Marx is committed to the route of reductionism, though for him it ends at a different destination—with class struggle and economic alienation rather than the needs of society or the neurotic personality. In their differing ways, and sometimes taken together, all three of these ambitious reductionist theories have exercised an enormous shaping influence on modern thought.[24] Their tide of influence on interpreters of religion can be said to have reached a crest in the decades of the 1960s and 1970s, and while it has in a measure receded, it has by no means disappeared. They still have much to say, but they certainly do not have the last or only word—as our next chapters will show.

Notes

1. Friedrich Engels, "Speech at the Graveside of Karl Marx," in *Karl Marx and Frederick Engels: Selected Works*, tr. and ed. Marx-Engels-Lenin Institute, 2 vols. (Moscow, 1951), 2: 153.

2. Marx's major work in economic theory, *Capital*, was published in 1867 as the first of three volumes to be printed by a German publisher in Hamburg; the initial edition was 1,000 copies. Most of Volume 3 and much of Volume 2 had already been written before the first volume appeared. Marx continued his work on revisions of these volumes after 1867, but he never finished them.

3. For an appraisal of Marx from the long perspective of a century after his death, see Betty Matthews, ed., *Marx: A Hundred Years On* (London: Lawrence & Wishart, 1983); on the changing critical estimate of his system, see Paul Thomas, "Critical Reception: Marx Then and Now," in Terrell Carver, ed., *The Cambridge Companion to Marx* (Cambridge: Cambridge University Press, 1991), pp. 23–54.

4. There are, of course, numerous biographical studies of Marx. The authoritative work in English, recently published, is now Jonathan Sperber, *Karl Marx: A Nineteenth-Century Life* (New York: Liveright, 2013). Among other works David McLellan, *Karl Marx: His Life and Thought* (New York: Harper & Row, 1973) is still of considerable value. An earlier and classic intellectual biography that analyzes the development of Marx's thought in the context of the Europe of his day is Isaiah Berlin, *Karl Marx* (New York: Time Inc., [1939] 1963).

5. Karl Marx, *A Correspondence of 1843*, in *The Early Texts*, ed. David McLellan (Oxford: Oxford University Press, 1971), p. 82.

6. Karl Marx and Friedrich Engels, *The Communist Manifesto*, in *Selected Works* (Moscow: Foreign Languages Publishing House [1935] 1955), 1: 34.

7. A work that is especially helpful on such key concepts in Marxist theory as "mode of production" and "relations of production" is Terrell Carver, *A Marx Dictionary* (Totowa, NJ: Barnes & Noble Books, 1987).

8. Karl Marx, *Capital*, 3 vols., ed. Friedrich Engels (New York: International Publishers, 1967), 1: 645.

9. Marx and Engels, *The German Ideology*, Parts 1 and 3, ed. R. Pascal (New York: International Publishers, 1947), p. 39.

10. *The Class Struggles in France* (1850); *The Eighteenth Brumaire of Louis Bonaparte* (1852); *On the Civil War in France* (1871).

11. For the meaning of the term see, again, Carver, *Marx Dictionary*, under "ideology," pp. 89–92.

12. Karl Marx, "Doctoral Dissertation," in McLellan, *Early Texts*, p. 13; see also McLellan's comments in *Karl Marx* (1973), p. 37.

13. These were *Preliminary Theses on the Reformation of Philosophy* and *Principles of the Philosophy of the Future*, both published in 1843.

14. Karl Marx, "Preface," *Economic and Philosophical Manuscripts*, in T. B. Bottomore, ed., *Karl Marx: Early Writings* (New York: McGraw-Hill, 1964), p. 64.

15. Karl Marx, "Contribution to the Critique of Hegel's Philosophy of Right: Introduction," in *Karl Marx and Friedrich Engels on Religion*, intr. Reinhold Niebuhr (New York: Schocken Books, 1964), p. 41.

16. Marx, "Critique of Hegel's Philosophy of Right," in Niebuhr, *Marx and Engels on Religion*, p. 42.

17. Karl Marx, "Theses on Feuerbach," in Niebuhr, *Marx and Engels on Religion*, p. 72.

18. Karl Marx, "The Communism of the Paper *Rheinischer Beobachter*," in Niebuhr, *Marx and Engels on Religion*, pp. 83–84.

19. Marx, "Critique of Hegel's Philosophy of Right," in Niebuhr, *Marx and Engels on Religion*, p. 42.

20. One of the most thorough recent expositions of Marx on religion, accompanied by a penetrating analysis, can be found in Alistair Kee, *Marx and the Failure of Liberation Theology* (London: SCM Press, 1990), particularly Chapters 1 through 5.

21. Marx did briefly address this in several articles written while serving as a correspondent for the *New York Daily Tribune;* see Trevor Ling, *Karl Marx and Religion in Europe and India* (New York: Harper & Row, 1980), pp. 68–80.

22. On this point, see R. N. Carew Hunt, *The Theory and Practice of Communism: An Introduction* (Harmondsworth, Middlesex, UK: Pelican Books, [1950] 1963). A thorough study of this problem both in the French Revolution and in other radical revolutionary movements in the West is J. L. Talmon, *The Origins of Totalitarian Democracy* (Boston: Beacon Press, 1952).

23. Eugen Böhm-Bawerk, "Unresolved Contradiction in the Marxian Economic System" [1896], in *Shorter Classics of Eugen Böhm-Bawerk*, tr. Alice Macdonald (South Holland, IL: Libertarian Press, 1962).

24. See the study by J. Samuel Preus, *Explaining Religion: Criticism and Theory from Bodin to Freud* (New Haven, CT: Yale University Press, 1987), which argues that the most convincing scientific, naturalistic explanation of religion to date is to be found in a combination of the theories of Durkheim and Freud.

Suggestions for Further Reading

Albritton, Robert. *Economics Transformed: Discovering the Brilliance of Marx.* London: Pluto Press, 2007. A major figure in political philosophy today, Albritton shows the continuing relevance and importance of Marx and argues for the value of Marxist concepts and theory in present-day political debate.

Arnold, N. Scott. *Marx's Radical Critique of Society: A Reconstruction and Critical Evaluation.* New York: Oxford University Press, 1990. A sophisticated, thorough, and detailed modern analysis of Marx's economic concepts and formulations.

Barnett, Vincent. *Marx.* Routledge Historical Biographies. London: Routledge, 2009. A recent biography that offers Marx without the distortions of the left and the right; integrates thought with personal life and shows how Marx's thinking developed over time; oriented toward nonspecialist readers.

Böhm-Bawerk, Eugen. *Karl Marx and the Close of His System,* ed. Paul M. Sweezy. London: Merlin Press, 1974 [1896]. Analyses by the foremost early economic critic of Marxism.

Carver, Terrell, ed. *The Cambridge Companion to Marx.* Cambridge: Cambridge University Press, 1991. Instructive essays on the changing estimates of Marx, his political theories, views of science, economic analyses, and other topics.

Carver, Terrell. *A Marx Dictionary.* Totowa, NJ: Barnes & Noble Books, 1987. A useful reference work especially for key concepts in Marx's thought.

Eagleton, Terry. *Why Marx Was Right.* New Haven, CT: Yale University Press, 2011. One of several spirited current defenses of Marxism challenging theorists who have buried it in the wake of the Soviet collapse and the Chinese turn to capitalism. Cites the recent Western financial crisis and argues that the most common critiques of Marxism arise from distortions of communist theory and history.

Goldstein, Warren. *Marx, Critical Theory, and Religion: A Critique of Rational Choice.* Leiden: Brill, 2006. Though Marx was dismissive of religion, this collection offers the work of scholars who use Marxist and critical theory to assess religious belief and practice sociologically and frame an alternative to rational choice theory.

Gottlieb, Roger S. *Marxism, 1844–1990: Origins, Betrayal, Rebirth.* London: Routledge, Chapman, & Hall, 1992. An earlier attempt by a sympathetic mind to rehabilitate Marxism in the aftermath of the Soviet collapse.

Kee, Alistair. *Marx and the Failure of Liberation Theology.* London: SCM Press, 1990. A wide-ranging recent critique of Marxism and the mostly Latin American theology that seeks to combine Marxist theory with Christian belief.

Knapp, Peter, and Alan J. Spector. *Crisis & Change: Basic Questions of Marxist Sociology.* 2nd ed. London: Rowman and Littlefield, 2011. Introduces Marxist theory using a question-and-answer format that is especially suited to students. Addresses a wide variety of themes with a global perspective and in a manner that invites energetic debate.

Le Blanc, Paul. *Marx, Lenin, and the Revolutionary Experience.* New York: Routledge, 2006. A wide-ranging discussion of democratic revolutionary movements in action from the 1930s to the present; argues for the ongoing importance of Marx and Lenin; considers the American civil rights movement and the global encounter between Marxism and religion.

McLellan, David. *Karl Marx.* Modern Masters Series. Harmondsworth, Middlesex, UK: Penguin Books, 1976. A brief biographical account of Marx's career, controversies, and ideas; provides a clear and succinct overview.

McLellan, David. *Marxism and Religion.* New York: Harper & Row, 1987. One of the best accounts of the subject in English, this analysis extends beyond Marx and his early followers to recent Marxist theory.

Plamenatz, John. *Karl Marx's Philosophy of Man.* Oxford: Clarendon Press, 1975. A subtle, scholarly examination of the ideas and arguments at the core of Marx's thought.

Rockmore, Tom. *Marx After Marxism.* Oxford: Blackwell, 2002. Another attempt, occasioned by the great collapse of 1989, to recover the voice of Marx the political philosopher who reacted against Hegel and thereby free the real Marx from later "Marxisms."

Sperber, Jonathan. *Karl Marx: A Nineteenth-Century Life*. New York: Liveright, 2013. This expansive, ambitious biography has been widely praised and is destined to be the standard discussion for years to come. Written by a leading historian of Europe, it draws on the recently released complete edition of the writings of Marx and Engels and covers all aspects of Marx's life and personal affairs, along with his work as a theorist, brilliant controversialist, formidable intellectual colleague, and committed activist.

5

A Source of Social Action: Max Weber

Man is an animal suspended in webs of significance he himself has spun.
Clifford Geertz on the guiding theorem of Max Weber[1]

If we take Freud, Durkheim, and Marx together, one thing seems clear: each develops a decidedly functional view of religion. From their several perspectives, it is not enough to say that some Hindus worship Shiva because they believe in his power or that a Muslim follows the Quran because it holds truths revealed by God. They choose instead to show how these beliefs are traceable to conditions or needs that lie deeper—below the surface of the mind's assent. They further believe that such functionalist approaches lead logically to reductionist conclusions. This is not just a matter of explaining one aspect of religion while other theories explain other aspects. The premise of such functionalism is that it has found what is basic and fundamental. Religion—all of religion—can be fully accounted for by tracing it to a single underlying circumstance or elemental cause: to humanity's universal state of neurosis, to the universal claims of society on the individual, or to the world dynamic of class struggle. Such explanations reach wide to sweep evidence from all cases into the embrace of a single formula. That is the key to their appeal. Even so, we can still ask whether such accounts are the best accounts. Do these reductionist theories perhaps come to their bold conclusions too easily? What if we were to start instead from the stubborn complexity of religious behavior and ask whether such a dense compound can be so easily distilled to a single substrate?

At the turn of the last century, no theorist was more intrigued by the baffling intricacy of human behavior than the German social scientist Max Weber, a man who began his studies, like Marx a half century earlier, at the University of Berlin, where his main interest was not in religion but in economics and law. Though he is often paired with Durkheim as one of the twin founders of modern sociology, the term "sociologist" does not do justice to the wide array of Weber's intellectual interests. His mind was encyclopedic and absorbent, steeped in learning that embraced not only law and economics but also history, philosophy, art, religion, literature, and music. As he read and wrote, he worked methodically to find connections and outline contexts. He traced the links between politics, geography, and cultural history; explored the roots of class conflict; described the features of social status groups; distinguished types of human action and forms of social authority; examined the role of administrative institutions; and intuitively grasped the power of religious behavior and belief in social life. Society, as he saw it, is best understood as a tapestry of quite different but tightly interwoven strands of human activity, each strand twisting over and under the next. The status of religion in this regard is equivalent to that of other human behaviors. For Freud, Durkheim, and Marx, it seems obvious that religion should always be considered an effect and never identified as a cause. For Weber, that is not so obvious. In human affairs, causal trains do not travel on one-way tracks; explanation is more complicated. As a thoroughly human endeavor, religion is neither always cause nor always effect; it may be either or both as only the specific circumstance can determine.

Background: Family, Politics, and Scholarship

Karl Emil Maximilian "Max" Weber (1864–1920) was the oldest of eight children born to Max (senior) and Helene Fallenstein Weber. Although the Weber family had long prospered as linen manufacturers in the region of Westphalia, Max senior chose a career in law and became active in government. While his first son was still a young child, he moved to Berlin, where he enjoyed a long parliamentary career, serving first in the Prussian House of Deputies and later in the German Reichstag as a member of the National Liberal party. Outgoing, self-assured, and supportive of the empire's "Iron Chancellor" Otto von Bismarck, he fit well into the social and political life of the city, opening his home regularly to colleagues and friends. Helene, the daughter of a government minister in Berlin, also came from wealth. Highly educated for a woman of her time, she was more introspective than her husband and devoutly religious, with a strong social conscience keenly attuned to the hardships of the poor.

These contrasting parental temperaments converged, somewhat uneasily, in the personality of their son. Max junior shared his father's active interest in politics and government but inherited his mother's reflective demeanor, as well as her ethical sensitivity and humanitarian idealism. To describe his early life as "cerebral" would be an understatement.[2] From early on, reading was as routine as breathing. At age thirteen, his idea of a Christmas gift to his parents was a pair of essays: one on medieval German history, another on the later Roman Empire. The Weber household made little distinction between learning and leisure. Visits from Berlin's political and intellectual elite were a regular occurrence. In rooms alive with intersecting discussions of economics and society, politics, law and history (suitably spiced with society gossip), Weber as a teen met some of the most glittering figures in a golden era of German learning. The philosopher Wilhelm Dilthey, the eminent Roman classicist Theodore Mommsen, historian Heinrich von Treitschke, theologian Ernst Troeltsch—all of these and others were not just authors on a page; they were family friends personally encountered.

Weber's formal education was no less stellar. At preparatory school in Berlin, he took an interest in philosophy and in both ancient and medieval history. He read widely in classical authors—Homer, Herodotus, Virgil, and Cicero—while also working his way through all the works of Goethe, mostly as a personal diversion from unexciting classwork. In 1882 he entered Heidelberg University to study legal and economic history as well as philosophy and theology. He also joined a fraternity, where, like Marx, he learned to duel and drink—both with more vigor than wisdom, to judge by his mother's unhappy reports. After a year of combined study and military service in Strasbourg, where he formed a friendship with the historian (also his uncle) Hermann Baumgarten, Weber returned to further university work in Berlin. There, over the next eight years and while still living with his parents, he pursued advanced studies in legal and economic history. In 1889 he took a doctoral degree with a dissertation on medieval Italian trading companies; soon afterward, he completed his work in law and took a position in the Berlin courts. In 1892 he earned his *Habilitation*, or license, as a university lecturer with a study of agriculture and law in ancient Rome. At about this time he also became engaged to Marianne Schnitger, a distant cousin; they were married a year later, just as Weber was entering professional life.

With his marriage at age twenty-nine, Weber's life story divides into a tale of two selves. Professionally he had established himself as a scholar of exceptional promise; positions awaited him in both government and the academy. He had become active in the *Verein für Socialpolitik*, or Union for Social Policy, an organization of professional economists for which he prepared an important study of immigration and farm labor in eastern Germany. He also published an analysis of the newly established German stock exchange.[3] In 1895 he accepted a university appointment (remarkable for a scholar of his age) as a full professor of political economy in Freiburg, and in the following year he accepted a similar post, with greater prestige, at the University of Heidelberg.

On a personal level, however, his life took a disturbing turn. The marriage to Marianne turned out to be unusual, at least by normal measures of affection.

Though he and his new wife were ideal personal and intellectual companions, they chose, apparently by mutual consent, a marital relationship that was to be not just childless but almost certainly also asexual. It is not clear just why. Weber's capacity for self-denial was well known, and it appears to have converged with something similar in his wife—an apparent aversion to physical sexuality. The full truth of this intimate matter is probably beyond discovery. (Marianne, who wrote the first biography of her husband, had all personal papers burned after his death.[4]) But it doubtless set the stage for emotional unsettlement, which was further complicated by other tensions. Though he respected both of his parents, Weber as an adult drew closer to his mother and felt a need to support her against his father, who could be personally domineering. On the occasion of a fierce quarrel over his mother's right to visit her newly married son and daughter-in-law, now living away from Berlin, Max junior took his mother's side, angrily opposing his father. A few months later, before they could reconcile, his father suddenly died of a heart attack. Whether or not feelings of guilt were involved, Weber soon found himself slipping into serious emotional collapse. From 1897 to 1901 and even beyond, he struggled with episodes of paralyzing anxiety that left him by turns exhausted, restless, sleepless, and unable to function in his role as a professor. After taking several leaves for health reasons, he resigned his appointment at Heidelberg, effectively withdrawing from any professional position.[5] Not until 1918 did he bring himself again to accept an academic post, this time at the University of Vienna. Less than two years later, he was stricken with pneumonia. Inadequately treated, it took his life at the young age of fifty-six, in the very prime of his intellectual career.

Although the nervous disorder deflected him from his university duties, Weber over time managed gradually to regain his capacity for scholarly labor. He coped well enough to travel in both Europe and the United States, where he participated in conferences on social theory and policy. While no longer in a professorial position, he was able by 1904 to accept an editorship (alongside economists Werner Sombart and Edgar Jaffe) at an important scholarly journal, the *Archiv für Sozialwissenschaften und Sozialpolitik* (*Archive for Social Sciences and Social Policy*). This step was both emotionally therapeutic and intellectually opportune. Aided by family funds and (after 1907) by a comfortable inheritance, Weber began to work as a private scholar, pursuing a program of research that grew more productive each passing year, even amid the occasional nervous relapse. He made the *Archive* the forum where some of his work, including most of his important research on religion, was published. During sixteen remarkably productive years from the date of his editorship to the day of his death in 1920, he produced in its pages and elsewhere a steady stream of articles, critical reviews, and extended essays of extraordinarily high quality. Not all were intellectual landmarks, but they routinely advanced striking and original ideas, supported by close historical analysis and thorough social research. The more important of these will claim our attention in a moment. Before turning to them, however, we should attend to a preliminary matter that Weber held to be of paramount importance: the methods employed in sociological research.

Three Tools of Sociological Inquiry

Methods are to scholars what tools are to craftsmen. All need them; few give them much thought. Weber, however, is one of those few. Amid the recovery from his illness, he wrote a number of articles, including a first editorial essay for the *Archive* (1904), which centered on the main issue of sociological method: How do we proceed when we try to explain human social actions? Weber developed his answers to this question in several technical essays that outline three guiding principles of social inquiry.[6]

Verstehen

Weber's first and fundamental principle is best stated in the single word *Verstehen*, the German term for "understanding." He was not the first or only scholar of his time to stress this idea, the hallmark of what would later be known as interpretive sociology, but he made it decidedly central to his labors. On the surface, it is a notion easy enough to grasp. The principle of *Verstehen* presumes that we cannot explain the actions of humans as we explain occurrences in nature. Natural science centers on non-mental objects and processes; social science explains the mentally driven activities of human beings. It is true that within nature, humans too can be called objects, but clearly they are objects of a special kind. Unlike stones and trees, they are conscious; they assign meaning to the things they do. Their behavior is guided not just by external forces such as gravity but by internally held ideas such as the belief in freedom and inwardly experienced emotions such as the feeling of love. This distinction may seem a matter of mere common sense, but applied to complex social issues and institutions, it can become controversial.

In Weber's day, scholarly debate over this issue of explanation grew so heated that it acquired its own name: the great *Methodenstreit*, or "dispute about methods." At the center of the argument stood the undeniable success achieved in fields like chemistry and physics by framing universal laws of cause and effect. Why, some asked, could not laws like these, with their wondrous applications in medicine and industry, also be framed to explain human affairs? Economists were the first to make this case, claiming some success in applying scientific "laws of the market" to human action. Similar views soon sprouted elsewhere, suggesting that perhaps an entire natural science of all human behavior could be created. Others sharply dissented. The philosopher Wilhelm Windelband asserted that while science deals with processes that repeat themselves, allowing us to explain things "nomothetically" (Greek for "making rules"), human actions are singular events, requiring explanations that are "idiographic" (Greek for "uniquely descriptive") in character. On this view, there is a fundamental divide between *Natur-* or *Gesetz-wissenschaft* ("sciences of nature or of laws") and *Geistes-* or *Kultur-wissenschaft* ("sciences of the spirit or of human culture"). Wilhelm Dilthey went even further, contending that we cannot really "explain" such things as human action at all, at least in the scientific sense of the word "explain." We must use *Verstehen* to "feel our way" intuitively, one might say, into the minds of others. By acts of imagination rather than reason, we recreate their thoughts in our own minds.

Weber participated in this spirited quarrel by taking a position somewhere in the middle. His views leaned toward those of Dilthey, but he felt it a mistake to suppose the process of *Verstehen* is purely intuitive, an exercise in the art of imagination. We cannot possibly recreate by imagination the complicated mixture of ideas and motives that may have played in the mind of, say, Socrates while on trial in ancient Athens or of Lincoln when he decided to free the Southern slaves. The only thing we can do is proceed rationally. We describe a historical circumstance or set of conditions, and based on that knowledge we envision a probable sequence of next events; we try to isolate what it was that made one sequence occur when the others did not. *Verstehen* is thus a form of science: a systematic, rational method of accounting for human actions by discerning the role of motives or meanings where they figure as causes.

To say *Verstehen* is a rational procedure is not to say that human beings always act in rational ways. Weber was well aware that there are very different forms and degrees of rationality. In his later landmark work *Economy and Society*, he observes that actions can be either instrumentally rational (seeking the means to achieve a goal) or value-rational (seeking a goal as good in itself); they can also be affectual (driven purely by emotions) or traditional (done purely out of habit).[7] In this way social science reaches useful explanations; it infers the inner motives that affect outward actions.[8]

Although Weber's main interest was to explain social rather than personal behavior, his stress on the inner motives of human actions has led others to describe his perspective as "methodological individualism"—a term that is instructive. For him, social values or beliefs acquire reality only insofar as they gain assent in the minds of individuals. Whenever he refers in abstract terms to a moral value such as, say, physical courage, Weber reminds us to think of the specific individuals or subgroups in a society whose leadership or influence makes them what he calls the "bearers" of such an ideal. Ideas and values, in other words, have effects only because certain people embrace them and induce others to follow their lead. This accent diverges from that of Durkheim, who tends to think of society as an abstract entity, standing apart from its individual members and imposing duties upon them from above. Weber is disposed instead to think of the community as a mixed assemblage of individuals in which the many defer to the few, to those who by tradition, privilege, or personality claim the authority to lead them. They are the custodians of cultural values; they shape society as much as it shapes them and others.

Ideal-Types

Individuals may carry the ideals of society, but sociology does not center only on individuals; if it did, it would be neither social nor scientific. Making valid statements about general classes of things is the entire purpose of the endeavor. To clarify the role of these general categories in social research, Weber employs another technical German term—*Ideal-Typus*. An ideal-type is a general concept, but it is different from what is known as a generalization in natural science. Generalizations identify a single trait or characteristic common to a group, as when we say, "All kings have countries." A country to rule is a kind of bare minimum qualification for a king. When we create an ideal-type of a king, however, we form almost the very opposite of a generalization. We frame a sort of purposeful exaggeration, or maximum outline, of what a ruler should be, adding to the country he rules a large set of further attributes: royal birth, male gender, rule by "divine right," a queen, a palace with courtiers, nobles sworn to fealty, and so on. No real-world monarch, past or present, will possess all of these characteristics. Some have most of them and others only some, but that does not matter. The key is that the ideal-type furnishes a conceptual framework into which all cases can be brought for analysis. With it, we can compare kings over time and across locales. We can trace changes from one type of monarchy to another, and we can make inferences about cause and effect, as in the French Revolution, when an assault on religion demolished the idea that kings rule by "divine right."

Almost everything we meet in social analysis can be fashioned into an ideal-type, and the formulas can vary greatly in kind and scope. A concept like "revolution" is an obvious example from politics; "democracy" might be another. So are the forms of rational action we noted earlier. Broad historical concepts such as "Greek civilization" and "modern capitalism" and terms such as "Renaissance" and "Impressionism" from the history of art can all serve the purpose, but so can quite specific types comparable to "king," such as "artisan" or "merchant." The same is true in the realm of religion for types like "priest," "mysticism," "church," or "sect" or any similar conception that supports the explanatory process.

One of Weber's most celebrated ideal-typologies offers an apt illustration. In *Economy and Society*, he singles out three main types of social authority: traditional, legal, and charismatic. All three express what he calls "legitimate domination." In the case of traditional authority, people acknowledge a pattern of power that seems to have "always existed," as in tribal societies where rule of the elders has been accepted from time immemorial. Similar forms include "patriarchalism" and "patrimonialism," where a single person or family inherits power to rule. Conversely, the authority most common to modern societies can be defined as legal, or rational. It finds purest expression in the modern bureaucracy, which presumes consent among all to abide by a set of rules consistently applied by trained, specialized, paid officials who work in a graded hierarchy and with a sense of professional duty. Weber's writings on bureaucratic authority have generated serious discussion among analysts of public and corporate administration. He finds bureaucracy the most rationally ordered form of authority, offering great efficiency, though often by suppressing creativity. By contrast, the third of the types—charismatic domination—is the most dynamic, and it holds special importance in the sphere of religion. It is on clear display in the prophets and sages of world history, though it applies as well to warriors or to statesmen. In such cases, leadership is acquired through a single characteristic: the compelling personal magnetism of one or a few individuals. The prophets of Israel, Gautama and his community of monks, Confucius and his followers, Jesus and his apostles—all of these cases demonstrate the social impact of an exceptional personality, the spiritual hero, the singular gifted person who alone can work miracles, deliver an oracle, or energize disciples. When such a figure appears in a society, he or she can, on the sheer strength of a claim to power, wisdom, or divinity, win a following and alter the course of civilization. Charisma is the most compelling agent of change in society and history.

Abstractions like "bureaucracy" are not the only kind of ideal-type; historical processes qualify also. One of Weber's widely cited types defines the process of cultural "disenchantment," by which faith in the supernatural realm of magic and the gods, long anchored in a traditional society, gradually dissolves under the pressure of systematic and rationalized patterns of thought. Another is the "routinization" of charisma, the gradual transformation that occurs when, after a prophet's passing, the fiery intensity of his message begins to cool and fix itself into institutions if it is to survive. Types like these, which depict historical developments, can naturally be blended with types of other kinds to frame cause-and-effect explanations when social or cultural changes occur. An illustration (though not one of Weber's own) might be the process of Christianization of the ancient Roman Empire. Around the year 100 CE, the dominant religions of Rome were polytheistic; by about 500 CE, they had been almost entirely replaced by Christian monotheism. If we think of polytheism and monotheism as differing ideal-types of religious belief, we can frame an explanation of the change. Between the two pure ideal-types, we can locate a kind of bridge belief that figured in the transition. Some converts, such as the Roman general Constantine, were superstitious and opportunistic; he embraced "Christos" as the one god out of many most able to help his army in battle. Neither his faith nor his monotheism was very pure, but the ideal-types of each enable us to understand the form-in-between that drew the emperor and others along the path from pagan polytheism to Christian monotheism. Here, as elsewhere, the explanatory benefit lies not so much in the kind of ideal-type we use as in the service it provides in framing comparisons and explaining actions.

Values

Weber's third principle of inquiry addresses the issue of values. From early on he took the position that social science, like other sciences, must be a value-free endeavor. Like others of his day, he held that facts and values are quite separate things; confusing them is an error of the first order. Every true scientist (natural or social) seeks a factual account of the real world as he experiences it, and personal value judgments should be kept out of the process. The purpose of science is to describe things as they are, not to promote personal views on what ought to be. The same distinction applies in the university classroom; the vocational duty of a professor requires that personal value judgments not be mixed into classroom lectures.

If this were all to be said on values, we could end here and move on. But almost always for Weber, things are not as simple as they may seem. He recognizes that there are certain value-relevant considerations no one can avoid. The basic decision even to become a social scientist expresses a value choice. To choose sociology over, say, medicine or carpentry is a decision to place a career value on social science rather than another vocation. The choice of what to study within sociology is the same. To make a study of class differences rather than suicide rates is to make a value-relevant decision about the issue most in need of one's attention. If we think about it carefully, the commitment to follow the principle of "value-freedom" is itself a value-conditioned choice. In promising to explain reality as accurately as possible, without inserting personal opinions into the accounts, we affirm the value that science places on factual truth over the value of our personal or political interests.

Value choices appear also to affect social science more than natural science. Physicists and mathematicians work with closed sets of concepts—like the axioms of algebra or theorems of geometry—that remain fixed over time. Euclid in ancient Greece used the same postulates as those applied by a geometry student in a modern high school. But it is not the same, says Weber, in open-ended disciplines like social science, where new ideas, issues, and formulations continuously appear as new observers bring in the perspectives of later ages and differing cultures. Further, as the principle of *Verstehen* shows, when we try to explain human activities, we find ourselves negotiating between at least two sets of values: those of the people whose actions we are interpreting and those of the culture—our own—within which we are working.

Consider in this regard the early years of the Industrial Revolution, when workers known as Luddites (followers of the folk hero King Ludd) raided factories to destroy the new textile machines, which had left them jobless and poor. They saw no future for laborers in a world ruled by machines. A Marxist historian of the early 1900s, writing their story with an ear attuned to worker exploitation, might well regard the Luddites as prophetic; they alone foresaw the coming final phase of corrupt capitalism and worker enslavement. Today's neoliberal free-market historian, on the other hand, is inclined to see them as sadly deluded souls, vandalizing the very technology that would spare their grandchildren long hours of hard labor and make them prosperous, not poor. Certainly, Marxist and free-market interpreters can both try to put personal views aside, but the questions they bring and explanations they offer seem almost unavoidably shaded by value-relevant factors tied to the culture of their own time and place.

This point is underscored by what we know of Weber's own deepest convictions about society and values. He had been influenced by Marx and by the philosopher Friedrich Nietzsche, both of whom fiercely rejected any thought of universal moral values binding on all of humanity. In wrestling with their radical ideas, he developed a more complex stance on these questions that has generated pages of commentary from later theorists. Some say his views are contradictory; others say he failed to show how values affect social more than natural science.[9] Still others contend that "value-freedom" of any kind is a myth, citing Weber himself as a proof of the point. When he joined the Union for Social Policy, he strongly argued that its research must be strictly "value-free." But the study of farming in East Prussia that he did for the Union actually passed a severe judgment on the landowners, whose self-centered practices encouraged Polish immigration and weakened German ethnic identity.[10] Clearly, that verdict—offered by an intense German nationalist—hardly qualifies as "value-free."

Writings on Religion

Criticisms aside, Weber put his principles of method diligently to work as he turned to his main program of research. Its guiding theme, as we have seen, was the interweaving of economics and society. Yet the closer he looked at this issue, the more it appeared that the role of religion in that relationship was pivotal. This fact came to light decisively in the first of his major works, *The Protestant Ethic and the Spirit of Capitalism* (1904–1905). It can be said to have become even more central to his interests as time went on.[11] Since here, as in other chapters, our discussion must center on a few signature texts, *The Protestant Ethic* is an obvious first choice. Its title alone is recognized widely in popular conversation. Quite apart from the agenda it set for so much of Weber's subsequent work, it remains his most famous and widely debated book. The second choice—less obvious, but no less important—is the blueprint he laid down for scientific study of religion in a long section of *Economy and Society*. Later translated and published separately in English as *The Sociology of Religion*, this analysis has become a standard reference for current theorists of religion. It outlines some of Weber's most suggestive typologies and conceptual comparisons. Third and finally, we can take some notice—admittedly brief—of an ambitious multipart series of studies Weber projected as "The Economic Ethic of the World Religions." Less than half this work was finished at his death, but the three books that did appear offer a window on the wider landscape of his thinking.

The Protestant Ethic and the Spirit of Capitalism (1904–1905)

Few scholarly books have made their authors more of an intellectual celebrity than this striking venture in cultural analysis, which Weber first published as a pair of articles in the *Archive* just after becoming one of its new editors.[12] Debate over its famous argument, known almost everywhere as "the Weber thesis," has continued for more than a century, with little reason to think it will not go on for another. At its core is a startlingly bold but fundamentally simple thesis. It claims there is a close connection between religion, the rise of economic capitalism, and the birth of modern civilization in Western Europe.

Weber begins by noticing, as had others, an odd fact of life in modern Germany: in proportion to their numbers, Protestants were much better represented than Catholics among the class of business leaders, capital investors, and skilled corporate managers. To account for this fact, some had suggested that perhaps Catholics are just more spiritually inclined people, while Protestants tend to be more materialistic. Such explanations, says Weber, will not satisfy anyone who intimately knows Protestant attitudes, both past and present. If we look closely at their history, we see that the most successful of these enterprising Protestant businessmen have often also been the most intensely religious, keeping diaries that carefully recorded their daily efforts to follow the will of God in their lives. If anything, we could better suppose that something in the religiosity itself of these Protestants is what urged them toward serious enterprise in business. So inquiry can better begin with Protestantism's founders: Martin Luther in Germany and the French-speaking theologian John Calvin in Switzerland.

Though religiously revolutionary, Luther was socially and politically conservative. He did not directly advance new ideas about business, but he did assert the equality of all people before God—a principle that entailed a quite unconventional view of everyday human labor. In the Catholic culture of medieval Europe, the daily labor of ordinary people received no special recognition; it was merely what people must do to eat and have shelter. Specifically religious work of the kind undertaken by monks, nuns, and priests was another matter. People who choose lives such as these do much more than everyday labor. They are specially called by God to their duties. They take solemn vows of poverty, chastity, and obedience. Their divinely appointed vocation (from the Latin *vocare*, "to call") assures them of exceptional rewards in heaven. To Luther, this notion that some believers are more religious than others was unacceptable; he insisted adamantly on the complete equality of all believers before God. The effect of his teaching was to dissolve the Catholic concept of a special religious vocation simply by expanding it to include everyone. In Weber's words, Luther "secularized" the idea of vocation, thereby giving as much importance to the everyday work of a peasant or tradesman as the Church had given to the devotional exercises of the parish priest or cloistered nun. This idea—that even the humblest tasks are solemn duties assigned by God himself—invested everyday work in the world, no less than prayer in the convent or chapel, with real religious importance, a spiritual value that it had never before held. All work, not just religious work, was a calling from God; it should not just be done but done well, as faithful service carried out (in the words of the great Puritan poet John Milton) under "the great Taskmaster's eye."

Luther's idea of a "secular calling" offers a start in understanding Protestant energy and success in business, but only that; it does not explain how a particular kind of economic activity seems to have predominated. Protestants chose a distinctive lifestyle marked not only by habits of discipline, thrift, simplicity, and self-denial, but also by a systematic lifelong pattern of effort in enterprises designed to earn a profit. Moreover, it is just this kind of endeavor, whose sole motive is the orderly and incremental increase of wealth, that expresses the frame of mind we associate with the modern, and uniquely Western, economic phenomenon of capitalism. Is there, then, a connection?

Weber says emphatically "Yes." But to explain it, to account for the distinctive ethic behind the spirit of capitalism, he turned from Luther to Calvin, the most cerebral of the reformers.

Calvin was a brilliantly systematic thinker, the main architect of the Protestant doctrinal system. But it was he especially who also stressed the dark teaching of predestination, which held that God, and God alone, determines the eternal fate of all mankind, choosing some ("the elect") to reach Heaven and eternally condemning others ("the reprobate") to Hell. Calvin was not the first to hold this view; St. Paul, St. Augustine, Luther, and numbers of others taught the doctrine, but it was Calvin who made it a centerpiece of his system. He also found it a personal source of deepest assurance. No matter the circumstance, he knew with certainty that he could never be separated from the love of his God, whose divine decree could never be undone. For Calvin's followers, however, things were more unsettling. Not sharing his natural self-confidence, many were subject to intense anguish about their eternal fate, which God alone determined. The deep psychological effect of this anxiety, says Weber, must be properly appreciated. We need to realize that the early Protestants occupied a unique time and place in Western history. Like medieval Catholics before them, they lived in an intensely religious world, well before the modern era, with its now weakened sense of the supernatural. For them there was a fearsome reality in the prospect of an eternity spent either in Heaven or in Hell. On the other hand, Protestants were no longer fully medieval. They were disciples of reformers—again, Luther and Calvin—whose revolt had stripped out of Catholicism its supporting web of "magical" beliefs and customs through which the Church affirmed God's presence and mediated his love and forgiveness to his people.

Here we should recall Weber's ideal-type depicting the disenchantment of the world. The medieval church was a nursery of the supernatural. Relics, pilgrimages and indulgences, stained glass and sculpture, the wonders of the martyrs and saints, priestly absolution dispensed in the confessional, the miracle of the wafer and wine turned to Christ's body and blood in the Mass—all of these formed a vast supernatural support system that mediated God's forgiveness to the simplest believer. To Luther and Calvin, conversely, this entire system was little more than a mass of Satanic superstition. They systematically reduced it to rubble. Consequently, the ordinary Protestant was left without the usual mechanisms to reassure the soul or channel divine love to the heart. They felt instead only the deep inner anxiety of the individual soul, alone in fear before a God who in sovereign mystery decides the destiny of all. This keen personal anxiety was so troubling that Calvinist pastors in later generations groped for a way to offer at least some reassurance. They counseled their congregations to live in the world as true faith requires—soberly, frugally, and with discipline, offering themselves up wholly to God through hard work as his servants in their worldly tasks. If they so lived, they could be reasonably expected to prosper, and prosperity amid simplicity could be taken as the sign of election.

This pastoral guidance, framed to reassure troubled religious souls, was momentously important. Within it, says Weber, lay the psychological key to the economic future of Europe. For indirectly (and quite without intention) it ushered in a profound change of attitude toward worldly effort and the acquisition of wealth. Prior to the Reformation, in almost every place and age of Catholic Christendom, any activity aimed at an increase of money or property stood under the shadow of moral disapproval. In the eyes of the Church, the pursuit of riches was at best regarded as neutral, but more commonly as vile avarice, one of the seven deadly sins. It was the poor whom Jesus loved and the rich he condemned. Both the Bible and the Church strictly prohibited usury because a loan of money and its return with interest amounted to exploitation of the poor by those who are rich. The Church's discomfort with the pursuit of great wealth by those not born into it could be read in its cathedral architecture. Why were cathedral walls lined with chantries where prayers could be said for the souls of those who endowed them? So that those who had committed themselves to the pursuit of wealth in this life could secure unceasing prayers of forgiveness for the sin of avarice that had brought them their gold. In Catholic theology, the poor always are near to the heart of God, while the rich live under suspicion.

Among the theological disciples of Calvin, however, this moral framework was subjected to a most remarkable reconstruction. The pursuit of wealth acquired an entirely new moral status: What was once a vice now became a virtue. The clearest evidence of the change is apparent—in varying degrees, of course—among the main branches of Protestantism in Europe of the early modern era. Weber specifically cites the Puritans, Presbyterians, and Methodists in Britain and America, as well as other Calvinist groups in Germany, Switzerland, the Netherlands, and elsewhere. In these communities we find aphorisms that urge thrift and self-discipline; diaries and autobiographies that record entire lives lived in private struggles against softness and self-indulgence; and sermons that strike the recurring themes of restraint and sober self-denial, discipline and hard work, thrift and investment, the wise use of both time and money. It is a frame of mind aptly depicted in the adages that Benjamin Franklin made popular across colonial America: "Time is money; sloth is sin." "A penny saved is a penny earned." These homespun phrases distill the essence of the spirit of capitalism, even as they mirror the moral reversal that produced it.

Weber's chosen term for this new ethic was "inner-worldly asceticism"—self-denial within everyday society rather than apart from it. The "otherworldly asceticism" of the medieval Church idealized withdrawal from the world to the seclusion of the convent or monastery. The new ethic of Protestantism was just as ascetic, just as self-denying, just as intense and lifelong as the sacred vow of any medieval monk, but its execution was different. It required disciplined mastery of the self *within* the arena of the everyday world. God's call was not to a spiritual practice performed while in hiding from the world but to a disciplined mastery of the world while active in it. That inner-worldly asceticism is the Protestant ethic. As applied to economics, it is hard to mistake; it is the spirit that drives all of modern capitalistic enterprise.

As he unfolded this argument, Weber was careful to address certain objections and clarify points of confusion. One obvious problem centers on the meaning of the term "capitalism." If all we mean by that concept is "striving to get rich," then what is so special about the Protestant connection? Old-fashioned greed certainly can be found anywhere in the world, long before Protestants came along and far from Europe.

Weber answers this point by making a distinction. Loosely speaking, capitalism can indeed mean any effort to gain wealth; driven by greed or opportunism, it can even take criminal forms like piracy or theft, and these, certainly, are things we find in all times and places. Long before the Reformation, ancient merchants and conquerors practiced buccaneer capitalism, traveling "through hell itself should it singe the sails" to get rich. But true capitalism, the economic ethic created in Europe at the dawn of modern times, is something quite different. The merchant or buccaneer seeks wealth for one purpose—to indulge it, to live in luxury and buy pleasures. The principles that guided the Calvinist businessman in London or Rotterdam of the 1600s are virtually the exact opposite. He earns money with the intent to *save* it, not to spend it. God calls him to a serious, restrained life of self-denial, so he has no interest in luxuries or expensive personal pleasures. His focus is on making a profit as a duty of his calling and a mark of divine election, not on spending money on self-gratification. It is true that this habit of saving leads to the creation of even more wealth—what modern economists call new capital formation—because there is no other place for it to go. But that comes not because of any vice in the heart of the Calvinist; it is, on the contrary, a natural (if unintended) consequence of his virtues. Instead of spending, he saves, reinvests, and thus increases his wealth. Modern capitalism, therefore, is not the everyday greed of all people and places; it is a distinct and different phenomenon that first appeared in one place, Western Europe, and for historical reasons quite specific to the faith and values of Protestantism.

Weber was clear also about another issue. This spirit of capitalism is the key thing, but not the only thing, that makes up this unique modern form of economic activity. In framing the ideal-type that guides his discussion, he lists other elements that define it: rational bookkeeping, separation of the workplace from the home and of corporate from personal property, decisions based on careful calculation, use of free (rather than slave) labor, dependence on mathematical and experimental science, and reliance on a social structure shaped by the rule of law and orderly administration. All of these elements belong to a wider pattern of "rationalization" in Western society, on which Weber placed great importance. Although it is intimately tied to this larger process, it is clear nonetheless that capitalism could not have appeared without the specific impulse that came from the Protestant ethic. It is this idea that has led some to refer to Weber as the theorist who "stood Marx on his head." Weber himself found that assessment too simplistic. But it bears a kernel of truth—applicable as well, we might add, to the reductionism of Freud and Durkheim. In the case of one of the most important socioeconomic revolutions in world history, Weber concludes not that religion is a mere reflection of social structure or economic forces, but precisely the reverse. For him, it is the new religious ideas and behaviors of Protestantism that usher in a reversal of attitudes toward acquiring wealth, and from that reversal has come the culture of commerce, markets, and capitalism that defines Western civilization as we know it today.

Finally, Weber is careful to distinguish the original capitalism of the early modern centuries (1550–1750) from capitalism of his own day and ours. Today Catholics as well as Protestants are capitalists, and among Protestants, most have no awareness or even memory of the old religious motives. The new ethic is now ingrained and thrives purely on the power of its own economic efficiency; once introduced to a culture, it drives out all rivals, as history has shown. Over the centuries from 1500 to 2000, capitalism has traced a steady rise to dominance both in the West and the world beyond it. Today it governs all economic practice, long after its original Protestant coloring has faded.

From almost the moment it appeared, *The Protestant Ethic* sparked a vigorous intellectual debate that has never really ended. It is quite alive today, a full century after the essays were first published. Weber himself participated in the first phase of discussion, offering various responses and clarifications to criticisms that appeared, mainly in Germany, over the next five years. By 1910, however, he had run out of patience with the critics and turned from defending his ideas to developing them.

The Sociology of Religion

The Sociology of Religion is a more difficult text to summarize than *The Protestant Ethic*. It does not so much assert a thesis as embark on an exploration. It moves far beyond Protestantism to offer a broader set of interpretive categories—Weberian ideal-types—and applies them to the whole spectrum of world religions. Weber had written most of this discussion by 1914, but it was not published on its own; he chose instead to include it as a book-length chapter in *Economy and Society*, which was published after his death.[13] The exposition in these pages is at times densely tangled and makes multiple turns; it wanders on occasion into intriguing side roads and sometimes loses its way. Here we will follow only its main path, which travels through four general topic areas. It begins with the role of religious leaders and then addresses the influence of social classes and groups; it turns next to the forms of religious belief and behavior; and it last explores the interaction of religion with other aspects of social life. Each of these topics merits some comment here.

Religious Leaders: Magician, Priest, and Prophet

Magician. Religion for Weber is rooted in special experiences, what he calls "ecstatic states," that put people beyond the realm of everyday activity and disclose to them another level of reality. Anyone may have such an experience on occasion, but those who can manage it on a regular basis are naturally regarded as having special talent in spirituality. They have "charisma" (a key term for Weber, as we have seen); they possess a gift that gives them a claim to the role of religious leader. In early societies, the magician was the person the tribe regarded as "permanently endowed with charisma." When the need arose, people called on the magician to cure illness, to make the hunt succeed, or to assist the crops in their growth. Frazer, we may recall, spoke in a similar fashion, but Weber does not see magic as a form of primitive science, different from religion. Magicians, he says, do not rely only on impersonal principles of contact and imitation; and they do engage the gods or spirits, something Frazer reserved only for religion. Nor is there a sequence in which religion emerges after magic fails. Magical interest in miracles and healings may be more common in earlier, simpler cultures, but it can appear at any time, even in complex, modern religious systems, because it offers things ordinary people need or want in everyday life.

Priest. Magic tends to be an occasional thing, focused on immediate concerns; normally people call on the magicians when the practical need arises. That is not the case with religious leaders who function as priests. In general, we find a religious priesthood where there is some kind of permanent system of worship at fixed times and places and associated with a definite religious community. If we encounter the same ritual performed in a certain temple daily at dawn or weekly at dusk, we normally find a specialized priesthood in charge. The priest, even in most primitive societies, is a permanent, paid official. We can think of him as having charisma, like the magician, but it is something derived from his office rather than from his personal magnetism. The priest's "professional" status is defined by the rites he controls and by the religious community of ordinary people, the laity, he directs. In more complex societies, as we might expect, priests fit into Weber's category of bureaucratic domination. They are "professionals" in religion; they have assigned duties and are arranged in ranks with differing levels of responsibility; they are conscious of their special status, dispensing religious guidance and benefits to clients; and above all, they prize social and religious order. In ancient India, for example, it was the community of priests that promoted Varuna and Mitra, the gods of cosmic law and order, against Rudra, the chaotic god of storms.

This concern of priestly religious leaders with structure and stability is one source of a key development in most civilizations: the emergence of the concept of a vast cosmic order that imposes on human beings a universal ethic, or value system, leaving behind the narrow ethic of the primitive village, in which good and evil are defined entirely by the interests of one's own family or clan. The precise concept of cosmic order may vary from one culture or civilization to the next, but whatever the form, priests have often played a part in either shaping it or conveying it to a wide community of followers.

Prophet. The notions of cosmic order and a universal ethic bring us to the third ideal-type: the prophet. Among those who become social leaders, says Weber, there is hardly a single type—statesman, artist, intellectual, or conqueror—more consequential to the course of civilizations than the commanding figure of the prophet. He is a person recognized as "a purely individual bearer of charisma."[14] The prophet may appear at any time in a culture, acting on a powerful sense of mission, to proclaim for all a comprehensive "religious doctrine or divine commandment." A prophet is not a magician, centered on securing everyday practical benefits—foretelling the future, curing illness, changing the weather. He may have some magical appeal, but the center of his life is his mission; he has been specially called by either the voice of God or a vision of Truth to proclaim a life-altering message. He would find it absurd to be paid for his labors. His calling sustains him, and he is content if need be to live in poverty, accepting only what people voluntarily give him to subsist. A prophet is also unlike a priest. His authority is not derived from his religious office. It anchors itself in the revolutionary power of his personality and his message. It is clear that most of the great world religions trace their origin to a transforming prophetic figure whose charismatic life and compelling message revolutionized the world of his day.

Historically, prophets have been of two main types. The "exemplary prophet"—the wise man who teaches by his own powerful example—has predominated in the Far East. In India, Gautama the Buddha belongs to this type, as do the teachers Lao-tzu and Confucius in China. Each offers a path of wisdom and truth meant for all, even if only some have the full capacity to follow it. In contrast, the "ethical prophet" has predominated in the Near East and in Western civilization. Zoroaster in ancient Persia, the prophets of Israel, Jesus of Nazareth, and Muhammad in Arabia fall within this distinctive type. Here too the prophets offer a universal ethic, reaching beyond self-interest and the ties of family or tribe. But on an essential point they differ from the great Oriental sages, who shared the world views of Asian civilizations that found the ultimate Reality of the universe to be impersonal, as in the Chinese *Tao*, or "Way of Nature." Western prophets embrace monotheism. They present themselves not as wise men modeling the life of wisdom but as instruments chosen by an almighty and personal God to proclaim his will. Their mission is to deliver his oracles and to demand obedience to the universal ethic he imposes. They reject magic as a useless exercise, addressed only to petty interests; they are suspicious also of priests, whose concern with ritualized ceremonies and orderly administration tends to smother the vital flame of religion. That holy fire is something found only in a deep inner commitment carried out in obedience to a moral code; it is neither selfish nor tribal but is anchored in the sovereign universal will of the world's Creator and Lord.

Prophets, of course, are exceptional people—capable of living an entire life at the highest level of personal commitment. The prophet's followers, being normal human beings, are less likely to possess such total dedication. So in any religious community, if it is to sustain itself over time, the charisma of the founder must somehow be kept alive by successors. As noted earlier, the ideal-type Weber frames for this important process is the "routinization" of charisma—the transformation of the prophet's inspirational gift into something permanent, something fixed in the bureaucracy of an institution.[15] After the death of Jesus, for example, it fell to the twelve apostles, then to the Church fathers, and later to the priests and bishops of the Catholic Church to make his charisma routine by molding it into institutional systems, by giving it fixed forms that would make it last. In this way, the priestly bureaucracy, by nature opposed to the unpredictable inspirations of prophecy, can become the prophet's best ally after his death. Only a conservative bureaucratic system—aimed at maintaining the prophet's truth (now that it has won a following)—can frame his message into a system of teaching and administration that will be able to guide an ever-enlarging community, or "congregation" (Weber's preferred term for this ideal-type), of followers through the ages. This structural support comes at a price, for bureaucracies do tend to smother the fires of the spirit. Reformers with charisma of another kind will on occasion need to challenge priestly authority and restore the original vigor of the prophet's message. Episodes of tension are to be expected, for the vitality of the original message is always put at risk by the "dead hand" of bureaucracy.

Social Classes and Groups

In speaking of the religious congregation, Weber calls attention to the key role of the laity—ordinary people who hold no offices but form the vast majority of participants in any religious community. Charisma, in prophetic or any other form, does not exist unless a community of laypeople comes to recognize and reinforce it, so an appreciation of their role is essential. It is important to grasp not only the place of social classes and groups in religious communities but especially the role they play in responding to the demands of the great prophetic religions. Weber's dissent from Marx in this connection is significant. For Marx, one issue, the division of classes into rich and poor, determines all others; for Weber, things again are considerably more complex. Social groupings are formed not just by economic separation according to class but also by such things as location (rural or urban), vocation (craftsman, farmer, or warrior), and, notably, social respect or honor (status group). As we saw earlier, one element of bureaucracy as an ideal-type is the claim to respect made by those who belong to it; they are "professionals." In Weber's analyses, intellectuals, or "literati," who earn honor for their impressive learning or cultivation often acquire distinctive status as a bureaucracy in the same manner as the elders in a tribal society.

Depending on the place and time, each of these varied social groups has a distinctive part to play in the religious enterprise, and social science can discern certain typical patterns of action. Rural peasants, for example, live close to nature and depend on the weather. Almost always, therefore, they are drawn toward magical practices, looking for help in day-to-day life and labor. Even where a great prophet has established an ethical type of congregational religion, peasants find themselves subtly drawn back toward magic and miracles. Despite Confucius' promotion of prophetic ethical religion, magic has for centuries mattered most to the simple farmers of China. Despite the moral precepts of the Sermon on the Mount, the Christian Church's relics, icons, and miracles of the saints have long been the main interest of Europe's rural classes: peasants, serfs, and day laborers. Rarely do they give undivided loyalty to a prophetic faith; more often, they mix it with magic.[16]

As it happens, the privileged classes, protective of their advantages, have also shown resistance to prophetic religion, though from other motives. Their sense of honor and prestige is easily affronted by the demand that they change the course of their lives or ask forgiveness from a priest or some other social inferior. Similarly, bureaucratic elites do not always welcome the prophet or his message; they are disposed to find it irrational unless, as among China's Confucian mandarins, it can serve the useful purpose of taming the masses. Even so, prophetic religion does sometimes show the power of breaking through such resistance. Especially among warrior nobles and knights, who must summon the courage to face death, prophetic religion has been enlisted to give an ultimate meaning and purpose to warfare. This was especially the case with Islam, where the warrior class became the main bearer of the crusade mentality that has left its mark on most Muslim civilizations. The middle class, on the other hand, shows considerable diversity in its religious responses. The "commercial patriciate," composed of wealthy upper-middle-class merchant families, normally shows little serious interest. But a different response appears farther down the social scale among the artisans and craftsmen of the cities, the heart of the populous lower middle classes. Among these industrious groups—separated enough from nature to be freed of interests in magic and motivated strongly by an ethical sense of fair reward for fair labor—prophetic religion has had its most powerful appeal. From its earliest centuries, Christianity was known as the religion of the cities, not the countryside.

With the exception of Confucianism, prophetic religions have also developed into what can be called "salvation religions." They offer people a comprehensive program for achieving inner spiritual resolution or final escape from life's limitations and sorrows. This element is so central for Weber that we need to revisit it shortly. For the moment, we should note that while a salvation religion does not necessarily need to present some specific savior at its center, someone of that kind almost always appears among the masses. The lower the social class, the more intense becomes the need to frame a redemption story in which a god takes human form to bring deliverance to the faithful. Thus, in later Buddhism the concept of a bodhisattva, a divinity who assists people in the search for enlightenment, replaces the austere original practice of meditation, which leaves all of humanity entirely on its own. Similarly in India, the savior cults of Rama and Krishna replace the old and obscure Vedic rituals. Because ordinary people have traditionally found it hard to align themselves with some abstract and impersonal cosmic order, or have feared intimacy with a transcendent all-powerful God, most religions, both East and West, have also developed various cults of the saints, heroes, or minor gods and goddesses to give people assistance in their spiritual searches and struggles. (The two main exceptions seem to be Judaism and Protestantism, both of which place an emphasis on self-reliant individual enterprise.)

The poor are drawn to savior cults in part by the hope of a future reward, righting life's injustices either in the immediate present or in a future life. Another motive, not unlike the hope of reward, appears wherever there is a status group of elite intellectuals:

> The intellectual seeks in various ways . . . to endow his life with pervasive meaning. As intellectualism suppresses belief in magic, the world's processes

> have become disenchanted, lose their magical significance, and henceforth simply "are" and "happen" but no longer signify anything. As a consequence, there is a growing demand that the world and the total pattern of life be subject to an order that is significant and meaningful.[17]

Nearly everywhere among educated elites there is a deep yearning to find some true cosmic purpose to human existence in the world as we encounter it. In Asia most notably, "all the great religious doctrines . . . are creations of intellectuals," and they tend to become the special possession only of intellectuals.[18] The West strongly resisted elitism of this kind. Christianity, though it certainly has had an intellectual component, rejected the Gnostic teaching that true knowledge of God is the exclusive preserve of an intellectual elite. The urban craftsmen and tradesmen, who were the main bearers of Christian ideas and values in ancient Rome, declared their Gospel open to all classes, groups, races, and nations.

Belief and Behavior

Whatever the interests of intellectuals as a group, all of the world's prophetic religions must deal with one overriding intellectual problem—the mystery of evil or theodicy (Greek for "justifying God"). They need to explain how any idea of ultimate goodness can fit together with a day-to-day world that is so deeply flawed and filled with suffering. With this challenging topic as the transition, Weber turns to examine religious belief and behavior. His discussion is, again, difficult and inaccessible in places, so we will follow just the main themes.

The responses that religions make to the problem of evil divide into three ideal-types. One formula proposes that the problem will be solved either *within* this world at some future time when justice at last will triumph (as held by early Judaism) or *outside* of this life in another realm or a future existence when all will be made right (as held in later Judaism, Christianity, Islam, and other faiths). Alternatively, one can say with the book of Job and some of Islamic theology that God, or the universe, is simply inexplicable; our moral reasoning can never fathom ultimate questions. Or one can claim that there are two ultimate realities in the universe: two gods—one evil, one good, as the ancient Zoroastrians held, or a realm of spirit that is pure and eternal and a realm of material things that is subject to death and decay, as Hindu Brahmins have long maintained. Few religions offer these choices in the pure forms of these ideal-types. Most tend to mix different elements from each type in distinctive ways, and most (as we have noted) do so by offering as part of the solution a comprehensive program of human salvation, a formula that describes how everyone can find final peace or deliverance either in this world or beyond it. Weber thinks it possible also to divide these salvation programs into types—two in particular: the first assumes the need for some kind of human effort; the other declares that human effort is pointless and that salvation must come from the outside, as a gift from some extraordinary hero or from a divine being who assumes human form to assist.

Salvation Through Human Effort. One of the oldest avenues to salvation is ritualized action. Performing a ceremony or achieving a mental state, as in ancient Buddhist meditation, brings a person at that instant into enlightenment, or near to a god. Since these moods are momentary, the emphasis more often centers on various good works done over time. Credits are either tallied up at the end of life and weighed in the balance, as the prophet Zoroaster taught, or seen as expressions of an "ethical total personality."[19] Across almost all cultures, this pattern comes to clearest expression in certain exceptional people who practice what Weber calls "virtuoso sanctification"; they seek to be supreme artists of the moral life. In their differing ways, Buddhist and Christian monks, Pharisaic Jews, saints like St. Francis, Sufi mystics in Islam, and Puritans driven by the Protestant ethic all exhibit this trait. They claim an elevated status as spiritual athletes; disdaining "average morality," they seek living perfection instead.

Among these perfectionists, says Weber, we need to make some further distinctions, for not all heroes are the same. The term "asceticism" best describes one type of perfectionist practice, while "mysticism" better fits the other. The kind of strenuous ethical activity practiced by most Catholic monks in the Western world illustrates ascetic perfectionism. They see themselves as "instruments of God," actively engaged in a spiritual struggle that demands all of their strength to overcome weakness and resist temptation. Others, like the monks of earliest Buddhism, are just as perfectionist but adopt instead a passive, contemplative spiritual posture, and they are better described as practicing mysticism. They see themselves as vessels that receive spirituality rather than as instruments that actively achieve it. Their mission is not to follow a path of spiritual striving, but to contemplate, to achieve a quiet state of profound peace, filled with either truth or divinity.

There are, further, two settings in which each of these two forms of spiritual heroism can be pursued: either within the world of daily life or in isolation from it. The natural preference of the mystic is to reject the world and seek escape to a place of isolation, such as the forest retreat or the hermit's cave. There one can be alone and claim the joy of nothingness or swim in the oceanic peace of the divine being. Asceticism faces the same pair of options: it can either reject or embrace the everyday world as the scene of its activities. Most medieval Christian monasteries housed monks who worked together in isolation from the outside world and saw themselves as spiritual heroes actively engaged in the service of God. They were not passive mystics in the manner of Buddhist monks. They cleared forests, planted fields, and took the vow of St. Benedict that required them both to pray and to work—*ora et labora*—as they built their spiritual communities separated from the rest of society. The self-perfecting Calvinists who conducted their business in cities like London and Amsterdam were equally ascetic and spiritual—but with a crucial difference: their arena was not the monastery, but the everyday workplace. Like the medieval monk, the Puritan merchant enlisted in a life of spiritual struggle and self-restraint, but it came to expression through an "inner-worldly asceticism," a program of disciplined spiritual living that he applied *within* the realm of everyday life and business. In practical effect, the Calvinist Protestant sought nothing less than "to transform the world in accord with his ascetic ideals."[20] We can recall here for the purpose of comparison Durkheim's picture of the ascetic who by his self-denial serves as a model of how others too should give up selfish desires for the sake of society. The Protestant spiritual hero is different. The worldly ascetic denies himself in the service of God, but the unintended effect of this act is not to preserve the existing social order but to overturn it through a revolutionary change of attitudes toward both wealth and labor.

For Weber, this distinction between asceticism and mysticism is of major cultural importance. It highlights a central difference between religions of the East and the West. Typically, the Oriental religious ideal is mystical contemplation, while the West throughout history has tended toward activist asceticism. Even where mystics do appear in the West, they lean still toward a stress on conduct—what people actually *do* with their lives. Weber offers a complex set of philosophical and historical reasons for this circumstance, stressing especially a fact we noted earlier: Western salvation religions (Judaism, Christianity, Islam) all affirm a transcendent all-powerful Creator God who is wholly separate from the world that he has made. God and his creatures cannot be merged. The mysticism of the East is different; it promises a pathway of spiritual ascent by which humanity can, in the end, either merge with the divine or know the joy of perfect escape from the world.

Salvation as a Gift. Weber gives less attention to the belief that salvation is a gift (the other of the two formulas that religions apply to describe how salvation is secured), and we can spend less of our time on it as well. Some voices in the salvation religions have insisted on the claim that humans can do utterly nothing to win their own salvation. Ultimate peace comes only, and completely, from the outside. It can arrive as an unmerited gift, earned for us by a divine savior such as the Buddhist bodhisattva or Christianity's risen Christ. It can also arrive as an act of "institutional grace," such as the absolution given the sinner by a Catholic priest. Or, as in religions that affirm a God, it may come as divine grace bestowed in response to a simple, heartfelt, and utterly personal faith of the type seen in early Islam and some Protestant sects, such as German Pietism. Or, again, it may come to certain people and not to others through a mysterious act of divine predestination, as in later Islam and the austere Calvinist predestinarian doctrine of "divine decrees" enacted "before the foundations of the earth."

Religion and Other Spheres of Life

The fourth and last set of topics Weber addresses in *The Sociology of Religion* is the interaction of religion with certain other aspects of social life—namely, economics, politics, sexuality, and the arts. In the sphere of economics, he finds that the common rule of kindness to neighbors appears almost universally as the doctrine of charity or alms—giving freely to help others in need. This principle explains, among other things, the deep-seated distrust of usury in some religious traditions, which hold that to loan money while collecting interest is a way of exploiting, not helping, the poor. In keeping with its new ethic, Calvinism boldly challenged this principle. It prohibited charitable giving to beggars because not all were truly in need, as were the deserving poor: the disabled, widows, and orphans. Charity was not meant for those who can answer God's calling to work. Those who beg when they can earn clearly violate the law of love by accepting what is not rightly theirs. Conversely, usury may be seen simply as a payment from earnings generated by labor that could not have occurred without borrowed funds. Usury, then, does not exploit poverty; it creates opportunity.

As for politics, sexuality, and the arts, Weber observes that religion has most commonly found itself in a measure of tension, and then compromise, with each of these endeavors. Whenever prophetic religions have stated a universal doctrine of salvation or love, they cannot help coming into conflict with the state, which always puts first the interests of a political entity, whether that is a city, territory, nation, or empire. Religion can seek to subdue the state to its interests, as in the early wars of Islam or the exploits of Cromwell's Protestant army in England, but most often it must pursue compromises, accepting or ignoring the independence of the political order. The same holds true for sexuality and the arts. In the great religions with a salvation ethic, both mysticism (which seeks to lose the self) and asceticism (which seeks to discipline it) are in competition with the one human drive most able to distract from the goal of the former and break the constraints of the latter. In general, therefore, religions distrust sexuality; women are assigned secondary status, and marriage in all ethical systems is primarily a legal rather than an erotic or a romantic institution. Artistic expression should, by contrast, have a natural affinity with religion through the value it places on imagery and symbolism. But when art ceases being a craft in service of a religious purpose and asserts aesthetic values independently, proposing that people can find ultimate meaning through created beauty, a clash with religion is unavoidable.

"The Economic Ethic of the World Religions"

In its final pages, *The Sociology of Religion* does not really come to an end; it simply breaks off midway through a new chapter (the rest of which survives in notes) that examines the great religions of the world. Those pages can perhaps best be understood less as a conclusion to *The Sociology of Religion* than as the introduction to Weber's last and most ambitious enterprise, also left unfinished at the time of his death. He projected a series of studies that would include *The Protestant Ethic* and continue through no less than eight volumes dealing comparatively and in sequence with the world's major religions. There is no space in our discussion to give this project the full attention it deserves, but we can offer a brief sketch of the parts that Weber did finish, along with some observations on the general theme it was designed to explore. We will pass entirely over two important and complex essays he included at the beginning and in the middle of the sequence. Since the time of their translation, they have been read widely by English-speaking sociologists of religion; here they can be left to more advanced inquiries.[21]

"The Economic Ethic" proposes to explore all of the "five religions, or religiously determined systems of life-regulation which have known how to gather multitudes of confessors around them."[22] Weber adds Judaism to this group because of its historical importance to two other religions: Christianity and Islam. Of the volumes he planned, three—on Chinese religions,[23] Indian religions,[24] and Judaism[25]—were completed. The two on Asian systems were prepared during the years of World War I, and the essays that made up the volume on Judaism were completed between 1917 and 1919. Weber's first aim in these works was to return in much greater depth to the economic question that he had first asked, and provisionally answered, in *The Protestant Ethic*: Why did capitalism, the economic system that has transformed the world, arise in Europe and North America and *only there* in the two centuries after the Reformation? The proper strategy for answering this question requires a broad comparative analysis, starting with civilizations of the Far East.

The Religion of China (1916)

From time immemorial, China has been predominantly an agricultural society ruled at the top by the emperor, who controlled the river systems crucial to agriculture and transport, and managed at the bottom by local village elders. The emperor asserted his authority through an elite class of public administrators—the literate mandarins schooled in the great Confucian writings—who resided mainly in the cities. Privileged and cultivated, they pursued an ethic of refinement and comfortable "adjustment to the world" that shaped Chinese elite culture for two millennia, but without notable impact on the attitudes of the masses. In both city and countryside, ordinary life was governed by ties of family and clan and by religious attachment to age-old magical rites and ancestral spirits, which the elite made little effort to challenge or to change. China's cities never developed features of many cities in the West: self-government, charters of independence, legal rights, guilds and fraternal societies. They remained patrimonial institutions that deferred to the emperor and willingly accepted rule by the Confucian elite. The only protest against this traditionalism came from the Taoists, followers of the teacher Lao-tzu, who urged a life of self-denial and escape from the world. Lao-tzu called for retreat into the unspoiled forests, where the spirit could attune itself to the *Tao*, the great and mysterious flow in all existing things. Taoists sought a life of simplicity, but because they prized life so highly and took such keen interest in techniques they believed could extend it, their doctrines often blended naturally with popular magic, even reinforcing its grip on the masses. So although it did enter a protest against the mandarins' learning and privileged urban lifestyle, Taoism was no more disposed than Confucianism to promote a universal ethic among the masses; on the contrary, the stress on quiet, selfless drift in the stream of nature left Taoist teachers as much at ease as Confucians with a civilization shaped mainly by peasant traditionalism.

This dominant posture of traditionalism and passivity meant that neither the folk traditions nor the great philosophical systems of China furnished a religious incentive for people to seek profit in business or trade. Despite certain early advances in mathematics and technology, China's cultural blend of traditionalism and patrimonialism discouraged the kind of rational impartiality (the refusal to "play favorites" to help friends or family) in business dealings that is crucial to rational profit-oriented activity. More decisively, the indispensable element, the *spirit* of capitalism, failed to appear. The learned mandarin, proud of his Confucian training, thought mostly about his personal dignity, not about fulfillment of any divine calling, as Luther had taught. As disciples of Confucius, the literate and cultivated elite showed no inclination toward the asceticism that drove Calvinists to see themselves as instruments of God at work in the world. If one's life is seen as already a polished and perfected achievement, there is little point in striving to gain greater self-control or to prosper in the marketplace. Confucianism did not seek mastery of the world through a life of disciplined self-denial; it was content with its ethic of adjustment to the world as it was and had always been: traditional, stable, and unchanging.

The Religion of India (1916–1917)

In India, successive invasions and conquests had created divisions in the social order that appeared in the system of caste, which was dominated by two elite groups. The Brahmins were a caste of priests privileged alone to read the sacred texts of the Vedas; the Kshatryias, a warrior class, held military and political power. Beneath these two groups, which claimed their status as an inherited charisma (or family gift), lesser castes arranged themselves downward on a scale fixed by birth and vocation. At the bottom were the very lowest of the slaves, literally "out-castes." Rules against marriage or even association at meals kept the lines of separation distinct, but the most powerful support of the system was religious. Brahmin intellectuals, who were the main bearers of the ideas that shaped Indian civilization, wrote caste divisions into the very script of the universe. They held that all of life is subject to the cosmic law of *samsara*, or rebirth, which governs both nature and society on the principle of *karma*, the cumulative weight of one's spiritual (or unspiritual) deeds. Those in the Brahmin caste, placed high, deserved their fortune as a reward for spiritual achievement in an earlier existence; those placed low equally deserved theirs as a natural consequence of prior lives too entangled in material attachments and sensual pleasures. This system was intellectually persuasive, explaining with a kind of cold logic just why social differences that seem unfair are not so because they are built into the very framework of the world. But it was also deeply disheartening. To the ordinary person, it promised one life after another lived on the great "wheel of rebirth." Human existence was defined chiefly by a continuous struggle to slip free from the coils of reincarnation and by (mostly failed) efforts to overcome the allurements of sexuality, luxury, and even family.

This great world system, gray at best and grim at worst, colored the entire development of both religion and society in India. Brahmin leaders, originally masters of the sacred chant, introduced ascetic practices of yoga and withdrawal to impose discipline on the body's urges and to cultivate a form of spirituality pure enough to give the soul its final release. The same motive of determined search for release gave rise to India's two great protest religions: Buddhism and Jainism. Both accepted in full the system of *samsara*, but they broke the grip of caste by offering hope of escape to all who could either manage a Buddhist life of total ascetic discipline and meditation or travel the Jain path of total respect for life in all its forms. Still, for the ordinary masses, none of this was realistic. They were not spiritual athletes; they could not hope to reach the heights of a virtuoso in spiritual performance. Because such self-denial was unachievable for the great majority of people, they accepted second best, gaining merit by supporting the communities of monks. While the Brahmin, Buddhist, and Jain elite practiced spiritual heroics, the great masses lived as religious stepchildren. On the surface of life, they could interest themselves in the "garden of magic" that was filled with popular saviors and superstitions, but deep within, at the level of ultimate questions, they were resigned to a fate that promised little more than seemingly endless discouraging new births on the ever-turning wheel of reincarnation.

All of this resignation left a visible imprint on economic life. As in China, capitalist enterprise in India failed to take root, even though the prospects were quite favorable. There was a system of arithmetic using zero and positional numbering; there were thriving centers of handicraft and trade, as well as specialized laborers with guilds to support them; there were independent merchants; and taxation was not oppressive. But in contrast to Europe, Indian society remained chiefly rural and traditional, so true capitalist enterprise did not develop. It did not help that free, self-governing cities, the nurseries of capitalism in the early modern West, had failed to emerge. The main cause was caste, which prevented the unification of different guilds and classes into a single community of citizens, all possessing equal rights under an impartial legal and moral system that rejected any favoritism based on family or class ties. Further, the problem of caste was in the end the problem of the Indian religious system that served to anchor it. The classic teachings of Hinduism held, and still today hold, that there is in the end no enduring, positive value to be placed on human activity in the physical world and present life. The messages of the Brahmin elite and of prophets such as Buddha and Mahavira (the founder of Jainism) were essentially the same: spiritual peace comes only through withdrawal from the world and release from its toils, cares, and even joys.

Such teachings differ sharply from those of the Jewish prophets, who offered a message received directly from God, a divine revelation that disenchanted the world of its magical spells and spirits. Their oracles demanded obedience to the moral law of a sovereign Lord rather than ceremonies and sacrifices to please the spirits of the field or village. India abounded with elite ascetics and mystics skilled in withdrawal *from* the world, but again, as in China, there was no program that called for self-denying obedience to the will of God through systematic engagement *with* the world, such as we see in the Puritan merchants of London or the settlers in Massachusetts Bay. For all their other achievements, the civilizations of China and India did not produce an equivalent of

Europe's Protestant ethic. And without it, neither the true spirit nor the genuine practice of modern capitalism ever managed to emerge.

Ancient Judaism (1917–1919)

As he turned from Asia to the West, Weber planned his next volumes, which were to center on the great Western religions: Judaism, Christianity, and Islam. Unfortunately, the first, on ancient Judaism, was the only one he lived long enough (almost) to complete. It is a dense, thoughtful work; we, again, cannot do it justice. But we can touch upon its central ideas.

As with China and India, Weber begins by offering a close review of the material circumstances in which Judaism arose: the geography, politics, and culture of the ancient Near East. Even before the age of kings, the Hebrew confederation of tribes had united around a shared faith in Yahweh, the personal Lord of the covenant and Creator of the world. Out of all humanity he had chosen the Jews as his children by contract. His favor was theirs for the taking; only their loyalty was expected in return. All subsequent Jewish history was to be interpreted, by priest and prophet alike, in terms of this sacred covenant, which was to shape the theologies of both Christianity and Islam as well.

The contract was shattered in the age of monarchy. The kings brought wealth to Jerusalem, but along with their success came dynastic marriages to non-Israelite princesses and the worship of foreign gods of fertility. Resentment flared among the rural and traditional poor, bringing civil war and eventually the destruction of the tribes in the North. In time the kingdom was reconstituted in the South, and under King Josiah, prophets and teaching priests made the books of the law—the Torah rather than temple sacrifices—the centerpiece of Jewish life. They called for a new individualized religious faith: obedience to the precepts of the Torah out of a sense of personal devotion to Yahweh, the covenant Lord, no longer conceived only as Israel's God but as the God of all nations. This obedience consisted of more than just isolated good deeds; it was to be a complete "ethic of commitment." The prophets who proclaimed it—Amos, Hosea, Isaiah, Jeremiah—demanded both purity of faith in Yahweh and social justice for the poor. Differing from the exemplary prophets of the East, they made no personal claim for themselves of supreme wisdom or divinity. But in another sense they asserted something far greater: the message of ethical monotheism. They proclaimed the sovereign majesty of God and demanded total obedience to his will. More than almost anything else, that message is what separates Judaism and its successor religions of the West from the traditions of the East. Unlike the great Asian systems, Judaism and its disciple faiths insist that salvation is not won through contemplation that leads the soul out of the everyday physical world; it comes instead through faith and lifelong obedience that seek to achieve a divine purpose within that world.

Equally important in this connection was prophetic opposition to the ways of magic, which was widely tolerated among the masses in the Far East. As the prophets conceived him, Yahweh, the Lord of creation, is utterly beyond manipulation by rituals and spells of the kind offered to the Canaanite deities of fortune and fertility. Personal devotion and ethical obedience, not magic and divination, are the things that please him. In place of mysterious forces and occult manipulations, the prophets urged ordinary people to a life freed of magic, a path of action governed solely by personal obedience to the Mosaic law. This new ethic of commitment was not reserved only to an elite circle of specialists, as in Hinduism and Buddhism. It placed before all Jews the ideal of a "total ethical personality," of an entire individual life molded into habits of obedience to the Torah's commands. Through preaching from texts of the Old Testament, this ideal of an entire life lived in service to God made its way ultimately into the ethic of modern Protestants as they pursued their sacred vocations in the world.

As these paragraphs reveal, Weber keenly appreciated the historical significance of Judaism to both religion and civilization in the Western world. There is, however, a troubling element in his discussion. Although he treats Judaism no differently than he does Christianity or Buddhism, and although he fiercely opposed the mistreatment of Jews he saw in German universities, some of his ideas on Judaism have been linked nonetheless to later German anti-Semitism. The issue arises from his description of later Jews as a "pariah people" of the ancient Near East. After the exile in Babylon, he claims, Jews gradually became a "community of outcasts," partly of their own making. They adopted a form of self-isolation in Christian Europe (similar to that of the outcastes in India) by refusing either to intermarry or to associate with members of the wider gentile community. Inevitably, then, they found themselves disprivileged—the victims of suspicion, hatred, and exploitation. Burdened further by an "ethic of resentment" against their oppressors, they embraced a kind of dual morality, applying a high moral standard in all dealings with fellow Jews and a lower one for commerce with others. Jewish enterprise thus became "pariah capitalism," as illustrated in practices associated with usury. Because the Torah prohibited the practice, interest-bearing loans could not be made to other Jews, yet they could be offered to gentiles. In part this divided ethic also helps explain why Protestantism, and not Judaism, is the real parent of Western capitalism. Protestants demanded wholly neutral and rational standards of conduct in commerce—a principle that was alien to the Jewish pariah ethic.

Some critics have vigorously attacked this "pariah" theory of Jewish identity, challenging Weber's evidence and noting how easily such words could later be conscripted to support Nazi racism—barely more than a decade after they were written. Had he lived longer, we might well have had a chance to read Weber's responses to such critics and measure his words by the judgments he himself would have been compelled to render as he witnessed the patriotism of his generation descend into the fascism of the next. Unfortunately, his early death in 1920 has left no chance of discovering what his response might have been. Nor can we know what his wide erudition might have offered in the remainder of "The Economic Ethic" had it been brought to completion; certainly it would have made a suitable capstone to a career of extraordinary scholarly achievement.

Analysis

1. Weber and Durkheim

Weber's writings are notoriously difficult to summarize because he weaves such an abundance of historical and sociological detail so seamlessly into his theoretical discussions. With him the forest does seem hard to see for the trees. Even so, we can find a path if we work comparatively, placing Weber's methods and his achievements over against those of neighboring theorists, especially his nearest intellectual rivals, Durkheim and Marx. With respect to Durkheim, we should notice that between him and Weber there is a clear similarity of interest combined with a sharp difference in method. As noted, Durkheim and Weber were not just pioneers in the field of social theory; they were also responsible for turning the focus of professional sociology in its earliest years specifically toward the sociology of religion. Durkheim's *Elementary Forms* was pivotally important in placing religion at the center of social investigation and theory. In the same way, Weber, though primarily interested in the economic aspects of social life, found himself steadily drawn toward the central importance of religion to society. By the time of his death, comparative study of civilizations, anchored in research on world religions, was the main focus of his labors.

This shared interest in religion did not carry over into agreement on the methods most suitable to the inquiry. Durkheim's agenda, as we saw, was to begin from a single case of religion in its near-original state—among the Aborigines of Australia. From their tribal practices he broke out the "elementary" forms of ritual activity—and proceeded to show how all of religion exhibits them. Weber, by contrast, starts less with a religious community than a cultural problem: How did a new, revolutionary form of economic behavior arise to transform Western civilization in the early centuries of the modern era?

The search for an answer to this question leads him to a religious change—the emergence of the "Protestant ethic," which became the animating spirit of modern capitalism. Unlike Durkheim, Weber then proceeds (in works like *The Sociology of Religion* and "The Economic Ethic of the World Religions") to explore the widest possible range of cultures, practices, and beliefs. Also in contrast to Durkheim (and, for that matter, Tylor and Frazer as well), he does not privilege primitive religion as containing the seed from which all later institutions have grown. He thinks that at least as much (and indeed much more) can be learned from the actual histories of the great world religions as from the field studies of anthropologists centered on primitive tribes.

There is a further difference over the matter of cultural evolution. As we saw earlier, Durkheim, because of his central focus on religion in its earliest forms, allowed for some forms of later development. He could entertain the notion of religious institutions changing over time from the simple to the more complex. Clearly, this was not the view of Weber. When he sets out to explain ideal-types, he is careful to notice how expressions of those types may appear in one epoch, fade in the next, and return again thereafter, depending on each new cultural or historical circumstance. He finds magic, for example, more common in earlier societies but concedes its enduring appeal among the masses—the peasants and poor—in any society. He notices too how it can revive in places where once it had faltered. Magic was probably more widespread in medieval Christian Europe than it was a thousand years earlier in ancient Judaism after the message of the prophets had taken effect. Accordingly, there is also for Weber no such thing as a natural intellectual evolution of the kind Frazer imagines when he puts magic, religion, and science into historically successive stages. Finally, and significantly, Weber departs from Durkheim's functionalist reductionism. As we have already seen in several connections, he does not believe that religious beliefs and practices are mere reflections of a controlling and more fundamental social reality. Since Weber diverges from Marx on this issue even more acutely than he does from Durkheim, we can turn to that comparison next.

2. Weber and Marx

When we compare Weber with Marx, there seems at first an obvious similarity. Both are historically oriented social theorists who build arguments from close analyses of complex social and historical relationships. They draw on encyclopedic understandings of culture and civilization, and they energetically search out causes and effects. Marx, however, confines most of his historical work to Western civilization, where, among other things, he finds decisive evidence that the fantasies of religion arise from economic exploitation. Weber, on the other hand, attends to religious activities worldwide, a strategy that makes him more cautious than Marx about advancing, for nearly all events, only one form of explanation: class struggle born of economic oppression. The complexity and differences in world religious systems suggest to him that interpreters need to draw on explanatory theorems that are not singular but multiple and interacting.

It is, further, just this sense of the great complexity in human endeavors that draws Weber back from reductionist functionalism. As we have seen, Freud, Durkheim, and Marx readily assume that religious actions and beliefs always trace to nonreligious causes, whether psychological, social, or socioeconomic. What sets Weber clearly apart from their approach is the conviction he articulates in the principle of *Verstehen*. Human ideas, beliefs, and motives deserve to be counted as real and independent causes of human action. An idea in the mind of one human agent (or shared by a group of agents) is as much a real cause of human action as the application of heat to water is the real cause of steam. Conscious thoughts affect human action at least as much as unconscious urges or needs. When he unfolds the argument of *The Protestant Ethic*, Weber does not, like Marx, look first to economic distress, tracing the theological doctrine of predestination to class conflict in Calvin's Geneva. His inquiry takes him in the very opposite direction, unearthing as the key cause of the capitalist revolution not some material circumstance but a new form of economic behavior that in fact followed from a new religious idea. The self-constraining ethic of Protestantism was the animating spirit of capitalism. It is historically significant that in two decades after 1900, as Freud, Durkheim, and the disciples of Marx were extending their intellectual influence, Weber steadfastly pressed on with his approach. For him, meanings matter; the webs of significance that human beings spin do effectively shape and change the material and social structures that underlie them. In taking this view, Weber certainly was not given to overstatement. He appreciated in full the dense tangle of causes, events, conditions, ideas, and motives that enter into all of human action, both individual and social. He makes a special note of this point in an introduction later added to *The Protestant Ethic*, where he grants that Calvinist worldly asceticism was by no means the *only* cause that accounts for the rise of modern capitalism. Clearly, a complex array of factors converged at its creation. He states that he has addressed

> the side of the problem which is generally most difficult to grasp: the influence of certain religious ideas on the development of an economic spirit, or the *ethos* of an economic system. In this case we are dealing with the connection of the spirit of modern economic life with the rational ethics of ascetic Protestantism. Thus we treat here only one side of the causal chain.[26]

That "one side of the causal chain" was the powerful imprint of Protestant religious ideas on human behavior. Certainly that factor was not the only cause, but just as certainly it *was* a cause, and arguably the most important one. This firm but carefully modulated antireductionist stance, which Weber maintained as a feature of his approach through all his later research, is a prime reason why his analyses draw new appreciation (and of course new criticism) to the present day. Because social endeavor is for him always complex, and explanation is almost never singular or simple, Weber on principle refused membership in the club of reductionist theory. He could not join Marx or Freud or Durkheim in diminishing the role of ideas, intentions, and beliefs while still remaining true to the evidence that history and society presented to him.

Critique

Normally, it is no compliment to describe a theorist as someone whose work has been widely and roundly criticized. The case of Max Weber, however, is a notable exception. As with Marx, the scale of the criticism Weber's ideas have received is a sign of their importance and influence. If the real merit of a theorist is measured by the commentary he provokes, then Weber's stature is secure. As noted earlier, *The Protestant Ethic* is still starting arguments more than a century after its publication. Similarly spirited critical discussions center on the concepts, distinctions, and connections advanced in *Economy and Society*, *The Sociology of Religion*, and the separate studies of "The Economic Ethic of the World Religions." The controversy over Judaism as a pariah religion is just one example. Weber's ideal-type of "bureaucracy" is another. Both have produced vigorous discussion among social psychologists, as well as experts on industrial organization and public administration. Economists and historians of business still debate the definition of capitalism; others have disputed Weber's ideas on power, on law, and on political institutions, as well as his commentaries on the arts, eroticism, science, and music. More recently, intellectual historians have focused on his discussions of "rationalization" in human societies over the course of history. Some think this is actually the grand interpretive theme that underlies Weber's program, linking religion, economics, and society.[27]

With regard to religion, the stormiest debates have swirled, not surprisingly, around the famous thesis advanced in *The Protestant Ethic*. Many critics accept that the concepts of both the Protestant ethic and the distinctive spirit of capitalism are illuminating. Some, however, claim that Weber fails to establish the connection he asserts. Others point to factors more important than religion that account for the capitalist revolution. Still others contend that the economic behavior Weber thinks so new and so distinctively Western can be found to have existed both long before the arrival of Protestantism and well outside of Europe. These debates, which turn on sociological and historical details, can be left for specialists to settle. But there are two other issues to address that bear more directly on Weber's general program both as a theorist of human action and an interpreter of religion.

1. Consistency

The first is a criticism leveled primarily by disciples of Marx, though it could just as well have come from the circle of Durkheim or of Freud. It applies well beyond *The Protestant Ethic* to the whole spectrum of Weber's work on religion, and it pits against Weber a most formidable opponent—himself. The issue is consistency. Weber, we have noticed, insists that religious ideas must be accorded an independent, causative place in the process of understanding human history and society. In discussing Protestantism, for example, he considers the Calvinist concepts of "vocation" and "worldly asceticism" to be compelling religious ideas that caused people to adopt a distinctively new form of behavior. But in other discussions (and elsewhere even in that study), Weber's practice appears to depart from his precept. *The Sociology of Religion* offers an interesting example. When he discusses there the origin of monotheism, he writes:

> [T]he personal, transcendental and ethical god is a Near-Eastern concept. It corresponds so closely to that of an all-powerful mundane king with his rational bureaucratic regime that a causal connection can scarcely be denied.[28]

He adds that the model of the monarch who owned the vital irrigation systems "was probably a source of the conception of a god who had created the earth and man out of nothing, and not procreated them, as was believed elsewhere."[29]

This explanation of a crucially important religious idea—the sovereign Creator God—looks almost as if it could have come from Marx. The discussion adduces a purely material economic circumstance—a basic need for water provided by a mighty and distant monarch—as the fundamental reality and turns the religious conception into a reflection of political power and geography. To be sure, Weber can reply that he finds the desert king to be only *a* source, not *the* or *the only* source, of the idea of God. But even so, the tenor of his exposition here certainly suggests what Marx might have said: Religious ideas arise naturally as reflections of socioeconomic realities. Weber's correlations of certain class interests or status group concerns with specific religious ideas proceed in similar fashion. He finds the Muslim notion of God a concept characteristic of the "warrior nobility" of early Arabia, and he thinks the Hindu doctrine of samsara reflects the need of an intellectual elite to offer a cosmic rationale for the birth of some to wealth and privilege while others are fated to poverty and hardship. With this, Marx could readily agree.

This pattern of explanation occurs also in the studies that make up "The Economic Ethic of the World Religions." Before he turns attention to the religious beliefs and teachings of China or India or ancient Judaism, Weber offers an exhaustive examination of the material, political, and socio-economic contexts in which the religions arose. In principle, he articulates an anti-reductionist position, saying of India, for example, that the course of development in religious thought proceeds independently of material circumstances and social influences. But in the actual process of explanation, he is disposed to treat those ideas differently: as bound to their historical framework and as naturally mirroring the specific social, cultural, and economic settings in which they appear.

2. Social Science and Religion

Criticism of another kind attaches to Weber's idea of a social science as applied to the subject of religion. As we noticed in our discussion of his methods, Weber (no less than other theorists) is keenly committed to developing accounts of religious activity that can claim to be *scientific*. The whole purpose of devising the concepts he designates as ideal-types is to offer, as in all science, some kind of generalized conceptual framework that can be applied uniformly across cultures. The approach is somewhat similar to that of Durkheim, who draws the elementary forms out of one religious instance and applies them to all others. For a genuinely historical sociologist like Weber, however, this strategy is more problematic. Historical precision, after all, is not the easy friend of scientific generalization. Whatever the religious phenomenon—event, person, process—he addresses, Weber's habit is to bring to the issue the full array of his wide learning, often outlining an intricate network of material circumstances, political influences, economic conditions, social forces, and class or status group interests, as well as religious ideas and activities, in the course of his analyses. All of this labor is instructive, at times even dazzling, in its effect. But there is a complication: the aim of sociology as a science, presumably, is to find patterns and categories that can be applied generally to most, or many similar cases. Yet that is the very thing that Weber's delicately complex historical descriptions make it exceedingly difficult for him, or anyone interested in social scientific theory, to do.

A specific instance can illustrate. In one section of his *Religion of India*, Weber explains the beginnings of Buddhism. He describes it as the product of an urban aristocratic setting, not the pastoral world of the Hindu Brahmins.

It teaches reincarnation, as does Hinduism, but leaves out any doctrine of the soul or Brahman-atman (the world soul). It is a salvation system, but only for cultivated intellectuals. It shows none of the asceticism of the Jains. In almost every way, "it is the polar opposite of Confucianism and of Islam."[30] It is an ethic that rejects both active conduct in the world and ascetic exercises. Despite this fact, its monks gradually acquired permanent residences and estates, becoming landowners and farm administrators like the Christian monks of the West. Unlike the Western monks, however, Buddhist leaders had no real authority, and ordinary monks were not formally attached to any one monastery. These and many other explanatory details are carefully presented as the discussion proceeds.[31] But the end result of this process is a kind of paradox. On the one hand, we have been given the historian's dream—a remarkably rich, detailed, and specific account of Buddhist life and culture in early centuries after Gautama; on the other, we have (one could almost say) the sociologist's nightmare—an economic, social, cultural, and religious portrait of early Buddhism so carefully shaded, precise, and detailed that any attempt to place it in a category, any effort to bring it under some general sociological pattern or draw from it an analogy applicable to a religious community of another time or place, seems nearly futile. Weber's cabinet of ideal-types does offer a set of tools to classify and compare, but their value to the aims of social science is limited. The historian's task, certainly, is to explain particulars, to trace events or actions to a convergence of causes and conditions specific to one time, place, and circumstance. Social science, by Weber's own account, is not history. Like natural science, it seeks theoretical constructs that have some kind of general applicability to most (if not all) reasonably comparable cases. In his actual practice, however, Weber seems unable to deliver this general applicability. Despite his best efforts toward the goal of empirical sociology, his inquiries wear the look of outstanding history rather than successful, generalized social science. His analyses are useful, instructive, illuminating, and original, but they are not general, or generally applicable, in the way that scientific sociology presumably would want them to be.

Present-day theorists working in Weber's lineage do offer responses to these complaints, but here we must leave them aside, with an invitation to further debate at another time in another place. Whatever the residual misgivings critics may harbor, Weber's contribution to the theory of religion is most impressive. The marks of his achievement are to be found in the great range of his learning and interests, in the precision of his concepts and subtlety of his analyses, in the firmness of his resistance to reductionist functionalism as represented by Freud, Durkheim, and Marx, and most emphatically, in his keen appreciation of the great complexity involved in the task of explaining human behavior, both religious and otherwise.

Notes

1. Clifford Geertz, "Thick Description: Toward an Interpretive Theory of Culture," in *The Interpretation of Cultures: Selected Essays* (New York: Basic Books, 1973), p. 5.

2. A brief but detailed factual account of these early years and education is provided in Dirk Käsler, *Max Weber: An Introduction to His Life and Work*, tr. Philippa Hurd (Chicago: University of Chicago Press, 1988), pp. 1–25.

3. Descriptions and discussions of these early studies can be found in Reinhard Bendix, *Max Weber: An Intellectual Portrait*, 2nd ed., rev. (Berkeley: University of California Press, 1978), pp. 13–48.

4. Her richly anecdotal but also rather formal and protective memoir is Marianne (Schnitger) Weber, *Max Weber: A Biography*, tr. Harry Zohn (London: John Wiley & Sons, 1975).

5. A noteworthy (if also controversial) attempt to provide a "psycho-historical" account of Weber's life and thought that pivots on his emotional crisis is Arthur Mitzman's *The Iron Cage* (New York: Alfred A. Knopf, 1970).

6. English translations of these essays can be found in two collections: Edward A. Shils and Henry A. Finch, *Max Weber on the Methodology of the Social Sciences* (Glencoe, IL: Free Press, 1949), and Max Weber, *Roscher and Knies: The Logical Problems of Historical Economics*, ed. and tr. Guy Oakes (New York: Free Press, 1975). A clear and very instructive recent study of Weber's ideas on method is found in Sven Eliaeson, *Max Weber's Methodologies: Interpretation and Critique* (Cambridge: Polity Press, 2002).

7. Max Weber, *Economy and Society: An Outline of Interpretive Sociology*, ed. and tr. Guenther Roth, Claus Wittich et al., 2 vols. (New York: Bedminster Press, 1968), 1: 24–25.

8. Fritz Ringer, *Max Weber: An Intellectual Biography* (Chicago: University of Chicago Press, 2004), p. 100.

9. On this issue, see especially the analysis of W. G. Runciman, *A Critique of Max Weber's Philosophy of Social Science* (Cambridge: Cambridge University Press, 1972), pp. 33–78.

10. On this early sociological research for the Union, see Bendix, *Max Weber*, pp. 13–48.

11. This point is part of an important revisionist assessment of Weber's achievement by Wolfgang Schluchter, *Rationalism, Religion, and Domination: A Weberian Perspective*, tr. Neil Solomon (Berkeley: University of California Press, 1989). He argues that the center of Weber's lifelong interests is not to be found in *Economy and Society*, as most have thought, but in the unfinished multivolume "Economic Ethic of the World Religions."

12. The English translation of this study was first published in 1930 by Harvard sociologist Talcott Parsons, who worked not with the original articles but with revised German versions that included an introduction and other materials Weber added later. This revised edition was published in German with other works by Weber's wife, Marianne, after his death. See Talcott Parsons, "Translator's Preface," in Max Weber, *The Protestant Ethic and the Spirit of Capitalism*, tr. Talcott Parsons (New York: Charles Scribner's Sons, 1958), pp. ix–xi.

13. On the composition and publication of *The Sociology of Religion*, as well as its inclusion in *Economy and Society*, see Sam Whimster, "Translator's Note on Weber's Economic Ethics of the World Religions," *Max Weber Studies* 3, no. 1 (2002): 80 and n. 1; Weber, *Economy and Society*, "Introduction," pp. lix–lx, xciv–xcv.

14. Max Weber, *The Sociology of Religion*, tr. Ephraim Fischoff (Boston: Beacon Press, 1963), p. 46.

15. Weber, *The Sociology of Religion*, p. 60.

16. Weber, *The Sociology of Religion*, pp. 80, 82.

17. Weber, *The Sociology of Religion*, p. 125.

18. Weber, *The Sociology of Religion*, p. 120.

19. Weber, *The Sociology of Religion*, p. 155.

20. Weber, *The Sociology of Religion*, pp. 164–165.

21. They are found in *From Max Weber: Essays in Sociology*, ed. and tr. H. H. Gerth and C. Wright Mills (New York: Oxford University Press, 1946) under the titles "The Social Psychology of the World Religions," pp. 267–301, and "Religious Rejections of the World and Their Directions," pp. 323–359. There is a good recent analysis of the first of these discussions in Whimster, "Translator's Note," pp. 75–98. The second is in part a more elaborated discussion of the asceticism-mysticism typology discussed on pp. 165–166.

22. Gerth and Mills, *From Max Weber*, p. 267.

23. Weber, *The Religion of China*, tr. Hans Gerth (Glencoe, IL: The Free Press, 1951).

24. Weber, *The Religion of India*, tr. Hans Gerth and Don Martindale (Glencoe, IL: The Free Press, 1958).

25. Weber, *Ancient Judaism*, tr. Hans Gerth and Don Martindale (Glencoe, IL: The Free Press, 1952).

26. Weber, *The Protestant Ethic*, p. 27.

27. On this, again, see Schluchter, *Rationalism, Religion, and Domination.*

28. Weber, *The Sociology of Religion*, pp. 56, 57.

29. Weber, *The Sociology of Religion*, pp. 56, 57.

30. Weber, *The Religion of India*, p. 206.

31. Weber, *The Religion of India*, pp. 204–230.

Suggestions for Further Reading

Andreski, Stanislav. *Max Weber's Insights and Errors*. London: Routledge and Kegan Paul, 1984. A short, highly substantive analysis filled with penetrating observations on all aspects of Weber's thinking.

Barbalet, J. M. *Weber, Passion and Profits: 'The Protestant Ethic and the Spirit of Capitalism in Context*. New York: Cambridge University Press, 2008. A recent reassessment of one of the most widely discussed theorems in economic and social history. The author links Weber to Adam Smith and others in the previous century.

Bendix, Reinhard. *Max Weber*. 2nd ed. Berkeley: University of California Press, 1978. A perceptive intellectual biography in English, widely read and cited by scholars in America.

Collins, Randall. *Max Weber: A Skeleton Key*. Beverly Hills, CA: Sage, 1986. A very brief introduction to the whole of Weber's life and scholarly career; valuable for those making a first encounter with Weber.

Eliaeson, Sven. *Max Weber's Methodologies*. Cambridge: Polity Press, 2002. A fairly recent, thorough, and clear assessment of Weber's difficult writings on sociological method.

Freund, Julien. *The Sociology of Max Weber*. New York: Pantheon Books, 1968. An earlier study, but lucidly written; one of the most readable of all introductions to Weber.

Honigsheim, Paul. *On Max Weber*. Translated by Joan Rytina. New York: The Free Press, 1968. A fascinating personal memoir by a student of Weber who knew him personally, rich with insightful anecdotes illuminating Weber's life and intellectual associations.

Käsler, Dirk. *Max Weber: An Introduction to His Life and Work*. Translated by Philippa Hurd. Chicago: University of Chicago Press, 1988. An English translation of a thoroughly researched German study; difficult in places, but important.

Kivisto, Peter, and William H. Swatos, Jr. *Max Weber: A Bio-Bibliography*. New York: Greenwood Press, 1988. A comprehensive annotated guide to the entire literature on Max Weber in English; contains nearly 1,000 entries. Now slightly dated, but still indispensable for non-German readers.

Lehmann, Hartmut, and Guenther Roth, eds. *Weber's Protestant Ethic: Origins, Evidence, Contexts*. Cambridge: Cambridge University Press, 1993. Essays by a group of international experts addressing multiple aspects of the "Weber thesis" controversy.

Max Weber Studies. Sheffield, UK: Academic Press, 2002–. A relatively new journal offering careful studies, notes, and book reviews on all aspects of Weber's life and career.

Mitzman, Arthur. *The Iron Cage: An Historical Interpretation of Max Weber*. New York: Alfred Knopf, 1970. A provocative "psycho-history" that seeks to understand Weber's life in terms of the tensions arising from his family relationships, his marital arrangement, and the effects of his anxiety disorder.

Mommsen, Wolfgang. *Max Weber and German Politics: 1890–1920*. Translated by M. S. Steinberg. Chicago: University of Chicago Press, 1984. An important revisionist study by a major German historian who centers on Weber's politics and German nationalism.

Radkau, Joachim. *Max Weber: A Biography*. Translated by Patrick Camiller. Malden, MA: Polity, 2009 [2005]. The publication of this long-awaited biography in 2005 was a major event in German cultural history; now in English, it offers an in-depth account of Weber in multiple dimensions; new sources allow a rich portrayal of the man and his achievement.

Ringer, Fritz. *Max Weber: An Intellectual Portrait*. Chicago: University of Chicago Press, 2004. Though now surpassed by Radkau, a still useful, briefer account of Weber's life and ideas in English, written by an accomplished historian of universities and intellectual life in pre–World War I Germany.

Schluchter, Wolfgang. *Rationalism, Religion, and Domination: A Weberian Perspective.* Translated by Neil Solomon. Berkeley: University of California Press, 1989. A major reinterpretation of Weber's complete intellectual project, shifting emphasis from his work on economy and society to his comparative studies of civilizations and world religions.

Turner, Stephen, ed. *The Cambridge Companion to Weber.* Cambridge: Cambridge University Press, 2000. More than a dozen current essays on specific dimensions of Weber's work by leading authorities on his life and thought.

Weber, Marianne. *Max Weber: A Biography.* Translated by Harry Zohn. New York: John Wiley & Sons, [1926] 1975. A long, rich, informative but also protective account of Weber's life and thought, written by his wife and published six years after his death.

Wrong, Dennis, ed. *Max Weber.* Englewood Cliffs, NJ: Prentice Hall, 1970. Short, highly informative essays on specific Weberian concepts contributed by leading international authorities and complemented by the editor's informative, wide-ranging introduction.

6

The Verdict of Religious Experience: William James

Religion is the great interest of my life.

William James, *Letter to Henry W. Rankin*, 1897[1]

If among sociologists Weber offers a counterpoint to Durkheim, can we find something similar in the case of psychology? Is there in the psychology of religion a voice to dissent or differ from the reductionism of Freud? The answer to both of these questions is: Yes. But in this instance—and for the first time in our discussion—we need to travel beyond Europe to locate the theorist who offers the most instructive case to consider. We need to reach across the Atlantic to Harvard University, where we find in its lecture halls at the turn of the century the energetic, engaging figure of William James. Scientist, essayist, moralist, philosopher, and by official title psychologist, James was seen in both his time and in the decades after his death in 1910 as one of the leading lights in American cultural and religious discussion. His career spanned the decades of the nation's Gilded Age, capturing notice in the later 1870s and extending through the first full decade of the twentieth century. Throughout this entire epoch, he cut a visible profile on the Harvard campus as a thoughtful conversationalist, genial colleague, lively classroom lecturer, and mentor to scores of students, private inquirers, and personal friends. He did as much as anyone in its early years to establish psychology as a major field of study in American universities; his *Principles of Psychology*, published in 1890, provided a much-needed introduction to the discipline and definitive summary of its research as it stood on the edge of the twentieth century. When the American Psychological Association held its diamond anniversary in 1977, the opening speaker publicly declared William James the father of psychology in America.[2] At the same time, James was not the kind of theorist to be contained by a single discipline, however new and promising. With his Harvard colleague and philosopher Charles Sanders Peirce, he introduced pragmatism, a perspective on knowledge and truth that to this day can claim to be the most distinctively American contribution to modern philosophy.[3] In the same vein, we can credit James with a gift of comparable value to the study of religion: his signature work, published in 1902 as *The Varieties of Religious Experience*. This ambitious project, which marshalled the empirical methods of science to catalogue instances illustrating the subtle power of religion to alter individual human lives, secured James's place as a theorist of enduring importance. Appearing at the dawn of the twentieth century, it has since become a classic text, addressing present-day concerns with an immediacy that rivals the wide interest it generated among thoughtful readers when it first came to print. It will claim the better part of our attention here as well.

Early Life and Learning

William James belonged to one of the most well-known and widely heralded families in American arts and letters. He was the eldest, but arguably not the most accomplished, of five children born to Henry James Sr. and Alice Walsh in the decade of the 1840s.[4] Their second son, Henry Jr., is considered by many the finest American novelist of the post–Civil War era; two other sons were wounded serving in the Union Army during the conflict; the youngest sibling, their sister Alice, who was in persistent ill heath, produced a diary that emerged (after her early death in 1892) as one of the late century's most candid and shrewdly perceptive commentaries on morals, customs, and personalities in the circles of American privilege. Their father, Henry Sr., was born to wealth, inheriting part of a vast fortune earned by his father (also named William) from property ventures along the route of the Erie Canal. Without a need to work, Henry Sr. gave most of his time to two interests—religion and family. Though not trained formally, he aspired to be a theologian, and such he became, if of a rather marginal kind, embracing the peculiar mysticism of the Swedish visionary prophet Emanuel Swedenborg and mixing it in equally peculiar ways with the utopian ideas of the French socialist Charles Fourier and support of the quixotic communal living experiment at Brook Farm in Massachusetts. There was nothing odd or marginal, however, about the social circle in which the James family moved. At their townhouse near Washington Square in New York City, they entertained a variety of elite guests, including notables from both the New England and Atlantic intelligentsia that included Ralph Waldo Emerson, Henry David Thoreau, Bronson Alcott, Horace Greeley, and others of sufficient talent or means. When the family traveled to Britain, Henry Sr. made sure the children were taken to meet Thomas Carlyle, Alfred Lord Tennyson, and John Stuart Mill; similar meetings occurred with French and German intellectuals placed on the European continent. These prestigious encounters came about in part because of their father's other personal passion—the education of his children, which was almost as eccentric as his theology. In singular pursuit of this goal, Henry Sr. not only moved his family to new places in America; he also took up travel to Europe in search of the most intellectually challenging educational forums available.

In consequence, throughout much of their childhood and most of their youth, the five James children were moved from school to school, and from teacher to tutor or governess, first in New York, then in Europe, and back again in the United States. In 1855, when William was thirteen, the family traveled to London, Geneva, Paris, and Boulogne (to name some but not all of the destinations), then again to London, and finally back to America—a three-year odyssey in good measure inspired his father's search for new and better mentors wherever they could be found. This unusual experiment in pilgrim learning was a measure of both the family intimacy and the deep sense of intellectual mission that pervaded the James household, even if it did not always demonstrate the best in parental judgment. In the end, the results were somewhat mixed. The travels offered some pleasures that all of the family enjoyed, but in the longer term and in its main purpose, it did little for the younger sons; only Alice and the two eldest, most gifted brothers saw clear benefits. William acquired complete mastery of French and would later do the same with German. He and Henry Jr. both also developed exceedingly broad, cosmopolitan tastes; they came to relish the best of Europe's art, literature, and thought; William read incessantly, choosing the finest in literature, poetry, science, and philosophy that the Western tradition had to offer. Only a year after the family's return to America, he could be found back in Europe on his own, working with private tutors in Germany and Switzerland and developing contacts of lifelong value across the Atlantic. Henry Jr. was more reserved and contemplative; he preferred isolation. Leaving America behind, he chose Europe as his home, settling into a reclusive life in England, where most all of his fiction was to be written.

The personalities of the two brothers, who corresponded continuously in perceptive, mutually critical, and yet personally affectionate and candid letters throughout their lives, were quite different in a variety of ways. William was and remained always outwardly more social and engaging than Henry, though he was inwardly prone to tensions and misgivings. He was generally active, ambitious, and energetic, but with recurring episodes of depression that, in the language of present-day psychology, suggest a personality uncomfortably near to bipolar syndrome. These darker moods were aggravated by assorted physical ailments—some real, others perhaps imagined—that he wrestled with unevenly for all of his adult life.

The active, optimistic side of this dual personality appears in a letter written near the end of the European educational experiment, when James was just sixteen:

> What ought to be everyone's object in life? To be as much use as possible. Open a biographical dictionary. Every name it contains has exercised some influence on humanity, good or evil, and 99 names of out 100 are good. . . . I want to be a man and to do some good no matter what.[5]

To a degree, this kind of earnest moralism was not atypical in the circles of privileged, well-educated young men in America and Britain of the Victorian era. Often enough the sentiment passed. In James's case, however, it was quite consciously carried into later years, with a direct bearing on the perspective he would adopt in his analyses of both psychology and religion. Initially, however, the two areas in which William felt that he could "do some good" were the arts and natural sciences. In Paris he was captivated by the vast canvases of the painter Eugene Delacroix, and he had shown real skill of his own with sketches and drawings. So in 1860, when back from Europe, he made a try at art, entering the studio of the notable American portrait and landscape artist William Morris Hunt. After some modest early success, he abruptly changed course. Though he had both talent and interest, he seems to have concluded he had not enough of either, and so turned to his other passion—science. In 1861 he entered the Lawrence Scientific School at Harvard, and three years later was admitted to the School of Medicine, where from the beginning he made clear that his goal would be medical science, not practice. While enrolled in the program, he joined a scientific expedition to Brazil led by Harvard biologist Louis Agassiz, whose aim was the collection of tropical fish, wildlife, and foliage samples. James was utterly fascinated by the exotic beauty of the tropics but found the circumstances physically harsh; among other ailments, he contracted a minor form of smallpox that affected his vision. Even so, he was greatly impressed by Agassiz, whom he regarded as a wonderful team leader and a model of the scientific intellect. On returning, he committed to continuation of his medical studies at Harvard, where in 1869 he took his M.D., the only graduate academic degree he ever earned. In the meantime, his father had funded a return to Germany for rest and recuperation. The darker, depressive side of James's personality had begun to manifest itself; both mind and body were in need of healing.

A Personal Crisis

Over a five-year interval from about 1867 to 1872, both during and after his medical studies, James wrestled with recurring, serious attacks of mental depression. As recounted in his letters, he became at moments even suicidal. It was the onset of what physicians of the day called "neurasthenia," a mentally paralyzing state defined by pessimism and a sense of futility, a debilitating incapacity to act, and the loss of all energy and motivation. In James's case, multiple factors probably converged to bring this condition on. He had chosen medicine as a professional interest, but with no taste for clinical practice, there was little promise of a career. At age twenty-six, any further dependence on his father was nearing the point of embarrassment. He was personally alone, with no prospect of a spouse or plans to marry. More troubling still for someone of his young age were his health concerns. There was the eye problem acquired in Brazil; there were digestive ailments, and more acutely, recurring back pain, from which he hoped to find relief in Germany's famous thermal baths. But beyond these issues, there was something more emotionally critical. To friends he confided his need to resolve a disconcerting philosophical problem, an intellectual dilemma with an unsettling personal dimension.

Just as he was turning—still with some hesitation—to science for a career, James felt compelled to address the theory of scientific materialism, which he encountered directly in a book entitled *Force and Matter* (1855), published in German by physiologist-philosopher Ludwig Büchner. Büchner, who lost his academic post in the controversy he generated, was a leading advocate of materialism in its starkest form. On this view, all of nature, every element, structure, and organism—including human organisms—could be explained as a product of matter and motion; nothing more or other was needed, or even conceivable: no soul, no mind or spirit, no human feeling, emotion, or free action. All of nature, even human nature, behaves as an automaton: a field of mindless energy-and-matter-driven material mechanisms. For Büchner materialism required this determinism. If human organisms are only matter in motion, then we are robots. That is the very meaning of "automaton." The decisions made by our minds are in fact made by our bodies, by our biology. The soul that we think we have is not consciousness, but chemistry. It is clear from the language in James's letters and diary that he felt keenly the full force of this thesis, which was both intellectually and personally disconcerting. At the very moment when he was making an important life decision about his future in science, science itself was telling him that whatever decision he might make was meaningless—a mere illusion. Further, science construed in these terms seemed to undermine the very purpose of any human effort in life and in society, the sphere in which, by freely taken choice, he had made it is mission "to do some good." Determinism appeared to make action for any cause meaningless. For both these personal and intellectual reasons, a satisfactory answer had to be found. Without it, action for a purpose was a meaningless charade.

Amid bouts of depression and after some distressed searching, James in time encountered the writings of the philosopher Charles Renouvier, who furnished the response he was so urgently seeking. A French disciple of the German Immanuel Kant, Renouvier was a figure little known in America, but a reasoned defense of the idea of human freedom was central to his thinking, and it spoke directly to James's concerns. In his diary for April 30, 1870, he wrote: "I think that yesterday was a crisis in my life. I finished the first part of Renouvier's 2nd Essay, and saw no reason why his definition of free will—the sustaining of a thought *because I choose to* when I might have other thoughts—need be the definition of an illusion. My first act of free will shall be to believe in free will."[6] These words might not have been persuasive for everyone, but somehow, they took effect with James. For him, Renouvier's argument provided the anchorage needed to weather the determinist storm. He could build his life, and much of his life's work, on a resolute commitment to the freedom of the human will.

With the resolution of this intellectual issue, James's depression began partly to lift, and other positive developments followed. In 1872 he received his first academic appointment, being named an Instructor in Physiology at Harvard. Five years later, he married Alice Gibbens, a girls' school teacher who lived in Boston. Over the decades, her even temper and exceptional patience brought happiness, stability, and children into his personal life. Their thirty-two years of successful married life ran a course that mirrored the thirty-five years of almost unbroken success and growing recognition that James enjoyed on the Harvard faculty. The physical ailments did not disappear, nor did occasional further bouts with depression, but both became more moderate and manageable as the years moved on. In time, invitations to prestigious lectureships arrived, and other accolades followed. At Harvard, James's march upward in rank culminated in 1889, when President Eliot awarded a promotion that brought him—with an M.D. as still his only professional credential—the coveted title of Professor of Psychology. There he remained in rank until his resignation (for reasons of health) in 1907, the year that marked a reluctant professional end to an impressive (and still unfinished) intellectual journey.

Harvard Career: Psychology, Religion, Philosophy

While at Harvard, James's career passed through three phases, each centered on a different intellectual project. Each in turn brought an achievement of considerable note—a book, a collection of essays, or both. Impressively, the work was also done in three disparate fields. The first twelve years, 1878 to 1890, were taken up with the teaching of his Harvard classes, his initial studies in psychology, and work on *The Principles of Psychology,* his ambitious introduction to the field that grew to a book of imposing proportions. Published in 1890 and regarded by some as his finest achievement, it ran to more than 1,200 pages.[7] During the next phase, 1890 to 1902, his interests in moral philosophy and religion moved to the foreground. A collection of lectures he delivered both before and during this interval came to print in 1897 under the title *The Will to Believe*, and the capstone to this phase of his endeavors was put into place in 1902 with the publication of *The Varieties of Religious Experience,* his chief endeavor in what he defined as the science of religion. Although his intellectual legacy as a theorist of religion rests on his achievement in *Varieties*, it was not his last noteworthy accomplishment. In the final decade of his life, James turned more fully toward philosophy, and despite faltering health, he managed to complete several projects that some contemporary philosophers have come to admire as his most genuinely original work, defending the merits of pragmatism as a philosophical outlook. In addition to *Pragmatism* (1907), the book that gave definitive expression to his ideas on truth and value, both *A Pluralistic Universe* (1909) and the posthumously published *Essays in Radical Empiricism* (1912) have won new appraisals as both provocative and underappreciated works. In the pages that follow, *The Will to Believe* and the *Varieties of Religious Experience* will naturally claim our main attention, but not without also attending to the studies in psychology that came earlier and those in philosophy that came afterward.

The Principles of Psychology

In 1878 James was asked to write a book summarizing current knowledge in the field of psychology for the "American Science Series" offered by publisher Henry Holt. He thought he could finish the task in two years; it took all of twelve, expanding along the way into an early landmark overview of the discipline. *The Principles of Psychology* did considerably more than introduce and summarize. It took readers into each of the major area of the field, offering substantive discussions and thorough analyses of the issues as they stood at the time.

As James's approach to religion relies on his psychology, a closer look at this first and only major book he published in the field is in several ways instructive. It begins by defining psychology as the scientific study of human mental activities. It explains that in the past this kind of inquiry belonged to theologians and philosophers, but in the modern era psychology has become a science: it proceeds by observation and experiment, and by classification and comparison of data. Examining mental activity requires introspection, an inward form of close observation similar to what is done with a microscope in biology or chemistry, but without instruments and only a trained, attentive intellect to assist. Psychology explores all things affecting the mind: obviously the structure and physiology of the brain, where mental life is centered, but also the various forms of mental activity, including such things as sensation and perception; the sense of space and of time; the nature of habit, attention, and instinct; and the roles of imagination and conception, and of memory, will, and emotion. Most of these discussions do not bear specifically on James's ideas about religion, but in indirect ways they are relevant, and on some matters offer essential background.

To start with a negative, James explains that there is one quite common and traditional idea that modern scientific psychology simply cannot accept. It rejects the notion, long embraced by nearly all of religion and much of philosophy, that human beings are composed of a body and a soul. From the time of Plato to earlier modern times, theologians and philosophers have routinely relied on these paired concepts to understand the mental and physical sides of the human self.[8] Ordinary people almost invariably use the same language. They assume bodies have souls; they think the soul controls the body; they believe that the two can be separated at death, and (for most Jews, Christians, and Muslims at least) that they can be rejoined at the end of time. In brief, they conceive of the body and soul as two substances: one material and mortal, the other nonmaterial and eternal. But that is not how science sees them. Body and soul are not separable entities. They are two intimately interwoven aspects of the same living organism. Every smallest element of activity in what we call the soul, or mind—every sensation, perception, or thought—mirrors an associated and simultaneous process in the chemistry of the brain. In human life, brain and mind are so inseparable that a better (if still not perfect) word to use for the latter is "consciousness." We must think of the soul not as a thing, but as a process: as a tumbling river of feelings, ideas, and images pouring over, in, and through the physical network of the brain. As James said in a famous phrase he is now credited with coining, the mind is a "wonderful stream of consciousness," an ever-changing flow of ideas, images, and sensations continuously affecting and affected by the physical body through which it passes, as water over the riverbed moves among its rocks, shifting or slowing or turning, then sweeping ahead, taking silt and stones along with it. The physical and mental aspects of the self are fitted to each other like river and valley.

James believed that thinking of the self in this interwoven manner offers real advantages to psychologists, whose task is to explore the subtle interplay between the mental and physical sides of the human person. For him the model of a physical organism suffused and saturated with consciousness offered to science exciting new paths of research. At the same time, it is just this model that had led others, including some of James's own Harvard colleagues and mentors, to draw the conclusion that he himself had resisted when confronted with the works of the German scientist-philosopher Büchner. They were inclined to endorse physiological materialism, the view that the physical is all that is real, that there is nothing other than body, and that the idea of "mind" or even "consciousness" is an illusion. Among some scientists, this materialist perspective gained further support as the century progressed. The watershed moment, of course, was Charles Darwin's publication of the *Origin of Species* in 1859. As his version of evolutionary theory took hold, biological materialism found outspoken new advocates in both England and America. In the 1880s T. H. Huxley, the man who became famous as "Darwin's bulldog," took the position that physical processes fuel and drive all of human mental life; our thoughts, he wrote, are like the steam that issues from the smokestack of a locomotive. The churning body is real; the mind is a mere vaporous appearance totally dependent on the body. Huxley's slightly less combative but no less outspoken scientific colleague John Tyndall took the same point of view. Moreover, as Huxley affirmed without flinching, materialism logically requires determinism. The body's processes determine the mind's thoughts. Most people prize what they like to call the freedom of the will, but there is no such thing.

To many people of religious faith, this doctrine of materialist determinism was utterly unacceptable. How, they naturally asked, could a person believe in immortality of the soul if the soul—if "consciousness"—is as completely interwoven into the body as Huxley and Tyndall suppose? When the body dies, the soul, it seems, will die also. And more than just immortality is at stake. Even more than Marxism, scientific materialism reduces religious beliefs to empty words; in fact, it reduces all beliefs about human motives and actions to empty words, and distills all decisions into biological processes.

As we would expect from his earlier struggle with materialist determinism, James shared such concerns. But as a psychologist he also recognized that the materialist principle is needed for scientific explanation; scientists address physical reality, and naturally look for material, physical causes to explain the workings of the brain. That principle cannot just be ignored. At the same time, it is true that beyond science, the debate over freedom and determinism is exceedingly complex; the issues are so difficult to decide that the quarrel likely will never be resolved. And if neither view can persuade, James argues, it is entirely reasonable outside of the laboratory to endorse freedom. Because it is crucial to almost every form of human endeavor, we are justified in making freedom the presiding postulate of our lives. Put in simplest terms, James could allow materialism for his work as a psychologist, but as a person, he just as firmly held to the principle he had seized upon when reading Renouvier: the first act of free will is to believe in free will . . . even when science seems to oppose it.

If to others it seems arbitrary—even an outright contradiction—for a scientist to accept determinism in his profession while assuming freedom elsewhere in life, James is prepared to explain himself. Choosing and deciding, he reminds us, are from the very beginning a part of the human physical organism. The brain is not some passive thing that just responds and never initiates. Even in its primitive animal forms and earliest human stages, the brain's consciousness is defined by its active, choosing properties. When a child is born, sensations come to it from the outside world as a great "blooming, buzzing, confusion," but at once consciousness starts to work; it attends to some things in that confusion—the face or touch of the mother—and filters others out completely.[9] It "makes sense" of the world precisely by centering on some sensations and disregarding others. Then as we mature, our consciousness continues the process. We live by continually selecting from impressions, organizing experiences, and placing some things in focus while moving others aside. As we become adults, we gradually confront the most complex of these choices, most notably those that create and shape our human character. When consciousness reaches the level of rational and moral choices that affect personal conduct, it is only natural to embrace our freedom and dismiss the thought of determinism. The momentous matters of personal and social morality require that we accept, as a moral principle of the universe, that "what ought to be can be." We know that where evil occurs, it is possible that good could have been done in place of it.[10] Without the critically essential belief in mental freedom, we cannot make moral decisions, so the mind must assume its truth. And if the demands that arise from our moral experience take us beyond the materialism of science, then so be it. "Science," says James, "must constantly be reminded that her purposes are not the only purposes, and that the order of uniform causation which she has use for . . . may be enveloped in a wider order, on which she has no claims at all."[11] In this intriguing manner James blended his moral convictions with his scientific aspirations. Just as in his personal crisis as a young man who wanted to "do good in the world," he had to overcome determinist thinking, so James argues here—as a principle of moral psychology surpassing the claims of science—that only the idea of freedom can make human moral conduct meaningful and possible. That is a principle that science, even if it needs materialism and determinism, cannot be allowed to undermine. Nor is this all that can be said. In different and later discussion, James affirms a further tie between freedom, morality, and religion. He of course agrees that religion is not necessarily needed for moral conduct; there are many non-religious people who behave morally, and may in fact behave better than many religious people do. But there are different kinds of moral action. Passive morals, the conduct of the vast majority of people who obey the law and live decently, is one thing; active, strenuous moral effort is another. Only a very few people are capable of heroic morals, of showing exceptional sacrifice and dedication of their lives to others in the manner, as we might say today, of a St. Francis, a Gandhi, or a Martin Luther King. And in that respect, religion does make a difference. Faith in a divine order can furnish the inspiration for lives of great sacrifice, and great endeavors of love, in a way that no other human resource seems able to deliver.[12]

One final point should be made before leaving *The Principles of Psychology* behind. Its discussions presume, and in some places clearly state, that there should not be a separation between human "knowledge" on the one hand and "feelings" on the other, as if the part of the human self that is our rational intellect is one thing and the sensing, feeling side of our selves is another. Some thinkers James encountered in his time (and some very much active today) claimed that ideas are grasped only by the human intellect; feelings, on the other hand, are the emotional qualities that accompany knowledge but do not in themselves convey any conceptual content. For example, sadness is a general emotion, and as such it is an undefined feeling, nothing more; I can "feel sad" about many different things. Only when a concept provides content can I have a "specific" emotion, as when I feel sad about "my lost dog" or my "bad investment." Significantly, James here takes a different view of this matter. For him, human feelings can actually carry intellectual content; the ideas are, we might say, bound into, or bound up from the start with, our emotions. Feelings can provide us with "preconceptual" knowledge in the very moment we experience them. This principle will be worth recalling, and assessing, when we turn to James's discussion of religious experience in *Varieties*, where, in an echo of what is said here, he will tell us that such experience "has a noetic component" ("noetic" being Greek for "knowledge"). Religious experience, therefore, is not empty; it conveys knowledge without the help of concepts supplied by the intellect.[13]

"The Will to Believe"

After finishing *Principles* James turned his attention increasingly to questions of moral philosophy and religion. He began lecturing and writing for a wider, more general audience, choosing articles and occasional papers as his preferred format. In 1897 he published ten of these essays, collected in book form under the title of the lead entry, "The Will to Believe," which had been prepared just a year earlier.

"The Will to Believe" was first presented as a lecture to college students, members of the Philosophical Clubs of Yale and Brown Universities. It soon made a wider impression, and as it provides an instructive path into James's general perspective on religion, it is worth some effort on our part to follow where it leads. Designed as a justification of religious faith, James proposes "a defence of our right to adopt a believing attitude in religious matters, in spite of the fact that our merely logical intellect may not have been coerced."[14] The argument begins with some context. In any circumstance where we are faced with the choice to accept or reject a belief, James tells us, three things naturally affect the decision. The alternatives before us can be described as (1) "living or dead," (2) "forced or avoidable," and (3) "momentous or trivial." As to the first of these, if you ask me whether I seriously would worship the nature gods of ancient Greece or the warrior gods of early Scandinavia, I am likely to chuckle rather than answer. Ancient mythology is intriguing, but in the modern world, polytheism is not a "living" option. Secondly, we all recognize that some choices are forced and others are avoidable. If you ask of a concert I've attended: "Was it good or bad?" I might just answer: "No comment." I could offer an answer, but the choice you've given me is avoidable. But if you say: "Either catch this train or wait a full day for the next," I cannot avoid a decision. Either I will catch the train, or I will need to wait a day. If I try to say: "No comment" and put off an answer, the deferral will be a decision; today's train will be missed. Some situations compel us to make a choice; there is no way to avoid it. Finally, some choices are trivial, others momentous. If you ask me whether I want Italian biscotti or English crumpets with my tea, that is hardly a critical matter; either will do. But if I am in urgent need of a heart transplant, and the donor heart is not the best match, I face a momentous choice. If this heart is taken, the transplant could fail; if it is passed over, it may be too late for another. That decision is hardly trivial: life or death hangs in the balance.

To these three initial considerations, says James, we need to add another. Some thinkers, influenced heavily by modern science, have said there is an "ethic" of belief. We have a moral obligation not to believe just anything we want; our beliefs should have rational support. James points to W. K. Clifford, the noted British mathematician of his time, who said that we should, as a matter of moral propriety, only believe things "upon sufficient evidence." If the evidence is not good enough, we cannot consent; it is morally wrong to do so. Above all, we should not allow ourselves to be duped into obviously foolish, misguided beliefs. Religion belongs among those beliefs.

Now in some respects, James observes, Professor Clifford's advice makes sense and is easy enough to follow. If there is a technical, scientific question at hand, and I do not have technical knowledge, I should naturally decline to answer. A nontechnical person who does not understand electricity should not try to wire a complicated circuit. He does not have sufficient evidence to make electrical judgments.

But suppose we move from electrical circuitry to larger moral and personal issues. In matters such as these, we do need to ask—do we not?—how one is to judge when and whether Clifford's standard of "sufficient evidence" has been met. Both philosophers and scientists disagree intensely on this matter. And even if we could agree on what evidence is sufficient, another question needs to be asked: how did Clifford come up with his idea that to hold a mistaken belief is, morally, the worst of all options? It seems to come from what James calls his "passional" nature. Clifford believes from the start, as an article of his own personal faith, that avoidance of error at all costs is required as our "duty to mankind"; it is for him a moral precept. We have an ethical obligation to follow it as the only behavior fitting and proper to human beings.

But if we accept that view, says James, if we accept that our "passional" nature—anchored in our most basic values and wishes—is to be allowed a voice in deciding these questions, then we are in the realm of moral judgments about what is good, not just scientific conclusions about what is true. And if that is so, then certainly other judgments, other deeply held views about what accomplishes our duty to mankind, have a right also to be heard.

Religions believe that the best things are eternal things, and that we as humans all are better off holding to such beliefs. So let us consider them, says James, by the criteria set out earlier: (1) Is religious belief a "live" option? Yes. For thoughtful people in the modern world, the choice of theism or atheism presents itself as very much a live option. (2) Is the choice for or against belief a momentous one? Unquestionably it is momentous. It is not like deciding on biscotti or crumpets with tea; it bears upon all of life and its meaning. (3) Further, and most critically, is belief a choice that is forced or avoidable? It would certainly seem that it is forced: either you embrace belief or dismiss it. You cannot easily "wait and see." So, when Clifford says: "My duty is not to believe without proof," he is making a choice from which it follows that he will not believe. By deferring he is in effect choosing not to believe. Presented with the religious option, he insists that "to yield to our fear of its being error is better and wiser than to yield to our hope of that it may be true."[15] But if so, then this clearly is not a choice between the clear rationality of science and the "blind passion" of religion. It is rather a disagreement between one kind of faith, one moral passion, and another. In that circumstance, and in a matter this momentous, James says that the believer, no less than the skeptic, has a right, equally grounded, to choose faith. Belief is no more "passional," and no less rational, than disbelief.

In the course of his discussion, James readily acknowledges a similarity in his reasoning to that of Blaise Pascal (1623–1662), the brilliant, devoutly

Catholic French mathematician-physicist of an earlier time who formulated the famous "wager" argument for belief in God. Pascal had ingeniously argued for faith from the law of probability. Since giving one's life to God promises the infinite gain of eternal life at the price of only small sacrifices in this present life, while disbelieving entails the opposite—eternal loss in return for short-term self-indulgence—the rational choice always will be to commit to belief in God. If God does not exist, the wager brings limited loss; if God does exist, it brings infinite gain. Anyone who calculates rationally would take the wager.

Though not identical to Pascal's, James's reasoning bears a certain resemblance to it. He does not focus on eternal life, and he does not go so far as to claim, as Pascal does, that "wagering" on belief is logically superior to choosing disbelief. Instead he argues more indirectly, striving to show that people who do believe stand on ground equally as firm as that on which disbelievers like Clifford choose to stand. Believers are not gullible or superstitious; they are not being duped. By any fair measure of rationality, they are in are a position quite comparable to that of those who choose not to believe. Holding to religion out of hope of its truth is no less justified, psychologically and rationally, than rejecting religion out of fear it is in error.

It is not hard to see why this essay struck a resonant chord with an audience of educated Christian readers in America. It ingeniously placed the prestige of science and profession of religious faith on a roughly equal footing, and predictably enough, it has generated both warm approval and stiff criticism ever since. For present purposes we do not need to take sides in the Clifford-James debate itself or discuss the similarities to Pascal, however intriguing to theologians and logicians such arguments along the lines of game theory or wager transactions have proved to be. There are two other points that we can better notice instead.

First, as he moved to the second phase of his career, turning from his narrower professional interest in psychology to wider questions of philosophy and morality, James expressed a more openly favorable attitude toward religion. As a professional psychologist in a university, he had been in frequent conversation with intelligent atheist colleagues, whom he held in high regard. But as he turned seriously to the investigation of moral values in society, his doubts about the superiority they claimed for the nonreligious world view grew steadily deeper and more insistent. He was not persuaded. Secondly, the reason for these doubts lay in his steadily deepening commitment to the logic of pragmatism, his growing personal conviction that we discover the truth of our beliefs when we assess them by their value to our actions, by examining how they "pay off" when we apply them in our lives. In *Principles*, this is the logic he applies to justify belief that we have freedom of the will, despite the need of science to rely on materialist determinism. In the same way, the argument for religious faith as "The Will to Believe" articulates it is also pragmatic in character: it is at least as beneficial to mankind, James says, to live by a faith that we hope to be true as it is to live in fear that it might be false. Further and finally, if measuring benefit to mankind is a relevant matter, then surely it is part of the theorist's duty to make the effort. Let us try, as best we can, to measure those effects (both personal and social) of religious faith as reported by those who experience it. What actually happens when people encounter the divine? In fairness, no person of scientific mind should answer that question dismissively. We should instead turn to the kind of objective, empirical study that is worthy of science. We should examine religion scientifically and let the evidence speak for itself.

The Varieties of Religious Experience

The invitation to pursue just such a scientific inquiry came soon enough. In 1900, three years after publishing *The Will to Believe,* James was invited to give the prestigious Gifford Lectures in Edinburgh, Scotland. The Gifford Trust required a treatment of religion that appealed to natural evidence, not to supernatural revelation; it stipulated an argument that draws on evidence acceptable to all interested parties, and not to some special revelation found only in the Bible or church doctrines. James welcomed this opportunity, for it enabled him to work just as he wished—scientifically and empirically. Under the title *The Varieties of Religious Experience* he proposed a two-part project. First, he would assemble evidence—testimonies from people of every type or inclination, great or small, wise or weird, young or old, ordinary or exceptional: people who had encountered "the divine" (as they saw it) in some powerful, life-affecting form. Second, with this substantial array of evidence in hand, he would offer a wider philosophical assessment of the beliefs, issues, and questions raised by those experiences. The project did not quite turn out as planned, for as he worked, James saw the first of his tasks grow into almost the entire effort, leaving only the last several lectures to address the work of assessment. Clearly, he had set himself a daunting assignment.

Defining Religion

After some preliminaries, James begins his inquiry by proposing a definition of religion that can lead the way. For the purposes of his investigation, religion should be defined as "the feelings, acts, and experiences of individual men in their solitude, so far as they apprehend themselves to stand in relation to whatever they may consider divine."[16] This formula is less than elegant, but the main idea is clear. Such a definition intentionally puts much of what we normally associate with religion to the side. By design, says James, the focus of a book from a professor of psychology ought not to be on institutions or assemblies, not on churches, temples, or mosques, not on ministers or monks, and not on rituals or ceremonies, pertinent as these things undoubtedly are to the religious life. Nor should the focus be on creeds, confessions, or theological doctrines. All of these features—the beliefs, the practices, the organizations—should be seen as matters that are secondary; they come after, and arise from, the primary fact, which is to be found in the personal experience of individuals. The center of religion appears in those decisive, deeply felt moments when human beings feel they have directly encountered God (or whatever else they may think of as the divine). Those experiences are the heart of faith, the center of all religion. They are not superstition; they do not involve some bargain with a spirit of the field to make crops grow, or some sacrifice to win favors from the gods of battle. They are serious, moving encounters with the divine as an overarching, enveloping power, a primal reality. True religious experience elicits a response of solemnity and gravity, along with a feeling of surrender and overwhelming joy; it spurs an impulse to embrace all things, and allows the self to feel profoundly affirmed and inwardly renewed. In that connection, James says that we should attend especially to the reports of those people who appear to have had experiences of this kind in unusually intense or decidedly dramatic form. We can learn most about religious experience not from people who are conventionally religious, people who follow custom or obey routine, but from those who live at the edges of ordinary life—the mystics, seers, prophets, and saints: those who have seen visions or heard voices. They are the people who may even be counted as "'geniuses' in the religious line."[17]

Judging by conventional measures, our first impulse would be to dismiss such personalities as unbalanced: a collection of the eccentric, unstable, and slightly strange. But in fact, we need to look carefully at these examples, not ignore them, for they often disclose in pure, unmixed form what is not easily noticed in the personalities we call normal. Further, we should not be put off our task by people who want to dismiss religious beliefs, especially strange or mystical beliefs, on the basis of human physiology. "Medical materialists" are quick to attribute religious experience to purely physical causes or psychophysical disorders, such as sexual tension, epileptic seizure, or nervous dysfunction. These physical causes can be introduced to explain almost anything humans claim to experience or believe; we can explain atheism or faith with these same causes. So they prove nothing negative or otherwise about the actual content of religious beliefs. If we were to learn that the genius Isaac Newton suffered from chronic depression or epilepsy, that fact would hardly be a reason to reject his laws of motion or theory of gravitation. "In the natural sciences and industrial arts," James notes, "it never occurs to anyone to try to refute opinions by showing up their author's neurotic constitution. Opinions here are invariably tested by logic and experiment, no matter what their author's neurological type. It should be no otherwise with religious opinions."[18] We should therefore dismiss alien causes and judge these religious opinions on their own terms, where different measures apply: "*Immediate luminousness, . . . philosophical reasonableness,* and *moral helpfulness* are the only available criteria."[19]

The first attribute of all religious experience is an intuition, a certitude that beyond our conventional experience, beyond the routine events of daily life, stands another, unseen order of reality. This reality does not immediately stand out in the specific events or occasions of ordinary life because it lies in, under, around, and beyond them. It impinges invisibly on visible things, calling us to look past the dreary round of daily tasks and troubles and seek harmony with what lies beyond.

Two Kinds of People: Healthy-Minded and Sick Souls

Religious experience of every kind affirms this unseen reality, but there are certain differences in the way people respond to it. Drawing a distinction that has since become famous, James says we must recognize two kinds of personality, two differing temperaments. Some are fundamentally "healthy-minded," affirming and optimistic; others are more darkly disposed—more inclined to notice evil, to lean toward pessimism. They are the "sick souls."

For those born with a "sky-blue" spirit, a positive, welcoming view of life and its experiences comes naturally and spontaneously. The beloved St. Francis of Assisi was one of these "healthy-minded" souls. He loved, embraced, and was made wondrously happy by all he encountered—by brother sun and sister moon, by all things bright and beautiful, by all things located or living in the beneficent Creator's world. Others, perhaps not as naturally healthy as St. Francis, achieve a similar contentment by conscious effort and practice. They set a course of purposeful self-surrender and acceptance of life; they welcome things as they come, and they do so with an embrace that disposes them to dismiss all bad things as invisible or deceptive, and to attend only to what is positive. James cites as examples of this more studied optimism the new religious movements of his day: the system of self-help known as "mind cure," or "new thought," and the program of Mary Baker Eddy and her disciples, known as Christian Science. Nor are these innovative movements alone. For some this inner peace can be found in the older theologies, in the release that the teachings of Martin Luther and John Wesley promise to those who accept God's grace in their lives. The spirit they all share is a determination to think positively, to look away from evil and place it on the periphery of life, and to attend only to things that are good. And they are convinced that good is genuinely achieved in their lives by doing so. By their accounts, some who think this way experience such things as better health; physical "cures" can take effect because of their mental optimism. In this they could even be commended as near to the attitude of modern science. They prove their hypothesis by its effects, finding the experimental evidence of healing in their own lives. And who are we to dismiss them instantly, without at least considering the evidence they offer? When we dismiss their claims abruptly, looking in on them and passing judgment from the outside, are we outsiders not in fact the ones who behave unscientifically?

The other temperament—what James describes as the "sick soul"—presents a less appealing portrait on first sight. This is the personality inclined to maximize, rather than marginalize, the presence of evil in the world. People of this type find the attitudes of the healthy-minded superficial and shallow. They insist on an undeniable fact: suffering, sorrow, and death are stamped indelibly on the world's architecture as we encounter it. This is a sober truth that the ancient Greeks, for all their playful mythology, knew very well. They recognized that no one can escape fate; their Epicurean and Stoic philosophers did not pretend otherwise. Similarly Tolstoy, the great novelist, claimed to see with acute vision the utter pointlessness of human activities, the triviality of interests and pleasures that are certain to end—for all people—at their death. An even more personalized form of this despair can be seen in the English preacher John Bunyan, author of the famous book *Pilgrim's Progress.* He described himself as a man in double despair: "weary of life, and yet afraid to die." To these more troubled souls, evil is ingrained in the world. And though most of us could wish to be in the club of the happier and healthy-minded, it must be admitted that the wider, more truthful grasp of life belongs to these more pessimistic minds. The simple fact of all existence is that while it can offer joy and wellness, it is also framed irretrievably by defect and danger, by disease, and ultimately by death. In all lives, these grim elements appear at one time or another, and they invariably bring dark, despairing moments with them. Correspondingly, the religions that most completely address the human situation are those that most fully appreciate this reality of evil and center on deliverance from it. The best known of these religions of salvation are Christianity in the Western world and Buddhism in the East.

Most people of pessimistic temperament do not give up on life; only a few become utter nihilists and fatalists. The others become what James calls Divided Selves. They seek wellness and true inner peace, but they know it will only come by struggle. This was the case with the early Christian theologian Augustine of Hippo. Only after great inner struggle did he give up his self-indulgent life as a young man to find the gift of eternal joy and peace. Only through an extreme agony did his restless heart come to rest in God. All pessimistic minds know that somewhere in life there must be a turning, a clear and true reversal—something that puts life back on firm ground. A profound experience of life wholly changed is what the personality needs in order to regain a secure equilibrium.[20] Such transitions do not necessarily need to be religious; they can occur in other ways, as when a person turns toward some new goal or purpose, even in some cases what may seem a less admirable purpose. People can turn from a life untouched by the temptations of wealth to one of avaricious greed, or vice versa; we can fall in or out of love, and if we are religious, we can also turn away from religion, as was the case with the French philosopher Theodore Jouffroy, who found relief in renouncing his faith and adopting atheism.

When such a major turning happens, it is not a kind of minor and momentary shift of interest, as all human beings pass through when they prefer—for a time—a new trend in clothing, a novel diet, or a different football team; it is instead a shift at what James calls "the habitual center" of a person's self, the core of one's being. Some feeling or belief, perhaps once at the margin of a personality, moves unmistakably, and sometimes suddenly, to the commanding center. It occurs as something deep and fundamental, reshaping a person's entire life from that moment forward. The religious word "conversion" is the most suitable term we have to describe this kind of experience. Certainly conversion can occur in different ways. Sometimes it happens in a manner James calls "volitional." Gradually over time, yet still in a decisive way, the orientation of a personality changes. In other instances it takes the form of a spontaneous and sudden experience. In either form, the key point in any conversion appears in the moment of self-surrender, the instant of "letting go." No matter how studied and strenuous any prior religious efforts may have been, the classic cases of conversion involve at some key point a state of exhaustion with all previous efforts, a sense of being spent, and often physically weak, just before the moment of self-surrender and rebirth.[21] In certain American and British Protestant communities, especially the Baptist and Methodist churches, there has also been an accent on "revivalism"—events specially arranged to promote a dramatic, emotional, and instantaneous conversion experience. In the archetypal revivalist conversion, James writes, "you must first be nailed on the cross of natural despair and agony, and then in the twinkling of an eye be miraculously released." He adds that "it always seems, after the surrender of the personal will, as if an extraneous higher power had flooded in and taken possession."[22] Along with surrender, the drama of spontaneous conversion is accompanied by other characteristic features: a sense of "higher control," a release from worry and concern, and a deep feeling that all is well. There is also a sense of perceiving truths unknown before, of seeing the world itself as changed in appearance and accepting life as suffused with a secret joy and inner tranquility.

James suggests also that in these extraordinary cases what we may well be seeing is an eruption of the "subliminal" consciousness recently proposed by Freud and Breuer. "*If there be* higher spiritual agencies that can directly touch us," he observes, "the psychological condition of their doing so *might be* our possession of a subconscious region which alone could yield access to them."[23] Even so, the validity of such experiences should in the end be measured not by where they originated, but by what they have produced. This does not mean, of course, that those who have had conversion experiences are presumed to be better people, or can be expected to do more good, than those who have not. But at least this much can be said: There is broad and vigorous testimony from those who have had such experiences that they feel they are better people, emotionally and morally, than they would have been without them. Their lives offer exhibits of the Bible's promise: "By their fruits ye shall know them."

Saints and Saintly Lives

If the value of the conversion experience is to be seen in its effects, what do those effects look like? And how do we assess them? James responds as follows: We know that conversion leads to "saintliness," so in addressing these questions, we can hardly do better than listen to what the saints themselves have chosen to tell us. Here he puts to full use the remarkable inventory of personal confessions that has made the narrative of *Varieties* so rightly famous and irresistibly fascinating to readers of almost every persuasion. For after all, who better to tell their story than the converted ones themselves? And how better to hear them than in their own words as shared in the treasury of their letters, diaries, sermons, books, and meditations, their musings, poems, prayers, and songs?

It should not be surprising, in light of these questions, that the descriptions, accounts, and assessments of "saintliness" that James provides for us take up no less than five lectures in their entirety and a good measure of the others as well. There is a rich, remarkable diversity in the deeply personal and emotional statements that he draws upon, though it needs to be noted that they in most cases come from Christian experience, both Protestant and Catholic. (Examples from Asian, Jewish, Muslim, and other religions do appear, but they are rare.) Whatever the source, there is in these stories from the saints a striking personal candor, an unvarnished and intimate honesty, a sense of singular joy newly discovered and placed on a wide canvas for full display. Most are touchingly emotional, tender, and sometimes beautiful; others are stunning in the level (for their time and place) of self-disclosure; still others suggest personalities near to the neurotic and behaviors bordering on the bizarre. Yet amid all the variations in quality and peculiarities of expression, certain shared patterns naturally emerge.

In their inward character, the emotions that claim the central place in the lives of saints follow naturally from their experience in the conversion moment. There is a feeling of surrender, of being swept into something wider and grander than mere personal concerns—a welcome embrace of the greatness of the divine that dwarfs all things human. Along with the feeling of release from all constraints and stress, a true joy and elation in "letting go," there is a desire to affirm others and join in harmony with them. These inner spiritual qualities come to visible expression in the distinctive behaviors of the saints. In some cases the quality of self-surrender expresses itself in asceticism—the visible practice of self-denial and, in more extreme cases, even self-punishment. Others among the converted are moved to practice some or all of the classic religious vows: poverty, chastity, and obedience. The most enthusiastic try to practice all of the disciplines. The saints strive also for purity in life, strongly opposing cruelty and sensuality. Above all, there is in the saints a noticeable "increase in charity." Their testimonies show decisively that religious experience moves believers to a renewed sympathy for others, a love even for enemies, and a selfless compassion for the poor and downtrodden. Not that religious experience makes all who have found it to be alike. In some these qualities and behaviors are more evident; in others less so. But almost all of the traits can to some extent be seen in almost all of the saints.

Of course it is not enough just to describe the motives and manners that arise from religious experience. We need also to appraise the outward effects and measure as we can the actual good that comes from saintly lives. And here, James argues, we ought to test saintliness by common sense; we should "use human standards to help us decide how far the religious life commends itself as an ideal kind of human activity. If it commends itself, then any theological beliefs that may inspire it, in so far forth will stand accredited. If not, then they will be discredited, and all without reference to anything but human working principles."[24] We need of course to allow that individuals differ considerably from one to the next; just as there are varieties of religious experience, there are varieties in the individual aims and actions that such experience may lead to. Judgments need to be broadly drawn, and we can only say what is "on the whole" good or not good. By no means, for example, can we say that the truly strange and excessive behaviors of some of the saints actually commend themselves to our common sense. Clearly, devotion can on occasion become fanaticism, as when Martin Luther saw no reason to protest the torture of the

Anabaptists he disagreed with. Or it can go to absurd extremes. Sister Mary Margaret Alacoque became so consumed with her visions of the Sacred Heart that she was of no use to others in her convent—unable to work in the kitchen, attend to the sick, or perform any other useful task. Saint Louis of Gonzaga was so obsessed with his sexual purity that he refused to have a conversation with a woman, or even look up from the pavement to see one. But on the whole, and even with the excesses, the record of religious experience is undeniably positive. If we measure by the impulse toward charity, for example, the saints have been by all accounts "a genuine creative social force" in the world. They are people who in countless instances have turned lives filled with despair or mired in evil into beacons of hope and forces for good. They have moved out of enslavement to vice or addiction and into exemplary civility and compassion; or they have escaped habits of cruelty, violence, and self-centered malice to embrace generosity, self-sacrifice, and love of others. As with acts of charity, so too with asceticism, the spiritual practice of self-denial. When applied in reasonable measure, asceticism has enabled saints in their multitudes to liberate themselves from the debilitating worship of money and material possessions. It has taught them to value life and the others in their lives, rather than allow possessions and properties to become obsessions of the kind that disable compassion and deflate all spiritual aspirations. Asceticism has also provided welcome release from lives dominated by silly pretensions, envious competition with rivals, and incessant worries about whether wealth is increasing or decreasing. By these measures, the beneficial effects of religious experience are indisputable and everywhere visible.

Mysticism

No discussion of saintly lives transformed by conversion can be complete without a consideration of mysticism, which some consider the premier form of religious experience. It is found across the globe. In almost every one of the world's major traditions, we can find a focus on mysticism as the pinnacle of the religious life. In Christianity, both Protestant and Catholic, mystics have seen themselves as a select and special few—spiritually favored souls—to whom God has given the ultimate gift of being drawn into the wonders of His immediate presence, of being absorbed, through Christ or the Virgin or some relic or symbol, into the full, unmediated glory of divinity. Those in the elite Sufi sect of Islam feel the same way. In Asian religions like Hinduism and Buddhism, mystical experience is even more prevalent; the most profound Hindu sacred texts and the most highly regarded teachers of yoga offer the mystical experience of "Samadhi"—oneness with Brahman—as the ultimate goal for all. The most revered of Buddhist monks stress the supreme value of "dhyana"—meditative contemplation of the highest order—as the ultimate path of release from the cycle of rebirth. There is a set of shared features that define these mystical encounters wherever they appear. They are the same across cultures. Thus, mystics of almost every kind report their breathtakingly beautiful experiences as "ineffable"—beyond the power of words to describe; if we suggest to them a description, their most likely response is: "No, not that; so much more; more than speech can say." Though words cannot capture it, mystics are nearly always certain that they have acquired some profound new knowledge; they instinctively sense they have found truth of a kind that is deep and hidden, truth of a type that the ordinary rational mind does not grasp. The mystical moment is, to be sure, a passing thing. The peak phases rarely reach to even an hour in length, but in those brief intervals, new dimensions of divinity, new waves of wonder, come flooding in. And they come seemingly without effort, for another feature of mystical experience is its passive character. Strenuous efforts are sometimes made in preparation for the experience, but when the mystical moment comes, the feeling is one of being utterly overwhelmed. The self is nothing; it is helpless; the divine is all and is overpowering; the self is completely engulfed by such experience, joyfully submerged in transcendent beauty and peace. To be sure, most ordinary people never reach these mystical heights; they have neither the gift nor the discipline to get there. But through more conventional means, through sacrifice, confession, and especially prayer, they can achieve at least a faint approximation of the mystic's peace and joy in embracing the divine.

When we turn to the matter of assessing these mystical experiences, James says that there are limits that apply. In describing the union of the human soul with God, a mystical poet like St. John of the Cross shares a deep experience that to him is of surpassing value and undeniable truth. His poetry sings of his encounter with God. We who have not had his experience have no ground for denying him the validity of his visions. They are his; they are truth for him. At the same time, he cannot impose his truth on others. However powerful his poetry, he cannot require those of us without his mystical gifts to accept his revelations as valid for all merely on his word. Neither can the Hindu yogi or the Buddhist sage. The truth is theirs; the value is theirs. We cannot make it fully ours. But even if not ours, such truth can still be of spiritual use. For the great majority, those of us who are not mystically inclined, mystics can be tutors. They provide the world with clues, with hints and suggestions of a reality that is there for all of us even if we are less able than they to access it. Compared to everyday rational thinking, the visions of mystics suggest a vastly wider spiritual reality; they serve as "windows through which the mind looks out upon a more extensive and inclusive world"; they open portals that disclose "the truest of insights into the meaning of this life."[25]

The Heart of Religious Experience

The issue of mysticism and truth brings us to the final chapters of *Varieties*, where James turns at last to the philosophical questions raised by religious experience. Mysticism, we can agree, offers truth for the mystic. Religious experience offers truth for those who have been favored to have it. But even so, we still need to address the question of truth for everyone. When a scientist affirms the truth of the law of gravitation, she means that gravity applies to all; it is not truth just for herself. So we do need to ask whether there is any way that we can say the same thing for religion. Is there anything about religious experience that we can say is true for everyone—for all religions and even all who are not religious? That is the more difficult question. The confirming of objective, general truths—truths that all can accept—has in the past been the business of philosophy to address, using its tools of logic, analysis, and argumentation. But as applied to religion, says James, philosophy has been of little use. It has led only to endless, futile arguments about such things as the existence and attributes of God. So by far the better course is to apply (as far as they can take us) the methods of science: to continue on the path of these very Gifford Lectures, and draw conclusions from the observation of actual religious experiences. Better to make judgments only after we have made all of the effort needed to gather evidence, to classify and compare it, and to frame proper categories and generalizations.

Clearly, there are things that a truly scientific study of religious experience can tell us. But also, we need to proceed carefully. Science can make mistakes. Some who have thought themselves scientific about religion have been confused, and seriously mistaken. They see religion as the opposite of science because it appeals to the personalities of the gods to explain the world rather than the uniform, impersonal laws of nature that are the pride of scientific inquiry. It hardly needs saying that James has theorists like Tylor and Frazer in mind here, and he is underscoring their mistake. To understand religion scientifically, we must "subordinate the intellectual part" and realize that "it is founded on feeling"; that is the only place where "we catch real fact in the making, and directly perceive how events happen." The heart of religion is not to be found, as Tylor and Frazer think, in belief in gods or in the prayers and sacrifices offered to please them. If we think that way, we will of course conclude, as they do, that religion is simply a "survival," a set of ancient superstitions now properly replaced by science. But that is a grave mistake. For what the pages of *Varieties* illustrate in abundance is that the heart of religion is to be found in the realm of human feeling, along with the undeniable change in moral conduct that it produces. That, if anything, should be clear from all of the reports that come to us from the saints. That is the center—the enduring core—of religious experience. What Tylor and Frazer dismiss as the superstition of primitive religions is a quite marginal and dispensable thing; it is merely the "theory," or theology, that primitive peoples place upon their religious experience to try to account for it. Such theories are changeable and replaceable, while the experience and actions at the core of such theories are changeless and abiding. As James puts it,

> When we survey the whole field of religion, we find a great variety in the thoughts that have prevailed there; but the feelings on the one hand and conduct on the other are almost always the same, for Stoic, Christian, and Buddhist saints are practically indistinguishable in their lives. The theories which Religion generates, being thus variable, are secondary; and if you wish to grasp her essence, you must look to the feelings and conduct as being the more constant elements. . . . This seems to me the first conclusion which we are entitled to draw from the phenomena we have passed in review.[26]

In sum, religious ideas and beliefs invariably change and differ. Religious feeling—along with the conduct it produces—is different: it is always present and constant—the same across the borders of cultures and in both the great religions and the small.

So, if all of this is the case, can we say anything more precise about these "feelings" at the core of religious experience? What do they consist of? In broad strokes, James says we can mark out the following. Religious experience finds the visible world to be part of a larger, more spiritual universe; it sees our uniting with that spiritual realm as the goal of human life; it conveys knowledge of that realm; and it draws on practices like prayer and meditation to channel that spiritual energy into the present world; finally, religious experience inspires and uplifts, even as it offers the believer a profound sense of safety and peace.

Wherever we observe these feelings, these sentiments and emotions, along with the habits and actions they inspire—there, says James, we can detect the "more constant elements" that define the essence of religion. In addition, if we consider the structure of religious experience, we can say more. In its most universal and compelling form, religious experience almost everywhere consists of a crucial two-part sequence. There is first a personal feeling of uneasiness, a deep sense that something about ourselves as we naturally stand is discordant, dissonant, broken. Then there is the feeling of rescue: a wonderful, flooding sense of a solution found, a salvation discovered. In the moment of conversion we feel a sense of resolution and escape that has been achieved by somehow "making proper connection with the higher powers." This transition, this compelling experience of reversal and recovery, is religion's pivotal centerpoint. In every one of us, says James (shifting as he occasionally does to parent-and-child discourse) there is a "wrong part" and a "better part." The crucial turn occurs as the individual person connects his or her "real being" with the "higher" and "better" part. Further, those who pass through a religious experience discover that "this 'higher part' is coterminous and continuous with a MORE of the same quality, which is operative in the universe" outside of ourselves.[27] James here goes back to more abstract language, but if we attend closely to it, his meaning becomes clear. In the moment of religious conversion, of renewal, enlightenment, or discovery—whatever we may call it—and as individual persons move inwardly from distress to relief, from being "lost" to being "saved," they are enabled to make this change through contact with the "more," which is divinity, however theologians or spiritual leaders may say this "divine" should be conceived. In other words, through religious experience human beings repair their broken selves with help they see as coming from beyond, from the realm of ultimate reality. This pivotal experience, however it may occur, is the permanent emotional core of religion. After that conversion moment, or conversion process, the self recovers; a sense of well-being suffuses the mind, and good actions follow. On that most basic transaction, James argues, there is virtually unanimous agreement among the world's religions.

Religious Experience, Theologies, and Truth

Of course there is also genuine disagreement among religions, but it should be now clear to everyone just why this is so. It is in their differing efforts to explain religious experience that divergent religious cultures, traditions, and theologies arise. The work of theologians and the wisdom of spiritual teachers has always been to propose ideas and frame systems of thought *about* religious experience that help to convey and explain it within their distinctive cultural communities. In each instance they connect the core experience of conversion with doctrinal teachings that are built out and up from it. James assigns to these systems of thought the word "over-belief"—each religion in its different way constructing its own system of ideas on the common psychological foundation of the conversion experience. The Christian theology of creation, fall, and redemption is a system of over-beliefs. The Hindu system of imprisonment in matter, self-denial, meditation, and release is a different over-belief. The Muslim framework of infidel irreligion, submission to Allah, and heavenly reward is another. The Buddhist sequence of karma, moksha, and nirvana (imprisonment, release, and the bliss of extinction) is yet another. In each of these systems there is, obviously, a different set of over-beliefs governed by differing personal temperaments, cultural assumptions, and religious ideas. But these varieties of religious over-belief do not alter the psychological core, which remains the same across cultures, behind theologies, and underneath traditions.

To identify this core of religion is a major step, but it is not the last step. There is still the matter of the general truth of religion for all. Does the "more" that James finds at the heart of religious experience enable believers to say that their beliefs are universally true? After all, the core of religious experience may well be universal, but it could be a universal delusion. That is what Freud has said: the obsessional neurosis of religion is universal. Further, even a fully scientific consensus can be mistaken. Before Copernicus nearly all of science held that the sun circles the Earth. There was consensus, but it was mistaken. Why not the same for all of the religious experience that has been so thoroughly documented in these lectures?

In response to this final question, James offers first a suggestion and then an argument, the former psychological, the latter both philosophical and personal. To make the suggestion, he turns—in part at least—to Freud for help. From their very different perspectives, Freud and James's sometime associate F. W. H. Myers, who promoted psychical research into the supernatural, stood in agreement on psychology's most impressive achievement: the discovery of the subconscious self.[28] James had already alluded to this intriguing domain as the source of religious ecstasy. Could it be, he suggests, that Freud's unconscious—what Myers calls "the subliminal self"—is the hidden corridor by which the divine directly enters the human personality? This speculative notion did not rest on a very clear or full understanding of Freud, and James does not really offer it as much more than an intriguing possibility. It nonetheless shows his willingness to enlist and engage creatively with newer theorems that might be applied to religious experience.

About the philosophical issue James is more definite. He turns again to the pragmatic principle that has guided his earlier thinking. As before in the *Principles of Psychology* and "The Will to Believe," he argues that the final test of truth is to found the value it offers when we translate belief into action. We measure the meaning, the truth-character, of an idea or an experience by the result it delivers when we actually put it to use—whether in the laboratory or in life. And in those pragmatic terms, we certainly can speak of the truth of religious experience, can we not? In light of the manifold evidence assembled in *Varieties*, evidence which emphatically shows the immense power of religious experience to alter lives—almost invariably for the better—we are certainly entitled to speak of the truth of religious experience. Measuring by pragmatism's standard of value when applied in action, religious experience can be judged on its many merits to be true. Experience that has done so much to heal wounded souls and morally inspire sacrifice of self for others cannot be other than the experience of truth.

As the Gifford Lectures come to a close, their author candidly—and commendably—offers his own personal view of religious experience, including a statement on his own over-belief, to be placed alongside all the others. Not surprisingly, James asserts that as a Christian, steeped in the heritage of his cultural tradition, he finds the term "God" to be the best way to describe the MORE, the divine reality that accompanies religious experience as he has known it. He announces that faith as his own, but not with the voice of dogmatic certainty. Instead, he chooses just the words we would expect from the author of "The Will to Believe." He describes his faith as "my personal venture," a choice attended by risk, but with prospect of reward. As he writes on the final page of *Varieties*' final chapter:

> I believe the pragmatic way of taking religion to be the deeper way. It gives it body as well as soul, it makes it claim, as everything real must claim, some characteristic realm of fact as its very own. What the characteristically divine facts are . . . , I know not. But the over-belief on which I am ready to make my personal venture is that they exist. . . . By being faithful in my poor measure to this over-belief, I seem to keep myself more sane and true.[29]

Analysis

Intellectually, William James was a man of two profiles. It has been said, with a trace of both wit and truth, that he pursued psychology as a philosopher, and philosophy as a psychologist. If so, we can best understand his work as a theorist by looking at him from each side of the porous border he straddled between those two fields.

1. Psychology

It is plain to see that as a psychologist, James takes a view of religion that is not just different from Freud's, but emphatically opposed to it. The two theorists start from a measure of common ground, but from there they move in decidedly different directions. Both sought to unlock secrets of the human mind; both turned to psychology after starting with medicine and physiology; and both readily moved beyond psychology to address wider philosophical issues: the nature of the mind, the connection between beliefs and emotions, the role of religion in the personality and society. Despite these shared interests, the conclusions they reached were polar opposites. James endeavored lifelong to appreciate and affirm the religious life; Freud summarily dismissed it. James looks to faith as a source of meaning, as a healer of the afflicted personality, and as a force for good in the world. Freud finds belief in God a neurotic delusion—the chief symptom of mental illness that, with the help of psychotherapy, we must try to cure. James assembles an array of evidence to show that people of all kinds have found in religious experience a lifeline to mental health, a true and timely rescue for sick souls. For Freud nothing could be more absurd; nothing could lead us farther from the truth than the conclusion that religion should be favorably associated with mental health.

A part of this sharp divergence obviously lies beyond psychology, in two very distant personal and cultural worlds. Freud was a European Jew who had become an atheist early on in life. James, as we have seen, was raised in an affluent American Protestant home; his father, though unconventional, was deeply religious and emotionally close to his eldest son, who in return appreciated a parental faith that enriched relationships, anchored morals, and affirmed democratic values. Beyond these personal motives, it is apparent also that James and Freud saw the enterprise of psychology from different vantage points. James saw the field as a far-reaching, formal discipline newly emergent from a mere province within philosophy. To him it was a broad and promising form of inquiry equipped with the tools of science and capable of shedding new light on the mysteries of the brain and mind. His work on *The Principles of Psychology* brought him into acquaintance with the newest paths of research, from brain physiology to laboratory studies and methods of mental introspection. Freud's work by contrast was that of a brilliant innovator working with small circle of peers to explore a quite unconventional subject; his research was concentrated primarily on studies of neurotic patients that had led him and his associates to pioneer the theory and methods of psychoanalysis. When Freud first advanced his revolutionary ideas in Vienna, James expressed genuine interest. He helped introduce Freud to American discussion. We have already seen how he found Freud's general idea of the unconscious to be highly intriguing. At the same time, he thought of psychoanalysis as only one among several promising paths of inquiry that made the landscape of modern scientific psychology so inviting. More so than Freud, James's intellectual travels took him to multiple points of interest in the discipline.

2. Philosophy

By the time he began his medical studies, James was well acquainted with the broad intellectual currents of the Victorian age. He had read widely, not only in the classics, arts, and literature, but among the main texts in Western thought and the newest research in the sciences.[30] He certainly knew that in philosophy the leading figures of his day were gathered into two major, and opposing, schools of thought. The one—already encountered early in his personal life, as we have seen—was scientific materialism, the perspective of Büchner and Huxley, bolstered by Darwin's evolutionary theory. Materialists affirmed the primacy of matter over mind. Those in the other camp, in James's day often called philosophical monism, took as their starting point precisely the reverse: the primacy of mind over matter. As some may recall from our earlier discussion of Marx, monism can be traced to the German philosopher Hegel, who in the early decades of the century advocated Absolute idealism. The monists of James's day were late-century disciples of Hegel. Like him, they held that behind the many material appearances and forms of the physical world, there is a singular and immaterial ultimate reality, a supreme cosmic Mind, to which they gave the same title that Hegel used: "the Absolute." Although the prestige of science was rising rapidly, philosophical monism still claimed the high ground among academic philosophers almost up to World War I.[31] Its spokesmen held prestigious positions in both European and Anglo-American universities. In Britain, F. H. Bradley commanded wide respect, while in America James's Harvard colleague and close friend Josiah Royce held pride of place. Like Hegel, Bradley and Royce held that the Absolute, as supreme Mind or Idea, discloses itself and its designs in the material world with a kind of perfect rationality, just as, we might say, our own human minds express themselves unfailingly in the actions of our bodies, or (to use a different analogy) just as an architect can be said to bring the concept of a structure to expression in an actual physical building that perfectly mirrors the design it was created from. We could almost call these idealists theologians, given how nearly the concept of the Absolute approximates to the Judeo-Christian concept of the Creator God. But their monism was not monotheism. The Absolute is supreme mind, but it is not a personality; it does not reveal itself in the Bible with personal qualities like anger or love; it is absolute rationality—with neither personality nor emotions. Nonetheless, the Absolute does express itself in a cosmic order that unfolds in the forms of the material world—exhibiting a grand coherence that our finite human minds can in their small way conceptually grasp.

To materialist philosophers, of course, these monists had managed to get the whole question of mind and matter both backward and upside down. Matter—physical reality—is fundamental; what we call mind is a mere product of matter. To theorize about some great abstraction called the Absolute is to embark on a fool's errand. The only path to real understanding of the world leads through Darwin, materialism, and experimental science, not through Hegel, idealism, and airy webs of speculation. Materialism claimed not only gifted, aggressive spokesmen like Huxley, but more than a few other, more quietly sympathetic adherents, including two of James's most admired Harvard mentors in the sciences—Chauncey Wright and Jeffries Wyman. But monism also had powerful spokesmen, one of whom, as noted, was James's other colleague Josiah Royce. In lectures and papers, over coffee or wine, on walks in the country, Royce could be seen with his friend strenuously arguing the case for idealism. James had great respect for Royce; he listened, and listened more, but in the end was not convinced. He rejected monism just as firmly as, years earlier, he had rejected materialism. And for largely similar reasons.

Both perspectives, he insisted, follow the perilous path of abstraction. They are framed in the study or the laboratory, places very distant from the realities of life as it is lived by ordinary human beings coping with everyday concerns. Materialism entails determinism and undermines freedom of the will. Life in the real world, however, requires us to assume that we are free agents, who can act responsibly in making moral decisions. From the start, therefore, materialism disqualifies itself. As James had concluded early in life, it is a philosophy no one can actually live by. But then monists are no better off. They spin their silver web of abstractions to prove that the world as we find it is exactly as it should be. They explain that it unfolds in keeping with the perfect rationality scripted by the Absolute. But such a system can only be proposed by thinkers utterly out of touch with the actualities of human life, which is scarred by horrific episodes of evil. No philosopher, no human being who has experienced real physical suffering, known the devastation of a flood or famine, or seen the death of a child can truthfully say such a world is "just as it should be." Such things cannot be accepted as needed, logical, and natural, any more than a building with faulty foundation could be seen as an essential part of an architect's plan. Such a calm, icy acceptance of evil as a logical and natural feature of world and true expression of the perfectly rational Absolute is absurd. Monism may entertain philosophers at a distance from life's realities, but like materialism, it does not make sense of moral thought or action; it cannot speak to life as we actually experience it.[32]

It was this dissatisfaction with both monism and materialism that led James to propose, as a new departure, his philosophy of pragmatism, where the truth and value of ideas should be judged by their usefulness, by what happens when we apply them to our actions in the real world. In that world, we know that a belief is true "if it pays" when we adopt it. To use a simple, real-world carpenter's analogy: If we define wood as "a natural substance that is solid and strong," we determine the truth of that definition when we act upon it to build a house. It is in our use of wood that we discover the truth that it is solid and strong. Similarly so in other aspects of life: we assess the truth of beliefs by their value to us when we make use of them.

James did not develop this core idea fully until the very final phase of his career, publishing near the end of his of his life the collection of essays entitled: *Pragmatism: A New Name for Some Old Ways of Thinking* (1907). Nearly a decade earlier, however, in a well-known address given at the University of California in Berkeley just two years prior to his Gifford Lectures, he publicly introduced pragmatism as the distinctively new philosophical outlook that he would personally champion. He would turn his back "resolutely and once for all" on other philosophies, giving the last years of his career to the exposition and defense of the pragmatist program. He acknowledged his Harvard colleague C. S. Pierce as its pioneering thinker and, in part, his mentor. From that lecture it was also evident that he was giving a preview of the central role that pragmatism—the principle of measuring truth by its effects—would play in the scientific study of religion that he was about to begin. If we were to propose a long philosophical subtitle for *The Varieties of Religious Experience*, we would not be mistaken to suggest: "Neither Materialism nor Monism, but Pragmatism as the Key to Understanding Religion."

Critique

No less than other theorists, William James has acquired his share of critics, not only in his day but certainly also in the century following. The more noteworthy of the criticisms vary considerably in scope and character. Some center on matters of evidence; others focus on assumptions and definitions; still others address the logic of certain arguments, both in *Varieties* and in some of the shorter discussions James offers in his lectures and essays. In addition, some criticisms come close to the core of James's overall approach; others, while not unimportant, address matters somewhat less central to his program. We can look briefly at both types.

1. Marginal Concerns

Unconsidered Evidence

James commits to studying religion scientifically, so it is fair to ask how scientific he is with his evidence, especially as assembled in *The Varieties of Religious Experience*. There he proposes to make a universal argument, applicable to all of human religious experience and anchored by direct evidence—the personal reports of people who testify to an encounter with the divine. By quite a significant margin, however, the reports he considers can be seen to come from Protestant Christians, especially those of evangelical persuasion, placed in either England or America. These are religious cultures that by tradition are most disposed to make the moment of "conversion" a central element of their religious life. James does also adduce Catholic instances, citing the cases of St. Theresa of Avila, St. John of the Cross, and occasionally others. But that still leaves the discussion framed chiefly by Christian voices.

Reports of Asian Buddhist or Hindu experiences, for example, or texts drawn from Jewish or Middle Eastern Islamic experience are almost nonexistent. The lack of examples from these more distant cultures does not necessarily discredit James's analyses, but it certainly opens the way to questions about just how widely grounded his claims are and how definitive his conclusions can be. At the very least, we would like to hear more from these large, ancient, and important religious cultures outside of the Western world. Conversely, James gives perhaps too much attention to certain rather marginally religious movements in Britain and America. He refers, for example, to the short-lived "mind cure" and new thought movements of his day. James himself was a founding figure of one such group. Following the British example of F. W. H. Myers, who was keenly interested in "spiritualism" and belief in the occult, James promoted the American Society for Psychical Research, which he cites in his exposition. Among these groups there was a keen interest in religious experience based on the (quite unproven) premise that better emotional health will guarantee better physical health or that one could make contact with deceased loved ones on "the other side." They were thus open to manipulation by charlatans claiming dubious psychic and spiritual powers. One can certainly ask why such movements receive attention when little notice is taken of, say, the mysticism of the Hindu Upanishads or the rich Buddhist literature on meditation and enlightenment. To be sure, in James's day Asian materials were just beginning to be translated on a scale sufficient to be of use, but certainly some Asian writings and not insignificant numbers of Islamic and Jewish mystical religious texts already in translation might well have been more closely considered and cited.

Unfinished Arguments

Leaving aside evidential issues and the case of *Varieties,* we can also notice questions that have been raised about James's occasional writings, which often were initially presented as public lectures for general audiences. This circumstance naturally required simplification and compression, which in some instances came at a cost. Consider the argument we traced in "The Will to Believe," certainly one of James's most well-received and provocative lectures. There we found him defending belief in God along the lines of Pascal's wager argument. Over the three centuries since it was penned, however, Pascal's claim that belief in God is worth the risk has elicited a variety of criticisms from later philosophers and theologians. In the course of his presentation, James properly acknowledges Pascal, but he then makes no real effort to engage the subsequent criticisms of the wager theorem, some of which are quite relevant to his own version of it, or to modify his discussion to take account of them. We can perhaps excuse the oversight on the immediate occasion of the public lecture, but less so afterward. There is no sign that James returned to his discussion to amplify or amend it by addressing at least some of those criticisms before allowing it to go forward for publication. Instead, he moved on to other topics and allowed it to be published it as it stood—still intriguing, still provocative, but certainly less compelling than it might have been. James in fact later conceded that there were weaknesses he had left unaddressed.[33] Perhaps not surprisingly, his Harvard colleague Santayana offered the final, somewhat sardonic word on the matter, suggesting that James himself was less than persuaded by his own arguments. There was "no sense of security," he wrote, "no joy, in James's apology for personal religion. He did not really believe; he merely believed in the right of believing that you might be right if you believed."[34]

2. Core Concerns

Difficulties of the kind noticed above are not trivial, but at the same time, they do not go to the center of things. There are, however, at least two criticisms that come nearer to the core of James's theoretical agenda and thus carry greater weight. They are definitional in the one instance and conceptual in the other.

Defining Religious Experience

In *Varieties*, we may recall, James develops his thesis in a way that we can restate as follows: at its core, religious experience occurs in individual persons who pass through a crucial psychological event, from unsettlement to resolution, from a sense of "something wrong" to that of "something made right." With this change comes a new state of mind in which they feel buoyant, revived, and morally energized, motivated to do good. Amid these welcome emotions, the self feels in touch with something "MORE"—with the source of this renewal, perceived as powerful and active in the universe. This pivotal psychological change is the center of religious experience, which is then, secondarily, described and explained in the many varieties of theological belief that are found across the world's cultures and religions. Those beliefs, obviously, are particular and specific, not universal; only the experience is universal.

At first sight, this is an attractive argument to anyone who wants to respect differences but still think of all humanity as religiously in harmony. But if we look at the formula very closely, there is a puzzling element to it. The world's theological beliefs and belief-systems are exceedingly diverse. The Christian may define her religious experience as "being saved by the grace of God in Christ." The Hindu yogi may describe it as "the absorption of the soul (atman), or self, into Brahman-atman (the Supreme Soul)"; the Buddhist speaks of "the release (moksha) of enlightenment leading to the bliss of Nirvana." Some of these theological ideas do not just differ minimally or modestly from each other; they differ fundamentally—in ways that sharply diverge or directly conflict. In Buddhism, "Nirvana" means "nothingness"; the Buddhist monk longs for non-existence, for non-being. The Christian concept of "Heaven" is precisely the opposite; it means not just existing, but existing eternally, with God, in a perfected state. Buddhist and Christian can perhaps agree *that* there is a "more" that is the source of conversion or enlightenment, but they can hardly be said to agree on what that "more" is, if it is to be anything other than a mere empty word. If anything, the Buddhist idea of the "more" appears to be just what the Christian idea is not. So in order to be truly common, in order to be universal to all, religious experience needs, it would seem, to be entirely empty of content, devoid of specific definition.

To put this matter a little differently, the fact of religious diversity discloses something paradoxical about James's idea of universal religious experience. He describes it as the profound feeling of escape and resolution uncolored by competing religious beliefs and belief-systems. But we seem to need those religious ideas, those divergent sets of beliefs, if we are in any way to define the experience as religious. The moment we remove those beliefs, the feelings at the heart of the experience would seem to have no identity of their own. And if so, how can we call the experience "religious"? Without any theological concepts to define it, it may well be a feeling of transformation, a sense of personal wellness newly discovered, but not an identifiably *religious* transformation. James understandably centers his attention on religious experience as the powerful and welcome feeling of renewal—a sense of personal joy, contentment, and surrender alongside a new surge of empowerment. But as soon as we try to define these feelings as religious, we encounter a problem: we need the ideas and beliefs in order to do so. After all, a morning walk can yield a soaring sense of joy; a glass of wine brings contentment; falling in love brings blissful surrender. None of these things is religious. "Religious" experience thus seems to need—somewhere, somehow—a religious belief or idea to define it. James, however, does not provide any. In fact, he seems in this connection studiously to avoid mentioning concepts or ideas—something that is especially puzzling in light of what he had said earlier in *Principles*. There, we may recall, he insisted that human feelings can, even without help from the intellect, provide us with "pre-conceptual" knowledge. Similarly, in *Varieties*, when discussing mystical experience, he tells us it has "noetic" character; it gives us knowledge. But here, when separating pure religious experience from the theologies that explain it, there seems to be nothing left in the way of knowledge that would allow us to define it as religious. It seems a feeling that is empty, like feeling happy without anything to define what we are happy about. In the end, then, we are left with a puzzle. To the degree that an experience is religious, it must be quite specifically religious (that is, "theological") to some, and cannot be universally religious to all, while to the degree the experience is universal and valid for all, it must be without ideas and so cannot be specifically religious to some or any. Putting it more pointedly, James seems to insist on a kind of experience that cannot be religious if truly universal, and cannot be universal if truly religious. We seem to be in a definitional quandary—with little in the way of a path to escape it.

3. Pragmatism, Belief, and Truth

A final point of criticism pertains chiefly to James as a philosopher, but with relevance also to his understanding of religion. The key issue is how we judge the truth of our beliefs, particularly religious beliefs. If pragmatism is to be our guide, it follows that we will apply to religions the pragmatic criterion of truth. In James's own later words, published after *Varieties* had been written: "If the hypothesis of God works satisfactorily in the widest sense of the word, it is true."[35] The register of religious testimonies we find in *Varieties* is assembled to illustrate that very principle. The "hypothesis of God" confers psychological benefit, a wellness of mind, on all of those souls—healthy or sick—who have affirmed it. And evidence abounds that such selves are then moved to do good for others. The narrative of *Varieties* enables us to see in vivid colors how the truth of religion emerges from the good things that flow into the souls of the saints and the equally good things that flow out of the lives they live.

Not surprisingly, both in James's own day and ours, this pragmatic test of truth has drawn a great deal of scrutiny from the analytical eyes of philosophers. Does the pragmatic criterion, they ask, really serve the purpose James assigns to it? Does it in fact lead us from the benefits of religion to the truth of religion? The earliest and most skeptical questioners in this regard were two British philosophers, younger contemporaries of James, who at the time were offering the world of philosophy a new departure of their own in the form of language analysis.

In several articles published in the leading British journals of philosophy, G. E. Moore and Bertrand Russell subjected James's pragmatism to a rigorous analytical critique. What, they asked, does James actually mean when he claims that we measure truth by its utility, when he says that we discover what is true by determining that it is good? It can be generally agreed, wrote Moore, that most of the things we know to be true are useful, and many things known to be false are not. But that is evident enough. Presumably James wants to say more than that. If we read his language attentively, he appears to make utility the *sole* criterion of truth, so that only useful beliefs should be judged true, and false beliefs judged useless. But clearly, that principle is a problem if James means to apply it in all cases. We can certainly think of instances where true beliefs are not always useful—as when a detective attends too much to certain things known to be true about a crime and becomes distracted from other things that would better lead him to the real culprit, rather than the innocent man that he now has under suspicion. Conversely, we can think of obvious cases where believing, or leading someone to believe, what is false can be very useful—for example in war, when deception of an enemy with a lie can save the life of a friend in hiding.[36] Russell adduces another instance, this with a sly and more pointed application to religion. Using James's own language, he says, "I have always found that the hypothesis of Santa Claus 'works satisfactorily in the widest sense of the word'; therefore 'Santa Claus exists' is true, although Santa Claus does not exist."[37] It would seem that the pragmatic criterion of truth leads to absurdities.

The Santa Claus example, while amusing enough, is not entirely fair. James does not in fact say that we can believe just about anything we want if we happen to think it beneficial. A belief under consideration does need to be compatible with our other true beliefs if we want to accept it also as true. And certainly there are some true beliefs—about the inability of reindeer to fly, the constraints of narrow chimneys on overweight men, and the poor aerodynamics of sleighs—that are incompatible with belief in Santa Claus. But still, as Russell might respond, we would then want to ask how *those* beliefs were established. On the pragmatist criterion of utility also? Or on factual grounds? If the latter, then, it appears that we must somewhere allow a separate determination of facts to intrude on the test of utility after all, and we cannot apply the pragmatic criterion universally, as James seems to assert. The problem with using utility as our sole, or even chief, guide to the truth of religious belief, Russell concludes, is that it "omits as unimportant the question whether God really is in His heaven."[38] James is content to accept belief in God as something that has good effects, but he fails to see that for people of faith, belief in the good effects requires that the belief in God be a factually true belief—true, that is, in a sense other than being simply useful.

These matters of fact and utility are not the only complications of pragmatism. Russell further explains that we face with James's pragmatic formula the very difficult task of deciding what the "good effects" of a belief actually are, and for whom they would be good effects, before we can go on to determine its truth. If the effects of the French Revolution are judged to be good, then we can say that the beliefs of the men who led it were true; if bad, then they were false. But the consequences of the French Revolution for our time are exceedingly mixed and complicated. How do we judge whether even in the most general terms they are good or bad? And of course our own present views are very likely to affect our judgments. Leftist historians have thought the Revolution overall to have been good; many rightists and Catholic historians think it was disastrous. So no clear answer is possible. At the very least, such circumstances suggest that judging the truth of a belief by "how it works in action" is itself highly problematic and, as it would seem, pragmatically unworkable.[39] Moore and Russell are not alone in their misgivings; subsequent analysts have raised either the same or quite similar questions. Of course, it is true also that more recently some impressive arguments have been offered in James's defense.[40] Nonetheless, the key issue remains difficult and much disputed. To think of truth as a matter of utility without somewhere addressing truth as factuality requires for most contemporary philosophers a substantial leap in logic that they are not willing to make. And as James makes the pragmatic test central to his assessments of religious faith, is it no surprise to learn that theorists of religion express very similar reservations. The path of pragmatism may not be entirely closed to future theorists, but certainly it is not without certain imposing obstacles to overcome.

Conclusion

Serious as some of these misgivings may be, they have neither altered the impact nor reduced the importance of William James's rich investigations into the nature of religious experience. Like Freud, he unquestionably opened new paths to follow in excavating the close ties between psychology and religion. If it is true that Freud assessed one pole of that relationship and found faith chilling, crippling, and destructive, James clearly laid a strong claim to the other pole, where he found in religious experience a remarkable power to heal the wounded personality, inspire vigorous moral action, and assert the cause of good against evil wherever it was present in the world. In time, both Freud and James were to find devoted disciples; and in consequence, their opposing views are still very much alive, not just as intellectual legacies, but as living theoretical options for some—a circumstance all the more impressive when we consider how much the field of psychology has transformed itself in the century since they both were among the most celebrated of its early patrons and, in their ambitious explorations of religion, among the most adventurous of its pioneers.

Notes

1. *The Letters of William James*, vol. 2: 58, as quoted in Ellen Kappy Suckiel, *Heaven's Champion: William James's Philosophy of Religion* (Notre Dame, IN: University of Notre Dame Press, 1996), p. 3.

2. Cited in Jacques Barzun, *A Stroll with William James* (New York: Harper & Row, 1963), p. 298. The opening speaker was experimental psychologist David Krech.

3. There are many introductions to pragmatism as a philosophical method, including James's own book *Pragmatism*, published in 1907, which contains a collection of eight essays on the subject. He gave a great deal of time and effort to explaining the pragmatist program and defending it against misconceptions in the last phase of his career, from 1902 to 1910.

4. One of the best accounts of William James's early life and the unique character of the James family is still the two-volume biography, supplemented with extensive citations and quotations from the intra-family letters, written by Ralph Barton Perry, who was one of James's most accomplished students at Harvard. Though now itself very old, this book, published in 1935, reflects an intimate knowledge not only of William James but also the James family and William's many associates and colleagues. Few modern biographers can match it in the immediacy of its knowledge of the man, his times, and those who knew him best.

5. Letter to friend Edward B. Van Winkle, from Boulogne-sur-Mer, March 1, 1858, quoted in Ralph Barton Perry, *The Thought and Character of William James*, Briefer Version (Cambridge, MA: Harvard University Press, 1948), p. 52.

6. William James, Diary, April 30, 1870, cited in Daniel W. Bjork, *William James: The Center of His Vision* (Washington, D.C.: The American Psychological Association, 1997 [1988]), p. 89.

7. George Santayana, *Character & Opinion in the United States* (New York: George Braziller, 1955), p. 41.

8. William James, *The Principles of Psychology*, 2 vols. (Mineola, NY: Dover Publications, 1950 [1890]), 1: 344.

9. James, *The Principles of Psychology*, 1: 488.

10. James, *The Principles of Psychology*, 2: 573; see also the article "The Dilemma of Determinism," in *The Will to Believe and Other Essays in Popular Philosophy* (Mineola, NY: Dover Books, 1956), p. 146.

11. James, *The Principles of Psychology,* 2: 576.

12. William James, "The Moral Philosopher and Moral Life," in *The Will to Believe*, pp. 213–214.

13. An assertive defense of James's view that feelings or emotions provide such preconceptual knowledge can be found in Suckiel, *Heaven's Champion*, pp. 39–75, and throughout.

14. James, "The Will to Believe," in *The Will to Believe and Other Essays on Popular Philosophy*, pp. 1–2.

15. James, "The Will to Believe," in *The Will to Believe and Other Essays on Popular Philosophy*, p. 27.

16. William James, *The Varieties of Religious Experience: A Study in Human Nature*, The Modern Library (New York: Random House, 1936 [1902]), pp. 31–32 (italics removed).

17. Ibid., p. 8.

18. Ibid., p. 19.

19. Ibid.

20. Ibid., p. 173.

21. Ibid., p. 210.

22. Ibid., p. 224.

23. Ibid., p. 237.

24. Ibid., pp. 324–325.

25. Ibid., p. 420.

26. Ibid., p. 494.

27. Ibid., p. 499 (italics removed).

28. On James's support of Myers and the British Society for Psychical Research and his founding of the American equivalent, see Gerald E. Myers, *William James: His Life and Thought* (New Haven, CT: Yale University Press, 1986), pp. 10, 374, 472, 613.

29. James, *Varieties of Religious Experience*, p. 509.

30. For rich portraits of James's unusual early years and education, see the engaging accounts by Gay Wilson Allen, *William James: A Biography* (New York: The Viking Press, 1967), and Linda Simon, *Genuine Reality: A Life of William James* (Chicago: University of Chicago Press, 1998).

31. A comprehensive recent account of monism in Anglo-American discussion is W. J. Mander's *British Idealism: A History* (London: Oxford University Press, 2011).

32. William James, *Pragmatism: A New Name for Some Old Ways of Thinking*, Popular Lectures on Philosophy (London: Longmans, Green and Co., 1928 [1907]), pp. 20–32.

33. Myers, *William James*, pp. 451–461; see also n. 16.

34. George Santayana, *Character and Opinion in the United States* (New York: George Braziller, 1955 [1920]), p. 46.

35. James, *Pragmatism,* p. 299.

36. G. E. Moore, "Professor James' Pragmatism," *Proceedings of the Aristotelean Society*, New Series, Volume 8 (1907–1908), pp. 47–48.

37. Bertrand Russell, *A History of Western Philosophy: And Its Connection with Political and Social Circumstances from the Earliest Times to the Present Day* (New York: Simon and Schuster, 1945), p. 818.

38. Ibid.

39. These and other objections were raised by Russell in two early essays: "Pragmatism," published in 1908 in the *Edinburgh Review*, and "William James's Conception of Truth," also published in 1908 under the title "Transatlantic 'Truth'" in the *Albany Review*. Both were republished in *Philosophical Essays* (New York: Simon and Schuster, 1996 [1910]), pp. 79–111 and 112–130.

40. For a sophisticated and relatively recent analysis of James's pragmatic justifications of belief, which shows that some critics have too easily dismissed the arguments, see William J. Wainright, "William James, Rationality and Religious Belief," in his

Reason and the Heart: A Prolegomenon to a Critique of Passional Reasoning (Ithaca, NY: Cornell University Press, 1995), pp. 84–107.

Suggestions for Further Reading

Allen, Gay Wilson. *William James: A Biography.* New York: The Viking Press, 1967. A brief, well-respected biography focused chiefly on James's life rather than his thought.

Barzun, Jacques. *A Stroll with William James.* New York: Harper & Row, 1983. An engaging, literate reflection on James's life and thought by a man of comparable stature in American life, one of the nation's most accomplished humanist thinkers.

Bixler, Julius Seelye. *Religion in the Philosophy of William James.* Boston: Marshall Jones Company, 1926. The earliest study specifically of James's ideas on religion; argues for the unity of his thought as woven from strands of empiricism, realism, and romanticism and as expressed in his ideas of the will, immortality, mysticism, and deity.

Bjork, Daniel W. *William James: The Center of His Vision.* Washington, D.C.: The American Psychological Association, 1997 [1988]. A more recent study of James's intellectual agenda, emphasizing his introspective approach to psychology and his disposition to see the world as a scene of constantly moving, changing relationships; provides a valuable bibliographical essay.

Bordogna, Francesca. *William James at the Boundaries: Philosophy, Science, and the Geography of Knowledge.* Chicago: University of Chicago Press, 2008. A recent study that interprets James as a thinker who felt impelled to cross the boundaries of traditional disciplines.

Carrette, Jeremy. *William James's Hidden Religious Imagination: A Universe of Relations.* New York: Routledge, 2013. An innovative, well-researched study reflecting the current state of discussion, as well as the author's effort to achieve a more interdisciplinary and integrated understanding of James's personal and intellectual life.

Cooper, Wesley. *The Unity of William James's Thought.* Nashville, TN: Vanderbilt University Press, 2002. Sees James's thought as an integrated whole in which two levels of truth, scientific and metaphysical, are united by his concept of pure experience.

Cotkin, George. *William James: Public Philosopher.* Baltimore: The Johns Hopkins University Press, 1999. An examination of James's inquiries in philosophy, psychology, and religion as affected by American politics and society.

Gale, Richard M. *The Divided Self of William James.* Cambridge: Cambridge University Press, 1999. A well-received recent consideration of James's philosophy that finds multiple themes, such as two different empiricisms in creative tension with each other.

Levinson, Henry Samuel. *The Religious Investigations of William James.* Chapel Hill: University of North Carolina Press, 1981. A monograph centered specifically on

James's inquiries into religion; meant for the more advanced reader; provides an extensive bibliography.

Myers, Gerald E. *William James: His Life and Thought.* New Haven, CT: Yale University Press, 1986. The definitive modern intellectual biography; a major study, comprehensively conceived and exhaustively researched, but not easily accessible to the novice.

Perry, Ralph Barton. *The Thought and Character of William James: As Revealed in Unpublished Correspondence and Notes, together with his Published Writings.* Volume 1: *Inheritance and Vocation.* Volume 2: *Philosophy and Psychology.* Boston: Little, Brown, and Company, 1935. The first comprehensive study of James's life and thought; winner of the Pulitzer Prize in biography, Perry was one of James's students who became himself a philosopher of considerable note. Written with support from the James family, Perry makes extensive use of James's diary and private correspondence. Its 1,500 pages were reduced to about a third of that length in a subsequent *Briefer Version.*

Proudfoot, Wayne, ed. *William James and a Science of Religions: Reexperiencing* The Varieties of Religious Experience. Columbia Series in Science and Religion. Ithaca, NY: Columbia University Press, 2004. A collection of six essays by scholars recognized for their expertise on James, religion, and the scientific study of religion; includes a contribution from the editor, who has published an important study of religious experience.

Putnam, Ruth Anna, ed. *The Cambridge Companion to William James.* Cambridge: Cambridge University Press, 1997. Thorough, thoughtful, original essays on multiple aspects of James's intellectual enterprise contributed by leading figures, mainly in philosophy, but also from the fields of literature, history, and religion.

Russell, Bertrand. *Philosophical Essays.* New York: Simon and Schuster, 1966. A collection that contains Russell's two trenchant essays: "Pragmatism" and "William James's Conception of Truth."

Simon, Linda. *Genuine Reality: A Life of William James.* Chicago: University of Chicago Press, 1998. A personal, rather than intellectual, biography that draws on a large cache of letters to capture the several sides of James's personality and the many relationships he cultivated.

Suckiel, Ellen Kappy. *Heaven's Champion: William James's Philosophy of Religion.* Notre Dame, IN: University of Notre Dame Press, 1996. A sustained analysis and defense of James's appeal to religious experience as a legitimate source of "preconceptual" knowledge and a justifiable ground of religious belief.

Taves, Ann. *Religious Experience Reconsidered.* Princeton, NJ: Princeton University Press, 2009. A rich interdisciplinary study exploring the concept of religious experience in the light of recent research in the natural sciences, social sciences, and study of religion.

7

The Reality of the Sacred: Mircea Eliade

> My duty is to show the grandeur, sometimes naive, sometimes monstrous and tragic, of archaic modes of being.
>
> Mircea Eliade, *Journal III: 1970–1978*[1]

For Max Weber explanation is a kind of integration. Human endeavor is complex; when we explain it, we cannot privilege one explanation (or kind of explanation) to the exclusion of all others. Religion, no less than economy or society, is sometimes mover and sometimes mirror of the forces that shape human behavior. William James thinks similarly for psychology. On occasion religion may reflect mental disorder, as Freud claims; but for most of humanity, it anchors the self and is the agent of healing. But if these things are true, can we go farther? Can we claim that in truth the best way to explain religion is to explain it "religiously"?

If Marx can explain religion by offering a purely economic explanation of it, could we not just as well offer a purely religious explanation—as religious people themselves presumably do? Perhaps we best account for religion not as something neurotic, socially determined, or driven by class struggle, but as something normal, natural, even central to the human condition. That, in essence, is the position taken by the next theorist in our sequence, the influential Romanian (and later American) comparativist and historian of world religions: Mircea Eliade.

A genuinely multicultural scholar who spoke and wrote in several European languages, Eliade was born and educated in Romania, studied and taught in Western Europe, and completed his career in the United States. Although he had an array of intellectual interests and was also a talented writer of fiction, he chose to devote his life to the comparative study of religion, a field that, in keeping with European practice, he preferred to call "history of religions." As a young man he studied for a time in India, then carried on further research at home in Romania and elsewhere in Europe. For a time he held a university position in France. In the 1950s he moved to the United States, where, as a professor at the University of Chicago, he played a pivotal role promoting the study of religion in American universities. From the outset, Eliade developed his ideas in direct opposition to reductionist theories, which in his view seriously misunderstood the role of religion in human life. He advocated what he called a "humanistic" approach, and throughout his long career as a scholar he held steadfastly to the thesis that religion must always be explained "on its own terms." His program thus deserves our attention not just on its own merits, but because it goes beyond both Weber and James, issuing a more explicit and direct challenge to reductionist accounts.

Background

Mircea Eliade was born in Bucharest on March 9, 1907, the son of an officer in the Romanian army. As a boy, he loved quiet places, science, stories, and writing. In his autobiography he reports how at the age of eighteen he celebrated with friends the appearance of his one hundredth published article![2] Already at this young age, he was hired by a newspaper to write feature stories, opinion columns, and book reviews. Also among his recollections is a memorable incident from early childhood. He tells how one day at home, on entering an unused room of the house, he was startled by sunlight filtering through green curtains in a way that gave the entire space an unearthly emerald-golden glow. Dazzled and entranced, he felt as if he had been transported into an utterly different, transcendent world. Later, in words identical to those he used in his accounts of religious experience, he chose to describe his memory of this event as a profound "nostalgia"—a longing for a beautiful space of otherworldly perfection.[3] This theme of otherworldly ideals was to run through his education as well. At the University of Bucharest and in Italy, he studied the mystical Platonist thinkers of the Italian Renaissance. While doing this work, he discovered Hindu thought, with its stress on spiritual union with the Supreme Soul beyond the world. Soon he was setting off for India to study with the noted sage and scholar Surendranath Dasgupta. Arriving late in 1928, Eliade enrolled at the University of Calcutta and worked with Dasgupta in his home. On a somewhat less spiritual plane, he also began an affair with his mentor's daughter. An unpleasant separation from his teacher followed, and he moved on to train in yoga with a guru in the Himalayas.

Looking back in later years, Eliade declared that this stay in India had a decisive impact on his life. In particular, he says, he discovered three things: that life can be changed by what he called "sacramental" experience; that *symbols* are the key to any truly spiritual life; and, perhaps most important, that much could be learned from India's countryside, where there was a broad and powerful heritage of folk religion—a deeply felt form of spiritual life that had been in existence since time beyond memory. Simple peasants saw things sacred and eternal in the mystery of agriculture; they viewed the world as "an unbroken cycle of life, death, and rebirth." In addition, this "archaic religion," as he came to call it, was a perspective on life that seemed to be shared across much of the world. It could be found to stretch from the villages of India to the rural corners of his own Romania, from Europe and Scandinavia to East Asia, the Americas, and other locales where primitive peoples tilled the soil as ancestors had taught them for generations. In India, he wrote, he first discovered "cosmic religious feeling."[4]

In 1931, after three years away, Eliade returned to Romania to complete his military service. He continued to write, and in 1933, at the young age of twenty-six, he became a national celebrity by publishing a prize-winning novel, *Maitreyi* (in English, *Bengal Night*), based on his romance with Dasgupta's daughter. This decade was eventful in other respects as well. His doctoral dissertation, *Yoga: An Essay on the Origins of Indian Mystical Theology* (1936), was published in French, the first of several works on the subject. On receiving his degree, Eliade began teaching at Bucharest as an assistant to the influential philosopher Nae Ionesco, who was also a leading figure in a Romanian nationalist organization known as the Legion of the Archangel Michael. Some members of this group, whose violent, terrorist wing was known as the Iron Guard, saw their role in Romania as similar to that of the Nazi party in Germany, and they showed some sympathy for Hitler. Eliade had other friends as well in this circle, though for his part he seems to have preferred intellectual life, editing a journal, writing, and arranging discussions of current issues and movements in literature, philosophy, and art. About any other activities he was always disinclined to speak, describing himself as a largely nonpolitical person.

During the years of World War II, Eliade was assigned by the Romanian government to a diplomatic post in Lisbon, Portugal. When the fighting ended, he chose not to return to Romania and took up residence in Paris, where he was given a chance to teach at the École des Hautes Études. There he completed research on two important books that set the course for most of his later study and thought. *Patterns in Comparative Religion* (1949) explored the role of symbols in religion, while *The Myth of the Eternal Return* (1949) investigated the concepts of history and sacred time, as well as the differences between archaic religion and modern thought. Both books were published in French. As his work progressed, Eliade drew further inspiration from Carl Jung, the notable Swiss psychologist and Freud's former associate, whom he met in 1950 at Ascona, Switzerland, during a regular gathering of European intellectuals known as the Eranos Conference. Until Jung's death in 1960, Eliade visited him regularly, finding in this aged scholar not just a supporter of his ideas on archaic religion but a kind of living exhibit of them as well. Of their discussions, he wrote, "I felt I was listening to a Chinese sage or an East European peasant, still rooted in Earth Mother yet close to Heaven at the same time."[5]

The 1950s brought the last important change in Eliade's scholarly career. After lecturing at the University of Chicago, he accepted a professorship in its Divinity School; in 1962, he became one of its Distinguished Service Professors. His position at Chicago, where he remained for the rest of his life, enabled him to serve as mentor to a full generation of talented younger scholars who were inspired by his example, even when, as was common, they proceeded to disagree with his views. He chose to measure his own impact by citing a simple statistic. When he came to Chicago, there were three significant professorships in the history of religions in the United States; twenty years later, there were thirty, half of which were occupied by his students. On the intellectual journey from Romania to India to Chicago, Eliade traced a career—and life—that saw many opposites converge: East and West, tradition and modernity, mysticism and rationality, contemplation and criticism. He continued his research and writing in retirement until his death of a stroke on April 22, 1986.

Eliade's Starting Point: Two Axioms

Before considering Eliade's theory in its particulars, we ought to notice the foundation on which it stands. Two ideas especially serve as its axioms, or cornerstones; they are fundamental to everything else. The first, which has come into view already, is his strong stand on reductionism. Eliade believes adamantly in the independence, or "autonomy," of religion, which for him cannot be explained as the mere by-product of some other reality. "A religious phenomenon," he insists,

> will only be recognized as such if it is grasped at its own level, that is to say, if it is studied *as* something religious. To try to grasp the essence of such a phenomenon by means of physiology, psychology, sociology, economics, linguistics, art, or any other study is false; it misses the one unique and irreducible element in it—the element of the sacred.[6]

In the language of the natural sciences, we might rephrase this to say that religion should not be construed as a "dependent variable," the thing that always changes in any test or experiment. If anything, it must be taken as the constant or the independent variable; other aspects of life—social, psychological, economic—must be understood to depend upon *it*. As an element in human behavior, religion functions as active agent rather than a passive effect.

The second axiom applies to method. If religion is in fact something independent, something that cannot be explained purely through psychology or sociology, how, then, *should* we explain it? Eliade answers that we must combine two separate angles of vision. Because students of religion mostly study the past, their subject in one sense is simply history. Accordingly, like other historians, they gather evidence, make generalizations, criticize them, and try to find causes or consequences. In this respect, their discipline certainly is the *history* of religions. At the same time, the study of religion cannot be *just* historical either. We understand religion only when we also apply what Eliade calls "phenomenology" (from the Greek *phenomenon*, "an appearance"): the comparative study of things in the form, or appearance, they present to us. Any science is partly phenomenology. We know the color red in the spectrum because its appearance differs from that of blue or violet. By the same measure, one way we know a religious form—a belief or a ritual—is by comparing it with others. Eliade thus emphatically endorses the famous words of the philosopher Goethe on language, which Max Müller had already adapted to religion: "He who knows one knows none." Without comparison there can be no real science.

It is true that historians are suspicious of comparisons, especially when they are used to find similarities. The skeptical mind of the scholar is always inclined to think that no two things are ever quite the same; every time, every place is different from the next. Eliade disagrees: he thinks that certain general forms, certain broad patterns of phenomena, can be taken outside of their original time and place to be compared with others. Times and places may differ, he would say, but concepts are often the same. The mathematician Euclid was an ancient Greek, a man of his time; yet we can study his geometry as if he had taught it just yesterday. The man may be historical, but his theorems are timeless. The same applies to the concepts of religion. The worship of Zeus is in one sense tied to a single time and place in history; it is a practice belonging to ancient Greek religion. But if we notice that in the Greek stories of the gods Zeus has a wife, that he lives on Mt. Olympus, and that he is more powerful than other divine beings, it is not hard to see in him certain typical features of the "sky god" as he appears in many different times and places around the world. Zeus may belong only to the Greeks, but the phenomenon of the sky god does not. Because such gods appear in many cultures, we can learn a great deal by tracing their patterns—by noticing those features they share with one another and those they do not.

With these axioms in hand, we can turn to the main elements of Eliade's program, although here, as with Marx and Freud, we will need help from more than one of his books. Eliade tends in all of his writings to explore the same major ideas and patterns, but in none of them does he offer a sort of single, major exhibit of his theory. In addition, as a writer of fiction, he occasionally prefers the ways of the novelist even in his scholarly works; he offers winding commentaries rather than succinct arguments. That being so, we can best explicate his views by keeping to the main themes and exploring each by way of the one book that explains it best. We will consider in sequence each of the following:

1. Eliade's *concept of religion.* This is most clearly outlined in *The Sacred and the Profane* (1957), perhaps the best short introduction to his theory written for the general reader.
2. His *understanding of symbolism and myth.* This is best observed in *Patterns in Comparative Religion* (1949), the work that sets the agenda for most of his later works.
3. His *explanation of time and history* as seen by archaic and modern cultures. This theme is the focus of *The Myth of the Eternal Return* (1949), perhaps the most original and challenging of all Eliade's books.

Eliade's Concept of Religion: *The Sacred and the Profane*

The Sacred and the Profane (1957) is a short introductory work which makes it clear that in seeking to understand religion, the first move we make is probably the most important one. Eliade explains that the historian must step out of modern civilization, which, after all, accounts for only a small and recent fraction of human life on Earth, and enter the world of "archaic" humanity. Archaic people are those who have lived in prehistoric times or who live today in tribal societies and rural folk cultures, places where work in the world of nature—hunting, fishing, and farming—forms the daily routine. What we find everywhere among such peoples is a life lived on two decidedly different planes: that of the sacred and that of the profane. The profane is the realm of the everyday business—of things ordinary, random, and largely unimportant. The sacred is just the opposite; it is the sphere of the supernatural, of things extraordinary, memorable, and momentous. While the profane is vanishing and fragile, full of shadows, the sacred is eternal, full of substance and reality. The profane is the arena of human affairs, which are changeable and often chaotic; the sacred is the sphere of order and perfection, the home of the ancestors, heroes, and gods. Wherever we look among archaic peoples, religion starts from this fundamental separation.

For readers with a good memory, the first impression made by these words is likely to be one of déjà vu: Eliade here seems to be repeating the very thing we heard from Durkheim. Nor should that come as a surprise. Eliade was educated in the French intellectual tradition, where, largely because of Durkheim, this way of defining religion came to be widely accepted. A closer look, however, will show that in fact there is a difference. As we saw before, when Durkheim speaks of the sacred and profane, he is always thinking of *society* and its needs. The sacred for him is the social (that which matters to the clan); the profane is the opposite (that which matters only to the individual). For Durkheim, sacred symbols and rituals *seem* to speak of the supernatural, but all of that is just the surface appearance of things. The purpose of symbols is simply to make people aware of their social duties by symbolizing the clan as their totem god. When Eliade speaks of the sacred, this clan worship clearly is *not* what he has in mind. In his view, the concern of religion is with the supernatural, plain and simple; it centers on the sacred in and of itself, not on the sacred merely as a way of depicting the social. Though he uses Durkheim's language and agrees that the term covers more than just personal gods, Eliade's view of religion is closer to that of Tylor and Frazer, who conceive of it first and foremost as belief in a realm of supernatural beings.

Instead of Durkheim, Eliade invites us to think of another scholar as his guide: the German theologian and historian of religion Rudolf Otto. In 1916 Otto published on this very subject a famous book entitled *The Idea of the Holy* (in German, *Das Heilige*), where he too uses the concept of the sacred but *not* as applying to society or social needs. He writes instead about a distinct and dramatic kind of individual human experience. At one time or another in their lives, he writes, most people encounter something truly extraordinary and overwhelming. They feel gripped by a reality that is "wholly other" than themselves—something mysterious, awesome, powerful, and beautiful. That is an experience of "the holy," an encounter with the sacred. Using Latin terms, Otto calls it the *mysterium* that is both *tremendum et fascinans*, a mysterious something that both frightens and fascinates at the same time. Another name he gives it is the sense of "the numinous" (from the Latin *numen*, a "spirit" or "divine being"). When people have such an encounter, he says, they invariably feel that they themselves are nothing, no more than "dust and ashes" as the Bible puts it, while the sacred seems just the opposite: something overpoweringly great, substantial, sublime, and truly real. Otto believes this awe-inducing sense of the numinous is unique and irreducible. It is unlike any other encounter with things beautiful or terrible, though they may vaguely resemble it. It is the profound emotional core of all that we call religion.

Eliade's concept of the sacred bears a strong resemblance to Otto's. In an encounter with the sacred, he says, people feel in touch with something otherworldly in character; they feel they have brushed against a reality unlike all others they know, a dimension of existence that is alarmingly powerful, strangely different, surpassingly real, and enduring.

> For primitives as for the man of all pre-modern societies, the *sacred* is equivalent to a *power*, and in the last analysis, to *reality*. The sacred is saturated with *being*. Sacred power means reality and at the same time enduringness and efficacity. . . . Thus it is easy to understand that religious man deeply desires *to be*, to participate in *reality*, to be saturated with power.[7]

Readers of a Judeo-Christian or a Muslim background naturally suppose that Eliade is referring here to an encounter with God, but his idea of the sacred is much wider than that. It could mean the realm of many gods, of the ancestors or immortals, or of what some Hindus call "Brahman," the Supreme Spirit beyond all personality. However the sacred is conceived, the role of religion is to promote contact with it, to bring a person "out of his worldly Universe or historical situation, and project him into a Universe different in quality, an entirely different world, transcendent and holy."[8] Further, the sense of the sacred is not an occasional thing, found only among certain people or at certain times. In the secular societies of modern Western civilization, people display it in surprising, unconscious ways, such as through dreams, nostalgias, and works of the imagination. Yet however disguised, suppressed, or obscured, the intuition of the sacred remains a permanent feature of human thought and activity. No human being is without it. When eyes are open to notice it, it can be seen anywhere.

Among archaic peoples, Eliade continues, this idea of the sacred is more than just common; it is regarded as absolutely crucial to their existence, shaping virtually every aspect of their lives. They refer to it even when they think of something so basic as the time of day or the place where they live. When the ancient Greeks thought of their daily routine, they turned naturally to the myth of Phoebus Apollo, the god who each day drove the chariot of the sun across the sky. When they rose at dawn, they assumed that the light would be with them because Phoebus was just then harnessing his horses; they did their work as he traveled, knowing from him how much of the light had passed and how much still remained; and when, at the end of the journey, he rested his horses, they too could sleep and restore their strength for the next day's dawn. While to us such mythological tales are merely entertaining, to archaic peoples they mean a great deal more; they provide the very framework within which they think, the values they admire, and the models—Eliade sometimes calls them "archetypes"—they choose to follow. Such sacred patterns govern all sorts of archaic activity, from the grand and ceremonial to the ordinary and even trivial. In some ancient cultures, which had myths similar to the story of Phoebus, every chariot had to be built on the model of the chariot driven by the god of the sun. In others, similar rules applied. Among the early peoples in Scandinavia, for example, boats for fishing and transport could not be made in just any way; they had to follow a sacred model, that of the ship on which the dead were placed for their funerals. Such rules existed because archaic peoples insisted on the precept that the ways of the gods are best; divine models show how life should be lived.

In *The Sacred and the Profane*, Eliade draws upon numerous examples from a wide range of cultures to show just how seriously such traditional peoples take the business of following the patterns set by the gods. The authority of the sacred controls all. When they set up their villages, archaic clans do not choose just any convenient place to build. A village must be founded at a place where there has been a "hierophany" (from the Greek *hieros* and *phainein*, "sacred appearance"). Once it has been confirmed that this particular place has, in fact, been visited by the sacred, perhaps in the form of a god or ancestor, the location receives a ritual blessing that establishes it as the center point of a "world" (in Greek a *cosmos*, "place of order"). Around this center, the community can then be built in such a way as to show it has a definite divinely ordered structure; it is a sacred system. Because this constructed society extends outward from a ceremonial center point, it stands clearly separate from the disorder of the desert, forest, or open plain that normally surrounds it. Instead of a chaos, the village, built according to the blueprint given by the gods, is a cosmos; in a world of danger and disorder, it is a scene of security and design.

In many cultures, this sacred center is marked with a pole, pillar, or some other vertical object that plunges into the ground and rises up to the sky to join the three great regions of the universe: Heaven, Earth, and the underworld. That is because this point, which may also be marked by a tree or even a mountain, is regarded not just as the center of the village but as an *axis mundi* (Latin, "centerpost" and "world"); it is the very axle, the central pillar, around which the whole world is seen to turn. If we remember the stories of the Bible, the tale of Jacob's ladder fits into this pattern. The biblical patriarch Jacob, tired from his travels, chooses to sleep outdoors and lays down a stone as a pillow. During the night, he dreams of a ladder extending from the place where he sleeps all the way to Heaven, while angels rise up and come down upon it. When he wakes, he is afraid, for he has here encountered the sacred. "How dreadful is this place!" he says, "This is none but the house of God, and this is the gate of heaven."[9] Significantly, he then sets his nightstone vertical, turning it from pillow to pillar, so that it will mirror the angelic ladder. For Jacob, this special place is the *axis mundi*, the point where one finds the sacred pole that connects Heaven to Earth, the holy place where the separate worlds of the sacred and the profane are joined.

In medieval Christianity and early Islam, in ancient Babylon and modern Java, among the native peoples of the American Northwest and in the villages of Vedic India—almost everywhere we may look—we find this recurring pattern, says Eliade. Life orients itself around a sacred center, a vertical "symbol of ascent" that links Heaven to Earth, the sacred to the profane. Around such sacred poles or atop sacred mountains, great temples have always been built. And from them also the surrounding world is divided into its different sectors, usually the four directions of the compass. Just as the universe itself starts from a center and spreads out to four horizons, so, in Bali and parts of Asia, villages must be built at a crossroads, so that they can reflect the four main sectors of the world. In some tribal cultures, the ceremonial house in the village center is supported by four columns, which represent the four main directions, while the roof symbolizes the vault of Heaven, and an opening in the center allows prayers to rise along the sacred pole up to the gods.

In all of these shapes and ceremonies, which naturally vary in minor ways from one culture to the next, the role of divine patterns, or models, is plainly evident. Eliade explains that the archaic village, temple, or even house must be an *imago mundi*, a mirror image of the entire world as it was first fashioned by divine action. When such places are built, the process of construction is just as important as the structures themselves. Things must not only *be* a reflection of the sacred; they must *come into being* in a sacred manner as well. And that is, again, because human structures and activities must trace out the very process by which the gods brought the world itself into existence. Archaic peoples thus place great significance on "cosmogonic" myths—their stories of how the world first came into being, whether by divine command or by some struggle in which the gods overcome chaos to defeat an evil monster. Whenever something new is begun—when a temple is built, a child is born, or new phase of life is entered—that process must be a repetition of the creation, a reenactment of the original deeds and struggles by which the gods brought the world into being. Eliade offers a fascinating instance of this imitation of the gods from ancient India, where, before building a house, an astronomer shows the masons exactly where they must lay the first stone: "This spot is supposed to lie above the snake that supports the world. The master mason sharpens a stake and drives it into the ground . . . in order to fix the snake's head." There the foundation stone is laid, at the point now regarded as the exact center of the world. The act of piercing the snake is profoundly sacred because it repeats the very work of the gods Indra and Soma as described in the sacred texts. These gods were the first to strike the snake, who "symbolizes chaos, the formless, the unmanifested." By destroying it, they brought into existence an orderly world where once there was only a formless confusion.[10] So, when the home is built, the work must exactly mirror the work of the gods. Elsewhere, Eliade points to other examples of the same process. In many myths, for instance, the dragon fills the role played by the snake in India; he is the great ocean monster, the symbol of watery chaos, who rises from the dark fluid depths and must be subdued by a hero or a god before an ordered system of nature, as well as a human civilization, can come into existence.

In Eliade's view, this intense effort to imitate the gods is part of an even deeper desire that archaic peoples have. They wish not only to mirror the realm of the sacred but somehow actually to *be in it*, to live among the gods. A full discussion of this issue must be deferred until we come to *The Myth of the Eternal Return*; for the moment we can simply note Eliade's comment that all archaic peoples have a sense of a "fall," of a great tragic loss in human history. By this he does not mean just the fall of humanity into sin as told in the biblical story of Adam and Eve. Archaic people know a fall in the sense of a profound separation. They hold that from the first moment human beings become aware of their situation in the world, they are seized by a feeling of absence, a sense of great distance from the place where they ought to be and truly want to be—the realm of the sacred. Their most characteristic attitude, in Eliade's words, is a deep "nostalgia for Paradise," a longing to be brought close to the gods, a desire to return to the realm of the supernatural.

Archaic Religion: Symbol and Myth

It is one thing to sense or seek the realm of the sacred; it is quite another to find and describe it. Although archaic peoples, like any others, strive to depict it, the very nature of the sacred, which is something utterly different from the profane, would seem to make this impossible. How can one describe that which is "wholly other" than anything in normal experience? The answer, Eliade explains, lies in *indirect* expression: the language of the sacred is to be found in symbols and in myth.

Symbols, we know, are rooted in the principle of likeness, or analogy. Certain things have a quality, a shape, a character that strikes us as similar to other things. In the realm of religious experience, certain things are seen to resemble or suggest the sacred; they give a clue to the supernatural. Myths are also symbolic, but in a slightly more complicated way; they are symbols put into a narrative form. A myth is not just one image or sign; it is a sequence of images put into the shape of a story. It tells a tale of the gods, of the ancestors or heroes, and their world of the supernatural. That seems clear enough.

But just what is it that this indirect language actually tells us about the sacred? It is said to be something real, but what kind of reality is it? What are its qualities, its characteristics? These are questions that Eliade spent most of his career addressing in his many studies of symbolism and myth. Our plan allows space to examine only the most important of these works, *Patterns in Comparative Religion*, which was first published in 1949, while Eliade was working in France.

Patterns is a book designed to explain and explore religious symbols on a very wide scale. It examines the nature of symbolic thinking, showing what symbols are, how they work, and why archaic peoples in particular make use of them. It also shows, with the help of many examples, just how systems of symbol and myth tend to follow certain recurring patterns throughout the world. Eliade claims that regardless of the location we choose or epoch in history we select, certain common symbols, myths, and rituals turn up again and again.

In observing how symbols work, the first thing to notice is that just about anything we encounter in the world can serve as a symbol. Most of the things that make up ordinary life are profane; they are just themselves, nothing more. But at the right moment anything profane can be transformed into something more than itself—a marker or sign of that which is sacred. A tool, an animal, a river, a raging fire, a star or stone, a cave, a blossoming flower, or a human being—anything can become a sign of the sacred if people so discover or decide. Once recognized as such, moreover, all symbolic objects acquire a double character: though in one sense they remain what they always were, they also become something new, something other than themselves. At the shrine known as the Kaaba Muslims revere a sacred black stone. Though on one level that object remains to this day just a stone, no faithful follower of Muhammad would ever recognize it as that. From the instant of hierophany—from the moment, that is, when Muslims saw it as something touched by the sacred—this profane object was transformed; it became no longer a mere stone but a holy object, an imposing package, we might say, that carries the sacred within. Eliade calls this infusion of the supernatural into natural objects the "dialectic of the sacred." Though concrete, limited in shape, and perhaps even movable from place to place, a sacred stone can—through another of its qualities, its solidity—convey to the eyes of a believer features of the sacred that are precisely the opposite of its limitations; it can suggest, as the sacred stone of the Kaaba does for Muslims, a God who is immovable and beyond change, the almighty, infinite, and absolute Creator of the world. In common logic, of course, such a combination of opposites strikes us as irrational. If the profane is truly opposed to the sacred, how can it become its precise opposite? How can the natural also be the supernatural? It can do so, says Eliade, because in such matters human reason is not in charge of the transaction. Symbol and myth make their appeal to the imagination, which often thrives on the idea of contradiction. They grip the complete person, the emotions, the will, and even subconscious aspects of the personality. And just as in the personality impulses collide, just as in dreams and fantasies all sorts of illogical things can happen, so in religious experience opposites like the sacred and profane do converge. In an intuitive burst of discovery, the religious imagination sees things otherwise ordinary and profane as more than themselves and turns them into the sacred. The natural becomes supernatural.

It is interesting to notice that, like Max Müller, Eliade finds the main supplier of materials for symbolism and myth to be the world of nature. To the archaic mind, the physical world is a veritable storehouse of prospective images, clues, signs, and analogies. All that we see in the world is part of a grand framework that the gods brought into existence at the beginning of time, and everywhere in it, the sacred waits to shine through. In all of its beauty and ferocity, its complexity, mystery, and variety, the natural world is continually opening windows to disclose the different aspects of the supernatural—what Eliade calls "the modalities of the sacred." This, by the way, is what makes traditional cultures so rich in imaginative figures and symbols and their world so wonderfully alive with folklore and legend, with creation accounts, flood stories, and epic tales of heroes, monsters, and gods. As collections of symbols put in narrative form, all of these can be broadly associated with myth. They are tales of the sacred, stories that bring the supernatural world of divine life closer to the natural world of humanity.

Over the centuries, of course, human beings have generated countless new myths, symbols, and variations of both. No scholar could hope to find them all. Nor is it necessary to try. Eliade thinks a great deal can be learned just from the major symbolic patterns and systems, which are the only ones he chooses to trace out in detail. It will repay our efforts to notice a few of them.

Sky Symbolism: Sky Gods and Others

One of the most common elements of archaic cultures is belief in sky gods, divinities whose character is suggested by the very nature of the wide heaven above the Earth. The sky conveys a sense of transcendence, of a span raised high above us, something infinite, sovereign, and eternal—full of authority and reality. Fittingly, the sky god is often imagined in just this fashion. The god Iho among the Maoris is "raised up"; Olorun among the African Yoruba tribes is "owner of the sky"; the great god Ahura-Mazda in early Iran is the giver of all laws and enforcer of moral order in the world. Because the heavens are high, these gods are, in fact, often portrayed as almost too elevated and distant, too far away to care about mere human beings. Australian myths tell the story of the withdrawal of the sky god, while in other primitive societies as well, the god of the sky seems so far beyond human reach that other religious conceptions must come in to replace him. Often these new conceptions are gods of the rain and storm, deities who are more concrete and personal, more directly involved in human life because they specialize in one task. Here the early Hindu god Rudra is an example. Virile and violent, surging with life, he was for the villagers of ancient India the bringer of rain as well as the source of sexual energy. He and others like him had female partners or entered sacred marriages; they stood at the center of lavish ceremonies, which often included bloody sacrifices and orgies. Their imagery is exceedingly powerful and their influence extremely widespread. In fact, says Eliade, in words that remind us of Frazer, "this structure made up of the rainy sky, bull, and Great Goddess was one of the elements that united all the protohistoric religions of Europe."[11]

It is not hard to guess why such a change from sky to storm gods may have taken place. Eliade explains that the appeal of rain and fertility gods was closely linked to one of the most important events in all of early civilization—the development of agriculture. Plowing the soil, planting seeds, and harvesting crops—all of these activities brought a new pattern of life, and with it an occasion for new hierophanies and symbols of different kinds. In an agrarian world, the great "fecundators," the gods of storm and sex, conveyed the sacred with greater power and more vivid appearance than the distant god of the sky.

"Son" gods, like Dionysos in Greece and Osiris in Egypt, also made their appearance in the age of agriculture. Like storm gods, they were dynamic, but differently so. Their role was rather to suffer and die. The so-called mystery religions, which were enormously popular in the ancient Mediterranean world, centered especially on these deities, which in name were vegetation gods but figured more prominently as divine saviors. In these gods especially, Eliade discerns an important psychological aspect of religious symbols. They not only tell us about the world and the sacred but also show "the continuity between the structures of human existence and cosmic structures."[12] Their myths do not just reflect the cycles of life and death in nature; they reenact as well the personal struggle that takes place in the life of each human individual: the drama of birth, life, and death as well as the hope of rebirth or redemption. Eliade tells us that no symbol brings divine life so near to human as the figure of the savior-god, the divinity who "even shared mankind's sufferings, died and rose from the dead to redeem them." Precisely because of his marked "humanity," this type of god plays a crucial role in the history of religion.[13]

Sun and Moon

Eliade notes that sun worship, which some earlier theorists (especially Max Müller) thought the center of all mythology, is in fact very rare.[14] Much more prominent and widespread are myths and symbols associated with the ever-changing moon. The moon moves through cycles; it grows, becomes full, then for a time completely disappears. Its phases connect readily to other events, such as the ebb and flow of the ocean tides, the coming and going of the rains, and through the latter, to the growth of plants and the fertility of the Earth. Since it always returns to its beginnings, the moon furnishes the archetypal image of ceaseless renewal. Its dominant theme is "one of *rhythm* carried out by a succession of contraries, of 'becoming' through a succession of opposing modalities. It is a becoming . . . that cannot take place without drama."[15]

Lunar symbolism also shows a remarkable power of expansion; it keeps reaching out to make new connections. Besides waters and vegetation, the moon is often linked to death, the last phase of life; to the snake, which regenerates itself by shedding its skin; and to woman, whose power to renew life by giving birth arises from the "lunar" phases of the menstrual cycle. In fact, "the intuition of the moon as the measure of rhythms, as the source of energy, of life, and of rebirth, has woven a sort of web between the various levels of the universe, producing parallels, similarities, and unities among vastly differing kinds of phenomena."[16] Because of a long linkage that takes the form moon–rain–fertility–woman–serpent–death–regeneration, a person can tap into the lunar network at any one of its points. A simple rain ritual, for instance, or a serpent charm worn on the wrist, can engage this entire system of cosmic associations, all of which play upon the fundamental theme of opposites that alternate and converge.

Like the "son" gods, the moon has both a cosmic and a personal dimension. On the one level, it is treasured "in what it reveals of the sacred, that is, in the power centred in it, in the inexhaustible life and reality that it manifests."[17] On the other, it reminds us psychologically of the double nature of our human condition: rooted in the realm of the profane, the place of shadows and death, we nonetheless long for the sacred, the sphere of things real and undying. In earlier ages, amid disease and death, the hopes of archaic peoples for their own personal renewal and immortality "gained confirmation from the fact of there being always a new moon."[18] The moon is in one sense a display of dualisms: light and dark, full and empty, old and new, birth and death, male and female. Yet by its alternations and changes, it also suggests the overcoming of all dualisms. Eliade here points to myths of androgyny, which suggest that the first human beings, who lived close to the gods, were neither male nor female but a unity of both sexes. This theme, moreover, is just one in a whole family of myths of reintegration. Common throughout the human race, these stories express a powerful hope for the end of all opposites, the dissolution of all separations, the return to the original unity of the sacred.

Water and Stones

In addition to the great symbols of the sky and moon, archaic cultures abound as well in lesser signs and images, which often link up with the more dominant ones. Water, for example, everywhere expresses the shapeless, unformed nature of things before they were ordered into a world by the gods. It starts the process of renewal. Neither the world nor the human self can be reborn until each has first returned to chaos by plunging into the watery depths, thence to emerge as a new creation. In ritual initiations and in rites of purification, water is the agent that cleanses and erases all, taking us back to the unformed, the primeval, the "clean slate," where a new beginning can be made.

The symbolism of stones, by contrast, suggests the opposite. Unlike water, the substance of stones is hard, rugged, and unchanging. To the primitive person, "rock shows . . . something that transcends the precariousness of his humanity; an absolute mode of being. Its strength, its motionlessness, its size . . . indicate the presence of something that fascinates, terrifies, attracts, and threatens, all at once."[19] If we put these words into the Latin *fascinans* and *tremendum*, we actually have Rudolf Otto's very words for the sacred. A normal stone would hardly attract our notice; a sacred stone generates awe and fear.

Other Symbols: Earth and Fertility, Vegetation and Agriculture

The symbolisms of life, growth, and fertility have played a large role in the religion of archaic peoples, both before and after the dawn of agriculture. Of the many patterns Eliade considers in this category, we can notice just a few.

A very early image is that of the Earth as sacred mother, the source of all living things. The sacred marriage of the divine sky father and Earth mother is found in many mythologies, from the South Pacific to Africa, the Mediterranean, and the Americas. The sky fertilizes the Earth with rain, and the Earth produces grains and grass. With the coming of agriculture and cultivation of plants and grains, the earlier symbol of the Earth as mother is often overlaid by that of the great goddess—again, a more dynamic, emotional divinity who, like the "son" gods considered above, personally lives out the fate of the crops in her life cycle of birth, sexual encounter, fertility, and death.

More widespread than that of either the Earth mother or the goddess, however, is the symbolism of trees. Sacred trees can be found "in the history of every religion, in popular tradition the world over, in primitive metaphysics and mysticism, to say nothing of iconography and popular art."[20] Some, like the cosmic tree Yggdrasil in Norse mythology, combine the symbolism of the *axis mundi*, the world's centerpost, with a second theme: the tree as the sacred source of life. As great vertical objects that are alive, trees represent "the very life of the entire world as it endlessly renews itself." Further, since trees live a long time, the life within them is considered inexhaustible; they become a focus of human hopes for immortality. Frazer, we should remember, found the soul, the source of life, to be closely associated with both the mistletoe and tree worship in northern Europe. And in the many ancient myths of a tree of life, we read of a hero who must face a test, as did Adam and Eve in Eden. By defeating a dragon or resisting temptation, the great man wins the prize of immortality. Trees tell us that the sacred is the fount of all life, the one true reality, and, to those who can pass the test, the giver of immortality.

Eliade reminds us that to appreciate vegetation myths we must recall how primitive people lived in ongoing fear that at some point the powers of the natural world would weaken and begin to run out. For the archaic mind, all things—whether plant, animal, or human—are energized through "the same closed circuit of the substance of life," which passes from one level or creature to another.[21] When planted, the grains that die at harvest give their life to the next year's crop. When harvested, ground into flour, and baked, they transfer their life to humanity, for they then become the force of life in the bread that is eaten at meals. This tight connection shows why in so many legends we read of a murdered human being who is changed into a tree, or of plants that spring directly from the blood of a slain god or hero. When the power of life leaves one living thing, it must move to another; when it runs down, it must be recharged. Always there is an ebb and flow, a fading and renewal. For archaic peoples, "the *real* is not only what *is* indefinitely the same, but also what *becomes* in organic but cyclic forms."[22] In that connection rites of initiation, purification, and redemption, by their gestures and procedures, recreate the first of all renewals—the creation of the world itself as it arises out of chaos by the powerful commands or mighty struggles of the gods.

The Structure and Character of Symbols

From fertility and vegetation Eliade turns next to the symbolisms of space and of time. The first of these we have already noted earlier, and the second will come our way shortly, so we can pass over them here to observe something else. Although most of the discussion in *Patterns* is taken up with individual symbols and myths from around the world, Eliade takes time along the way to consider two broad features of all symbolic thinking. One is the structural, or system-like, character of most symbolism and mythology; the other is the matter of ranking symbols—placing some above others in value.

Throughout his discussion, Eliade explains that symbols and myths rarely exist in isolation. It is their nature always to be part of larger symbol systems; they "connect up" with other images, or other myths, to form a pattern. The thought world of archaic peoples is thus filled with associations, linkages, and repetitions that keep extending the sense of the sacred, if possible, to almost every dimension of life—from the noblest occasions and ceremonies to the simplest daily task. A pair of examples may help to illustrate this process. In a first appearance of the sacred—an original hierophany—a religious person finds, let us say, a vision of the one true God in the sun, as did the Egyptian Pharaoh Akhenaten. (Freud, we may recall, thought Akhenaten was the religious genius who inspired Jewish monotheism.) Soon the round solar disk is declared the symbol of the divine. It is carved into walls, worn as jewelry, and required on flags at palace ceremonies. These gestures naturally expand the occasions for thinking about the sun; they "sacralize" places, people, and events quite beyond the occasion or place of the first sacred encounter. In time, still more connections may be made. The sun is personified, and the stories of the sun and its adventures come to expression in myth. Akhenaten or his followers may claim that because it "defeats" the night, the sun is the lord of battle; or they may see in each morning's sunrise a sign of personal renewal and immortality. Because of its warmth, the sun can be tied to the return of vegetation each spring; it can be connected with plants, like the sunflower, or substances, like gold, that resemble its shape or possess its color. With each of these new connections, the sacred reaches out to capture a new aspect of life.

Another vivid example of this systematic extension is the cycle of lunar myths and symbols noted earlier. From its center in the phases of the moon, this symbolic system continually spreads out its net to convey a sense of the sacred to many other dimensions of life: the waters and rains, fertility and woman, serpents and human redemption, even shells and spirals and bolts of lightning. There may be no formal rule of logic that compels people to connect lunar phases with spiral shells; yet intuitively and imaginatively, there is a certain "logic of symbols" that makes the connections. Symbols always lead naturally to other symbols and to myths in such a way as to create a framework, a world that is a complete, connected system, rather than a chaotic jumble.

In addition to noticing their systemic character, a second general issue Eliade alludes to is that of comparing symbols and myths. Are some symbols perhaps better in character than others? Can we rank myths on a scale of value? And if so, what standard would we use? In *Patterns*, he does not address these questions as directly as one would like, but it is plain that he does in fact feel some images and myths to be superior to others. The main standard he applies seems to be that of their scale or size. The "bigger" the symbol, the more complete and universal it is, the better it conveys the true nature of the sacred. Here again, a specific example may help. If the people of a primitive village encounter something supernatural in a nearby tree, that can be called a hierophany; the tree manifests the sacred. If, in the course of time, however, the council of elders should rethink this symbolism and decide that this sacred tree is in fact the cosmic tree, the center of the world, that too is a hierophany, but of a higher order. It is a better representation of the sacred because it is wider in extent, grander in scale than the original sacred tree. By means of the elders' decision, then, the first sighting of the sacred in the local tree is "revalorized" (as Eliade likes to say) into a far more impressive image of the sacred than it originally was. The new symbolism of the world tree surpasses the old symbol of the simple village hierophany.

Again, one type of hierophany is a *theo*phany (from the Greek *theos*, "deity"): the appearance of a god. A theophany can occur in something as simple as a stone. At the same time, drawing on his own tradition of Romanian Orthodoxy, Eliade points out that Christianity finds God to be incarnate in the man Jesus of Nazareth. This human theophany is superior to the stone theophany, not—as missionaries once would have said—because Christianity is true and other religions false, but because a human person, possessing intelligence and emotions, is by nature a richer, fuller being than an animal or stone. Thus, as a symbol, the figure of Christ, the God-man, captures more of the fullness and reality of the sacred. In addition, Christians make universal claims about the incarnation; they say that never has there been or will there be a theophany as final or as world-embracing. Christ is to other theophanies as the great cosmic tree is to the village tree—a wider, grander, and consequently better image of the divine. As the human form of the all-powerful Creator, he better conveys the full extent of the sacred than, say, the Greek god Pan, who is pictured only as god of the pastures and forests.

These concepts of replacement and "revalorization" of symbols play an important role in Eliade's theory. They show that he is interested in examining not just the timeless forms of religion but also their historical changes. In his view, human beings throughout time have been continually at work restating their perceptions of the sacred in original ways, fashioning new myths, discovering fresh symbols, and rearranging them into wider or different systems. Accordingly, the mission of the "history" of religions is first to discover symbols, myths, rituals, and their systems, then to trace them through the human past as they have been changed and interchanged from one age or place to the next. After that—and just as importantly—the more phenomenological side enters in. The historian seeks to compare and contrast these materials to determine their different levels and types of significance as carriers of the sacred.

And he observes how in different ages and places, symbols, myths, and rituals are perpetually subject to change. Through history, they are constantly being created, revised, discarded, and created again. Were he an evolutionary thinker, we might find Eliade claiming that all these changes are improvements, that each new myth or symbol is progressively better than the last. But that is not really his view; he believes the natural logic of symbols and myths pushes them always to become more universal, to shed the particulars of a single time and place and approximate ever more closely to a universal archetype, as when a local goddess acquires more and more of the features of the archetypal great goddess of fertility. But the reverse happens also; symbols can decay and degenerate. History presents occasions when cultures move counter to the logic of the sacred—say, by losing or corrupting a great world creation myth or by replacing more universal symbols with *less* universal ones, as when the smaller storm god replaces the earlier sovereign sky god. When that happens, certain new dimensions of the sacred may be discovered, but others are lost. Then again, while that is happening in one culture, in another the figure of the sky god might reappear. The natural tendency of symbols and myths is to grow, to spread out their significance in new associations; but in different times and places there are also variations that "flow simply from differences in the mythological creativity of the various societies, or even from a chance of history."[23]

Throughout the ages, then, archaic and other peoples have enjoyed a certain freedom of imagination in selecting sacred symbols and myths. Eliade notes that there seems scarcely a single natural object that has not at one time or another become a symbol or figured in a myth. And yet, for all of this creativity, religious imagery has never been purely random or chaotic. The point of *Patterns* is to show just the opposite: that regardless of place, time, or culture, archaic peoples have shown a remarkable constancy in returning to the same types of symbol, the same themes in their myths, and the same universalizing logic in both. The closer we look at the historical specifies of religion, the more clearly we see its ever-recurring, ever-expanding patterns.

History and Sacred Time

For the scholar inquiring about the symbolism, the historical record is of considerable value. It shows us how people have conceived the sacred in different places and times. Archaic believers themselves, however, assess their situation in history to be less than fortunate. For them, the events of ordinary profane life, the daily rounds of labor and struggle, are things they desperately wish to escape. They would rather be *out* of history and in the perfect realm of the sacred. Eliade's term for this desire, as we noted earlier, is the "nostalgia for Paradise." It is a concept central to his theory. Though he refers to it in many places, he explains it best in the third of the three texts we have taken as our guides: *The Myth of the Eternal Return: Or, Cosmos and History*, first published along with *Patterns* in 1949.

Eliade considered this book one of his most significant, and even his critics have tended to agree. In it, he sets out a strong thesis: the one theme that dominates the thought of all archaic peoples is the drive to abolish history—all of history—and return to that point beyond time when the world began. The desire to go back to beginnings, he argues, is the deepest longing, the most insistent and heartfelt ache in the soul of all archaic peoples. The distinctive mark of archaic ritual and myth is the wish "to live in the world as it came from the Creator's hands, fresh, pure, and strong."[24] That is why myths of creation play such a central role in so many archaic societies. It is also why so many rituals are associated with acts of creation. We have not said much about rituals so far, but Eliade does find them important, especially in association with creation accounts. Usually they involve a reenactment of what the gods did *in illo tempore* (Latin for "in that time")—at the moment when the world came into being. Every New Year's festival, every myth of rebirth or reintegration, every rite of initiation is a return to beginnings, an opportunity to start the world over again. When in archaic festivals of the New Year a scapegoat is sent out and purifications are done to rid the community of demons, diseases, and sins, this event is not just a rite of transition from one year to the next but "also the abolition of the past year and of past time." It is an attempt "to restore—if only momentarily—mythical and primordial time, 'pure' time, the time of the 'instant' of the Creation."[25] In India, coronations follow patterns set at the beginning of the world. And in sacrifices as well, "there is an implicit abolition of profane time, of duration, of 'history.'"[26]

Eliade thinks it important to notice the motives that inspire this myth of return. He explains that archaic peoples, like all others, are deeply affected not only by the mysteries of suffering and death but also by concerns about living without any purpose or meaning. They long for significance, permanence, beauty, and perfection as well as escape from their sorrows. Life's minor irritations and inconveniences are not the problem; they can be borne by anyone. But the idea that the human adventure as a whole might be merely a pointless exercise, an empty spectacle with death as its end—that is a prospect no archaic people can endure. Eliade calls this experience "the terror of history." It explains why people have been drawn so powerfully to myth, especially the myth of eternal return. Because ordinary life is not significant, because real meaning cannot be found *within* history, archaic peoples choose to take their stand *outside* of it. In the face of life's drab, empty routine and daily irritations, they seek to overcome all in a defiant gesture of denial; through symbol and myth, they reach back to the world's primeval perfection, to a moment when life starts over from its origin, full of promise and hope. "The primitive, by conferring a cyclic direction upon time, annuls its irreversibility. Everything begins over again at its commencement every instant."[27]

This "terror of history" has been felt not only by archaic peoples but also by the great civilizations of the ancient world, where a cyclical view of time was predominant. In India, for example, the oldest teachings held that human beings were destined to live without hope in a world that passed through immense cycles of decay and decline until all was finally destroyed and again remade. The reaction to this deeply pessimistic outlook eventually took the form of the classic Eastern version of eternal return—the doctrine of rebirth, or reincarnation. We find it chiefly in the famous Hindu Upanishads, as well as in the teachings of Gautama the Buddha and Mahavira, the founder of Jainism. Seeing humanity as hopelessly enslaved by these endless cycles of nature, these teachers pointed to a path of purely spiritual release from history's triviality and terrors. They announced that the soul, or true self, could free itself from the body, which is its main tie to history, by struggling patiently through a long series of rebirths until a purely spiritual escape was ultimately achieved. In different ways, each offered meaning through the doctrine of *moksha*, the soul's final release from nature and history. Elsewhere, the doctrine of return appeared in other forms. Among certain Greeks and the followers of the great prophet Zoroaster in ancient Persia, it was expressed in the belief that human history consists only of a single cycle, which has come out of eternity and will one day end forever in fire or some other great catastrophe. Against this backdrop of finality, Zoroaster's followers found liberation by way of the last judgment and the reward of Heaven that came to all who had remained faithful to Ahura-Mazda, the great god of goodness and light. The pattern of these religions is thus quite clear. Though culturally more advanced than archaic peoples, the great civilizations of the Mediterranean and Near East, no less than those of India and Southeast Asia, faced the very same problem of history and labored just as strenuously to chart a path of escape.

The Revolt Against Archaic Religion: Judaism and Christianity

Almost everywhere in archaic and civilized ancient cultures, then, the problem of history was central, and the solution, the escape, was found in some form of the myth of eternal return. The pattern is so widespread, says Eliade, that only in one place—among the Hebrews of ancient Palestine—can something different be found. It is in ancient Israel that, apparently for the first time on the world scene, a new kind of religious outlook emerges. While not entirely rejecting the idea of a mythical return to beginnings, Judaism proclaims that the sacred can be found *in* history as well as outside of it. With this insight, the whole equation of archaic religion is altered. In Judaism, and later in Christianity, which derives from it, the pointless cycles of nature are pushed into the background, while human events come to center stage, where they take shape along the line of a meaningful story—a history—with the sacred, in the form of the God of Israel, a participant in its scenes. In place of endless, purposeless world cycles, Judaism asserts a meaningful sequence of sacred historical events. This striking innovation was fashioned chiefly by the great prophets of Israel—Amos, Isaiah, Jeremiah, and others. When disasters fell on their people, they presented these troubles not as miseries to be escaped but as punishments to be endured—*in* history—because they came from the very hand of God. In their oracles and speeches, says Eliade, the prophets affirmed the idea

> that historical events have a value in themselves, insofar as they are determined by the will of God. This God of the Jewish people is no longer an Oriental divinity, creator of archetypal gestures, but a personality who ceaselessly intervenes in history, who reveals his will through events (invasions, sieges, battles, and so on). Historical facts thus become "situations" of man in respect to God, and as such they acquire a religious value that nothing had previously been able to confer upon them.[28]

That the encounter of a people with this personal God of history is something quite new can be seen also from the famous biblical story of the patriarch Abraham, who prepares to kill his son as an offering to God. If Judaism were an archaic religion, says Eliade, this fearsome act would be an instance of human sacrifice, a killing of the firstborn to renew the sacred power of life in the gods. Within Judaism, however, the event has a quite different character: Abraham's encounter is a very personal transaction in history with a God who asks him for his son simply as a sign of his faith. This God does not need sacrifices to renew his divine powers (and indeed he does spare Isaac, the son), but what he does require from his people is a heart loyal enough to make that ultimate sacrifice if asked. Christianity inherits this same perspective. The sequence of events that make up the life and death of Jesus forms a singular and historic instance, a decisive moment that, occurring once only, serves as the basis for a personal relationship of forgiveness and trust between Christian believers and their God. In celebrating the life, crucifixion, and resurrection of Christ, the Christian faithful do not engage in a ritual of seasonal rebirth; they do not act out an eternal return to beginnings. They remember a specific and final historical event, one that requires from them an equally singular and final decision of personal faith.

Of course, this new historical religion did not win an instant victory over the older, archaic attitudes, which are deeply rooted in human psychology. The tremendous attraction that fertility religions like the cult of Baal had for ordinary people in ancient Israel is proof of this in the case of Judaism. In Christian cultures also, archaic seasonal ceremonies of rebirth survive and blend in with the more purely historical elements. And both traditions have been routinely susceptible to messianic movements. These passionate groups, which expect a return of God's chosen one, a catastrophe at the world's end, and the coming of a perfect world, bear again the marks of the archaic mind; they tolerate history, but only because they believe "that, one day or another, it will cease."[29] In consequence, both sides of the Judeo-Christian tradition have unfolded amid some considerable tension and compromise. They have found the sacred both within history and outside of it.

The Revolt Against All Religion: Modern Historicism

The Judeo-Christian turn to historical religion is for Eliade an event of momentous importance. It marks the beginning of a shift away from archaic attitudes, a first revolt against the myth of eternal return. Yet it is not the only seismic shift in the world's religions. A second revolt—of equal or even greater proportion—has just recently begun to take shape in the very centers of Western civilization, notably modern Europe and America. Over the past few centuries, Eliade explains, we have once again seen something quite new in human history: the wide acceptance of philosophies that deny the existence and value of the sacred altogether. Advocates of these views claim that it makes no difference where we locate the sacred, whether in history or beyond it, for the simple reason that human beings do not need it. The truth, they say, is that there are no gods, there are no "sacred archetypes" that can show us how to live or what ultimate purpose to live for. We must learn to live without the sacred altogether. There is no such thing.

We can put aside for a moment the question of whether this modern, wholly unsacred view of the world is good or bad. Eliade's first concern is to show where it came from. He thinks, interestingly, that the door to this second revolution was in fact opened by the very same shift of ideas that created the first: the coming of Judeo-Christian historical religion. This seems puzzling at first sight, but for Eliade the sequence is clear. It comes into focus the moment we place everything within the original context of archaic religion and the myth of eternal return. We must remember that to the first archaic peoples, the world of nature was of pivotal importance. It was able at any instant to come alive with the sacred. Symbolism clothed it in the supernatural; legend and myth sang of the gods behind the storm and rain. Clues and hints of the sacred could be found in a tree, a stone, or the path of a bird in flight. Nature was the garment of the divine. This was not to be the case, however, in Judaism and Christianity. The prophets of Israel and writers of the New Testament pushed nature into the background and brought history up to the front of the stage. The seasons, storms, and trees were "desacralized," for the God of Israel and of Christian faith chose to reveal himself chiefly in the twists and turns of dramatic *human* events: in the Hebrews' escape from Egypt, in the battle of Jericho, or in the birth, death, and resurrection of Jesus Christ. To be sure, nature still had a part to play, but only in a supporting role. Israel's prophets still saw the great wind that parted the Red Sea as a sign of the sacred, but—in the light of their historical perspective—they read it quite differently. For them it disclosed the divine not because it was a wondrous natural event—as archaic peoples would have said—but because it advanced God's aims for the people he had chosen; it delivered them from the hands of their enemies.

As Eliade sees it, this change of religious sensibility is a significant one, not only on its own terms, but because of the momentous consequences that follow from it. For gradually, and almost imperceptibly, this original move from religions of nature to religions of history laid the groundwork in the present era for a further shift—from the religions of history to philosophies of history and society that discard religion altogether. Through the long passage of centuries, and especially in Western civilization, the removal of the divine from nature has slowly opened the way for entire societies to adopt a style of thought that only a few isolated individuals ever seriously considered until the coming of the modern era. That style is secularity: the removal of *all* reference to the sacred from human thought and action. Eliade states that in explaining the logic behind their move entirely away from religion, secular thinkers can argue as follows: If biblical religions like Judaism and Christianity made one great change in the world's religious consciousness, does that not license us to make another if we should so wish? If the prophets felt they had a right to take the sacred out of nature and find it only in history, why can we not follow their own example and dismiss it from nature and history both? There is, in short, nothing indispensable about the idea of the sacred. For Eliade, this is the form of reasoning at work in nearly all of the secular, nonreligious philosophies that have arisen with such powerful appeal during the past three centuries of the modern era. We might call them the unwelcome stepchildren of Judaism and Christianity.

Eliade describes these secular creeds as forms of "historicism," a type of thought that recognizes only things ordinary and profane while denying any reference at all to things supernatural and sacred. Historicists hold that if we want significance, if we want some sense of a larger purpose in life, we obviously cannot find it in the archaic way—by escaping history through some doctrine of eternal return. But neither can we find it in the Judeo-Christian way—by claiming that there is in history some great plan or purpose of God. We can find it only in ourselves.

Examples of this historicist thinking can be found in any number of modern systems and thinkers, among them several we have already met in our chapters. Eliade notes the developmentalism of the German philosopher Hegel, the communism of Karl Marx, and the perspectives of twentieth-century fascism and existentialism. Modern capitalism might be included as well. What all of these systems share is the fundamental belief that if human beings want meaning and significance in their lives, they must create it entirely on their own—in the profane realm of history and without assistance from ideas about the sacred. This can be done in different ways, of course. Fascists and Marxists believe that even without gods or the sacred, history is still "going somewhere." It will end in the triumph of a nation or race or in the victory of the proletariat. Existentialists tend to think that history as a whole has no central purpose; it is "going nowhere," so only the private lives and choices of individuals matter. The capitalist entrepreneur may make a similar choice by finding purpose only in money and other material goods. For such people, only personal freedom or achievement matters, and they can even argue that they are better off than archaic peoples, who do not have freedom because their lives must always conform to patterns provided by the gods.

In the contemporary world, these nonreligious philosophies have been extremely attractive, winning followers not only in Western civilization but around the world. Eliade, however, has serious doubts about all of them. Is it really the case, he asks, that they offer a greater degree of meaning and purpose than archaic religion or Judeo-Christian faith? Is the modern fascist, who must obey every command of his leader, really more free than the archaic woman, performing her household ritual of renewal? Does the life of the communist, bound absolutely to the cause of the party, really have more significance than that of the archaic tribesman or medieval monk? Is the existentialist philosopher, whose prized individual freedom could be destroyed in a moment if a brutal army were to march through his streets, truly more content and fulfilled than the archaic villager who celebrates the seasonal feast of fertility, hoping thereby to bring life to his crops each spring?

The Return of Archaic Religion

Despite his misgivings, Eliade does not carry on an extended argument with these modern philosophies. He merely voices his doubts as to whether they can ever be truly satisfying. And he tries, by contrast, to show how in hidden ways archaic thinking has persisted up to the present day. He notes that creative artists like T. S. Eliot and James Joyce display in their works a remarkable attachment to forms of the myth of eternal return. Athletic events, the great public spectacles of our time, show similar affinities; they generate intense emotions and center on a single "concentrated" game time, very much like the sacred moments of primitive ritual. The dramas of theater, television, and film play out life in a compressed interval of "sacred" time that is wholly different from normal hours and days. The images and stories of popular culture resemble archaic myths, creating character archetypes on which ordinary people pattern their lives: "the political or the military hero, the hapless lover; or the cynic, the nihilist, the melancholy poet." These and others play for us the same roles filled for archaic people by the heroes and gods of myth. Even the modern habit of reading can be seen as a replacement for the oral traditions remembered and recited by primitive peoples; it mirrors the archaic desire to create an "escape time," free from the pressures of daily life.

Finally, and quite apart from its disguised modern versions, Eliade observes that even in its original form, the archaic nostalgia for paradise has never fully disappeared. Christianity, we have seen, is committed to finding the sacred only in history. Yet among the Christian peasants of Romania and other central European lands, one finds a remarkable blend in which archaic habits of mind virtually sweep aside the residue of history in the church's creeds. In this "cosmic Christianity," it is accepted that Jesus of Nazareth was a man in history, but that fact fades from view once it is taken up into the peasants' image of Christ as the great Lord of nature, the eternal divinity who in sacred folklore continues to visit his people on the Earth, just as the high gods do in the myths of other archaic cultures. Significantly, the liturgies and ceremonies of this cosmic Christianity tend to celebrate not the historical Jesus but the eternal Christ, the cosmic ruler who renews the powers of nature and returns humanity to the time of beginnings. To its followers, this archaic faith offers a depth of meaning that the historical perspective inherited from Judaism can never provide.

It is worth noticing that this cosmic Christianity with which Eliade concludes *The Eternal Return* bears a marked resemblance to the peasant religion he found so strongly appealing when he first encountered it in the villages of India as a young man. He is always careful not to make any open endorsements, but it would seem that in the end his own strong sympathies lie nearest to this sort of cosmic folk religion and the satisfactions offered by the archaic frame of mind.

Analysis

Eliade pursues a program of inquiry that dissents, more sharply than those of either Weber or James, from the functionalist reductionism of Freud, Durkheim, and Marx. At the same time, his interest in comparisons on a global scale and his commitment to explaining religion "on its own terms" recall the intellectualist perspective of the Victorian anthropologists Tylor and Frazer. Three of the elements in this theoretical agenda call for more specific comment.

1. Critique of Reductionism

From the outset Eliade announces his strong dissent from the reductionist approaches favored in his day and still attractive in ours. In opposition to Freud, Durkheim, and Marx, he strongly asserts the independence of religious ideas and activities. He accepts that psychology, society, economics, and other forces affect religion, but more even than Weber or James he refuses to see such influence as largely determinative, still less exclusively so. Religion, he insists, can be understood only if we try to see it from the standpoint of the believer. Like Roman law, which we can grasp only through Roman values, or Egyptian architecture, which we must see through Egyptian eyes, religious behaviors, ideas, and institutions must be seen in the light of the religious perspective, the view of the sacred that inspires them. In the case of archaic peoples especially, it is not profane life—social, economic, or otherwise—that controls the sacred; it is the sacred that controls and shapes every aspect of the profane.

2. Global Comparativism

Another main feature of Eliade's theory is its broad and ambitious design. He is of course not the only theorist to try to assemble data from a wide variety of sources, places, and times, but he is certainly more ambitious in this regard than most. He takes very seriously his double mission to be both a serious historian and a precise phenomenologist, and he strives for a genuinely comprehensive understanding of religion in all its forms. The research that lies behind his analyses is far-reaching in extent. The three central texts on which we have focused here represent just a part of his labors, which include not only his several books on Indian yoga but studies as well of Australian religions, European folk traditions, and Asian shamans, or prophet-mystics. Other works focus on alchemy, initiation rituals, and witchcraft; on dreams, myths, and the occult; on symbolism in the arts; on methods of studying religion; and on a variety of related other topics. Even in retirement, Eliade continued to work on a full-scale *History of Religious Ideas*, which was almost complete at his death. These wide-ranging global interests have won Eliade endorsements, especially among some of his American followers. Skeptical critics, on the other hand, wonder whether this agenda is rather *too* global, and perhaps therefore superficial. In tones that hardly suggest a compliment, some see his approach as "Frazerian," as a retreat to the doubtful aims and methods of *The Golden Bough*.[30]

3. Contemporary Philosophical Engagement

Third and last, as we saw in his comments on what he calls modern "historicist" philosophies, Eliade does not regard himself as a detached scholar, solely interested in the obscure customs of people from distant ages. Though his professional life is taken up with scholarship, ancient texts, and archaic ideas, he sees himself as very much a man engaged with the ideas and culture of his own time, a theorist who draws from his knowledge of the past to address important philosophical issues that confront society in the present. He is quite frank, for example, in arguing that scholars and intellectuals of the modern era have greatly underestimated the psychological merits of archaic thinking, which has sustained human endeavors for so much of the history of civilization. While, again, some greatly appreciate this "philosophical" side of Eliade, there are others who say it damages any claim he may have to scientific objectivity. There is undoubtedly more to be said on this matter, but as it stands, it has already taken us into the final task of this chapter, which is to turn from Eliade's theory itself to the main complaints of his critics.

Critique

Eliade's theory of religion is warmly welcomed in some quarters and strongly contested in others. This is hardly surprising, given the bold stance he takes against reductionist approaches and the broad scope of his interests. As should be apparent from the discussion we have just concluded, Eliade is not afraid to tackle large questions and take sides on controversial matters of current interest, though both of those policies have a way of placing other scholars in a very skeptical mood right from the start. Among the charges of Eliade's detractors, it is helpful to make a distinction between minor complaints and those that are more serious. Certain misgivings expressed about his work seem quite marginal or even mistaken. It has been said by some, for example, that evidence from Chinese religions and Islam is missing from most of his writings, even though he claims to be a "global" comparativist. Others claim that examples which might discredit his claims can never be found in his books; that he does not carefully evaluate the texts and scholars he relies on; and that he applies our modern concepts to ancient peoples.[31] Still others have claimed that his views are a throwback to Victorian social evolutionism and that his methods are largely intuitive and speculative rather than scientific.[32] In fairness, we should first note that some of these criticisms could be made of almost any theory as broad as Eliade's, while others could, in part, be answered or even corrected. Failing to speak at length about Islamic or Chinese religions, for example, would not be a serious oversight unless significant evidence from these traditions could be found to contradict the general conclusions Eliade draws from his other evidence in some significant respect. After all, no one who seeks to make general observations can possibly know *all* of the available evidence. Again, it does not seem accurate to say Eliade is some sort of old-school social evolutionist. He recognizes the fact of change in history, but for him change is by no means to be equated with irreversible evolutionary progress.

These points aside, questions about Eliade's approach still can be raised on several other, more important matters. Specifically, reservations have been raised about the issues of theology, history, and conceptual precision, or clarity.

1. Theology

A number of observers have claimed that the key problem with Eliade is a religious one. Hidden within his theory, they say, are certain prior assumptions, both religious and philosophical, that undermine its objectivity; therefore, it cannot be scientific. In recent years, several outspoken critics have claimed that Eliade is really a Christian theologian—or even missionary—in disguise. He believes in God and presents all religions in a favorable light, so that he can then show Christianity to be the true and best form among them.[33] As one might guess, this charge is a source of considerable controversy, which Eliade's own statements unfortunately do not always help to clarify. Though he published both a journal and an autobiography and discussed his career in a wide-ranging published interview, he has always remained elusive about his personal religious convictions. Another issue is that even if he were to admit to a Christian motive behind his work, we could not discredit his arguments and analyses for that reason alone, any more than, earlier on, we could dismiss the theories of Marx and Freud merely because these were inspired by decidedly antireligious motives. The question that must be asked is whether such prior beliefs, on either side of the issue, *actually enter the theory* in such a way as to make it invalid for anyone who does not accept them. Once we put the matter this way, perhaps the best that can be said is this: Although it might be true that Eliade allows his own religious sympathies to intrude on his science, none of his critics has so far proved that point to general satisfaction. Interestingly, one of the most objective and careful observers to write on this issue argues that Eliade's theory does in part rely upon what may be called a "normative" religious point of view, but this stance is closer to that of antihistorical Eastern religions like Hinduism than it is to Christianity.[34] Others argue that Eliade's personal creed is in fact the cosmic religion of the archaic peoples he so much appreciates, and that because of this he fails to do justice to the nonarchaic, historical perspective of Judaism and Christianity or to the nonreligious modern perspective when he raises doubts about their value.

2. Historical Method

Another set of critics claims that troubles lie in the path not of theology but of history. As we noted earlier, Eliade feels he has succeeded in making the study of religion both a phenomenological and historical enterprise. He claims not only to explain the timeless symbolic forms of religion but also to show how they change with each new historical situation. His historical critics, however, are not so sure. They point out, often quite persuasively, that in reality only the timeless forms seem to count for Eliade; their special historical contexts, each with its small but significant variations of, say, the great tree, the moon cycle, or the eternal return, seem to count very little in his interpretations. In framing his generalizations, Eliade draws examples from very distant places in space and time; he lifts them out of their setting, finds certain similarities, and on that basis concludes that they form a significant pattern. Regardless of whether he turns to Vedic India several thousand years ago, to European peasants of the Middle Ages, or to people living in tribal communities today, he finds in all of these religions the same basic categories of thought. Everywhere, it seems, he is able to find the same types of symbol and the same forms of myth, all expressing the same core of ideas: the reality of the sacred, a reliance on its archetypes, the escape from history, and the symbolism of return. The conclusion easily drawn from this argument is that Eliade's research program is subject to just the sort of criticism first leveled at Frazer more than half a century earlier. It may well be that some method of this kind must be followed by anyone who attempts a truly universal theory of religion, but that does not necessarily mean Eliade's is sound. As was the case with Frazer, each time a careful anthropologist or historian who has closely studied a certain society shows that one of its symbols or myths cannot be fitted into Eliade's grand patterns, another crack appears in the theory's foundation. One or a few may not weaken the structure, but the effect of such cumulative weakening cannot be lightly dismissed.

3. Conceptual Confusions

Alongside both of these problems, there is finally the matter of certain key concepts that seem, if not confused, at least somewhat imprecise and unfocused. It is troubling that at just those moments when we want him to be very clear, Eliade's discussions can turn out to be rather disappointingly vague and elusive. Instead of sharp, clear lines, we tend to find a mist. On the question of symbolism, to give just one example, anthropologist Edmund Leach has pointed to a significant confusion. Eliade tells us that myths often present the division between the sacred and the profane and then introduce a third thing that connects them: a boat, a bridge or ladder, a pole, or "great tree." What is important, Eliade explains, is not the content of the symbols but their structure, the linkage they make between the sacred and profane. Whether the connecting object is a boat rather than a bridge does not really matter, since the important thing is the form, or framework, of the symbols—the relationships between them—rather than the actual content of the symbols themselves. At the same time, we are in other places told with equal emphasis that certain connecting symbols—like the great tree as *axis mundi*—must be considered superior to others. But surely that can be true only if the content of the symbol *does*, in fact, matter after all. So we have a confusion. Could it be, Leach asks, that Eliade has from the start decided—perhaps for his own religious reasons—that certain symbols which he personally prefers must come out of the analysis as better than others? Could it be that content is more important than formal relationships after all? Whether or not Leach is correct, the matter of symbols and their precise significance is too important in Eliade's theory to be left in this kind of uncertainty.

A similar point can in a sense even be made about the concept of the sacred itself. Whenever we try to specify just what the sacred is for archaic peoples, that task turns out to be quite difficult. Eliade says it can be symbolized by the image of a center that is hard to reach, but also by a center that is easy to reach. He says that stones represent the sacred because they are solid and changeless; yet the moon, with its changing phases—its cycle of birth, death, and reappearance—is said also to represent it because "the *real* is not only what *is* indefinitely the same, but also what *becomes* in organic but cyclic forms."[35] Elsewhere we learn that "all divinities tend to become *everything* to their believers."[36] In other words, the content, or character, of the sacred as Eliade conceives it would seem subject to considerable change. But if so, if the concept of the sacred must be this formless and changeable to do its job, how useful can it really be? How instructive is it to build a theory on the notion of the sacred if, in the end, there is relatively little that can be specified about it other than the fact that it is the opposite of the profane?

Despite these problems, Eliade deserves a measure of commendation for being one of the few thinkers to speak assertively against the spirit of his age, laying a strong claim to the independence of religious behavior over against the various forms of functionalist reductionism. He can also be commended for at least attempting an approach that draws its data from almost every world religion and tries to account for all the evidence within the framework of a single comprehensive system. Whether he has succeeded, or ever could succeed, with such an ambitious program is of course another matter. Interestingly, among those who think not, it is sometimes suggested that a more promising approach would be simply to abandon Eliade's hopes of a "global" theory and refocus the aims of inquiry altogether. They claim that just as much can be learned not by looking for general patterns but by doing the very opposite: by centering upon the religion of a single place or people and exploring it in painstaking depth and detail. As we shall see next, that is just the path taken, and made exemplary, by the renowned English anthropologist E. E. Evans-Pritchard.

Notes

1. Mircea Eliade, *Journal III: 1970–1978*, tr. Teresa Lavender Fagan (Chicago: University of Chicago Press, 1989), p. 179.

2. *Autobiography: Volume 1, 1907–1937, Journey East, Journey West*, tr. Mac Linscott Ricketts (San Francisco: Harper & Row, 1981), p. 94. In addition to Eliade's own autobiography and journals, accounts of his life include Ioan Culianu, *Mircea Eliade* (Assisi, Italy: Cittadella Editrice, 1977), and Ivan Strenski, *Four Theories of Myth in Twentieth-Century History: Cassirer, Eliade, Lévi-Strauss and Malinowski* (Iowa City: University of Iowa Press, 1987), pp. 70–128. The most extensive account of Eliade's early years is Mac Linscott Ricketts, *Mircea Eliade: The Romanian Roots, 1907– 1945*, 2 vols. (New York: Columbia University Press, 1988).

3. Mircea Eliade, *Ordeal by Labyrinth: Conversations with Claude-Henri Roquet* (Chicago: University of Chicago Press, 1978), pp. 6–8.

4. Eliade, *Ordeal*, pp. 54–56.

5. Eliade, *Ordeal*, pp. 162–163.

6. Mircea Eliade, *Patterns in Comparative Religion*, tr. Rosemary Sheed (New York: Meridian Books [1949] 1963), p. xiii.

7. Mircea Eliade, *The Sacred and the Profane: The Nature of Religion*, tr. Willard R. Trask (New York: Harcourt, Brace & World [1956 French], 1957), pp. 12–13.

8. Mircea Eliade, *Autobiography, Volume II: 1937–1960: Exile's Odyssey*, tr. Mac Linscott Rickets (Chicago: University of Chicago Press, 1988), pp. 188–189.

9. Genesis 28:17.

10. Eliade, *Sacred and Profane*, pp. 55–56.

11. Eliade, *Patterns*, p. 91.

12. Mircea Eliade, "Methodological Remarks on the Study of Religious Symbolism," in *The History of Religions: Essays in Methodology*, ed. Mircea Eliade and Joseph Kitagawa (Chicago: University of Chicago Press, 1959), p. 103.

13. Eliade, *Patterns*, pp. 98–99.

14. Eliade, *Patterns*, p. 124.

15. Eliade, *Patterns*, p. 183.

16. Eliade, *Patterns*, p. 170.

17. Eliade, *Patterns*, p. 158.
18. Eliade, *Patterns*, p. 158.
19. Eliade, *Patterns*, p. 216.
20. Eliade, *Patterns*, p. 265.
21. Eliade, *Patterns*, p. 315.
22. Eliade, *Patterns*, pp. 314–315.
23. Eliade, *Patterns*, p. 322.
24. Eliade, *Sacred and Profane*, p. 92.
25. Mircea Eliade, *The Myth of the Eternal Return: Or, Cosmos and History* (New York: Harper Torchbooks [1949], 1959), p. 52.
26. Eliade, *Eternal Return*, p. 35.
27. Eliade, *Eternal Return*, p. 89.
28. Eliade, *Eternal Return*, p. 104.
29. Eliade, *Eternal Return*, p. 111.
30. William A. Lessa, review of *The Sacred and the Profane*, in *American Anthropologist* 61 (1959): 1147.
31. For a full accounting of these criticisms and their merits, see John A. Saliba, *"Homo Religiosus" in Mircea Eliade: An Anthropological Evaluation* (Leiden: E. J. Brill, 1978).
32. On the claim that he is an evolutionist, see Dorothy Libby, review of *Rites and Symbols of Initiation*, in *American Anthropologist* 61 (1959): 689. On the other criticisms, see Anthony F. C. Wallace, *Religion: An Anthropological View* (New York: Random House, 1966), p. 252; and Annemarie de Waal Malefijt, *Religion and Culture: An Introduction to Anthropology of Religion* (New York: Macmillan, 1968), p. 193.
33. Among the most vocal of these critics is Canadian scholar Donald Wiebe, who, in a number of articles and books, repeats the claim that Eliade's opposition to reductionism is not a scientific principle but a religious prejudice; see, among several of his writings that make this point, *Religion and Truth* (The Hague, Netherlands: Mouton Publishers, 1981).
34. Douglas Allen, *Structure and Creativity in Religion: Hermeneutics in Mircea Eliade's Phenomenology of Religion and New Directions* (The Hague, Netherlands: Mouton Publishers, 1978), pp. 221–245, especially pp. 221–222.
35. Eliade, *Patterns*, pp. 314–315.
36. Eliade, *Patterns*, p. 262.

Suggestions for Further Reading

Allen, Douglas. *Structure and Creativity in Religion: Hermeneutics in Mircea Eliade's Phenomenology of Religion and New Directions*. The Hague: Mouton Publishers, 1978. A substantive analysis, difficult in places, but written by a scholar with a wide and deep knowledge of Eliade's life and works.

Cave, David. *Mircea Eliade's Vision for a New Humanism*. New York: Oxford University Press, 1993. A sympathetic, but not uncritical, discussion of the humanist perspective that in the author's view guides all of Eliade's thinking about religion.

Dudley, Guilford, III. *Religion on Trial: Mircea Eliade and His Critics*. Philadelphia: Temple University Press, 1977. An instructive discussion, with a critique of the assumptions and major themes in Eliade's works.

Eliade, Mircea. *Autobiography: Volume 1, 1907–1937: Journey East, Journey West*. Translated by Mac Linscott Ricketts. San Francisco: Harper & Row, 1981. *Autobiography: Volume 2, 1937–1960: Exile's Odyssey*. Translated by Mac Linscott Ricketts. Chicago: University of Chicago Press, 1988. In these volumes Eliade himself provides a narrative of his life and thought up through his first years at the University of Chicago.

Leach, Edmund. "Sermons by a Man on a Ladder." *The New York Review of Books*, October 20, 1966. A sharply critical review of Eliade's works from the perspective of professional anthropology.

Olson, Carl. *The Theology and Philosophy of Eliade: A Search for the Centre*. New York: St. Martin's Press, 1992. A good introduction to the major themes in Eliade's work.

Rennie, Bryan, ed. *Mircea Eliade: A Critical Reader* (Critical Categories in the Study of Religion). London: Equinox, 2006. Essays that introduce students and non-specialists to key concepts and themes in Eliade's work; also considers developments in his life and criticism of his theories.

Rennie, Bryan, ed. *The International Eliade*. Albany: State University of New York Press, 2007. The editor assembles a wide array of scholars from Asia, South America, Europe, and Scandinavia, whose global appraisals measure Eliade's strengths and weaknesses.

Ricketts, Mac Linscott. *Mircea Eliade: The Romanian Roots, 1907–1945*. 2 vols. New York: Columbia University Press, 1988. The most extensive account of Eliade's earlier years in Romania, Italy, India, and other places.

Saliba, John A. *"Homo Religiosus" in Mircea Eliade: An Anthropological Evaluation*. Leiden: E. J. Brill, 1978. A modern anthropological assessment that mixes appreciation and criticism.

Strenski, Ivan. *Four Theories of Myth in Twentieth-Century History: Cassirer, Eliade, Lévi-Strauss and Malinowski*. Iowa City: University of Iowa Press, 1987, pp. 70–128. Contains a perceptive and provocative exploration of Eliade's ties to Romanian culture and its nationalist movement between the wars.

Wedemeyer, Christian, and Wendy Doniger. *Hermeneutics, Politics, and the History of Religions: The Contested Legacies of Joachim Wach and Mircea Eliade*. New York : Oxford University Press, 2010. Papers presented at a conference marking the death of Wach and birth of Eliade offer the most recent perspectives on their legacies, along with reappraisals of their achievements.

8

Society's "Construct of the Heart": E. E. Evans-Pritchard

> If he could alter the categories of his own generation's universe so that primitive peoples would rank in it as fully rational beings, that change would entail others, among them a higher status for religious knowledge.
>
> Mary Douglas, *E. E. Evans-Pritchard*[1]

E. E. Evans-Pritchard is one of the great figures in modern anthropology, a field he claimed as his profession for a period of nearly fifty years, from the 1920s to his death in 1973. Were he to have seen his name alongside the others in this book, this unassuming Englishman doubtless would have expressed some surprise, insisting that if theories of religion are the subject, he had proposed no such thing. Certain observers, in fact, might even prefer to describe him as an "antitheorist" of religion, for in one of his most widely noticed books, *Theories of Primitive Religion* (1965), he takes it as his mission to dismantle the ambitious schemes of explanation put forward by the pioneering figures in anthropology and the study of religion, including several of the theorists already discussed in these pages. It may be recalled that on occasion in earlier chapters we noted some of his perceptive criticisms of their views. Evans-Pritchard's role in the enterprise of explaining religion, however, has been much larger than that of a critic whose main interest is to find the faults in the work of others. His considerable reputation rests on the very impressive work he was able to do "in the field"—as anthropologists prefer to say—preparing studies he carried out as a trained, professional observer of actual tribal peoples.

Of the theorists we have so far met in this book, almost all have readily offered an opinion on the nature of primitive, or tribal, religion, yet only one—Eliade in India—records even so much as a passing contact with people living in circumstances remotely similar to a real primitive society. This is emphatically not the case with Evans-Pritchard, who did far more than just meet or speak with a few "native" peoples. He made it his mission fully to engage with two different primitive societies, learn their languages, live for a time by their customs, and carefully study them in action. The significance of his work can therefore hardly be overestimated. His approach differs from that of earlier "armchair" anthropologists just as experimental science does from speculation. Further, while he was critical of most theories he had encountered, Evans-Pritchard was by no means opposed to them in principle. He felt that among anthropologists, in fact, not enough effort had been put into this enterprise, and he saw his own work among tribal peoples of Africa as—if not a way of framing a full theory of his own—a necessary step in the right direction.

Life and Career

E. E. Evans-Pritchard was born in 1902, the second son of a Church of England clergyman, Rev. John Evans-Pritchard, and his wife Dorothea.[2] The parish his father served was at Crowborough, Sussex, not too distant from Hampshire, where Evans-Pritchard took his secondary education at Winchester College, one of England's elite public schools. He then entered Exeter College, Oxford University, continuing his studies for four years and graduating with an M.A. in modern history. By then his interests had already begun to turn in the direction of anthropology, so in 1923 he began graduate study at the London School of Economics. As noted earlier, the study of anthropology in England had evolved from the older armchair-and-library research practiced by Müller and Frazer into a discipline that required at least one apprenticeship of study devoted to a society very different—meaning "primitive" usually—from those of modern Europe and America. This was precisely the kind of work Evans-Pritchard was determined to do. In London he was able to study with C. G. Seligman, who had been the first professional anthropologist to do fieldwork in Africa. At the same time, Bronislaw Malinowski came to London and became a second mentor. Malinowski, a noted figure, had spent four years studying the people of the Trobriand Islands, where he was the first anthropologist to do his research in a native language and immerse himself fully in the daily life of a primitive community. He strongly encouraged Evans-Pritchard to do what he had done, studying the culture of a single people in great depth; Seligman encouraged him to choose a tribal society in Africa.

Taking the advice of both tutors, Evans-Pritchard traveled to the Sudan region of East Africa, the area where the Nile and Congo rivers find their source. Under the joint control of Egypt and Britain at the time, this area was known as the Anglo-Egyptian Sudan. Between 1926 and 1931, while encountering a number of tribal communities, he settled among a people known as the Azande in the southern Sudan. In all, he spent almost two years with them and learned their language thoroughly, all the while writing his doctoral dissertation and other articles on their social life. Between 1930 and 1936 he did further fieldwork among the Nuer people of the region. In 1935 he became Research Lecturer in African Sociology at Oxford, and four years later he married a South African, Ioma Nicholls, with whom he had a family of three sons and two daughters. In 1937 he published his first major work, *Witchcraft, Oracles, and Magic among the Azande*. Though it made a modest impact at first, this book acquired great importance in the years after World War II, being called by at least one authority "the outstanding work of anthropology published in this century."[3] It was followed by the first of three volumes he was to publish on the other tribe he had studied in depth. *The Nuer: A Description of the Modes of Livelihood and Political Institutions of a Nilotic People* appeared in 1940.

During World War II, Evans-Pritchard served in the British army, leading a Zande (this is singular; "Azande" is the plural) band of warriors on a campaign against certain Italian army defenses in East Africa. Later, while serving at a post in Cyrenaica, Libya, he did further research that led to a study of a Muslim Sufi religious order known as the Sanusi. It was at this time, in the year 1944, that he converted to Roman Catholicism. After the war, he returned to England, where he settled first at Cambridge and then became professor of social anthropology at Oxford, taking the chair occupied by the noted advocate of functionalist theory, A. R. Radcliffe-Brown, on his retirement.

At Oxford Evans-Pritchard rose to even greater prominence as perhaps the leading figure in British social anthropology. During these years he published, alongside numerous articles on anthropological subjects, the results of his work in Libya, *The Sanusi of Cyrenaica* (1949); the second and third of his Nuer studies, *Kinship and Marriage among the Nuer* (1951) and *Nuer Religion* (1956); and major books on the methods and history of the field, including *Social Anthropology* (1951), *Essays in Social Anthropology* (1962), and *A History of Anthropological Thought* (1981). The last of these appeared a number of years after his death. Evans-Pritchard's worldwide renown in anthropology was almost matched by his fame in and about Oxford as one of the university's most engagingly eccentric characters. Unpretentious, retiring, and often dressed in clothes that allowed him to be easily mistaken for a handyman, his close associates marveled at his acid tongue and what one described as his "awesome, Celtic prowess at drinking."[4] In 1970 Evans-Pritchard retired from his post, and the following year, against his wishes, he was knighted. He died two years later, in 1973.

Intellectual Background

Evans-Pritchard's approach to anthropology—and consequently religion—took shape against the background of three earlier traditions. The first was older Victorian anthropology, the second was French sociology, and the third was the newer British school of fieldwork anthropology. We have already met the last of these, at least briefly, in the form of his teachers Seligman and Malinowski, who stressed close study of a foreign society. We can understand why this type of research was considered important if we look at the two other traditions as Evans-Pritchard saw them when he began his work.

Older Anthropology

As we noticed earlier in the case of such figures as Tylor, Frazer, and their associates, the Victorian founders of anthropology imagined a new science of human affairs. They felt they could study such things as religion and the rise of human culture as scientists, methodically collecting, comparing, and classifying facts. They thought also that this science could demonstrate social evolution, humanity's march of progress. And though they were less aware of it than of the other principles, they preferred an approach that was intellectualist and individualistic.

Looking back on this enterprise, Evans-Pritchard, like others in the early years of the twentieth century, gave it a quite mixed review. The ideal of science he found the easiest to accept, and even improve upon, chiefly by using the Victorians' research, gathering more facts, and refining the methods for studying them. The evolutionary conclusions, however, were another matter. He recognized that certain technical improvements in history were obvious: a better plough, a faster loom, a stronger wheel. Cultural progress as a whole, however, was a much larger, more elusive issue. And though it may have seemed self-evident to Tylor and Frazer, Evans-Pritchard insisted that such a theory contradicted the very scientific principles upon which it supposedly was based. Darwin, after all, had provided *evidence* to prove the physical evolution of animal species; unfortunately, evidence was precisely what the older anthropologists did *not* have for their broad theories of cultural progress, including their views on the origin and development of religion. Most theorizing about the first humans—what their marriage customs were, what their religion was, and so forth—consisted mainly of speculation about an era from which there were no historical records, nor could there ever be. The ideas were interesting, but there was no way they could be proved or, for that matter, even disproved. So any theory of social evolution was problematic from the start.

With regard to the other feature of older anthropology, its individualist intellectualism, the appraisal was more mixed. Insofar as Tylor and Frazer explained primitive belief as the ideas of isolated ancient thinkers, they had clearly failed to see that humans always live *in society*, which conditions and colors their thought in a fundamental way. Insofar as they explained religion intellectually, their emphasis was rather one-sided; however, they were partly correct. All human beings, even uneducated ones, do approach life to some extent in intellectual terms; they want to explain their experience; so they frame concepts, connect them to others, and relate them to the activities of daily life.

French Sociology

Evans-Pritchard felt strongly that the proper corrective to the individualism of Tylor and Frazer could be found in the field of sociology as it had recently developed in France. As noted earlier, the French tradition of interpreting human affairs in social terms went back to the period before the Revolution and could be seen in the works of the Baron de Montesquieu, especially his *Spirit of the Laws* (1748). This approach had been further developed by figures like Henri de Saint-Simon and Auguste Comte in the early nineteenth century and further refined at its close by Durkheim and his disciples. Evans-Pritchard expressed real admiration for Durkheim, whom he called "the central figure" in the development of social anthropology, not just because of his own work but because of the way in which he formed a circle of talented associates and students to work with him.[5] He was the leader of the French school, which had shown definitively that human social life, which included religion, could never be understood merely as what individuals think and do, though in associations and numbers; there was more to the formation of social groups than merely private thoughts and emotions in assembled form. Durkheim's disciples demonstrated that the framework of life is fixed for every person by society even before birth and remains in place through the generations. Accordingly, in their view, it was society that created much of the individual. A child born in France will speak the French language, feel obliged to obey French laws, and observe French customs. So too in thought: a French child will understand the world with French ideas. Everyone knew these things more or less, but until Durkheim not everyone knew their full importance.

The colleague and sometimes critic of Durkheim who sought to explain the influence of these social factors on how people think, both religiously otherwise, was Lucien Lévy-Bruhl (1857–1939), a philosopher who was very much aware of social considerations and took a special interest in the thought of primitive peoples. When they were translated into English in the 1920s, two of his books, *How Natives Think* (1926) and *Primitive Mentality* (1923), drew considerable attention in Britain. Evans-Pritchard thought these works, like Durkheim's, were extremely important for anthropology. Unlike Tylor and Frazer, whom we have seen referring to early peoples as rational but also as ignorant, superstitious, and childish, Lévy-Bruhl sought to show how primitive thought is not weaker or more immature than ours but simply different from it. It is a reflection of an entirely different social system, which places value on a type of thinking best described as "prelogical." Primitive people live in a world of "mystical participations" that do not follow our rules of logical connection or our law against contradiction. Because they obey these different rules of thought, primitive people can quite literally think of themselves as one thing and something else at the same time. When, in the report of a European explorer, a South American native declared, "I am a red parakeet," those words were meant literally, yet the native was not demonstrating that he was deranged or even weak in reasoning power; he was demonstrating a different kind of thought, a type that is irrational to us because it accepts as normal the "mystical participation" of one thing in another.

Evans-Pritchard thought the work of Lévy-Bruhl to be brilliant, even though, on the key point of the primitive prelogical mind, it would need correction. Not only had it shown that the ideas and attitudes of nonliterate peoples must be understood within the context of their culture—the whole sea of values, habits, and assumptions in which they swim—but it also marked a most important change in the attitude of modern thinkers toward primitive people. In Lévy-Bruhl's perspective, early peoples were not mentally deficient, subhuman, or childish; they were equally but differently mature, human, and intelligent beings. To Evans-Pritchard, this was a perspective every anthropologist should take with him into the field.

British Empirical Anthropology

Evans-Pritchard was not the only one in the Britain of his day to appreciate French sociology. Its importance had already been recognized by A. R. Radcliffe-Brown, whose ideas dominated anthropological discussion at the time. From Durkheim and his colleagues, Radcliffe-Brown had borrowed and then further developed the functional theory of society as a complete, interconnected, working organism: no part of it could be understood without the whole. Explaining primitive religion without addressing primitive class divisions or economic needs was like explaining the human heart without ever referring to the blood or lungs. Evans-Pritchard, along with almost every other aspiring younger anthropologist of the time, heartily endorsed this view, as well as the important practical conclusion that followed from it. To do his work, the anthropologist could no longer stay in a library or read the reports of missionaries about this strange notion or that odd habit. He must go out into the field and make a *complete* study of a single culture, observing not just its religion, but its law and economics, its class divisions, family structure, and kinship connections—all of these aspects as they come together in a unitary, organic whole. This conclusion, endorsed and implemented by all of his most important teachers, is what led Evans-Pritchard in 1926 to the interior of the Sudan—and to his first major anthropological study.

Witchcraft, Oracles, and Magic among the Azande

In this chapter as in the others, our plan of action requires that we focus our attention on the main books in which Evans-Pritchard developed his key ideas on religion. These are chiefly *Nuer Religion* (1956) and, to a lesser degree, his critical study *Theories of Primitive Religion* (1965). Before doing so, however, we must take note of his extremely important earlier work on the Azande people, in part because of its great significance for anthropological research as a whole but also because it provides the key link between the initial assumptions we have just noted and Evans-Pritchard's views on religion as they were developed in his later years.

As its title indicates, *Witchcraft, Oracles, and Magic among the Azande* (1937) deals with a topic that anthropologists since Tylor and Frazer had taken to be closely related to religion: namely, magic. For Evans-Pritchard, magic is the belief that certain aspects of life can be controlled by mystical forces or supernatural powers. Since most educated members of modern Western societies—and Evans-Pritchard includes himself in this group—think the belief in such forces is wholly mistaken, the natural question is: Why then do the Azande believe in them? Evans-Pritchard found it unacceptable, as we have seen, to say with Tylor and Frazer that they are partly irrational and childish. And outside of the realm of magic, there was abundant evidence to support him. On their own terms, he wrote, the Azande are logical, analytical, and inquiring. In social and practical affairs, they are clever and perceptive. They are skilled craftsmen; they are poetically imaginative, and in matters of survival and daily living extremely resourceful. On the whole "they are unusually intelligent, sophisticated, and progressive."[6] Still, a surprisingly significant part of life among the Azande is given over to oracles, magic, and other ritual performances. They refer to mystical ideas and ritual practices on a daily basis; they speak freely about them and without fear, even though addressing practical matters still takes up most of their daily conversation.

The precise nature of Zande witchcraft seems strange to a Westerner, but it is not difficult to describe. The term "witchcraft" actually refers to a physical substance that some people have in their bodies, unknown to themselves. It is inherited and can be discovered in their bodies after death. Evans-Pritchard states his own belief that this substance, which the Azande can find *post mortem* as a dark mass in the small intestine, is nothing more than undigested food. Yet the Azande believe that while this substance looks to be merely physical and natural, it operates in a mystical fashion to bring misfortune, and especially sickness, on other people. It is a mistake, Evans-Pritchard cautions, to suppose the Azande are so obsessed with witchcraft that they spend most of their time making and responding to accusations that they have it in their bodies; they do not. But references to it are made in every aspect of their life, especially in connection with almost any unfortunate turn of events that cannot be directly explained by ordinary mistakes or misjudgments.

Evans-Pritchard observes that if a blight hits one of the crops, if animals are not found in the hunt, if a wife and husband quarrel, if a commoner is turned away by his prince, there are always mutterings of witchcraft, though very little is done about it. Nonetheless, when a truly serious misfortune makes an appearance—say, the presence of a wasting disease that seems to be taking the life of an individual—there is no doubt in the Zande mind that such occurrences must be due to witchcraft. The person whose witchcraft caused them must be found—and confronted.

In such cases the Azande regularly consult what they call the poison oracle. In this—again, to us quite strange—procedure, a man forces poison into the throat of a chicken while at that very moment asking a question that can be answered with a yes or no. The death or survival of the chicken then determines the answer. For example, concerning the sick friend: "If x has caused his illness, poison oracle, kill the fowl."[7] If the bird dies of the poison, the person whose witchcraft has caused the illness has been found. There then follows a procedure of accusation, a ritual of "blowing water," in which the accused agrees to "cool" his witchcraft, which is devouring the soul of the sick person, and all is considered to be at an end—unless of course the victim of the witchcraft dies after all. In that case, vengeance must be taken. Evans-Pritchard points out that at one time in the Zande past, this act might have involved the murder of the accused witch. Now, however, it is usually a matter of offering compensation to the family or, even better, of discovering, again through oracles, that another person in the community, now deceased, was in fact the witch and has thus already suffered a fitting punishment for his witchcraft. Vengeance, moreover, cannot be claimed until the verdict of one's private oracle has been confirmed by the secret poison oracle of the local prince, for Zande society is an aristocracy in which the ruling class makes all final decisions. If the logic of these oracles, deaths, and acts of vengeance were analyzed publicly, Evans-Pritchard notes, it would reduce itself to an absurdity, because every new death would have to be attributed to yet another act of witchcraft in an endless circle. The Azande—significantly—choose not to address this problem in any abstract or theoretical manner.

Alongside witchcraft and the poison oracle, there is an array of associated magical practices. There are minor oracles that function like the poison oracle but are less accurate and need its confirmation in important matters. There are all sorts of medicines that witch doctors can apply as good magic to ward off the effects of witchcraft. And there is sorcery, which is done in secret and regarded as a crime if discovered. In addition, Evans-Pritchard notes that the class of the nobility is largely exempt from the entire business of witchcraft. Commoners do not accuse the ruling class; conversely, the poison oracle of the prince, which gives the final determination on all serious witchcraft charges brought by commoners, is the anchor of the society's entire legal system; it is both constitution and supreme court.

The painstaking detail with which Evans-Pritchard describes these magical practices is one reason for the extraordinary praise *Witchcraft* came to receive from experts in the field. It is a classic piece of what anthropologists call scientific ethnography. The details have great theoretical importance, for through them Evans-Pritchard is able to show how, from the Zande perspective, the seeming absurdities of witchcraft and magic form not only a coherent and rational system, but one that plays a central role in social life. It offers a plausible account of all personal misfortunes. It also works alongside what we would call explanation through natural causes, for the Azande also believe in these and appeal to them often as well. In certain cases, witchcraft helps to explain why the natural causes act as they do. It does not explain why fire burns, but it does explain why, on this particular unfortunate occasion, fire, which never bothered me before, now has burned my hand. The Azande, therefore, see no competition between science on the one hand and their system of magic, oracles, witchcraft, and religion on the other. Significantly, the notion of a struggle between these two forms of knowledge—which is so central to views of Tylor, Frazer, Freud, Lévy-Bruhl, and so many other theorists of the primitive mind—seems totally foreign to their experience. Magic and religion are not replaced by science; they simply operate alongside and with it.

In addition to its task of explaining misfortune, witchcraft works along with magic to achieve other useful social purposes. It not only serves as the foundation of legal affairs but also governs Zande morals and softens the rough edges of social life. The chances of violence, for example, are reduced because there is a routine procedure for determining the identity of those who are believed to have caused misfortune and an expectation that, in the appropriate way, they will be punished. Again, since witches are thought to be naturally disagreeable, uncooperative, unhappy people, there is a strong incentive not to behave in that way lest other people suspect you are a witch and bring your name before their oracle after the next bad event. As Evans-Pritchard puts it in concise form: "The concept of witchcraft . . . provides them [the Azande] with a natural philosophy by which the relations between men and unfortunate events are explained and a ready and stereotyped means of reacting to such events. Witchcraft beliefs also embrace a system of values which regulate human conduct."[8]

All of this also puts Evans-Pritchard in the position to make a clear statement about how the Azande reason as compared with thinking in a modern scientific culture, and here it is worth quoting him at length. Although the Azande clearly do not see the theoretical weakness in their system of witchcraft belief,

> their blindness is not due to stupidity, for they display great ingenuity in explaining away the failures and inequalities of the poison oracle and experimental keenness in testing it. It is due rather to the fact that their intellectual ingenuity and experimental keenness are conditioned by patterns of ritual behaviour and mystical belief. Within the limits set by these patterns they show great intelligence, but it cannot operate beyond these limits. Or, to put it in another way; they reason excellently in the idiom of their beliefs, but they cannot reason outside, or against, their beliefs because they have no other idiom in which to express their thoughts.[9]

Having said this, Evans-Pritchard then turns the argument around. He states that if we look closely at Zande witchcraft in the context of the society in which it functions, we find it a system of thought that shows certain quite striking similarities to our own nonmagical system. Certain beliefs—like the idea that there is such a thing as witchcraft—are fundamental and beyond dispute. Once these are accepted, other inferences, connections, and ideas follow from them quite logically and consistently. Moreover, the fundamental ideas are always affirmed in a way that allows for certain adjustments and protections of them if they *do* happen to be contradicted by the facts.

Toward the end of *Witchcraft*, Evans-Pritchard provides a long list of considerations that affect Zande thinking and of the defenses they readily adopt to "save the system" when needed. When a poison or type of magic does not work, they declare that it may have been inappropriately used or that it was applied against mystical powers whose action is beyond the natural realm and so cannot be contradicted by events within nature. If a medicine fails, the Azande set against it the apparent successes of others. They may also claim that magic seldom produces a result by itself but acts only in combination with other actions. Moreover, their medicines are never actually tested and some are always used, so there is no way to tell what would happen if they were not. These are only a few examples of the way in which the fundamental assumptions of the Zande world view are very well protected against facts that might disprove them; indeed, they form a system of belief impossible to shake. From our perspective the Azande may be wrong, but from theirs it is clear that they think quite rationally within the limits their culture chooses to allow. Their small beliefs rest very logically on certain large ones, and these important basic principles are extremely well guarded. The attachment to the major beliefs is so fundamental to their life that the Azande cannot imagine them to be in error. Without them, their entire social order would be inconceivable, and no one could endure that.

As students of contemporary culture have come to realize, what Evans-Pritchard shows to be true for the Azande holds consequences for the assessment of belief and doubt in our own social circumstance. The case of the Azande suggests that in any culture, certain fundamental beliefs *must* at all costs be preserved; they are too precious and crucial to lose.

Nuer Religion

In 1930 Evans-Pritchard began a series of visits to the land of the Nuer, a people living just to the north of the Azande but very different in their character, culture, and traditions. He at once set upon the difficult work of learning their language and began questioning his hosts, a task that proved more difficult than with the Azande, who had volunteered information freely. Over a period of about six years, to 1936, he put together the equivalent of a year in the Nuer camps, questioning, observing, and writing. This research led in time to three impressive books—and numbers of articles—published between 1940 and 1956. The first of the books, entitled *The Nuer*, focused on economic and political life. Among other notable features of Nuer community life, it explores the central place of cattle in the tribal economy and examines the role they play also in people's personal affections. It offers as well a fascinating discussion of the way the Nuer have constructed their ideas of time and space in relation to their way of life. In 1951 *The Nuer* was followed by a more specifically social study of the community's patterns of kinship and marriage. The trilogy was then brought to completion in 1956 with *Nuer Religion*, the book that calls for our attention here.

The Concept of "Kwoth"

Evans-Pritchard begins *Nuer Religion* at the very center of its subject. On a first look, he notes, one would almost say that the Nuer are a people without religion; they seem to have no formal dogma, no developed liturgy or sacraments, no organized worship, not even a system of mythology. But those appearances are misleading. The Nuer have all of these things, but they appear in the culture in such an informal, almost hidden way that the casual observer can easily miss them.

Nuer religion centers chiefly on the concept of *kwoth*, or spirit (in the plural, *kuth*). Foremost in their thought is God, the being they know as *Kwoth nhial*, the "spirit of (or, in) the sky." He is the creator of all things, invisible and present everywhere, the sustainer—and taker—of life, the upholder of *cuong*, or what is morally upright, good, and true. A being with qualities of human personality, *Kwoth nhial* is preeminently a God who loves unselfishly the human beings he has created.[10] Nuer are keenly aware of God's control of their lives, often uttering quiet prayers to the effect "God is present." And though proud in their attitudes to other people, they regard themselves as nothing before him. They are dumb and small, mere ants in his sight.

The Nuer have a strong sense of God's complete control over the great natural events that happen in the world. Floods, storms, drought, and famine—all of these are in his hands and must be accepted as they come. If, as happens not infrequently, someone is killed by lightning in a thunderstorm, they do not mourn or hold a normal rite of burial; they accept that God has just taken back what is his own. At the same time, the lesser, if still significant, misfortunes that arise in the course of daily social life are another matter. Unlike the Azande, the Nuer do not see them as caused by witchcraft, which must be discovered through oracles so the witch can be pointed out; they feel strongly that such things are their own fault: reversals caused by their own wrongdoing. And they believe that life cannot go on, nor can their community prosper, until matters have been made right before God—until the pollution of their wrongs has been purged. To this idea we will return shortly.

Spirits of the Above

In addition to God, the spirit of the sky, the world of the Nuer embraces other, lesser spirits. They fall into two main groups: the "spirits of the above" (spirits who live primarily in the air) and "spirits of the below" (those associated strictly with Earth).

Spirits of the above include *deng*, the son of God; *mani*, the spirit who leads in war; *wiu*, the god of the clan assembled; and *buk*, a female spirit, called the mother of *deng*, who is associated especially with rivers and streams. Though their primary dwelling is the air, these spirits can seize and enter the bodies of human beings. When this happens in a temporary way, the sign of it in the person possessed is sickness. But there is also a more lasting kind of possession experienced by those who are recognized as prophets. Such persons are actually described as permanent possessors, or owners, of a spirit. Historically, the main role of these figures was to serve as inspired leaders in battle, especially during cattle raids upon the neighboring Dinka tribe. But in the modern era, Evans-Pritchard notes, that duty is seldom carried out. In no case does the spirit of the sky, *Kwoth nhial*, ever stoop to possess a human being; he is far, far above anything like that.

If we ask what is the relation of these secondary *kuth*, or spirits, to God, we meet one of the most complex and subtle elements in the whole of Nuer theology. Characteristically, Evans-Pritchard makes a very close comparative analysis of Nuer speech patterns in order to determine exactly how, and in just what contexts, they use the terms *Kwoth nhial* (God) and *kuth nhial* (spirits of the air). The usage patterns show that in certain contexts the Nuer clearly think of the air spirits as beings with their own identity, separate and distinguishable from each other. Just as clearly, they fall between God and humanity; they are lesser spirits, beings whom the people often regard more with annoyance than fear. At the same time, being *kuth*, they are in other respects thought of as inseparable from *Kwoth nhial*, the supreme God. In other words,

> they are many but also one. God is manifested in, and in a sense is, each of them. I received the impression that in sacrificing or in singing hymns to an air-spirit Nuer do not think that they are communicating with the spirit and not with God. They are, if I have understood the matter correctly, addressing God in a particular spiritual figure or manifestation. . . . They do not see a contradiction here, and there is no reason why they should see one. God is not a particular air-spirit but the spirit is a figure of God. . . . Nuer pass without difficulty or hesitation from a more general and comprehensive way of conceiving of God or Spirit to a more particular and limited way . . . and back again.[11]

Among other things, this short sample of Evans-Pritchard's analysis shows why his work has been so much admired. He was an anthropologist who worked with analytical precision, respect, and self-awareness. Not content to find out in a general way what the Nuer think, he can be seen here, as in many other places, striving to catch each connection, sort out confusions, and make clear each shade of difference or emphasis. In the process, he was also able to win from many Western scholars a respect for Nuer thought that had rarely been given to primitive peoples in the past. Instead of a culture marked by savagery and superstition, he presents a people whose material life may be very simple but whose theology is abstract and sophisticated, a creed suggestive of both Jewish monotheism and medieval Christian mysticism.[12]

Among the spirits of the air, those called *colwic* are a special class; they are the spirits created directly from the souls of human beings struck down by lightning. When lightning strikes a hut and kills its occupants, the Nuer regard this awesome event as a direct act of God, who has chosen to take back these souls for his own purposes. The bodies of such people, as we noted, are not buried in the normal way, for they have been instantly transformed into spirits. In their air-spiritual form, however, they often keep their connection to their original human families, serving as their patrons and protectors.

Spirits of the Below

As family guardians, the *colwic* spirits provide the Nuer with a link between one form of their gods and one part of their social structure: the family, or lineage. We find further connections of this sort the moment we turn to the other main class of divinities: the "spirits of the below," whose natural ties are to the Earth rather than the sky. These spirits are held in much lower regard than those of the air; in fact, they seem hardly even to qualify as *kwoth*, though that is what they are called. It is of interest to notice that after all the attention lavished on the controversial practice of totemism by earlier theorists of religion, this is where it finally appears in Nuer religion—much farther down the scale of importance than Frazer, Durkheim, or Freud could have imagined. The Nuer do recognize totem spirits, which they associate with animal species, such as the crocodile, lion, lizard, snake, and egret, and even plants, gourds, rivers, and streams. Consistent with totemic customs elsewhere, members of a specific tribe or clan are said to give "respect" to their totem animal. They do not eat it; they acknowledge it when seen; and they bury it if they should happen to find it dead in the wild. The totem animal, however, is not the same as the totem spirit. The Nuer clearly think of these two as separate, though they are, of course, closely related. They take the totem animal to be a physical symbol of the totem spirit, which is a manifestation of *Kwoth*. The totem animal is always less important than the totem spirit. But totem spirits, in turn, are always less important than spirits of the air; unlike the air spirits, they must remain connected to their physical symbol, the totem animal.

Nuer theology holds finally that there are mystical objects, persons, and powers on a still lower level than spirits of the air—so low, in fact, that they take us to the margins of tribal life. There are diviners, and there are healers of a sort. The concern of these figures is with minor ailments and anxieties, like fortunetellers in our own society. In the same class are the people who control fetishes and nature sprites. These are mystically charged objects or beings under the control of an individual person. In general, however, the Nuer have a dislike or at least a healthy low-grade fear of these things. There is a general suspicion that they are alien entities, which have entered Nuer life through tribes they dislike, especially the Dinka.

Religion and Refraction in the Social Order

Totemic and *colwic* spirits both exhibit what Evans-Pritchard calls the "social refraction" of religion. As white light is split by a prism into different colors, so the Nuer seem to think of Spirit, or God, as in these cases "refracted" into different bands, or levels, of divine power that apply in a particular way to different clans or social groups. In these cases, though the Nuer feel they are still worshipping God, they worship him as figured, or symbolized, in association with one lineage, clan, or social group in particular. Spirits of the air sometimes also assume this role when they possess a prophet who becomes a public spokesman for a clan, or when they are called upon in a special way by a certain lineage. So too with fetishes and nature sprites, which often are owned and even inherited by families. Interestingly, Evans-Pritchard notes that the lower we travel down the scale of Nuer spirits, the nearer we come to ritualized ceremonies of the kind normally associated with religion in the West. God, the spirit of the sky, is worshipped through simple prayer and sacrifice, while such things as hymns, possessions, and divination become more common as we descend through the spirits of the air and down to the spirits of the below.

This hierarchy of spirits shows itself in other ways as well. There is a political dimension, with God conceived as ruler and spirits of the air as aristocracy; below them come the totem spirits, which fill a middle rank, in essence spiritual but on display in animals and plants; and last, fetishes fall into the undesirable position of outcast or foreign objects, however mystical their powers. In similar fashion, the Nuer trace a persistent contrast between the light and darkness, the first belonging always to the spirits of the air, the second always associated with those of the below. Even age comes to figure in the contrast. God is the eldest of the spirits; spirits of the air are his children; totemic spirits are the children of his daughters; and so on.

It is only natural to think of Durkheim when we follow these connections between layers of divinity and levels of society. In some respects, Nuer spirits obviously mirror social groups and attachments. But to Evans-Pritchard, this is hardly the complete picture. "An interpretation in terms of social structure," he writes, "merely shows us how the idea of Spirit takes various forms corresponding to departments of social life. It does not enable us to understand any better the intrinsic nature of the idea itself."[13] In language that recalls Eliade's strong opposition to reductionism, we are told that the value of a sociological model "is limited, for it does not help us to understand the specifically religious facts any better." Evans-Pritchard then adds,

> Were I writing about Nuer social structure this is the feature of the religion that it would be most necessary to stress. But in a study of religion, if we wish to seize the essential nature of what we are inquiring into, we have to try to examine the matter from the inside also, to see it as Nuer see it.[14]

Symbolism

After discussing spirit in its multiple forms, Evans-Pritchard turns to an important—and now famous—discussion of Nuer symbolism. He points out that this is the subject on which the primitive mind has been most commonly misunderstood. He begins with a very careful analysis of language, particularly what the Nuer mean when they say one thing "is" another. When a bird, for example, perches on top of a hut, they are known to say, "It is *kwoth*," or spirit. Or they may say that a crocodile is spirit, meaning that it has the significance of spirit for people who call the crocodile their totem and give reverence to the crocodile totem spirit. Again, they sometimes say that an ox is a cucumber, but only in situations where an ox must be sacrificed and none can be found or spared, so custom allows for a cucumber to be substituted—to be placed, that is, in the role of the ox. To all appearances the cucumber is still a fruit, and no one would pretend to deny it. Conceptually, however, it is in this situation given a new role, that of a (substitute) ox in sacrifice.

Again, in words remarkably like the phrase "I am a red parakeet," which so interested Lévy-Bruhl, the Nuer will say, "A twin is a bird." Lévy-Bruhl believed that such contradictory phrases show the prelogical, primitive mind at work. But do they? Evans-Pritchard shows what this phrase really means in Nuer culture. Birds, as the only creatures that fly in the air, are regarded as particularly close to spirit, which as we have seen is also associated with the air in the cases of both the spirits of the air and God, the "spirit of the sky." On the other hand, the birth of twins, because it is a quite unusual event, is in its way also a sign that spirit is present in a special form. Twins are given special treatment in Nuer culture, being thought of on some occasions as one personality even though they are two separate physical individuals. Twins do not receive the same sort of funeral as ordinary people, for they are said to be "people of the air" rather than, like all others, "people of the below." Both twins and birds, in other words, are in an unusual way *gaat Kwoth*, "children of God," and it is in that respect that they are identical.

Against the full background of Nuer theology, then, it is clearly true, and not a contradiction, to say that twins are birds. But if so, then there is also no need to claim, as Lévy-Bruhl did, that people like the Nuer have a prelogical mentality; their thought, in their terms and in ours, is logical enough.

Evans-Pritchard tells us further that Lévy-Bruhl was not the only one to fall into this kind of error. Earlier investigators like Müller and Tylor tended to make the same mistake when they claimed that primitive people believed the sun or moon was a divinity. Being uninformed about the larger context in which primitive or ancient peoples make such statements, they fail to make allowance for metaphors, figures of speech, and multiple meanings of words. When some primitives name the sun a divinity or spirit, they may mean no more than that such an object *suggests* or *symbolizes* divinity to them, or that it simply shares one of the qualities of divinity—its grandeur or brightness or beauty. In Evans-Pritchard's view, most anthropological writers have been sorely deficient in appreciating the richly poetic habits of speech adopted by primitive peoples. In their imaginative way of describing the world, analogies, figures, symbols, and metaphors are the rule of language, not the exception.

Ghosts and the Soul

The Nuer believe that there are three parts to the human being: the flesh, the life (or breath), and the soul (or intellect). At death, the first of these goes into the ground and decays; the second goes back to God, who gave it; and the third lingers for a time near the realm of the living until it eventually disappears. The Nuer are not happy if it stays for long. They have a true horror of death, in part because all of their attention is centered on this life, which they wish to have and enjoy in abundance. Says Evans-Pritchard, "They neither pretend to know, nor, I think, do they care, what happens to them after death. There is an almost total lack of what in Western religions falls into the category of eschatology."[15] The Nuer prefer not even to talk about death. Their main concern at funerals is to make sure that the souls of the dead are given their full status as ghosts, so that they can be separated completely from the affairs of those who remain on Earth. The only way a ghost can trouble the living is through *cien*, or vengeance, which may come if a person were wronged while alive and then died before a reconciliation could occur. When this situation arises, it is necessary to make a sacrifice to God and a gift of reparation to the ghost. Since only wrongs done in life can lead to *cien*, the living can at least rest assured that only the recently dead will ever try to bother them. The dead, and their ghosts, are rather quickly forgotten in Nuer life.

For the Nuer, "soul" is something that only humans possess, and Evans-Pritchard notes that this fact bears directly on Tylor's famous animistic theory of religion. Tylor, as we saw earlier, thought that early peoples developed their idea of spirits and demons out of the idea of the human soul, which they got from dreams and visions. This primitive concept of a soul led naturally to that of a spirit and thence to gods. If we look closely, however, that is not the case with the Nuer, who find these two to be very different and even opposed things. Soul is a part of all human beings, and it is created; spirit exists outside of human life, and when it enters a person, it always does so as an invasion from the outside. Even in the case of the *colwic* spirits, those persons taken by lightning, the Nuer are careful to say that their souls must be replaced by spirit at the moment they are taken. The one is so different from the other that any idea of derivation seems impossible. And in that Evans-Pritchard finds a lesson. We should notice, he warns, how Tylor's theory, which seems perfectly reasonable and natural when it is pieced together out of scattered fragments of mythology and folklore, looks very different when brought up against the concrete evidence of an actual system of primitive religious thought.

Sin and Sacrifice

The idea of sin—including the suffering that is associated with it—is central to understanding the human side of Nuer religion. The Nuer conceive of wrongdoing in two basic forms, both of which are defined by the concept of *thek*, or "respect." Among the Nuer as in other tribal cultures, various things are prohibited out of respect for others. A man, for example, ought not to be seen naked by other women in his wife's family; a new wife avoids her husband's parents; engaged or newly married couples ought never to eat in each other's presence, and so on. When these rules are broken, even unintentionally (as they most often are), the acts are considered faults, and they bring a measure of shame upon those responsible for them. In other cases, however, breaches of *thek* are more serious; they may involve such things as adultery or incest, and they are known as *nueer*, acts regarded as "death." These are usually intended actions, and they are not just shameful but sinful. Their consequence is sickness, which in Nuer thought will lead to death unless there is an appropriate sacrifice to God, who is the guardian of the entire moral order.

Though it has its human effects, all sin ultimately is sin against God, and its main consequence is to bring God, by way of his punishments, into the affairs of the community. This is a dangerous situation, for, ideally, the Nuer want God to rule but at a safe distance, looking after his world and his creatures with pleasure and not needing to enter it with punishments. The only way the danger of such divine involvement can be cleared is through sacrifice. The ceremony of sacrifice is almost the only element of Nuer religion that might qualify as a full-scale religious sacrament, though even here the most important instances are largely personal affairs—transactions between one or a few persons and God.

Sacrifice in Nuer life is of two kinds: personal and collective. The second of these—group sacrifice—seems to be the less clearly religious and perhaps less important. It occurs in connection with rites of passage, especially weddings and funerals, and its purpose is to make sacred an otherwise secular event. "It sacralizes the social event and the new relationships brought about by it. It solemnizes the change of status or relationship, giving it religious validation. On such occasions sacrifice has generally a conspicuously festal and eucharistic character."[16] The level of attention given to sacrifice on these occasions, and the emotions on exhibit, vary greatly from one person to the next; some are indifferent and almost bored, others are serious, while still others may be happy and jovial. Their attitudes do not offer much support, Evans-Pritchard claims, for the views of theorists who find the essence of religion in some unique feeling of awe, ecstasy, or fear. Many kinds of emotion seem acceptable.

Unlike the group rites, personal sacrifices are more seriously religious, occasioned by a sin or crime. They properly require the death of an ox—the most precious possession any Nuer can claim. The ceremony, which can be held at any location, is conducted by an older male, preferably the head of a family, and occurs in four stages. There is a presentation of the designated victim to God; a consecration, in which ashes are rubbed on the back of the animal; an invocation, in which the celebrant "states the intention of the sacrifice and matters relevant to it"; and finally the immolation, in which the ox is killed, usually with a quick single spear thrust from the side into the heart.

The roles of the ox and of the spear in this ritual are quite important, for the Nuer identify themselves closely with both. For the Nuer man, the spear in his right hand communicates power, virility, authority, and goodness. It is "a projection of the self and stands for the self"; by extension, it also serves to represent the clan or lineage group, which in fact is called by its spear name.[17] The spear represents the clan in its unity and strength—the clan as prepared for war. The ox, on the other hand, represents a more strictly personal attachment. From the moment of initiation, when each Nuer boy is given his own ox, it is an animal he becomes extremely close to, an animal he identifies with, almost as a second self. And that identification is particularly important when, later in manhood, the occasion arises for personal sacrifice, for then the ox may have to be killed. In the rite of sacrifice, the rubbing of ashes on the back of the ox seems to fix the identification of the man with the beast. It is done always with the right hand, the spear hand, symbolizing the whole self, which is thus united to the animal in the last moments before it is slain. In the gesture of sacrifice to God, a man may be said to be enacting, through the victim, his own personal death.

It is not sufficient, in Evans-Pritchard's view, just to describe the procedure of Nuer sacrifice for his readers. Turning once again to a close analysis of language, he probes and explores to discover its meaning. He observes that anthropology has in general proposed two main views of primitive sacrifice: the gift theory and the communion theory. The latter was put forward in connection with totemism by Robertson Smith, who by now has become a familiar name in our discussions. Smith believed that by killing the animal and eating it, people engaged in an act of social communion, or solidarity—a sacred sharing of food and friendship with each other and with God. There were no "bargains" or trade-offs involved. The gift theory, on the other hand, proposes just that: an exchange, or trade, in which something is given to God, who gives his favor in return. Nuer ceremonies, Evans-Pritchard tells us, clearly belong in some sort of "gift" category. Their central purpose is to give something very precious to God, even though God, of course, does not get anything he does not already have. The important thing is that a human being, responsible and at fault, undergoes a loss, a denial of the self, that connects deeply with a personal sense of guilt for wrong and expresses the desire for evil to be expiated and expelled. It is not a case of God being angry and needing to be pleased; it is a case of the human need to make a transfer of that which is evil in oneself to the ox as a representative, "so that in its death that part may be eliminated and flow away with the blood."[18] Dramatic as the ceremony may be, the key thing is not the ritual but the inward intention. In this serious and necessary transaction, the person who sacrifices—and the community about him—finds a release from the dangerous visit of spirit to human affairs. With the atonement complete, God can at last "turn away" and be finished with the entire matter. The family, clan, or tribe can again feel out of danger.

Evans-Pritchard closes his discussion with a short account of prophets and priests, none of whom is central to Nuer religion in the way that they are for religions like Judaism and Christianity. The most important is the leopard-skin priest, who performs his role mainly in connection with a murder or some other circumstance in which a human life is taken. His task is to provide sanctuary for the killer, to begin a process of reconciliation with the victim's family, and to arrange compensation for the act, so as to prevent any one such terrible event from spiraling into a destructive blood feud. He is thus a valuable figure, but more for social than religious reasons. Other figures include the cattle man, or cattle priest, and the prophet. In the past these figures, who claim to possess (or be possessed by) certain spirits of the air, acquired political significance among the Nuer clans and therefore were suppressed by colonial authorities. They are not rivals of the priests, but the keen interest of some in material things, and the unusual behavior of most, have caused the Nuer people as a whole to view them with mixed feelings.

As with *Witchcraft* and the other Nuer books, one cannot read *Nuer Religion* without coming to appreciate the careful and thorough work of its author. Only the most patient study in the field could yield the precise, sympathetic, and systematic account of primitive beliefs and rituals that appears in its pages. From its narrative two things clearly emerge: (1) a picture full of correctives for nearly every one of those theorists who has framed a personal concept of "primitive religion" without ever having come into contact with the real thing and (2) the portrait of a complex, well-ordered religious system, one that seems almost surprisingly Western and even "modern" in character.

Theories of Primitive Religion

Early in the 1960s, Evans-Pritchard was invited to give a short series of lectures at the University College of Wales. He took the occasion as an opportunity to revisit several issues first raised in the conclusion of *Nuer Religion* and build them into a general discussion addressed to theories of primitive religion. In 1965 the lectures were published as *Theories of Primitive Religion*, one of Evans-Pritchard's shortest but most engaging books—a work whose pages glisten with clear analyses and penetrating criticisms, often adorned with his stinging wit. In addition, by way of its judgments on others, the analyses in this book indirectly profile his own fully ripened views on the matter of explaining religion. Though we have space here to look at this work only briefly, we can at least trace the general line of its discussion.

Theories of Primitive Religion opens with a word of caution and some candid comments about earlier approaches to the subject. Most of the interpretations it considers were developed when little was known and much was misunderstood about the actual facts of primitive religion. Few people who addressed the issue had even seen a primitive culture, let alone studied one. But not for a moment did that stop them from writing on the subject, with all the confusion and distortion one would naturally expect in the process. Evans-Pritchard notes that nearly all of these theorists start with the premise that most of religion, like most of magic, is something quite strange to modern people, who think scientifically, but quite normal to primitive people, who have no difficulty accepting absurd and incredible ideas. They see primitives as "quite irrational" people, "living in a mysterious world of doubts and fears, in terror of the supernatural and ceaselessly occupied in coping with it."[19] The challenge they thus find themselves facing is to give a reasoned and plausible explanation of why early peoples held these beliefs, and why, despite the progress of science, so many other people still do. The explanations they propose, which include those considered or mentioned in our own earlier chapters, are of two main types: psychological and sociological. Those taking the path of psychological explanation include Müller, Tylor, Frazer, Freud, and others. Numbered among the sociological theorists are Marx and Durkheim, naturally, as well as Durkheim's disciples, Lévy-Bruhl, and a sequence of others.

In framing their psychological accounts of religion, Evans-Pritchard contends, these interpreters have almost without exception resorted mainly to clever guesswork. Each has simply asked himself how he, an educated Westerner, might have come to hold a religious or magical belief if he were walking in the footsteps of some primitive person who one day put a hand to his chin to reflect upon the world around him. Müller, a sentimental and romantic gentleman, says he would have been dazzled and intrigued by nature's great displays of power; accordingly, he finds the origin of religion in nature worship. Tylor, a flinty rationalist, thinks he would have been puzzled by the human figures he sees in dreams; so he produces the animistic theory. Frazer, both a rationalist and evolutionist, thinks he would have started with magic, then changed to religion, and finally adopted science. Being intellectuals, they all offer psychological explanations we can call intellectualist. They think that primitive people, like themselves, wanted to explain everything and so settled upon religious beliefs as a way of showing how the world works.

Other psychological interpreters, alert to the fact that while not all people are thinkers, all do have feelings, have put forward a type of theory best called emotionalist. Freud, for example, imagines that early people were gripped by anxieties and fears that could be eased only by concluding there was a divine Father above them. The English scholar Marett and the anthropologists Lowie and Malinowski suppose that primitives felt a certain profound awe and wonder about life and took this as a sign of some awesome Being or Power who had created it. Regardless of the specifics, however, one common feature is apparent in every one of these theories: they are pure speculation. Evans-Pritchard calls them examples of the "If-I-were-a-horse" mistake. Because these interpreters do not really know how a primitive person thinks, they imagine he or she would think as they do. Some make matters even worse by supposing that they can actually reconstruct the thoughts not just of today's primitives but of the very people who thousands of years ago first created religion, even though these ancient believers have left us not a single written word about anything in their lives, let alone their thoughts about a god or gods! Needless to say, the unsparing verdict Evans-Pritchard renders on such psychological theories is that they are for the most part worthless.

Sociological thinkers, Evans-Pritchard continues, have done a somewhat better job, but not by much. The more interesting are the theories that follow paths traced by Robertson Smith, the French scholar Fustel de Coulanges, and of course Émile Durkheim. These theorists have noticed, quite correctly, that however primitive people think, they do not do it on their own, any more than civilized people do. They are part of a culture, a society, that shapes their language, values, and ideas. Yet even with this insight at their disposal, sociological theorists have been no less inclined to guesswork than their psychological rivals. Because none of them actually knows a real primitive society, each chooses to create one in his imagination out of the scraps of evidence about totemism, sacrifice, or some other custom that happens to float in conveniently from Australia or other remote parts of the globe. As a result, even the most brilliant of the sociological theorists, Durkheim, constructs a theory that, however fascinating, begins to totter the moment new evidence comes along to show that totemism is something very different, and much more diverse in kind, than he thinks it is. For all their promise, then, sociological theories come in the end to something only slightly better than psychological ones; they still tend toward the fallacy that begins, "If I were a horse."

In contrast with these efforts, Evans-Pritchard finds it refreshing to note the achievement, limited as it is, of Lucien Lévy-Bruhl. He, too, scarcely left the comfort of his study, and he was mistaken to think that the primitive mind is prelogical while the modern mind is not. But he was a penetrating thinker, who, almost alone among modern theorists, recognized the crucial principle that we cannot understand the culture or religion of primitives until we concede that their whole world may be a very different one from ours, and that this world cannot be properly explained until we have worked very hard and very long to understand how it functions *from the inside*.

With so many failures and only Lévy-Bruhl to admire, one is inclined at this point to ask whether even attempting to explain religion is any longer worth the effort. Interestingly, and despite the record, Evans-Pritchard very much thinks it is. He believes, in fact, that more explanation, not less, should be offered, so long, of course, as theorists are ready to learn from the mistakes of their predecessors. There is, after all, at least a grain or more of truth in these earlier theories. There can be no question that religion involves the intellect, that it engages the emotions, and that it is closely associated with social organization. But it cannot be explained by any one of these factors alone. It must be explained comprehensively, in terms of its relations with all other factors and activities in a given society. In addition, though the guesswork of the past has compelled current anthropology to turn toward careful, specialized studies of specific cultures like the Azande and the Nuer, interpreters do need to move beyond specialized work. At some point, theorists need to "take into consideration all religions and not just primitive religions."[20] In this connection, Evans-Pritchard notes, one promising general path of inquiry has already been charted by the Italian social theorist Vilfredo Pareto, the French philosopher Henri Bergson, and the German sociologist Max Weber, all of whose writings seem to converge on a common theme. Instead of regarding religion and magic as forms of primitive thought, while science is assumed to be modern, they suggest that these two types of thinking are perhaps best seen as complementary configurations—forms of understanding that are clearly different but equally necessary in all human cultures, primitive and modern alike. No society can survive without something like science *and* something like religion; all cultures will always need both science's constructs of the mind and religion's "constructs of the heart."[21]

Evans-Pritchard does not completely commit himself to this last view, but he does suggest that it should be pursued as a hypothesis—to be confirmed or disproved through further work in the comparative study of religion, which has been sadly lacking to date. Moreover, such study should center not on theological writings, which carry the ideas of elites and leaders, but on encounters with ordinary people, on religious faith as it is actually lived and practiced. That is a difficult enterprise, he notes in conclusion, and the scholar without any personal religious commitment is unlikely to succeed in it. For the study of religion is not entirely like other disciplines. Scholars who reject all religion will inevitably be looking for an explanation that reduces it, for some theory—biological, social, or psychological—that will explain it away. The believer, on the other hand, is a person much more likely to see religion—including other people's religions—from the inside and to try to explain it on terms that are its own.

Analysis

One way to measure Evans-Pritchard as a theorist of religion is to place his work next to that of Eliade, who is almost his exact contemporary. Both men began their work in the decades between the two world wars, at a time when functionalist interpretations were dominant and when, in European culture as a whole, reductionist Freudians and the followers of Marx were regarded as the leading lights of the age. Both came to reject this reductionist perspective and anchor their work in a more sympathetic approach to the religion of primitive (in Eliade's word, "archaic") peoples. Both also repudiate the idea of social evolution. It misreads human cultural activities, and besides, it never fails to put primitives at the bottom and beginning of history while Western culture is placed at the end and at the top. Finally, both men—it is not irrelevant to add—exhibit a natural sympathy for religion that arises in some measure out of their personal heritage or commitment: Eliade presumably to Romanian "cosmic" Christianity, Evans-Pritchard to Catholic Christianity after his conversion in 1944.

Agreed as they are against certain attitudes of the age, Eliade and Evans-Pritchard nonetheless choose to carry out their programs of opposition in quite different ways. Starting from a resolute rejection of all reductionism, Eliade sets out to draw a global portrait of "the religious mind" in all, or at least most, places and times. He is also a man of the library, who thinks religion can still best be understood through its recorded history and mythology. Evans-Pritchard's stance is quite decidedly different. He too comes to reject functionalism, at least in its more extreme reductionist form, and the whole thrust of his research is to show that there really is no need for it. After all, if primitive magical and religious systems are in their terms just as rational as ours, we certainly do not need a reductionist theory to explain why people believe irrational things. At the same time, he is not nearly so emphatic about all of this as Eliade, especially in the case of sociologically functional approaches to religion, which played a strong role in his training and earlier work. He opposes any sociological determinism, to be sure, but, as we have seen, he also has the keenest appreciation for the merits of the French school—for Durkheim and especially Lévy-Bruhl. In addition, he has no wish to make claims about "the archaic mind" on some sort of worldwide, all-embracing scale. In his view, a theory of that sort comes near another instance of "If-I-were-a-horse" speculation. Not that there is anything necessarily wrong with the *ideal* of a broad, general theory embracing all of religion; at the close of *Nuer Religion*, Evans-Pritchard describes his own work as a step toward "building up a classification of African philosophies" that will make for the even wider comparisons needed to construct a theory of religion as a whole.[22] But to be done right, such things take time, patience, and a great deal more research. They simply cannot be done as readily as theorists like Eliade, and those of the past century, have supposed. Nor can they be done in the same way. Regardless of whether it is a world religion or primitive cult one studies, Evans-Pritchard insists that in the future the real work must be done outside of libraries and theological texts. A valid theory will have to explain religion as it is lived by ordinary people, not as it is taught by priests and theologians. That is where the real source of its power and remarkable resilience will ultimately be found.

If we draw a comparison with economics, we can see that Evans-Pritchard's great achievement lies on the plane not of macro- but micro-theory of religion. In his detailed account of Nuer belief and practice, he is able to show, just as he did for Zande magic, how religion "makes sense" for a specific people, in a specific kind of tribal society, at a specific point in time. He shows how this religion is intellectually coherent, how it "fits together" within itself. And he shows that it is culturally connected; it fits into the patterns of Nuer life in ways that answer both personal and social needs. When we compare Evans-Pritchard's own very solid, small-scale achievement in *Nuer Religion* with the grand theoretical balloons he floats by us from the past, puncturing them as he writes, it is not hard to see which kind of work, in his eyes, carries the greater weight. On the issue of how best to construct theories that reflect a true "science" of religion, his work represents an unmistakable turning point. No subsequent interpreter can afford to ignore his achievement.

Critique

As Freud's theory of religion depends in part on the strength of his psychology, so the value of Evans-Pritchard's theory rests in part on the nature and quality of his anthropology. As we have noted above, the judgment of most anthropologists on the value of his fieldwork and his interpretation of cultures is impressively favorable. Some regard him as the greatest ethnographer ever to have worked in the field. Though there have been criticisms, the more persuasive of them do not pertain to the religious dimensions of his work.[23] So we can perhaps pass over them here and note for our purpose the following points, which bear more specifically on his approach to religion.

1. Assessments of Other Theories

There are places where Evans-Pritchard shows considerably less patience with the theories of his fellow scholars than he does with the thought of the Azande and the Nuer. In discussing Nuer sacrifice, for example, he criticizes as "inept" those thinkers—like Rudolf Otto—who find the origin of religion in a distinctive emotion of awe or solemn wonder. The crowds at Nuer collective ceremonies show all kinds of emotions: attention, indifference, solemnity, amusement, whatever. Having said this, however, Evans-Pritchard in the very same context also points out that these collective sacrifices occur on occasions that are barely religious at all; they are largely social events, where one would expect a great variety of emotions, including, of course, at least a few serious moments. When, on the other hand, he discusses personal sacrifices, which by his own account are more purely religious occasions, the emotional state of the participants seems to be quite different. They are expected to show a grave and serious disposition—not unlike the emotions Otto calls religious. They exhibit a demeanor of solemnity and awe, a sense—one might almost say—of the numinous. This is not to say that Nuer religion offers a confirmation of theories like Otto's; it is meant only to suggest that when dealing with other theorists, Evans-Pritchard shows an occasional rush to judgment. The same tends to be true when he demolishes other theories with his favorite hammer: the "If-I-were-a-horse" fallacy. In a sense, the method of "If-I-were-so-and-so" is the only one we have when we wish to understand the motives and actions of other people, just as the detective does when trying to rethink the actions of a person who has committed a crime. The real problem with this kind of argument, which Evans-Pritchard does not strive as hard as he might to detect, is not *that* it is used (we really have no other) but *how* it is used, especially when theorists merely guess about how tribal peoples think instead of carefully reconstructing their thought on a solid foundation of evidence.

2. The "Primitive" Mind

Evans-Pritchard's great achievement has been to give theorists of both religion and human society a greater appreciation of what we can call "the normality" of the primitive mind. In the light of his work, we can say that the world of non-Western, tribal thought seems to make sense; it no longer strikes us as absurd or childish, as it once seemed to Tylor, Frazer, and others. But even so, we can legitimately ask whether Evans-Pritchard has solved as much of the problem of the primitive mind as he seemed to think. In the case of the Azande, for example, it is curious that after analyzing a particular item of witchcraft, he writes the following: "Azande have little theory about their oracles and do not feel the need for doctrines."[24] Elsewhere he observes that the idea of testing general beliefs against actual experience is simply foreign to Azande practice. On reading this, the question that naturally comes to the mind of the reader is: Why? *Why* do the Azande have little theory? *Why* do they fail to test their beliefs? Evans-Pritchard's answer to this question is clear but not entirely persuasive. He says magic is something too fundamental and too important in Zande life ever to be questioned—as are some of the inconsistent and seemingly illogical notions that many people hold in our civilized cultures as well. In short, they and we are the same, neither of us being in the sum of things either fully rational or wholly irrational. But here there is a further question to be asked: We and they do not seem to be exactly the same, do we? For our world, unlike theirs, is quite clearly a divided one. Some people in our civilization—scientists, philosophers, mathematicians, even some theologians—do stress theoretical understanding of the world, while others of us do not. Zande culture, on the contrary, seems curiously undivided. In it, we seem unable to find *anyone* who wants to defend theoretical knowledge and testing, or anyone who believes in critical, logical, and experimental thought. In that sense, their society *is* different, and we would very much like to know why. Evans-Pritchard does not really pursue this question, even though it is clearly important to the defense of his view that our culture and theirs stand on intellectually equal footings.

3. The Need for Theory

The last complaint we might bring against Evans-Pritchard is in some ways the most obvious and important—and yet the one to which he would most readily plead guilty. He does not really have a full theory of religion, or even of primitive religion, but only a theory of *a* religion—that of the Nuer—along with a few suggestions as to how thoughtful scholars might begin to work so as one day actually to arrive at something more general. Far better, he tells us, to do the small-scale foundational work that in the future will yield a solid general theory than to rush into the groundless speculations that were the trademark of theories past. This is a point no one can dispute. Yet Evans-Pritchard himself concedes that this is not an entirely satisfactory way to leave things. In the concluding pages of *Theories of Primitive Religion* he writes:

> During [the] last century . . . general statements were indeed attempted . . . in the form of evolutionary and psychological and sociological hypotheses, but since these attempts at general formulations seem to have been abandoned by anthropologists, our subject has suffered from loss of common aim and method.[25]

We could almost wonder, in light of these comments, whether Evans-Pritchard's weakness is just the opposite of his predecessors'. Could the study of religion have been done an even greater service if someone as well grounded as he in the evidence were perhaps *more* willing to generalize—even if only on the order of suggestion and hypothesis? Could he not himself have possibly contributed something to this much-needed "common aim and method"? At the least, a book from his hand with a title such as "Notes Toward the Construction of a General Theory of Religion" certainly would not have gone unread.

Even without such an effort, however, Evans-Pritchard's influence on thought about religion, especially in anthropological circles during the middle and later decades of the past century, has been unparalleled in scope and consequence.We shall see an instructive parallel to it in the next theorist, Clifford Geertz, the contemporary American advocate of interpretive anthropology.

Notes

1. Mary Douglas, *Edward Evan Evans-Pritchard*, Modern Masters Series (New York: Viking Press, 1980), p. 93.

2. There is no complete biography of Evans-Pritchard. T. O. Beidelman offers a brief account in "Sir Edward Evans-Pritchard, 1902–1973: An Appreciation," *Anthropos* 69 (1974): 553–567. There is also a measure of biographical information in a critical study,

noted earlier, by anthropologist Mary Douglas, who has been strongly influenced by Evans-Pritchard; see her *Edward Evans-Pritchard*, pp. 1–22 et passim.

3. John Middleton, "E. E. Evans-Pritchard," *The Macmillan Encyclopedia of Religion* (New York: Macmillan & Co., 1987), 8: 198.

4. Beidelman, "Appreciation," p. 556.

5. See his comments in *Social Anthropology and Other Essays* (Glencoe, IL: The Free Press, [1951] 1962), pp. 51–53; also in *Theories of Primitive Religion* (Oxford: Clarendon Press, 1965), pp. 53–69, where he is, however, also severely critical.

6. E. E. Evans-Pritchard, *Witchcraft, Oracles, and Magic among the Azande* (Oxford: Clarendon Press, 1937), p. 13.

7. Evans-Pritchard, *Witchcraft, Oracles, and Magic*, pp. 299–312.

8. Evans-Pritchard, *Witchcraft, Oracles, and Magic*, p. 63.

9. Evans-Pritchard, *Witchcraft, Oracles, and Magic*, p. 338.

10. Douglas, *Evans-Pritchard*, pp. 91–113, points out that Evans-Pritchard prepared himself for writing on Nuer religion by reading extensively in the Western theological literature he found in his father's parsonage study. She adds that the description of *Kwoth nhial* as a god of selfless love seems to draw upon *Agape and Eros* (1936), a classic study of the concepts of love in Western religious thought by the Lutheran theologian Anders Nygren; Evans-Pritchard acknowledged this book and its influence in other works.

11. Evans-Pritchard, *Nuer Religion* (Oxford: Clarendon Press), pp. 51–52.

12. To those familiar with the mystical theology of the early and medieval Eastern church, the Nuer hierarchy of spirits reflecting God, but not identical to him, resembles the modalistic language used by the theologian Sabellius to explain the Trinity. Their beliefs about the *kuth nhial* also bear a likeness to the mystical doctrine of the heavenly angelic hierarchy as presented in the widely read early medieval treatises of Pseudo-Dionysius the Areopagite.

13. Evans-Pritchard, *Nuer Religion*, p. 121.

14. Evans-Pritchard, *Nuer Religion*, pp. 121–122.

15. Evans-Pritchard, *Nuer Religion*, p. 154.

16. Evans-Pritchard, *Nuer Religion*, p. 199.

17. Evans-Pritchard, *Nuer Religion*, p. 239.

18. Evans-Pritchard, *Nuer Religion*, p. 281.

19. Evans-Pritchard, *Theories of Primitive Religion*, p. 10.

20. Evans-Pritchard, *Theories of Primitive Religion*, p. 113.

21. Evans-Pritchard, *Theories of Primitive Religion*, p. 115.

22. Evans-Pritchard, *Nuer Religion*, p. 314.

23. For a discussion of some of these criticisms, see Adam Kuper, *Anthropology and Anthropologists: The Modern British School* (London: Routledge & Kegan Paul, 1983), pp. 88–98.

24. Evans-Pritchard, *Witchcraft, Oracles, and Magic*, p. 314.

25. Evans-Pritchard, *Theories of Primitive Religion*, p. 114.

Suggestions for Further Reading

Beidelman, T. O. *A Bibliography of the Writings of E. E. Evans-Pritchard*, pp. 1–4. London: Tavistock, 1974. Provides a brief biographical note on Evans-Pritchard's career. There is no comprehensive biography.

Beidelman, T. O. "Sir Edward Evans-Pritchard, 1902–1973: An Appreciation." *Anthropos* 69 (1974): 553–567. An account of Evans-Pritchard's achievements and importance in his chosen field of anthropology.

Burton, John W. *An Introduction to Evans-Pritchard*. Fribourg, Switzerland: University Press, 1992. A welcome supplement to the earlier study by Mary Douglas.

Douglas, Mary. *Edward Evans-Pritchard*. Modern Masters Series. New York: Viking Press, 1980. A short but informative analysis, combining biographical information with critical assessment, by a well-known anthropologist strongly influenced by Evans-Pritchard's research.

Evans-Pritchard, E. E. "Fragment of an Autobiography." *New Blackfriars*, January 1973, pp. 35–37. The author's own brief account of his life, addressing among other things his midlife religious conversion.

Geertz, Clifford. *Works and Lives: The Anthropologist as Author*. Stanford, CA: Stanford University Press, 1988. Observations on Evans-Pritchard's works and his personal style alongside essays on other leading figures in anthropology.

Karp, Ivan, and Kent Maynard. "Reading *The Nuer*." *Current Anthropology* 24, no. 4 (August–October 1983): 481–503. A wide-ranging discussion of the impact of Evans-Pritchard's research among the Nuer in Africa; comments on the article and on Evans-Pritchard by other anthropologists are included.

Kuper, Adam. *Anthropology and Anthropologists: The Modern British School*. London: Routledge & Kegan Paul, 1983. Examines Evans-Pritchard's important role in the British tradition of fieldwork anthropology.

Lienhardt, Geoffrey. "Evans Pritchard: A Personal View." *Man*, n.s. 9, no. 2 (June 1974): 299–304. Comments on Evans-Pritchard's career by a distinguished fellow anthropologist who did similar fieldwork with a different African tribe.

Siegel, James T. *Naming the Witch*. Stanford, CA: Stanford University Press, 2006. An examination of witchcraft in East Java, Indonesia, by an ethnographer whose long acquaintance with the practice leads him to re-engage and reconsider Evans-Pritchard's work among the Azande, as well as Lévi-Strauss's work in South America. He shows how modernization and witchcraft can coexist.

Wilson, Bryan R., ed. *Rationality*. Oxford: Basil Blackwell, [1970] 1984. Essays by distinguished philosophers debating the questions of rational thought and action addressed in Evans-Pritchard's study of the Azande.

Winch, Peter. "Understanding a Primitive Society." In *Rationality*, edited by Bryan R. Wilson, pp. 78–111. Oxford: Basil Blackwell, [1970] 1984. A celebrated and controversial essay that begins from Evans-Pritchard's analysis of magic and witchcraft and challenges it by claiming that he did not take his sympathy for Azande ideas and customs far enough.

9

Religion as Cultural System: Clifford Geertz

Cultural analysis is not "an experimental science in search of a law but an interpretive one in search of meaning."

Clifford Geertz, *The Interpretation of Cultures*[1]

The next theorist in our sequence is American cultural anthropologist Clifford Geertz. If Evans-Pritchard was until his death the leading figure in British anthropology, many would say that Geertz held a similar place among anthropologists in America. For more than three decades from the early 1970s to his death in 2006, he was arguably among the most influential social scientists actively working. And like Evans-Pritchard, Geertz took a keen interest in religion, even though it is only one of many issues in cultural analysis that drew his close attention. The themes addressed in the numerous essays and noteworthy books published over the course of his career fall across the entire spectrum of human social life: from agriculture, economics, and ecology to kinship patterns, social history, and the politics of developing nations; from art, aesthetics, and literary theory to philosophy, science, and technology. The phrase "Renaissance man" is seldom used in the contemporary world of specialized learning, but it is not too far from accurate in describing Geertz's remarkably wide circle of interests and investigations. His chief concern was to press for a serious rethinking of fundamentals in the practice of anthropology and other social sciences—a rethinking that bears directly on the enterprise of understanding religion. With keen insight and a kind of baroque eloquence, he argued that human cultural activities are quite unusual and distinctive things, and that we will therefore get little benefit if we try to "explain" them in the way scientists explain the nonhuman aspects of the natural world. Whether we like it or not, human beings are different from atoms and insects. They live within complicated systems of meaning, which anthropologists call "cultures." So if we wish to understand these cultural activities, one of the most important of which certainly is religion, we must adopt a method that suits them. And that method is "interpretation." In matters human, we are clearly better off if we abandon the "explanation of behaviors" approach that a natural scientist might apply to a colony of bees or species of fish and turn instead to the "interpretation of cultures." Not surprisingly, that phrase forms the title of Geertz's most famous book.

Although Geertz recommended this new approach for all of anthropology and social science, he himself led the way in applying it specifically to the study of religion, which he helped to revitalize in the process. Indeed, with perhaps the sole exception of Mircea Eliade, there is probably no American scholar who has done more than Geertz to show how valuable a well-crafted study of religion can be to an understanding of almost all other aspects of human life and thought. It is perhaps needless to add that this interpretive stance, which strives to see all religions through the eyes and ideas of the people who practice them, marks a further step on the path already entered by Weber, James, Eliade, and Evans-Pritchard. It charts a course that leads away from functionalism and reductionism and toward an accounting of religion's distinctively human dimension: the ideas, attitudes, and purposes that create it.

Life and Career

Clifford Geertz was born in San Francisco, California, in 1926.[2] After completing secondary school, then military service in World War II, he attended Antioch College in Ohio, where in 1950 he received his B.A. degree in philosophy. From Antioch he went on to study anthropology at Harvard University. By this time, of course, fieldwork had become the cornerstone of anthropological training both in Britain and the United States, so while still a graduate student, Geertz chose to take his plunge. During his second year at Harvard, he and his wife Hildred traveled to the island of Java in Indonesia and remained there for two years, studying the complex multiracial, multireligious society of a single town. After returning to Harvard, he took his doctorate in 1956 from Harvard's Department of Social Relations with a specialization in anthropology. He and his wife then set out on a second term of fieldwork in Southeast Asia, this time on the island of Bali. Like Java, Bali was a part of the new Indonesian Republic, which had been established late in the 1940s, shortly after World War II and the end of Dutch colonial rule. Unlike Java, where Islam was the dominant faith, Bali possessed its own religion, a colorful and fascinating network of beliefs and rituals derived mostly from Hinduism. In both Bali and Java, Geertz's first mission as an anthropologist was to do ethnography—to prepare detailed and systematic descriptions of these non-Western societies, noticing especially how the different aspects of life blended into a cultural whole. In the same way that Evans-Pritchard's work among the Nuer and Azande formed a basis for his theoretical writing, this work in Java and Bali provided the foundation for most of Geertz's later essays and analyses. In terms of religion especially, his close contact with these Indonesian communities served as both source and stimulus for many of his most original ideas. It led him early on to the view that if, as functionalists claim, a religion is always shaped by society, it is no less true that a society is shaped by its religion.

In 1958, after completing his fieldwork in Bali, Geertz briefly joined the faculty of the University of California at Berkeley; he then moved to the University of Chicago for ten years, from 1960 to 1970. In 1960 he published *The Religion of Java*, an extensive account of the beliefs, symbols, rituals, and customs found in the town where he had conducted his first term of fieldwork. This study exhibited an attention to detail rivaling that of Evans-Pritchard, but it also attempted to be more wide-ranging—and needed to be, for the society Geertz had chosen was considerably more complicated by the collision of cultures than were the largely isolated African communities of the Azande and the Nuer in the interior of the Sudan. In Java's culture, Islam, Hinduism, and native animist traditions all claimed a place in the social system. Alongside his work on Javan religion, he pursued research on other aspects of society in the region. *Agricultural Involution* (1963) examined the ecology and economics of Indonesia and assessed its troubles and prospects in the postcolonial era. *Peddlers and Princes*, published in the same year, compared the economic life of a town in Java with another in Bali. And *The Social History of an Indonesian Town* (1965) told the story of the community in which Geertz had done most of his fieldwork—Modjokuto in Java—tracing the close interplay among economics, politics, and social life during the passage from colonial rule to independence.

We may recall that Evans-Pritchard's one venture outside of tribal Africa occurred during his stay in Libya, when he studied the Muslim community of the Sanusi. Interestingly, after his work in Indonesia, Geertz made a similar move to expand his base of field research by doing further work in the Islamic culture of Morocco in North Africa. Beginning in the 1960s, he made five field trips to this area, enabling him to observe a second Muslim religious community in a part of the world decidedly different from Southeast Asia. As a result, he was able, in *Islam Observed* (1968), to make a comparative study of a single major religion—Islam—as it had taken shape in two very different cultural settings. Later we can look more closely at this book.

In 1970 Geertz became the only anthropologist ever named a Professor at the famous Institute for Advanced Study in Princeton, New Jersey, where he continued his research until his retirement. This singular honor, which brought him to the institution where Einstein once worked, did not come in recognition of his ethnographic research, which could have been done—if not quite as well—by a number of other professionals in the field. It occurred because in the decade of the 1960s, while doing his ethnography, Geertz caught the attention of thoughtful people in many fields with a series of striking critical essays that addressed some of the most important theoretical issues in modern anthropology. In these probing, analytical discussions he set out his reservations about most earlier social science, claiming that many of its aims and methods were seriously misguided. In the course of these studies he was able to make a forcible argument for his newer style of "interpretive" anthropology. In America especially, Geertz's theoretical writings have been read with interest not only by other anthropologists but by scholars across all fields in the academy and by more than a few thoughtful general readers as well. Though some have left their mark individually, most of these critical essays have made their main impression in gathered form, chiefly in the collection entitled *The Interpretation of Cultures* (1973), a work that was widely acclaimed, and in *Local Knowledge* (1983), a later assemblage that earned similar approvals. A proper appreciation of Geertz's approach to religion requires that we pay attention to both sides of his work: the ethnographic and the theoretical.

Background: American Anthropology and Social Theory

To understand Geertz's perspective, we should notice first that he acquired his professional training neither in Durkheim's Paris nor Evans-Pritchard's Oxford but at Harvard University in the United States. His ideas on culture and religion were thus developed under two main influences: a strong and independent American tradition of anthropology and a perspective on social science he encountered at Harvard under the prominent theorist Talcott Parsons.

Since about the turn of the twentieth century, a truly professional style of research in anthropology had been established in the United States under the leadership of the German immigrant scholar Franz Boas (1858–1942) and his younger contemporaries Alfred Louis Kroeber (1876–1960) and Robert Lowie (1883–1957). At the time when Tylor and Frazer in England were still promoting grand theories built on the comparative method, these pioneering figures had already seen its error and abandoned its ways. Ahead of their time and, like Evans-Pritchard, sharing the view of Bronislaw Malinowski (1884–1942) on the value of field research, they insisted that any general theory must be rooted in rigorous "particular" ethnography, the kind of study that centers on one community and may take years or decades to complete. In America, these men had natural access to the many tribal cultures of native American peoples, and they used it to good advantage, learning tribal languages and doing fieldwork in their communities. Boas made a lifelong study of the peoples along the

Canadian Pacific coast; Kroeber and Lowie worked among the tribes of the American plains.

In addition to fieldwork, Boas, Kroeber, and Lowie stressed "culture" as the key unit of anthropological study. They insisted that in their field studies they were investigating not just a society—as some European scholars preferred to think—but a wider system of ideas, customs, attitudes, symbols, and institutions, of which society was only one part. "Society," these Americans tended to think, was a term weighted too heavily toward the purely material and structural components of human communities, while the appropriate term for their more comprehensive concept, which searched for hidden attitudes and emotions that lay behind and within the social order, was "culture." To some degree, the difference was verbal. For the most part Europeans seem to have meant by "society" and "social anthropology" something rather close to what American anthropologists meant by "culture" and "cultural anthropology."

In her widely read *Patterns of Culture* (1934), Ruth Benedict, a talented student of Kroeber and Boas, explained that culture was the key to understanding even individual human personality traits. When in her fieldwork she noticed a difference of temperament between the gentle, restrained Pueblo Indians and more combative tribes like the Pima and Kwakiutl, she traced it to the fundamental character of Pueblo culture, which stressed harmony, while the others did not. Such a view departed significantly from that of theorists in the school of Durkheim, who had considerably less interest in the psychology of individuals because it was not something concrete and objective in the way social facts like families and clans are. Benedict found individual psychology important, for it showed that a culture was a pattern, a kind of "group personality" that each of its members held in the mind.

While still a student, Geertz seems to have absorbed ideas from Boas, Kroeber, and Benedict quite naturally into his own anthropological perspective. Though he chose Indonesia rather than any of the native American communities as his locale, he immediately enlisted in two substantial terms of fieldwork, as we have seen. In addition, he fully endorsed the American commitment to particular studies; they were much to be preferred over the bad science of general theories built on poorly gathered evidence. Anthropology, Geertz heartily agreed, must be ethnography before it can be anything else. Its focus must fall on specific places and peoples, so that general conclusions come, if at all, only from these closely studied single instances. Further, and finally, he embraced the American view that the objects of anthropologists' inquiries are "cultures," not "societies." He recognized that the door to other peoples' lives could not be unlocked only by examining such social units as the family, kinship patterns, clan structures, or legal systems; it was necessary to search beyond these for the entire interconnected pattern of ideas, motives, and activities that we call a culture.

With regard to this last point, we should notice that Geertz did have some reservations about the newer stress on culture and showed rather more sympathy for the sociological approach of the French school than did others. For if, as Benedict claimed, culture was nothing more than a kind of group attitude, a communal "personality" passed on in the minds of individual persons, then there was really nothing very objective about it for the social scientist to study. In the American view, one tended to argue that individual behavior is an expression of culture, while defining culture merely as the way in which individuals have learned to behave.[3] Such circular statements might be true, but they were not very enlightening. If the concept of culture was to be usable in scientific research, the French were right in saying that it had to refer to something objective, not just to elusive psychological states like the Pueblo "feeling of harmony" or another tribe's attitude of aggression. In addressing this difficulty, Geertz found help in the work of Talcott Parsons, his Harvard teacher and at the time one of the leading sociologists in America.

American Social Theory: Parsons and Weber

It is hard to know how direct his influence was, but Talcott Parsons seems to have affected Geertz in two ways. First, Parsons himself had come under the influence not of Durkheim primarily, as many others had, but of Max Weber, whom we have now had a chance to consider at some length. In the decade of the 1930s, well before many Americans (including many professional sociologists) had even read Weber, Parsons had translated some of Weber's works, most notably *The Protestant Ethic*, and had explored certain key themes of his agenda. So in the circle of Parsons's students and readers, at least, there was familiarity with concepts like "worldly asceticism" and its connection with capitalism, with sociology construed as the study of rational human action, and especially with the method of *Verstehen*, which was of key importance in distinguishing Weber's stress on the meaning systems that shape the actions of individuals from Durkheim's focus on the determinative role of social structure.

In addition to serving as a channel for the ideas of Weber, Parsons provided Geertz with something else: a way of resolving the problem of culture as it had been left by anthropologists like Ruth Benedict. In *The Structure of Social Action* (1934), his most important book, Parsons built upon Weber and developed the view that all human groups function on three levels of organization: (1) individual personalities, which are shaped and governed by (2) a social system, which is, in its turn, shaped and controlled by (3) a separate "cultural system." The last of these, which is a complex network of values, symbols, and beliefs, interacts with both the individual and the society, but for purposes of

analysis it can be separated from them. To many, this thesis was a breakthrough. If Benedict's idea of culture as a group personality was too vague and subjective to be of much scientific use, Parsons's concept was not. A "cultural system" was an objective thing, a collection of symbols—objects, gestures, words, events, all with meanings attached to them—that exists outside the minds of individual people yet works inwardly to shape attitudes and guide actions. As we shall see soon, Geertz clearly shared this idea of a culture as an objective system of symbols, so much so that some observers prefer to call his approach not interpretive but "symbolic" anthropology.[4]

Interpretive Social Science: Principles and Precepts

Weber, Parsons, and the tradition of American anthropology all provide components of Geertz's perspective. To see how he assembles them into a complete program of interpretive anthropology, we can now turn to his own writings, especially the theoretical essays and other works published mostly in the two formative decades of his career, the 1960s and 1970s. Since we obviously cannot cover all of these in our discussion and since some are theoretical and others ethnographic, it will be best if we work in stages. We begin by looking at two of Geertz's best-known theoretical essays: the first explains his interpretive anthropology in general terms, and the second directs it specifically to religion. With these in hand, we then turn to some samples of the way in which Geertz applies his perspective to actual religions.

Culture and Interpretation: The Method of "Thick Description"

In 1973 Geertz published his award-winning collection of essays entitled *The Interpretation of Cultures*. Most of these pieces had first appeared in various scholarly journals during the previous decade. But as an introduction to the others, Geertz provided a new essay that has since become the classic statement of his point of view. He entitled it "Thick Description: Toward an Interpretive Theory of Culture." In it, he points out first that although the term "culture" has tended to mean many different things to previous anthropologists, the key feature of the word is the idea of "meaning" or "significance." Man, he says, referring explicitly to the perspective of Max Weber, is "an animal suspended in webs of significance he himself has spun." If therefore we wish to do what anthropologists are paid to do, namely, explain the cultures of other human beings, we have no choice but to use a method that is described by the English philosopher Gilbert Ryle as "thick description." We must describe not only what happens but also what people *intend* by what happens.

Ryle gives the example of two boys: one experiences a muscular twitch at the eye while the other winks at a friend. In a purely physical, or "thin," description, both of these movements can be identically described. But the minute we take into account the element of meaning, the *significance* of the physical motion, no two actions could be more different: the one means nothing, the other means a great deal. "Thick" description, which includes the meaning of the motion, shows the wink to be decidedly different from the twitch. It must be clearly understood, says Geertz, that ethnography, and so all of anthropology, is always a matter of thick description. Its aim is never just to describe the mere structure of a tribe or clan or the bare elements of a ritual. Its task is to discern meanings, to discover intentions, to detect the *significance* people attribute to their rituals, institutions, and beliefs.

It is important to notice that when we speak of "meanings," most people think of something quite private—an idea in an individual person's head. But a moment's further thought makes it clear that there is nothing necessarily private at all about meaning. I cannot wink privately at you unless there is something public—a context of meanings—shared by both of us that enables you to take from the wink the same meaning I give to it. We should therefore understand that the culture of any society is just this shared context of meanings. Or, to use Geertz's own words, "culture consists of socially established structures of meaning in terms of which people do such things as signal conspiracies and join them or perceive insults and answer them."[5] A culture is not something physical, but it is there—objectively there—nonetheless. And it is the one thing that, more than any other, anthropologists must try to reconstruct when they study a community or people of any place or time.

By the same token, we should notice that a culture is not *just* about meanings, as if it were a purely self-contained system of symbols, like mathematics. Behavior, or action, must also be observed "because it is through the flow of behavior—or, more precisely, social action—that cultural forms find articulation."[6] This may mean that on some occasions the description of a culture will not always be completely consistent. People sometimes behave in ways that clash with the system of meaning prescribed by their own culture; or, perhaps more accurately, cultural systems sometimes present multiple and conflicting patterns within which people choose diverse courses of action. It also means that anthropologists can never do more than *re*construct what their subjects think and do by writing down their own best interpretation of it. Cultural analysis is, for the interpretive anthropologist as for every other careful theorist, always a matter of "guessing at meanings, assessing the guesses, and drawing explanatory conclusions."[7]

None of this difficult work can be done well unless it is done microscopically, so to speak. Interpretive anthropology attends to "ethnographic miniatures," small-scale subjects like clans, tribes, or villages, whose cultural systems can be mapped out in all the minute detail characteristic of each. For Geertz, this means too that any attempt to make broad, general statements about all of humanity must be viewed with the strongest suspicion. In the past, he notes, anthropologists have tended to say things like "Middletown, which I have studied, is the United States in miniature." The answer to that is: In some respects it may be; in others it most probably is not. So such general statements are just as likely to mislead as to inform. Again, it is sometimes said that a certain society is a "test case" through which we can prove something about all others. Here we can cite (though Geertz does not) Durkheim's "crucial experiment" with Australian totemism. But we need to ask: What kind of test case can we really make when almost none of the important conditions can be controlled? We can never compare two human cultures as we can—with a control—two laboratory cultures, placing them in identical dishes and adding a chemical to one and not to the other. The findings of any one such cultural test case, says Geertz, are "as inherently inconclusive as any others."[8]

In light of all this, anyone interested in explaining human activities must understand that the day when scholars set as their goal some "general theory of cultural interpretation" is now past—and most likely gone forever. For the unavoidable fact is that analysis of culture is not "an experimental science in search of a law but an interpretive one in search of meaning."[9] Does this mean that the interpretation of cultures can never give us wisdom that is of any general value? Well, not quite. But what we can learn from it, says Geertz, is probably more like the diagnosis a doctor makes in determining a type of illness from certain symptoms. Anthropology is never fully predictive, never able to offer the certainty that is available in fields like physics or chemistry, which center only on physical processes that follow the laws of motion or the rules of molecular reactions. The anthropologist cannot forecast with certainty what will happen in a culture, any more than a doctor can definitely predict that a child will catch or resist a virus. But like a diagnosis, a theory should in some measure try to anticipate what will happen elsewhere or be in some way applicable to other cases. In interpreting one culture, a theory ought in some way to be capable of being "tried out" on another, and then be either kept for further use or discarded. In that connection, anthropologists do have a variety of general ideas at their disposal—abstract concepts expressed in words like "structure," "identity," "ritual," "revolution," "world view," "integration," and so on. These allow a theorist to stretch a single example into an idea that might apply in several or many cases. They may not seem like much, but in fact such concepts are extremely valuable, and in any case, they form the only kind of general observation a good theorist would ever want to make. Anything more ambitious might be interesting, but it is also likely to mark the return of the old mistakes: bad science pretending to be anthropology.

Cultural Interpretation and Religion

If interpretive anthropology is a matter of seeking out the system of meanings and values through which people live their lives, then it stands to reason that in any culture religion will command serious anthropological attention. That Geertz firmly believes this is evident in the first study that came out of his fieldwork—and for that matter the first of his career—*The Religion of Java* (1960). This book is an ethnography in the best tradition of American anthropology; it is a particular study of a specific people whom Geertz came to know in depth through his immersion in their language and culture. It explores in detail the complex interweaving of Muslim, Hindu, and native animistic (the Javan name is *abangan*) religious traditions. And it looks at religion as a cultural fact in its own right, not as a mere expression of social needs or economic tensions (though these are certainly noticed). Through its symbols, ideas, rituals, and customs, Geertz finds the influence of religion to be present in every crevice and corner of Javan life. His study is so microscopically detailed, so closely tied to the particulars of Javan culture, and so careful to avoid generalizations that he might well have used it as the very model for the kind of "thick description" anthropology we have just seen him recommend. For that very reason, however, the book does not try to tell us very much of a theoretical nature about the aims of an interpretive approach to religion. Typically for him, Geertz chooses to do that instead with an essay, "Religion as a Cultural System," first published in 1966 and later included in *The Interpretation of Cultures*. Though almost as celebrated as "Thick Description" and just as widely noted or commented upon, this is not the easiest essay to understand or to summarize. But it is important, so we need at least to trace its outline.

Geertz begins by telling us, as his title indicates, that he is interested in "the cultural dimension" of religion. Here he also helps by providing a fairly clear and complete idea of what he means by a culture. It is "a pattern of meanings," or ideas, carried in symbols, by which people pass along their knowledge of life and express their attitudes toward it. As there are within a culture many different attitudes and many different forms of knowledge to pass on, so there are also different "cultural systems" to carry them. Art can be a cultural system, as can "common sense," a political ideology, an ethnic heritage, and the like.

What does it mean to say religion is a cultural system? Geertz offers an answer to this question in a single, heavily packed sentence. Religion is:

> (1) a system of symbols which acts to (2) establish powerful, pervasive, and long-lasting moods and motivations in men by (3) formulating conceptions of a general order of existence and (4) clothing these conceptions with such an aura of factuality that (5) the moods and motivations seem uniquely realistic.[10]

This is not a description anyone is likely to find brief and clear, but it is not quite as forbidding as it first may seem. In the rest of his essay, Geertz actually does us the service of breaking down his account (which serves as both a definition and theory) by explaining in detail each of its elements. We can start with the first. By "a system of symbols" Geertz means just about anything that carries and conveys to people an idea: an object like a Buddhist prayer wheel, an event like the crucifixion, a ritual like a bar mitzvah, or a simple wordless action, like a gesture of compassion or humility. A Torah scroll, for example, conveys to Jews the idea, among others, of God's revelation. The image of a saint in a hospital room may convey the idea of divine concern for the sick. As we have seen before, the important thing about these ideas and symbols is that they are not purely private matters. They are public—things that exist outside ourselves in the same way that, say, a computer program exists outside of a computer as well as within it. As program codes can be examined and read objectively apart from the physical machines they are installed in, so religious symbols, though they enter the minds of private individuals, can be grasped apart from the individual brains that think them.

When it is said, secondly, that these symbols "establish powerful, pervasive, and long-lasting moods and motivations," we can abbreviate this by saying that religion makes people feel things and also want to do things. Motivations have goals, and they are guided by an enduring set of values—what people think is good and right. The Buddhist monk feels a strong negative motivation, an aversion, when presented with a generous midwestern American steak dinner. For him, it is wrong both to eat meat and to eat in such quantity, because attachments to food weigh him down in his struggle for a better rebirth and ultimate escape from life in the natural world. His motivation here is a matter of morals, of choosing for himself the good over the evil. Jews wishing to see Jerusalem and Muslims hoping to visit Mecca will also arrange things so as to reach their goal, which is to attain the morally good experience of being in the spaces sacred to their traditions. Moods are more temporary than motivations, also less defined and less clearly directed. When Hindu pilgrims arrive at Benares or Christians at Bethlehem, they may well experience, even unexpectedly, a feeling of joy, an inner peace that inspires for a time and then gives way naturally, at a later time, to a different mood.

The power of these moods comes from their source; they are not occasioned by trivial or minor things. They arise because religion occupies itself with something truly important; it formulates "conceptions of a general order of existence." By this Geertz simply means that religion offers ultimate explanations of the world. Its main interest is not to tell us about stocks and bonds, sports and games, fashions in clothing, or forms of entertainment. Its intent is to provide an ultimate meaning, a great ordering purpose to the world. Everyone knows when the disorder, the chaos of the world makes itself felt. It does so when people face things that, intellectually, they just cannot comprehend; when, emotionally, they face sufferings they cannot bear; or when, morally, they encounter evil they cannot accept. At these moments they see that what is collides with what ought to be.

On the one side, then, stand conceptions of the world, and on the other a set of moods and motivations guided by moral ideals; taken together, these two lie at the core of religion. Geertz abbreviates the two elements by referring simply to "world view" and "ethos"—to conceptual ideas and behavioral inclinations. He then adds that religion "(4) clothes these conceptions with such an aura of factuality that (5) the moods and motivations seem uniquely realistic." In simpler terms, this means that religion marks out a sphere of life that has a special status. What separates it from other cultural systems is that its symbols claim to put us in touch with what is "really real"—with things that matter to people more than anything else. And it is in rituals that people are seized by the sense of this compelling reality. In rituals, the "moods and motivations" of religious believers coincide with their world view in ways that powerfully reinforce each other. My world view tells me I must feel this way, and my feelings tell me, in turn, that my world view must be right; there can be no mistake about it. In ritual, there occurs "a symbolic fusion of ethos and world view"; what people want to do and feel they should do—their *ethos*—joins with their picture of the way the world actually is.

Geertz explains that a vivid example of this fusion, this blending of ethos and world view, can be found in one of Indonesia's most remarkable ceremonies. On certain occasions the people of Bali stage a colorful performance of a great battle between two characters from their mythology: the fearsome witch Rangda and the comical monster Barong. As these two struggle, the audience itself gradually comes into the great spectacle, with some members taking the parts of supporting characters and others swooning into states of trance. As the performance proceeds, it becomes clear that for the Balinese this drama is "not merely a spectacle to be watched but a ritual to be enacted."[11] At its height, the great drama of the performance, the intense emotion, and the crowd involvement bring the whole scene almost into chaos. The struggle always ends without a clear winner, but that is irrelevant. What is important is the way this theatrical event evokes from the Balinese the attitudes and emotions—a mixture of playfulness, exhibitionism, and fear—that are emblematic of their culture. In and through the turbulent, emotion-filled process of observing and joining this ritual, they experience a deep confirmation of their view of the world as an always uncertain struggle between the evil and the good. Further, these religious moods and motivations, fitted to the world view, carry over from the ceremony into the rest of society, giving all of Balinese life the features that set it apart from the lives led in other cultures.

From all of this, we should be able to see again how unwise it is, in religion no less than any other sphere of culture, to leap toward quick general conclusions. Balinese religion is so distinctive, so specifically its own sort of thing, that there is hardly anything about it that we could turn into a general rule for all religions—other than the fact that all traditions somehow manage to combine, like the Balinese, both a world view and an ethos. Accordingly, as Geertz explains in his conclusion, any useful study of religion will always require a two-stage operation. One must first analyze the set of meanings found in the religious symbols themselves—a difficult task in itself. Then comes the even more difficult but equally important second stage: since the symbols are tightly connected to both the structures of the society and the psychology of its individual members, those connections must be traced along a continuous circuit of signals given, received, and returned. If we think of wires strung in a triangular configuration among three poles, one standing for symbol, another for society, and a third for individual psychology, we have a fitting image of the steady flow of influences and effects that pass among and through all three of these centers in any religious system.

Interpreting Religion: A Balinese Example

If this is what Geertz's approach to religion looks like on its theoretical side, what shape does it take when applied to actual cases? Although his writings on Bali, Java, and Morocco give us more than enough examples to choose from, we have space here to consider just two: one, a short essay on religion in modern Bali, and the other, as noted, Geertz's comparative study of Muslim culture in Indonesia and Morocco, published as *Islam Observed* (1968).

The article "'Internal Conversion' in Contemporary Bali" (1964) begins with an idea proposed (not surprisingly) by Max Weber. In one of his interesting comparative discussions (which we could only mention in our earlier chapter), Weber distinguishes between traditional and rationalized religions. We have already noticed the importance he attributes to the broad process of rationalization that has propelled the advances of Western civilization. Traditional religion, which is characteristic of primitive peoples, tends to gravitate toward magic and polytheism. The natural inclination in these "enchanted" cultures is to see divinity everywhere. There is a spirit in every rock and a ghost in every tree, while ritual, often with a magical purpose, frames almost every aspect of life. Primitive peoples find themselves so immersed in dealings with this spirit or that demon that they scarcely realize they even have such a thing as a religion; such things are just what they always do.

Rationalized religion, by contrast, is what we find at the core of the great world religions. Though traditional elements are invariably included, Judaism and Christianity, as well as Confucianism and the Brahmin and Buddhist sages of India, all center attention on just one or a very few universal spiritual principles: the one God of the prophets, the Way of Nature, Brahman, the Supreme Spirit, or Nirvana (absolute nothingness). By a logic of one kind or another, rationalized religions execute a process of "abstraction," lifting their ultimate being or cosmic principle above the little things of life. The effect of this "internal conversion" process is to leave ordinary life "disenchanted"—left bare of its helpful or spiteful little gods and the little ceremonies that connect people to them. Instead of these numerous everyday ceremonies and spells, rationalized religion offers everyone a single path to the divine, such as through mystical experience, which the sages of India taught, or through Judaism's demand of obedience to the moral law. And in distinction from traditional cults, the followers of these rationalized religions are fully aware of what they are doing; they know quite self-consciously that they "have a religion." They know, and are taught to know, that they are giving personal assent to an ordered system of teaching that embraces all of the world and life.[12]

Rationalized and traditional religions also differ in one other important respect: the way in which they deal with the great problems of life. Traditional religions, as Evans-Pritchard explained in the case of Zande witchcraft, address these great questions—what life means, why there is pain, why there is evil—in very particular, specific ways. They do not ask, "Why do people suffer?" They ask, "Why is my father sick?" And they look for very particular answers as well: "Father is sick because his enemy has used witchcraft." Rationalized religions, however, always raise such questions to a cosmic scale; they include the whole world. In the case of suffering, they point not to a single witch but to Satan, who brought sin into the world, or to the dark, cool side of the Tao; they appeal, in short, to great realities that affect everyone.

Rationalized religions typically have appeared in periods of social upheaval, at those critical cultural moments when the local practices of magic and the traditional religions of field and village appear insufficient to meet the cultural and emotional demands placed on them. Christianity, for example, arose amid the great social turmoil caused in the ancient Mediterranean world by the rise and spread of Greco-Roman civilization. Confucianism appeared amid the chaos of China's destructive ancient civil wars.

Granting the value of this broad conceptual framework, says Geertz, we can apply it to modern-day Bali. Anyone who approaches its culture with Weber's contrasts in mind will at once notice several interesting things. Though in name it is Hindu, the religion of Bali is not the mysticism of India's intellectuals but the everyday polytheism and mythology of its villagers; that is to say, it fits

Weber's category of a traditional religion. There is in it almost no rationalized theology, whereas rituals and a sense of nearby divinity can be found everywhere. There are thousands of temples in the landscape, and a person can belong to dozens of them at the same time. Often people have no idea which gods are worshipped in them, but for each one they insist that an appropriate ritual be performed exactly according to a set plan. The ceremonies, moreover, are also tightly woven into the social structure. Local priests who belong to the Brahmin caste find their high social rank reinforced by their special spiritual status; each "owns" a group of lower-caste followers who associate him with divinity, while he calls them his "clients." In addition, one of the main enterprises of the various princes, kings, and lords on the island is to hold large-scale religious festivals, spectacles that require time-consuming labor, sometimes employing hundreds of peasants and other laborers. The ceremonies remind all people of their proper place on the social scale; the highborn host the celebrations, while the lowborn do the work. Finally, in the true manner of magical religions, the cult of death and witches, which we saw above in the dramatic combat of Rangda and Barong, penetrates to every aspect of Balinese life. Although over the years they have encountered both Christianity and Islam, the Balinese have never seriously considered conversion to either of these outside faiths. So their traditional religion has been able to survive the centuries largely untouched by the entry of any rationalized world religion.

As Geertz viewed it in 1964, however, Bali was an island confronted with dramatic social changes, many brought on by the coming of independence to all of Indonesia in 1949. Modern education, political consciousness, and improved communication had opened the channels of contact with the outside world. The growth of cities and of population had added to the pressure, so that what happened in ancient societies like the Roman empire when social turmoil brought the disenchantment of the world and the end of magical religion seems to have anticipated what was happening in modern Bali. If one were to look closely, in fact, it would seem that the people of modern Bali were at that very moment engaged in Weber's process of internal conversion, transforming their traditional ways of worship into something that, gradually, was beginning to assume the features of a rationalized world religion. Geertz states that in the course of his fieldwork, he was particularly struck one evening when, at a funeral, an intense philosophical discussion of the meaning and purpose of religion broke out among certain young men of the town. Almost unknown in traditional cultures, such discussions are the hallmark of rationalized religion; yet here just such a vigorous exchange was taking place on the street in Bali. Almost as unheard of in a traditional situation is the development of scriptures, doctrines, religious literacy, and an organized priesthood. But there were signs that each of these things was now coming into Balinese culture. Interestingly, too, the nobles and princes, perhaps seeing their old privileges threatened by the coming of democratic government, had actually put themselves behind this initiative, hoping they could keep their status by being in the forefront of a new, more defined and self-conscious Balinese religion. The new movement, says Geertz, had only recently acquired the most visible badge of any rationalized faith: an organization. In opposition to the Indonesian government's Muslim-dominated Ministry of Religion, Bali had recently chosen to establish its own, locally supported, purely Balinese ministry, which had assumed the task of certifying Brahmana priests and creating an authorized class of professional clergy.

In essence, Geertz explains, all of those processes and changes that Weber discovers behind the growth of the great rationalized religions of the world could be found in evidence on the island of Bali in the postwar era. Bali in 1964 seemed to stand where Rome did in the time of Jesus and China did in the days of Confucius. That being so, the question that comes naturally to mind is: Can any more general conclusions be drawn from Bali's experience? Is there a theory to connect ancient Rome with modern Bali, and perhaps other places as well? Geertz does not propose one. What will happen in the future, he concedes, is something no one can predict. Nonetheless, if there is no theory, there is clearly much insight to be gained from general paradigms, and ideal-types such as Weber's, along with the promise that the case of Bali may help us further to apply and refine them. In conclusion Geertz observes, "By looking closely at what happens on this peculiar little island over the next several decades, we may gain insights into the dynamics of religious change of a specificity and an immediacy that history, having already happened, can never give us."[13]

Islam Observed

Our second example of Geertz's interpretive approach in action takes us into a larger subject, his comparison of two kinds of Islam. At the outset of *Islam Observed* (1968), he proposes, ambitiously enough, to lay out a "general framework for the comparative analysis of religion" and apply it to one faith, Islam, as it exists in the two quite different countries that his fieldwork enabled him to know best: Indonesia and Morocco.[14] In addition to being Muslim, he notes, both of these cultures have in modern times passed through great social change. At one time traditional societies of rice farmers in the one case and herdsmen in the other, both became colonies of Western powers (the Dutch and the French) and have only recently won independence (Indonesia in 1949, Morocco in 1956). Religion, needless to say, has often been at the center of the social transformations that have come over both of these nations.

The Classical Styles of Islam

Morocco took shape as a Muslim nation during four important centuries from about 1050 to 1450 AD, when the society was dominated by aggressive tribesmen from the desert and strong-minded merchants in the towns. The two main figures in this culture were the warrior, or strongman, and the mystic, the Muslim holy man, who sometimes came together in the ideal form of the warrior-saint. Idris II, who built the city of Fez in the ninth century and was the first Moroccan king, cut such a figure; he was a fierce fighter and reformer who claimed direct descent from the Prophet Muhammad. Later in time, holy men so devout that they were known as "marabouts"—from the Arabic word *murabit*, "lashed" or "shackled" to God—attracted bands of followers who split the land into militant sects, each fiercely loyal to its sacred leader. In Indonesia, by contrast, Islam arrived later and took a different form. Long a prosperous farming culture whose abundant rice fields supported peasant, prince, and merchant alike, Indonesia had little use for the boldness and nerve that were key to survival in Morocco. The virtue prized above all was quiet diligence in the fields, a personality trait supported for centuries by Hindu-Buddhist ideals, which stressed meditation, inwardness, and personal composure. Not until the 1300s did Islam begin to reach the Indonesian islands, and then it came quietly through trading contacts and in a tolerant Indian form that allowed it to blend with the Hindu, Buddhist, and animist beliefs already in place. Indonesian Islam accordingly developed flexible features; it was "adaptive, absorbent, pragmatic, and gradualistic"—very different from the "uncompromising rigorism" and "aggressive fundamentalism" of Morocco.[15] While the one evolved into something gradualist, liberal, and accommodating, the other took a shape that was perfectionist, puritanical, and uncompromising.

These characteristic religious attitudes, rigorous in the one case, relaxed in the other, Geertz calls "the classical styles" of Islam in each nation. Both are "mystical," because they find religious truth through immediate contact with God, but there are significant differences, which Geertz explains through the stories of two legendary religious leaders. In Indonesia's sacred legends, Sunan Kalidjaga is the hero said to have brought Islam to the island of Java. He was born into the court of a ruling family during the age of the great Hindu-Buddhist "theater states"—that is, at a time when the ruling classes, as members of the highest caste, were seen as the spiritual elite of the country. In the royal and princely courts, elaborate religious ceremonies were held to demonstrate the political power and religious authority of the kings. As a young man, however, Kalidjaga cared little for religion until one day he met a Muslim mystic whose precious cane and jewels he tried to steal. The holy man only laughed at his foolish desire for material things and suddenly transformed a nearby banyan into a tree of gold, hung with jewels. Kalidjaga was so astounded by this miracle and the man's indifference to wealth that he asked to become a Muslim as well, then proved his Islamic self-discipline by remaining in one place, in a state of obedient meditation, for an interval that stretched to several decades! He thus became a Muslim without ever seeing the Koran or visiting a mosque. Significantly, however, after embracing Islam, Kalidjaga did not abandon the theater-state culture of his childhood. Instead, he helped to establish a new royal city at Mataram, and there used his high personal position and the ceremonies of the king's court to promote Islam, just as they once served the purposes of the older Hindu-Buddhist religion.

The legend of Kalidjaga is of course more than the tale of a man. It is the story of all Islam as it came to Indonesia, merged with the older religions, and adapted itself to the culture of the theater states. Such syncretism, or blending, of religions was very typical of Indonesia, but it did not last. It began to break down in the modern era, as Islam came to be the dominant faith of the merchants, whose power grew stronger, and as the Dutch, who arrived at the same time to colonize the islands, pushed the ruling class out of power. Under pressure from the European conquerors, the delicate mixed religion of these earlier days broke up into the three separate traditions—Hindu-Buddhist, Muslim, and native animist—that we find in Java today.

In a fashion similar to the case of Kalidjaga in Java, the features of Islam in Morocco can best be seen in the life of the Muslim holy man known as Sidi Lahsen Lyusi, one of the last of the marabouts, who lived in the 1600s. Like the others, Lyusi too saw himself as "tied to God." A wandering prophet, scholar, and pilgrim, he was a man of intense morality and great learning, a mighty figure who in Moroccan stories is revered as the saint who faced down a sultan. It happened that while a guest of none less than the Sultan Mulay Ismail, founder of the great Alawite dynasty, Lyusi one day began to insult his host by breaking all of the serving dishes in the palace. The purpose of this ungrateful display was in fact a noble one: a protest against the backbreaking labor the sultan imposed on his slaves. For this, the sultan expelled Lyusi from the palace and attempted later to kill him. But when he charged the holy man's tent, his horse miraculously began to sink into the ground. At once the sultan admitted his wrongs, acknowledged Lyusi's demand to be recognized as a holy man and a *sherif*, a descendant of the Prophet, and allowed him to go his way.

The quality that Lyusi triumphantly demonstrated in this confrontation was *baraka*: a kind of spiritual charisma. His supernatural power to stop the sultan's horse was a sure sign that he possessed this divine blessing. Further, Islam's other way of proving one's authority is to be accepted as a *sherif*. Even though Lyusi performed a miracle, he required that the sultan recognize in him this second proof of his holiness as well. We thus find centered in this one holy man the great question that faced all of Islam in Morocco: How is the spokesman for God to be known? Does *baraka* come simply through a holy man's personal charisma and miraculous powers? Or must one be a descendant of the Prophet Muhammad? Or are both required? In the tension between these two principles, Geertz explains, we can see one of the key issues that animated Moroccan Islamic culture throughout its history. Over time, the ruling families of the country established descent from the Prophet as the dominant principle, but the appeal of *baraka*—as expressed in the charismatic qualities of holiness, moral intensity, and wonder-working power—never disappeared. It remained very much alive in various cults of the saints and—significantly for later history—in popular opinion. The people tended to hold that the sultan should possess both qualities: personal religious charisma *and* descent from the Prophet's line. As a result, both heredity and spirituality had to be in evidence to speak or act with divine authority.

In both Indonesia and Morocco, then, the classical styles of Islam are "mystical"; they try to bring people into the immediate presence of God. But the stories of the Muslim saints show how different in form even mystical Islam can be. The passive "illuminationist" mysticism of Kalidjaga stands in sharp contrast to the aggressive "maraboutist" piety of Lyusi. To borrow from Geertz's own definition, the religions of Indonesia and Morocco, though both Islamic, show decidedly different "moods and motivations." On the Indonesian side, there is "inwardness, imperturbability, patience, poise, sensibility, aestheticism, elitism, and an almost obsessive self-effacement . . . ; on the Moroccan side, activism, fervor, impetuosity, nerve, toughness, moralism, populism, and an almost obsessive self-assertion."[16]

The Scripturalist Revolt

Whatever these differences, Islamic Indonesia and Morocco have in recent times both had to cope with two major challenges: colonial rule and the coming of modernization. In both lands the high point of colonial domination fell roughly in the century between 1820 and 1920. And in both, this experience made people distinctly more aware that they were Muslim while their Christian masters were not. Islam became identified with protest, nationalism, and the hope of independence. In the process, however, the faith itself began to change. The classical styles—Indonesian illuminationism and Moroccan maraboutism—found themselves under challenge from a powerful new movement that claimed to be very old. This was "scripturalist" Islam.

In the case of Indonesia, this scripturalist revolt took shape in the 1800s, at the high point of Dutch control and at a time when national sentiment turned strongly against colonial powers. Inspired by new opportunities for pilgrimage to Mecca, Indonesians began to discover in Arabia a different, more rigorous and militant Islam, which soon came to be taught in newly founded schools. In these *santri* (Javanese for "religious student") institutions, the older and more flexible illuminationist Islam was pushed aside to make room for the "purer," original tradition, which centered on the example of the Prophet, the first caliphs, and above all the literal truth of every word in the Koran. Mosque and marketplace, moreover, were always natural allies; so in the growing number of trading centers throughout Indonesia, this new, scripture-based Islam rapidly spread, all the while contributing its strength to a growing nationalism and the cause of resistance to colonial rule. Interestingly, says Geertz, at almost the very same moment, scripturalism also made its appearance in Morocco. Known as the cause of the Salafi, or "righteous ancestors," and led by fierce, passionate nationalists such as Allal Al-Fassi, this new movement had by 1900 come into open conflict with the older style of maraboutist—or "holy man"—Islam. As in Indonesia, these new scripturalists opposed both French foreign rule and the earlier classical Muslim style.

Scripturalist Islam in both Indonesia and Morocco thus provides a background to the struggle for national independence that engaged both countries throughout the middle years of the twentieth century. This struggle can be followed in the careers of the two national leaders at the time, Sultan Muhammad V in Morocco and President Sukarno in Indonesia. Muhammad V rode to power on the strength of the nationalism inspired by the scripturalist revolution in his country. Personally devout as he was, Muhammad V found himself nonetheless uneasy with the fundamentalism of the scripturalists. He preferred the older-style maraboutist Islam, which recognized the sultan as the chief holy man of the country. When, in the course of the 1950s, the French took a number of unpopular measures, Muhammad V refused to be their puppet and resisted. He was deposed and exiled, but two years later managed to return in triumph as head of the new, independent Moroccan state. In Muslim eyes, his defiance and devotion were clear proof of divine favor; he had shown the same *baraka* as Lyusi, and he measured up fully to the prized maraboutist ideal of the warrior-saint. Nonetheless, says Geertz, it is hard to see his success in uniting the old religious ideals with the new postcolonial age as anything more than a holding action against the running tide of scripturalist fervor.

Sukarno's story in Indonesia is a less happy one, since it ends with his overthrow by the military in 1965. Yet in the long struggle that he led from the 1920s to the year of independence in 1949 and then as president of the new nation, we can see a similar mix of religious and political concerns. Sensitive to the religious diversity of his people and resisting both communism on the left and the Muslim scripturalists on the right, he tried to unify all parties with his famous Pantjasila (Five-Point) Creed: nationalism, humanitarianism, democracy, social justice, monotheism. When this eventually failed, he made a last effort at unity that seemed to turn the clock back to the time of the hero Kalidjaga. He tried to revive in modern form the ancient "theater state," building the world's largest mosque, a colossal sports stadium, and a national monument. He also instituted a number of grand state ceremonies.

In the last analysis, both Sukarno and Muhammad V knew well the power of religion in their societies; both sought to harness it constructively to the national cause. Significantly, both decided that an Islam of the classic rather than scripturalist style offered the best hope of success. Just as significantly, neither was completely successful. Although Muhammad V achieved more than Sukarno, Geertz claims that in neither case could the older forms of faith survive unchanged in the modern circumstance.

Conclusion: World View and Ethos

What, then, is the significance of the parallel Islamic histories that can be traced in Indonesia and Morocco? That question can be answered by recalling the central point of "Religion as a Cultural System": religion consists of a world view and an ethos that combine to reinforce each other. A set of beliefs people have about what is real, what gods exist, and so forth (their world view) supports a set of moral values and emotions (their ethos), which guides them as they live and thereby confirms the beliefs. In both of these cultures up to at least the year 1800, world view and ethos supported each other, meeting people's religious needs in a natural way. In Morocco, Islamic belief gave support to the ethos of maraboutism, which "projects a style of life celebrating moral passion," and this ethos, in turn, reinforced the Muslim creed.[17] In Indonesia, the same balance held; the world view of blended Islam and Hinduism supported the gentle, meditative mysticism of figures like Kalidjaga, while the ideal of conduct and emotion he provided gave support to the world view. During the last century, however, and in both lands, the arrival of nationalism and the protests of scripturalism have brought serious challenges. Doubts of the world view and changes in ethos have appeared in ways that leave people uncertain about each and dimly aware that the one is often at odds with the other.

With regard to world view, the root problem is a clash of ideas. In both lands, secular attitudes have entered the scene with the spread of science in industry, the universities, and professional classes. At the opposite extreme, the determined "ideologization" of religion in the hands of the scripturalists, who either isolate the Koran from all other knowledge or claim that all knowledge is somehow already in the Koran, has had the same unsettling effect. Collisions between these two seemingly incompatible faith perspectives have fostered deep, troubling doubts where once there was only quiet assurance.

The effect of modern developments on the ethos component of religion in both countries has also been significant. To prevent misunderstanding, Geertz notes that a distinction must first be made between the *force* a religion may have and the *scope* of its influence in any given culture. Moroccan Muslims regard the encounter with God as an extremely intense, all-consuming experience; yet for them, most of ordinary life in the market or village square is discernibly unreligious. Conversely, in Indonesia, few religious experiences are as intense, as full of force, as those that are prized in Morocco, but the range of religiosity is far wider: there is scarcely a single aspect of life that is not in some way tinged with a sense of the supernatural. Still, despite these differences, it is clear that in both countries a significant erosion of ethos is under way. In small, subtle ways, the religious moods and motivations in both cultures have begun to weaken. People may still be "religious-minded," wishing to keep their sacred symbols, but they are less immediately religious. They are moved less by the direct presence of their gods than by the more indirect feeling that they would somehow like their gods to be present. Increasingly, theirs is becoming a religion one step removed from a direct encounter with the Reality it claims to worship.

Islam Observed offers a particularly good illustration of Geertz's approach to religion primarily because of what it does *not* do. It does not offer a crisp logical argument in defense of a definite thesis about religion, Islamic or otherwise. It is instead a kind of exploration, a journey into cultural systems led by a guide who is keenly interested in comparing landscapes and less concerned with reaching a specific destination. Along the way, three things come into focus. The first is the particularity of each culture under scrutiny. While Morocco and Indonesia are both Islamic nations, a central theme of Geertz's discussion is the marked difference in the character and texture of the two forms of Islam they present.

Second, there is the characteristic stress on meaning, the "thick description" of a religion in terms of what is significant to those who live it. The Islam of Morocco and Indonesia is governed by the same formal theology in both places, but within that common system, the ideas that are emphasized and the attitudes and emotions that are prized differ in marked degree. In Morocco, the stress on the holy man, on moral passion, and on intensity of experience creates a pattern of meaning and values manifestly different from the more passive, tolerant, gently diffused sense of the supernatural found in Indonesia. Thus, although both nations are Muslim and both encounter the identical challenges of nationalism and scripturalism, each responds in its own way, and with varying degrees of success in the outcome. Morocco's Muhammad V succeeded in preserving a style of classical Islam in the new age of nationalism; Indonesia's Sukarno did not.

Third and finally, despite all of the attention to specifics and differences, Geertz does venture to suggest at least the prospect of more general conclusions. He notices, for example, that whatever their differences, neither Morocco nor Indonesia seems able permanently to reverse the tide of doubt created by the rise of secularism and scripturalism. For him, this is the kind of similarity that may serve, like the categories of Max Weber, as at least the beginning of a theorem that can be "tried out" elsewhere to discern if it will apply more widely to religions in other places and times.

Analysis

We can best measure Geertz's achievement as an interpreter of religion by noticing two things: (1) where he stands among the theorists we have considered in this book and (2) what he represents as a leading recent spokesman for interpretive anthropology.

1. Geertz and Other Theorists

Geertz's program is best seen as an effort to blend the sociological theory of Weber with the fieldwork of Evans-Pritchard. He clearly shares their misgivings, and those of Eliade, about functionalist reductionism—rejecting it not only as an explanation of religion but as a misleading account of any cultural system. Contrary to Marx, Durkheim, and Freud, Geertz insists that a general reduction of all religion to the product of hidden neurosis, social need, or economic conflict can claim no more credibility than any other grand theory—which is to say, very little. To explain a religion without trying to grasp the system of meanings it conveys is not unlike trying to explain a computer without mentioning a program, or writing a book without using sentences. It cannot be done.

While Geertz may share their suspicions of reductionism, he harbors doubts of another kind that set him apart from Evans-Pritchard and Eliade. We noticed, for example, that Evans-Pritchard cherishes the thought of one day framing a general science of religion whose theories can be built up from the small, specific studies that ethnographers in the present and in the future still need to complete. Geertz thinks that time spent in pursuit of such a dream is wasted, for what it imagines will simply never happen. Eliade's program is, of course, quite different from Evans-Pritchard's, but he too is inspired by the hope of finding something universal: the human response to the sacred as expressed in certain enduring images and symbols shared by religious people of all times and places. Geertz, in sharp contrast, is a declared and passionate particularist;

to him, a theory of the "universal forms" of religion is as much a mirage as any "general science" of it. The reason for this lies in the very nature of anthropology as he understands it.

2. The Interpretive Anthropologist

In assessing Geertz the anthropologist, we need to recall again the two sides of his intellectual career. He was from the beginning both an ethnographer and a theorist: on one side, a careful student of quite specific cultures in Indonesia and Morocco; on the other, an innovative thinker, intrigued by the broad issue of how to understand human behavior. His ethnography, though not of first interest to us here, is widely praised and admired. Ordinary readers and most professional scholars applaud the sensitivity, insight, analytical skill, and intricate style of his essays on Balinese religion and field studies like *The Religion of Java*, as well as the other works. They feature the trademarks of his craft: original observations, inventive comparisons, important ideas, and connections drawn from seemingly insignificant details.

Ethnography of such high quality is interesting in its own right, but in Geertz's case it also supports—in an indirect way—the central point of his interpretive theory. Most scholars of any kind—not just theorists of religion, anthropologists, and social scientists—make an effort to know one or a few things in great depth, so that from this foundation they can build to broader claims. Freud's psychoanalysis started with a few individual patients and led in time to a full general theory of the human personality. From the specific case of Australian totemism, Durkheim produced an account of religion in all societies. In Geertz's case, however, this relationship between the specific and the general is different. Except in certain limited ways, he does not, like Durkheim or Freud, move from the specifics of religion in Bali or Morocco to general pronouncements on religion in all or even most other places. On the contrary, he as much as states that his ethnography—and that of others as well—cannot and should not be made into a general theory. The point of his method is to stress the opposite: particularity. In the interpretive approach, no two instances of humanly created meaning should be fitted to one rule. We might almost say that the better the ethnography, the worse its chance of becoming science, at least in the usual sense of that term. Geertz produces his finely etched accounts of Bali's rituals and Java's feasts much as a skilled painter does a portrait—to show us that the features and temperament of this duchess or that queen are truly individual; there is not, and will never be, another like her. After reading *The Religion of Java* or *Islam Observed*, we find ourselves saying that we now know a great deal about Indonesian and Moroccan religion. But Geertz does not strive to offer some more general theorem that ties them together. What he offers instead are cautious suggestions, the hint at a possible connection here, a fruitful comparison there. Beyond that we cannot go. In his opinion such distinctive cultural expressions cannot be tied together, at least not the way experimental scientists place under a single rule the facts of cell division or planetary motion. In human affairs, as he puts it in the title of his second essay collection, all knowledge is "local knowledge." That phrase is well chosen. It can stand as an apt motto for the only kind of interpretive anthropology he thought it possible to pursue.

Critique

Clifford Geertz's stature in American social science may not be beyond criticism, but it is imposing enough. Critics are well outnumbered by admirers. Questions have occasionally been raised about his literary style—sometimes so adorned with metaphors, allusions, and artful sentence structure as to obscure what would otherwise be clear and distinct. But that is a relatively minor matter. On a more substantive level, there are two issues that call for some attention: one centers on some of Geertz's rather puzzling claims about anthropology as a science; the other, on the apparent clash between his principles and practice as applied to the enterprise of interpretation.

1. Anthropology as Science

In promoting his program of interpretive anthropology, Geertz insists that he has no intention of abandoning the belief that his discipline is a science. Yet, as a number of anthropological critics have noticed, that appears to be what in fact he is doing. For example, in "Thick Description," the very same essay that states his commitment to science, he just as forthrightly declares that his form of cultural analysis is "not an experimental science in search of a law, but an interpretive one in search of meaning."[18] This is, to say the least, a puzzling statement. Paul Shankman, one of Geertz's sternest professional critics, finds it to be mere gamesmanship with words.[19] Shankman and others contend that if interpretive anthropology is only looking for "meanings," whatever those are, and not striving to develop scientific theories to explain what it finds, then Geertz's ideas may be interesting, but they certainly are not what we know as science.[20] Theoretical laws, after all, are what science is all about. So, say what he may, Geertz the interpreter of meanings is not practicing science; he is abandoning it, at least as a useful method in anthropology.

It should be clear from what we have seen of Geertz's position that these critics are partly right. Geertz *is* proclaiming the end of science in anthropology if by "science" we mean the making of ironclad predictive laws about human behavior in the way physicists speak of the law of gravity or biologists describe the laws of cell division. But he holds also that this is not the only form a science can take. For "science," from the Latin term *scientia*, can just mean a systematically acquired body of knowledge. Consider a comparable field of study like history. There is a sense in which historians are scientists. In evaluating a document, they work quite rationally to determine such things as the specific dates before and after which it could not have been written. In constructing the story of a battle or a parliament, they proceed quite critically, weighing the importance of different events and decisions. In explaining the rise of a nation or the fall of a king, they are always proposing theories, testing them with evidence, and then discarding or revising them as the case requires. All of these procedures are things we call scientific; they are rational, critical, and evidential. And as far as anthropology goes, those are precisely the things that good ethnographers do on every day of their field research. In that respect, anthropologists plainly work as scientists, even though their conclusions will always be stated in the probabilities that apply in human affairs, not under the binding laws applied to natural events.

Understanding that there can be two kinds of science, then, clears up some of the confusion. But even so, anthropologists who cherish the efforts of social science to approximate the natural sciences as their model of study still have their misgivings. They note that a further problem of the interpretive approach is its disabling effect on our motivation to explain. Another critic of the interpretive approach, Richard Franke, observes that in one of his articles Geertz reports how tens of thousands of Balinese peasants were massacred after the fall of President Sukarno in 1965. In seeking to account for this atrocity, Geertz refers it to a deep contradiction in the Balinese sensibility, a combination of a love for high art and a darker love of extreme cruelty. But in the process, says Franke, he never really tries to find out

> who was killing whom, who benefited from the massacre. . . . Instead of asking about the possible roles of . . . foreign business elements, the United States CIA, wealthy Indonesian military officers and their business allies . . . [and others], Geertz offers the "goal [of] understanding how it is that every people gets the politics it imagines."[21]

Other scholars have shown that there was in fact nothing uniquely Balinese at all about the sensibility that led to this slaughter. The killing arose from a power struggle between the communists and the military—a struggle quite typical of what occurred elsewhere in Asia. At times Geertz showed himself attuned to the risks entailed by an inclination to overinterpret meanings rather than explain facts. But in the view of the critics, the stronger tendency of his thought was quietly to forget the cautions that arose in his own better moments.[22]

2. Interpreting Religion

In the case of matters more specifically religious, we must keep in mind Geertz's central idea: that religion is always both a world view and an ethos. It consists of ideas and beliefs about the world and an inclination to feel and behave in accord with those ideas. Its peculiar chemistry comes from the support that each of these two elements gives to the other. Although Geertz throughout his discussions reminds us often of this point, it is not very clear, at least on the face of it, why such a statement should be regarded as particularly new, or freshly illuminating. It seems a truism: how could religion be anything *but* a set of beliefs and behaviors that relate to each other? It is hard to imagine a religion that announces to its followers, "God exists" as part of its world view but then recommends that they live as if there were no God, or makes no recommendation on a pattern of life. Similarly, an ancient Chinese sage who said, "The Tao holds the secret of life," but then recommended that people live as if no such thing as the Tao existed seems just as impossible to conceive. Geertz's well-phrased formulas at times appear to cloak the obvious.

In this same connection it is interesting to observe that when Geertz actually does seek to interpret religious behavior, only one of the two elements he thinks central to it ever gets detailed and thorough scrutiny. He tends to say a great deal about ethos—about conduct, values, attitudes, aesthetics, temperament, and emotions—but very little about world view. One critic perceptively noted this fact in the discussion of the dramatic Balinese spectacle of Rangda and Barong. Geertz writes eloquently of the Balinese ethos, the combined emotions of horror and hilarity that are on display, the moods of dark fear and playful comedy that ebb and flow through the performance.[23] But the narrative passes almost entirely over the native myths upon which the story is based. When it is said, for example, that the audience fears the witch Rangda, what is it precisely that they are afraid of? Her ugliness? Her threat to children, whom she is known to eat? Death in general, which she symbolizes? Or something horrible to occur *after* death? Is it perhaps just one of these things or several? Or could it be all? From Geertz's account, we just do not know. The "world view" side of the religious equation, which in his theory of interpretation is just as important as "ethos," is, in his practice of it, often curiously neglected.

In *Islam Observed*, the same tends to happen. While tracing closely the relationship between social context and religious life in both Indonesia and Morocco, Geertz writes at length about differences in ethos: the divergent values, moods, and temperaments that mark the contrast between the activist self-assertion of the Moroccans and the inward self-effacement of Indonesia. But in all of this we are told little about the Islamic world view: the belief in Allah, the five pillars of Muslim practice, the doctrines of fate and the last judgment, and so on. That omission leaves behind it a substantial trail of questions: Without any reference to world view, how do we know that the "temperaments" are even religious? Political revolutionaries are often self-assertive, while addicts of certain drugs can be quite inward and self-effacing. We would also like to know if the different social contexts that have had such a strong impact on ethos have made any similar impression on world view. Are there some things Moroccan Muslims believe that Indonesians do not? Or are the basic Islamic beliefs about God and the world still the same? If they are the same, then is there not a problem to address? If world view and ethos reflect and "reinforce" each other, and if the Moroccan ethos differs sharply from the Indonesian one, why are the world views not different as well?

All of these questions point to a rather curious feature of Geertz's interpretive approach, particularly in the case of religion. Though in theory he continually asserts that the hallmark of his method is its address to "meanings," the way it attends to the social symbols that carry ideas, he is at times rather surprisingly uninterested in these ideas. In practice, he seems much more excited about actions and feelings—feelings unattached to the beliefs that would seem to be necessary to inspire and shape them.[24] What is particularly puzzling about this stress on emotion and ethos—especially if we recall Geertz's American anthropological background—is that in some ways it brings his view of culture back to the subjective notion of a "group personality" found in the theory of Ruth Benedict—a theory that, under the influence of his teacher Parsons, he would seem to have rejected. Even in his much praised ethnographic writings, for all their attention to detail, there seems a noticeable hesitance on Geertz's part to track down the inner relationships between the specific beliefs in Islamic or Balinese theology. A comparison here with Evans-Pritchard's meticulous reconstruction of Nuer theology is instructive. If we truly wish to look at a religion in terms of its meanings and want to avoid the vagueness of concepts like the "group personality," then an attention to particular beliefs, a tracking of their minute connections and shades of difference, would seem to be a central part of the anthropologist's mission. Yet in his theoretical essay, Geertz gives it passing notice at best.

None of these questions is likely to tarnish the sheen on any of the numerous personal tributes paid to Geertz by his colleagues both in modern anthropology and in the wider circle of the social sciences, as well as by sundry admirers and observers from other fields of study. His success in establishing the "interpretive turn" in anthropological research, and in pointing that path out to students of religion as well, has left his reputation quite secure. The doubts do suggest, however, that other and future theorists who see promise in his approach would be quite mistaken to suppose that there is no need still to assess, revise, and improve it.

Notes

1. Clifford Geertz, "Thick Description: Toward an Interpretive Theory of Culture," in Geertz, *The Interpretation of Cultures: Selected Essays* (New York: Basic Books, 1973), p. 5.

2. To date the only full-length monograph on Geertz's life and thought is Fred Inglis, *Clifford Geertz: Culture, Custom and Ethics* (Malden, MA: Blackwell, 2000). Particulars of his career can also be found in Adam and Jessica Kuper, eds., *The Social Science Encyclopedia* (London: Routledge & Kegan Paul, 1985), under "Geertz, Clifford."

3. This was a criticism made by Talcott Parsons, which Geertz cites with approval in an essay entitled "After the Revolution: The Fate of Nationalism in the New States," in *Interpretation*, pp. 249–250.

4. See, for example, Sherry Ortner, "Theory in Anthropology Since the Sixties," *Comparative Studies in Society and History* 26 (January 1984): 126–166, especially 128–132.

5. Geertz, "Thick Description," p. 12.

6. Geertz, "Thick Description," p. 17.

7. Geertz, "Thick Description," p. 20.

8. Geertz, "Thick Description," p. 23.

9. Geertz, "Thick Description," p. 5.

10. "Religion as a Cultural System," in *Interpretation*, p. 90.

11. "Religion as a Cultural System," p. 116.

12. Geertz's summary of Weber's theory appears in "'Internal Conversion' in Contemporary Bali," in *Interpretation of Cultures*, pp. 171–175; the full article covers pp. 170–189.

13. "'Internal Conversion,'" p. 189.

14. Geertz, *Islam Observed* (Chicago: University of Chicago Press, 1968), p. v.

15. Geertz, *Islam Observed*, p. 16.

16. Geertz, *Islam Observed*, p. 54.

17. Geertz, *Islam Observed*, p. 98.

18. Geertz, "Thick Description," p. 5.

19. See Paul Shankman, "Gourmet Anthropology: The Interpretive Menu," *Reviews in Anthropology* 12 (Summer 1985): 241–248, and for a more extended critique, "The Thick and the Thin: On the Interpretive Theoretical Perspective of Clifford Geertz," *Current Anthropology* 25 (June 1984): 261–279.

20. Others who argue that Geertz's approach represents an unwise departure from scientific ideals include Richard Newbold Adams, "An Interpretation of Geertz," *Reviews in Anthropology* 1, no. 4 (November 1974): 582–588; William Roseberry, "Balinese Cockfights and the Seduction of Anthropology," *Social Research* 49

(Winter 1982): 1013–1028; and Robert A. Segal, "Interpreting and Explaining Religion: Geertz and Durkheim," and "Clifford Geertz and Peter Berger on Religion: Their Differing and Changing Views," in Segal, *Explaining and Interpreting Religion: Essays on the Issue* (New York: Peter Lang, 1992), pp. 77–101, 103–122.

21. Richard W. Franke, "More on Geertz's Interpretive Anthropology," *Current Anthropology* 25 (1984): 692–693.

22. See Paul Rabinow, "Humanism as Nihilism: The Bracketing of Truth and Seriousness in American Cultural Anthropology," in *Social Science as Moral Inquiry*, ed. Norma Haan et al. (New York: Columbia University Press, 1983), p. 73.

23. Henry Munson, Jr., "Geertz on Religion: The Theory and the Practice," *Religion* 16 (January 1986): 19–25. An early collection of essays is *Soundings: An Interdisciplinary Journal* 71, no. 1 (Spring 1988), where the entire number centers on Geertz. Newer essay collections are Richard A. Schweder and Bryon Good, eds., *Clifford Geertz by His Colleagues* (Chicago: University of Chicago Press, 2005) and Jeffrey Alexander, Philip Smith, and Matthew Norton, *Clifford Geertz: Cultural Investigation in the Social Sciences* (New York: Palgrave Macmillan, 2011).

24. Munson, "Geertz on Religion," p. 24.

Suggestions for Further Reading

Alexander, Jeffrey C., Philip Smith, and Matthew Norton, eds. *Interpreting Clifford Geertz: Cultural Investigation in the Social Sciences*. New York: Palgrave Macmillan, 2011. The most recent collection of articles reassessing Geertz's ideas and methods.

Asad, Talal. "Anthropological Conceptions of Religion: Reflections on Geertz." *Man*, n.s. 18, no. 2 (June 1983): 237–259. An unconventional discussion of Geertz, which is obscure in places, but focuses critically on his assumptions about the nature of religion and religious symbolism.

"Geertz, Religion, and Cultural System." Special issue of *Soundings: An Interdisciplinary Journal* 71, no. 1 (Spring 1988). An early set of essays by seven authors from different fields addressing Geertz's research, methods, and theories as well as his views on religion and other topics.

Inglis, Fred. *Clifford Geertz: Culture, Custom and Ethics*. Malden, MA: Blackwell, 2000. At present the only single-authored effort to appraise Geertz's intellectual achievement over the full course of his career.

Kuper, Adam, and Jessica Kuper, eds. *The Social Science Encyclopedia*. London: Routledge and Kegan Paul, 1985. Under "Geertz, Clifford." A brief account of Geertz's professional career and achievement.

Munson, Henry, Jr. "Geertz on Religion: The Theory and the Practice." *Religion* 16 (January 1986): 19–25. A thoughtful analysis, with persuasive criticisms of Geertz's actual practice as different from the principles of his interpretive approach.

Peacock, James L. "The Third Stream: Weber, Parsons, Geertz." *Journal of the Anthropological Society of Oxford* 7 (1981): 122–129. Traces the intellectual roots of Geertz's interpretive anthropology through his Harvard mentor to Max Weber's ideas and methods.

Rabinow, Paul, and William Sullivan. *Interpretive Social Science: A Second Look.* Berkeley: University of California Press, 1979. Essays by various scholars assessing the movement in anthropology for which Geertz is the foremost spokesman.

Rice, Kenneth A. *Geertz and Culture.* Ann Arbor: University of Michigan Press, 1980. A first step in the direction of a full-scale study of Geertz and his program, though it relies heavily on summaries of Geertz's works and extended quotations.

Roseberry, William. "Balinese Cockfights and the Seduction of Anthropology." *Social Research* 49 (Winter 1982): 1013–1028. An analysis of Geertz against the background of the opposing approach to anthropology taken by the school of "cultural materialism."

Segal, Robert A. "Interpreting and Explaining Religion: Geertz and Durkheim," and "Clifford Geertz and Peter Berger on Religion: Their Differing and Changing Views." In Robert A. Segal, *Explaining and Interpreting Religion: Essays on the Issue*, pp. 77–122. New York: Peter Lang, 1992. Terse, analytical, and critical essays on Geertz that shed light on his view of religion through comparisons of his approach with those of other leading social theorists.

Shankman, Paul. "Gourmet Anthropology: The Interpretive Menu," *Reviews in Anthropology* 12 (Summer 1985): 241–248. A stringent critique of Geertz by a younger professional in the field.

Shankman, Paul. "The Thick and the Thin: On the Interpretive Theoretical Perspective of Clifford Geertz." *Current Anthropology* 25 (June 1984): 261–279. Another aggressive critique of Geertz's interpretive approach, with responses from other anthropologists.

Shweder, Richard A., and Byron Good, eds. *Clifford Geertz by His Colleagues.* Chicago: University of Chicago Press, 2005. Assessments and appreciations of Geertz from leading figures in anthropology and the social sciences; published in the year prior to his death.

10

Sexism and the Sacred: Mary Daly

Patriarchy . . . is the prevailing religion of the entire planet.

Mary Daly, *Gyn/Ecology*

If she were alive today and told that she was about to be theorist number ten in this book, the American feminist Mary Daly likely would have replied, “Thank you, but I’d rather not. In fact, let me put that more clearly: Absolutely No. Not under any circumstance!” If then asked why, she doubtless would have pointed, with an arched brow, to the Table of Contents, noting that all nine of the other theorists in the book are male, and as if that were not enough, so is the author as well. Not the kind of company she wants to keep—the entire lot of them tainted by membership in the privileged club of male supremacy: women not admitted. That dismissal may seem harsh, but it is not surprising. Mary Daly took pride in declaring herself a truly “radical, lesbian feminist.” She was outspoken in her opposition to the perverse culture of “patriarchy”—the term coming from the Greek words *patēr* (“father”) and *archē* (“rule”)—in which men’s lives are all that matter, and women for all important purposes do not. She deplored what males (one half of humanity) have said of women (the other half) to degrade them and demand their deference over the long course of history. Clearly, then, she was too militant a feminist to want a place in these pages. But she is also too important as a theorist for us to accept her veto. The revolution she sought to lead has been compared in significance to the social upheaval caused by Martin Luther’s Reformation four centuries earlier. With good reason, she is seen by some as “a central figure in twentieth-century feminism.”[1] She was undeniably a leading light in the movement known as “second-wave” feminism that seized the attention of both Europe and America between the 1950s and 1980s, and she was no less a pioneering figure among feminists in training her focus specifically on religion. So here she stays—despite her preference—in a forum where she may have been unwilling to speak, but where her voice clearly deserves to be heard.

Background: Early Life and Academic Training

Born in 1928, on the eve of the Great Depression, and raised in upstate Schenectady, New York, Mary Daly was the only child of modestly middle-class Irish parents. Despite financial stress (the great crash of the stock market occurring in the year after her birth), they made sure she was educated entirely in Catholic schools, from elementary grades on through her undergraduate years at the all-female College of St. Rose in nearby Albany. In high school she proved an excellent student, especially—and to the irritation of the teacher who fielded her difficult questions—in the "boy subjects" of science and mathematics. Other instructors thought her equally stubborn, but they discerned academic promise as well. She had a gift for languages, and quite apart from school lessons, wrote extensively, publishing poems in national anthologies and columns in the diocesan newspaper. On arriving in college classrooms, she took an immediate (and what was to be lifelong) interest in philosophy, even though an undergraduate major in that subject was not offered. In later years she warmly recalled the dedication of the (mostly female) instructors from religious orders who taught her college courses, but also recorded a certain sense of "broken promise."[2] Though it was serious about educating women, St. Rose did not offer its students a serious education as measured by the best academic standards. Like other institutions of its time, it was (unknowingly) trapped in what she called "the foreground"—a favorite term—by which she meant the framework of American cultural, political, and social institutions shaped by men to subjugate women. By contrast, the true and free spirit of women was to be found in goddess-centered tales and myths of earliest antiquity—in the deep "background" of the human adventure, where we find early hints of true equality and collaboration, the feminist ideal of a community before it was disfigured by the malign imprint of male supremacy.

At St. Rose, the idea of a woman "breaking free" intellectually and aspiring to excellence or notable academic achievement was an utterly foreign concept. Consequently, Daly found it "imperative" that any young woman of academic talent and temperament move on to university-level graduate study. For her, the first step was to take an M.A. degree in English at the Catholic University in Washington, D.C. With funds limited, she next seized on the chance to enter a new program at St. Mary's College, Notre Dame, Indiana, which was offering a doctorate in religion designed specifically for women. There she pursued a rigorous course of study in the thought of Thomas Aquinas, taking her degree at the young age of twenty-five. But this was still not enough. She had earlier had a dream-like experience—a "Dream of Green," as she named it—which told her that she absolutely must "study philosophy."[3] Still, an unexciting interval of teaching at a two-year college followed. With little in the way of resources, and opportunities in America limited, she turned to Europe, and Switzerland responded. She received funding to teach American college students abroad while gaining admission to a program of study at the Catholic University of Fribourg. Over the next seven years she took a sequence of course work (much of it taught in Latin by the Dominican faculty) that enabled her to earn multiple degrees, including the European Licentiate in theology, a doctorate in sacred theology, and (her ultimate goal) a third, much-prized, doctorate in philosophy. The degree was awarded in the summer of 1965 with the acceptance of a dissertation on the French Catholic philosopher Jacques Maritain. The student cohort in Fribourg consisted mostly of young Catholic seminarians drawn from various parts of Europe. Most were of quite modest ability, preparing for the priesthood and, having taken the vow of celibacy, quite nervous about engaging with women, still less a woman of intellectual talents as formidable as those of their singular female American classmate. But if fellow students were less than scintillating, Fribourg was magical. Walking the old streets, climbing the steep local hills, listening to the cowbells, encountering the Alps, and staging travels throughout Europe from the country's ideal location—all of these formed a tapestry of ever-changing pleasures she found to be both intimate and grand. Only with multiple regrets were these attachments given up when the time arrived for a return to America to take up a lecturer appointment to the faculty of Jesuit-led Boston College.

The Feminist "Second Wave"

During her graduate years, Daly found occasion to read *The Second Sex* (1949), the path-breaking study of male oppression and call for female liberation penned by Simone de Beauvoir, the existentialist author, activist, and partner of Jean-Paul Sartre, then the leading philosopher in France. Appearing half a century after the first wave of feminism in the early 1900s, when the suffragettes in Britain and America campaigned for women's right to vote, fairness in family law, and protections against marital rape, de Beauvoir's ambitious two-volume book made the argument for the more far-reaching goal of full female equality, inspiring numbers of women across Europe and the Americas with new hope. For feminists of this second wave, securing the right to vote was only a beginning. More was needed, and clearly, more was about to come.

Even as *The Second Sex* was being written in Europe, an audience for feminist ideas was gradually taking shape in America. Out of necessity, large numbers of women entered the workforce during World War II, many of them—like the poster figure Rosie the Riveter—in jobs formerly held by men. As veterans returned from battlefronts in the postwar years, most of those women returned to the home to raise families, but many did not, or did so differently. They stayed or found part-time work, discovering the value of independence or a second income along with avenues to freedom and fulfillment outside of motherhood or alongside it. Their daughters—children of the postwar baby boom—were soon to discover freedom of another kind. The advent of the birth control pill in 1960, just as they were entering their mid-teens and twenties, enabled them to defer marriage and childbirth while enrolling in college or university classes and pursuing career paths in clerical posts, nursing medicine, or education. For younger women especially, a new spirit of exploration and self-development was in the air, while eyes were also opening to issues of equality and limited opportunity in workplaces, where control was in the hands of men.

In 1961 President John F. Kennedy, newly elected and alert to the winds of change, gave feminism new visibility by appointing a Presidential Commission on the Status of Women, with the revered earlier feminist icon Eleanor Roosevelt named as its chair. The Commission issued its report a year later, recommending initiatives aimed at greater equality in both education and the workplace. Two years later, lightning struck. Betty Friedan, a journalist and labor activist, published *The Feminine Mystique*, a feminist manifesto of sorts, stressing the priority of a woman's individual growth and self-fulfillment over marriage and family. The book, which appealed at once to women who felt trapped by sacrifices made for husbands and children yet with little sense of their own personal achievement or reward, soon became a bestseller. In 1966 Friedan cofounded the National Organization for Women and became its president. In 1970 another, even more militant work, *The Female Eunuch,* by Australian writer Germaine Greer, mirrored Friedan's success internationally. And just over a year later, American columnist Gloria Steinem founded a new monthly, a magazine named *Ms.* Against this backdrop of feminism gaining both strength and visibility, Daly found her encounter with Simone de Beauvoir to be pivotal. Her life and her learning had been framed by the traditionalism of the Catholic Church. The newer wave of feminism induced her to look at both with fresh, critical eyes.

The Church and the Second Sex

The occasion for this second look at herself and her tradition in the light of *The Second Sex* arose by way of an invitation early in 1965 from a British publisher whose editors had seen a magazine article Daly published on "built-in" bias in her Church. Later that year she traveled to Rome during sessions of the celebrated Second Vatican Council (1962–1965) convened by Pope John XXIII, finding her way into the Sistine Chapel and visiting the observer section with a borrowed identification card. The spectacle of it all left her unimpressed, especially with "the pompous cardinals, who seemed like silly old men in red dresses, droning their eternal platitudes."[4] Meanwhile, to the side and in stark contrast, the sight of some humble nuns in simple black habits moving toward an altar rail to take Holy Communion suggested "a string of lowly ants at a bizarre picnic."[5] What little inspiration she could draw from the spectacle came through encounters outside the council chambers with other Catholic feminists. With that energy at her back, she returned in the following year to Fribourg to travel and to work on the manuscript for her first book.

The Church and the Second Sex was published in the winter of 1968, with the homage paid to Simone de Beauvoir evident in its title. Its aim was to reconsider the place of women in the Catholic Church with the issue of equality at the center of discussion. From the beginning, the book argues, two strains of thinking have been evident in Catholicism, as well as the wider Christian tradition. The predominant one, as we would expect in a Church governed by male priests, bishops, and theologians, asserts that women are secondary and at all times subordinate to men. As institutionally "official," this voice of the faith draws on the Bible's creation stories in the book of Genesis to claim that Eve, the first woman, was fashioned from Adam, whom God made first, and tasked to support him. It recalls that the ancient prophets and kings of Israel were men, as were Jesus and his disciples. It notes that Paul, the first major theologian of Christianity, instructed women to keep silent in Christian gatherings, deferring to male elders as the proper leaders. And it argues further that these teachings were adopted by most all of the early fathers, who taught that just as the Church serves Christ as his "bride," so women, whose character they frequently also disparage, should show the same "bridal" qualities by serving their husbands and supporting them. The great majority of later Catholic theologians of stature and prelates of importance have said the same. From early fathers up to the Angelic doctor, St. Thomas Aquinas, on through a sequence of sacred teachers and examples that embraces Ignatius Loyola, Frances de Sales, and a long line of both medieval and modern popes, the message of female deference to male dominance has been clear.

At the same time, there is, for those diligent enough to discover it, another strand of thought in the Church, less publicly visible but no less religiously valid. It holds that man and woman are equal in humanity and dignity and equally prized by God (and the Church) as human persons. This line of thought contends that in the Genesis story Adam and Eve hold a shared place in Eden as human persons—equally responsible to God, equally punished, and equally promised a hope of redemption. Similarly, in the Christian gospel accounts, when Jesus meets women, he engages them as true and equal persons, not as inferior to men and somehow subservient. And though the Apostle Paul, a product of his age in history, may have insisted on deference, there was nothing deferential about women like the medieval mystic and Abbess Hildegaard of Bingen, or St. Teresa of Avila in the age of the Catholic Reformation. Still less can we speak slightingly of Christendom's powerful female ruling figures like Eleanor of Aquitaine. They offer exhibits of both spiritual and secular eminence that was anything but deferential. And whatever earlier papal pronouncements may have been, Pope John XXIII initiated a new appreciation of this equal role at the time of the Second Vatican Council as called in 1962. Under John XXIII, at least some prominent bishops and others have at last begun to listen with ears more attentive to these claims of equal dignity and fully partnered humanity in the eyes of God.

Some . . . but not most. Even with the modest sympathy shown by a few at the Council, advocates of male–female equality have encountered stiff resistance. Most in the priesthood and higher church offices have stood firm in their allegiance to patriarchal ways. Further, they have subtly kept many Catholics in the patriarchal fold with an appeal to the alluring idea of The Eternal Feminine. Women, they contend, have been given a truly special place in the divine plan. They are to be elevated and adored as maternal, virtuous, and spiritual; they embody an ideal that men cannot offer but ought to admire: the elusive blend of the sexual, the beautiful, and the submissive. Women are blessed with an exquisite sensibility of self-surrender that comes to unique expression in the virgin, the bride, and the mother. A woman's natural bent, her intuitive gift, is to defer gracefully, and thereby to win affection, even adoration. She is the symbol of purity imbued with holy submission.

Daly finds it sad to see this idea of The Eternal Feminine so deeply embedded and widely embraced in Catholic popular piety. For this seductive notion, seemingly so sublime and complimentary to women, is the polar opposite of the freedom, independence, and equal dignity that women—Catholic women, all women—truly should crave. It is a sacred stereotype whose psychological effect is to induce individual women into a kind of gender paralysis. By the same dynamic that afflicts other disadvantaged groups, such as African Americans and Jews, Catholic women who come under its spell choose willingly to play out the roles that are expected of them by men: their privileged superiors. It is a sacred ideal that subtly deceives. It stultifies all talent, suppresses all initiative, destroys independence, and freezes aspiration, leaving women no drive to assert their identity, master a skill, command an area of knowledge, or take control of their lives. "The Eternal Feminine is passive and purely relational. When they [women] do develop a sense of independence, or dominance, or initiative, society makes them pay a price for it."[6]

In sharp contrast to the dispiriting image of The Eternal Feminine, Daly finds the new, open spirit discernible among some of the voices at Vatican II to be encouraging. Some of the formal pronouncements could even be read as forward-looking.

The Pope himself had referred to "equal rights and duties for man and woman," while the Council's "Pastoral Constitution" did the same, speaking of the "fundamental rights of the person" and against discrimination based on sex—a position affirmed also in its "Decree on the Apostolate of the Laity."[7]

In keeping with this new spirit, Daly ends with some "modest proposals" for change in both the thought and practice of the Catholic Church. In the realm of theology, she urges that the unfortunate image of God as male be reconsidered, that doctrines fixed in forms that are centuries old be allowed naturally to evolve, and especially that those teachings which demean women and define their main role as sexual reproduction be discarded. Further, theologians need to restate the central idea of the incarnation, which holds not that God became man as male, but that God became human as a person. In the form of Jesus, God elevates not what is masculine, but what is human—both male and female. Similarly, from a practical perspective, "all automatic exclusion from any Church office or function on the basis of sex is to be eradicated."[8] Daly is realistic enough to recognize that the actual ordination of women as Catholic priests lies in the more distant future. But in the nearer term women should certainly be granted positions on Church councils and boards and acquire posts of importance in national organizations.

The Turn to Radical Feminism

Just a few months after *The Church and the Second Sex* was published, Daly received notice that her Boston College faculty appointment would not be renewed. She was personally stunned by the decision and convinced that her book was the cause of the action. Soon afterward an uproar of sorts occurred on the Boston College campus. There was a vocal student demonstration, a petition, a picket line at the home of the College president, and a cluster of graffiti scrawled on an administration building. Academic freedom became the issue, prompting an institutional task force to investigate. By the following summer, there was a quite remarkable reversal. Daly was not only reappointed but (somewhat surprisingly) granted both immediate tenure and promotion. Clearly, she had won an unexpected victory, but even so, real damage had been done. From that point forward, she expressed open distaste for her colleagues, along with disdain for the clergy in the Boston College administration; she coined the term "bore-ocracy" to describe the male functionaries whom she saw as tiresome placeholders cluttering the administrative ranks of higher education. Further, and whether as cause or coincidence, it was not long after this episode that she moved to sever all ties to the Church of her childhood, youth, and academic life.

Nor was that all. Daly also found herself beginning to move away entirely from Christianity as a meaningful system of personal religious belief. Within two years after the appointment reversal, she staged with friends an unusual exhibit of "performance art" at Harvard Memorial Church, where she had been invited to offer a sermon at the Sunday worship on November 14, 1971. She agreed to do so, but with a plan in mind. When the occasion arrived and she stepped to the podium, her gathered feminist friends and associates rose from the pews, and with Mary as their Moses, strode militantly down the center aisle and out of the assembly. What they had boldly staged was their own "Exodus" event, leaving for good and forever the Egyptian bondage imposed by the institutional Catholic Church and the enslaving doctrines of the Christian belief-system. From that day forward, like the ancient people of Israel, the journey that would take her and her associates out of patriarchal religious captivity had begun. With theatrical bravura, the transformation of the precocious Catholic schoolgirl into the radical, anti-Christian feminist had announced itself to be underway. The following year that change in selfhood found its complement in another; she openly affirmed what she called the discovery of an "Other dimension" of herself: her lesbian identity.[9]

The process of moving from inherited faith into full-on feminism was not just personal. It was accompanied by a change in scholarly focus as well. *The Church and the Second Sex* had been written by a Catholic theologian for fellow Catholics. As the 1970s arrived, it was clear that Daly would no longer engage with exclusively Catholic themes; her perspective expanded to Christianity as a whole and would eventually reach beyond Christianity to the world's other major systems of belief. Theologian and philosopher by training, feminist by conviction, she was on the verge of adding to her intellectual profile a new contour: theorist of religion.

Feminist Theory and Religion

In print, the first sign that Daly's new stance was intellectual as well as institutional appeared in 1973. By then it was clear that the author of *The Church and the Second Sex* was being left behind. Daly would in fact later write an autobiographical preface to its new edition in just that vein, commenting on the earlier book as if written by a different person.[10] The new Mary Daly was embarked on a new agenda. She had been called out of Catholicism to pursue—with all the zeal of the newly converted—the mission of radical anti-church feminism. Over time, that de-conversion and new agenda would produce a sequence of six additional books that came to print over the three decades and more of her subsequent career. We of course cannot consider all of those works in detail here. The first two, however, hold a kind of signature status, anchoring the others and allowing us to take a closer look at themes they develop while for the most part leaving the rest on the shelf. Accordingly (and following our practice also with earlier theorists), *Beyond God the Father* (1973) and *Gyn/Ecology* (1978) will have the chief claim on our attention in the pages that follow. In the first of the two, Daly goes beyond Catholicism to offer a feminist reading of Christianity in its full contours as world religion, with implications also for Judaism and Islam, the two major religions that share with Christianity both its monotheism and sacred texts. *Gyn/Ecology*, published five years later, then expands the horizon, taking feminist theory outside of Europe and the Middle East into the civilizations of India, China, and Africa before returning to early modern and contemporary developments in the West.

Beyond God the Father

With the publication of *Beyond God the Father* in 1973, Daly became something of a celebrity in two forums at once. Like a well-schooled gladiator, she stepped combatively into the arena of national debate over second-wave feminism. Closer to home, she enlisted herself as a subversive figure of controversy in the precincts of the Catholic Church, as well as corridors of her College. Outside of feminist circles, *Beyond God* is the first book that comes to the mind of general readers at the mention of Mary Daly's name. Its subtitle—"Toward a Philosophy of Women's Liberation"—suggests not just its own theme, but the course of things to come in future works. Both its design and substance deserve notice. The design is clear enough: Daly proposes to reconsider the central teachings of Christianity—no longer a faith claimed as her own—when they are seen, unfiltered, through feminist eyes. As for the substance, that is perhaps best described as an unyielding exercise in reversal, rejection, and revision: a harsh portrait of the Christian faith so framed that however much feminist eyes are opened, those of traditional believers could only be averted in dismay.

Daly opens her discussion by observing that on its surface, and as believers themselves embrace it, Christianity is both a way of life and a system of belief. The belief system is anchored in three main ideas, along with associated inferences and images. Christians believe in (1) one God, the Father in Heaven and Creator of the world; (2) the Fall of mankind, through disobedience to the Father's will, and (3) the Redemption, or rescue, of mankind from that Fall by a Savior: Jesus, the Christ, who is God in human form. For centuries, these basic articles of faith have been taught to ordinary Christians as the truths that frame all of life. However, what the watchful feminist at once discovers in these ideas is something few followers of the faith ever pause to notice—something both different and distressing. Every noun and name we see in these "articles of faith" is masculine. "God" is male, and he is "the Father." "Mankind" is masculine, leaving fully half of humanity excluded, and Jesus "the Savior" is, again, indisputably male. The word "woman" or "female" is nowhere to be found. In this regard, to be sure, Christianity is hardly unique; it is in fact emblematic of all world religions in that it divides its followers, and all of humanity, into two parts, or better said, two tiers. Men are in the upper tier; women, below. Men are primary; women, secondary. Men are to lead, command, and control; women are to follow, listen, and obey.

Consider the first and most basic article: belief in a Creator "God." The thing to notice about that concept is how Christians habitually finish it with "the Father." The classic Christian "Lord's Prayer" begins with "Our Father." Elsewhere in the Bible, God is often addressed as the masculine Lord, not as Lady; as Master, not Mistress; as King, not Queen. The Catholic priest who intones these words in worship is known to his parish as "Father." And the most celebrated sacred figure in the Christian world is known as the "Holy Father." These male images have dominated not just the Catholic Church, but almost every aspect of Western civilization for so long—two thousand years—that their subtle power goes almost unrecognized. And invisibly enough, they have imprinted on women a feeling of permanent inferiority to men. It is these doctrines that have helped to create, across all of Western civilization, the set of social arrangements that define the word "patriarchy," the rule of the male, the father, with the natural consequence that the role of the female, the role of women, is "to be ruled." Further, and to be bluntly honest, the chief accomplishment of patriarchy—anchored in this male imagery—has been to serve in ways both hidden and open as the agent of systematic female oppression, placing women at the margin not only of both family and church, but all of society as well. Like the air we breathe, female oppression is so much a part of the cultural atmosphere that even those who should see it fail to do so. Theologians, for example, write lengthy tomes on the issue of the moment—theologies of hope, or history, or racial discrimination and inclusion—failing all the while to grasp that the deep injustice underlying all of these others is sexism, the rank dismissal of the rightful claim to equality registered by women: that is, by fully half the human race.

The most obvious and universal illustration of this "sexual caste system" is the religious teaching—endorsed by Catholic and Protestant alike—that a woman's divinely sanctioned role is to support men both in society and at home. Socially, she does not belong; her primary place is at home, not in the world. And at home, her role is to create a family that will fulfill the hopes and carry on the name of . . . her husband. The principle that applies can be stated simply: "If God is male, male is God."[11] Conversely, if the woman is, say, Catholic and not married, she can fulfill her family purpose by committing herself to the service of others and, if able to take vows, choosing marriage to God himself by entering a religious order. No other options exist. Protestant Christians may not have religious orders, but their churches amply delineate other ways for women to perform their secondary role of service to God and men. A woman, as defined by Christian ideals, invariably finds her true fulfillment in and through a man, in support of either her family or her God, and ideally, both. These noble ideals "justify the social structures which have given rise to them and which sustain their plausibility."[12]

With sexist attitudes of this kind bolstered by religious faith and deeply embedded in Christian civilization, the difficult task that falls to all women, but especially women talented enough to think, speak, and write on the issue, is that of resistance, of revolt that can bring an end to this long captivity, both religious and social. "With the rise of feminism," we are told, "women have indeed come to see the necessity of conflict, of letting rage surface and of calling forth a will to liberation." To undertake such a mission is of course no easy task; it requires great courage, but brings enormous benefits, for "the women's revolution implies the liberation of all human beings."[13]

As a first order of business, women must be prepared to dismantle the "false gods"—that is, the distorted features of the Creator God—that are put forward by patriarchal religion. For example, religious leaders often recommend acceptance of suffering or social disadvantage as part of the "divine plan"; they stress hope of "the next life" and its heavenly rewards, drawing attention away from earthly evils; or they portray God as the judge who upholds the—male-controlled—social order, with moral guilt imposed upon those who disrupt it. At different times and in different places, each of these powerful divine sanctions has been applied to keep women in place. They show just how demanding the work of female resistance to the divinely approved logic and legacy of male domination promises to be. It requires that women never be passive. Borrowing from the terminology of the German-born theologian Paul Tillich, Daly insists that above all women must have "the courage to be." They must always embrace the process of being and more fully becoming themselves, refusing to accept the secondary status that males—male philosophers, theologians, and social critics, as well as the men encountered in everyday life—have so instinctively imposed upon them. They should reject not only the image of the "Father" as created by males. They should reject even the word "God," the stiff, frozen noun for divinity, and replace it with an ungendered and truly dynamic name: the term "Be-ing," understood as a verb. God should be viewed as the active principle of existence, the matrix in which all of us who are human equally live and move and have our own "be-ing" affirmed. "What we are about," Daly continues, "is the human becoming of that half of the human race that has been excluded from humanity by sexual definition." It is nothing less than "a real leap in human evolution, initiated by women." Clearly, she adds: "The unfolding of the woman-consciousness is an intimation of the endless unfolding of God."[14] In this connection, women can regard even atheism as a friend, for with their rejection of "God" atheists perform the service of also destroying masculine symbolism of the divine that oppresses rather than liberates. It is true, of course, that sophisticated theologians have long insisted that language about god as "Father" is merely imagery and analogy, but no one should be deceived by such subtle points. The plain effect of the male imagery is at least as influential as any male theologian's claims about a nongendered abstraction.

The Fall

If the image of the heavenly Father has done much to elevate men in the social order, nothing has, at the same time, done more to degrade women than the archetypal story of Adam and Eve in the Garden. By the accounts in the Biblical book of Genesis, Eve, the first woman, is not only secondary, derived from Adam's rib at her creation; she is the one key figure responsible for the greatest of all human catastrophes: Adam's Fall—with the included subsequent lapse of all of humanity in its aftermath. It was she who caused Adam's downfall, and "all his woe, with loss of Eden," as the poet Milton put it in his great poem *Paradise Lost*. Daly explains that the classic story of "the Fall" and the "original sin" of humanity places a double curse on the woman. Not only is Eve dependent on Adam and blamed for tempting him; she has given legitimacy to male disparagement of women throughout human history, leaving her female descendants perpetually afflicted with guilt. Accepting the Biblical story on faith, women have been forced to cope with a legacy of self-hatred, internalizing the fault that the patriarchal text of the Bible assigns to them. In brief, the "holy scripture" itself is part of the mechanism "through which women internalize the consciousness of the oppressor."[15]

The only way that this guilt complex, this deep female sense of inferiority and self-hatred, can be overcome is through an intense intellectual regimen—a self-directed process of conceptual change and psychological healing. Daly compares the process to an exorcism—expelling the near-demonic power of hatred and guilt turned in upon a woman's own self. A classic symptom of this female self-hatred is psychological paralysis. Women often become so immobilized personally that they are unable to see and address the problem. Another symptom, oddly enough, is feminine antifeminism, something often seen in the very women who have succeeded in the male world. Because they have "arrived" at their goal on male terms, they tend openly to adopt the male values and turn them against other women. They embrace their roles as virtual "token males" and demean other women as too weak, or too little talented, to achieve the same. Still another symptom of self-hatred is a kind of "false humility"—the tendency to avoid becoming "too much" of a success, or "to find every other cause more important than our own."[16] And sadly, self-hatred at times takes the form of extreme emotional dependence—the need always "to be with a man" in public, or always to "seek a man's advice" before trusting one's own judgment. In each instance of this kind, choosing instead to seek support from other females of like mind is at least one sure way that "women can raise each other's consciousness."[17] Still, psychological insight alone is not enough; self-discovery also needs weaponry. Feminist intellectuals must take up arms against the battalions of male theologians who have twisted the Genesis story along with other Biblical texts to denigrate and diminish Eve. To find in the world's first woman humanity's first villain is to turn all subsequent women into victims—defamed by a scholarly theological slander. Females in the academic world should devote their own deeper learning to a battle against just this kind of male interpretive outrage.

Jesus the (Male) Savior

The third key element of the Christian story centers on the person of Jesus, who as God-become-man has won redemption from the original sin of Eve and Adam, as well as all human wrongs that have followed. As with the ideas of God and the Fall, Christian teaching about Jesus offers a kind of pious and sexist distortion that places divinity in male form at the center of devotion, leaving females in the distant shadows. Sermons, homilies, and tomes of theology over the centuries have not hesitated to affirm that in Jesus God became uniquely *man*—not woman—to save mankind. From that as starting point, the supremacy of males nicely follows. In becoming human God could not possibly have chosen the "inferior sex," as any number of Christian theologians have openly described women. Further, this unmistakably masculine incarnation of the divine has led to a form of "Christian idolatry concerning the person of Jesus"—a religious sensibility that also "is not likely to be overcome except through a revolution . . . in women's consciousness." Daly then continues: "To put it rather bluntly, I propose that Christianity itself should be castrated by cutting away the products of supermale arrogance: the myths of sin and salvation that are simply two diverse symptoms of the same disease."[18] It is true that some male theologians—Tillich, for example—will admit that sacred symbolism has been used oppressively toward women, but they then quickly claim it does not have to be so. It can be applied, generically, to all of humanity. Such concessions are unpersuasive. If the symbol has a long history of being used oppressively, that fact suggests that the symbol is inherently deficient; it is by its very nature a distortion. And in just that connection, something much more decisive is needed. Whatever their historical role, religious ideas and images, whether of Jesus or others, need to be broken, not salvaged; they should be dismantled and dispensed with, not daubed with new paint or displayed with softer lighting. The model of Jesus as the incarnate God, and most other models created by the Christian patriarchy, all carry a common message of female inferiority. And if that is so, what is the purpose of using them at all? If the cloth of the Christian past is so deeply stained with ideas of patriarchy, there is no point in striving to launder the fabric. Rags do not need yet another washing; they need the waste bin.

The reason for taking such drastic action is that the "stains" left by the worship of Jesus in Christianity are by no means superficial; they have been damaging to the innermost threads of female identity, and in quite specific ways. For example, the sacrifice of Christ is portrayed in the Bible under archetype of the "scapegoat," the helpless animal described in the Old Testament texts as a victim sent away with the sins of the ancient Hebrew community laid on its back. The virtues idealized by this model—sacrificial selflessness, acceptance of suffering, voiceless humility, and expendability—are precisely what women, of all people, should *not* be emulating in a sexist male culture all too ready to treat them as subservient. They cannot possibly live up to an ideal which, even if they could do so, would only underscore their victimization. Further, not being male, they cannot claim the active dignity of restaging, in a more admired role, the sacrificial act itself, when repeated in the service of communion or eucharist. That gesture, more positively and courageously Christ-like, is reserved for priests or ministers, and they, of course, can only be male.

It is characteristic of patriarchal religion (Daly's other favorite words for it are "androcentric," from the Greek *andros* for "male," and "phallocratic," from the Greek *phallos* for "penis" and *kratos* for "power") to find subtle ways of not noticing these obvious patterns of male privilege. Thus, male religious leaders invariably generalize about women among others, so that female oppression is treated as hardly unique. Women, they say, should know their grievances are shared by the elderly, the disabled, the non-white races. They should know as well that some injustices belong to the past, while others limit themselves to minor aspects of life. Also, women should be intelligent enough also to know that the "maleness" of Christ is merely a symbol, and that spiritually speaking, the glory of the cross is that it extends divine love to all, thus equally to both women and men. And just as surely, they should be mature enough to know that there are many great human evils and crises that need attention, some of them certainly more urgent than whatever slights religion may have unintentionally delivered to women.

These considerations hold little merit in Daly's estimate. She dismisses them all as dishonest—as sly pieces of half-naive, half-intentional reasoning whose real aim is to mask the true, structured cruelty of patriarchal religion by offering its female victims a smokescreen of male distraction and deception.

Mary: The Blessed Virgin

But surely—we could ask in response—is there not at least one sacred figure, one feminine ideal that devoutly religious women in the Christian tradition can embrace? An ideal they can pattern themselves after? Think of the Blessed Virgin Mary, the Madonna, Mother of Jesus. To be sure, this image has held more appeal for Catholics than Protestants, but as the Biblical annunciation story and holiday nativity scenes amply testify, all Christians see in Mary the essence of holiness, purity, and sacred love. Surely her example can be followed by women with real benefit to their self-esteem, can it not? Well, unfortunately no. Here too Daly places the ideal of the Virgin in a very different light; she removes the religious halo, only to return it in a quite un-churchly fashion. First (and as with the scapegoat), the qualities we see in the Mary of popular Catholic piety are—once again—those imposed by males: mildness, humility, and deference, not strength or power. Second, this mild "saccharine" Mary, the figure addressed in servile acts of adoration and clutching of rosaries, cannot possibly be an ideal for women because she cannot begin to be humanly imitated. No woman could truly identify with someone so strange as to be revered simultaneously as a set of opposites: both a Virgin and a Mother. This Mary is not an attainable ideal; she is just strange. So instead of accepting it, women of true feminist intuition have been disposed in the past to think subversively. They have discerned in Mary something that tradition, poisoned by patriarchy, cannot. And here a curious thing has happened. We need to recall how Protestants have often described the Catholic "cult of the Virgin" as unchristian Mariolatry—the actual worship of Mary as a divinity. That criticism can be welcomed by feminists in reverse fashion as a gift. To envision Mary in that aspect—as virtually divine, as a Goddess, in other words—is to embrace a figure that in truth *is* empowering to women. To hold that divinity, or even near-divinity, can appear in the female figure of Mary just as well as in the masculine form of God the Father or Jesus the Son is, subversively thinking, a bold feminist idea. Further, modern Catholics go on to affirm the perpetual virginity of Mary, "before, during, and after the birth of Jesus."[19] By way of this doctrine—and again, thinking subversively—Mary holds a sacred status that is not merely derivative, not something acquired from her role as Mother of Jesus. To the contrary, her miraculous status belongs to her alone, wholly apart from any relationships to the (male) God the Father in Heaven or his (again, male) divine Son on earth. Unintentionally, then, the doctrinal claim of an unchanged virginity suggests something powerful and independent; it finds in Mary an emblem of true, female independence. In disguise, one could say, both the "virtual divinity" and "unaltered virginity" of Mary have offered a surprising hidden counterpoint to official—patriarchal—teaching: a subtly strong feminist ideal that "many women throughout the centuries have managed to take from the quite different, overtly sexist Marian doctrines" taught so insistently by the male hierarchy of the church.[20]

The same thing can in a sense be said for modern papal pronouncements affirming Mary's Immaculate Conception and her bodily Assumption into heaven. The feminist with a shrewd eye can find an equally hidden dissent from male patriarchy even in these products of deep old-school Catholic piety, which describe the "sinless" Madonna, standing opposite to the fallen Eve, along with Mary taken up "God-like" to reign as Queen of Heaven. In both these dogmas, the symbolism suggests its own subtext. "Conceived free of 'original sin,'" Mary is a female who "does not need to be 'saved' by the male."[21] And rising virtually deathless to heaven, she can be seen to offer women the very thing that patriarchy conveniently chooses to miss: the aura of divinity configured in gloriously female form.

Of course, we do not have to explore the crevices of Christian theology for hidden feminist gold. We can find it also in history, in the remarkable accomplishments of strong women whose legacy has too often been ignored. Word of these achievements has often gone unheard, largely because of "the Great Silence" quietly orchestrated by males who have owned the pages of history in science, culture, and the arts. In not a few cases, women have had to hide their identity—like the Bronte sisters—under male pennames if they were to be noticed at all. A distinctive episode of this silence can be discovered if we look behind history to human beginnings. Those who study prehistoric cultures have proposed that the earliest human communities were in fact matriarchies: the term anthropologists ascribe to societies ruled by females. They were also matrilineal, tracing family names and lineage through mothers, rather than fathers. In addition, while under female leadership, these early cultures were communally structured, stressing equality and sharing of control, rather than a steep hierarchy and harsh authoritarian rule. Those features arose only later, as the hallmark of the male-dominated societies that came to replace them in Greece and Rome, and in later Christian civilization.

The End of "Phallic" Morality

The mission of radical feminism includes more than just dismantling oppressive religious ideas and imagery. It faces an even greater task in the realm of ethics. Traditional Christian morality, relying upon Aristotle and the Bible, stresses a "prudential ethic," where the heart inspires but the head controls. It holds that moral goals follow from reason as prescribed by the scriptures and religious leadership. Followers are counseled passively to accept the goals set by those figures, who, as we know, are invariably male: priests, ministers, bishops, and theologians placed in religious authority. But when we consider the features of the moral system these leaders have sanctioned, the proper response can only be outrage. The truth is that the historical record of this "phallic" (again from the Greek *phallos*) morality over the centuries has been truly appalling. For women it has been nothing more than an "ethic of victimization," and for the world, even worse. Whatever its stated ideals, European-American Christian morality has turned out to be cruelly male-centered, giving quiet assent, or open approval, to discrimination against women and, beyond that, to a "Most Unholy Trinity" of evils: the violent crimes of rape, genocide, and war. These three closely related horrors show the true handiwork of male supremacy; they are afflictions nourished and spread by the viral disease of androcentric religion. The foundational crime of the three is rape. As the most deeply personal act of male violation and female victimization, it is the source from which all wider violence takes its energy, the epicenter from which the evils of humanity invariably spread. For rape is not just a crime of private violence; it is "an act of group against group; male against female," expressing the sinister structure of male domination, where abuse of the one naturally evolves into assault on others.[22] It is just such "group think" that animates both racial and gender prejudice and serves as the cold motive for greater, darker acts of violence. "It is rapism that has spawned racism. It is gynocide [murderous violence against women] that gives rise to genocide."[23] And by the same logic of collective hate, it fuels the age-old male attraction to warfare, the final third of the unholy triad. War and its cult of death follow naturally from the impulse that begins with rape and unfolds into genocide.

Meanwhile, with eyes closed to these crimes, male religious leaders proceed with astonishing hypocrisy to a reverse stand on the issue of abortion. Posing suddenly and strangely as defenders of life, they deny to a woman her most fundamental human right: the choice of what to do with her own body. How telling, Daly observes, that "one hundred percent of the bishops who opposed the repeal of anti-abortion laws are men, and one hundred percent of people who have abortions are women."[24] These spokesmen for morality shaped by male interests conveniently denounce the isolated physical procedure of an abortion despite the most minimal attention to "the assumptions, attitudes, stereotypes, customs, and arrangements which make up the fabric of the world in which the problem of abortion arises."[25] Somehow, women themselves do not count. But the feminist truth is that women do count. A feminist-sensitive ethic does not woodenly apply fixed categories of right and wrong; it offers "graded evaluations of choices in such complex situations" and considers "the needs of the woman as a person, the rights of women as an oppressed class, the requirements of the species in adapting to changing conditions, such as overpopulation," and more. Over against patriarchal authoritarianism, feminists offer "an ethic of courage to confront ambiguity."[26] This sensitivity to things complex and personal stands in sharp contrast to the unanswerable questions about when life begins that anti-abortion extremists prefer, or their absurd "domino" claims that abortion leads to Nazi-style genocide.

Given the distorted features of the traditional religious ethic, which is "the logical expression of phallocentric power," feminists really have no choice.[27] They must repudiate every element of it, root and branch, stem and leaves. They must overturn its corrupted values and install a new order of moral courage. In practical terms, what the moment calls for is the construction of an entire "counterworld" to patriarchy, led by what Daly calls the "Sisterhood as Antichurch." The emergence of such a true feminist community is the first step in overcoming the "divide and conquer" tactics which have allowed sexist churches and political institutions to weaken women, stifling their voices under structures that induce feelings of fear and guilt at any thought of questioning male domination. This sisterhood is rightly seen as a profound spiritual community. In religious terms, it resembles a true "covenant" as the Bible portrays it—a gathering of women centered on the discovery of deep agreement among themselves as to what they believe and what must be done. It is also "prophetic" in that it represents a revelation, a "breakthrough" of truth into life as the Hebrew prophets like Isaiah and Amos proclaimed it.

"Church," it needs to be said, is a term so tainted by patriarchy that it could never apply. Feminism needs to be anti-church because the word "church" is hopelessly scarred by its historic roots in patriarchy. The new sisterhood must declare itself Anti-christ as well as Anti-church. That is because the symbols and rituals of the Churches are best described as "Christolatry," an idol-worshipping formula—unnaturally and exclusively reliant on the male person of Jesus—that by definition depresses the status of woman, both overtly and unconsciously. And in this connection, it is the rituals of the churches, especially the Catholic Church, that are the most pernicious and corrupting. Rituals are re-enactments; they dramatically repeat and reaffirm key events and ideas in a religious story. But in the case of Christianity, these ideas and events are deeply alienating to women because they are thoroughly poisoned by patriarchy. There is nothing women can possibly "re-enact" that would not by its very nature be profoundly offensive. So radical feminism, the sisterhood as Antichrist, must declare an emphatic "No" to traditional Christianity—its entire assembly of rites and morals, no less than its doctrinal beliefs.

To all this Daly adds that by "sisterhood" she does not have in mind the sort of "women's initiatives" widely promoted in popular forums of the 1970s and 1980s. Too many women, she says, have thought of their cause in the most constricted and minimal terms. Accepting patriarchy, they meekly offer tiny adjustments. They seek funds for daycare, petition for an equal rights amendment, and seek to legalize abortions. But these are half-measures—far too small in scale. They amount to mere tinkering with tiny bolts in the ironwork of male oppression. They are even counterproductive, as they draw attention away from frontal warfare and waste energy on tiny skirmishes. Even more damaging is the mindless distraction of the sexual revolution as promoted in fashionable seventies magazines like *Cosmopolitan.* Nothing is as hollow as the thought that sexual self-indulgence is female liberation. Celebrating sexual freedom centered on multiple-partner sex and male approval is not to escape patriarchy, but to become even more captive to it. Transitory sex that pleases men may be less violent, but it is hardly less demeaning than to succumb to an act of rape. The difference is only one of degree. Freedom on those terms is the very opposite of a woman's liberation.

By contrast the truly radical feminism of the sisterhood sees that the cause of equality for women is crucial and revolutionary; it must demolish the entire cultural system, every strut and beam that supports the edifice of injustice erected by patriarchal religion. In opposition to the unholy male Trinity of rape-genocide-war, feminism must affirm the precise opposite: a "Most Holy Trinity" of power, justice, and love—a value system framed not under hierarchy but in a true spirit of male–female equality. Such a displacement is a truly momentous thing: a sweeping intellectual and moral revolution. Mirroring with good the evil triad of patriarchy, the pre-eminent virtues of the sisterhood should be thought of not as separate things, but as a mutually reinforcing complex. Each element of this moral formula must be seen to strengthen the other. Love, for example, cannot be purely a private good, while power and justice are defined as public and political. Each ideal must infuse the other with its distinctive energy. Love involves more than staging trivial neighborhood "charity bazaars." It must be the kind of love that enlists power to lift the downtrodden and force justice upon the male world—thus upending forever the androcentric culture of the privileged and unwilling. True feminism will accept no less.

Gyn/Ecology

Although pointedly feminist in perspective, *Beyond God the Father* addresses only one of the world's major religions: Christianity. In *Gyn/Ecology*, the other major book with a close-up claim on our attention, Daly turns to the wider, global horizon. Published five years after the previous book, it offers a feminist assessment not just of what has been said or written, but of what in fact has been done to women, or imposed on them, across world cultures in the name of religion. The text of *Gyn/Ecology*, we could say, is the place where Daly's Western feminism acquires truly international scope, the site where the feminist theologian becomes fully engaged as a global theorist of world religions. So how does she proceed?

At the outset, the discussion in *Gyn/Ecology* picks up some of the feminist themes explored earlier, offering further arguments just in case there was any remaining doubt. Even before the coming of Christianity, male domination tainted the social order of Western civilization. The idea of male superiority filters through its earliest tales and texts. In Greek myths, themes that originally celebrated a goddess have had the feminine element erased or revised to glorify masculinity. Divinities like Athena and Dionysus have been portrayed in ways that stress male identity over female. In the prehistoric era there were almost no gods, only goddesses; yet by the end of the classical era the very opposite was in place. Gods claim reverence; goddesses of significance are pushed out of sight. Apollo, the male god of order and reason, is given priority over Dionysus, the god of turbulence and emotion, who is linked more closely to female identity and resistance. Christianity, in addition to the vices already seen, added to this damage. The Sacred Tree is a central ancient symbol of female fertility, an image of ever-growing life. In Christian theology the tree is in a manner still central, but no longer is it living wood; it becomes the dead wooden cross of the crucifixion. In similar fashion, and as first noted in *Beyond God the Father*, early Christian theology executes a kind of conceptual "rape" of the powerful ancient image of the triple Goddess, replacing her with a masculine Trinity and a meek, minimalist Virgin Mary.[28] These perversions have persisted right into the modern world. In children's literature like Shel Silverstein's *The Giving Tree*, the archetype of the female, a living tree, sacrifices everything, even its life, for a child who, of course, just happens to be male. In adult literature and the world of entertainment, we find across most every venue instances of sadomasochist fantasy, in which females invariably are cast as victims. Examples can be found throughout the media and public discussion. A mountain of evidence confirms it.

True as this all may be, the most compelling feature of *Gyn/Ecology* lies not in these classical and Christian examples, but in accounts of what has happened, and still happens, outside of Western civilization. Daly is keen to show that when it comes to sexist attitudes and social structures, Western society is hardly unique. In Asia, Africa, and beyond, the truly global extent of patriarchy and the measure of its destructive behaviors come fully into view. To make the point, Daly takes her readers on a journey of discovery through the cultures shaped by the world's major religions. As she proceeds, the mere description of the customs and rituals placed on exhibit amply demonstrates why, in her view, the response of anyone who sees what she shows should be visceral outrage, nothing less—anger exponentially raised to a level of abiding fury.

The excursion begins with a passage to India. Anyone who has examined Hinduism or explored the civilization of India knows that there is something in the history that no one likes to address. That is the ritual known as Suttee, or "Sati," the Hindu practice of "widow burning." Though strongly discouraged under British rule and outlawed in 1829, Hindu tradition has long held that a wife must go to her own death when her husband dies. If a rich or powerful family patriarch dies, the obligation may extend to multiple women—mistresses, sisters, female servants—in the extended family. This idea was deeply rooted in Indian culture prior to the modern era. Hindu sages (male, of course) traced its origin to texts in the ancient Rig Veda and wove it into the classic doctrines of karma and reincarnation. In this appallingly cruel and sexist form of human sacrifice, the wife was expected *willingly* to mount the funeral pyre of her husband and enter the flames as an act of either marital devotion or personal penance. In death, she could show how much she loved her husband or, in some cases, accept that her own bad karma—incurred in the present or a previous life—had put her at fault in the death. Poignant stories and legends out of old India show that many a woman did *not* go willingly to this grotesque fate; pathetic tales tell of weeping, terrified victims forced at spear point to enter the fires. And as for proving a lover's devotion, Daly pointedly observes that in all of India we see no instances of a widower going to *his* death in the flames of his wife's funeral pyre. Worse still, the practice of arranged marriage often created great disparities in age, so that child brides given to men of middle age and even older found themselves sentenced to likely death with less than half a life lived. Not that young brides fared much better should their husbands live on. To live as a young girl with an older or sometimes abusive husband, who could initiate sexual encounters when his obligated wife was as young as ten years of age, might have been less horrific than committing suicide on his funeral pyre, but not by much. Early on, the practice of Suttee was confined to the uppermost castes, but over the centuries and by imitation it filtered down into the lower caste tradesmen and merchants, gradually becoming more and more widespread. In certain regions, where a male of wealth or importance died, the numbers of women committed ceremonially to the fires could reach into the scores and beyond. There is no way to describe a standard ritual of this kind, Daly explains, other than by introducing the word "gynocide"—that is, "genocide" as applied only to women. Suttee fills India's historical landscape with "gynocidal atrocities" across nearly all its regions and ages.[29]

Almost as disturbing as the ritual itself is the guarded, unconscionable behavior of modern Western scholars, who choose to avert their eyes from this repellant legacy of religiously sanctioned male dominance. Incredible as it may seem, special efforts have been made to be "objective" or "culturally sensitive" in discussions of such a custom when "appalling" is the only appropriate word. Some scholars, both Western and Asian, have tried to argue that many, even most, Indian women have gone into the flames "freely" and even "heroically." Meanwhile, they say virtually nothing about the controlling ideas and structures of male oppression that for centuries left these women in the pathetic state of themselves internalizing the perverse values that worked to destroy them. So powerful and subtly intrusive are the assumptions of patriarchal dominance that have insinuated themselves into the cultures of both the West and East, that the horrors inflicted, with cultural approval, on Suttee's victims are either passed over in silence or described with a passionless, merely descriptive acceptance that no one would tolerate if the subject were the Nazi holocaust or Stalin's purges. The difference, of course is that India's holocaust has affected only women, so even if slightly troubling, no comparable outrage is needed.

Turning from India farther east to China, we meet a different religious world. There the major philosophies of Daoism and Confucianism have been more life-affirming than classical Hinduism, so we do not find anything like Suttee. Yet to think that in China women were treated as more nearly equal to men would be a serious mistake. Chinese male domination, anchored in Confucian reverence for "the gentleman," produced its own—quite peculiar—form of female oppression. For about a thousand years, from approximately the end of the T'ang dynasty in the 900s C.E. to the early twentieth century, the binding of a woman's foot was the way to achieve the ideal of feminine elegance and sophistication—the prized measure of physical beauty in the eyes of male suitors, admirers, and family members. Starting in early childhood, girls from the educated and upper classes were subjected by mothers, grandmothers, and others to the painful process of distorting their feet into the smallest possible size and most unnatural shape. The aim was to shrink the feet, breaking bones as needed, in such a way that the lesser toes were crushed underneath while the largest was turned upward to create the prized "lotus hook," the ultimate in female fashion and personal allure. Over an entire millennium, male poets and novelists waxed eloquent in their praise of women whose feet had been shaped into this minuscule and (to them) highly erotic ideal form. To the upper-class Chinese male, the foot as much as the face made a woman truly attractive. The pleasure thus belonged to men while the price was paid—wholly—by women. And a heavy price it was. This "ideal" of Chinese feminine grace, the woman judged most appealing to men, was condemned to an adult lifetime in which she was barely able to walk. At best she moved unsteadily—in a manner that men also found sexually appealing—on what were in effect twisted stumps of callused scar tissue and bone underneath her ankles. Often such women, as they aged, could not walk at all; they had to be carried by servants: a circumstance all the better of course for the husband, who owned the guarantee that none of his wives could "wander off" alone and into the arms of a lover. Male control was complete. Worst of all, the reach of patriarchy was so wide, and its social power so strong, that foot-binding became fully internalized as a subtle tool of domination in the female subculture of the home and community. As with Suttee in India, so in China male privilege self-servingly set the cultural ideals; subservient females obligingly, even eagerly, embraced them. Not until the Chinese revolution in the 1920s did foot-binding fall out of favor, in the process leaving an entire generation of Chinese women who had grown up with the practice hobbled, demeaned, and displaced as social outcasts.

In the case of China, and as also with India, Western (again, mostly male) scholars encountering this bizarre practice have shown the same casual "tolerance" and "objectivity" in addressing it, often with nothing more than mildly amused detachment. One authority has spoken of it as just another among multiple "small perversions" found in Chinese custom, and Arthur Waley, the great authority on Chinese language translation and literature, found it to be merely another instance of the strange things women do "in almost all cultures, in order to make themselves attractive to men."[30] Still another (male) scholar dismisses claims about detrimental effects on women's health as "often exaggerated."[31] It is telling that almost no one shows the courage to describe foot-binding as what in fact it was: male-imposed physical torture entailing nearly complete social captivity.

If we move from the ancient and complex societies of Asia to the tribal religious cultures of Africa, we find female subjugation on comparable display, though in a different, and specifically sexual, form that is no less callous, and in some ways even more grotesque, than what we see in the Far East. In most all regions of the continent, and across multiple nations and tribal attachments, we can find African societies that perform rituals of female genital mutilation. By no means is this a practice typical only of so-called primitive religions. It has been found in both Muslim and Christian modern nations, and in Christian missionary communities, both Catholic and Protestant. This intrusive surgical procedure commonly takes one of two forms: excision or infibulation. In the case of excision, the young woman's clitoris is cut away with a knife or other sharp object. The aim of the rite is to achieve purity; without the organ that provides female gratification, a woman will be less tempted by unapproved sexual pleasure, and more faithful to her (future or present) husband. In case that may not be enough, infibulation goes farther, cutting away both the clitoris and other vaginal parts, then stitching the sides of the open wound back together. As the girl becomes sexually mature, she must be cut open for intercourse and childbirth, then re-sewn, and further cut and re-sewn for new occasions of childbirth as needed. As anyone can guess, the medical complications that attend such a victimized woman throughout her child-bearing years are likely to be multiple and inescapable. The process is also highly ritualized, normally occurring at a specific young age designated by tradition and under specific rules that guide preparation, dress, body and facial coloring, clothing, and subsequent celebration.

As in both India and China, so in Africa any male responsibility for this horrific endeavor is erased; older women alone enact the ritual on the younger. And while the pleasure of sexuality is again preserved for males, the ritual process, along with its cost in pain, denied pleasure, deformity, infection, and chronic disability—all of that falls exclusively on females. "These women," Daly explains, "are 100% pure because 100% enslaved. Their perpetual pain (or the imminent threat of this) is an important condition for their perpetual purity, for pain preoccupies minds, emotions, imaginations, sensations, prohibiting presence of the Self."[32]

It may be hard for Westerners to grasp, but in many cultures, mothers inflict the excruciating pain of excision or infibulation on their own daughters—something that happens only because they have so fully internalized these twisted, self-gratifying male demands as their own. Often, to get the task accomplished, they need other females to assist. Daly cites a report from Guinea that no less than six women were needed to hold down a screaming ten-year-old girl till the cutting, done with a glass shard from a broken bottle, was complete. Afterward, and to the cheers of the surgical team, she was paraded, while in full hemorrhage, through the village in triumph and celebrated as now ready for marriage. Why the celebration? Because in Guinea "no man marries a woman who has not been excised." Nor is this just the ancient folk wisdom of the poor and uneducated. Jomo Kenyatta, the modern-day President of Kenya, said the same: "No proper Gikuyu would dream of marrying a girl who has not been circumcised [i.e., genitally excised]," for that is regarded as "the *conditio sine qua non* for the whole teaching of tribal law, religion, and morality." The cruel irony for the female, says Daly, is palpable: "By removal of her specifically female-identified organ . . . she 'becomes a woman.'"[33]

The continued existence of these torments is cause enough for outrage. Even more dispiriting, however, is the avoidance, indifference, and apparent cowardice of those in the modern West who have seen the blood and heard the screams yet say either nothing or very little. The World Health Organization and U.N. Agencies know it well and turn away. Anthropologists know; Christian and

Islamic religious leaders know; liberal reformers, socialists, population experts, and indigenous government officials all know. Yet most all (and most all of them male) have joined in a conspiracy of near silence on the matter. There are even African politicians, cosmopolitan in taste and well-versed in human rights, who have allowed mutilation rituals to be inflicted on their own daughters. They are blind to what every feminist can readily see. Few things better demonstrate the true, degraded position of women in a patriarchal world.

Daly cautions that before anyone should suppose Europe and America to be more enlightened about female repression, a look inward, and backward, is needed. In the early modern era, from the later 1400s to about the year 1700, the Western world found itself plunged into a frightening and ever-expanding "witch craze." In the very centuries known for the Renaissance and birth of science, assorted superstitions centered on witchcraft flourished throughout Europe and arguably left as indelible an imprint on everyday social life as did any of the brilliant thinkers and artists of the age. No doubt more Europeans saw in their village or close nearby the trial of a witch than knew of Galileo's experiments or had seen the art of Rembrandt. Further, and in most cases by far, the accused witch was a woman—a lonely spinster, neglected widow, or emotionally fragile young girl.

In the early years of Europe's witch-craze the book at the center of things had been written in Germany by two Dominican friars, Heinrich Kramer and Jacob Sprenger. They solicited papal support, and when it was given, proceeded to claim that the Pope had done the asking. In any case, the Pope's approval conferred special status on the work entitled *Malleus Maleficarum*, "The Hammer of Witches," published in 1486. Readers unfamiliar with Latin need to know that the gender of the word "Maleficarum" is feminine. Those who needed hammering were presumed to be women. Kremer and Sprenger provided the textbook and guidebook for finding, charging, and prosecuting witches of every type, whose dark engagements towered over every other sin. They had chosen to trade in the demonic or had bargained directly with the Devil himself. No one posed a greater threat to Christian civilization. The "Hammer" was soon supplemented by popular handbooks—*Teufelsbücher* (Devil's books)—detailing the hideous crimes that witches perpetrated against God, the Christian moral order, and basic human decency.

As elsewhere, sexuality and purity were central to witchcraft accusations and trials, but in a manner somewhat different from what appears in Asia and Africa. Suttee, foot-binding, and female mutilation all occur in the context of marriage—its anticipations and obligations. In the Western witch trials, however, the focus is not on purification of the individual for acceptance into the social order, but purification of society *from* the demonic individual. The witch is not a woman who must undergo suffering to be included in the patriarchal community; she embodies evil that threatens the community and must be excluded. It is as if an arm or leg of the Mystical Body of Christ had become infected; hence, the site of the disease must be discovered, and the limb amputated. "All witchcraft comes from carnal lust which is in women insatiable," write Kremer and Sprenger, and this sensual desire is what leads women to liaisons with demons.[34] Males, while not free of temptation, share their gender with Jesus, who was also male, and so are more naturally immune to lust than females. Further, women are by nature more credulous, impressionable, slippery-tongued, weaker in both mind and body, and more disposed to tell lies.

As if these groundless accusations were not enough, the judicial process for proving them stood outside of all procedures that normally guided the presentation of evidence and testimony in addressing other crimes. Even France's Jean Bodin, the greatest jurist-intellectual of the later 1500s, showed his patriarchal stripes by making an exception to normal practice for the pathetic, powerless women caught in the evil machinery of witch trials. Since witches had gravely sinned against God himself, not just their fellow Christians, their offense was too heinous to come under ordinary rules of justice. Bodin held their crimes to be so filthy that if full proof were lacking, "presumption should suffice for the sentencing of witches to death."[35] At a mere seven years of age, children were considered acceptable witnesses, and even desirable, as they were easily persuaded or compelled to testify—often against their own mothers. Indescribable tortures to secure confessions were also perfectly acceptable. And once a witch had been convicted, it was legitimate to seek accusations of others on the way to her execution. As is evident with Jean Bodin, the architects of these legal excesses were not poor, ignorant peasants; they were men of power, influence, and learning, the social elite that included priests, scholars, lawyers, princes, and prosperous merchants.

This last factor is most revealing. The true sin of witches, Daly tells us, is not that they failed their God; it was that they failed to fit into their male-dominated communities; they were judged socially indigestible by the rules of patriarchy, and so had to be expunged. Spinsters and widows came under suspicion because they were unattached; young girls, merely because they might be unsteady in temperament or emotionally fragile, became natural targets of distrust, as did mature women of intelligence and learning, whose considerable knowledge of herbal medicine and physical health challenged the privileged position of their male oppressors.

The witch-craze reached its height in the early 1600s, an era known for some of Europe's most widely acclaimed intellectuals and legal theorists: René Descartes, Francis Bacon, the English jurist John Selden, and Hugo Grotius, the learned Dutch scholar renowned for works on international law. It is deeply troubling that not one of these magisterial figures is known to have spoken a word about the ritual atrocities that were occurring publicly in villages and towns near them. Just as troubling are the comments of modern historians who excuse them. Hugh Trevor-Roper, England's admired historian of the witch-craze, can only say, lamely, that these heroes of the mind and the law had "more 'important'" matters to address. Appallingly, Montague Summers, the modern Catholic priest who has edited the text of *Malleus*, chooses to praise it as a "great work," with "inexhaustible wells of wisdom." And though the trials and burnings continued for a span of two centuries, they have earned so little notice from today's leading (and mostly male) historians that one would think the places where these crimes against women routinely occurred were invisible. This silence of modern scholars speaks volumes about their studied indifference to the dark European and American story of female repression and denigration.

To protest against this silence and to honor the generations of marginal women, including especially those who went to a cruel death as witches before crowds defaming them with curses and vulgarities, Daly decided to choose the most common words and names of female abuse and make them her own. From about the time of *Gyn/Ecology* on, she and her closest associates took pride—and a good deal of pleasure—in routinely referring to themselves as "Hags" and "Crones," or as "Harpies," "Furies," and "Spinsters." She took a devilish pleasure also in using them to coin new terms in combination. So, while male historians offer "chronology," she insists upon "Crone-logy." And in contrast to "hagiography," the Church's sacred stories celebrating the glorious deeds of the saints, she offers "Hag-ography," stories in praise of feminist heroines and their amazing (or, as she calls them in another coinage, "Amazon") adventures.

For its last exhibit of patriarchal oppression, the discussion in *Gyn/Ecology* turns from the early modern era to developments in present-day America. At first sight, no one familiar with the burning of widows and witches would think to associate modern medicine with such cruelties. But Mary Daly does. To the surprise of many, she sees in American medical gynecology and clinical psychology certain troubling parallels to the sexist cruelties of past eras and locales. Gynecology arose as a medical specialization in the later 1800s, alongside the first wave of feminism. While early feminists sought independence, and suffragettes pursued the right to vote, the new specialists in gynecology offered to improve women's health. But that "health" was conceived in anti-feminist, traditional terms, as enabling women mainly to fulfill their passive, submissive roles as mothers or as sexual objects. In brief, "better female health" supported the sexual caste system. Almost entirely male, these specialist physicians often did not hesitate to put their science ahead of their female patients. In the early decades of their specialized practice, they undertook procedures in unsanitary conditions. They performed misguided surgeries, such as the removal of ovaries to cure "insanity," along with hysterectomies and sometimes radical mastectomies or lobotomies for the same purpose. They also experimented on patients, applying new techniques with real risk and minimal consent. More recently, they have introduced a variety of drugs with serious side effects and prescribed chemically created hormone replacements to counteract the entirely natural effects of menopause. And of course, there is plastic surgery, an incredibly lucrative enterprise that has become a virtual industry designed to alter almost any part of the female body, so that it can conform to purely male sexual expectations. As experts in female physiology and anatomy, such specialists see the surgical knife as the tool to fix most every problem, and to address any male-imposed desire that women feel they must accommodate.

This general cadre of surgeons and clinicians, whom Daly calls the "body-gynecologists," have not acted alone in the business of imposing male "cures" on female patients. They were joined at the turn of the twentieth century by a second set of experts, the rising of ranks of psychologists, psychoanalysts, psychiatrists, and other therapists whose new specialty was "mind-gynecology." Led by German-speaking intellectuals like Freud in Vienna, Carl Jung in Switzerland, and others in Berlin and other major university centers, some in their circles took a dim view of the female personality, for the most part insisting that women's disorders were invariably self-created due to the basic emotional fragility and instability of the female temperament. Almost always, the diagnosis of a personal health concern came down to "blaming the (female) victim" or "blaming her mother." Never was it suggested that female anxiety or depression could have been caused by something as obvious as the demeaning social roles and repressive behaviors that males have inflicted on them. Freud and his disciples, who have so influenced American psychoanalysis and psychological therapy, showed a persistent distrust and denigration of both the intellect and emotions of women.

When seen in this critical light, the theories of modern gynecology in both its mind and body forms ought to arouse deep suspicion. Strange as it may seem, they bear a disturbing resemblance to the ways of the witch burners:

> We have seen that the legitimating theology of the witchburners, which erased their responsibility for the murder and torture of the witches, was Demonology. The witches were named victims, not of their torturers, but of the Devil, god's enemy. . . . Gynecology is of course streamlined Demonology, and the Devil is Disease, to which women are especially susceptible. Patients are named victims, not of the physicians, but of Disease, the doctors' enemy. The "fact" that the patients are under the influence of "Sickness" is built into the very phrasing

> of "problems." Thus modern witch-hunters speculate about the "untreated menopause" as "a possible contributory factor in the causation of cancer" and about the uterus as a "possible breeding ground for cancer." Since Disease is the "real" enemy, the gynecologists, as god's agents and representatives, can present themselves as acting for the good of the women they torture and kill, for the good of other women.[36]

If we want a name for it, both modern gynecology and the cold exploitations on exhibit in other ages and places can together be described as instances of the "Sado-ritual Syndrome": a pattern of subjugation and orchestrated cruelty that discloses more vividly than any other behavior the deep sexism that lies at the heart of patriarchy everywhere in the world.

This Sado-ritualism qualifies as a syndrome because it generally follows a recognizable pattern with certain evident features, such as (1) the aim of female purification, as women everywhere are believed to be in a significant measure unclean, sensual, unreliable, or unstable; (2) the erasure of male responsibility for actions taken to achieve that purification, as it is always another thing—disease or demons, or most often a woman herself that is at fault; (3) the spread of the rites of repression from the elite of society—that is, the male-dominated upper classes—down to the lower orders; (4) the use of women as scapegoats and their recruitment into supporting or (as in foot-binding) actually performing the acts of repression, thus serving as "token torturers," who inflict on other women the most horrific procedures; (5) the stress on an orderly, repetitive, routine process of preparation and execution; (6) the gradual acceptance of the ritual, however horrific, as an aspect of "normal" social behavior; and finally (7) the benefit of scholarly writings that pass over the sinister sexist truth of the syndrome and, by inattention or indifference, manage to sanction the entire process, so that what is sinister is conveniently sanitized into acceptance as routine and necessary.

For Daly, the record is clear. When we look with unshielded eyes at the "review of atrocities" *Gyn/Ecology* presents and the chilling features of the Syndrome it exposes, can anyone still deny or diminish the grievous legacy that male supremacy has left in its wake? The evidence adduced is historical, factual, and global. It does not quibble about what theologians say or how they debate the meaning of sacred texts. Instead, it presents a perfectly straightforward question and offers a disturbing answer. What have male-dominated societies around the world in fact *done* to and with women? The answer lies plain in the historical and global record, which fairly shouts its own tragic truth.

In the later pages of *Gyn/Ecology* the discussion draws on this ugly past to seek lessons for the future. The only way forward for women is to show courage, crying out against the cruelties, overcoming social denigration, and fiercely attacking male deception and domination. Daly makes a special point of underscoring this call to armed intellectual combat in the unusual spelling of the book's title. The slash symbol was placed in the title (itself typical of the split words she liked to invent) to represent an ancient labrys, the fearsome double-edged ax used by Greek warriors in combat. While working on the manuscript for the book, she had traveled to the Mediterranean, where she saw this huge battle weapon on exhibit in the Herakleion Museum on the Island of Crete. She seized on it at once as an emblem of the slashing hand-to-hand combat needed to win the battle against patriarchy and purchased a souvenir version—to be carried always and everywhere on her personal key chain.[37] She well knew, of course, that even with the fearsome, legendary labrys in hand, the feminist battle could not be won in singular combat. Consequently, she urges women always to find strength in sisterhood, in a female community of the kind first suggested in *Beyond God the Father*. All of this is, to be sure, more in the vein of inspiration than argument. But in her view, that is because no further argument is needed. The case has been made, and the verdict is clear. As any candid look at the Sado-ritual Syndrome in all its malicious aspects will show, the historical and global guilt of patriarchy lies beyond dispute.

Later Works

In 1984, six years after *Gyn/Ecology*, Daly published her next book, *Pure Lust: Elemental Feminist Philosophy*. At the same time, she entered a collaboration with a colleague on an innovative dictionary designed to support feminism with its own vocabulary and set of distinctive definitions. It was published in 1987 with a sly, puckish title: *Websters' First New Intergalactic Wickedary of the English Language, Conjured in Cahoots with Jane Caputi*. (Note that the first word of the title is a kind of pun; the reference is to feminists, in the plural possessive, as "Websters'"—those who "spin webs" in the tradition of early American spinsters—combined with an allusion to Noah Webster, the pioneering American educator and editor of the classic early American dictionary.) As a reference work, *Wickedary*—not surprisingly—puzzled some readers outside the ranks of radical feminism, while delighting those in the inner circle of Daly's admirers. Some feminist critics think it an important book precisely because it attacks patriarchal culture at its roots, which reach down into the soil and substrate of language, weaving sexist assumptions into the very words we select to express ideas. Feminism on this view must enlist itself in subterranean combat, quite literally, a "war of words"—that is, the choice and meaning of words—that must be fought even before debate with patriarchy can begin. Accordingly, *Wickedary* is written in the vein of Daly's other word and language experiments. These include not only the choice, noted above, of terms like "Hag" and "Crone" as feminist catchwords and coinages, but also the use of hyphenations to disclose the component parts of a word, such as "re-cognition," meaning not just "to recognize," but to "rethink." The entries and definitions in the book are often imaginatively original and, to say the least, defiantly "anti-patriarchal." *Pure Lust*, by contrast, follows the pattern of the earlier works, mounting a further militant offensive in the ongoing battle with androcentric manners and morals. Its arguments were supplemented later by two shorter, similar books aimed again at rallying sisters to the feminist cause. Placed just before and after the turn of the millennium, *Quintessence* came to print in 1998, and *Amazon Grace*, the last of Daly's books, followed in 2006. We cannot consider either *Pure Lust* or these two other books at length, but our account can perhaps benefit from a brief paragraph or two about each.

Pure Lust: Elemental Feminist Philosophy

Daly chose for this book (published in 1984) a rather unusual title, which was meant to have a double meaning. She wanted the word "lust" to refer not just to the vice of sexual aggression that she despised in men, but even more, to a specific type of virtue she wanted to instill in women. The feminist meaning of that term draws on the invigorating German word *Wanderlust*: the longing to break chains, the urge to wander and roam free. Pure "lust" of this kind stands for the female right to think and act boldly, to show courage in resisting social pressures, and to sail free of the self-doubts imposed by males who seek to crush female ambition and self-expression. In articulating these aims, Daly often returns to the complaints she registered earlier on, striving to restate them with new urgency or link them to more recent events. We are reminded that the battle against androcentrism must be fought everywhere, without rest and on all fronts, from the most basic word choices in everyday speech up to the heights of the culture—the institutions that shape religion, learning, and politics. The "phallic sensibility" must be everywhere attacked because it everywhere thrives on female degradation. It has effectively engineered a "sadosociety" by imposing iron regimens of self-denial and guilt on women, subjecting them to exploitation, and manipulating them through a network of deceptions that draws on a veritable "stockpile of lies." In addition to its sexist doctrines of the Fall, the Incarnation, and Virgin Birth as outlined previously, phallocentric Christianity can be described as especially perverse. It furnishes a religious rationale for male abuses in the delusion of supernaturalism, claiming that ultimate happiness is to be won by finding God beyond this world rather than in an active life filled with personal freedom, equality, and liberty here and now. All in all, the male mentality advocates ideas that are overwhelmingly "necrophilic" (from the Greek *nekros* "dead" and *philia* "love")—a world view "in love with those [women] who have been victimized into a state of living death."[38] This patriarchal mindset freezes itself in the status quo, while thriving on female denigration and removing all joy from the present life. In response to these perversities, women must have the courage to step forward and resist, to show themselves as they truly are: committed to "biophilic" thinking (from the Greek *bios* "life" and again, *philia* "love")—a frame of mind not only "in love with life," but also with one's self, with the sisterhood, and with the natural world as now given to us, rather than with some fantasy hope of a supernatural afterlife.

These expectations and ambitions go still further. Women are so fundamentally different from men that the very idea of a single common humanity can be challenged. "Female" is so contrary to "male" as almost to constitute a different species, and whether literally true or not, that distinct identity needs aggressively to be affirmed, for it is the only way to a better planet and a world community worth preserving. Women need to overcome the "unnatural programmed reflexes" inherited under patriarchy. They must not repeat the mistake of socially approved feminists, who merely strive for "equality" with men under the rules of the existing patriarchal system. That is a fatal weakness. The only real choice is radical, separatist feminism, which knows that it must detonate a virtual explosive under the entire paradigm of patriarchy, destroying it completely.[39] Such action requires that women first overcome fragmentation among themselves, the divisions that males so ingeniously orchestrate. What is needed instead is "elemental bonding" to create the closely knit, powerful sisterhood that seeks not only justice, but what the Greeks called "nemesis": a proper reprisal against males for multiple wrongs cruelly inflicted. Only by affirming and living in "radical connectedness" can the feminist community be a counterforce equal to the powerful male "sadostate." For without question, it is, again, the phallocracy at the core of civilization that is the root of "rapism, racism, gynocide, genocide, and ultimate biocide." Against this system, women need to cultivate their deep intuition of "otherness" from all that we find in the myths, symbols, ideas, emotions, and actions of male-dominated society. That is the essence of "pure lust"—the one true path to a genuinely radical feminist revolution that alone can secure the kind of just future that in their heart of hearts all women crave.[40]

Quintessence: A Radical Elemental Feminist Manifesto

The aggressive claims and feminist goals advanced in *Pure Lust* are revisited, along with others, in *Quintessence*, which appeared in 1998, as the year 2000 approached, and which featured a somewhat novel format adopted for the occasion. We are introduced to an imaginary conversation with a young feminist of the future named Annie and her mother Kate, to whom Daly appears—from the beyond—in the year 2048, a half century into the future and two full centuries after the America's watershed Woman's Rights Convention, first held in 1848. Together the three characters speak affectionately of the long feminist struggle from its beginnings to its present (now in the future) where Annie lives in a paradisal feminist community known as Anonyma, located on a "Lost and Found Island" with males nowhere in sight. There, in the feminist version of heaven, they recall the era of the courageous "foresisters" who fought the battles of first- and second-wave feminism. They review also the setbacks of the Ronald Reagan reactionary years of the 1980s and early 1990s, when the empire of patriarchy struck back, and finally the decades after 2000, when their radical feminist colony came at last to be established as a shining beacon of hope to women still engaged in struggles across the globe.

Alongside these moments of feminist nostalgia, *Quintessence* furnishes an update on the latest crimes and newer indictments of the phallocracy. And certainly, by Daly's account, there is no lack of new evils to report. They include the mass rape of Muslim women during the Bosnian genocide in the early 1990s, as well as the rise of profoundly sexist Christian and Muslim fundamentalism in the United States and the Middle East. There are also the new threats to women arising in the academic world—from biotechnology and cloning in the sciences to the invasion of Women's Studies in the humanities by scholars promoting "postmodern feminist theory," which threatens to erase some of the solid gains just made earlier on. Some women also have found themselves seduced away from the true cause of liberation by the distant lure of Eastern religions, even as feminist women's literature has been intentionally overlooked, with their books and their bookstores silently ignored.[41] These disturbing developments pose an imminent danger to what lives and lies at the heart of radical feminism: the very spirit of life, the vital activity that fills the universe. That living presence is what ancient Greeks called the fifth essence—hence the "quintessence"—of all things, the invisible agency that along with the properties of the four physical elements—earth, air, fire, and water—binds and animates all that exists. At every turn, patriarchy has repressed that spirit in women, and from that original sin has come a wider network of human evils, as male interests have sought to control, manipulate, deform, and poison all things natural as well. Radical feminists understand this tragedy. They take it as their sacred task not just to liberate women, but to celebrate and cultivate that quintessence, "the Integrity and Harmony of all creation."[42]

Amazon Grace: Re-calling the Courage to Sin Big

Mary Daly's last book, *Amazon Grace*, was published in 2006, four years before her death at age eighty-one. In it she draws again on the device of an imaginary conversation with future feminists (as well as a liberated heroine from the past, Matilda Joslyn Gage) to restate certain points made in *Quintessence* and earlier books. A good portion of its narrative centers on current politics and social policies, where developments since the turn of the millennium have, if anything, proved even more disappointing than in the years just before it. In rather downcast tones, Daly argues that on looking at the world candidly, we see that the wreckage left behind by patriarchy is much wider and deeper than most people realize. It extends well beyond the many specific male acts of discrimination and injustice that occur every day to the deep, and worsening, structural faults in the entire world order. This fact has always been on exhibit in the masculine attachment to warfare and violence. But in the most recent decade it has become alarmingly more evident, with new episodes of American-led international conflict and ever more reckless crimes against the environment that endanger life in all its forms. As civilization passes the year 2000, it faces the deforestation of woodlands, the reckless burning of fossil fuels, the wild spread of electro-magnetic radiation to accommodate wireless communication, the exhaustion of farmland by agribusiness, and not least, the distressing election and re-election of American President George W. Bush, who managed to combine backward personal sexism with military catastrophe in Iraq. All of these misfortunes contribute to the sad spectacle of patriarchy in command.

Nonetheless, in the face of this ugly male legacy, the female sensibility refuses to acquiesce and rises in protest:

> A major development in twentieth-century feminism is increasing recognition that the cause of women and the cause of ecology are profoundly interconnected. How could anyone not see this? It is essential to See and Name the Fact that the Earth and its inhabitants are now targeted for hideous destruction. Women are Lifegivers. We are targeted by necrophiliacs.[43]

The message here is unmistakable. Though under unceasing male attack, feminists must stand firm to fight with passion for the cause of women, which is the cause of life, which is also the cause of the environment and the planet.

Outercourse and Last Years

It can hardly come as a surprise that the passion Daly poured into her theoretical war on patriarchy would lead to recurring battles that broke out of her book pages and extended to fronts of combat both personal and professional. Over the years, she routinely came into skirmishes with colleagues and administrators in the halls of "academentia" (her term for her profession). Diplomacy is not a skill she was much inclined to cultivate. Most of these clashes, including the one that marked her first years of teaching, are recounted in one other book, of a quite different kind, that appeared alongside the others penned in her later years. *Outercourse*, published in 1992, is a personal memoir—so titled because it traces the course of her feminist journey along the "outer" side of patriarchy's imprisoning masculine walls. Among many things, it offers an engaging narrative, honest and self-revealing, of her controversies at Boston College, the one institution she knew—and clearly did not love—for the three decades and more of her professional life.

As noted earlier, Daly joined the Boston College faculty in the later 1960s. When in 1969 her contract was not renewed, she welcomed student demonstrations and protests that followed and later on brought a complete institutional reversal—not just a new contract, but the award of tenure and promotion. At the time, the College's president may have thought his troubles ended, but if so, he was sorely mistaken. The incident left Daly permanently embittered, and "the Mary Daly issue" turned out to be a matter not at all put to rest. It was just the beginning of a career-long personal battle with what academic feminism's spirited *agent provocateur* saw as the entrenched patriarchal privilege that had corrupted American universities—not only her own deviously led home institution, but all of American higher education. In the following years she made no effort to hide her derision, even as she still sought advancement. In 1975, having gained visibility with *Beyond God the Father*, she applied for promotion to the rank of full professor but was turned down. Angered again by what she saw as the malice of her colleagues and dishonesty of administrators, she joined supporters in a sequence of new campus demonstrations organized on her behalf, though this time, to no avail. The College stood firm. With that, her fury over specific incidents evolved into a kind of settled institutional contempt. Four years later, she was instructed to send a letter of apology to colleagues whom she had allegedly mistreated during an (unannounced) visit to her class. Several years after that incident, there was a 1982 inquiry into alleged anti-Catholicism in a speech given at a parish in LaCrosse, Wisconsin; her defiant response led to denial of a salary increase. In 1985, a new inquiry arose from a lecture given at the meetings of the American Academy of Religion, while in the same year students again petitioned the College administration, this time demanding that a close feminist associate be appointed to replace Professor Daly while she was to be on leave in the coming year. After an attempted compromise, the College refused. In 1989 she again applied for promotion to full professor, only to be again denied. After this instance, a new cohort of students picketed and petitioned the office of the College president, but once again the institution would not bend. During these years and afterward there were certainly some calmer intervals, though that might be attributable to Daly's own choice to take multiple leaves of absence. When asked why, with her wide recognition, she had not chosen to leave Boston College and place herself elsewhere, her response was revealing: "I was choosing to Fight/ Act (Stand my Ground) at that precise location . . . where the demonic patriarchal distortions of women's Archaic heritage are most visible and accessible to me, where my Craft can be most effective in the work of Exorcism."[44] Clearly for her, feminism was not just about interpreting religion theoretically; it was also deeply a personal and professional endeavor. Although colleagues and academic officers who denied her advancement insisted their judgments were objective, she knew better. In every aspect, their decisions and denials bore the telltale marks of patriarchy at its most disreputable.

The closing scene in this long-running professorial drama came about in the late fall of 1998, when Daly received a "frantic" call from her department chair, telling her that a student previously denied enrollment in her "Feminist Ethics" course would be forcibly enrolled, against her wishes, the following January, when it was to be taught again.[45] The student was male, and Daly had developed a policy that created a problem. Although she had once favored coeducational classrooms, her first years of teaching brought her to the opposite view. She disliked "the dulling of women's participation that occurred in mixed classes."[46] Consequently, from the early 1970s onward she insisted on teaching female and male students separately. Males could not enroll with the women, but she would teach them by segregation, placing them apart and meeting them at a different time. Knowing of this policy, the (male) student who presented the problem had tried to enroll with the planned intent of challenging her policy and with the support of a conservative organization known as the Center for Individual Rights. When enrollment was denied, he and the Center threatened to file a discrimination complaint under Title IX of the Amendments to the U.S. Civil Rights Act first passed in 1972. On hearing the specifics, Daly was infuriated, not only by what she saw as a cynical ploy on the part of the student and the Center but by her school's own administration, which seemed all too willing to comply. As discussions to resolve the matter proceeded, she stated that she would rather resign than give in to the student. Institutional officers, facing the prospect of lost federal support and finding no room for compromise, decided to take her statement about resignation as a verbal agreement to retire. Daly's legal request for the courts to intervene failed, and in subsequent discussions she was formally retired—"disappeared" as she put it—from the Boston College faculty. In the classroom, her seventieth year would turn out be the last in which she could freely swing her prized labrys—slashing through the serried ranks of patriarchy and splitting male from female students in her tutelage. In print the struggle could go on, but on campus, the days of feminist battle had ended, her souvenir weapon still on her keychain, but no longer usable in arming her student wards for new struggles to come.

Analysis

1. Feminism and Marxism

We can perhaps best grasp Mary Daly's explanatory agenda if we place her among the others considered in this book and look for her nearest theoretical neighbor. When we do so, the name that comes first to mind is Karl Marx. To be sure, a full century separates the German theorist of communism from the American feminist, but theoretically, certain evident similarities bring them together. In broad outline, both take it as an axiom that all of humanity, including its various religious communities, can be divided into two main groups, each placed in opposition to the other. Thus divided, the two have since antiquity lived together in a state of continuing conflict, a clash of aims and interests that has persisted throughout all of history, or at least for as long as anyone can remember. For Marx, of course, this separation is economic in nature; the human community is everywhere divided economically into two social classes: the rich and the poor, the owners of the means of production and the workers, who serve them. For Daly, there is a similar line of division, but it is drawn by gender: male and female, exploiters and exploited. For both Marx and Daly, one of these groups is clearly privileged, enjoying great benefits from the organization of society. The other, just as clearly, is disprivileged, enduring mostly hardship, discrimination, and sacrifice. In feminist theory, males are seen to dominate; females must acquiesce and accommodate. In Marxist theory, the rich are seen to rule and prosper; the poor are fated to obey and serve. Further, both theorists hold that the entire dynamic of human civilization is driven by this deep-running conflict, which governs social history, overriding and shaping all other concerns. Placed in this permanent state of struggle, the privileged gender (for Daly) or social class (for Marx) undeniably possesses distinct structural advantages. Social expectations, political power, legal precepts, moral ideals, inherited customs, and not least, religious beliefs and practices line up decidedly in their favor.

In both the feminist and communist instances, religion offers clear benefits to the favored group, at a cost to the disfavored others. Sacred scriptures and their interpreters, for example, can be readily enlisted to sanction the social divide and anchor claims of the privileged by issuing eternal rewards, such as a better next life or rebirth, or punishments as needed. So just as for Marx the Biblical promise of heaven with its gates of pearl and streets of gold teaches the poor to accept their suffering on earth, so—as Daly shows—the Genesis story of the Creation and Fall of mankind teaches women to accept their suffering as divinely imposed. They were created by God in secondary status as the gender "taken from Adam's rib," and they rightly bear the blame for the human fall into sin, Eve being first to seize the forbidden fruit and lure Adam into doing the same. Similarly, just as for Marx the Church as an institution requires poor believers to obey the laws of the state against theft, no matter how starving they may be, so for Daly, the Catholic Church requires women to acknowledge in the Confessional even the most personal of sins to the (male) priest who then offers absolution and assigns penance. In these, and scores of subtle and smaller ways, the religious authority structure functions as an enabler for those who are privileged and in power while keeping the thought of resistance safely out of mind for the poor and the weak.

There are of course certain differences in the arguments framed and evidence considered. Marx centers our attention almost exclusively on Western society and on its Judeo-Christian moral heritage, though we can readily guess how he would have extended his critique to Asian and other traditions. Daly proceeds differently, extending the reach of her inquiries, as Marx does not, beyond the West. In *Gyn/Ecology*, as we saw, she outlines the complicity of Hinduism, Chinese traditions, and African tribal religions in the atrocities their cultures have inflicted on women. Her argument runs parallel to that of Marx, but the scope of her discussion, and the evidence she adduces, is wider. Even so, their final judgments clearly agree; both cast the world's religions in an unfavorable light. They are grand systems of belief and practice that serve ultimately as agents of oppression.

Because of this shared judgment on religion as oppressive, there is a natural second point where feminism and Marxism converge. Both theories show an emphatic strain of moral censure; in fact, it is hard to see how that could not be so.[47] Marx is of course famous for his blunt indictment of human religious despair: "the sigh of the oppressed creature, the heart of a heartless world, and the soul of soulless conditions." For him religion's great harm is that it approves and anchors injustice, providing security for the rich and offering deception to the poor. It is also true that Marx does not in the end think religion important enough to address it at length; it is a mere illusion created by the class struggle, too easily dismissed to deserve serious attention. In that regard, it should be noted that Daly takes a rather different stand. An exception must be made for her very first book, *The Church and the Second Sex,* where she speaks from within Catholicism and holds out hopes of reform. In the subsequent books, the perspective is very different; religion stands at the very center of her indictments, which swing from distaste and displeasure to denigration and disdain, as well as moments of anger and outrage. The Catholic Church clearly is her first hate, but other faiths and religious cultures are not far behind. The papacy and specific popes come in for special scorn. Pope Paul VI is called Paul "the Sicksth,"[48] while John Paul II's 1980 declaration in support of motherhood is categorized as "papal pornography."[49] In a feminist event staged under Daly's leadership to ridicule male authority, an effigy representing the Pope and a prominent Cardinal is titled "His Nothingnesss of Rome and His Arrogance, Cardinal Flaw, figureheads for the Soul-killers of women."[50] In the same vein, Catholics favoring the right-to-life are called "a cast of vampires." The Immaculate Conception offers "the image of Mary as the model rape victim. From the moment of her conception, she is ineffably undermined by this sublime spiritual rape."[51] Going beyond Catholic dogma to Christianity as a whole, the fantasy of connecting with an eternal, omnipotent God arises from nothing more than "the phallocratic male's problem of impotence."[52] The doctrine of the Trinity can be dismissed as little more than "the ideal all-male family, the best boys' club, the model monastery, the supreme Men's Association, the mold for all monogender mating."[53] Worse still, the Christian era itself is best described as "the reign of the Torture Cross Society."[54] The rest of the world's religions are no better:

> All of the so-called religions legitimating patriarchy. . . are essentially similar, despite the variations. All—from buddhism and hinduism to islam, judaism, christianity, to secular derivatives . . .—are infrastructures of the edifice of patriarchy. All are erected as parts of the male's shelter against anomie. And the symbolic message of all the sects of the religion which is patriarchy is this: Women are the dreaded anomie. Consequently, women are the objects of male terror, the projected personifications of "The Enemy," the real objects under attack in all the wars of patriarchy.[55]

The references here to "a shelter against anomie" and "projected personifications" bring to mind Freud's critique of religion as humanity's "universal obsessional neurosis." And it is certainly true that he and Daly are equally as categorical as Marx in their dismissals of religious belief. But there is a difference also. Like Marx, Freud sees religion less as the cause of human distress than as the unhappy product of a deeper, underlying malady, an underlying emotional insecurity. His language is that of health and wellness; his prescription is that with the right therapy, people can be cured of the illusion of religion, just as for Marx the success of revolution will make the opium-fantasies of belief in God and the afterlife wither away. Daly, however, is inclined to see religion as something less superficial and more substantively detrimental: a willing accomplice of a male power structure that gives a holy blessing to chronic and cruel female repression.

2. The Ideal Feminist Society

Along with these comparisons on the level of what she rejects in patriarchal religion, analysis can benefit also by asking of Daly what she affirms: what a world shaped exclusively by feminism of her kind would look like. Assuming patriarchy could somehow be made to disappear, what would be the shape of the ideal feminist society once freed from its phallic oppressors? Obviously, by her accounts, it would be a better place than what we see now, but in what ways? We know from the start that she would want her "sisterhood of the anti-church" to be in charge, and as much as is possible, it should be empty of men. Beyond what is required for reproduction of the species, their presence is un-needed and decidedly unwanted. But then, what would the sisterhood want to do with the world once in charge of it? If patriarchal religion is to be destroyed, what should be built on the ruins? Daly is often so busy with the tasks of demolition that the work of reconstruction gets put into the shadows. Amid the recurring volleys of critique, an equal measure of affirmation is not easy to find. Presumably, though, we can draw on some hints in her memoir. In *Outercourse* she writes of certain spiritual moments in her years as a child and young woman. Notably, they did not occur in association with rites or ceremonies of the Church. They occurred instead during encounters with the natural world: her quiet adolescent surprise at the sight of a certain clover blossom, the chance notice of a lush green hedge on a college campus, and her delight in coming upon a hive of droning bees, a stray farmyard cow, or a playful pair of household cats. As noted earlier, during her university years, these fleeting sparks of spirituality seem to have found abstract expression in language drawn from theologian Paul Tillich, who rejected the traditional idea of God in his book entitled *The Courage to Be*. Tillich chose instead the term "Ground of Being," which Daly embraced. "God" is better conceived as "Be-ing," to which we relate by living, acting, and thinking in the present world, rather than by longing for a life in some supernatural realm beyond the present.

If we further ask how this philosophy of Be-ing comes to concrete expression, Daly makes multiple references to what she calls the "Archaic Past."[56] This is an epoch long before recorded history when the human community, led by women, lived in idyllic peace and harmony with the natural world. Theirs was a community that pursued lives of genuine be-ing, actively and equally collaborating, supporting, and nourishing each other, as well as blending into the world around them. Only later, in historic times, was this ideal world destroyed by violent, warring, necrophilic male conquerors—the makers of patriarchy. Accordingly, and especially in her later books, what most animates Daly's thinking is the belief that this ideal ancient community can be recovered, that it can experience a rebirth. In feminist hands the Archaic Past can become the Archaic Future, defying not just masculinity, but much of modernity as well. The false gods of violence and patriarchy can be displaced, and the ancient commune restored. The original religion of humanity was the worship of Nature as herself the Great Goddess. And only through the present-day recovery of that worship, only through that natively female bond with the environment and deep affection for all living things, both botanical and animal, can the human future and human well-being be preserved. Whether such a utopia would be achievable in practice is a question Daly does not address, but she has no doubt of its value as an ideal toward which all of society, led by women, should be striving. Amid the ruins of patriarchy, women must build a new, natural spirituality. Humanity needs a gathering of human hearts in perfect harmony with Nature, souls attuned here and now to all living things, all that thrives among and around us—that is the gift of all gifts that the feminine spirit offers the world. In that inspirational plea, voiced most clearly in her twilight years, Daly traces an arc that runs from feminism as a theory of religion to feminism as itself a virtual religion—a Goddess-centered nature mysticism she claimed as meaningful for all while also uniquely hers and uniquely suited to serve as a spiritual surrogate for the lost Catholicism of her birth.

Critique

The core of Mary Daly's feminist theory lies in the claim that humanity has been profoundly damaged by sexism, the pervasive evil of male supremacy. That fundamental injustice, which fatally divides men from women, is woven tightly into religious belief and behavior across the globe. Exposing the layers of injury inflicted by this chronic human fault is the main task of the two anchoring studies that Daly wrote during the prime years of her career. *Beyond God the Father* seeks to demonstrate just how deeply sexist attitudes about the inferiority of women are embedded in Christianity, the world's most widespread and influential religion. *Gyn/Ecology* expands this thesis from Western civilization, the home culture of Christianity, to the entire world community. It offers abundant proof that sexism is not just the primal sin of one religion; it is a vice of "planetary" dimensions, afflicting all times and places. Daly's subsequent works refine and reaffirm this thesis but do not noticeably alter it. She is content to let her case stand (or fall) on the evidence, which in some respects, certainly, is persuasive; in others, less so. Among the more problematical elements, we can take notice of the following.

1. Sexism and Medicine

More than a few readers of *Gyn/Ecology* have been surprised to find modern medicine and related fields placed among the crimes of patriarchy, alongside such cruel rituals as Suttee and genital mutilation. Daly singles out specifically both medical gynecology and psychological therapy, to the point even of drawing explicit parallels to witch-burning. Her argument for doing so, as we have seen, is that these modern, supposedly scientific endeavors are fundamentally patriarchal. As elsewhere on the globe and in history, medical and psychological science have treated women, and often enough abused women, by subjecting them to ideals of wellness, health, and appearance set solely, and wrongly, by men. Some of those men—Freud, for example—have been notorious in their dismissive attitudes toward the "weaker" sex. As noted, the record of both these so-called sciences furnishes ample enough evidence of women subjected to deplorable mistreatment: experimentation on patients without consent; prescription of drugs with often devastating side effects; the misinterpretation of emotional problems as physical, thus leading to tragic misdiagnoses and treatments; and such extreme surgeries as removal of ovaries to cure depression. Further, in some subfields, such as plastic surgery, rich rewards go to physicians who are all too willing to assist women who feel pressured to accommodate male standards of beauty.

All of that being so, we can still ask whether such judgments are entirely fair. Surely mistakes and misapplications of the kind Daly cites here, and even occasional abuses, need to be distinguished from the *intent* of these sciences and therapies, which in the main rest on science and set as their goal, at least, the life and better health of women. That is very different—in fact, the virtual opposite—of witch-burning or suttee, where the lives and well-being of women clearly were not primary, but secondary or worse. Those rites and practices, determined by males, are clearly framed on the premise that (some) women's lives and well-being are expendable in pursuit of male-endorsed social or supernatural values Daly deplores—such as defeating the Devil, pleasing a prospective husband, or sharing in his death. By contrast, modern health sciences are, in theory at least, committed primarily to values that Daly herself endorses—above all, the health and well-being of women. There is certainly merit in denouncing the obvious crimes of patriarchy as Daly lists them, but her indictments of modern gynecology and psychotherapy are not only puzzling, but by her very own moral logic, open to vigorous dispute.

2. Prehistoric Feminism

We have seen that the image of a true sister-led community, as Daly imagines it, can be assembled from certain qualities she sees in women but finds lacking in men. We should notice further that she seems to envision this social system as more than a purely mental construct. In multiple places she suggests that an ideal feminist society once actually existed at a real time in the human past.

During the prehistoric era, well before the earliest recorded civilizations in Egypt and Mesopotamia, there was an ancient, truly feminist society of the kind she commends. The social order in this era was ruled and shaped by women. Its worship probably centered on the Great Goddess, now a lost figure to whom there are still some trace references and cryptic allusions in Greek and other mythologies. As noted, this sisterhood, which was truly nonviolent, lived in close harmony with both the plant and animal life of the natural world. Corrosive ideas of male supremacy were nowhere to be found. Matriarchy predominated. Among early anthropologists, in fact, two notable figures from the nineteenth century, the American Lewis Henry Morgan and a German scholar, Johann Bachofen, described the circumstance. In a volume published in 1861, which he entitled *Mutterrecht* (in English: *Mother Right*), Bachofen contended that matriarchal communities were in fact the earliest forms of human social organization. These views were supported early in the twentieth century by Robert Briffault, who published a work called *The Mothers* in 1927. Then in the 1970s, while Daly was at work on her studies, the thesis gained two new supporters, Elizabeth Gould Davis, author of *The First Sex* (1971) and subsequently the Lithuanian-American anthropologist Marija Gimbutas, who specialized in early European archaeology. In *The Goddesses and Gods of Old Europe* (1974) and other books, Gimbutas drew on new archaeological evidence to propose, like Davis, the existence of an ancient European matriarchy that was later conquered by warring, male-dominated invaders.

We can well understand why Daly, who cites these sources with approval, would readily embrace their thesis. Evidence of such a prehistoric matriarchy, idyllic in form and features, offers a perfect confirmation of her feminist allegations against the repressive male-centered, violence-prone phallocracies of early history and later modernity. There could be no better support for feminism than concrete evidence of an actually existent, harmonious, equality-based primeval community, guided by female leaders and values, that was conquered and replaced by brutally warlike patriarchal clans, who appropriated and imposed a masculine reversal on its guiding feminine religious beliefs and social customs. On this view, when we think of human civilization in its very earliest stages, it is natural to conclude that females came first and did it best. Only later were those matriarchal ideas and customs cruelly stolen, reversed, renamed, and reappropriated—all to serve male interests.

Enticing as this narrative may be to militant feminism, claims of an early matriarchy have not fared well, unfortunately, in the wider realms of anthropology, archaeology, or feminist theory. Despite the considerable influence (for a time) of her book, Elizabeth Gould Davis was simply a local Florida librarian, who had no real expertise in anthropology or prehistoric archaeology. The older theorems of Bachofen and Lewis Morgan were never able to win serious assent from later field-working anthropologists. And the work of Marija Gimbutas, while creative and provocative, has also drawn heavy criticism. Although her archaeological findings have been found to be valuable, the conclusions she has drawn from them have been sharply questioned. The most notable critic of the thesis, feminist Cynthia Eller, claims that the entire idea is little more than a myth, built on the thinnest of evidence, that actually does a disservice to feminism by associating it—needlessly—with factual claims that are almost certainly false or, at the very best, unprovable.[57] Quite apart from the critique of Eller, it is well known that conclusions about beliefs and values drawn from prehistoric and fragmentary archaeological finds, often with little to nothing in the way of written texts among them, are notoriously difficult to either prove or disprove. They are invariably speculative and tenuous, often untethered to the beliefs or values supposedly affirmed, and derived indirectly from reference to historical sources that were written centuries, even millennia, after the happenings that are said to have occurred. Further and finally, the most recent consensus in professional anthropology has, if anything, moved away from the idea of matriarchy, not toward it. The great majority of specialists working in recent decades concede that they are unable to find good examples of an exclusively matriarchal culture in their field research; some add that none is actually known to have existed in the past, as the records adduced are unspecific or unreliable; and others go further still, contending just the opposite: that in societies of almost every kind and locale, men invariably dominate in matters relating to tribal or communal governance.[58]

3. Sexism as the "Original Sin"

The idea that a prehistoric, matriarchal society once existed may be a problem, but if so, it can be put to the side of the discussion, at least for purposes of argument. The central thread of the argument against sexism, at least as it has afflicted women in recorded history and the present, still holds. Further, the idea alone of a harmonious matriarchal community—matriarchy as a purely conceptual model, or aspirational ideal—can be instructive in theory, even if not anchored in fact. The same cannot be said, however, for a different issue that lies closer to the heart of the feminist agenda as Daly construes it. In *Beyond God the Father*, and elsewhere more indirectly, she issues a severe moral indictment of male dominance—what she calls "phallic morality"—that is deeply disturbing and if valid, ethically devastating. Sexism, as she explains it, is not just one form of evil among others; it is (to almost paraphrase the old proverb about money), the very root of all evil, the true "original sin" of humanity. Patriarchy is nothing less than the primeval wrong from which all others follow. Hence the patriarchal—or phallic—sensibility bears responsibility for the three most hideous evils found in human experience: the "Most Unholy Trinity" of rape, genocide, and war. Rape, the first of the three, is deeply tied to the male sense of possession, or ownership—the right to do whatever one wants with the body of a woman, as with a lifeless workman's tool or disposable object. A woman can be used for a purpose and without consent, but when worn, broken, or old, or just no longer wanted, she gets discarded. This attitude lies at the center of the grievous mass rapes we have seen in recent civil and tribal wars of non-Western cultures. But the same sinister attitude infects Western civilization as well. The Bible, in its Old Testament books of Numbers and Deuteronomy, includes women among the spoils of war, which the Hebrews can claim or discard after victory in battle. Such behaviors and texts, examples of which can be easily multiplied, show that there has always been a connection between the mentality of rape and the reality of violence and war. "The socialization of male sexual violence . . . forms the basis for corporate and military interests to train a vicious military force."[59] Similarly, there is a close association between the male ownership sensibility ingrained in the act of rape and the mass horror of genocide. Rape after all is not just an individualized crime. Its logical extension "is the objectification of all who can be cast in the role of victims of violence." It is "an act of group against group: male against female. . . . Rape is expressive of group-think, and group-think is at the core of racial prejudice, whose logical conclusion and final solution is genocide."[60] In other words, when we trace out their intimate linkage, the verdict on the related triple crimes of rape, genocide, and war is that they converge as

> a logical expression of phallocentric power. These are structures of alienation that are self-perpetuating, eternally breeding further estrangement. The circle of destruction generated by the most Unholy Trinity . . . will be broken when women, who are by patriarchal definition objects of rape, externalize and internalize a new self-definition. . . . The casting out of the demonic Trinities *is* female becoming.[61]

In considering this argument, we can certainly agree that rape, an act of sheer physical domination rooted in male sexuality, is a crime of appalling cruelty visited upon innocent women. But it is not clear how an act, or multiple acts, of rape—which Daly defines as male-on-female violence—should necessarily link to the phenomenon of war, which in most instances has consisted of violent actions inflicted by men on other men. To be sure, warfare entails death and destruction that may well fall upon women and children as well as men, but then those horrors are often also inflicted by both women and men together on other men and women together—that is, by adversaries who jointly enlist in battle for their clan, community, or nation and against each other. That war is violence inflicted often on the innocent is evident without question; that it is necessarily a gender-driven group crime of male against female is not. On the face of things, it would appear that ethnic prejudice or social tribalism, in which both males and females, bound by race or ethnicity or locality, do battle jointly against other males and females, is a more plausible cause than Daly's "rape mentality," which is gender-specific in victimizing women (and which also does not address instances of male-on-male rape that occur in warfare). Group psychology affecting male and female alike seems a better place to look if we want to find the deeper wellsprings of violence organized in the form of warfare. And the same would seem to apply to genocide, which also is inflicted not mainly as a crime against a gender, but as an act of violence visited by one community on another, with both sexes of one community united in horrific purpose against both sexes of the other. Daly presumably would respond that this happens only because the women of a given tribe or community are victimized by the men, internalizing the ethic of rapist violence that their own males have imposed on them. But why should we be obliged to think this is so? Instead of claiming that the rapist mentality leads to tribal violence, it seems just as reasonable, arguably even more reasonable, to say that things are the other way around: that tribalism (a joint male-female phenomenon) is primary, and that tribalist violence often leads to rape, in either individual or mass form. Though Daly may disagree, this alternative deserves at least to be considered, with reasons offered for rejecting it. In the same way, when she concludes that only women, as victims of rape, can break the rape-war-genocide cycle of destruction, we can reasonably ask why the fact alone of their experiencing one of these horrors—the individual and gender-specific crime of rape—should enable them, any more than men, to overcome or eliminate the horror of the other crimes, which are both communal and unspecified as to gender. This too would seem to be a point that needs to be argued—by offering evidence or refuting alternatives—rather than simply asserted. That sexism is an evil can be agreed upon easily. That it is the foundational evil, the singular original sin of humanity that comes to pivotal expression in the rapist mentality, from which the great evils of war and genocide are necessarily derived . . . all of that cannot be as readily assumed, or convincingly demonstrated, as Daly seems to think.

4. Feminist Dissent and Race

In the late spring of 1979, the year after publication of *Gyn/Ecology*, Daly received a personal letter from Audre Lorde, a prominent African American author and poet, who had been nominated for a National Book Award and would later be named Poet Laureate of the State of New York. Lorde wrote that she had just read *Gyn/Ecology* and found herself troubled and personally offended. Daly had discussed at length certain strong female divinities and images of the Goddess in Greco-Roman mythology, but had said nothing about the powerful warrior goddesses and female spirits of Africa, even though she had written at length about African women as victimized by the demeaning rites of genital mutilation. Lorde found her own non-white history and mythic background "distorted by the absence of any images of my foremothers in power." She continued as follows:

> As an African-american woman in white patriarchy, I am used to having my archetypal experience distorted and trivialized, but it is terribly painful to feel it being done by a woman whose knowledge so much touches my own. . . . What you excluded from *Gyn/Ecology* dismissed my heritage and the heritage of all other noneuropean women, and denied the real connection that exists between all of us. . . . So the question arises in my Mind, Mary, do you ever read the work of Black women? Did you ever read my words, or did you merely finger through them for quotations . . . ? This is not a rhetorical question. To me this feels like another instance of . . . women of Color being ghettoized by a white woman dealing out of a patriarchal western European frame of reference. . . . When radical lesbian feminist theory dismisses us, it encourages its own demise.[62]

Daly did not immediately reply to the complaints made in this unsettling letter. In the summer following, she did attend a reading by Lorde and spoke to her briefly about arranging a conversation. Then, in September, she wrote a letter that apologized for the delayed response and suggested they meet at the end of the month during a conference they both were planning to attend. They did in fact meet as planned, but Daly reports that Lorde was apparently not satisfied. Lorde, claiming that Daly had never responded to the private letter, chose for that reason to publish it as an open letter "to the community of women." The "Open Letter," which soon made its way into anthologies published for Women's Studies courses and circulated widely in the feminist community, became a source of more than minor embarrassment for Daly. The points it made were not easy to refute. She had (rightly enough) reported on the humiliations of African women, but the fact of the matter was that she had indeed passed over their goddesses—the compelling religious emblems of black female dignity and power. In addition, why had she not responded? Lorde was a black lesbian author of considerable stature, and on their face, her concerns had genuine merit; yet a response was nowhere to be seen. Daly's reputation was in some measure restored by a feminist scholar working on Lorde's biography some two decades later. Among the Poet Laureate's papers she found a hand-written letter of response, dated September 22, 1979. Daly had unfortunately not made a copy for herself, but the letter gave evidence that she had in fact responded; even so, we can plausibly also conjecture that Lorde felt a brief letter of that kind signaled an acknowledgment, but was hardly sufficient to consider it a genuine response. Clearly, the substance of her criticism had gone unanswered.

Beyond the personal issues and misunderstandings, the incident of Lorde's letter disclosed a challenge facing feminism in years ahead. Daly had often complained of patriarchy's perverse skill in "fragmenting" the sisterhood—breaking the double bond of feminist unity and loyalty that was key to success in achieving justice for women. But Lorde had held a mirror up to the face of white, middle-class feminism's champion and allowed her to see something else that was more than a little ironic: unconsciously perhaps, Daly had become just as divisive as the men she so ritually chastised. By passing over the cause of black feminism, it would appear that she had internalized the (overwhelmingly white) racial prejudice that was also part of patriarchy, allowing her own racial indifference to occasion the very fragmentation among women that she deplored. Patriarchy, one could almost say, had been handed a gift—its most outspoken adversary herself weakened by the self-inflicted wound of racial insensitivity.[63] In the years following, that convergence (or we perhaps should say, collision) of race and gender has acquired an even greater significance, taking the form of complicated, and sometimes acrimonious, conversations within the feminist family that have continued into the present moment.

It is understandable that university courses in feminist theory would include among their assigned texts Audre Lorde's "Open Letter." New generations of women certainly need to face the complicated question of feminism and race. But in another respect, it is also unfortunate. If the "Letter" is the only avenue by which educated younger women encounter the pioneering work of Mary Daly, something of considerable value clearly will have been lost. For Daly's wider achievement as a theorist of religion is considerable. It ought not to be too readily overshadowed by her failure—critical and serious as it certainly was—to appreciate the role of race in the feminist struggle. Here we can again recall the comparison to Karl Marx, himself a theorist with a bold, but not unflawed, agenda. Marx knew that a crucial part of his task was to "raise the consciousness" of societies that were blind to the fact of class struggle; exploitation of the poor could hardly be overcome if people were unable to notice that injustice even existed. In the same way, Daly knew that her main mission also was to "raise consciousness," to awaken men and women alike to the power of patriarchy deeply ingrained in the religious beliefs, cultural institutions, and customary practices of all humanity. She knew (as did Marx) that society can hardly overcome structural injustice unless the fact, and depth, of the problem has been at least discovered. Consequently, she gave all of herself—her imposing argumentative skills and the full force of her driven personality—to the (too often thankless) task of opening the world's eyes to what she saw as obvious. She made it her lifelong calling to expose androcentric prejudice wherever it could be unearthed: first in her own Catholicism, then in Christianity, the most widespread and widely followed of the world's religions, and finally in the entire spectrum of the world's religious communities—from antiquity to the present and across all continents, from Europe to the Americas, and to Africa and Asia alike. She could be truculent and combative, to be sure. But she also could say in her own defense that, as with Marx, the social world she encountered in the unliberated 1960s and early 1970s required nothing less than full-on intellectual combat; no other option would do. Her mission as a sometimes snarling "Hag" called her to take arms on behalf of women even as she sought to disarm powerful men. A final measure of the legacy she has left to feminist theory can be taken in the near cultic cadre of devoted feminist followers she acquired, and the keen endorsements received in all quarters from those who saluted and still salute her as a treasured "foresister," in the same way she honored her own intellectual mentor Simone de Beauvoir. It is that shaping influence, and those tributes from the sisterhood, that have rightly earned for Mary Daly this placement in the otherwise exclusively male company of modern major theorists of religion. For conferring upon her that unwanted recognition, those sisters, both past and present, presumably need ask their beloved mentor's forgiveness. They should know, however, that if true to form, she would not be disposed to grant it.

Notes

1. Robin Morgan, quoted in the *New York Times* obituary, January 7, 2010.
2. Mary Daly, *Outercourse: The Be-Dazzling Voyage* (New York: HarperCollins, 1992), p. 44.
3. Ibid., p. 49.
4. Ibid., p. 78.
5. Mary Daly, quoted in Sarah Corbett, "Mary Daly: Gyno-Theologian," *New York Times Magazine*, December 26, 2010.
6. Mary Daly, *The Church and the Second Sex* (Boston: Beacon Press, 1968), p. 172.
7. Ibid., pp. 119, 121.
8. Ibid., p. 195.
9. Daly, *Outercourse,* p. 144.
10. Mary Daly, "Feminist Postchristian Introduction," in *The Church and the Second Sex,* pp. 15–52.
11. Mary Daly, *Beyond God the Father: Toward a Philosophy of Women's Liberation* (Boston: Beacon Press, 1973), p. 19.
12. Ibid., p. 13.
13. Ibid., p. 21.
14. Ibid., pp. 35–36.
15. Ibid., p. 49.

16. Ibid., p. 54.
17. Ibid., p. 55.
18. Ibid., pp. 71–72.
19. Ibid., p. 85.
20. Ibid.
21. Ibid., p. 87.
22. Ibid., p. 118.
23. Ibid., p. 194.
24. Ibid., p. 106.
25. Ibid., p. 107.
26. Ibid., p. 110.
27. Ibid., p. 122.
28. Mary Daly, *Gyn/Ecology: The Metaethics of Radical Feminism* (Boston: Beacon Press, 1978), p. 85.
29. Ibid., p. 126.
30. Ibid., p. 140.
31. Ibid., p. 148.
32. Ibid., p. 159.
33. Ibid., pp. 163, 167.
34. Ibid., p. 180.
35. Ibid., p. 183.
36. Ibid., p. 264.
37. Daly, *Outercourse,* p. 219.
38. Daly, *Gyn/Ecology,* p. 59.
39. Hester Eisenstadt *Contemporary Feminist Thought* (Boston: G. K. Hall & Co., 1983), pp. 107–115, singles Mary Daly out as a leading figure in the shift from the more moderate "reformist" program of women's liberation to a more militant "separatist" agenda that left second-wave feminists divided in the later 1970s. While reformists felt there was a realistic hope of changing the male culture by engagement and persuasion, separatists like Daly came to the view that such hope was an illusion. For her and her separatist associates, male culture was so irretrievably tied to the vice of supremacy that there was no chance of change; it was "wholly evil." Conversely, female culture was "wholly good" (p. 111). Between two such adversarial communities, there could be no such thing as reconciliation.
40. While to some observers much of *Pure Lust* restates these themes as addressed earlier, feminist Anne-Marie Korte finds in it "a more profound exploration of women's lack of self-actualization." See "Deliver Us from Evil: Bad Versus Better Faith in Mary Daly's Feminist Writings," in Sarah Lucia Hoagland and Marilyn Frye, eds., *Feminist Interpretations of Mary Daly* (University Park: Pennsylvania State University Press, 2000), pp. 95–96.
41. Daly had already incurred the displeasure of the "trans" community with negative comments about transsexuality made earlier; see *Gyn/Ecology*, p. 238 n.
42. Mary Daly, *Quintessence, Realizing the Archaic Future: A Radical Elemental Feminist Manifesto* (Boston: Beacon Press, 1998), p. 23.

43. Mary Daly, *Amazon Grace: The Courage to Sin Big* (New York: Macmillan Palgrave, 2006), pp. 7–8.

44. Daly, *Outercourse,* p. 284.

45. The account of this final episode is found in *Amazon Grace*, pp. 65–77. In 1996, four years after the publication of *Outercourse,* Daly updated the story of her professional struggles in a brief, autobiographical article entitled "Sin Big," published in *The New Yorker* magazine (February 26, 1996), pp. 76–84.

46. Daly, *Amazon Grace*, p. 70.

47. Eisenstadt, in *Contemporary Feminist Thought,* p. 111, cites the suggestion of some reviewers that Daly's division between male as evil and female as good also recalls Manicheanism, the dualist sect from Persia that was a rival of Christianity within the Roman empire. Manicheans believed in a cosmic struggle between those loyal to a good God of Light and those captive to an evil God of Darkness.

48. Daly, *Gyn/Ecology,* p. 187.

49. Daly, *Pure Lust,* p. 55.

50. Daly, *Outercourse,* p. 395.

51. Daly, *Pure Lust,* p. 105.

52. Ibid., pp. 339–340.

53. Daly, *Gyn/Ecology,* p. 38.

54. Ibid., p. 190.

55. Ibid., p. 39.

56. Daly, *Amazon Grace*, pp. 4, 7, 14–15, 55.

57. Cynthia Eller, *The Myth of Matriarchal Prehistory: Why An Invented Past Will Not Give Women a Future* (Boston: Beacon Press, 2000).

58. Among other works, see J. M. Adovasio, Olga Soffer, and Jake Page, *Uncovering the True Roles of Women in Prehistory* (New York: Harper Collins, 2007); *Encyclopedia Britannica* (2007), s.v. "Matriarchy"; Joan Bamberger, "Why Men Rule in Primitive Society," in *Women, Culture, and Society*, ed. Michelle Rosaldo and Louise Lamphere (Stanford, CA: Stanford University Press, 1974), p. 263; and Donald E. Brown, *Human Universals* (Philadelphia: Temple University Press, 1991), p. 137.

59. Daly, *Beyond God the Father*, p. 117.

60. Ibid., p. 118.

61. Ibid., p. 122.

62. Audre Lorde, "An Open Letter to Mary Daly," in Cherrie Moraga and Gloria Anzaldúa, *This Bridge Called My Back: Writings by Radical Women of Color* (Albany: State University of New York Press, 2015), pp. 90–93.

63. AnaLouise Keating, "Back to the Mother: Feminist Mythmaking with a Difference," in Hoagland and Frye, *Feminist Interpretations,* pp. 378–379, comments instructively on the key point where the perspectives of Daly and Lorde diverged.

Suggestions for Further Reading

Ahranjani, Maryann. "Mary Daly v. Boston College: The Impermissibility of Single-Sex Classrooms within a Private University." *American University Journal of Gender,*

Social Policy, and the Law 9 (2001): 179–205. A review of the Title IX legal issues raised in the segregated classroom complaint that forced Daly's retirement; it concludes that her practice did violate the federal statute.

Anderson, Carol S., and Jennifer Rycenga, et al. "Mary Daly: Grand Agitator and Revolting Hag." *Feminist Theology: The Journal of the Britain and Ireland School of Feminist Theology* 24 (May 2000): 9–13. The first of six articles (pp. 9–40) produced from papers presented in a session of tribute to Mary Daly at the Annual Meeting of the American Academy of Religion, held in November of 1998. Other articles contributed by Jane Caputi, Carter Heywood, Mary Hunt, Jennifer Rycenga, and Peggy Schmeiser.

Berry, Wanda Warren. "Feminist Theology: The Verbing of Ultimate/Intimate Reality in Mary Daly." In *Feminist Interpretations of Mary Daly*. Edited by Sarah Lucia Hoagland and Marilyn Frye, pp. 27–54. State College: Pennsylvania State University Press, 2000. Stresses Daly's use of metaphor as entry to metaphysics.

Carr, Anne. "Is a Christian Feminist Theology Even Possible?" *Theological Studies* 43 (1982): 279–297. Explores the challenge that Daly's views present to more religiously conventional Catholics and other, more conservative feminists.

Corbett, Sara. "Mary Daly: Gyno-Theologian." *New York Times Magazine*. December 26, 2010, pp. 14–15. An obituary appreciation of Daly's life and work, highlighting her confrontations with Boston College and exclusionary attitudes toward men.

Culpepper, Emily Erwin, et al. "Special Section in Memory of Mary Daly." *Journal of Feminist Studies in Religion* 28, no. 2 (2012): 89–117. The first of eight brief articles forming a retrospective assessment of Daly's life and career from multiple feminist perspectives; includes contributions from Mary Hunt, Carol Adams, Xochitl Alviso, Judith Plasgow, Zayn Dassam, Laura Levitt, and Traci West.

Eisentein, Hester. *Contemporary Feminist Thought*. Boston: G. K. Hall, 1983. Offers two insightful chapters with comparative comment on Daly's agenda in the context of works by Betty Friedan and other second-wave feminists.

Gray, Francis. "Elemental Philosophy: Language and Ontology in Mary Daly's Texts." In *Feminist Interpretations of Mary Daly*. Edited by Sarah Lucia Hoagland and Marilyn Frye, pp. 222–245. State College: Pennsylvania State University Press, 2000.

Hedrick, Elizabeth. "The Early Career of Mary Daly: A Retrospective." *Feminist Studies* 39, no. 2 (2013): 457–483. Discusses aspects of Daley's career in terms of both achievements and failings, including the incident and controversy created by the letter from Audre Lorde.

Henking, Susan. "Rejected, Reclaimed, Renamed: Mary Daly on Psychology and Religion." *Journal of Psychology and Theology* 21, no. 3 (1993): 199–207. An appraisal of Daly's mixed views on the discipline of modern psychology, both as science and therapy.

Hewitt, Marsha. *Critical Theory of Religion: A Feminist Analysis*. Minneapolis: Augsburg Fortress, 1995. Provides an analytical chapter (pp. 113–146) on "Unreason and Revolution: Herbert Marcuse, Mary Daly, and Gynocentric Feminism."

Hoagland, Sarah Lucia, and Marilyn Frye, eds. *Feminist Interpretations of Mary*. State College: Pennsylvania State University Press, 2000. An instructive collection of essays offering a variety of analyses, criticisms, and appreciations of Daly's career and achievement as seen on the eve of her formal academic retirement.

Hunt, Mary E. "Biographical Sketch." In *The Mary Daly Reader*. Edited by Jennifer Rycenga and Linda Barufaldi, pp. xv–xix. New York: New York University Press, 2017. A warm and succinct appreciation of Daly's life, work, and achievements.

Karaganis, Maria. "Mary, Mary, Quite Contrary." *Ms.* 9, no. 4 (1999): 56–59. An assessment of Daly placed in feminism's leading popular magazine, which in the year prior had been reacquired and placed under independent ownership by its founder, Gloria Steinem.

Katherine, Amber I. "A Too Early Morning: Audre Lorde's 'An Open Letter to Mary Daly' and Daly's Decision Not to Respond in Kind." In *Feminist Interpretations of Mary Daly*. Edited by Sarah Lucia Hoagland and Marilyn Frye, pp. 266–297. State College: Pennsylvania State University Press, 2000. A detailed discussion of the "Open Letter" incident and debate that divided feminism in the 1980s and 1990s.

Liddle, Joanna, and Shirin Rai. "Feminism, Imperialism and Orientalism: The Challenge of the 'Indian Woman.'" *Women's History Review* 7, no. 4 (1998): 495–520. A critique of *Gyn/Ecology* and its negative portrayal of women as victims in Hindu culture in contrast to the positive portrayal of witches as defiant women in the West.

Lorde, Audre. "An Open Letter to Mary Daly." In *This Bridge Called My Back: Writings by Radical Women of Color*. Edited by Cherrie Moraga and Gloria Anzaldua, pp. 94–97. Watertown, MA: Persephone Press, 1981. The letter, to which Daly was slow to respond, suggesting that in *Gyn/Ecology* an implicit white racism affected the portrayal of African women as victims and occasioned a corresponding failure to explore and exhibit African goddess images as sources of strength.

Mann, Mark and David McMahon. "Mary Daly." In *Boston Collaborative Encyclopedia of Western Theology*. Edited by Derek Michaud. Accessed September 23, 2020. http://people.bu.edu/wwildman/bce. A brief, yet highly informative, overview of Daly's mission and agenda that offers perceptive observations about her use of unconventional language.

Messina, Gina. "Mary Daly's Letter to Audre Lorde." In *Feminism and Religion*, revised October 8, 2011. https://feminismandreligion.com/2011/10/05. A discussion that offers at least a partial vindication of Daly as regards her response to Audre Lorde.

Riswold, Caryn. "From a Babylonian Captivity to the Otherworld: Martin Luther and Mary Daly as Political Theologians?" *Currents in Theology and Mission* 24, no. 1 (February 1997): 50–58. A comparative study that finds in Daly's feminist revolt certain strategies and themes that offer parallels to Luther's momentous theological reform.

Riswold, Caryn. "Two Reformers: Martin Luther and Mary Daly as Political Theologians?" *Political Thelogy* 7, no. 4 (2010): 491–506. Further development of the Luther/Daly comparison.

Rycenga, Jennifer, and Linda Barufaldi, eds. *The Mary Daly Reader*. With a preface by Robin Morgan. New York: New York University Press, 2017. The most recent work on Daly, with excerpts from her major books arranged chronologically over the course of her career; includes informative introductions to its sections and an updated, comprehensive bibliography, richly populated with both primary and secondary sources.

Sharma, Renuka, and Purushottama Bilimoria. "Where Silence Burns: *Sati* (suttee) in India: Mary Daly's Gynocritique and Resistant Spirituality." In *Feminist Interpretations of Mary Daly*. Edited by Sarah Lucia Hoagland and Marilyn Frye, pp. 322–348. State College: Pennsylvania State University Press, 2000. A dense, thoughtful discussion that mixes carefully qualified dissent from Daly's judgments on suttee with just as carefully qualified appreciation.

Sturgis, Susanna. "Mary Daly: Revolting Hag." *Women's Review of Books* 27, no. 3 (2010): 30–31. An obituary appreciation, stressing how Daly's strong theological training in Catholic institutions furnished the analytical skills that exposed the Church's subjugation of women.

Suchocki, Marjorie. "The Challenge of Mary Daly." *Encounter* 41 (1980): 307–317. Explores how an intellectual attachment to Christianity might be salvaged for feminism despite Daly's radical rejection of that pathway for herself.

Weavcr, Mary Jo. "Who Is the Goddess and Where Does She Get Us?" *Journal of Feminist Studies in Religion* 5, no. 1 (1989): 49–64. A thoroughly researched inquiry into the claim of prehistoric Goddess worship to which Daly was drawn and which stands at the center of ongoing feminist debate.

Conclusion

It may be helpful to look back on the previous pages of this book as a kind of panel discussion. The invitees are an impressive group, needless to say. Each has had a fair opportunity to speak, and the sequence of the presentations is not unimportant. Some are best understood after we have heard others: we need a grasp of armchair anthropology to see the point of field anthropology; we need to see the questions left behind by Tylor and Frazer to appreciate certain answers proposed by Freud and by Durkheim; and only when we consider the nature of the reductionist functionalism urged by Freud, Durkheim, and Marx can we follow the reasoning that led Weber, James, Eliade, and others to dissent from it. Sequence, however, is not the same as succession. It would be a mistake to conclude from the review of theories just completed that those at the end of the sequence have solved all the problems discovered among those that preceded them. If so, we could easily conclude that Mary Daly has "won the debate" merely because she is placed in the final chapter. It is true that she is the theorist most recently active, but that does not mean her ideas are the only ones still standing. Theoretical constructs have a certain timeless quality, like the theorems of geometry. Their value lies in calling certain key questions continuously to mind for reflection and reconsideration. That being so, we can make best use of this final chapter in two ways: first, by looking beyond the classic formulations to the interpretive efforts undertaken by other theorists, chiefly in more recent decades; and second, by taking a final measure of our ten theorists, and implicitly all theories, with a set of general questions that enable us to compare their strategies and briefly appraise their prospects.

Recent Theoretical Interests

Currently, the modern research university is the home of most efforts to frame explanations or interpretations of religion. These endeavors are carried out mainly by academic specialists pursuing programs of research that are highly diverse and individualized. Even so, their work can be seen to cluster around certain shared general patterns—or paradigms—of explanation. Throughout much of the past century the paradigms of widest general influence have been those of Freud and Marx. Durkheim also has claimed a significant set of disciples, mainly among professional sociologists. Despite limited access to his work earlier on, Max Weber has also drawn a small, select following, while through the 1960s and after, discussion in America came increasingly to be influenced by the disciples of Mircea Eliade. In addition, feminists were drawn to Mary Daly and her associates or conversation partners. Throughout most of the century, however, no theory of religion could hope to be taken seriously if it did not engage the aggressive reductionist explanations advanced by Marx and Freud and refined by their disciples. Not until the 1980s and 1990s did that circumstance begin to change. In quite different, unrelated ways the achievements of both Freud and Marx came under severe challenge—the former from critics who questioned both the ideas and methods of psychoanalysis and the latter from the stunning popular revolts in East Europe and Russia against the oppressive regimes of Marxist socialism.[1]

Today, it is fair to say that no single theory exercises an influence comparable to that of these leading paradigms over half a century ago. There are instead various competing patterns of interpretation that have built upon the classic theories examined here, even as they have refined and applied them in novel ways. We can perhaps best describe these initiatives as centers of theoretical interest—as programs that give to certain kinds of explanation a kind of first conceptual priority, as inquiries that for differing reasons privilege certain types of explanation over others. Among these, we can distinguish a number of leading patterns, or dominant agendas: (1) humanistic, (2) psychological, (3) sociological, (4) politico-economic, and (5) anthropological. In each case, the adjective defines the kind of guiding axiom that directs the inquiries of those who work within its broad framework. In each case also, "industry" may be a better word than "inquiry" to describe these enterprises as they currently proceed. A century ago, scholars who attempted to theorize about religion formed a tiny guild of learned, solitary craftsmen; *Chips from a German Workshop* was actually the title Max Müller gave to a collection of his essays. Today, in the academies of the English-speaking world alone, the scholar working from one of these orientations is likely to think of herself as part of a technical team at a multisite production facility, conversing with dozens or scores of others in different locations, each with a complementary specialty or competing method that promises the best design and assembly. What follows is an effort to penetrate some of that complexity by offering a brief outline of these main approaches, attended by some examples that illustrate how the classic theories have left their imprint on other and later work.

Humanist Orientations

Humanist theory assumes that religious activity is first and foremost human behavior governed primarily by ideas, intentions, and emotions, just as in other human endeavors. We explain political behavior in terms of the political ideas that citizens naturally frame and act upon if they have an interest in politics. We explain artistic behavior in terms of creative ideas and expressive actions that move artists to paint, novelists to write, and musicians or actors to perform. In the same way, we explain religious endeavor by appealing to religious beliefs, intentions, and aspirations. This kind of explanation, which comes nearest to the way we explain our activities in everyday life, is anchored in theoretical axioms articulated most clearly by Weber and Eliade, also by Evans-Pritchard and Geertz. Its focus falls mainly on the conscious religious motives that account for obviously religious behavior such as worship and devotion, ritual and belief. Eliade, we may recall, insists that it is not just religion that should be explained religiously. For him, religious beliefs and attitudes stand at the center of general human experience, so they can offer a key to understanding activities of other kinds as well. A similar address to religion and the diversity of religious traditions on a global scale can be found in *An Interpretation of Religion: Human Responses to the Transcendent* (1989) by the eminent British philosopher of religion John Hick. He centers attention on belief systems and moral values, and on forms of religious experience. An exemplary instance of humanist explanation can also be found in the work of David Carrasco, a disciple of Eliade who has written extensively on the native religions of Central and South America before Columbus. His *Religions of Mesoamerica: Cosmovisions and Ceremonial Centers* (1990) demonstrates how the vision of the sacred, embodied in religious ideas, myths, and rituals, shaped almost every aspect of life in ancient Aztec and Mayan civilizations.

If we compare the work of Carrasco with that of Wendy Doniger, who has written extensively on the myths, rituals, and religions of India, we can see the same axiom applied to an Asian culture, though with a difference as well. Doniger commits also to a humanist approach; she appeals to religious motives, ideas, and values embedded in Hindu religion and mythology, but she is less disposed to privilege them as dominant. In works such as *The Origins of Evil in Hindu Mythology* (1976) and *The Implied Spider: Politics and Theology in Myth* (1998), she works more evidently in the vein of Weber than Eliade, using what she calls a "toolbox" approach ("whatever tool seems to work") to discover a web of causation in which religious ideas and motives mutually interact with historical, social, psychological, artistic, political, and other factors. A humanist toolbox of a different kind is on display in the work of the American cultural historian Thomas Tweed. His *Crossing and Dwelling: A Theory of Religion* (2006) offers the domestic ethnography of Cuban Catholic exiles in Miami as a localized clue to the crucial role of religion worldwide in orienting human thought and action at the intersection of the body, the home, the homeland, and the cosmos. These kinds of investigation, which freely adduce an eclectic mix of human ideas, motives, conditions, and causes to explain either religion or religion's impact on other spheres of life, are today so widely practiced as to be almost the "default setting" of most explanatory endeavors in the field. Most interpreters who do not self-consciously choose other orientations move toward this kind of mixed paradigm, in which the explanation may even start with an appeal to primarily religious factors but readily blends them with others as the actual case may require. Examples of scholars who work in broadly humanistic fashion, assigning primary or significant credit to religious ideas, values, and practices in their explanations, can be found across the whole spectrum of present-day scholarship. Most authors of articles and books on religion encountered in the academy or the marketplace do not attend greatly to the matter of theoretical presuppositions. But that does not mean they do not have them; they hold, mostly unawares, to axioms not unlike Tweed's placement-and-movement model, Doniger's toolbox, or even Carrasco's all-encompassing sacred and apply them intuitively with varying personal emphases.

Psychological Orientations

Theorists who give priority to issues of human psychology and personality have long been divided about the legacy of Freud. His path-breaking importance is readily acknowledged, but over the past half century especially, the mainstream of social scientific psychology has moved quite decisively away from the methods of psychoanalysis toward "hard science" models of data collection, correlation, and analysis. For this kind of research, Freudian theory is regarded as fundamentally unusable.

Elsewhere, judgments on Freud are quite mixed. Practicing psychoanalysts naturally remain closer to his founding principles, and some, certainly, continue to share Freud's dim view of religion as a tissue of illusion rooted in the dysfunctional personality. But there have been important countertrends as well. At the very start of the psychoanalytic movement, Freud's Swiss colleague Carl Jung took a decidedly more positive view of religion. Further, and as we have seen at length in the chapter on William James, the guiding thesis of *The Varieties of Religious Experience* is the power of religion to restore and energize the broken self. In the mid-twentieth century Gordon Allport's *The Individual and His Religion* (1951) and Abraham Maslow's *Religions, Values, and Peak-Experiences* (1964) also sought to make constructive reappraisals. Allport saw no need to presume there was some singular form of religious experience, whether that might be Freud's neurosis or James's conversion moment. He found that individuals draw on a variety of emotions and sentiments in adopting a religious perspective on life. Aligning with James, he argued that such experiences foster maturity if embraced "intrinsically," through a willing inward assent, rather than being forced upon the personality from the outside. Maslow concurred. He found that across the human race, religious sentiments have arisen naturally within individuals as they respond to peak experiences of a mystical type; to the extent that those experiences are the same, so are the goals of all the religions they inspire, regardless of the specific doctrines that arise to define them. Maslow's perspective here resembles that of James. Religion in this naturally and universally human form cannot be dismissed as pathological; it should be seen as natural.

Since at least the 1980s, the association of religion with mental health (rather than mental illness) has emerged as a promising new focus of psychological inquiry. Most of this effort has been centered on data-driven programs of research, often with human subjects, that have managed to acquire substantial funding from both private foundations and government agencies. In general, religion has emerged from these investigations as beneficial in nature, fostering both mental and physical wellness. It should further be noted that over time a significant change in method has occurred. Psychologists of William James's generation pursued "introspection" as their main avenue of inquiry, while later psychology has turned the focus to "behavioral" analyses, most recently supplemented by the technology of brain imaging. One example of the new trend, also illustrative of a turn away from Freudian hostility toward religion, is a major study by Kenneth Pargament, noted for his empirical inquiries by way of questionnaires and for his widely respected *Psychology of Religion and Coping* (1997). In this comprehensive study he charts the several mental pathways by which religion, particularly belief in a God, enables people, in both sickness and health, to manage situations and relationships affected by emotional stress. He also offers a map of the diverse perspectives on religion represented in both current research and clinical forums. The turn toward behavioral studies and affirmative themes can be seen also in newer avenues of research, especially the study of human relationships. *Forgiveness: Theory, Research and Practice* (2000), edited by Michael McCullough, along with Pargament and Carl E. Thoresen, gathers a number of recent studies centered on the intriguing theme of religion as an agent of human reconciliation, a resource for the repair of broken relationships. These theorists can almost be said to have stood Freudian reductionism on its head. For them religion is not a malady that psychoanalysis alone can cure; it is a therapy that psychoanalysis does not provide.

Sociological Orientations

Theorists working with a sociological orientation have in the main looked to Durkheim (or even Marx) rather than Weber as the main guide for their labors. This is not surprising if we recall the distinctive features of their work. Durkheim sought quite self-consciously to create a school of inquiry committed to the axiom of sociological interpretation; in *The Elementary Forms* he even offered a kind of template for future inquiries. By way of the *Verstehen* method and the appeal to ideal-types, Weber too searched for some kind of general theory that could be applied, in a manner resembling that of natural science, to all future work. But as we have seen, his feeling for cultural complexity, his vast command of evidence, and his keen appreciation of what is unique to each historical instance have made it difficult for others to draw on his work as a close model for their own. Accordingly, though some theorists of humanist orientation have found ideas and themes from Weber that they can use, most social scientists active in the professional guild and appearing in major journals have not.

Durkheim's legacy can be observed in Milton Yinger's *Scientific Study of Religion* (1970), a major summation of the state of social science published two thirds of the way through the past century. Like Durkheim, Yinger defined religion functionally, arguing among other things that it serves to control private passions for the good of the whole. Yinger also strongly endorsed Durkheim's claim that however it may change over time, religion is too well integrated into the patterns of social life ever to predict, as Freud and Marx do, that it will someday disappear. It would seem as enduring as society itself. Conversely, later theorists working also in the tradition of Durkheim have come quite sharply to disagree. Bryan Wilson's *Religion in Sociological Perspective* (1982) and Steven Bruce's *God Is Dead: Secularisation in the West* (2002) present modern secularization as a process destined to usher in the eventual disappearance of religion. Their arguments draw on Durkheim's distinction between the "mechanical solidarity" of unified primitive tribes and the "organic solidarity" of segmented, specialized modern societies. They contend that in any society, as modernization proceeds, the space left for religion grows steadily smaller. In the Western Middle Ages, the arm of the Christian Church reached into every sphere of social activity, from morality to art, economics, politics, literature, and science. In the modern era, religion's reach has gradually contracted; control of knowledge has been conceded to science, political power and social welfare have been given over to the state, the arts have their freedom, and so on. Religion today is at most simply one piece of a complex social package.

This "secularization" thesis is not new. It had been anticipated in Peter Berger's *Sacred Canopy* (1967), a work that blends some of Durkheim's emphases with others from Weber. For Berger, people living in a social community frame ideas and project them outward; those ideas then become objectified as truth outside of the self and society, only to be internalized again as programs of future action and belief. Modernization, however, tends to break up these connections, and so religion as an external belief system begins to lose its strength. The same theme was quite differently explored in *The Invisible*

Religion (1967), a work by Berger's sometime associate Thomas Luckmann, who disagreed with the secularization thesis and insisted on the power of religion to adapt and survive. Changing course, Berger came later to add his own critique of the secularization thesis in *The Desecularization of the World* (1999). In yet another key, and most recently, one of America's foremost sociologists of religion, Robert Bellah, turned his sights near the close of his career from modernity to earliest antiquity, probing the emergent interaction of social needs and religious claims as they took form in prehistoric times. *Religion in Human Evolution: From the Paleolithic to the Axial Age* (2011) embarks on a wide-ranging inquiry into religion's role in the rise of ancient civilizations in both the East and West. Blending sociology with archeology and ancient history, Bellah searches for religion as rooted in the deep human past—terrain where more cautious scholars in the field have been reluctant to tread. Both the novelty of this work and the ongoing vitality of the secularization debates, which are cited here as illustrative rather than definitive, suggest just how durable and fertile Durkheim's legacy has been, even apart from its impact on anthropological theorists, whom we have yet to consider.

Politico-Economic Orientations

Theorists whose explanations appeal primarily to socioeconomic conditions work in the long shadow of Karl Marx, regardless of whether they endorse all or only part of his economic theorem: that religion is an illusion born of the class struggle. Until the great collapse of 1989, it could be said that communist socialism had brought to Western civilization the greatest revolution in thought and society since Christianity overturned the pagan cultures of Greece and Rome. For many, Marx and Engels had unmasked the great fraud of religious belief—that it comforts the rich while deluding the poor. Further, the truth of the Marxist analysis was underscored by the political success of the communist movement it inspired. Through much of the twentieth century, it was reasonable to conclude that communism was indeed "on the march." It had captured Russia and China, two of the world's major nations; it was spreading in Asia and to Cuba in Latin America; even in Europe and the United States, strong socialist movements and left-leaning political parties supported the goals of communism, though not its violent methods. Marxist theory thus made a strong claim upon the assent of intellectuals, artists, journalists, academics, and politicians in nearly all Western nations. Within the Soviet and socialist states, however, it was a different matter; disillusionment arrived quickly under the rule of Stalin and became chronic thereafter. But outside the Eastern bloc, this was not the case. Neither the reports of purges nor the tales of famine and murderous atrocities that filtered out of the socialist states could shake the faith of true Marxist believers. In recent decades, consequently, the major spokesmen for the Marxist cause have been placed not in the old communist bloc, but in the universities of Europe, America, and the Third World. They are found not mainly among professional economists, as we first might think, but in humanistic fields such as history, literature, philosophy, religion, and the political or social sciences, as well as thematic fields centered on ethnic, environmental, or gender studies. In general, these scholars and critics offer variant forms of a common argument built on the premise of global injustice.

"Postcolonial theory" is one of the terms often used to denote this program of critical suspicion focused on the affluent, imperialistic cultures of the modern West, but it circulates under many labels in university classrooms and offices. Terms such as "cultural criticism," "critical theory," "postmodernism," "anti-hegemonism," "transgressive discourse," "subversive discourse," "alterity," and "subaltern studies" suggest just some of the initiatives associated, in varying ways of course, with this general posture of cultural critique. Marxist theory of this sort counts among its modern apostles and evangelists many of the most influential critics, scholars, and public intellectuals of the later twentieth and early twenty-first centuries in Europe and America. The most influential, though not the most profound, of all these figures may well have been the Algerian French writer Frantz Fanon, whose animated protest work *The Wretched of the Earth* (1961)—now more than a half century old—furnished these movements with both a bible and an early catechism.

Postcolonial and related theorists write on a far-reaching spectrum of subjects, and the literature as a whole is abundant. The best we can do here is notice, somewhat at random, certain recent efforts to advance the thesis as it bears particularly on the sociopolitical interpretation of religion. In *Orientalism and Religion in Postcolonial Theory: India and "the Mystic East"* (1999), Richard King argues that the category of "mysticism" employed so prominently in comparisons of Asian with Western religions is a distortion imposed on Indian religion by European scholars subtly determined to assert the superiority of the West. In *Genealogies of Religion: Discipline and Reasons of Power in Christianity and Islam* (1993), Talal Asad makes a similar point about religion itself as an abstract concept provincial to the Western world and unfavorably imposed on the Muslim East. His argument underscores a theme earlier articulated by Edward Said in *Orientalism* (1978), one of the most politically provocative critiques of the West and its imperialist ways written in the past four decades. The works of Michel Foucault, perhaps the most celebrated of France's radical theorists, have had an even wider impact. He was not exactly a postcolonial theorist, but his aggressive efforts to expose the mechanisms by which those who hold power in society manipulate institutions, language, culture, religion, and even science to maintain their control have had a similar effect. In works such as *Madness and Civilization: A History of Insanity in the Age of Reason* (1961) and *Discipline and Punish: The Birth of the Prison* (1975), he claimed to unearth within the society of the West the same social disparities, anchored in power and privilege, that postcolonial theory discerns between the West and other cultures.

Foucault's comments on knowledge as a means of oppression have found a parallel in the subsequent work of Gayatri Spivak. In such studies as *In Other Worlds: Essays in Cultural Politics* (1988) and *A Critique of Post-Colonial Reason: Toward a History of the Vanishing Present* (1999), she adds both an Asian and a feminist turn to the conventional critique of the West, bringing women as well as the poor and outcast into the growing army of those offering resistance to power. Feminist theory is certainly not the same as postcolonial theory, but Spivak's work illustrates how feminist literature also explores themes of protest, as we have seen here in the work of anti-church theologian and theorist Mary Daly. Similarly, Marsha Aileen Hewitt's *Critical Theory of Religion: A Feminist Analysis* (1995) assesses the implications of Frankfurt School's critique of the West and late capitalism, while looking beyond Europe to pursue themes of feminist and Latin American political liberation. Again, these works have been chosen merely to illustrate patterns; the complete literature on these issues runs to scores and more of volumes reflecting a wide array of academic fields and initiatives in social activism. Two recent, equally noteworthy studies provide instructive avenues into the complex and contentious issues at the center of the postcolonial debate. *Resistance to Empire and Militarization: Reclaiming the Sacred* (2020), edited by Jude Lal Fernando, brings together essays by scholar/activists from the Middle East, Asia, Africa, Latin America, and elsewhere who register a passionate protest against the fusion of religion and economic imperialism that has enabled oppressors in the capitalist West to exploit their peoples and their lands. Some of the same issues are insightfully addressed from a different vantage point in a magisterial new study by an accomplished American historian of Christianity. In the later chapters especially of *A History of Christian Conversion* (2020), David Kling judiciously appraises the complicated mix of altruistic idealism and distressing provincialism that marked the enterprise of modern Christian missions in the third world, where spiritual aims were found to be both entangled and embattled with imperial designs.

There is, finally, one case that can be cited here to illustrate that not all of politico-economic theory falls within the wide network of Marxist postcolonial criticism. That is the paradigm known as rational choice theory, which has emerged from behavioral analyses that originate among professional economists. It is rooted in the critical work of Marx's principal adversaries—economists from the Vienna school of free-market capitalism. These market theorists hold that economic behavior consists of rational choices made by individual people in their own self-interest. They argue the same point in regard to religion. In *The Future of Religion* (1985), Rodney Stark and Philip Bainbridge contend that the decision to believe in God or an afterlife can be explained in terms of cost–benefit calculations that human beings make every day in all aspects of their lives. A religious commitment is made on the ground that it offers rewards—including ultimate rewards—that are worth making other sacrifices to acquire. There are in this approach certain evident affinities to the views of Frazer and Tylor, who see religion as centered on the practical need to survive; there are similarities also to Max Weber's stress on explanation through *Verstehen*, the "understanding" of individual motives behind human action, and even to James's argument in "The Will to Believe." James would not have been surprised to learn that rational choice explanations also hold appeal for professionals in clinical psychology, where intervention theory stresses personal choice as a mechanism to overcome addictions on the principle of psychological self-interest. Rational choice theorists regard religion as more a matter of psychological than political or economic interest.

Anthropological Orientations

From their beginnings in the Victorian era, anthropological research and theory have trained attention chiefly on the customs and cultures of "primitive" peoples. Since these communities are invariably steeped in religion, it has naturally been drawn to the center of discussion. The approaches differ, however, in accord with the two kinds of anthropology we have encountered in these chapters: older Victorian and newer field-study investigation. As we saw earlier, the Victorian founders of the discipline—Tylor, Frazer, and their associates—came under stiff criticism in the early decades of the twentieth century. Their armchair methods, faith in cultural evolution, and narrow intellectualism were so strongly repudiated that their main legacy seemed to be that of bad examples. This critique has merit, but a distinction needs to be made. In and of itself, the Victorians' intellectualism—their idea that primitive religion, like magic, arises as an effort better to understand how the world works—can lay claim to some validity. Tylor and Frazer were mistaken in supposing their point could be proved through armchair research and a naïve idea of progress, of social evolution out of ancient savagery and upward to civilization. But if separated from those errors, it regains some credibility. That is the argument advanced in a series of decidedly original essays by African field-working anthropologist Robin Horton. In articles stretching over a quarter century and published in several collections, including *Patterns of Thought in Africa and the West* (1993), Horton has sought to demonstrate the value of what he calls "neo-Tylorian" theory: namely, that among the peoples of Africa he has encountered, religion is indeed an intellectual project, an effort to explain the world that places gods or spirits in much the same role that abstract conceptions such as atoms, molecules, and physical laws play in Western science. Horton's contrarian and original essays suggest that with regard to intellectualism, the last words on Tylor and Frazer have not yet been written.

This special case does not alter the fact that the general course of anthropology has moved in a direction apart from Horton, who for many years has seemed a lone but notable voice of dissent. Without doubt, most practice of modern anthropology has been molded by two dominant influences. The first is the principle of disciplined fieldwork, both as initiated by pioneers such as Bronislaw Malinowski and as brought to excellence by E. E. Evans-Pritchard and others (Horton certainly among them). The second, more theoretical influence has been the principle of primarily sociological explanation as set out by Durkheim in *The Elementary Forms* and other works. The central argument of Durkheim, as noted, is that religious ideas and rituals are mirror images of an underlying reality that is social. Social structures and constraints govern all that individuals think and do; they frame the beliefs and values, the practices, ceremonies, and even the categories of thought that determine human behavior.

In *Structure and Function in Primitive Society* (1952), published at the midpoint of the twentieth century, English anthropologist A. R. Radcliffe-Brown applied Durkheim's theorems to reach an understanding of a primitive culture as he had seen it in the Andaman Islands. His theoretical matrix, known as structural-functionalism, sought to demonstrate how the fixed components of a society contribute to its orderly function. In *Purity and Danger* (1966), Mary Douglas underscored the central importance of order in primitive societies by examining their elaborate systems of classification. Foods, animals, objects, other people, aspects of the human body itself—all are placed in a grid that specifies what is pure and what pollutes, what is permitted and what is taboo. People cannot conduct a social life without putting things into designated places, without imposing order on the naturally disordered flow of life as it comes along in daily experience. Religion sanctions the social grids that provide both spaces and boundaries, answering to the need for order. Edmund Leach's celebrated essays "Magical Hair" (1958) and "The Logic of Sacrifice" (1985) and his *Culture and Communication* (1976) are works in a similar vein; they explain how classifications serve the purpose of conveying important information in a society. The length of hair often serves as a sign of a person's social or religious status, and the ritual of sacrifice serves to mediate between different cultural categories as people move from one role to another. In *The Forest of Symbols* (1967) and *The Drums of Affliction* (1968), Victor Turner takes a similarly structural approach, showing how rituals resolve conflicts that threaten the stability of the community framework.

While these British anthropologists pursued their work chiefly along the rails laid down by Durkheim and Radcliffe-Brown, Belgian theorist Claude Lévi-Strauss, living in Brazil and conducting his fieldwork in its interior, developed an original approach to issues of social order, which he set out in provocative studies such as *The Savage Mind* (1966) and *The Raw and the Cooked* (1969). Brilliant but often maddeningly obscure, he applied structural linguistics to the myths and practices of tribal communities, contending that relationships among words, ideas, and objects, rather than their individual meanings or identities, are the truly important things in social communication. In the religious language we find in tribal mythologies, the key feature often is not the content or characters in the stories; it is the relationships between objects or terms or characters that matter; they reflect more universal categories of human thought. Though Lévi-Strauss spoke of himself as merely an "inconstant disciple" of Durkheim, his approach won an identity of its own as French structuralism.

In recent years American anthropologist Roy Rappaport has gained considerable attention for developing a new emphasis on the key role played by ritual in both religion and society. Rappaport began his studies in anthropology later than most, as a second career. He conducted field studies in Polynesia and Papua-New Guinea, where he observed the crucial role played by pig sacrifices in the proper functioning of a tribal society. Over a span of three decades given to continued research and analysis, he further developed his views on ritual, finding it to be the central element of religion, which he in turn saw as indispensable to social life. In the year after his death, the distilled product of these reflections was published as his signature study under the title *Ritual and Religion in the Making of Humanity* (1999). Earlier myth and ritual theorists had held that while ritual provides the action of religious life, myth furnishes the ideas—the conceptual content. Rappaport was prepared to argue that ritual is even more central, providing the content as well, thereby supplying the religious sensibility with all of its fundamental elements.

A New Paradigm?

Field studies anchored in structuralist sociology have thus marked one main path of inquiry. A new turn took shape, however, in the 1990s, as that decade became host to one of the most important reorientations in social science since the initiatives of Durkheim and Malinowski. Over the course of the past two decades, books and symposia, journal articles, research initiatives, and even popular magazine pieces have begun to trace a rising tide of interest in evolutionary biology and cognitive science. This arresting new turn has by no means been confined to anthropology or religion. Across both the human and natural sciences, brain scanning technology, advances in genetic research (including a now-complete map of the human genome), and the explanatory power of Darwin's evolutionary paradigm have converged to offer the prospect of striking new possibilities in explanation.

A certain intellectual excitement attending this shift to biogenetic theory has been understandable, but it is not an entirely sudden occurrence. An early spokesman for this path of study, certainly, was the Harvard sociobiologist E. O. Wilson. His *On Human Nature* (1978) was among the first works to pursue inquiries that trace not just human physical features, but also mental activities and behavioral patterns to Darwinian natural selection. Significantly, his book included a discussion of religion in that context. At the beginning of the 1990s, in *Rethinking Religion: Connecting Cognition and Culture* (1990), American scholars E. Thomas Lawson and Robert N. McCauley followed Wilson with an argument for a more concerted effort to incorporate the findings of cognitive science into theories of religion. Momentum has grown steadily since then, as anthropologists have begun to pursue the new possibilities implied in the evolutionary paradigm. One of the more notable advocates of the new approach is Stewart Guthrie. His *Faces in the Clouds: A New Theory of Religion* (1993) asserted that religion arises from the human tendency toward "systematic anthropomorphism," the urge to personify processes and events that is shared with animal ancestors and is rooted, at least partly, in evolved brain functions associated with survival and self-protection. In a subsequent study, *Religion Explained: The Evolutionary Origins of Religious Thought* (2001), Pascal Boyer drew on evolutionary biology to argue that religious belief is a kind of conceptual afterthought that arises in the brain from structures that evolved naturally into consciousness for general survival needs. The appeal of entities like the gods lies in their counterintuitive character, possessing both human and nonhuman features in a single striking image or concept that is easily captured and retained in memory. Ilkke Pysaiennen, in *How Religion Works* (2001), charted a similar argumentative path, while in *Darwin's Cathedral* (2002) David Sloan Wilson framed the case in terms closer to sociobiological theory, holding that religion has emerged from the evolutionary process as an adaptation that binds human groups into collaborative communities for the purpose of survival in a manner analogous to the function of animal herds or colonies of insects.

One of the most impressive and widely discussed works in this rapidly expanding genre has been *In Gods We Trust: The Evolutionary Landscape of Religion* (2002) by Scott Atran. Adept in cognitive psychology, evolutionary theory, anthropology, and other fields, Atran develops a complex theory that draws on all of these disciplines. He on the one hand presents religion as the evolutionary by-product of systems that evolved for other purposes, while insisting on the other hand that religion is neither trivial nor marginal. It is a matter of real importance in the lives of individual persons and the functioning of social communities. His rich suggestions and original ideas have produced some of the most interesting conversations to date about the role of evolution and the methods of cognitive science in bringing about greater understanding and appreciation of religion's role in human experience.

Less widely heralded, but intriguing in its own way, is the theory offered by South African cognitive archaeologist David Lewis-Williams and his associates. In *The Mind in the Cave: Consciousness and the Origins of Art* (2002), *Inside the Neolithic Mind* (2005), and other works, Lewis-Williams argues for a specific point in prehistory when human consciousness emerged, and along with it, both expressive art and religious thinking. He and colleagues anchor these claims in the symbolic and spiritual character of ancient rock images and in the distinctive activity patterns that brain scans reveal when people are in trance states. To express themselves in art of this kind, these early humans must have been capable of such trances, and thus knew a level of consciousness like our own. They had acquired the capacity to think, to express themselves in symbols and images; hence, they had become capable of religious thought and emotion—of thinking about their relationship to gods and spirits. Put briefly: in their art we see evidence of trance; in trance there is evidence of consciousness; and in consciousness, we have the presence of thinking that is religious. In all of this there is much that critics dismiss as speculative; but at a minimum, an argument framed from the linkage of prehistoric rock art to modern technology of the brain scan can be commended for a certain bold originality. However that may be, the common pattern of argument in these works arising from evolutionary theory and cognitive science is evident enough: genetically based mental structures and dispositions, distilled by the age-old evolutionary process of filtration into the present physical composition of the human brain, hold the explanatory key to human action and belief. There can be little doubt that theories of this kind mark an important shift in emphasis away from social to natural science—especially along the paths of genetics and neurobiology. Philosophers and neuroscientists have already charted some of this terrain in vigorous journal debates over the mind–brain relationship.

In this connection, and to no one's surprise, atheistic theory, drawing especially on Darwin, has also made itself heard, militantly and in multiple ways. Among those leading the assault on religion, with evolutionary theory as the key weapon in hand, is Richard Dawkins, perhaps the most celebrated of atheism's recent evangelists. He has made the case against religion in multiple works of polemical design, but perhaps most notably in *The God Delusion* (2006), which was published in the same year that his fellow atheist and philosopher Daniel Dennett joined him with *Breaking the Spell* (2006). Both have been outspoken in their rejection of religious belief as a tissue of falsehood and baseless wishful thinking. Even so, atheism has by no means been the sole owner of discourse on religion, evolutionary biology, and cognitive science. Theories that apply neurobiological data and evolutionary models to affirm religion have also entered the field. One entry into the discussion from the realms of psychology and medicine is *Why God Won't Go Away* (2001), jointly authored by Andrew Newberg, Eugene D'Aquili, and Vance Rouse. The authors draw on brain imaging to argue that religious experience finds an anchor in a very specific kind of brain activity that can be uniquely identified; from this data they argue for the universally human capability to enter mystical states and for a certain presumptive value in the experience. Along similar lines, *The God Gene: How Faith Is Hardwired into Our Genes* (2004), by geneticist Dean Hamer, suggests that the tendency toward religious belief and behavior may be traceable to the coding of DNA on a specific gene. If so, it would seem that faith is firmly rooted in our biology. Whether theorems of this kind will stand up to close scrutiny over time is unclear; at present the interpretations developed are as much speculative and inferential as they are experimental. Nonetheless, they deserve serious consideration, for the implications are important, even if not yet entirely clear. Should we be able to construct it, a theory holding that genes determine all or most of human behavior would go a considerable way toward displacing, or at least reshaping, several of the theories on offer in this book. At the farther limit, it offers the prospect even of a new determinist biological reductionism. Of course, a theory of that sort would embrace far more than the realm of religion; it would purport to account as well for all other forms of human thought and action. On the other side of that ledger, if religion truly is coded into our genes, then the prophecies of secularization theorists about the death of God or the end of faith will have been misstated as well. They will appear to have relied more on tenuous projections about the human future than the clearer portrait of human nature emerging from the evolutionary past. For if truly rooted in the biology of our species, religion may in the end prove nearer to eternal than ephemeral . . . and at the very least, well worth the continuing effort to understand both its durability and mystery.

A Final Exercise: Comparing and Appraising Theories

If nothing else, this cursory review of recent interpretive strategies suggests that the classic theories we have considered in these chapters are more than mere curiosities on display in a museum of discarded ideas. Within and behind almost every current theoretical orientation, it is possible to discern, whether in the shadows or the foreground, the insistent questions that were raised more than a century ago and have persisted under varying forms to the present day. No doubt it would be convenient if in our conclusion we could issue summary judgments of "right" or "wrong" on each of our theories, as a jury might decide a case in court. It would simplify things greatly if we could accept one, reject the others, and end the matter with that. In matters of explanation and interpretation, however, that is almost never the case. Categorical judgments come at too big a price.

Further, as all who seek explanations know, the value of a theory goes well beyond the simple fact of its being true or false. "Wrong" explanations that discover a new way of seeing a problem or break open a new path of inquiry are arguably just as important as "right" ones that do little more than restate what everyone already claims to know. In addition (and as should now be plain), the matters taken up by most theorists of religion are just too complicated to yield a direct up-or-down vote of confidence on any theory in its total profile. It is far more likely that certain parts of an interpretive program will be rejected and pieces of its argument questioned while other aspects are endorsed, amended, or usefully merged with other views. In general, the principal thesis of almost every theorist considered here (with the sole exception perhaps of Evans-Pritchard) is just too broad in scope to be either accepted or rejected in its complete form.

Clearly, questions of several kinds need to be asked if we wish to grasp the grammar of theories and read their syntax correctly. On that principle, here is a final set of five questions that can be asked of all our theorists, allowing us to sort agreements from differences as we go: (1) *How does the theory define the subject?* What concept of religion does it start from? (2) *What type of theory is it?* Since explanations can be of different kinds, what kind of account does the theorist offer, and why? (3) *What is its range?* How much of human religious behavior does it claim to explain? All of it? Or just some? And in that light, does it actually do what it claims? (4) *What evidence does it appeal to?* Does it try to probe deeply into a few facts, ideas, and customs, or does it spread itself widely to embrace many? Is the range of the evidence wide enough to support the range of the theory? (5) *What is the relationship between a theorist's personal belief (or disbelief) and the explanation that is proposed?* As we put these questions to the classic theories, the bearing of the answers on contemporary theorists should readily become clear.

Theories and Definitions

It is said often that religion is so individual, so elusive and diverse, that it defies definition; it can mean almost anything to just about anyone. That is not the view of the theorists considered here. Although they disagree sharply on explaining religion, they differ much less than one might suppose on the matter of defining it. If we look closely—and in a few cases read between the lines—it is apparent that they all come close to the view that religion consists of belief and behavior associated in some way with a supernatural realm of divine or spiritual beings. This is a point worth demonstrating.

Tylor and Frazer both choose to define religion in quite straightforward supernaturalist terms, as does Eliade with his concept of the sacred, which is the realm of the gods, ancestors, and miracle-working heroes. Tylor puts it perhaps most simply when in his well-known minimum definition he refers to "belief in spiritual beings."[2] Durkheim, on the other hand, seems at first glance to take a quite different view, for he explicitly rejects the concept of the supernatural. He defines religion instead as that which concerns the sacred; he then further identifies the sacred with what is social.[3] For him, society is worshipped as divine. Nonetheless, his view is actually closer to the others than he admits, for the whole argument of *The Elementary Forms* depends on the premise that in the eyes of those who subscribe to it, a religion normally consists of beliefs (in his language, "representations") and behaviors associated with a realm of reality that, even if the believers themselves do not see it so, we with our modern concept of nature clearly *would* call supernatural. When Durkheim turns to his primitive Australians, he does not discuss their trading habits or techniques of husbandry; he starts with beliefs and ceremonies that refer to the supernatural, the rites pertaining to the gods, and the stories of the ancestral spirits. He of course differs from a theorist like Eliade in claiming that although the inquiry *starts* with such rites and beliefs, that is not where it ends. His aim is to show that once the issue has been explored, the Australians' worship of the totem god will turn out to be their concern for the clan. But he cannot get to this conclusion without at least beginning his inquiry at almost the same place it starts for Tylor, Frazer, and Eliade—with the notion of the supernatural.

The views of Freud, Marx, and Daly on this issue need less explication. All three are quite content with a conventional definition: they see religion as belief in gods, especially the monotheistic Father God of the Judeo-Christian tradition, even though, like Durkheim, they insist that this is only religion on its surface. Underneath the appearances lies humanity's obsessional neurosis, economic injustice, or oppressive patriarchy that needs to be overcome.

Weber, James, Evans-Pritchard, and Geertz can be seen to follow convention as well, though each has certain problems with the term "supernatural." Evans-Pritchard prefers the term "mystical" because unlike the cultures of the modern West, the tribal societies he explores have no clear concept of an opposition between a natural world and a supernatural one.[4] Nonetheless, he makes it clear that the overriding concern of both Nuer religion and Azande witchcraft is always to arrange a proper relationship with this mystical realm that lies behind and beyond ordinary life. Before they can be at peace with themselves or at home in society, the Nuer feel deeply that they must have a clear conscience before the gods, while the Azande always must locate the source of the witchcraft that is causing their troubles.

As we might expect given their common lineage, the positions of Weber and Geertz are similar. Weber's definition is expansive; it embraces systems of belief in the supernatural that include both magical and salvation interests, without excluding even a nonsalvationist ethical system such as Confucianism. As for Geertz, it is true that the word "supernatural" does not appear in his well-known definition of religion as a cultural system, where he speaks in abstract terms of "a system of symbols" that conveys "conceptions of a general order of existence."[5] And his main interest, admittedly, is in the *ethos*, the "moods and motivations" of religious people, rather than in the supernatural beings they fear or love. But when we turn to the actual accounts he provides in his ethnographies of Java, Bali, and Morocco, it is clear that the key feature of religion as practiced lies in the emotional and social responses people make to their world views: that is, to the supernatural beings they believe in, whether that be the God, angels, and Satan of Islam or the spirits, deities, and demons of the traditional cults on exhibit in Java and Bali.

Thus, while the theorists we have examined may disagree on any number of things, the definition of religion is, generally speaking, not one of them. Though some say it less directly than others, all find religion centered, initially at least, on beliefs and practices associated with spiritual or supernatural beings. Even in the cases of Durkheim, Evans-Pritchard, and Geertz (each of whom does have reservations), the differences turn out to be mainly a matter of terminology and emphasis, not substance. On the matter of defining religion, all ten of our theorists can be said to start, broadly speaking, from common ground.

Types of Theory

Needless to say, the moment these theorists turn from definition to explanation, consensus rather quickly disappears, as we have had ample occasion to notice. By their nature, of course, explanations come in different forms, which in themselves can create confusion. As we noted early on, the same fact, event, or behavior can be explained in multiple ways, some easily confused with others. In *Theories of Primitive Religion*, Evans-Pritchard observes that when in the later 1800s the first spokesmen for the science of religion presented their work as a search for "origins," they were often less than clear on the meaning of that term.[6] Assuming we can ever find it, the *historical* or *prehistorical* origin of religion is one thing; its *psychological* or *social* origin is another. The first would be found in certain specific events belonging to the earlier (or earliest) ages of civilization, while the others are rooted in conditions presumably characteristic of human life in all times and places. The one is a past occurrence; the others refer to a timeless condition or aspect of all human existence.

The search for religious origins in the first sense of the word has been carried on especially by Max Müller, Tylor and Frazer, Freud, and even (to a certain degree) Durkheim and Daly. It is typically connected with the doctrine of human social evolution and holds that religion is the result of a long process that began with events lodged deep in the human past, like Freud's "murder of the first father." In tandem with the growth of civilization as a whole, it then slowly developed through stages of ever-increasing complexity until it arrived at beliefs and practices of the kind we know today. Such evolutionary theories naturally take a keen interest in primitive peoples because they are thought to display religion, as well as civilization, in its earliest, simplest, and purest form. In the words of the well-worn evolutionist analogy, they show us the acorn out of which the oak of religion has grown. In addition, the primitive form is commonly (but not always) regarded as inferior to what is modern. "Crude," "childish," "barbaric," and "savage" are favorite words of theorists like Tylor and Frazer.

As we have had several occasions to notice, this once-fashionable doctrine of social evolution eventually came to be rejected on all sides. Its chief problem was that it claimed knowledge of things that no modern inquirer could ever hope to know. The "earliest forms" of human religion and social life are subjects we can only guess about—and not with much skill.[7] With the failure of this historical evolutionism, theory in the twentieth century has turned chiefly to the other sense of the term "origins." Religion, it is held, is ultimately traceable to the enduring psychological needs or social circumstances that we find in every age and place of human existence. But that is not all. Within this second category one must further distinguish purely functional and even reductionist explanations such as we find in Freud, Durkheim, Marx, and (to a degree) Daly from the antireductionist positions of Weber, James, Eliade, Evans-Pritchard, and (in his unique way) Geertz. The motive of the reductionist approach is apparent. Since in the modern scientific world, religion cannot be considered either a rational form of belief or a normal type of behavior, reductionist accounts must appeal to something subconscious, sexist, or irrational to explain why it persists.

The opponents of reductionism insist that such theories rest on a serious misunderstanding. Weber contends that regardless of whether the theorist believes in them, systems of meaning are indispensable; it is in the very nature of human beings to create conceptual frameworks for their actions. James argues similarly but prefers to make religious experience primary and beliefs secondary. Eliade and Evans-Pritchard concur, arguing that when seen in its own terms, there is nothing irrational or abnormal about religion; thus, there is no point in seeking to explain it away through appeals to the subconscious, the social, the economic-material, or the gender-repressive. Evans-Pritchard shows that even when they seem absurd to outsiders, the religious beliefs (even of tribal peoples) form coherent, orderly systems; they are neither barbaric nor crude—just different from the systems that undergird modern nonreligious societies. Eliade takes this argument further, claiming that the archaic mode of thought characteristic of religion is actually more meaningful, and thus more "normal," than modern secular attitudes because it responds more fully to the deep human craving for cosmic order and significance in a world of disorder, evil, and suffering. The same is true for Geertz: from the perspective of interpretive anthropology, which appreciates the particular self-defining character of every culture, he contends that religious societies stand on a footing of coherence and normality comparable to that of our own semireligious scientific cultural order.

All things considered, and apart from the partial countercurrent of Daly's rather radical feminism, this antireductionist stance can be said to have gradually gained strength throughout the twentieth century, aided of course by the rather sudden and steep decline in the stature of both Freud and Marx. We can even note as a further contribution to this shift Robin Horton's revival of Tylor's intellectualist theory.[8] Clifford Geertz, incidentally, comes near to the same conclusion. Though he thinks that religion is more than a purely intellectual exercise and that it fills a variety of emotional and social needs, he reports that more than anything else, the people he met in Indonesia appealed to their gods simply to explain events they otherwise could not understand.[9] Needless to say, the debate between reductionist and antireductionist theory, between the irrationalist and the intellectualist paradigms, continues into the present.

Range of Theories

As we have noticed along the way, all of our theorists address themselves in some measure to the question of religion in general—religion taken "in the round"—but they do so in quite different ways. Like their predecessor Max Müller, Tylor and Frazer feel they can explain the entire history of religion as it first appeared and then developed through the long span of the human centuries. This goal strikes us today as exceedingly unrealistic, though for their part, they felt the principle of social evolution provided all the guidance needed. For Tylor, the spirit worship of primitive peoples, the polytheism of the Greeks and Romans, and the monotheism of the "higher" religions could all be explained as steps on the staircase of civilization; they mark the ascent of humanity to ever more rational forms of thought—the most rational of which, in his view, was the choice to discard religion altogether. Frazer, who includes magic as a preliminary stage, embraces essentially the same grand global sequence.

Nor are Tylor and Frazer alone. From their different perspectives, the three major reductionists—Freud, Durkheim, and Marx—show the same sort of general ambition. When they explain religion, they mean to explain all of religion. They choose one religious system as a sort of paradigm case, the supreme exhibit of an endeavor that appears in numerous other "lesser" or later forms. For Freud and Marx, the paradigm is the Judeo-Christian belief in God as Father, an idea that reveals the escapist role of religion worldwide. For Durkheim it is Australian totemism, which puts on display "the elementary forms" from which all others can be derived. Weber, James, Eliade, and Daly are just as ambitious but decline to rely on a single paradigm instance. Each considers the entire spectrum of world religions, though their emphases differ. They keep the evolutionism and comparative method of Victorian anthropology off their agenda, but as it happens, the scale of their inquiries is no less wide-ranging than the worldwide armchair travels of Tylor and Frazer. Weber is confident that he can make well-grounded but sweeping comparisons between Asian and Western religions, between asceticism and mysticism on a global scale, and among the economic ethics of entire civilizations. James leans heavily on Protestant accounts of conversion experiences but clearly sees the personal transition from distress to release as the emotional core of religion in all cultures and traditions. Eliade draws his evidence from every age and every locale of human civilization. In his search for the universal patterns of symbolism and myth, he moves freely from Hindu yoga and the shamanism of Asia to the aboriginal culture of Australia and the "cosmic Christianity" of European peasants; he draws as well on the texts and rites of many other times, places, and peoples, whether ancient or modern, Eastern or Western, simple or sophisticated. Daly finds in Christianity her initial archetype of patriarchal oppression, but then moves around the globe, finding phallocentric cruelty to be just as pronounced in India, China, and Africa. Her aims too are genuinely global.

In contrast with these others, Evans-Pritchard and Geertz have serious misgivings about any theory that aspires to universal claims about "all" of religion. From their standpoint, any theory with global ambitions comes uncomfortably close to the ways of Tylor and Frazer. We cannot visit other cultures and societies as if we were tourists, stopping briefly to gather up a myth here, a symbol there, and move casually on. Nor can we, like Freud, Durkheim, and Marx, center on one tradition and assume what is said about that case will apply by extension to others. For Evans-Pritchard and Geertz, the focus of the religionist, like that of the anthropologist, must fall on particular cases for the simple reason that myths, beliefs, rituals, and values are always embedded things, laced tightly to other strands in the social fabric.

Theories and Evidence

A theory is one thing; the way we try to prove it is another. If we look at all ten theories in terms of their approach to evidence, certain clear differences are not hard to notice. Because they believe that a truly global theory of religion requires an equally global array of evidence, Tylor, Frazer, Weber, Eliade, and Daly all set out with great determination to collect the widest possible array of information. The strength of this approach lies in its honest attempt to make a complete fit between theory and evidence. It assumes that if claims about all of religion are to be made, then evidence from all (or as close as we can come to all) religions ought to be provided. Nevertheless, its disadvantages are obvious. It is a program virtually impossible to pursue without conceding that our grasp of some texts or traditions will be better than others, that there will be barriers of language and limits to translation, and that there will be gaps to fill by inference rather than evidence. In addition, global inquiries almost by definition must make at least some of their arguments by drawing facts, customs, or ideas out of the natural context of the cultures that generate them. When that happens, the risks of distortion and misunderstanding are real.

These difficulties with evidence are rather neatly escaped by Freud and Marx, even though the claims they make about religion are in their way as universal as any made by the other globalists. Freud and Marx feel no need to search the world for data because they feel they have found something better—the fundamental mechanism in human beings that everywhere generates religion, regardless of the specific form it takes in one culture or the next. For Freud, there is no need to scan the globe when the source of all rites and beliefs can be traced directly to the oedipal tensions and neuroses that are characteristic of every human personality. If we have in hand the principle that generates all religions, we have no need for all the many labors of anthropology and comparative religion, other than to supply us with instructive supporting details. Similarly for Marx, it makes little difference whether we examine the tribal religions of New Guinea or the Christianity of Europe; beneath the particulars, he is certain he will find everywhere the same fundamental dynamic of class warfare—the struggle that generates the hope of a better world beyond for the poor while offering divine sanction of the laws that protect the persons and property of the rich.

The challenge for both of these theories, of course, is that they must demonstrate how all religions arise from wish fulfillment or the class struggle; they cannot just assume it. Since religions differ tremendously in both form and substance around the world, both Freud and Marx need to show us just how it is that, say, Chinese folk religion or Australian totemism is generated by the same psychological and social dynamic that has produced Judeo-Christian monotheism.

This expectation is not impossible to meet. The Hindu doctrines of caste and reincarnation, for example, would seem to invite Marxist analysis. But neither Freud nor Marx sees any compelling need to canvas multiple cases; both are content to apply their theories chiefly to Judeo-Christian monotheism and let the verdict in that case stand also for all others. Still, such a strategy is not a substitute for consideration of other relevant cases. The sharp focus of both Freud and Marx on one Western monotheistic religion constrains their accounts unless some effort is made to widen the scope of the evidence they are willing to consider. Universal claims cannot easily rest on mainly provincial arguments; the range of the evidence needs to be generally congruent with the range of the theory it is adduced to support.

Among the other theorists, Durkheim, Daly, and James think that the matter of theory and evidence can be settled only by some form of compromise, while Evans-Pritchard and Geertz doubt whether it can be settled at all. In differing ways, they together find the comprehensive approach of Tylor and Frazer and of Weber and Eliade dauntingly expansive, while the exclusively Western focus of Freud and Marx is too narrow. The resolution must be found either in between the two approaches, in some combination of a singular formula and supporting evidence, or in renouncing the effort entirely. In this connection Durkheim's solution, though differently developed, still somewhat resembles that of Freud and Marx. He too thinks he has found the mechanism that generates all of religion, not in the psyche or the class struggle but in the needs of society. Like Daly, however, he seeks to provide evidence outside of the Christian West to support his claim. To illustrate this mechanism he offers the account of a single primitive religious tradition that serves as his test case—in his own words, the "one well-made experiment" that is "valid universally."[10] The religion he chooses is primitive Australian totemism, for it best shows the "elementary forms" inherent in all religions. As Durkheim's critics have been quick to point out, however, Australian clan cults cannot offer a better foundation for a general theory than any other religion taken in isolation. Although he does try to be more genuinely scientific about his procedure than either Freud or Marx, Durkheim faces the same problem: the very specific nature of the (Australian) evidence is insufficient to support the universal claims of the theory. To her credit, Daly manages somewhat to deflect such criticism by combining the singular formula of patriarchy with evidence of sexism from several Asian and African cultures, so that the range of her evidence at least aspires to match the range of the theory. William James proceeds in a manner similar to that of Daly. He finds the core of religion—the psychological experience of spiritual healing—to be prospectively universal and not tied to the diverse theologies of different cultures that seek to explain it. Like Daly, he then provides evidence of such experience as reported by religious believers who have felt its transforming power in their lives. But in his case, this evidence is culturally limited. Most of the varieties of religious experience cited in support of the theory consist of Protestant Christian testimonies. Consequently, without a wider range of evidence from non-Protestant and non-Christian sources, it is difficult to tell how globally applicable that core psychological experience of release really is.

The methods of Durkheim, Daly, and James enable us to see, finally, why theorists such as Evans-Pritchard and Geertz have moved near to renouncing such efforts altogether. In their view, ambitious general claims about the nature of religion are quite simply an intellectual bridge too far. The problem lies in the evidence, which in their view must be patiently studied in individual cases before any kind of more general statement can even begin to be made. In that connection, Evans-Pritchard does express a kind of deferred hope that at some future moment scholars, building on studies done in the present, may be able to frame well-founded general interpretations. In the conclusion of *Nuer Religion*, he describes his own careful work in the Sudan as little more than a first step on the way to comparative studies that in the future will examine African systems as a whole.[11] From there, presumably, he would encourage interpreters to go on to even wider theories that embrace other continents and cultures, though all of that would no doubt occur well into the future.

Geertz, by contrast, is even more skeptical. The position he takes brings him very near to announcing the end of all general theories. He thinks the fault of earlier theorists lies not (as Evans-Pritchard claims) in the method or manner of reaching their goal but in the goal itself. Given the deep and sharp particularity of societies around the world, he argues, the whole idea of a general theory of something so culture-bound as religion must be called into question. What we can develop, as the title of his most important book states, is the interpretation of *cultures* (plural); what we cannot create is some generic theory of *culture* (singular). And what is true of culture is equally true of religion. We cannot reach some comprehensive general theory of religion worldwide—of *religion* "as a whole." The range of our evidence will always be insufficient to support the range of such a theory.

Among more recent interpreters the cautions of Evans-Pritchard and Geertz have in a measure been taken to heart. Some certainly wonder aloud whether generalizations of the kind normally sought by social science still hold the promise they were once thought to offer.[12]

Theories and Personal Belief

None of the theorists we have met in this book should be considered a purely detached scholar, writing on a subject of no personal interest or relevance to real lives; each is a human being who in addition to endeavors in theory can be presumed to hold personal convictions about religion as well. The relationship between those personal convictions and the explanations proposed is in some instances obvious, as with Marx, but in others it is a more subtle and complicated matter, which we cannot explore in any complete way here. Still, some final comments on this issue may turn out to be useful.

First, to recall a point made early in this book, there is a sense in which all of the theories we have considered here offer at least a possible challenge to religious belief because they choose from the start not to consider supernatural explanations. The devout Christian explains her faith as a gift of God; the Muslim explains the power of the Prophet through a miraculous vision that delivered the divine messages recorded in the Quran. By contrast, the theorist of religion appeals only to what can be described as "natural causes" or "nonprivileged accounts." This difference of approach need not necessarily create a conflict. Max Müller, a devoutly religious man, saw no reason why natural and supernatural explanations of religion should ever need to come in conflict; the two could converge without colliding.[13] But that was not the view of Tylor and Frazer, who set the terms for much of the theoretical sequence that we have followed here. Both were antireligious rationalists who took considerable pleasure in announcing that supernatural explanations of religion lose their purpose once we discover that belief in gods and spirits arises from a natural but mistaken way of explaining the operations of the world. That Muhammad claimed to receive revelations from Allah, they would say, is a fact no one need doubt; that he actually was so inspired is a claim no rational person can accept. Religion for Tylor and Frazer is thus a form of thought that arises from ignorance of the (true) natural causes of things. Now that civilization has evolved, and the ways of science are known to all, such crude explanations no longer apply.

The decidedly antireligious uses that Tylor and Frazer found for the comparative study of religion opened the way to the even more aggressive attacks of the three classic reductionists we have considered—Freud, Marx, and Durkheim—as well as the feminist Mary Daly. Like Tylor and Frazer, they too personally reject conventional religion and dismiss it as a survival from earlier ages of ignorance or as a cruel deception used to justify sexist discrimination. Going a step further, however, they proceed to explain how it has survived by tracing its origin to irrational, subconscious, or malicious motives. Since religion cannot possibly be a rational or morally just form of behavior, such functionally reductive or hostile accounts of its existence are the only ones available. Atheism in this connection seems naturally to entail some form of reductionist or similarly dismissive explanation.[14]

Even so, not all rejections of religion or reductionist accounts are the same. Freud and Marx think religion is not only false but (by their standards of morality and normalcy) also a pathology. It is something destructive or dysfunctional, a kind of perversion to be crushed or disease to be cured of. Daly thinks similarly; it is an evil to be exorcised. Durkheim, however, proceeds differently. Though just as much an atheist as Freud or Marx, religion from his perspective is not something abnormal, dysfunctional, or devious; it is, on the contrary, socially indispensable. Societies cannot function without it. In fact, should we try to create a society without religion, we can be sure that some equivalent system of rituals and beliefs would appear in its place. Thus, even though his approach is clearly reductionist, Durkheim's more affirmative assessment of religion in terms of its constructive social function needs to be distinguished from its diagnosis as an illness offered by Freud and the moral indignation of Daly and Marx. Durkheim's appraisal emerges as more neutral and disinterested, and in that respect, it bears a measure of resemblance to the antireductionism of theorists like Eliade and James, who depict religion as something that is just naturally human.

It is not hard to see why theorists like James, Eliade, and Evans-Pritchard, all of whom exhibit some sympathy with religious belief, would be inclined to take a stand in opposition to reductionism. Reductionist explanations, even in the less militantly antireligious form developed by Durkheim, tend to be so pointedly opposed to the normal stance of faith that it is hard to see how believers can abide them without discomfort. Almost invariably, religious people see reductionism as an alien form of explanation. Yet if believers instinctively oppose reductionism, at least of the strict sort, it does not follow that *only* believers oppose it, even though current theorists of religion sometimes make the mistake of thinking that must be so.[15]

On this point, both Weber and Geertz provide instructive examples. Weber describes himself as "religiously unmusical." Geertz describes his stance as agnostic; he has no personal religious commitments. Yet in their explanatory work, both oppose reductionist theories as pointedly as do Eliade and James. Weber and Geertz obviously do not do so because reductionists present any challenge to their personal beliefs, but simply because in their view such accounts do not adequately explain the phenomenon of religion. From their perspective the appeal to a single circumstance or process that explains all forms of belief—whether it be Freud's neurosis, Marx's class struggle, or Daly's patriarchy—simply cannot do justice to either the extraordinary diversity of forms in religious life or its true nature as we actually encounter it in human personal and social affairs. A circumstance such as class struggle may explain some aspects of some religions, but it does not explain fully all of what occurs in any of them.

Behind the scenes, then, it is apparent that personal commitments often and at the very least play a certain motivating role in the development of theories of religion. To those who, like Marx, Freud, and Daly, have written from a personal stance of antipathy toward religion or some specific form of it, aggressive reductionism seems only natural and right. To those who, like Eliade, have been moved by greater sympathy for the religious perspective, it naturally appears misguided.

Theorists, Theories, and Their Influence: Past and Present

New chapters on the role of belief and nonbelief in these discussions no doubt remain to be written. But the central question going forward is not likely to be what theorists think personally about religion; it is most likely to center on what they think professionally about theory. Here the debate finds itself taking shape as a new version of the old German *Methodenstreit* that formed a background to the work of Max Weber. We can recall also that when in 1870 Max Müller mounted the podium to lecture to his British audience, what he specifically proposed was a new "science" of religion. The methods of natural science in his day—observation, classification, and generalization to create laws of development and behavior—could be adapted to the study of religion, a human and social endeavor. Over the next century and a half, social scientific theory—anthropology, psychology, sociology, and economics—took up the challenge, working strenuously to form general theories of religion. That ultimately has been the goal not only of reductionists like Freud, Marx, and Durkheim, as well as the feminist Daly, but also of nonreductionist interpreters like Weber, James, and Eliade, though their methods tended toward either humanist inquiry or some mix of the humanistic and the social scientific.

Along the way, however, the rise of field anthropology put the status of general theory itself into some question. The work of Evans-Pritchard has been doubly significant in this regard. Not only did his studies of the Azande and Nuer demonstrate just how rich explanations of religion can be when they are rooted in close, detailed, and distinctive analysis of a single society; he went on also to offer a searching critique of the most celebrated generalist theories. A similar outcome emerged from the work of Clifford Geertz, whose equally careful ethnographic studies of religion in Bali and Java underscored the question raised by Evans-Pritchard's work: What happens when the first mission of a science—to acquire precise, accurate, and specific information—is pursued so thoroughly that its second task—framing broad and generalized theories with testable hypotheses and predictive power—becomes almost impossible to accomplish? Without a path through that dilemma as they discern it, the prospects for a usable and general social scientific theory of religion do not look especially promising.

The emphasis of field anthropology on particular and local features of religion does not of course mean that no statements at all of a more general sort can be made. Efforts to make connections and frame comparisons that show similarities or highlight differences will always remain useful, but those are, to be candid, methods and techniques more nearly associated with humanistic inquiry than the distinctive principles of social science. And they suggest what some observers long predicted: that future inquiry may well trend toward the particularist and historical methods of the humanities because that is turning out to be the path most suited to the subject. It is interesting to note in this regard an incident from the late 1800s, when anthropology first captured the imagination of the Victorians. Asked about this intriguing new science, the great legal historian F. W. Maitland is said to have remarked: "It will become history, or it will become nothing at all." For Maitland history was emblematic of humanistic, not scientific, inquiry, and he may well have proved himself an accurate prophet. At the very least, we need to ask: Could he have been right that the sheer difficulty in framing general social scientific theories that can apply to human institutions and behaviors leads us back mainly, though perhaps not exclusively, to the ways and means of humanistic interpretation? Possibly so.

Or then again, possibly not. If the original ideal of social science is proving in part out of reach for theorists of religion, could the intriguing new turn to natural science cited above presumably offer an alternative? That is a possibility that Maitland never imagined, but his contemporary Charles Darwin well might have. For the newer appeals to evolutionary biology and cognitive science bring theorists of religion into a realm of theory that is indisputably Darwin's legacy. The research initiatives in this field of study are still very new, gaining a firm foothold mostly, as noted, in the past two decades. But the possibilities deserve exploring; they pursue lines of inquiry that appear both instructive and provocative. Should those now working in genetics, neuroscience, and evolutionary biology find some success, should their inquiries open paths that convincingly trace religious behaviors to the physical body, the brain, and the biochemistry of its processes, that clearly would mark the passage over a significant threshold—a turn not just to new explanations, but to a new kind of explanation. At a minimum, theories offering such a "biology of belief," anchored in the evolutionary heritage of the human species, would slice through the current humanistic or social scientific alternatives, making a strong case instead for the material and physiological origins of religion. At present, a definitive theory of that sort is a distant prospect, to be sure, but if more progress is made along the lines now in place, then future books of this kind will need to be supplemented with a new and different final chapter.

Notes

1. For an account of Marxism's decline, see Lesek Kolakowski, *Main Currents of Marxism: The Breakdown* (Oxford: Oxford University Press, 1981).

2. *Primitive Culture: Researches into the Development of Mythology, Philosophy, Religion, Language, Art, and Custom*, 2 vols., 4th ed., rev. (London: John Murray, [1871] 1903), 1: 424.

3. *The Elementary Forms of the Religious Life: A Study in Religious Sociology*, tr. Joseph Ward Swain (London: George Allen & Unwin, Ltd., 1915), pp. 24–29, 47.

4. See *Witchcraft, Oracles and Magic among the Azande* (Oxford: Clarendon Press, 1937), pp. 80–83; for his definition of "mystical notions," see p. 12.

5. Geertz, "Religion as Cultural System," in *The Interpretation of Cultures* (New York: Basic Books, 1973), p. 90.

6. E. E. Evans-Pritchard, *Theories of Primitive Religion* (Oxford: Clarendon Press, 1965), pp. 101–102.

7. Evans-Pritchard, *Theories of Primitive Religion*, p. 101.

8. Horton has outlined his views in a number of well-known articles; see "The Kalabari World View: An Outline and Interpretation," *Africa* 32 (1962): 210–240; "Ritual Man in Africa," *Africa* 34 (1964): 85–104; and "Neo-Tylorianism: Sound Sense or Sinister Prejudice?" *Man*, n.s. 3 (1968): 625–634. His most recent work is *Patterns of Thought in Africa and the West: Selected Theoretical Papers in Magic, Religion, and Science* (Cambridge: Cambridge University Press, 1993).

9. See "Religion as Cultural System," in *Interpretation of Cultures*, p. 101, where he writes, "Certainly, I was struck in my own work, much more than I had at all expected to be, by the degree to which my more animistically inclined informants behaved like true Tyloreans. They seemed to be constantly using their beliefs to 'explain' phenomena: or, more accurately, to convince themselves that the phenomena were explainable within the accepted scheme of things."

10. Durkheim, *Elementary Forms*, p. 415.

11. E. E. Evans-Pritchard, *Nuer Religion* (Oxford: Clarendon Press, 1956), p. 314.

12. For comment on some of these issues, see the essays of Robert Segal in *Explaining and Interpreting Religion: Essays on the Issue*, Toronto Studies in Religion, vol. 16 (New York: Peter Lang, 1992); see also the exchange between Robert Segal and Donald Wiebe in their essay "Axioms and Dogmas in the Study of Religion," *Journal of the American Academy of Religion* 57 (Fall 1989): 591–605, and my response in "Axioms without Dogmas: The Case for a Humanistic Account of Religion," *Journal of the American Academy of Religion* 59, no. 4 (Winter 1991): 703–709. See also my "Explaining, Endorsing, and Reducing Religion: Some Clarifications," in *Religion and Reductionism*, ed. Thomas Idinopoulos and Edward Yonan (Leiden: E. J. Brill, 1994), pp. 183–197, along with the other essays in this volume.

13. See in this book the Introduction, pp. 8–9; chap. 1, p. 29.

14. On this, see Robert A. Segal, "In Defense of Reductionism," *Journal of the American Academy of Religion* 51, no. 1 (March 1983): 97–124.

15. See my "Reductionism and Belief," *Journal of Religion* 66, no. 1 (January 1986): 18–36.

Suggestions for Further Reading

Allport, Gordon. *The Individual and His Religion*. New York: Macmillan, 1951.

Asad, Talal. *Genealogies of Religion: Discipline and Reasons of Power in Christianity and Islam*. Baltimore: Johns Hopkins University Press, 1993.

Atran, Scott. *In Gods We Trust: The Evolutionary Landscape of Religion*. New York: Oxford University Press, 2002.

Bellah, Robert. *Religion in Human Evolution: From the Paleolithic to the Axial Age*. Cambridge, MA: Harvard University Press, 2011.

Berger, Peter. *The Sacred Canopy*. Garden City, NY: Doubleday, 1967.

Berger, Peter. *The Desecularization of the World*. Grand Rapids, MI: Wm. B. Eerdmans Publishing Co., 1999.

Boyer, Pascal. *Religion Explained: The Evolutionary Origins of Religious Thought*. New York: Basic Books, 2001.

Bruce, Steven. *God Is Dead: Secularisation in the West*. Oxford: Blackwell, 2002.

Carrasco, David. *Religions of Mesoamerica: Cosmovisions and Ceremonial Centers*. San Francisco: Harper & Row, 1990.

Daly, Mary. *Beyond God the Father: Toward a Philosophy of Women's Liberation*. Boston: Beacon Press, 1973.

Dawkins, Richard. *The God Delusion*. London: Bantam Press, 2006.

Dennett, Daniel. *Breaking the Spell: Religion as a Natural Phenomenon*. New York: Penguin Books, 2006.

Doniger, Wendy. *The Origins of Evil in Hindu Mythology*. Berkeley: University of California Press, 1976.

Doniger, Wendy. *The Implied Spider: Politics and Theology in Myth*. New York: Columbia University Press, 1998.

Douglas, Mary. *Purity and Danger*. London: Routledge & Kegan Paul, 1966.

Fanon, Frantz. *The Wretched of the Earth*. New York: Grove Press, [1961] 1963.

Fernando, Jude Lal, ed. *Resistance to Empire and Militarization: Reclaiming the Sacred*. Sheffield, UK: Equinox, 2020.

Foucault, Michel. *Madness and Civilization: A History of Insanity in the Age of Reason*. English tr. New York: Pantheon Books, [1961] 1965.

Foucault, Michel. *Discipline and Punish: The Birth of the Prison*. Translated by Alan Sheridan. New York: Pantheon Books, [1975] 1978.

Guthrie, Stewart. *Faces in the Clouds: A New Theory of Religion*. New York: Oxford University Press, 1993.

Hamer, Dean. *The God Gene: How Faith Is Hardwired into Our Genes*. New York: Doubleday, 2004.

Hewitt, Marsha Aileen. *Critical Theory of Religion: A Feminist Analysis*. Minneapolis: Augsburg Fortress, 1995.

Horton, Robin. *Patterns of Thought in Africa and the West*. Cambridge: Cambridge University Press, 1993.

King, Richard. *Orientalism and Religion in Postcolonial Theory: India and "the Mystic East."* London: Routledge, 1999.

Kling, David. *A History of Christian Conversion*. New York: Oxford University Press, 2020.

Lawson, E. Thomas, and Robert N. McCauley. *Rethinking Religion: Connecting Cognition and Culture*. Cambridge: Cambridge University Press, 1990.

Leach, Edmund. *Culture and Communication: The Logic by Which Symbols Are Connected*. Cambridge: Cambridge University Press, 1976.

Lévi-Strauss, Claude. *The Savage Mind*. Chicago: University of Chicago Press, [1962] 1966.

Lévi-Strauss, Claude. *The Raw and the Cooked: Mythologiques, Volume 1*. New York: Harper & Row, [1964] 1969.

Lewis-Williams, J. David. *The Mind in the Cave: Consciousness and the Origins of Art*. London: Thames and Hudson, 2002.

Lewis-Williams, J. David, and David Pearce. *Inside the Neolithic Mind: Consciousness, Cosmos and the Realm of the Gods*. London: Thames and Hudson, 2005.

Luckmann, Thomas. *The Invisible Religion: The Problem of Religion in Modern Society*. New York: Macmillan, 1967.

Maslow, Abraham. *Religions, Values, and Peak-Experiences*. Harmondsworth, UK: Penguin Books, 1964.

McCullough, Michael E., Kenneth I. Pargament, and Carl E. Thoresen, eds. *Forgiveness: Theory, Research and Practice*. New York: Guilford Press, 2000.

Newberg, Andrew, Eugene D'Aquili, and Vance Rouse. *Why God Won't Go Away*. New York: Ballantine Books, 2001.

Pargament, Kenneth. *The Psychology of Religion and Coping: Theory, Research, Practice*. New York: The Guilford Press, 1997.

Pysaiennen, Ilkke. *How Religion Works: Toward a New Cognitive Science: Cognition and Culture*. Leiden: Brill Academic Publishers, 2001.

Radcliffe-Brown, A. R. *Structure and Function in Primitive Society*. New York: Free Press, 1952.

Rappaport, R. A. *Ritual and Religion in the Making of Humanity*. Cambridge: Cambridge University Press, 1999.

Said, Edward. *Orientalism*. New York: Pantheon Books, 1978.

Spivak, Gayatri. *In Other Worlds: Essays in Cultural Politics*. London: Routledge, 1988.

Spivak, Gayatri. *A Critique of Post-Colonial Reason: Toward a History of the Vanishing Present*. Cambridge, MA: Harvard University Press, 1999.

Stark, Rodney, and Philip Bainbridge. *The Future of Religion: Secularization, Revival, and Cult Formation*. Berkeley: University of California Press, 1985.

Turner, Victor. *The Forest of Symbols: Aspects of Ndembu Ritual*. Ithaca, NY: Cornell University Press, 1967.

Turner, Victor. *The Drums of Affliction*. Oxford: Clarendon Press, 1968.

Tweed, Thomas. *Crossing and Dwelling: A Theory of Religion*. Cambridge, MA: Harvard University Press, 2006.

Wilson, Bryan. *Religion in Sociological Perspective*. New York: Oxford University Press, 1982.

Wilson, David Sloan. *Darwin's Cathedral: Evolution, Religion, and the Nature of Society*. Chicago: University of Chicago Press, 2002.

Wilson, E. O. *On Human Nature*. Cambridge, MA: Harvard University Press, 1978.

Yinger, J. Milton. *The Scientific Study of Religion*. New York: Macmillan, 1970.

INDEX